INTRODUCTION TO PSYCHOLOGY

FROM A CHRISTIAN WORLDVIEW

A customized version of *Psychology in a Complex World* by Jennifer Bonds-Raacke designed specifically for Liberty University.

Shawn George

Brian Kelley

Rachel Piferi

Kendall Hunt
publishing company

www.kendallhunt.com
Send all inquiries to:
4050 Westmark Drive
Dubuque, IA 52004-1840

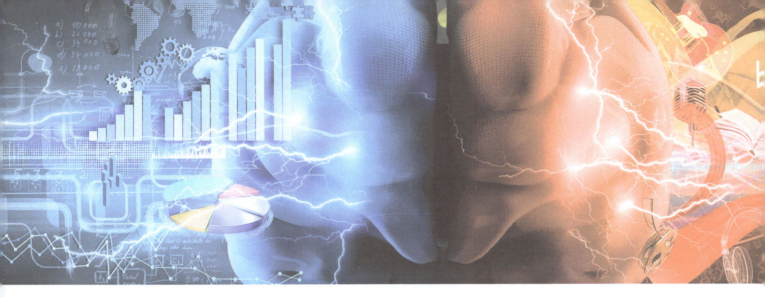

Brief Contents

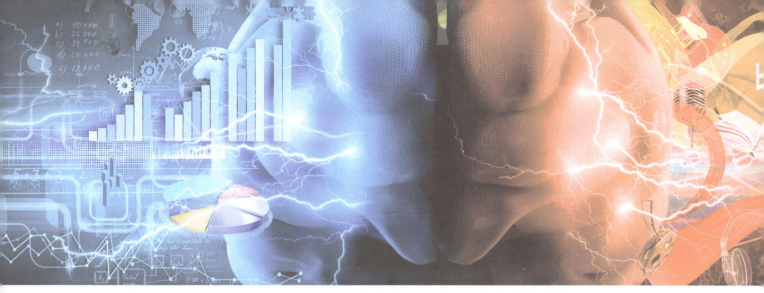

Contents

Chapter 2:   The Biology of Behavior   43

Chapter 3:   Sensation and Perception   95

Chapter 4:   Learning, Memory, and Intelligence   149

Chapter 5:   Motivation and Emotion   205

Chapter 6:   Developmental Psychology   247

Chapter 7:   Personality and Social Psychology   293

Chapter 8:   Psychological Disorders and Treatments   349

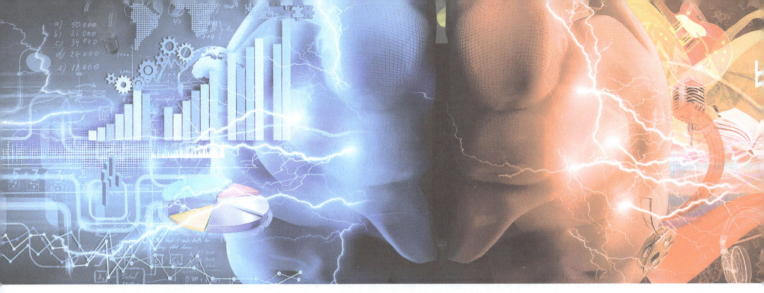

Acknowledgments

The development of this textbook truly was a team effort and the authors wish to offer their gratitude to several individuals, without whom this project would not have been as good, fulfilling, fun, or purposeful.

First, to our Lord and Savior, Jesus Christ, we offer immense thanks for the opportunity to write an introductory text that combines psychology and biblical teachings and who also has given us insight, grace, endurance, and guidance as we've written. Without Jesus, everything is meaningless, and this work is dedicated to Him and the advancement of His kingdom.

> *And whatever you do, in word or deed, do everything in the name of the Lord Jesus, giving thanks to God the Father through him (Colossians 3:17, ESV).*

Second, to our families who have always supported us and given us the space and time to write and learn, we are eternally grateful. Our families have stood by us, encouraged us, and in the case of one of the authors, have even grown during the writing of this textbook. We are extremely grateful for their constant support and understanding as we completed this work.

Additionally, we owe a debt that likely cannot be repaid to Bailee Robinson who has led our team with grace, humor, and accountability throughout the entire process. She was invaluable to the success of this project and it is not an overstatement to say that without her, it would still not be complete. Thank you for your wisdom, guidance, and for committing so many nights to editing as we worked on this project.

To Liberty University and the Department of Psychology, we are grateful for the opportunity to teach students about psychology and how God views the many topics explored in the field. It is a high privilege and calling to work at a university in which God's ultimate Truth is pursued and taught, as we all live a life as champions for Christ.

And finally, to the Kendall Hunt Publishing team, thank you for the opportunity to present the field of psychology from a biblical worldview. For your abundant resources and assistance in formatting, editing, and all that goes into putting a project like this together, we are grateful. Thank you also for the authors who contributed to this text before us. We are grateful for your expertise and work. May this textbook help introductory students learn the field of psychology and evaluate the many theories, constructs, and research findings in our field from a biblical worldview.

> *Trust in the Lord with all your heart and do not lean on your own understanding. In all your ways acknowledge him, and he will make straight your paths (Proverbs 3:5–6, ESV).*

A NOTE TO STUDENTS

Your book comes with access to a series of videos which provide further insights and discussion on a number of topics presented in the chapters. The play icon in the margin represents areas where you should watch one of these videos. To access the videos, review the information provided on the inside of this book's back cover.

Chapter

1

The Science of Psychology

LEARNING OBJECTIVES

- ❏ Define psychology.
- ❏ Identify major perspectives within the field.
- ❏ State types of degrees in psychology and common places of employment.
- ❏ Explain the roles of philosophy and physiology in psychology.
- ❏ ⌊Review⌋ the founding schools of thought.
- ❏ Identify key contributors to the founding of psychology.
- ❏ Describe the steps of the scientific method.
- ❏ Differentiate between experimental and nonexperimental research methodologies.
- ❏ List examples of nonexperimental research methodologies.
- ❏ Explain key terms for experimental research methodologies.
- ❏ Assess reliability and validity in research designs.
- ❏ Analyze limitations of various research methodologies.
- ❏ ⌊Emphasize⌋ the need for ethical behavior.
- ❏ ⌊Explore the relationship between psychology and Christianity.
- ❏ Evaluate research from a biblical worldview.⌋

THE INTERSECTION OF PSYCHOLOGY AND PURPOSE

▶ **CHAPTER 1 OVERVIEW**

An introductory psychology class is one of the most popular college courses at nearly every college in the country and this has been the case for many years. There is a good reason for why this is happening. Psychology offers tremendous value to students and that value is transferable to any job or relationship and is beneficial for self-improvement. In fact, in a recent ranking of college classes, *USA Today* rated an introductory psychology class as their number one most highly recommended course for all college students. They stated "You'll come out of a psychology class with a deeper understanding of the human mind, which in turn will help you interact and communicate well with others. Psychology prepares students for a wide range of careers, and students can use what they've learned to help them interpret behaviors and handle with a wide range of emotions" (Jones, 2015, para. 4). The prestigious publication *Forbes* suggests that, for even those focused on such fields as business or finance, psychology is a must-have class. "Understanding what motivates peoples' thoughts and behaviors, including how emotions impact finances, will lead to more valuable client relationships" (Forbes Finance Council, 2018, par. 11) says Jay Shah at Personal Capital. So, no matter what you plan to do as part of your educational or career path, an introductory psychology course can add a lot of value.

This course is important for other reasons as well. Instead of emphasizing the need for specific titles and experiences, organizations are shifting toward a focus on the skills that a potential employee may bring (Curtin, 2017). At tech companies, like Facebook, this is especially true as their definition of skills have shifted from things like computer programming to being able to work and support a team. "We actually value skills over experience in the grand scheme of things, skills really matter the most" (Hess, 2019), said Janelle Gale, Facebook's vice president of human resources. And, the experiences to which she was referring included things like programming classes. LinkedIn, the world's largest professional network focusing on career development, recently analyzed hundreds of thousands of job postings in order to determine the skills companies need the most. They found employers are looking for workers with both soft skills (e.g., soft skills are personal habits and traits that shape how you work, on your own and with others) and hard skills (e.g., hard skills are technical knowledge or training that you have gained through any life experience, including in your career or education). Their top five soft skills included (1) creativity, (2) persuasion, (3) collaboration, (4) adaptability, and (5) time management. All of these skills are covered in some way as part of an introduction to psychology course. Of their top five hard skills, three are especially relevant to this course and include (1) artificial intelligence, (2) analytical reasoning, and (3) people management (Hess, 2019). Furthermore, according to Indeed.com, advertised as the world's number one job posting site, their list of top in demand skills include:

1. Integrity
2. Dependability
3. Effective communication
4. Open-mindedness
5. Teamwork
6. Creativity
7. Problem-solving
8. Critical thinking
9. Adaptability
10. Organization
11. Willingness to learn
12. Empathy (Indeed Career Guide, 2020)

⌐This list of important skills are all relevant to psychology and, at various levels, will be covered in this course. It seems that psychology is also a good business.

⌐Psychology is not just important for career advancement. It is important because it is one of the few courses allowing you to apply material you are learning to yourself in real time—how you learn, how you think, and how you act, as well as potentially why. Psychology can equip you to gain a better appreciation for your unique skills and how those skills can be used to expand your life purpose. For Christians, all aspects of life are intended to be in service to God and to His glory. So, our vocation is also a key component of our ministry.

What Does the Bible Say?

⌐In the simplest possible explanation, our purpose is to love God with all that we have. This includes the work that we do to support ourselves and potentially our family and the preparation for that work through our studies.

Matthew 22:36–40 ESV

"'Teacher, which is the great commandment in the Law?' And he said to him, 'You shall love the Lord your God with all your heart and with all your soul and with all your mind. This is the great and first commandment'."

Colossians 3:23 ESV

"Whatever you do, work heartily, as for the Lord and not for men."⌐

⌐Our purpose in life is complex though, in part, because who we are and how we live is complex. Not everyone's work will be their life purpose but everyone should have purpose in their work. It is truly a blessing to be able to engage daily in work that feeds our soul as well as adds important value to the world. Our lives can be improved if the work we do aligns most closely with things we are good at and dedicated to. A recent study finds people who have a purpose in life have a surprising benefit in that they sleep better at night. Lots of other research has confirmed that having a purpose outside yourself is good not only for your mental health but also for your physical health, longevity, and even your genes (Lewis et al., 2017; Steptoe et al., 2015). It is an interesting question to ask why having a life of purpose might lead to all these health benefits. One big reason is that it takes the focus off ourselves, which seems to have a number of significant health benefits. Much of our mental anguish, stress, and depression is linked to rumination and worry-based, self-referential thoughts. Transferring your focus from yourself to others likely works to quiet worry and distress about one's own troubles, much in the same way meditation is known to reduce activity in the "self-focused-centers" of the brain. Such change in focus from "me" to "us" is also linked to better brain function, less depression, and improved immune function. Additionally, serving others helps build gratitude. Gratitude is the opposite of entitlement and a sense of entitlement produces the exact opposite of the negative behavioral outcomes noted above. Being part of something larger than yourself might be one of the best things we can do, both for others and ourselves. Some people seek out their purpose through jobs, titles, and the associated income. However, that does not lead to a satisfying life. Although our identity can be connected to our work, our value is not entirely vocational; it's not healthy to work and live like that.

⌐Figuring this out certainly won't occur without deliberate thinking and planning. In order to help you conceptualize the idea of purpose, consider it as an intersection of four important factors (Figure 1.1): (1) things you love to do, (2) things the world needs, (3) things that allow you to make a living wage, and (4) things that you are especially good at doing, thus bringing glory to God. From a vocational point of view, the diagram can be simplified to what you give the world (i.e., the top half, skills) vs. what the world gives you (i.e., the bottom half, money). A great activity would be to make a list of five to ten things for each of the four factors related to purpose. Because psychology touches on so many diverse topics, it is a great class to help you explore purpose. Throughout the course, continue to come back to the list in these four areas and add and subtract from the list as needed. By the end of the course, you might have more insight into your mission, vocation, profession, and passion as well as collectively, your purpose.

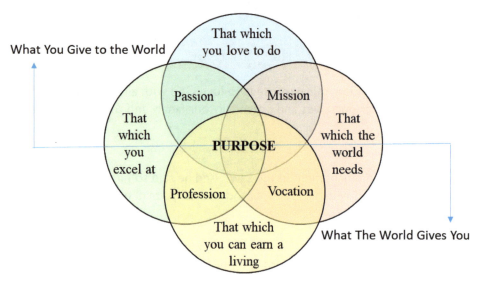

Figure 1.1   ⌊Intersecting areas that comprise purpose.⌋
Source: Brian Kelley

Quotes about Purpose

⌊"True wisdom consists in two things: Knowledge of God and Knowledge of Self."—— John Calvin

"There is no worse screen to block out the Spirit than confidence in our own intelligence."——John Calvin

"The mystery of human existence lies not in just staying alive, but in finding something to live for."——Fyodor Dostoyevsky

"True happiness… is not attained through self-gratification, but through fidelity to a worthy purpose."——Helen Keller

"Musicians must make music, artists must paint, poets must write if they are ultimately to be at peace with themselves. What humans can be, they must be."——Abraham Maslow

"If you can't figure out your purpose, figure out your passion. For your passion will lead you right into your purpose."——Rev. T. D. Jakes

"You don't create or design your purpose; you discover it. It's a process of looking inward and upward. Inward at the unique passions and talents you possess, and upward at your creator who promises to 'guide the humble in what is right.'"——Wesley Wiley

"Knowledge of the sciences is so much smoke apart from the heavenly science of Christ."——John Calvin

"Three things are necessary for the salvation of man: to know what he ought to believe; to know what he ought to desire; and to know what he ought to do."——Thomas Aquinas⌋

What Does the Bible Say?

The Bible has a lot to say about purpose. Our purpose is to serve God and others and to work diligently to accomplish those goals. Consider the following verses related to purpose.

2 Peter 1:3–8 ESV, Confirm Your Calling and Election

"His divine power has granted to us all things that pertain to life and godliness, through the knowledge of him who called us to his own glory and excellence, by which he has granted to us his precious and very great promises, so that through them you may become partakers of the divine nature, having escaped from the corruption that is in the world because of sinful desire. For this very reason, make every effort to supplement your faith with virtue, and virtue with knowledge, and knowledge with self-control, and self-control with steadfastness, and steadfastness with godliness, and godliness with brotherly affection, and brotherly affection with love. For if these qualities are yours and are increasing, they keep you from being ineffective or unfruitful in the knowledge of our Lord Jesus Christ."

Ephesians 2:8–10 ESV, By Grace through Faith

"For by grace you have been saved through faith. And this is not your own doing; it is the gift of God, not a result of works, so that no one may boast. For we are his workmanship, created in Christ Jesus for good works, which God prepared beforehand, that we should walk in them."

Romans 12:1–5 ESV

"I appeal to you therefore, brothers, by the mercies of God, to present your bodies as a living sacrifice, holy and acceptable to God, which is your spiritual worship. Do not be conformed to this world, but be transformed by the renewal of your mind, that by testing you may discern what is the will of God, what is good and acceptable and perfect. For by the grace given to me I say to everyone among you not to think of himself more highly than he ought to think, but to think with sober judgment, each according to the measure of faith that God has assigned. For as in one body we have many members, and the members do not all have the same function, so we, though many, are one body in Christ, and individually members one of another."

INTRODUCTION TO PSYCHOLOGY

The study of behavior and mental processes is exceedingly complicated—life can feel like a seemingly endless maze of reactions, choices, and dead ends. This should not be surprising though because we (i.e., humans) are exceedingly complicated. Just think about how many behaviors and thoughts you experience across a single day. More specifically, consider all the decisions you make from second-to-second (e.g., while driving), hour-to-hour (e.g., while working), and day-to-day (e.g., engaging in relationships)—easily, in culmination, thousands upon thousands of decisions in just one day. Trying to manage, understand, and plan for just your own life seems at times not just daunting but impossible.

How do we weigh all of the information available to make good decisions? For example, why did you pick out the clothes you are wearing now? Why

© ra2 studio/Shutterstock.com

did you select one thing for breakfast over another (i.e., if you even had breakfast and, if you didn't, why?)? Why did you stay up late watching television while simultaneously playing on your phone, when you had so much work to do? Is it hard to answer these rather simple questions? Often, in fact more often than not, we don't have direct access to the underlying mental processes involved in our own decision-making. This means we rarely know why or how we make our own decisions. So, if this is true, how do we even begin to understand the behavior of other people? If it is hard to understand people we know well, like family and friends, then how do we begin to understand the behavior of strangers or groups of people, especially if those people seem very different from ourselves? To this end, how do we begin to understand such behaviors as to be able to understand, explain, and predict them?

Predicting behaviors is one of the essential goals of behavioral science because prediction allows for future planning. The same way you like to check the weather so you can plan your day accordingly, we embrace the comfort of being able to do the same with people. Of course, weather predictions are not always right nor are even well-researched predictions about the behavior of people, but with good methods and data, the accuracy of both can be increased. While people are all different, special, and unique, we operate through similar underlying mechanisms from biological make up, to learning styles, and to cultural influences. Across the planet and across time, people have more similarities than dif-

© Who is Danny/Shutterstock.com

ferences. These similarities make systematic studies of behavior and mental processes possible.

Behavioral scientists study behavior and mental processes to help answer important questions on such contemporary topics as addiction, obesity, loneliness, grief, trauma, memory, attention, perception, and depression as well as many other topics. The study of behavior, psychology, is a scientific discipline. As a scientific field of study, it uses the same approaches as any other area of scientific inquiry. Thus, in order for psychology to be considered a science, it requires psychological conclusions to be based on evidence collected according to the scientific method. The **scientific method**, which will be discussed more in-depth later in this chapter, is a set of orderly steps used to analyze and solve problems—it is universally applied regardless of the specific scientific discipline. However, there are unique challenges to doing research in different disciplines and different perspectives within those disciplines. Additionally, this method uses objectively collected observations as the basis for drawing conclusions. This is important because behavior is the means by which living things respond to an ever-changing environment. **Behavior** is also defined as an action, that is, something observable and measurable; however, just because it can be observed and measured doesn't mean it is easy to interpret and understand. The goal of behavioral scientists is to understand a particular subject, which can be a person, a mouse, or a chimpanzee. Behaviors, or actions, are often under the direct control of mental processes, that is, the inner workings of the brain. So, behavioral scientists are interested in understanding events such as thinking, planning, reasoning, creating, and dreaming and the behaviors that emanate from the processes.

Scientific method: A set of orderly steps used to analyze and solve problems universally applied across scientific disciplines. The framework for the systematic study of behavior and mental processes.

Behavior: An action; something observable and measurable.

ᴸIn research, controlling behavior doesn't imply one is being denied choices. Instead, psychologists view controlling behavior as a means to empower people with the ability to control or manage their lives more effectively. For example, psychologists may use a particular intervention to help people eliminate unhealthy behavior, like cigarette smoking. Similarly, different parenting practices have different effects on children, so teaching parents better ways to control their own behavior could make them better parents. Finally, strangers tend to be reluctant to help people in certain emergency situations. By understanding this pattern of behavior, one might be capable of overcoming these feelings and offer help. Thus, control is generally something that is passed on to individuals, not some unique power that psychologists alone are capable of yielding. Understanding behavior doesn't make you better at controlling others so much as it makes you better at anticipating different outcomes, increasing motivation, building resiliency, enhancing group/team dynamics, and being a better consumer of information.

ᴸUnderstanding behavior and being able to affect the behavior of individuals and groups is a high demand skill. This is true because we are never separated from managing our own behaviors nor do we accomplish much on our own. While the idea of control can be seen as ominous, it is not. Just like a great coach is able to strategize, what is equally important is the ability to motivate and challenge the players as well as bring their best attributes together for a collective goal—literally and figuratively. Wouldn't you be happier and more successful if you and the people around you understood this? Many future employers think so as psychology is a top recommended course for undergraduate students.

ᴸIf behaviors can be observed, then they can be measured. If they can be measured, then they can be studied and researched. When research is conducted in a specific area and that research is verifiable and has predictive value, then it can generate a scientific fact. This book and all other academic textbooks are full of facts. How much time and money, as well as other resources, are you investing to learn these facts? These facts must be rather valuable to extract so many of your and others' resources. This begs the question, what is a fact and how are they created? This question is one of the most important yet challenging questions for this course. The question is so simple but understanding it is quite complicated.

The Benefits and Limitations of Facts

ᴸIn the simplest description, facts are objective observations of the world and they do not change over time. Examples of such observations include your height or weight and skin or hair color. Each of the aforementioned characteristics can be measured and described with amazing precision. But wait, each can also change across time. So, does that mean that facts easily change over time? Not really, your height and weight on that day and time will always be your height and weight, but it can change. The next time your height and weight is measured, those new numbers become new facts. So, while it can be argued that if facts are unchangeable and things like height and weight change, then how do we reconcile this? It goes to show that sometimes the content and the context is important in deciding about a fact and its value.

© Kheng Guan Toh/Shutterstock.com

There are different types of facts. **Empirical facts** are things we can assert about the way the world operates based upon observational evidence. **Conceptual facts** are things we assert about the way the world operates based on strongly held views often derived from experience. A simple everyday example would be someone saying their tea has a lot of sugar in it versus someone saying the tea is very sweet. It might seem like it is the same thing, but amount of sugar is something that can be empirically determined; that is, the amount of sugar (i.e., weight) in a specific amount of tea (i.e., volume) can be quantified. Conceptual facts tend to be confirmed by reference to the perceptions or ideas whereas empirical facts tend to be confirmed by reference to experience. It is also likely that more empirical facts are based upon direct, measurable experiences, whereas conceptual facts are shaped by reference to concepts. Concepts can be more fluid as they are more dependent and influenced by the individual's unique experiences (e.g., the tea is sweet versus very sweet). However, saying the tea is very sweet relies on an assertion that may not be held by everyone. Even excellent, detailed, and articulate ostensibly factual positions can be wrong—like saying the tea is very sweet. Perhaps, the one person who thought the tea was very sweet consumed some very bitter food or drink just before drinking the tea making it seem very sweet when it was just sweet. It shows that our unique, individual experiences are highly fallible (i.e., imperfect) and our individual experiences can impact our interpretation of the world around us.

Often in science, and especially in research, these types of facts fall along a continuum more so than a clear dichotomy. We often start with conceptual facts and as we engage in the topic area our ability to understand and define the topic in more detail increases, making our observations more accurate and repeatable. This becomes even more challenging as it can be hard to differentiate between a fact versus an opinion or the combination of the two, which could be an assertion based on a fact. Too often, people like to represent their view of the world as a fact when it could very well be a preference or an assumption; this can be true for research findings as well in which the fact is translated into potential value or perhaps policy. For example, about a decade ago, signs at Glacier National Park were installed noting the park's signature, tourist attracting glaciers would be completely gone by 2020. The signs were installed to note the fact that the glaciers would be gone and that fact was supported by an abundance of scientific evidence—empirical evidence. Some went so far is to state the science was entirely settled; climate change (i.e., warming) is occurring, humans caused it, and it is irreversible—the disappearing glaciers were the scientific representation of this fact. In 2017, the park was informed the glaciers would not be melting by that time and the signs should be revised to reflect this new fact (Maxouris & Rose, 2020). It is 2020 now, and the glaciers are still there, and new evidence is showing that they are in fact now expanding not shrinking; so what does that say about the science and about this fact? This fact was presented to guests of the park and featured in other places—like textbooks.

> **Empirical facts:** Things we can assert about the way the world operates based upon observational evidence.
>
> **Conceptual facts:** Things we assert about the way the world operates based on strongly held views often derived from experience.

© Pung/Shutterstock.com

In a similar way, what do we know about the relative safety of lead exposure or prenatal alcohol exposure? What is the safe level of lead in drinking water? What is the safe amount of alcohol to consume while pregnant? These are important and potentially life changing questions. You might be surprised to discover the safe amount of lead in drinking water and alcohol consumed during pregnancy has always trended downward according to research. In the 1960s, the allowable and safe amount of lead was about 60 micrograms per deciliter. By the late 1970s it was dropped to 30 micrograms per deciliter.

© Jean Faucett/Shutterstock.com

Moving to the early 1990s that number was dropped again to 25 and by 2012 it was dropped even further to just 10. The current recommended amount is below 5 micrograms per deciliter (Agency for Toxic Substances and Disease Registry, 2017). The reason for this dramatic shift in concentration over time is because new information—that is, observations—emerged about the neurological, reproductive, and cardiovascular toxicity of lead. As the research on the topic became more sophisticated and the measurements more precise, more harmful effects were discovered and appropriate recommendations and public policy positions followed. This is important because lead can cause serious development problems in exposed children and those problem can be irreversible.

Additionally, it wasn't that long ago that is was considered normal, acceptable, and sometimes encouraged to have a glass of wine while pregnant or perhaps even several glasses. People didn't think much about the consequences of drinking during pregnancy and later child development and dysfunction. Again, over time the safe amount of alcohol recommended during pregnancy dropped and now the recommended amount is zero. That is a radical change from some casual drinking to zero (CDC, 2015, 2018). If you were to read textbooks from different decades past, the facts about lead and alcohol would be reflected in the books but they would be wrong according to today's data and today's facts might be wrong in 5 to 10 years. The fact that science changes is an extremely important point and philosophical concept.

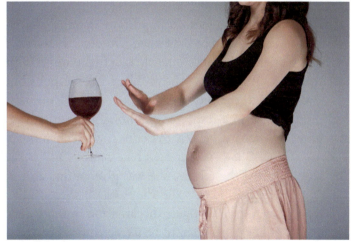

© InnerVisionPRO/Shutterstock.com

Scientific Mistakes and Misconduct

Expanding on the concept and definition of scientific facts, it is further complicated by individual factors like ethics, motivation, and bias as well as just mistakes. Science is actually very competitive and very fast paced. To maintain a successful career as a scientist there are grants to support research, laboratory management of people and equipment, and presentations and publications. With such pressure, there can be challenges and sometimes those challenges are met with short cuts at best and out right cheating and deception at worst. Mistakes can occur in many places along the path from an idea to dissemination of results.

© peterschreiber.media/Shutterstock.com

Considering again the concept and definition of facts, what does it mean to study, learn, and apply facts from a textbook only to find later the research was compromised and shown to be false? Does this happen? Sadly, too often and, even worse, generally after that false information—fake facts—were used to influence or create policy. So, while the study might be retracted and the lead scientist might suffer professional and legal consequences, the policy positions that emerged from the research are rarely retracted or even changed.

For example, just recently, Frances H. Arnold, PhD, who won the Nobel Prize in Chemistry in 2018 and who had a cameo in the hit television show *The Big Bang Theory*, officially retracted one of her prestigious papers in the Journal *Science* (see below). She stated, "It is painful to admit, but important to do so. I apologize to all. I was a bit busy when this was submitted and did not do my job well."

> After publication of the Report "Site-selective enzymatic C—H amidation for synthesis of diverse lactams" (Cho et al., 2019), efforts to reproduce the work showed that the enzymes do not catalyze the reactions with the activities and selectivities claimed. Careful examination of the first author's lab notebook then revealed missing contemporaneous entries and raw data for key experiments. The authors are therefore retracting the paper.

This example provides an important example that mistakes can happen in science and while this mistake could ultimately have been avoided, there is a difference between an oversight and error and deliberate scientific misconduct. It is actually quite impressive in today's culture for such an esteemed scientist to so quickly note the problem, take responsibility, and formally retract the paper.

In contrast to the earlier example, at Duke University in 2013, a researcher working in the lab of a well-known and well-respected pulmonary scientist was arrested for stealing more than $25,000 from the Duke University Health System. The stolen funds were used for purchasing merchandise from a variety of stores. She even created fake receipts to help legitimize her personal shopping spree. Despite the seriousness of the crimes, she was given a fine and sentenced to probation and community service. One quick question is how did the research successfully move forward with those funds removed? The University began to investigate the situation in more detail and discovered a variety of serious problems. In fact, 15 of her papers had to be retracted not because of an accidental error but because of fraudulent data, that is, deliberate misconduct. This same data was used in the procurement of numerous grants in sum worth more than $200 million. The lawsuit is ongoing and could result in the University having to pay back those funds plus penalties, which could be up to three times the amount of the grant awards. Similarly, in 2009 and 2012, Weill Medical College of Cornell University settled cases involving scientists misusing research funding and falsifying data (McCook, 2016; Worrall, 2016). Besides the legality of these cases, what does it say about the nature of scientific facts? While the articles were retracted, they were not removed from textbooks nor were the findings removed from any medical protocols or public policy positions. So, it is likely that many students, researchers, and clinicians have been operating on the positive factual findings from these studies and not even knowing that the information is categorically wrong.

If something is factual and true, then it should be regardless of place or time or investigator. Simply put, if a research study yields a factual outcome through appropriate application of the scientific method, then that same outcome should occur again and again. If that study occurs in the same laboratory a month or year later as well as in a laboratory across the country or globe, then you should see the same outcome. This is no different than following recipes when cooking or baking. No matter where or when, if you follow that recipe, then you should get the same delicious meal.

© everything possible/Shutterstock.com

If not, then there must have been human or mechanical error. Alternatively, perhaps the recipe was never correct. It would be frustrating to work hard at an important meal to have it ruined by a flawed recipe. Similarly, science is dealing with an absolute crisis with replication. Media doesn't help as it elevates and sensationalizes select findings but rarely, if ever, notes retractions or modifications because of ongoing findings (Bohannon, 2015).

A recent study—the largest effort yet to replicate historically important psychological studies—found only 39% could be reproduced. Some scientists might argue that this issue is more common in the behavioral sciences. However, the journal *Nature* carried out a large-scale study on reproducibility of research in the physical and medical sciences and of 1,576 researchers who participated in the study more than 70% reported trying and failing at reproducing another scientist's study. Also, in this study, 52% of the respondents agreed that there was a significant crisis of reproducibility. The top five reasons reported for the lack of irreproducible research was, in order, (1) selective reporting, (2) pressure to publish, (3) low statistical power or poor analysis, (4) not replicated enough in the original lab, and (5) insufficient oversight/mentoring. Also, in the top 10 factors impacting research quality included concerns over fraud (Baker, 2016). This is truly a crisis because so many fundamental facts throughout numerous textbooks read by millions of students are likely to be wrong and those wrong studies might also serve as the stimulus for creating ideas for future research. How much of what you learned so far in your academic and professional life is wrong?

Using Science to Form Conclusion in the Behavioral Sciences

If science is so fallible and it is because it is run by people, then how do we rely on it? Even with all of its problems, it clearly works as the human experience in many ways has drastically improved because of science. Today we have better diagnoses, better treatments, better parenting approaches, better technology, and so on. The appropriate application of scientific methods is a gift that changes lives, but no amount of science, regardless of how great and even if it could be done perfectly, can provide the human experience with absolute truth. Science doesn't work in absolute truths and it never will. It works with people, processes, and probability. However, studying God's creation through science can help us understand His truth.

It is also important to understand how we reach conclusions and define facts from different fields. So, while each field might employ the same scientific method, the factors underlying exactly how a study is carried out can be quite difference across disciplines. Psychology, with goals of explaining, predicting, and controlling behavior is influenced by (1) how well the study variables can be controlled, (2) how complex the study variables are on that behavior—keep in mind that psychology has to take into account biological, behavioral, and sociological factors and all of these across the life span— and (3) how many potential confounds are influencing the outcomes. All of these factors have to be weighed when determining the ultimate conclusions of the research findings.

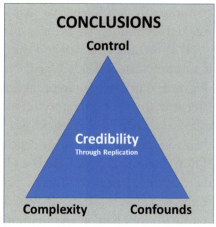

Source: Brian Kelley

⌐The combination and culmination of these factors allow conclusions to be reached based on various levels of confidence, and that confidence is based in part on statistical probabilities. Contrast psychology with physics, for example. Physics while being complicated has considerably more control and many fewer confounds; as such, replication of such work is much easier compared to psychology. For this reason, the facts in physics are often weighted differently compared to facts in psychology. Psychology could be argued to be more complex than physics considering how hard it is to control all of the factors around behavior; there are also considerably more potential confounds, both known and even unknown. Because of these factors, there is just less ability to control all of the needed factors in a psychological study. Less control, greater complexity, and increased confounds results in less potential credibility of the empirical findings, thus impacting the factual conclusions that can be reached. This should translate into greater reliance on replication. Meaning, stating something is a fact in psychology should really only occur after replication and only if those results demonstrate the same outcomes. This does not mean that psychology is less of a science compared to other sciences. It just means there are more challenges and those challenges impact the ability to draw more credible conclusions. So, a fact in psychology would likely have more disclaimers around it compared to a fact in physics. However, we rely on advances in both fields to help improve the human condition.

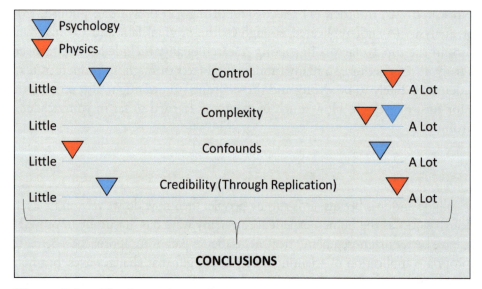

Figure 1.2 ⌐The figure depicts how psychology and physics approach common issues differently.⌐

Source: Brian Kelley

How should we approach behavioral science specifically, and science more generally, given all these limitations? The answer is with both enthusiasm and skepticism. It is an exciting time in history to be able to be engaged in psychology and to use the scientific method to gain information, knowledge, and wisdom, particularly if your goal is to improve the human condition. There are so many questions that still must be asked and answered. There is so much we still don't know. With each new advancement and innovation, there are numerous questions about its impact and application. For example, consider the research being carried out right now on the impact of modern mobile technology on child development. This field didn't even exist 10 years ago and there is so much we don't know and so much we need to know.

It would be easy to look at the limitations of science and decide to discredit such efforts, but would you really want those efforts discredited when you go to the doctor or when taking a new medication? Do you expect the safety of your car or the plane you fly in to undergo rigorous (scientific) safety testing? You might argue that you have no intention of being a behavioral scientist, so this level of detail and rigor won't apply. This is a disadvantageous position to take because, as noted previously, results from behavioral science research is used for decision-making and policy positions in nearly every field but especially so in mental health and substance treatment, education, child development, parenting, criminal justice, and prevention. It is to your personal and professional advantage to be equipped to better understand behavior as you are never separated from it.

Everyone can benefit from a greater understanding of scientific processes and critical thinking. Noted in Figure 1.3, there is a systematic and stepwise structure to understanding and applying scientific information with the goal of being equipped to not only understand scientific content but to also effectively evaluate it. Furthermore, with greater investments in content knowledge and critical analysis, one can begin to create new findings in science which could result in a life changing idea, process, or product. On the other hand, studying psychology specifically could help you be a better version of yourself and thereby positively impact the people around you.

Increasing Knowledge and Insight

RESEARCH IN ACTION: FORGIVENESS

The scientific method and studying in general allow for a systematic increase in knowledge and insight. In fact, most programs of study tend to follow this approach from undergraduate studies to graduate studies. Typically, across scholarly academic development, there is a predictable way in which learner's gain knowledge and insight. This process is noted in Figure 1.3. Although scientific processes and increased content knowledge can radically change the way we function in the world, no amount of this work can produce discernment or absolute truth. Furthermore, no amount of scientific advancement can determine the purpose or value. This is true of ideas as well as people. To that end, how much are you worth? Can money be attached to someone's worth? Because science is always in the process of revising and refining as well as founded on probabilities, it cannot produce absolute truth. It can obviously add tremendous value to our lives in the form of improving the way in which we interact and understand the world, but it can never fully inform us of our worth in the world. The Bible is uniquely positioned to address issues of truth, value, and purpose. So, while science can help us elevate our thinking, its processes, while impressive, are limited. Also, uniquely the Bible allows us to discern from the top of this process down and can serve as a filter when it comes to evaluation of scientific information.

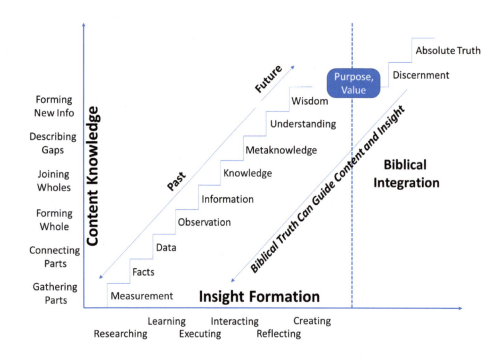

Figure 1.3 ⌊The stepped progression of knowledge and insight.⌋

Source: Brian Kelley

⌊Figure 1.3 captures the complex relationship between developing content knowledge and forming insights. A tremendous amount of work is required to develop knowledge and wisdom on just one general topic let alone in many topic areas. Even after about 13 years of formal education (K-12), many individuals continue on with their education. In fact, formal education beyond high school includes associates level (2 years), bachelors level (4 years), masters level (6 years), doctoral level (9 or more years), and even postdoctoral training (another 2–3 years). To become a real expert on a topic, it may very well require 12 years of intense study after high school. If one went straight through, he or she would be nearly 30 before truly being recognized as an expert in a specific field. That is just a tremendous investment in formal education to be an expert on a subject. During that process of formal study, it is likely that one would work their way up the above graph and along the way learn to apply their studies to creating new facts, information, and knowledge. Certainly this process would produce knowledge, and optimistically this process would produce wisdom; at least, wisdom around a specific area. That wisdom though doesn't always guarantee good outcomes. Unfortunately, biases and other individual factors can interfere with interpretation of observations and impede good decision-making (or one can only see their decision as good when they may not be).

⌊So, while science is extremely useful as it allows a planned and objective approach to problem-solving, it is not able to define something's or someone's purpose or value. Fortunately, a biblical worldview can provide a formal framework around content knowledge and insight formation and that view can help guide the process from the top-down as opposed to just the bottom-up.

Table 1.1A ⌐Stepped Definitions for Figure 1.3

Term	Definition
Measurement	Measurement is the act of operationalizing an object or event and then determining the best way to quantify the amount, degree, length, etc., of that object or event.
Fact	A fact is a generally accepted occurrence or event. Ideally, this would be measurable and falsifiable. However, a fact is true only for a limited amount of time because the emergence of new information or data can change how a phenomena is understood.
Data	Data is the result of measurement where there is some sort of qualitative or quantitative information collected.
Observation	Observation is the act of recognizing the data and noting patterns, themes, and specific occurrences within the data.
Information	From measurement, data, and observation, stems information, Information is the raw data, numbers, and raw quantities with no subjective attachment or observation.
Knowledge	Knowledge is the meaning that an individual applies to the information and the maintenance of this information with the intention to generalize it to other situations.
Metaknowledge	Metaknowledge is the awareness of what is known and unknown. This requires a great deal of awareness and content knowledge in order to assess and evaluate the actual degree of knowledge on a topic.
Understanding	Understanding is a sort of "mental grasp" on a concept. Understanding a concept is the power to make experiences intelligible by calling on previous knowledge and recognizing that they may not know all aspects of the situation, to move toward deeper comprehension and meaning through situations.
Wisdom	Moving from understanding to wisdom, wisdom is the ability to draw connections between understandings, and with an awareness of metaknowledge, an individual uses wisdom to influence the present and future.
Discernment	Discernment is the application of biblical wisdom in specific settings for the purposes of making virtuous decisions. The ability to determine the best course of action within a situation with complex dynamics and nuances.
Absolute truth	Truth is absolute. Truth comes from two sources: God's word and God's works. That is, the truth can be discerned through the scientific discovery (God's creation/works) and research process; however, truth is ultimately revealed through his word, the Bible. All truth is ultimately God's truth. Absolute truth exists and is unchanging whether it is believed or not.
Purpose, value	Purpose is the reason for which something is done or created or for which something exists, whereas value is the regard that something is held to deserve: the importance, worth, or usefulness of something. Science is not capable of determining the purpose or value of things; however, God has already determined that every human has infinite and eternal value.⌐

Table 1.1B   Content Knowledge for Figure 1.3

Term	Definition
Gathering parts	Gathering parts is the foundation of every well-constructed position. This consists of being immersed in the current information, knowledge, and wisdom on any particular topic.
Connecting parts	After gathering information, theoretical constructs emerge that are intertwined and show overlap in practice. It is seeing the potential benefit of uniting ideas.
Forming wholes	Forming wholes is taking the parts one has connected and join them together in a theoretical construct. In this step, with observations, facts, and measurement, one can create a new hypothesis for how things might work together.
Joining wholes	Next, with information based on the formation of wholes and how they are connected, theories can be formed combining constructs. This can also occur when two seemingly disparate ideas are brought together in a new way to address a problem.
Describing gaps	Even when constructs are joined, they do not explain the entire phenomenon. It is critical to knowledge gain to note the limitations in ideas and practices as a means to develop knowledge or skills to address those gaps.
Forming new info	As we measure new constructs, establish facts, collect data, observe the patterns to form information and create knowledge, our understanding of what we don't know about these concepts helps us create research and apply it to new settings. Thus, forming new information is really about a cumulative process that results in the dissemination of new findings into information ready to be tested in a real-world setting.

Table 1.1C   Insight Information for Figure 1.3

Term	Definition
Researching	The act of researching is systematically investigating all sources of information for data, observing your own data, inspecting, and utilizing measurements. One researches with the intent of learning, creating, and utilizing the data.
Learning	Learning is the natural by-product of researching and acquiring information through observation, data, and measurement.
Executing	Executing is carrying out a plan that is created through learning, based on the information and decided upon by knowledge that is acquired. It is hypothesis formation.
Interacting	Assessing the impact of hypothesis testing and determining the relative impact of one variable on another or the interplay between ideas.
Reflecting	To think deeply and carefully about the ideas and outcomes. To integrate information into the existing literature or database of ideas and theories. Innovation is a result of introspection and critical analysis with the goal of advancing an idea.
Creating	Creating occurs after much research, information, and critical analysis of presuppositions occurs. Creating is bringing new information (data, measurements, knowledge) into existence. Innovation is often the direct result of tremendous content knowledge and testing of numerous ideas to build something new.

In order to understand psychology and increase your knowledge and insight, you must begin thinking like a behavioral scientist. Do not naively believe everything you read and hear about human behavior. During this course, you must keep the following critical thinking questions in mind:

1. What am I being asked to believe or accept as true and factual?
2. What evidence is available to support this assertion and how was it collected?
3. Are there alternative explanations or other ways to interpret the evidence?
4. What additional evidence would help in evaluating other explanations?
5. Has the finding been appropriately replicated in the same and different research settings?
6. What conclusions are most reasonable, most logical, and most practical?
7. Do the facts through conclusions align with biblical principles?

Evaluating the Value of Information

How should we consider the experimental methods, data collection, research conclusions, and policy positions on controversial issues such as:

1. Genetic engineering
2. Climate change
3. Gun control
4. Child discipline
5. Gender studies
6. IQ testing
7. Minimum wage
8. School choice
9. Loneliness
10. Income inequality

To address any of the issues above, or any other complex topic, it is likely that you would have to work through the steps provided in Figure 1.3 as you try to make sense of the large volume of information available on any given subject. An Internet search on stress yields 1.8 billion results, a search on depression yields over 800 million results, a search on loneliness yields over 640 million results, a search on drug abuse yields over 600 million results, a search on anxiety yields 400 million results. Having lots of information is seldom the problem; however, being able to determine that information's value is going to be a lot more difficult. There is a typical way in which people process and think about information. It takes a lot of time, energy, and focus to become an expert on a topic. It is worth the investment and learning is never wasted.

What Does the Bible Say?

The Bible has a lot to say about learning and wisdom both as encouragement and as warnings! Consider the verses below.

Ecclesiastes 9:16–18 ESV

"But I say that wisdom is better than might, though the poor man's wisdom is despised and his words are not heard. The words of the wise heard in quiet are better than the shouting of a ruler among fools. Wisdom is better than weapons of war, but one sinner destroys much good."

Ecclesiastes 12:9–13 ESV

"Besides being wise, the Preacher also taught the people knowledge, weighing and studying and arranging many proverbs with great care. The Preacher sought to find words of delight, and uprightly he wrote words of truth. The words of the wise are like goads, and like nails firmly fixed are the collected sayings; they are given by one Shepherd. My son, beware of anything beyond these. Of making many books there is no end, and much study is a weariness of the flesh. The end of the matter; all has been heard. Fear God and keep his commandments, for this is the whole duty of man."

James 1:5–6 ESV

"If any of you lacks wisdom, let him ask God, who gives generously to all without reproach, and it will be given him. But let him ask in faith, with no doubting, for the one who doubts is like a wave of the sea that is driven and tossed by the wind."

Ephesians 5:15–21

"Look carefully then how you walk, not as unwise but as wise, making the best use of the time, because the days are evil. Therefore do not be foolish, but understand what the will of the Lord is. And do not get drunk with wine, for that is debauchery, but be filled with the Spirit, addressing one another in psalms and hymns and spiritual songs, singing and making melody to the Lord with your heart, giving thanks always and for everything to God the Father in the name of our Lord Jesus Christ, submitting to one another out of reverence for Christ."

While it is important to gain knowledge and wisdom in this world, no amount of worldly wisdom can replace the smallest bit of biblical truth.

Matthew 16:26 ESV

"For what will it profit a man if he gains the whole world and forfeits his soul? Or what shall a man give in return for his soul?"

Ecclesiastes 7:5 ESV

"It is better for a man to hear the rebuke of the wise than to hear the song of fools."

1 Corinthians 1:18–31 ESV

"For the word of the cross is folly to those who are perishing, but to us who are being saved it is the power of God. For it is written, 'I will destroy the wisdom of the wise, and the discernment of the discerning I will thwart.' Where is the one who is wise? Where is the scribe? Where is the debater of this age? Has not God made foolish the wisdom of the world? For since, in the wisdom of God, the world did not know God through wisdom, it pleased God through the folly of what we preach to save those who believe. For Jews demand signs and Greeks seek wisdom, but we preach Christ crucified, a stumbling block to Jews and folly to Gentiles, but to those who are called, both Jews and Greeks, Christ the power of God and the wisdom of God. For the foolishness of God is wiser than men, and the weakness of God is stronger than men. For consider your calling, brothers: not many of you were wise according to worldly standards, not many were powerful, not many were of noble birth. But God chose what is foolish in the world to shame the wise; God chose what is weak in the world to shame the strong; God chose what is low and despised in the world, even things that are not, to bring to nothing things that are, so that no human being might boast in the presence of God. And because of him you are in Christ Jesus, who became to us wisdom from God, righteousness and sanctification and redemption, so that, as it is written, 'Let the one who boasts, boast in the Lord.'"

1 Corinthians 2:6–11 ESV

"Yet among the mature we do impart wisdom, although it is not a wisdom of this age or of the rulers of this age, who are doomed to pass away. But we impart a secret and hidden wisdom of God, which God decreed before the ages for our glory. None of the rulers of this age understood this, for if they had, they would not have crucified the Lord of glory. But, as it is written, 'What no eye has seen, nor ear heard, nor the heart of man imagined, what God has prepared for those who love him'—these things God has revealed to us through the Spirit. For the Spirit searches everything, even the depths of God. For who knows a person's thoughts except the spirit of that person, which is in him? So also no one comprehends the thoughts of God except the Spirit of God."

Lilienfeld et al. (2010) recently published a book examining myths in popular psychology. Take a look at some of the chapter titles below:

- "Most People Use Only 10% of Their Brain Power"
- "Extrasensory Perception Is a Well-Established Scientific Phenomenon"
- "Subliminal Messages Can Persuade People to Purchase Products"
- "Playing Mozart's Music to Infants Boosts Their Intelligence"
- "Most People Experience a Midlife Crisis in Their 40s or Early 50s"
- "Intelligence Tests Are Biased Against Certain Groups of People"
- "The Defining Feature of Dyslexia Is Reversing Letters"
- "Researchers Have Demonstrated That Dreams Possess Symbolic Meaning"
- "Opposites Attract: We Are Romantically Attracted to People Who Differ From Us"
- "People's Responses to Inkblots Tell Us a Great Deal About Their Personalities"
- "People with Schizophrenia Have Multiple Personalities"
- "Most Mentally Ill People Are Violent"

© iQoncept/Shutterstock.com

And, other myths that have been perpetuated include:

- Psychology is pretty much just common sense wrapped in fancy words
- People are more left- or right-brained
- There are many different learning styles, and everyone is a genius in their own way
- Really smart people tend to be crazy
- Lie detectors never lie—they are always right
- Eyewitness testimonies are highly accurate
- Hypnosis is a great tool for uncovering repressed memories
- Always go with your gut instinct

- Holding in angry emotions can give you a heart attack
- Stress is always bad
- Adolescence is a time of rebellion

⌐Being able to differentiate between facts and truth provides the necessary foundation to think critically about psychology.⌐

PSYCHOLOGY DEFINED

Psychology is the systematic investigation of human behavior and thought. This means psychologists study what people do and think and they study this in an organized and consistent manner. In the next section, we discuss the origins of psychology and how the field has evolved over time. For example, even the definition of psychology

> ⌐**Psychology:** Systematic investigation of human behavior and thought.⌐

has grown and it is important to note psychologists now recognize the importance of studying behavior and thought (commonly referred to as cognition) and not just overt actions. In addition, psychologists are not limited to studying humans. Frequently, psychologists study animals, too.

⌐Many people enter the study of psychology thinking it is mostly going to reveal or explain commonsense phenomenon or serve as a precursor to counseling. Both assumptions are completely wrong. Usually, students figure this out on their own within the first 3 chapters of an *Introduction to Psychology* textbook (e.g., like you are reading right now). Psychology is an increasingly complex area of study and unique compared to the other science because it integrates many subdisciplines and perspectives to help explain behavior and mental processes. For example, the study of psychology is simultaneously a **natural**, **social**, and **behavioral science**. **Biological psychologists** are interested in how genes, the brain, the nervous system, and the endocrine system impact on behavior. Because drugs influence one or

more of these processes, they would be of interest to biological psychologists. **Social psychologists** are interested in how interpersonal and group dynamics as well as more specific topics like social media, prejudice, religion, bullying, criminal activity, and substance abuse as well as the application of this information to change attitudes, public perceptions, and behavioral economics. **Behavioral psychologists** study important phenomena like learning, memory, decision-making, reward, and behavioral modification. What makes these areas of study even more complicated is that the biopsychosocial approach of psychology is also embedded within a lifespan perspective, which means that each approach has to give attention to how an organism changes across its life. In summary, every psychological issue should be addressed from a biological, social, and behavioral approach while simultaneously giving consideration to how changes across age might impact one or more of those approaches.

⌐Psychology is also unique as a field of study because it is simultaneously a **basic, translational, clinical science, and prevention science**. The goal of basic scientists is to describe, explain, predict, and control behavior and this occurs without any clear clinical

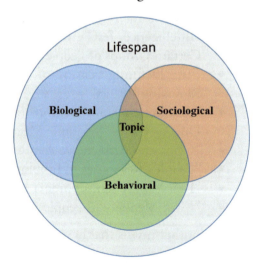

FIGURE 1.4   ⌐Areas of science within psychology.⌐

Source: Brian Kelley

objective—often, it is referred to as research for the sake of knowledge gain. Research in basic science helps explain the big "why" meaning why does this phenomenon operate this way. It is more focused on describing behavior. Translational science is an effort to build on basic scientific research to create new therapies, medical procedures, or diagnostics. The applied psychologists also share each of these goals, but also includes an additional goal, which is to improve the human condition or one's quality of life often through improving or creating a better treatment. Thus, applied researchers are concerned with the big "how" meaning how can we use information to make treatments or interventions better. It is more concerned with solving practical problems. Prevention science is a framework for studies on how to prevent and/or reduce negative medical, social, and emotional impacts before they occur; it is often an extension of clinical work in the sense that scientists work to prevent the occurrence or reoccurrence of a particular problem like depression or substance abuse. However, prevention science could also be focused on community issues such as human trafficking, gang activity, or teen pregnancy. Almost always, advances in basic science lay the groundwork for translation science that works to advance clinical science.

© Gorodenkoff/Shutterstock.com

GOALS OF THE FIELD OF PSYCHOLOGY

⬥ RESEARCH
ND STATISTICS:
FOUNDATION
PSYCHOLOGY

There are two main goals of the field of psychology:

1. Conduct research in psychological phenomena for the purpose of understanding, explaining, predicting, and controlling human behavior, cognition, and experience.
2. Use the knowledge gained from psychological research to promote human well-being (through counseling, interventions, social programs, etc.).

These two goals of the field of psychology can be seen in the goal statements of the leading professional organizations in the field. According to the Association for Psychological Science (APS), psychological science "has the ability to transform society for the better and must play a central role in advancing human welfare and the public interest" (Association for Psychological Science, p. 1). Through promoting psychological science, the APS seeks to further our understanding of psychological principles for the purpose of improving the welfare of individuals. Similarly, the American Psychological Association (APA) states that they promote research in psychology for the purpose of making a positive impact on social and individual issues (APA, 2020). Additionally, the Christian Association for Psychological Studies (CAPS) states they aim to study the integration of Christianity and the behavioral sciences at both theoretical and applied levels and promote research and educational opportunities that advance the mental health disciplines as avenues of ministry in and to the world (CAPS, 2020).

As is reflected by each of these national organizations, the field of psychology aims to understand psychological phenomena for the purpose of improving the welfare of all people. As a student in psychology, you will learn about the major theories and principles that relate to a variety of human experiences as you grow in your understanding of how to use psychological knowledge to help others.

In fact, in addition to goals for the field, the APA has set five goals for you, as a student in a psychology course. As you go through the material in each chapter, keep these goals for psychology students in mind (APA, 2020):

- **Goal 1. Knowledge Base in Psychology**
  You will demonstrate fundamental knowledge and comprehension of the major concepts, theoretical perspectives, historical trends, and empirical findings to discuss how psychological principles apply to behavioral problems.
- **Goal 2. Scientific Inquiry and Critical Thinking**
  You will demonstrate scientific reasoning and problem-solving, including effective research methods.
- **Goal 3: Ethical and Social Responsibility in a Diverse World**
  You will apply ethical standards to evaluate psychological science and practice and you will develop ethically and socially responsible behaviors for professional and personal settings in a landscape that involves increasing diversity.
- **Goal 4: Communication**
  You will demonstrate competence in writing and in oral and interpersonal communication skills.
- **Goal 5. Professional Development**
  You will apply psychological content and skills to career goals and develop meaningful professional direction for life after graduation.

If you are interested in learning more about the mission and work of different organizations in psychology, please visit the following websites:

- American Psychological Association (APA): www.apa.org
- Association for Psychological Science (APS): www.psychologicalscience.org
- Christian Association for Psychological Studies (CAPS): www.caps.net

---

Majors Perspectives, Types of Degrees, and Common Employment

Psychology is a diverse field. Although most of us might think of a psychologist as someone who provides therapy to individuals, this is not a complete picture of the field of psychology. As seen above, the field of psychology is both a scientific field and an applied field. Scientists in the field study various aspects of human behavior and they do so from a variety of perspectives. Counselors, social workers, clinical psychologists, and other applied psychologists then use this research to help individuals through counseling, community interventions, and in the business world. Table 1.2 highlights the various subareas of the field of psychology.

© iQoncept/Shutterstock.com

Table 1.2

Clinical psychologists	Work with individuals who have ⌊psychological⌋ disorders
Cognitive and perceptual psychologists	Study human memory, thinking, and perception
Community psychologists	Work to improve the lives of individuals within a community and assist individuals in locating needed community resources
Counseling psychologists	Work with individuals to help with everyday life stressors
Developmental psychologists	Study human development throughout the life span, from birth to death
Educational psychologists	Study how people learn and ways to make teaching practices more effective for learners
Engineering psychologists	Study how people work with machines, commonly referred to as human factors
Environmental psychologists	Study the interaction of the person and the environment (including the physical and social settings)
Evolutionary psychologists	Focus on how evolution impacts thoughts, feelings, and behavior
Experimental psychologists	Use experimental methods to study a wide range of topics
Forensic psychologists	Apply psychological theories and research findings to the legal setting
Health psychologists	Study factors that impact an individual's health and wellness
Industrial/organizational psychologists	Apply psychological theories, methodology, and findings to workplace settings and issues
Neuropsychologists (and behavioral neuropsychologists)	Study the brain and its relation to behavior
Quantitative and measurement psychologists	Focus on designing experiments and analyzing data for a wide range of topics
Rehabilitation psychologists	Work with individuals with disabilities to address rehabilitation needs
School psychologists	Deliver a variety of psychological services to those in the school setting
Social psychologists	Study how behaviors and thoughts are influenced by others
Sport psychologists	Work with athletes, especially on motivational issues to improve performance

As you can see from this list, psychology is a very broad field and you can do almost anything! There are three main types of degrees in the field. The most basic degree is a bachelor's degree. The bachelor's degree is normally attained in 4 years, requiring over 30 hours in the field. This provides a general overview of the disciplines and graduates have strong communication and research skills. The next degree is the master's degree. At this level, students begin to specialize in the perspectives we discussed in Table 1.2. The master's degree typically requires an additional 2 years of course work beyond the bachelor's degree and for many ⌞counseling or applied⌟ specialty areas, a practicum or internship is required. Finally, individuals can obtain a doctorate degree in psychology. This can take an additional 2 or more years beyond the master's degree. It is important to know what the job outlook is like for a discipline before you consider a career in that area.

What Can Be Done with a Psychology Degree?

⌞If you are looking for more information about the field, and types of career options you could have with a psychology degree, check out these additional resources.

- www.apa.org/careers/resources/guides/careers
- https://www.psyccareers.com/
- https://www.apa.org/gradpsych/2011/03/cover-sunny
- https://www.psychologydegree411.com/careers/#bach
- Bureau of Labor Statistics Occupational Outlook Handbook

For more information about how others are already solving problems and utilizing psychological research in the field, check out these major organizations.

- Substance Abuse and Mental Health Services Administration (SAMSA)
- National Institute of Mental Health (NIMH)
- National Institute on Drug Abuse (NIDA)
- National Institute on Alcohol Abuse and Alcoholism (NIAAA)⌟

Due to the diverse interests of ⌞those with psychology degrees,⌟ the workplace setting varies across the field. As you can see, there is not one predominant setting. Rather, ⌞those with psychology⌟ are employed in many places.

Beginnings of Psychology

Psychology as a discipline is a paradox in that the field is both old and new. Although the formalization of the discipline did not occur until the latter part of the 19th century, the subject matter of psychology has been studied by many people for thousands of years. Historically, the origins of psychology have been grounded in two separate fields: philosophy and physiology. Philosophy is the field from which psychology gains much of the subject matter we study today, while physiology provides researchers in psychology the tools

© michaeljung/Shutterstock.com

to study the subject matter. ⌐While the modern field of psychology would ascribe its beginning to these two foundations, the Bible is also an important foundation to consider when examining human behavior and psychological well-being.⌐

Philosophy

Plato, Aristotle, and other philosophers contemplated questions about human nature and behavior some 2,500 years ago, confronting issues still raised in contemporary psychology. Plato spent much of his life discussing the need to ignore sensory information by looking inward to understand the true nature of the soul. Only by using the rational powers of the mind could one truly gain understanding of the world. As a student of Plato, Aristotle took a different approach and was known to contemplate many issues in regard to human behavior that were externally influenced. For example, Aristotle studied the topics of human memory, motivation, perception, sleep, and dreams (Hergenhahn & Henley, 2014). Over the next several thousand years, the teachings of Plato and Aristotle would impact society as topics for exploration.

In the early 17th century, a French philosopher, Rene Descartes, changed the way people thought about the mind. Specifically, his work on the mind–body problem became, arguably, one of the most important early contributions to the field of psychology. Descartes reshaped people's thinking that the mind–body was unidirectional; that is, in which the mind controlled the body. Rather, Descartes concluded that not only do they interact, but that the body (physical) has more influence on the mind (mental) than was previously thought. In discussing the nature of the body, he described the theory of reflex action, in which an external object can bring about an involuntary response (Hergenhahn & Henley, 2014). For example, when someone scares you, you react to the external stimuli without having to think, "I should be scared and react this way." Rather, you react without the use of mental processes. Like Descartes's mind–body problem, those in contemporary psychology still investigate many of the same topics that Plato and Aristotle both viewed as important to understanding mental processes.

Physiology

Much of the early work on psychological principles was based in thought about philosophical constructs, as mentioned previously. During the latter part of the 18th century and the early part of the 19th century, a new breed of medical doctors, physiologists, and researchers became interested in psychological principles. Specifically, this new breed began to use their training in physiology to research psychological principles that previously had only been thought about in philosophy. These psychological principles included things such as memory, sensation, perceptions, and the influence of mental processes on behavior. However, although the subject matter being studied was not unique, it was the use of the scientific method (which we discuss later in this chapter) to systematically test these psychological principles that was the hallmark of this new breed of researchers. Whereas early philosophers built theories based on their own thoughts and observations, the use of the scientific method in physiology allowed these new researchers to empirically evaluate many of the historical topics in psychology. Research showing the impact of brain damage on behavior, as well as the discovery of basic brain physiology, began to shed light on the link between the brain and behavior. Thus, a new age in psychological discovery was underway.

Wilhelm Wundt and Early Schools of Thought

Wilhelm Wundt (1832–1920) was one of the early aforementioned physiologists to study psychological principles. Following graduation from medical school in 1855, Wundt worked as an assistant in many early psychophysics and physiology research laboratories in Western Europe. It was during this time that Wundt began to develop his ideas for a new scientific discipline, psychology. Although others helped to contribute along the way, Wundt is considered the founder of modern psychology due to his publication of the first psychology book, *Principles of Physiological Psychology,* in 1874. Thus, much of modern psychology can trace its academic lineage back to Wundt. Five years later, Wundt established the world's first psychological laboratory at the University of Leipzig in 1879, which remained active until 1910. It was from this laboratory that Wundt trained the first generation of psychologists who would go out into the world and make psychology the discipline it is today (Benjamin, 2008).

In addition to establishing the field of psychology, Wundt also made several contributions that led to the separation of psychology from philosophy. In order to make this separation complete, Wundt stressed the scientific exploration of conscious experience through the use of empirical methods. To do this, Wundt developed an empirical method he called **introspection**. Introspection is the examination of one's own mind to inspect and report on personal thoughts or feelings about conscious experiences. In order to properly use this technique, Wundt would rigorously train individuals over months and sometimes years. During the introspective process, individuals were presented with a physical stimulus and were to report on the size, intensity, and duration of their conscious experience. Wundt used the results of each experiment to draw inferences about the elements and processes of conscious experience.

> **Introspection:** The examination of one's own mind to inspect and report on personal thoughts or feelings about conscious experiences.

Can you see any problems with this technique? Unfortunately, much of the criticism of Wundt's early work centered on his use of introspection. Many researchers disapproved of the introspective method. Specifically, researchers argued there were problems with a method in which results could vary by different observers for the same stimulus. This led people to wonder which introspection was correct. Furthermore, since introspection is a private, personal method of study, how can the results be replicated? Despite these issues, Wundt is still considered to be the most important figure in the history of psychology, primarily as a result of founding psychology as a science, rejecting nonscientific thinking, publishing extensively on the topic, and training the first generation of psychologists.

Wilhelm Wundt.
© Nicku/Shutterstock.com

Structuralism

Edward Titchener (1867–1927) established the first brand of psychology (or school of thought) known as **structuralism**. Titchener developed structuralism at Cornell University in New York shortly after receiving his PhD from Wundt in 1892. Titchener believed psychology was to be used to study the structure of the mind. Structuralism

> **Structuralism:** The study of breaking down conscious experience into its fundamental elements: sensations, feelings, and images.

is the breaking down of conscious experience into its fundamental elements: sensations, feelings, and images. As did Wundt, Titchener sought to use introspection to accomplish this task. However, unlike Wundt who was interested in the whole of the conscious experience, Titchener was more concerned with the parts of the experience that made up the whole (Goodwin, 2008). Titchener's work suffered from the same criticism as Wundt's, and when Titchener died, so did structuralism.

Functionalism

Around the same time that Titchener was developing structuralism, William James (1842–1910) and colleagues at the University of Chicago were developing the second school of thought in psychology; **functionalism**. Functionalism was a deliberate protest against the work of Wundt and Titchener. Functionalists believed that the work of Wundt and Titchener was narrow in scope and could not be applied to the real world. James and colleagues adapted their work from the work of Darwin and his principles of evolution. Specifically, rather than focusing on the conscious experience only, functionalism

> **Functionalism:** The study of how the mind of an organism adapts to its current environment.

sought to study how the mind of an organism adapted to its current environment (Goodwin, 2008). This was a major change from Wundt and Titchener, who did not care about the outside environment, only the internal state. With the advent of functionalism, psychologists were able to expand the scope of psychology to children, animals, and the mentally impaired. These populations were not used with structuralism because researchers believed they were unable to be trained in introspection. Unfortunately, as with structuralism, functionalism lost ground around the 1920s with the death of Titchener and the introduction of behaviorism. However, some similarities do exist between functionalism and a contemporary perspective known as evolutionary psychology.

Psychoanalysis and Sigmund Freud

Sigmund Freud (1856–1939) is probably the most recognized name in psychology. Whether you are in the field or not, Freud is synonymous with psychology. Although his name is famous, there are mixed opinions as to his impact on the field. At roughly the same time as Wundt, Titchener, and James were working on their theories of psychology, Freud was heading in a different direction altogether. Whereas the other individuals were focused on learning about conscious experiences, Freud was more interested in the unconscious.

© Georgios Kollidas/Shutterstock.com

Freud graduated from the University of Vienna in 1881 with a medical degree and began work in neurology. Soon after starting his own practice, Freud developed the idea of a "talking cure." Freud believed individuals who suffered from psychological distress could be released from this distress by talking with a trained doctor. This process became the basis for Freud's theory called **psychoanalysis**. Psychoanalysis is a psychotherapeutic technique based on the belief that humans face psychological distress as a result of unconscious conflicts and desires (primarily sexual or aggressive) brought on during childhood. And it is these desires that influence negative behaviors exhibited in individuals. Freud's therapy was designed to bring these conflicts and

> **Psychoanalysis:** A psychotherapeutic technique based on the belief that humans face psychological distress as a result of unconscious conflicts and desires (primarily sexual or aggressive) brought on during childhood.

desires from a patient's unconsciousness to their consciousness through discussion. Freud believed that once the patient was aware of the conflicts or desires, the patient would have a chance to resolve these issues (Hergenhahn & Henley, 2014).

At the time, Freud's theories and beliefs were groundbreaking and popular across the globe. Today, despite the prevalence of psychoanalysis in pop culture, very few psychologists subscribe to the foundations of Freud's psychoanalysis. Although some of Freud's theories (such as the impact of the childhood on adult behavior) were correct, much of Freud's original work has not been supported when tested empirically. In particular, researchers have been critical of Freud's theories for relying too much on unconscious sexual and aggressive desires, as well as for ignoring the impact of conscious decisions on behavior.

Behaviorism

In the early 1920s a major shift occurred in psychology with the introduction of behaviorism by John Watson (1878–1958). Watson and colleagues (such as B. F. Skinner, 1904–1990) believed psychology should move away from using subjective procedures (i.e., introspection) and begin to engage in objective procedures. Watson's solution was **behaviorism**. Behaviorism is the scientific study of the prediction and control of behavior. In behaviorism, anything that could not be observed, such as mental processes like thoughts and feelings, could not be studied.

> **Behaviorism:** The scientific study of the prediction and control of behavior.

Behaviorists were focused on how humans and animals acquired and modified behavior as a result of their environment, which they called learning. Behaviorist believed people's development is little more than a result of learning that occurs in their world. While seemingly similar to functionalism, behaviorism focused solely on the behavior and ignored the mind or mental interaction with the environment. However, behaviorist like Watson and Skinner differed on the type of learning that led to the development of people (Goodwin, 2008). Behaviorism was the dominant theory in American psychology until the early 1960s when other contemporary ideas began reshaping the psychological landscape.

Other Key Contributors

In addition to Wundt, Titchener, James, Freud, Watson, and Skinner, there were many notable early psychologists that helped to shape the field. Even though we do not have time to discuss all of them, we highlight a few important people in the following (Goodwin, 2008; Hergenhahn & Henley, 2014).

- **G. Stanley Hall (1844–1924)**—Known by many in the field as "Mr. First," Hall is credited with starting the first experimental psychology lab in the United States, the first journal of psychology in the United States, founded APA (in 1892) and was its first president, and was the first to recognize adolescence as a separate stage of development.
- **James McKeen Cattell (1860–1944)**—Influenced by his work with Sir Francis Galton in eugenics, Cattell was the first to use the term "mental test" (although incorrectly as you will learn in later chapters). He spent much of his time professionalizing psychology, producing many famous PhD students while serving as head of the psychology program at Columbia.
- **Mary Whiton Calkins (1863–1930)**—Based on a recommendation by William James, Calkins attended Harvard University, successfully completing all requirements for a PhD in psychology. However, at the time Harvard did not accept women into graduate programs. Calkins never received her PhD despite her work in memory leading to breakthroughs in cognitive psychology.

Calkins was recognized by her peers when she was elected the first female president of APA in 1905.

- **Christine Ladd-Franklin (1847–1930)**—Similar to Calkins, Ladd-Franklin completed all of her degree requirements for her PhD in mathematics but was not awarded the degree upon completion. Ladd-Franklin went on to develop the earliest theory of color vision, becoming the world authority on the topic until her death. Interestingly, 44 years after completing the requirement, Johns Hopkins University awarded Ladd-Franklin her PhD 4 years before her passing.

- **Margaret Washburn (1871–1939)**—Washburn was the first woman to earn a PhD in psychology; she received her degree in 1894 from Cornell University. She is best known for being a leading comparative psychologist and wrote the standard comparative text of its day. Washburn was also elected an APA president as well as to the National Science Academy.

- **Francis Sumner (1895–1954)**—Sumner was the first African American to receive a PhD in psychology, awarded in 1920 from Clark University under the direction of G. Stanley Hall. Long considered the father of African American psychology, Sumner established a psychology department at Howard University. At Howard, Sumner pushed the psychology department to become the most outstanding department at all historically Black universities, producing many notable students who would all make contributions to the field.

- **Mamie (1917–1983) and Kenneth (1914–2005) Clark**—The Clarks, both graduates of Howard University under Sumner, contributed to the field of psychology during the civil unrest of the 1960s. Mamie and Kenneth began working on the effects of segregation on children, empirically showing the psychological damage segregation inflicted during that time. Their work, along with others, was considered by the U.S. Supreme court in the decision *Brown v Board of Education*.

- **Jorge Isidore Sanchez (1906–1972)**—Sanchez is considered the father of Hispanic educational psychology. Sanchez's research was instrumental in showing the racial biases in intelligence testing. His methodologies and models are still used today in research in bilingualism and educational testing.

THE SCIENTIFIC METHOD: THE SCIENCE OF PSYCHOLOGY

The research process in psychology can be broadly divided into two major categories, which include discovery and justification. Discovery, forming an idea, and then testing it; justification, which usually occur in sequence, are the initial steps in the research process. This process may be as simple as just observing some behavior and then speculating some cause.

The **scientific method** provides a framework for the systematic study of behavior and mental processes; more specifically, it is intended to provide a means to produce and reproduce controlled observations with the intent of being able to derive cause and effect relationships between a manipulation and behavior. The scientific method offers an objective approach for scientific experimentation resulting in unbiased interpretations of the world and refined knowledge. More specifically, the scientific method is a process for gathering

> **Scientific method:** A set of orderly steps used to analyze and solve problems universally applied across scientific disciplines. The framework for the systematic study of behavior and mental processes.

data and processing information. It provides well-defined steps to standardize how scientific knowledge is collected through a logical, rational problem-solving method that can be readily shared and replicated. Figure 1.5 shows the steps of the scientific method. The scientific method allows psychological data to be replicated and confirmed in many instances, under different circumstances, and by a variety of researchers—it takes this depth and breadth of work to confirm the relationship between variables and provide scientific facts. Through replication of experiments, new generations of psychologists can systematically reduce errors while simultaneously broadening the applicability of theories. It also allows theories to be tested and validated instead of simply being conjectures that could never be verified or falsified. All of this allows behavioral scientists to gain a stronger understanding of brain–behavior relationships. The use of the scientific method is one of the main features separating modern psychology from earlier philosophical inquiries about the mind.⌐

There are ⌐eight⌐ steps in the scientific method psychologists use when conducting research. The steps are ⌐(1) observation and problem identification, (2) asking a research question, (3) hypothesis formation, (4) make a prediction about the relationship between variables, (5) conduct study and collect data, (6) analysis of data, (7) conclusion—confirm or reject hypothesis, and (8) report findings (Figure 1.5). All studies should be replicated prior to their finding being generally accepted as fact.⌐

The first steps in the scientific method ⌐include identifying⌐ the problem. This step involves identifying a topic to research, as well as doing an initial review of the literature to determine what previous research

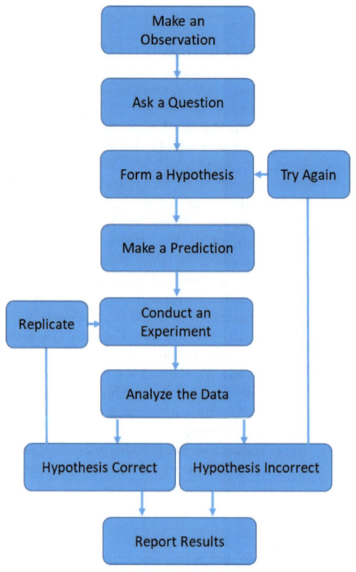

FIGURE 1.5 ⌐Working through the scientific method.⌐
Source: Brian Kelley

has been conducted on the topic ⌐and using that information to generate a research question. From there the next step is to⌐ formulate a hypothesis. A popular definition of a hypothesis is an educated guess. However, a more useful definition is that a hypothesis is a ⌐testable⌐ statement about the relationship between variables ⌐(e.g., the easiest to consider it is as an If…then…statement; if adolescent depression is associated with social media use, then increasing social media exposure should result in elevated risk for depression). While consistency, reproducibility, and validity are important components to variables, a key to each of those terms is having an exact, precise description of how the study is going to be conducted and exact, precise definitions for each variable that is being used. The next step is to make a prediction about the relationship between variables—anticipated outcome of the study. Thereafter, the next step is to⌐ collect data on the topic to test the hypothesis. To do this, researchers typically design an experiment or develop a study in which the variables of interest can be tested. The fourth step is to take the data collected and conduct data analysis. Data analysis involves the use of statistics. The results the statistical analysis yield are used to guide the fifth step, conclusion. The ⌐following⌐ step is very important in the research process. This is the step where a researcher revisits the hypothesis. At this point, the researcher, using the results from the analysis of the data, will make a judgment about the hypothesis. Based on the results of the study, a researcher will then decide to either support or reject the earlier hypothesis. ⌊This could also result in revising the study if the results do not support the hypothesis.⌋

The final step is reporting your findings. Research must be shared in such a way that the experiment or study can be replicated. Replication occurs when a research experiment or study is reproduced using the exact methodology and procedure. Thus, when reporting findings, the procedure and methodology need to be clearly communicated, with no ambiguity. Researchers prefer to publish their findings in what is known as peer-reviewed sources. This means that other scholars have reviewed the content of the manuscript and judged it to be worthy of publication and free from error, ⌊bias, and/or conflict of interests. The scientific process must be open to criticism. Another way to state this is that the scientific process must be open to peer-review, which means that other scientists must be allowed to evaluate the data, methods, and conclusions reached by their colleagues.⌋

NONEXPERIMENTAL (DESCRIPTIVE) RESEARCH METHODOLOGIES

One way to differentiate among types of research is by describing if the research is experimental or nonexperimental. Experimental research involves the manipulation of a variable of interest and the assignment of participants to treatment conditions. **Nonexperimental research** does not rely on manipulating variables; rather, it makes observations about how variables are related to one another and describes the findings.

> **Nonexperimental research:** Makes observations about how variables are related to one another and describes the findings.

As mentioned, nonexperimental research does not manipulate variables of interest. However, even without direct manipulation, you can still explore relationships between variables using correlational research methods. **Correlational research methods** are very important to the field. This methodology provides us with information on the initial link between variables of interest.

> **Correlational research methods:** Provides information on the initial link between variables of interest.

When you have a correlational research method, your results will tell you if the two variables are related. Variables can be either positively or negatively related. Do not be confused by the labels of positive correlation and negative correlation. This does not mean that positive correlations are good and negative correlations are bad. Rather, positive correlations have variables that vary in the same direction and negative correlations have variables that vary in opposite directions.

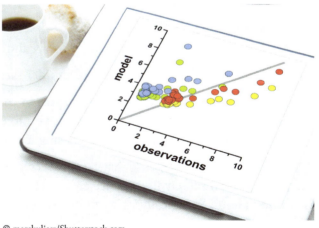

© marekuliasz/Shutterstock.com

To make this clear, we give some examples of positive and negative correlations. We have also provided Figure 1.6 to visually represent each type of correlation. Two variables that are positively correlated are years of education and salary. This is a positive correlation because as scores on one variable increase so too do scores on the second variable. Similarly, as scores on one variable decrease so too do scores on the second variable. In this situation, the greater number of years of education a person has, the higher the salary.

Conversely, the fewer number of years of education a person has, the lower the salary. In both instances, the two variables either increased or decreased together, making this a positive correlation.

With negative correlations, the two variables of interest are related to one another as well. However, as one variable increases, the other variable decreases, or as one variable decreases, the other variable increases. An example of a negative correlation is marital satisfaction and likelihood of divorce. As marital satisfaction

FIGURE 1.6 Arrows for positive and negative correlation.

increases, the likelihood of divorce decreases, and as marital satisfaction decreases, the likelihood of divorce increases.

As with any research method, there are advantages and disadvantages to examining correlations between variables. One major advantage of correlational research is that it allows us to make predictions. For example, if we know marital satisfaction and likelihood of divorce are negatively correlated, it can help us in counseling couples who are experiencing low marital satisfaction. Many times, examining correlations between variables is a great starting point to researching a topic. Plus, it is a useful method when conducting a true experiment would not be ethical.

This brings us to a limitation of the method— determining cause and effect. Did you know as ice cream sales increase, so do murder rates? This is a true correlation. So, should we stop buying ice cream so we can reduce the number of murders committed? Let's hope not! But we can ask ourselves questions to better understand the situation. When you have a correlation, you must think about the directionality of the correlation and ask yourself the following questions:

© HandmadePictures/Shutterstock.com

- **Is X causing Y?**
- Is Y causing X?
- Is there a third variable causing both X and Y to be related?

In the example of ice cream sales and murder rates, you would ask yourself the following questions:

- **Does eating ice cream (X) cause you to commit murder (Y)?**
- Does committing murder (Y) cause you to eat ice cream (X)?
- Is there a third variable that is causing ice cream sales (X) and murder rates (Y) to be related?

It really does not make sense that eating ice cream would cause you to commit murder or that murdering people would cause you to eat ice cream. However, it does make sense that a third variable (like heat) is related to both. Specifically, as it gets hotter, ice cream sales increase. Also, as it gets hotter, murder rates increase. Therefore, in this example, it is likely that a third variable was influencing both variables.

So far, we have provided you with introductory information that will be helpful as you learn about nonexperimental designs. Next we discuss naturalistic observation, case studies, and surveys. It is important to note that these nonexperimental designs can examine relationships among variables, as mentioned previously under correlational methodologies.

Naturalistic observation is when you observe people or animals in their natural settings. These observations can occur in the field (sometimes called field studies) or in the laboratory (referred to as laboratory observations). One of the most famous naturalistic observations was conducted by Jane Goodall. In the summer of 1960, Goodall went to East Africa to live among the chimpanzee population. There were many aspects about chimpanzees that Goodall wanted to learn, such as if chimps used tools. She believed the best way to understand chimp behavior was to observe them in their natural environment. Goodall's work has led to numerous publications on the life of chimps. Another example of a naturalistic observation comes from developmental psychologists who routinely use laboratory observations to study children. Important developmental information has been gained by bringing children into the lab and observing their interactions with their moms and dads. Examples include information on attachment style and stages of development such as object permanence.

> **Naturalistic observation:** Observe people or animals in their natural settings.

There are many advantages to this methodology. To begin with, the behavior being observed is natural and spontaneous. For the most part, participants being observed in naturalistic observations are just doing what they normally do in life. However, this method also has several disadvantages to be considered. One main disadvantage is how the observer changes people's behavior by his or her presence. Another disadvantage is that the researcher has to wait for events to occur. Goodall waited months before seeing chimps use tools. Researchers also need to be careful not to introduce bias in their observations. For example, researchers might be looking for a particular behavior and report "seeing it" when others would not. A well-known example of this has occurred with observation research of chimps using sign language. Some researchers reported seeing animals use sign language, while other researchers reported the animals were not signing. Finally, cause and effect cannot be determined from naturalistic observations.

© Ferenc Szelepcsenyi/Shutterstock.com

The next nonexperimental research method that we want to discuss is a **case study**. A case study is an in-depth observation of an individual, animal, event, or treatment method. Typically, an intensive observation is done and a detailed account is taken because the event is extremely rare and unusual. One example of a famous case study in the field is that of Phineas Gage. Phineas Gage provided us with information on the link between personality and parts of the brain. Specifically, in 1848, an explosion sent a tamping iron through Gage's skull. Surprisingly, Gage survived the explosion but his behavior changed greatly due to the damage in the frontal lobes of his brain. Researchers have long been interested in providing a detailed account of what took place and how Gage's behavior changed as a result.

> **Case study:** An in-depth observation of an individual, animal, event, or treatment method.

The major advantage to case studies is we can study rare events that would be unethical to study otherwise. Therefore, case studies provide us with unique opportunities to better understand situations that we could not study experimentally. Despite this advantage, there are limitations to this method. First, we do not always know the cause of the behavior. Second, these unusual events might not influence everybody in the same manner. Furthermore, not all people would have experienced the same resulting behavior. Thus, when using case studies, it is important to keep in mind the limitations of the findings.

The last type of nonexperimental research that we will cover in this chapter is **survey research**. Survey research is when a questionnaire is designed to obtain information regarding individuals' behaviors,

> **Survey research:** A questionnaire is designed to obtain information regarding individuals' behaviors, attitudes, or opinions.

attitudes, or opinions. This questionnaire can be administered in a variety of formats, but the most common format may be the written format. Questions are typed up and can be administered to participants in person by having them answer on paper or computer, through a mailed survey, and even over the internet. Another format of administering the questionnaire is via telephone. You can ask people questions verbally in person, which is known as a face-to-face interview, or gather a small group of people together to discuss the questions, which is known as a focus group. Each of these formats has its own advantages and disadvantages. A lengthy discussion of each is out of the scope of this book.

What are some of the potential problems associated with this approach, particularly the methodology? Self-report measures are verbal answers, either written or spoken, to questions asked by a researcher. These measures can include questionnaires, interviews, or surveys. One problem with this methodology is that it cannot be used with certain populations like children, animals, and people who cannot read or speak the language on the form. Other problems are that people may lie or exaggerate in order to look good. The questions may be posed poorly, or the interviewee may be biased and frame the questions in a certain way. Finally, the test may not be reliable or even valid.

© zimmytws/Shutterstock.com

Surprisingly enough, developing good self-report measures is actually quite difficult. Why even conduct studies through this method given all of the challenges? Questionnaires tend to be very cost effective because they can be mailed out, conducted via the Internet, or e-mail. Even if you are able to get really good and accurate data about behavior, you are relying on people who do not always have access to what controls their behavior, and when they do, they may not be honest about what drives their actions.

EXPERIMENTAL RESEARCH METHODOLOGIES

Experimental research involves the manipulation of a variable of interest and assignment of participants to treatment conditions. A variable is an event or characteristic with at least two possible values. For example, what would be the variable if we were to ask you, "How stressed are you about taking general psychology?." In this example, the condition with an assigned or attached value is your level of stress. Furthermore, the amount of stress you indicate in your answer is the value associated with the variable. There are two variables essential to research. These two variables are the independent variable and the dependent variable.

The independent variable (IV) is the variable in a study manipulated by the researcher. It is being manipulated because it is the variable the researcher believes will produce a change in his or her study. The other variable of interest is the dependent variable. A dependent variable (DV) is the variable within a study being observed or measured. Specifically, the dependent variable is the variable a researcher believes will change or will be influenced in the study. Usually, any change seen within the dependent variable is a result of the independent variable. In other words, any measurable change from the independent variable's influence will be seen in the dependent variable.

> **Experimental research:** Involves the manipulation of a variable of interest and assignment of participants to treatment conditions.
>
> **Variable:** An event or characteristic with at least two possible values.

> **Independent variable:** Variable manipulated by the researcher.
>
> **Dependent variable:** Variable observed or measured.

Let's look at an example. A pharmaceutical company has developed a new drug to help reduce the number of migraines experienced by individuals who report suffering from frequent migraines. To determine if the drug is effective, one group of participants takes the new drug daily and the other group does not. After 30 days, the participants report how many migraines they had during the time period. In this example, the independent variable was the new drug for migraines. It was manipulated by having some participants take the new drug daily and others not. The researchers at the pharmaceutical company manipulated the new drug because

© 9nong/Shutterstock.com

they believed it would reduce the frequency of migraines. The dependent variable was the number of migraines participants reported in the 30-day period. This was the variable the researchers measured and observed for change.

There is another type of variable used in research with some of the same qualities as the independent variable. This variable is known as a **subject variable**. A subject variable is a characteristic or attribute of a participant that can impact the participant's behavior or thoughts within a study. Subject variables are often traits specific to a participant, such as sex, age, or ethnicity, and these traits can influence the dependent variable. In the

> **Subject variable:** Characteristic or attribute of a participant that can impact the participant's behavior or thoughts.

migraine example, the pharmaceutical company might also want to know if the new drug works equally well on men and women. Thus, sex of the participant could be a subject variable added to the study.

An independent variable will always have at least two conditions. These are referred to as treatment conditions. Typically, the treatment conditions are the experimental and the control group. The **experimental group** is the group exposed to the independent variable. In other words, the experimental group is the group of participants given the independent variable and is the group where we would expect to see a measurable change occur. The **control group** is the group of participants not exposed to the independent variable. This group does not

> **Experimental group:** Group exposed to the independent variable.
>
> **Control group:** Group of participants not exposed to the independent variable.

receive the independent variable, and, therefore, we do not expect to see any measurable change in the participants.

To revisit our earlier example, the group of participants who took the new migraine drug each day would be the experimental group. This is because those participants are exposed to the independent variable, the new drug. The participants who did not take the new drug daily would be the control group. This is because the participants are not exposed to the independent variable.

In addition to the experimental and control groups, there is another group often used as a treatment condition in research. This group is known as the placebo control group. The **placebo control group** is similar to the control group in that participants assigned to this condition are not exposed to the independent variable. However, the placebo control group is different from the control group because the participants are exposed to a placebo. A **placebo** is an inert substance or object similar to the independent variable but having no direct effect.

> **Placebo control group:** Participants are exposed to a placebo.
>
> **Placebo:** An inert substance or object.

Essentially, the placebo control group acts as an insurance policy. Sometimes researchers see measurable changes in the experimental group that are not due to the independent variable but to the participant's belief that a change will occur. Therefore, the placebo control acts as a way for the researcher to determine how much measurable change is due to the independent variable and how much change is due to the participant's belief in a change occurring. If the pharmaceutical company wanted to be sure the reduced frequency of migraines was due to the new medicine and not participants' belief in the effectiveness of the medicine, the company could add a placebo

© Johan Larson/Shutterstock.com

control group to the research design. Participants in this group would take a daily pill. The participants would believe the pill to be the new drug but in reality it would be an inert substance like a sugar pill. The table below summarizes the different treatment conditions:

Table 1.3 ⌐Explaining Treatment Conditions⌐

Treatment Condition	Exposure
Experimental Group	Receives the new drug (IV)
Control Group	Does not receive the new drug (no IV)
Placebo Control Group	Receives the placebo (a sugar pill)

When conducting research, a researcher can have a single or double blind study. In a **single blind study**, the participant has no knowledge of the group to which he or she has been assigned—only the researcher knows. Although it is advantageous that the participant does not know to which group he or she has been assigned, there is a drawback. Specifically, the threat of demand characteristics may affect your study results. **Demand characteristics** are various hints and cues that participants use to tell themselves how the researcher wants them to behave, or at least how they think the researcher wants them to behave. If participants are responding to these demand characteristics, rather than the independent variable, this could explain the changes in the dependent variable.

Single blind study: Only the researcher knows to which group the participant has been assigned.

Demand characteristics: Hints and cues participants use to tell themselves how the researcher wants them to behave.

However, in a **double blind study** neither the participant nor the researcher interacting with the participant knows into which experimental group the participant has been placed. Thus, you reduce the likelihood of the participant or experimenter behaving in a way that can influence the study, because neither knows which group the participant is in.

Double blind study: Neither the participant nor the researcher knows to which group the participant has been assigned.

⌐One of the reasons why the scientific method along with double-blind designs are so important is because of observer bias. Observer bias is a particularly serious problem in psychological research. **Observer bias** is an error due to the personal motives and

⌐**Observer bias:** An error due to the personal motives and expectations of the viewer.⌐

expectations of the viewer. What are some of the means by which psychologists control this problem? This problem can be minimized by two methods. First, psychologists can rely on standardization. Standardization simply means using the uniform, consistent procedures in all phases of data collection. For example, using a written test would be more easily standardized then having the questions read out loud. Second, psychologists utilize operational definitions when defining variables. Operational definitions are precise, exact parameters for measuring and manipulating variables (e.g., independent and dependent variables). Without proactive approaches to controlling bias, it would likely impact every study. Good scientists recognize their own biases and design studies to make sure their and other participants' biases do not influence the outcome of the study.

⌐If experiments are the only way to truly demonstrate cause-and-effect relationships, why don't psychologists rely on them exclusively? It would certainly be nice if that were in fact possible. Psychologists would certainly prefer to demonstrate cause and effect relationships rather than demonstrating the strength of two or more variables. However, experiments are not always possible, because of ethical limitations. For example, imagine that you wanted to conduct an experiment on the long-term effects of prenatal cocaine exposure. How could you ethically carry out such an experiment? You would have to randomly assign one group of mothers to a control/placebo group and assign other mothers to various cocaine exposure conditions. I cannot imagine that many mothers would volunteer for such a study. For this reason, as well as others, psychologists need to be creative and find other ways to study this phenomenon.⌐

RELIABILITY AND VALIDITY

Regardless of the specific research methodology a psychologist might use for research, the discipline values the use of reliable and valid measures. Reliability of a variable is very important when conducting research. **Reliability** is the consistency of your measure to produce similar results on different occasions. Therefore, reliability is primarily concerned with being able to replicate or reproduce the findings. **Validity** is defined as the ability of your measurement to accurately measure what it is supposed to measure. This is different from reliability, which is about being able to replicate scores on future instances. To better understand these terms, let's look at an example.

> **Reliability:** Consistency of your measure to produce similar results on different occasions.
>
> **Validity:** Ability of your measurement to accurately measure what it is supposed to measure.

Remember the migraine drug example from earlier in the chapter? Researchers are currently working on this problem. Specifically, researchers are developing migraine drugs (independent variable) that are specifically designed to be more effective in reducing the number of migraines a person suffers in a month (dependent variable) as compared with current migraine medications. During the initial trials of the new "designer" migraine medication, the researchers saw a 63% drop in the number of days a person had a migraine in a 30-day time period. These results were seen as extremely promising and thus the researchers are looking to continue the study (Norton, 2014).

If you were the researcher, how would you best determine the reliability of the measure (i.e., the effectiveness of the drug as measured by a reduction in migraine days)? The simplest way would be to expand the initial trial and conduct another study to see if you can produce similar results on a different occasion. Should the new "designer" drug show similar results again (i.e., a 63% or so drop), then you could argue the measure of reduction in migraine days is reliable since the obtained results in the second study are consistent with the initial study. However, should the change in the measure be significantly different on each occasion, then the measure would show low reliability.

Likewise, how would you determine the validity of the measure (i.e., the effectiveness of the drug)? On the surface, the reduction in the number of days one has a migraine is straightforward. And, if the drug reduces the days significantly, a researcher would argue the measure is valid. However, it could be the case the measure is missing the greater impact of the drug. Specifically, the drug may reduce the length of a migraine from a full day to a few hours. While this difference may result in the number of days without a migraine changing only slightly, the overall length of time in which a person suffers

© wavebreakmedia/Shutterstock.com

from a migraine may change dramatically. In this case, a researcher would say the measure of a reduction in the number of days is not valid and the measure should be length of time when assessing effectiveness of the drug.

RESEARCH ETHICS

APA has developed a set of ethical guidelines all psychologists follow. These guidelines (most recently revised in 2010) are broken into 10 sections covering ethical issues: competence, human relations, assessment, therapy, and so on. For the purposes of this section, we will focus on a small part of Standard 8.0: Research and Publication and its 15 guidelines (see Figure 1.7).

The topic of deception is continually debated to this day. Specifically, researchers and others have debated whether deception is helpful or harmful in research. APA states psychologists may use deception in research if it is needed to study a particular topic and if its use is justified by the knowledge gained. When deception is used, participants should be told about the deception as soon as possible and it should be clearly explained why this method was used and the anticipated benefits. Participants are given the opportunity to withdraw their data if desired. Although deception is permitted in special cases, APA has made it clear that psychologists are not allowed to deceive participants with regard to physical or emotional pain. According to the APA, there are the four acceptable reasons to use deception in research. The first is that the study must have sufficient scientific and educational importance. Second, the researchers must demonstrate that no equally effective protocol is available. Third, participants should never be deceived about aspects of the study that would affect their willingness to participate. Finally, the deception must be explained to the participants by the conclusion of the study. Furthermore, such studies have to be approved by an institutional review board and participants must have the option of removing themselves from the study at any time.

Informed consent means that the subject fully understands the risk and benefits of the experiment, and has given the researcher his or her permission to be included in the study. Children, mentally ill, and prisoners often cannot give informed consent or demonstrate that they are willing participants in a study, which is why it is often very difficult to use such groups in research.

Approach of Textbook

As stated toward the beginning of this chapter, the goal of the field of psychology is to understand human behavior with the purpose of improving the human condition; and, as you will see throughout our textbook, this includes studying a variety of topics related to the human experience. Each chapter in this book is dedicated to a different subfield of the field of psychology. In Chapter 2, we explore the biological bases of behavior and you will be introduced to the research in neuropsychology, sleep and other biological processes. In Chapter 3, will explore sensation and perception and you will learn about how different sensory systems process information and make sense of the world around us. In Chapter 4, we introduce research and theories related to learning, memory, and intelligence, while in Chapter 5 we discuss theories of motivation and emotion as we examine what motivates our behaviors. In Chapter 6, we investigate development and how we grow cognitively, socially, and morally. In Chapter 7, how psychologists describe and understand personality is presented as well as research in social psychology. Finally, in Chapter 8, we present the current state of our understanding of psychological disorders and treatments that help individuals suffering from a variety of mental health issues.

It is very important for you, as an introductory psychology student, to understand the breadth of the field of psychology and how researchers in psychology have come to understand a variety of topics in our field. As you go through the material, you will be introduced to many different careers in our field, as well as see many different areas of life that are impacted by psychological research. You also will likely notice how much there is still to know about human behavior and the processes that guide our behaviors.

Institutional Review Board (IRB)

A committee that reviews proposals of intended research and evaluates if the research is ethical and if the rights of the participants are being protected.

IRBs can be found on college campuses, in hospitals, government agencies, and private corporations..

Use of Animals in Research

When conducting research with animals, researchers must follow APA guidelines and additional government (local, state, and federal) policies and guidelines.

For more information about research with animals, visit the website for the Institutional Animal Care and Use Committee (IACUC) www.unmc.edu/iacuc.

Use of Deception in Research

Active deception: Deception by commission is when a researcher deliberately misleads a participant. Example: A researcher embeds a **confederate**, a participant who is also part of the research team, in the study.

Passive deception: Deception by omission is when a researcher withholds information about the nature of a study from the participants. Example: At times researchers don't fully explain the purpose of their research design at the onset of a study; doing so might change the way participants respond in the study.

Debriefing

Researchers provide participants with information about the study immediately after the data are collected. If the results are not yet available, participants can be provided with the researchers' contact information so the they can learn of the findings when ready.

If it's necessary to delay debriefing until all participants complete the study, researchers are to reduce the risk of harm to the participants. If a one has been harmed during the study (physically or emotionally), researchers should immediately try to minimize the harm.

Informed Consent

A consent form must be given to all participants in a research study & must

- Tell information about the research being conducted.
- Give an estimate of how long it will take to participate and a brief overview of what will be required.
- Clearly inform that participation in the study is voluntary.
- Explain the consequences of withdrawing from or not participating in the study along with any potential risks or benefits of participating.
- Clarify whether responses are **anonymous** or **confidential**.

Anonymous research ensures no identifying information is gathered and participants can't be identified once the study is concluded.

Confidential research allows for participants to be identified by the gathered information. Information is kept in a way that responses aren't shared with others.

FIGURE 1.7   Terms in research ethics.

Source: Bailee Robinson

Additionally, in this textbook, you will be encouraged to think about the various topics in psychology from a **biblical worldview**. As you are presented with research and theories on various concepts, you will also be challenged to ask, "What does the Bible say?" In fact, throughout the textbook, you will see boxes that ask that very question and you will be provided with biblical answers and perspectives on many of the topics presented throughout the text.

> **Biblical worldview:** A comprehensive and integrated view of the world from a biblical perspective. Also defined as a conceptual framework centered on the Bible by which people consciously or unconsciously interpret or judge reality; the Bible is viewed as the written Word of God.

 **WHAT IS A BIBLICAL WORLDVIEW?**

What Is a Biblical Worldview?

Everybody has a certain way they look at the world—certain truths and frameworks by which they operate to understand the world around them. According to Wolters (2005), a worldview is, "the comprehensive framework of one's basic beliefs about things." It may sound pretty broad, but that is truly the purpose of this definition. Your worldview, according to Wolters, "speaks centrally to *everything* in our life and world, including technology and economics and science."

It is your basic framework of *everything*. It is what you believe to be true about everything and anything in life.

A biblical worldview asserts that truth originates with God. Someone adhering to a biblical worldview believes that God created the world and the order by which it operates, and He has revealed truth through His Word and through His Works (or the world around us that can be studied and truth about its order discovered). Holding a biblical worldview states that God reveals truth to us and we need to seek Him in the Bible and in His creation for it.

This is in contrast to the dominant worldview in society today that truth comes from science, logic, and critical thinking. Someone with a secular modern worldview values data we collect from the natural world over spiritual authority. Someone who would say they hold this worldview puts stock in empirical, evidence-based ways of justifying beliefs about what's real. They would claim that beliefs based in evidence (or science) are more reliable and more objective than those based in uncorroborated intuition, revelation, religious authority or sacred texts, like the Bible. This belief in science as the foundation for truth has truly dominated the modern era. Chances are, even if you come from a Christian background, you have modern thinking about the authority of research in your thinking patterns!

As a Christian in psychology, it is important to recognize that God has shared many truths about human behavior in the Bible. Due to our belief in the authority of God and His Word, we can receive those truths with confidence. We also can study His creation, with good science, and see how He has created us and the truths in human behavior. As a Christian student studying psychology, knowing what the Bible says and knowing what good research shows about human behavior is important to understanding psychological phenomena.

For the Christian student, it is important to understand what the field presents about human behavior. But, you also need to be aware that science is not the ultimate source of truth. As described earlier in this chapter, science is the study of the world around us and is dependent on measuring constructs well, analyzing data well, and coming to the correct conclusions. Because science is a human phenomenon, it is prone to error. And, as you will notice, scientific findings and conclusions on topics change frequently as new evidence emerges or as new theoretical perspectives emerge. Therefore, we must always be cautious and critically thinking when evaluating research. One way we can be critically thinking is by comparing it to the Word of God. Using the "What Does the Bible Say?" boxes throughout the textbook, you will be shown how to do that in various research areas.

In addition to the "What Does the Bible Say?" boxes, you also will be given definitions of terms in boxes throughout the chapters. One thing you will notice is that psychology involves a lot of terms, and these definition boxes will help you understand and organize the psychological terms as you learn about the various subfields.

The field of psychology is a diverse and exciting field. Nearly everything that is involved in human experience is studied within the field. When the study of human behavior is combined with the Bible, we can make an enormous difference in the world around us. We can glorify God, and, as stated earlier, we may just find our purpose. So, let's get started.

Chapter 2

The Biology of Behavior

LEARNING OBJECTIVES

- ⌞Explain the⌟ principal biological advantages and disadvantages of humans relative to other species.
- ⌞Understand⌟ the main components and functions of nerve cells.
- ⌞Describe⌟ the most important neurotransmitters relate to behavior.
- ⌞Review how⌟ drugs influence neurotransmitters and behavior.
- ⌞Describe how⌟ the human nervous system ⌞is⌟ organized.
- ⌞Define⌟ the key brain structures and their functions.
- ⌞Compare the frontal lobe to the limbic system.⌟
- ⌞Investigate⌟ the nature and purpose of sleep.
- ⌞Elaborate on the⌟ functions dreams ⌞likely⌟ serve.
- ⌞Explain how⌟ hypnosis ⌞is⌟ a distinct state of consciousness.

The very nature of consciousness, the mind, is an area of study that encompasses all others. Since psychology deals with how we perceive and understand the universe, it could be argued that this scientific disciplines brings all the other disciplines together. Ultimately, all scientific advancements and all human achievements are housed in the mind. Consciousness is fundamental to the psychological study of perception. Studying perception means studying how we construct and extract meaning from simple, isolated, physical stimuli (e.g., light, sound, smell, taste, and touch). Drugs are also a type of stimuli and people ingest drugs for all sorts of reasons. However, nearly all of these reasons involve alterations of consciousness.

▶ CHAPTER 2 OVERVIEW

Neuroscience is the study of brain–behavior relationships. Advancements in this field have furthered our understanding of how we perceive, remember, and respond to the world around us and within us. Considering how far our understanding of neuroscience has developed in the last 25 years, it begs the following question: How far will neuroscience take us, and do we really want to take that journey?

Imagine our understanding of the brain advances so much that we can program the brain as readily as we can program a computer. While this idea might seem ridiculous, again, consider how the idea of a mobile phone would have sounded 300 years ago. Scientists have already implanted electrodes in a pigeon's brain to control its flight. The implants activate specific areas of the pigeon's brain using electrical signals. These signals are sent by the scientists via computer, mimicking the natural signals generated by the brain (Huai et al., 2016). Even now, scientists are making enormous strides in understanding and replacing natural organs with artificial ones. For example, those who have lost their hearing can be fitted with an artificial cochlea. Those who have lost their sight can have an artificial retina implanted in their eye. People who have lost an arm or a leg can have a new, bionic one fitted to their body. While these devices are relatively crude at this point in time, in the near future, they may even surpass our body's natural abilities.

While much of our knowledge of brain–behavior relationships can be used to improve the human condition (e.g., the point of this textbook), this knowledge can also detract from it. Advances in neuroscience and chemistry have enabled humankind to further develop and refine the chemicals used to alter consciousness—often with terrible consequences. These consequences can include crime, violence, addiction, health problems, economic burdens, family breakdowns, job loss, and death. Overall, the individual and societal costs to getting "high" get higher every day. Even small declines in the number of people using abused substances could provide enormous benefits for society—and for you. While we often view complex problems in collective terms, the very best prevention strategies always center around a single fundamental issue—one individual making a decision to make the world a little bit better. As spoken by Mahatma Gandhi, "Be the change you want to see in the world."

Why focus on biology in a psychology course? Consider what factors make someone successful at academics, sports, music, or theater. It would be difficult to argue that for basketball players, simply being tall and strong would provide all of the necessary prerequisite attributes for success—if that were the case, all tall, strong people would be making millions of dollars playing basketball. That is to say, biology (i.e., genetics) alone does not make one an athlete. Certainly opportunity, coordination, endurance, motivation, training/coaching, and equipment would be necessary for competitive play. On the other hand, no amount of coaching or training would by itself make someone a professional basketball player. However, even the very best basketball players often make for poor cross-country runners, gymnasts, ice-hockey players, or wrestlers. So, being good at sports is not a universal phenomenon; that is, being good at one sport does not often translate into being good at all sports. This also holds true for other complex activities like music; having excellent hand–eye coordination and/or a good ear for pitch does not alone create a world-class violinist, pianist, or singer. Similarly, there are many very smart people who end up doing very poorly in school; so just looking at intelligence, as defined by an IQ test, is not always the most meaningful way to examine academic aptitude.

Complex behaviors almost always have a biological component and thus tend to fall along a "bell-curve" with few people on the extremes and a large number of people showing intermediate or average ability. So, while there is considerable variation in biology, motivation, and environment, often all three have to act on someone to decrease or increase the likelihood of a certain behavior—like athletic ability or musical talent. Hence, there are very, very few exceptional basketball players, a lot of just average players, and, again, very few who just can't play at all.

So, putting this together, if someone is naturally inclined toward sports, what sport is he or she most likely to play and excel at? If someone loves music, what instrument or type of music will he or she most likely play? In academics, what major or area of study is one most likely to pick? The answer to all of these questions is the one that is most rewarding or advances the easiest. Although there also has to be availability of that specific activity and, over the long run, a certain degree of social support (e.g., family, coaching, peers, etc.) there is always an important genetic or biological component.

EVOLUTION

In science, most notably in biology and psychology, evolution theory is a widely accepted position regarding the origins of and differentiation of species. The theory posits that all species are related and gradually change (i.e., advance or improve) over time. Evolution assumes that random genetic variations occurring in DNA in some organisms within a large population can affect the physical characteristics of those organisms and in rare cases, those changes can result in advantages in a small number of those organisms compared to other organisms. Those small and cumulative changes over many, many years would provide advantages. Reproduction would carry those changes onto future offspring. This is effectively where natural selection and survival of the fittest come together. Adaptions that provide a more competitive advantage in a particular environment are more likely to be passed along to offspring --being stronger, faster, taller, camouflaged, etc. In contrast, organisms less able to adapt to their environment would also be less likely to survive and similarly less likely to pass on those genes to future offspring. Therefore, while adaption and survival of the fittest are universally discussed concepts in evolution, the only thing that really matters is fitness. Fitness is simply defined as an organism's ability to produce offspring who produce offspring with the fittest organisms producing the most offspring and thus passing along more advantageous genotypes. While this quick introduction to evolution is obviously simplifying complex concepts, it does not change what the end goal of evolution is, which is producing many offspring that should also go on to produce many offspring.

So, how are humans so advanced above other species according to the theory of evolution? How did we, as *Homo sapiens*, (the self-named wise one), come to have such a well-developed "new" brain, opposable thumbs, upright gait, and our ability to communicate through the use of arbitrary symbols?

We don't have clever thumbs just because we decided they would be an advantage; we did not invent our brains; we made no conscious decision to shift from a four-legged to a two-legged form of locomotion, thereby making our front legs obsolete and eventually changing their names to arms. Nor did we, in council one day, decide that a language would be superior to the grunts and gestures we might previously have been using. Most scientists believe these revolutionary happenings resulted from **evolution** (Darwin, 1859). Evolution, the adaptive progression of species from their origins, might at first glance seem an inappropriate topic for a study of human behavior. We are, after all, concerned with understanding our current behavior. But perhaps something in

> **Evolution:** A scientific theory that holds that present life forms have developed from preexisting species through a series of modifications governed by laws of natural selection and diversification of species.

evolution might help our understanding. Certainly much in our behavior is related to biology; and much of our biology seems to be the product of evolutionary processes.

⌐The notion that something in evolution might help our understanding of our current behavior is the foundational idea of the perspective of evolutionary psychology. For a primer on this area of study, go to the following URL: http://www2.newpaltz.edu/~geherg/ep_expl.htm

For a more detailed primer, go to this URL instead: http://www.cep.ucsb.edu/primer.html⌐

⌐While it might seem that belief in evolutionary principals is university accepted, this is not the case—in fact, far from it. Many modern scientists have doubts about the ability of Darwinian or Neo-Darwinian evolution to explain the origins of any living organisms let alone humans. For example, a poll of medical doctors suggests a significant minority (34%) support intelligent design over evolution. However, upon examination of the details of survey itself, one finds that actually a majority of doctors favor intelligent design over Neo-Darwinism. More specifically, when questioned about the origin and development of human beings, only 38% agreed with the Darwinian story that "humans evolved naturally with no supernatural involvement–no divinity played any role." In contrast, 42% said "God initiated and guided an evolutionary process that has led to current human beings." Another 18% of doctors said "God created humans exactly as they appear now." In total, it means that 60% of doctors take an intelligent design/creation position (Pew Research Center, 2009a, 2009b, 2020). One such doctor who takes such a position is the famous Johns Hopkins pediatric neurosurgeon Ben Carson. Similarly, geneticist Francis Collins, the founder of the Human Genome Project as well as President Barack Obama's choice to head the National Institutes of Health, has *spoken* publicly about how he believes his evangelical Christian faith and his work in science are compatible.

⌐This position is not unusual. The Pew Research Center for the People & the Press (2009b) conducted a poll specifically focused on scientists who are members of the American Association for the Advancement of Science and found that 51% of scientists believe in God or a higher power. This number is much lower compared to the general public; however, while at first it might seem the difference is a factor of education or insight, there may in fact be other explanations that account for such differences. Academic pressure and an environment of overt and/or subtle coercion to adhere to this belief may also play a role in positive response rates to pro evolution positions.

⌐More recently, David Gelernter, who has taught computer science at Yale University *for* many decades, wrote a controversial article detailing his struggle of coming to believe that Darwinian evolution, for which he still believes is brilliant and beautiful, is wrong. He explained that no one should doubt Darwin's explanations about the small changes in organisms in which they adapt to their surroundings over time, adjustments like wing style, fur density, or the shape of the beaks of birds. Yet larger, more macro changes in biology that Darwinism posits, such as the emergence of new species as opposed to the micro adjustments in old ones, should be doubted, he said. "The origin of species is exactly what Darwin cannot explain" (Gelernter, 2019, p. 104), he emphasized. He further noted that the math just doesn't work out.

Consider the whole history of living things—the entire group of every living organism ever. It is dominated numerically by bacteria. All other organisms, from tangerine trees to coral polyps, are only a footnote. Suppose, then, that every bacterium that has ever lived contributes one mutation before its demise to the history of life. This is a generous assumption; most bacteria pass on their genetic information unchanged, unmutated. Mutations are the exception. In any case, there have evidently been, in the whole history of life, around 10^{40} bacteria—yielding around 10^{40} mutations under Axe's assumptions. That is a very large *number of chances at any game. But given that the odds each time are 1 to 10^{77} against, it is not large enough. The odds against blind Darwinian chance having turned up even one mutation with the potential to push evolution forward are $10^{40} \times (1/10^{77})$—$10^{40}$ tries, where your odds of success each time are 1 in 10^{77}—which equals 1 in 10^{37}. In practical terms, those odds are still zero. Zero odds of producing a single promising mutation in the whole history of life. Darwin loses (107).*

He further explained in an interview that his public rejection of Darwinism is taken among many of his colleagues as a personal, existential threat. Although his fellow academics remain his friends and are courteous to him, he noted, "when I look at their intellectual behavior, what they publish, and, much more important, what they tell their students, Darwinism has indeed passed beyond a scientific argument." "As far as they are concerned, take your life in your hands to challenge it intellectually. They will destroy you if you challenge it" (HooverInstitution, 2019). So, to be clear, believing in evolution is not necessarily a position of the intellectuals. In fact one could argue the true intellectual would be open to exploring different approaches to the origins of life. True intellectual freedom warrants having an open mind. This book and the underlying origins framework is decidedly Christian. While this is the case, it is important to understand alternative positions.

According to Albert Einstein, "Science without religion is lame, religion without science is blind." This famous maxim has been the source of continuous debate between believers and nonbelievers wanting to claim that one of the greatest scientist of the 20th century as their own. This debate between the value of science and religion especially as it pertains to evolution is not trivial. For example, the fundamental assumption of evolution is that humans are animals and a natural extension of this belief is that like animals, humans don't have free will. The behavior of animals—all animals—is a product of biology and environmental factors. Because humans are animals, evolution would posit that humans also don't have free will. An interesting series of question extend from this position and include: can an animal murder another animal? Can an animal rape another animal? Can an animal commit a crime or a sin? Probably the answer to these questions is no. But, the problem is humans are animals—perhaps, with better brain processing capabilities but animals nonetheless. So how do we reconcile moral positions with evolution?

To accept a totally secular view of origins simultaneously subsumes a view of moral relativism—all truth, value, purpose, or right or wrong is based on an individual's beliefs and no one belief system is necessarily better or worse than another. Belief in evolution played a fundamental role in changing the debate about what is right and what is wrong from one of searching for truth to one in which everyone simply defines their own truth. One extension of this truth resulted in the Nazi's killing millions of perceived inferior beings. It can be argued that the Nazi movement was a direct application of evolutionary principles played out at the global level. Even more recently, it resulted in the belief and application of eugenics—the science of improving the human population through controlled reproduction. This generally resulted in those viewed as inferior being sterilized. Keep in mind that the same line of research that led to pesticides also gave rise to nerve gas. Similarly, the same research that created nuclear energy also gave us the atomic bomb. Biomedical research that developed modern pain medication also helped usher in the worst addiction crises in all of history. The same research helping to create genetic treatments for diseases could also lead to genetic engineering. Humans have amazing creative potential but should that creative energy occur in a moral vacuum?

This is a science book, first and foremost. However, it is grounded on a biblical framework and filtered through a biblical worldview. This is in contrast to most approaches that presume to be purely scientific and objective, not adhering to any particular worldview, but that is impossible. Whether people admit or not, people's beliefs impact the way they approach controversial topics. At least this book is being transparent about those beliefs.

What Does the Bible Say?

⌐The Bible speaks clearly about humankind. We were created in the image of God, to be male or female, and to be above the other animals. We should value all human life as it is special and eternal.

Genesis 1:26–28 ESV

"Then God said, 'Let us make man in our image, after our likeness. And let them have dominion over the fish of the sea and over the birds of the heavens and over the livestock and over all the earth and over every creeping thing that creeps on the earth.'

So God created man in his own image, in the image of God he created him; male and female he created them.

And God blessed them. And God said to them, 'Be fruitful and multiply and fill the earth and subdue it, and have dominion over the fish of the sea and over the birds of the heavens and over every living thing that moves on the earth.'"

1 Corinthians 3:16–17 ESV

"Do you not know that you are God's temple and that God's Spirit dwells in you? If anyone destroys God's temple, God will destroy him. For God's temple is holy, and you are that temple."⌐

Early Homo sapiens

In some ways, it is astonishing that our species of humans survived, as defenseless as we were against the fangs and claws of the large carnivorous predators of those prehistoric times. We are a relatively slow species, endowed with unexceptional hearing and with a laughable sense of smell compared with that of many other species. Also, we are inadequately protected against both heat and cold, awkward at climbing trees or digging holes, clumsy in the water relative to dolphins, and incapable of flight without artificial means.

So, why have we *H. sapiens* thrived as a species? Why is the world population of humans growing at an extremely rapid rate compared to other species on this planet? The answer is that we are more intelligent! Prehistoric *H. sapiens* were not able to outfight or outrun their prehistoric enemies; they outwitted them! An additional but inconspicuous reason for our success is that we evolved to stand upright. And although becoming bipedal did not make us as fast as most four-legged animals, it freed our arms and hands for purposes other than locomotion. We became an animal that could walk quite nicely on just two of its legs, freeing our arms for making tools, striking enemies while in full flight, making hand gestures to aid in communicating, and blowing our noses—an undertaking that was not at all hampered by the fine opposable thumbs that we now take for granted. Although many other primates also have opposable thumbs, no other animal can boast the manual dexterity that we have at our fingertips. And no other animal possesses as complex a **brain** as we have.

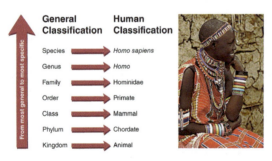

Figure 2.1   Biological classification of humans. We are the only species of the genus *Homo*, ⌐but⌐ there are more than 300 known living primate species in the world.

Photo on right: Photolibrary/Peter Arnold Images/Martin Harvey

Brain: A complex clustering of nerve cells that is centrally involved in coordinating activities and events in various parts of an organism. The human brain is reputedly the most complex structure in the universe.

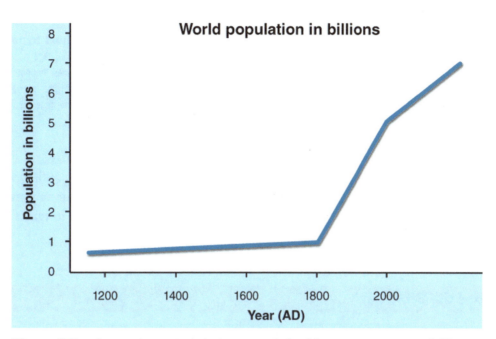

Figure 2.2 Approximate population growth for *Homo sapiens* on earth. The part of the graph to the left that is not shown would extend about 1 mile if it reached back to the time when humans first appeared.

Based on World Population Prospects: The 2008 Revision Population Database, United Nations Population Division. Retrieved July 20, 2010, from http://esa.un.org/unpd/wpp/index.htm; U.S. Census Bureau, International Data Base, June 2010 update. Retrieved June 20, 2010, from http://www.census.gov/ipc/www/idb/worldpopgraph.php

These adapted abilities are clues as to what tasks the mind of a *H. sapien* has developed to do, and how our brains have evolved into a system of "psychological faculties or mental modules" (Pinker, 1997).

Brains, Language, and Thinking

With such complex brains, we eventually were able to develop primitive tools, agricultural and hunting strategies, and inventions such as the wheel, the rocket, and the computer. But perhaps more important than all of those, the capacities of the human brain gave way to the development of language and culture.

Useful though they may be for a variety of purposes, our fine opposable thumbs aren't our biggest evolutionary advantage: Our enormously complex brains are.

© teerayuth oanwong/Shutterstock.com

Thinking and language are very closely related. In fact, a school of thought that was widely popular among anthropologists a few decades ago maintained that language is *essential* for, and determines, thought—a belief labeled the **Sapir-Whorf hypothesis**. This hypothesis maintains that different languages lead people to see the world differently and to think and behave differently (Whorf, 2012). For example, some early research suggested that the Inuit, who seemed to have many different words for snow, could actually perceive types of snow of which others were unaware. Similarly, cultures that had a different vocabulary for colors were thought to see colors differently. These beliefs have now been discredited (Pullum, 1991).

> **Sapir-Whorf hypothesis:** The belief that language is essential for and determines thought (strong form); or the belief that language limits but does not determine thought (weak form).

Experimental research has not supported the Sapir-Whorf hypothesis (Koerner, 2000). It seems that language is not essential for thinking. For example, there is evidence of thinking among preverbal infants (Gleitman & Papafragou, 2005). And it is also true that adults sometimes think in terms of images or other symbols rather than with language.

What Does the Bible Say?

⌐Humans are unique on the planet when it comes to complex language. The Bible has a lot to say about how we use language. What we say can have long-lasting consequences, so we are to be careful about what we say.

Ephesians 4:29 ESV

"Let no corrupting talk come out of your mouths, but only such as is good for building up, as fits the occasion, that it may give grace to those who hear."

Proverbs 12:18 ESV

"There is one whose rash words are like sword thrusts, but the tongue of the wise brings healing."

Matthew 12:36 ESV

"I tell you, on the day of judgment people will give account for every careless word they speak…"

Hebrews 4:12 ESV

"For the word of God is living and active, sharper than any two-edged sword, piercing to the division of soul and of spirit, of joints and of marrow, and discerning the thoughts and intentions of the heart."

Proverbs 15:1 ESV

"A soft answer turns away wrath, but a harsh word stirs up anger."

Proverbs 16:24 ESV

"Gracious words are like a honeycomb, sweetness to the soul and health to the body."

Proverbs 17:27–28 ESV

"Whoever restrains his words has knowledge, and he who has a cool spirit is a man of understanding. Even a fool who keeps silent is considered wise; when he closes his lips, he is deemed intelligent."

1 Peter 3:10

"For 'Whoever desires to love life and see good days, let him keep his tongue from evil and his lips from speaking deceit…'"⌐

Introduction to Brain–Behavior Relationships

The brain is obviously extraordinary. It is supporting your efforts to read and understand this sentence right now. All of the amazing capabilities of the brain are derived from the activity and interactivity of cells called **neurons**. Neurons, which are specialized cells, are the building blocks of the brain. Each neuron is like a sophisticated computer carrying out specific, predetermined activities. Very broadly, neurons can be divided into three categories: sensory, motor, and interneurons. Sensory neurons are involved in process like seeing, smelling, tasting, and hearing. Motor neurons are involved in generating a physical response, like running, kicking, throwing, or typing. Lastly, interneurons are involved in the processing and storage of information and serve as a link between the two aforementioned neurons—these neurons more generally would be involved in what we typically associate with "thinking."

> **Neurons:** Specialized information-processing cells that make up the brain; they control sensations, thinking, and movement. A single nerve cell, the smallest unit of the nervous system and its basic structural unit. The function of the neuron is to transmit impulses, which are basically electrical but are made possible through chemical changes.

While a computer by itself is rather impressive, an exciting transformation occurred when computers were linked together through the Internet or World Wide Web. The interactivity resulted in an amazing increase in processing complexity and related applications. Like the Internet, the brain has many individual "computers," but the true processing complexity is derived from the astonishing interconnectedness of these cells—some cells interface with hundreds of thousands of other cells. The connections in the brain play a very significant role in the brain's overall capacity for adapting, learning, and thinking. In fact, as we age, we ultimately have fewer and fewer neurons; but those remaining neurons, which are still astronomical in number, tend to increase in complexity over time. The good news is that neurons are able to "learn." The result is greater efficiency and interconnectivity. Increased interconnectivity makes subsequent learning easier; that is, as we learn more, learning more becomes easier. The brain is also supported by another category of cells. **Glial cells** support the brain in a number of vital and complex ways but are not directly involved in information-processing. Just like computers are supported by batteries, fans, and casings, the brain is supported by cells that make sure the brain is maximally operating and well protected.

> **Glial cells:** Cells that support neural functioning. Among other functions, they clean out debris and form protective coatings around nerves.

Neurons serve as the functional building blocks for the brain. They are the most amazing, unique, and complex cells in the body. Neurons provide meaning for the aspects of our lives that most valuable to us: moving, sensing, perceiving, remembering, thinking, and enjoying life. The essence of who we are, ultimately, resides in our neurons because they store our autobiographical information, our unique histories, and serve as the substance underlying our consciousness. All of the other cells in the body function to sustain and protect these cells. Unfortunately, neurons are also the site of action for all abused drugs. Understanding how neurons work, therefore, is critical to understanding how abused drugs and chemicals work.

> **Nervous system:** All parts of the body composed of nerve cells, the function of which is to transmit messages. The major components of the human nervous system are the brain, the spinal cord, receptor systems associated with the major senses, and other nerve cells implicated in the functioning of muscles and glands.

Inrodution to the Nervous System

The brain is part of our **nervous system**. In a simple sense, our nervous system is the electrical and chemical communication system within our bodies. It is because of our nervous system that our right hand knows what our left hand is doing, that our legs alternate rather than compete when we walk, and that we are sensitive to our environments. In fact, it is because of our nervous system we can even think about such matters; hence its tremendous importance in psychology.

The nervous systems of insects also provide an interesting evolutionary contrast to that of humans. In some insects, primitive clusters of nerve cells coordinate simple functions, such as a cockroach's brain telling it when and where to run (Bender et al., 2010), but in many insects, there is no single "command area"—no brain to oversee all functions or to be aware of what is going on in all parts of the body. Cut off the head of a wasp and it will continue eating even though it has lost its abdomen and there's nowhere for the food to go. In much the same way, the male praying mantis will continue to copulate even as the female systematically devours him from the head down (Prokop & Vaclav, 2008).

The more advanced nervous systems of fish, reptiles, and mammals differ from these more primitive nervous systems. Not only is their functioning more complex, but their activity is coordinated by an increasingly larger brain. Furthermore, brains in more advanced animals have become highly specialized: A large portion of the bat's brain is devoted to hearing (essential for echolocation); the olfactory (smell) area of a dog's brain is far more developed than that of a human's brain; those parts of the brain that control rapid movement are more predominant in a bird's brain; and in humans, the area of the brain devoted to thinking is larger, proportional to the remainder of the brain, than in any other living creature (Figure 2.3). It is this brain, the command center of our nervous system, that is largely responsible for producing the behaviors and qualities we believe make us uniquely human.

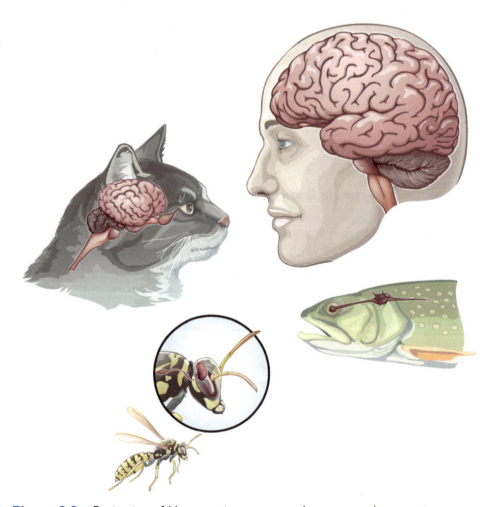

Figure 2.3   Brain size of *Homo sapiens* compared to many other species.

Interesting Facts About the Brain

1. ⌐The human brain at birth weighs about 400 grams (14.1 ounces) and about 1,450 grams (51.1 ounces or 3.19 lbs) at maturity.
2. After the age of 30, the human brain begins to lose weight until about age 75. At this point the brain has lost about 100 grams.
3. The brain is made up of 180 billion neurons.
4. There are about 10 million sensory neurons and about 0.5 million motor neurons. This provides a ratio of about 20:1 between the combined input and output channels. There are many times more channels available for analyzing the data and providing an appropriate response.
5. Each cell in the brain receives about 15,000 to 150,000 connections from other cells.
6. There are an estimated 300 trillion synapses in the human brain.
7. Each and every brain is functionally and morphologically distinct.
8. You are born with nearly all of the brain cells you will have in your lifetime.
9. Neurons can carry an impulse at speeds of nearly 400 miles per hour.
10. Neurons can fire up to 1,000 times per second.⌐

THE NEURON

The human nervous system is a *communication* system; its function is to transmit messages (impulses). Many of the messages it transmits go from sensory **receptors** (such as the skin, eyes, nose, tongue, ears, muscles, joints, and tendons) to the command center (the brain). Impulses also go from the brain to what are termed **effectors** (such as muscular and glandular systems).

> **Receptors:** Specialized cells or groups of cells that respond to sensory stimulation.
>
> **Effector:** A specialized cell or organ that carries out a response to a nerve impulse.

The cells that make up the nervous system, and whose specialized function is to transmit impulses, are called neurons (or *nerve cells*). Estimates vary widely, but scientists believe there are approximately 86 ⌐to 100⌐ billion neurons in the human brain alone, with the bulk of these—some 69 billion—being in the part of the brain called the *cerebellum* (Azevedo et al., 2009). The spinal cord contains at least a billion more, and several billion more are concentrated in sensory receptors and in muscular and glandular *effector* systems. Other neurons are *connectors:* They serve as links between receptor and effector systems (Figure 2.4). Most of the connectors are located in the brain.

Like all other living cells, neurons consist of a nucleus and surrounding matter. This matter is made up of the cell body, **axon**, and **dendrites**. The axon of a neuron is surrounded by a protective coating, called a **myelin sheath** (made up of glial cells), which speeds up neuronal communication and provides an efficient mechanism for one neuron to talk to another neuron. Without this very important myelin, your brain would not function properly. In extreme cases, our bodies can be tricked into attacking and destroying our own myelin, leading to what is known as *multiple sclerosis.* The destruction of myelin can also significantly affect the mind's ability to send messages to the muscles, which can lead to a loss of muscle control (Fields, 2008).

> **Axon:** The elongated part of a nerve cell. Axons ordinarily transmit impulses from the cell body to adjoining dendrites.
>
> **Dendrites:** Hair-like extensions emanating from the cell body of the neuron. Dendrites ordinarily receive impulses from adjoining axons.
>
> **Myelin sheath:** An insulating, protective coating that surrounds nerve fibers and facilitates neural transmission.

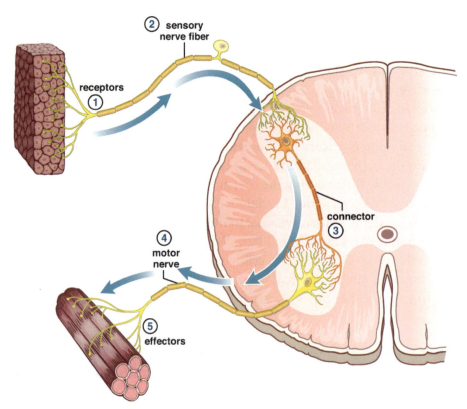

Figure 2.4 (A)   Schematic conception of the components of the sensorimotor arc. *Receptors* (1) in eyes, tactile organs, nose, ears, taste buds, and kinesthetic senses send signals (2) to *connectors* (3) in the spinal cord, brain, and other neural pathways. Signals are then sent (4) to *effectors* (5) in muscles and glands.

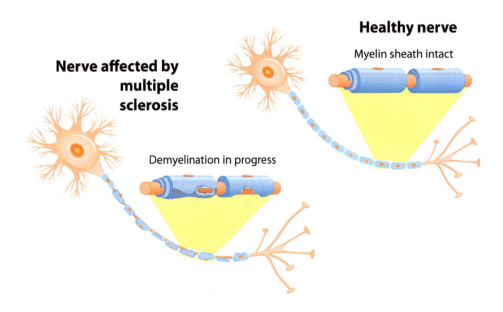

Figure 2.4 (B)   Schematic conception of a healthy nerve cell and a nerve cell affected by multiple sclerosis.

The axon is the elongated part of a neuron: It may be microscopically short or, as is the case for some neurons located in the spinal cord, as long as 2 or 3 feet! Dendrites are hair-like extensions emanating from the cell body of the neuron. These dendrites receive messages that other nerve cells, or neurons, send to them. The space between the ends of one cell's axon and another cell's dendrites is a **synapse**. At the synapse, one neuron can communicate with another neuron by sending little chemical messengers, called neurotransmitters (discussed in detail in a bit), across the synapse. The type and amount of these neurotransmitters can influence the likelihood of subsequent neural communication, which can alter our moods and behaviors. Bundles of neurons make up **nerves**. The typical configuration of a neuron is shown in Figure 2.5.

> **Synapse:** A microscopic gap between the end of an axon and an adjacent dendrite, axon, or other cell across which neural impulses (neurotransmitters) travel.
>
> **Nerve:** Bundles of fibers consisting of neurons, whose functions is the transmission of neural impulses.

Neural Transmission

The transmission of impulses from neuron to neuron involves both electrical and chemical activity. Think of each neuron as a tiny battery that can generate an electrical impulse. Electricity is the flow of negatively charged particles (called *electrons*) toward a positively charged pole. In the neuron, electrical impulses operate in exactly the same way. A neuron at rest (*resting potential*) is like a charged battery with the switch off. Stimulation brings about a series of chemical changes that effectively open the switch, causing a flow of charged particles called an **action potential**. And about 2 milliseconds later, the neuron again regains its *resting potential*. But for a brief period, termed a **refractory period**, it is essentially discharged and therefore

> **Action potential:** A pulse-like electrical discharge along a neuron. Sequences of linked action potentials are the basis for the transmission of neural messages.
>
> **Refractory period:** A brief period after firing during which a neuron is "discharged" and is incapable of firing again.

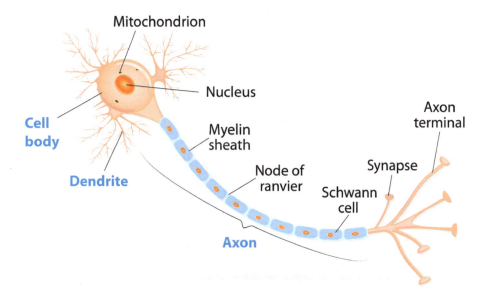

Figure 2.5   Anatomy of a typical human neuron. Neural transmission typically proceeds from the cell body, down the axon, across the synapse, and to the dendrites and cell bodies of adjacent cells.

© Designua/Shutterstock.com

puts the neuron into a state that makes it physically impossible to produce another action potential until its normal resting potential is again achieved (Figure 2.6).

Note the electrical impulse involves the entire neuron and is equally strong throughout the neuron, hence the expression "all-or-none" firing. The level of stimulation needed for a neuron to fire is referred to as the **threshold**. Think of threshold as pulling a trigger

> **Threshold:** The minimum level of stimulation needed for a neuron to fire an action potential.

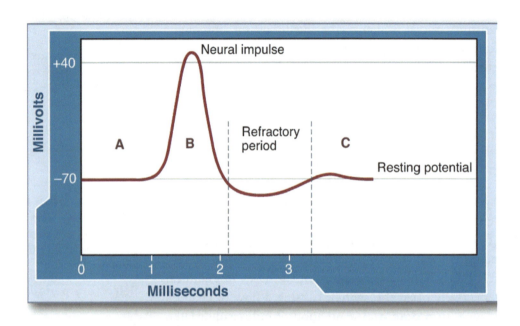

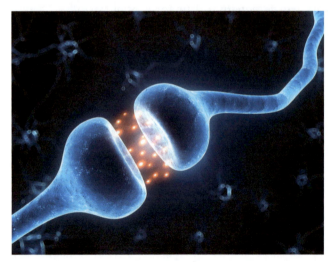

Figure 2.6

Representation of a neural impulse. At point A, there exists a state of readiness (*resting potential*). At B, a stimulus leads to an electrical impulse (*action potential*), which is followed immediately by a *refractory period* during which the cell cannot fire. A few milliseconds later, the cell is restored to its resting potential (charged) state. As shown in this photo of a synapse, certain chemical substances, as illustrated by the yellow and white dots located in this synapse, are the neurotransmitters (e.g., dopamine and serotonin), which play an important part in the "opening" of neural membranes to allow the passage of the electrical impulse.

Image on bottom: © Sebastian Kaulitzki/Shutterstock.com

on a gun, or a popcorn kernel about to pop. The amount of squeezing pressure you apply to the handle and trigger will eventually reach a level that causes the gun to fire. Likewise, the temperature inside a kernel will eventually reach a temperature that will cause the kernel to pop. Both of these instances reach a time in which there is a point of no return: The level of stimulation will or will not cause the action potential (all-or-none firing). Just like a popcorn kernel or gun, the stimulation intensity applied to a neuron will or will not cause it to fire: It all depends on the intensity of the stimulus.

To illustrate the process of an action potential, imagine stubbing your toe on a piece of furniture. Unfortunately, axons are efficient transmitters of electrical signals, and you will soon feel pain as a result of the transmission from your toe to your brain. Unfortunately, the "pain" sensation will not reach your brain immediately. Although electricity travels at the speed of light (186,300 feet per second), the thinnest axons transmit impulses at only around 3 feet per second! Larger axons might transmit at speeds up to 10 feet per second (Kalat, 2009).

So, less than a second after you stub your toe, you will know that you did so, unless something has happened to disrupt the flow of electrical impulses in relevant nerves. That is basically what happens when your dentist uses *novocaine* to "freeze" you. Nothing is frozen in the literal sense, but novocaine does effectively block the flow of electrical impulses between neurons. So, pain signals are being sent, but nothing is reaching the end of the line. Basically, no matter how desperately the receptors in your tooth yell, "It hurts," the message simply does not get to your brain.

The process of neurotransmission is made possible by certain chemicals called **neurotransmitters**, which are released by neurons, changing the electrical potential of cells and thus leading to neural transmission. These chemicals are then reabsorbed by the releasing neuron—a process referred to as **reuptake**.

The significance of the synapse in understanding drugs cannot be understated. The synapse is the location where drugs principally interact with nervous system tissue (i.e., brain). Drugs do this by simply modifying existing processes, often by mimicking or blocking existing neurotransmitters. **Agonists** increase the effectiveness of neurotransmitters, either by stimulating neurons to produce more, by increasing the sensitivity of receptor cells, or by preventing the reuptake of the neurotransmitter, thus making more available. **Antagonists** block or reduce the effects of a neurotransmitter. The synapse is also the structure in the brain that has the highest level of plasticity. **Plasticity** is defined as the ability to change. Basically, all learning could be defined as plasticity at the synapse because learning requires changes in the function of the synapse.

Because drugs have a direct impact on synaptic activity, they generally produce rapid changes in the function of the synapse. Generally, the alteration beyond normal levels is forcing the synapse to adapt (i.e., learn). Thus, drugs that cause stimulation of postsynaptic receptors (e.g., agonists) often result in long-term deactivation of these same receptors. This is generally referred to as down regulation. Long-term blockade of receptors (e.g., antagonists) often result in an increase in postsynaptic receptors, which is more generally referred to as up regulation. These adaptive responses, due to long-term drug

Neurotransmitters: Naturally produced chemicals that are released by nerve cells and that initiate or facilitate transmission of messages among nerve cells (e.g., serotonin, dopamine, norepinephrine, and acetylcholine).

Reuptake: The process by which a nerve cell recaptures some of the neurotransmitters it has released. Some medications and drugs function to increase neurotransmitter effectiveness by blocking reuptake.

Agonists: An agent or drug that enhances the activity of some naturally occurring substance. For example, cocaine is a dopamine agonist in that it appears to stimulate the activity of dopamine.

Antagonists: A drug that blocks the effectiveness of a neurotransmitter. For example, beta blockers are antagonists that reduce blood pressure by impeding receptivity of adrenaline receptors.

Plasticity: The ability to change.

exposure, serve as the neural foundation of what we consider to be tolerance and withdrawal. Of special interest in the treatment of a variety of emotional and physical disorders are drugs that have been developed to increase or impede the functioning of the neurotransmitters.

Of the more than 100 different neurotransmitters that have now been identified, four are especially important in the study of psychology: dopamine, norepinephrine, acetylcholine, and serotonin. The table at the end of this section includes a more complete list of neurotransmitters along with their proposed role in brain function.

Comparison between Graded Potentials and Action Potentials	
Graded Potentials	**Action Potentials**
1. Graded responses; amplitude is proportional to the initiating event.	1. All-or-none response; once membrane is depolarized to threshold, the amplitude is independent of the initiating event.
2. Graded responses are summated both spatially and temporally.	2. All-or-none responses cannot be summated.
3. Has no threshold.	3. Has a definite threshold (usually about a 10 to 15 mV change in the resting potential).
4. Has no refractory period.	4. Has a refractory period.
5. The strength of conduction decreases as the impulse moves along the dendrite.	5. The speed of the action potential does not decrease over distance.
6. Can be a depolarization or a hyperpolarization.	6. Is only able to depolarize.
7. Can be initiated by environmental energy or by neurotransmitter activity or can fire spontaneously.	7. Initiated by membrane depolarization.

Review of Neuronal Communication

1. The neuron synthesizes chemicals that serve as neurotransmitters.
2. The neuron transports these chemicals to the presynaptic terminals of its axon.
3. An action potential causes the release of the neurotransmitters from the terminals.
4. The released neurotransmitters attach to the postsynaptic receptors and alter the activity of the postsynaptic neuron (or muscle or gland) resulting in a graded potential.
5. The neurotransmitters separate from their receptors and are converted into inactive chemicals by either reuptake receptors on the presynaptic terminal or enzymes located within the synaptic gap.
6. The presynaptic neuron reabsorbs some of the neurotransmitters, and some are broken down whereas others are repackaged into vesicles to be used again.

Dopamine

Dopamine plays a key role in the functioning of neurons associated with pleasure and reinforcement. In fact, almost all abused drugs can attribute their abuse potential and feel-good effects to the increase in

Dopamine: A neuro-transmitter centrally involved with pleasure and reinforcement and also implicated in some instances of drug addiction as well as in conditions such as Parkinson's disease.

dopamine activity in certain areas of the brain. Some research (e.g., Asensio et al., 2010; Self & Staley, 2010) indicates individuals who normally have low levels of dopamine are more likely to become addicted. And in some cases, there appear to be genetic differences between addicts and non-addicts related to this neurotransmitter (Levran et al., 2009).

A disease associated with low dopamine levels in areas of the brain where dopamine is usually most concentrated is **Parkinson's disease**. It is characterized by uncontrollable shaking, generalized weakness, slow movements, constipation, sleep disturbances, and depression. On the other end of the spectrum, too much dopamine in different regions of the brain is thought to be a contributing factor to many of the positive symptoms of schizophrenia.

> **Parkinson's disease:** A central nervous system disease characterized by tremors, slow movement, and other symptoms; associated with low dopamine levels in the brain.

Almost all abused drugs are effective because they increase the release of dopamine in the brain and/or prevent its reuptake.

© Marco Govel/Shutterstock.com

Norepinephrine

The neurotransmitter **norepinephrine** (also called *noradrenaline*) increases blood pressure and triggers the release of glucose (sugar) from energy stores. Consequently, it is the neurotransmitter most closely linked with crises. In an emergency, parts of the brain are suddenly flooded with norepinephrine, a signal that prepares the body to respond, perhaps by fleeing, perhaps by fighting. If you have ever heard of, or experienced, an "adrenaline rush," norepinephrine is the primary neurotransmitter responsible for the feelings of the rush, which can accompany activities like skydiving or base jumping for some.

Norepinephrine is not just involved in extreme physical activities or flight-or-fight responses. Research indicates that norepinephrine levels may be implicated in some instances of **attention-deficit hyperactivity disorder (ADHD**; Bhaduri et al., 2010). One of the effects of drugs (such as Ritalin) commonly used to treat ADHD is they act as norepinephrine/dopamine reuptake inhibitors, increasing available levels of norepinephrine and dopamine in the *synapse* (Cohen-Yavin et al., 2009). This improves the person's ability to concentrate and to think clearly about what is being focused on, thus alleviating one of the main symptoms of ADHD.

Some manifestations of depression are also linked with norepinephrine. Many common antidepressant drugs (e.g., *tricyclic antidepressants* such as Elavil, Norpramin, and Pamelor) are agonists that increase norepinephrine levels by blocking its reuptake (Craig, 2006). One of the effects of increased norepinephrine levels is a speeding up of neural activity, which counters the "slowing down" sensation that often accompanies depression. Interestingly, an overabundance of norepinephrine has been linked with *mania*, the opposite mood to depression (Narayan & Haddad, 2011).

> **Norepinephrine:** A neurotransmitter linked with arousal, memory, and learning. Anomalies in the functioning of the norepinephrine system may be linked to manifestations of depression. Also called *noradrenaline*.

> **Attention deficit hyperactivity disorder (ADHD):** A disorder marked by excessive general activity for a child's age, attention problems, high impulsivity, and low frustration tolerance. Also termed *hyperactivity*.

Acetylcholine

Acetylcholine is a neurotransmitter involved in the largely unconscious functioning of the *autonomic* nervous system (concerned with functions such as heart and respiration rates). It is also importantly involved in conscious activity such as muscle movement, as well as in arousal, reinforcement, learning, and memory (Arnulf & Leu-Semenescu, 2009). It can also serve to increase the reactivity of neurons or to inhibit their responsiveness. Drugs that stimulate the

> **Acetylcholine:** A neurotransmitter present in the peripheral as well as central nervous system, involved in voluntary activity as well as physiological functions (such as heart and respiration rates).

acetylcholine system or that block its functioning have a variety of medical uses, including the treatment of Alzheimer's disease (Zhang et al., 2010).

The venom of a black widow spider acts as an *agonist* for acetylcholine. Meaning, when one gets bitten by a black widow spider, acetylcholine neurotransmitters and receptors are highly activated. This high activation and abnormally high release of acetylcholine can cause muscles to remain painfully contracted. Conversely, botulin (a poison found in small amounts in Botox treatments to get rid of wrinkles), is an antagonist for acetylcholine. *Antagonists* for acetylcholine can cause muscle paralysis (Gomez & Queiroz, 1982).

Serotonin

Serotonin is involved in neural transmission in much of the brain, especially in areas having to do with emotion. Its other functions include regulating sleep, appetite, and cognitive activity related to learning and memory (Pothakos et al., 2010). Depressed levels of serotonin have been linked with depression, aggression, and even violence. Accordingly, many antidepressants and anti-anxiety drugs are *agonists*

> **Serotonin:** A neurotransmitter, the bulk of which is found in the gut, where it regulates intestinal activity. Too low levels of serotonin may be associated with depression.

that affect serotonin levels by acting as selective serotonin reuptake inhibitors, or SSRIs (Arnone et al., 2009). Similar drugs are also sometimes used to control impulsive, violent behavior (Butler et al., 2010).

The Psychobiology of Drugs

The simplest way to clarify how drugs work is to first understand that drugs do not have any magical or mystical properties. All drugs work solely by altering existing physiological (i.e., biological) processes. More specifically, drugs work to increase or decrease an already occurring physiological process. The exact process that is being changed and how that process is being changed refers to the drug's mechanism of action. **Pharmacodynamics** is a more sophisticated term used to describe the mechanism of action of drugs and their corresponding effects. Because drugs have effects that are limited across time, there must also be some mechanism or process to deactivate them. Similarly, drugs are nearly always self-administered. There is a predictable route by which drugs move, as they enter and exit our body. **Pharmacokinetics** is a term used to describe the path that drugs take through our body, from start to

> **Pharmacodynamics:** The mechanism of action of drugs and their corresponding effects.
>
> **Pharmacokinetics:** The path that drugs take through our body, from start to finish.

finish. Another way to conceptualize the distinction between pharmacodynamics and pharmacokinetics is that pharmacodynamics explains the relationship between the dose of the drug and its effect; that is, a drug dose and a response. In contrast, pharmacokinetics explains the relationship between the doses of the drug across time; that is, how long the drug lasts. Stated plainly, what drugs do to our body is called pharmacodynamics, and what our body does to the drug is called pharmacokinetics.

Various recreational and addictive drugs can provide ways of altering the biological mechanisms in our brain and can effectively shape our reality. Most people do not develop crippling addictions to drugs because they can manage when and how much of a certain drug they should take. Like following a doctor's prescription, a person who experiences frequent mild headaches most likely does not become

© Velimir Zeland/Shutterstock.com

addicted to Advil or Tylenol. They don't *need* these pain killers to function properly throughout the day. Most people who use over-the-counter medication or other various prescriptions do not become **dependent** on these drugs.

Other people, however, do become dependent, and do need these substances to function properly, and at times, survive. These people more likely than not have become addicted to a **psychoactive drug**, a chemical substance that alters their perceptions and moods in such a way that either feels good to the user, and/or prevents the user from feeling bad. Here we briefly discuss a few of the more common psychoactive drugs, their effects on the brain and neurotransmitter systems, and how they can influence behavior. They are identified as being either a **stimulant** or a **depressant**. Stimulants are drugs that speed up bodily functions, whereas depressants are drugs that slow down bodily functions.

The problem with classifying drugs behaviorally is we don't always behave the same way after taking a drug; meaning drugs have such complex effects that it can be challenging to predict how a person might react to a given drug at one point in time based on their reaction at a previous point in time. Drugs, like other stimuli with which we interact, do have some powerfully predictable effects at specific dose ranges. For example, at a high enough dose of alcohol, everyone reacts the exact same—coma followed by death. On the other end of the continuum, everyone reacts the same to a very low dose of a drug—no effect at all. In order to understand how a drug impacts behavior, it is important to understand not only the broad classification of that drug, but also the behavioral state of the person prior to taking the drug. Drugs affect people's behavior differently depending on, among other factors, the frequency, intensity, and duration of the behavior prior to the drug exposure. So, to that point, simply referring to drugs as depressants or stimulants is actually too simplistic a way to categorize drugs just as calling a drug legal or illegal doesn't change its abuse potential.

The reasons for drug abuse are many. People use drugs to elevate the mood, decrease anxiety, reduce pain, increase energy, focus attention, or produce delusions. However, the primary purpose of substance

Dependent: A state of being characterized by the compulsive desire to have a substance, such as a drug, in order to feel "normal" and postpone the effects of withdrawal.

Psychoactive drug: A chemical substance that has the ability to alter perception, mood, behavior, and/or physiological function.

Stimulant: A type of drug that speeds up physiological functions. Cocaine is an abused stimulant and it speeds up the heart rate.

Depressant: A type of drug that slows down physiological functions. Alcohol is a commonly abused depressant and it slows down respiration.

use was and continues to be associated with alterations in consciousness. These alterations can be produced by a variety of drugs, each capable of exerting a unique profile of effects (Hopkins, 1998). Although there are many different abused chemicals, they tend to fall into eight major categories; these categories are based, in part, on the drug's mechanism of action. Drugs in each of the categories below tend to influence similar brain chemicals and structures.

1. Psychostimulants—cocaine, amphetamine, methylphenidate
2. Tobacco products/nicotine—cigarettes, chewing tobacco, cigars
3. Opioids—heroin, Oxytocin, Percocet, morphine
4. Depressants—alcohol, benzodiazepines, barbiturates
5. Inhalants—nitrous oxide, ethyl ether, toluene
6. Cannabinoids—marijuana
7. Psychedelics—lysergic acid diethylamide (LSD), mescaline, psilocybin
8. Dissociative agents (Arylcyclohexylamines)—phencyclidine (PCP), ketamine, dextromethorphan

⌐**Rebound effects** are another important aspect of drug effects over the course of time. A rebound effect occurs because the body is trying to bring itself back to a normal (pre-drug) level of functioning. Rebound effects tends to overcompensate, thus producing an exaggerated effect that often lasts longer than the initial drug effect. In other words, if a drug activates a particular process (e.g., increased heart rate) and the drug is removed, that particular process shows an inverse effect (e.g., decreased heart rate). The rebound effect will cause a longer lasting effect (i.e., decreased heart rate will last longer

> ⌐**Rebound effect:** Drugs exert acute, immediate effects as the drug wears off, an equal but opposite effect generally takes place. Taking a drug that produces sedation can result in increased arousal when it is deactivated by the body.⌐

than increased heart rate.) As is the case with abused drugs, the exact experience or problem that the drug user is trying to stimulate or eliminate, like euphoria or fatigue, respectively, backer-emerges when

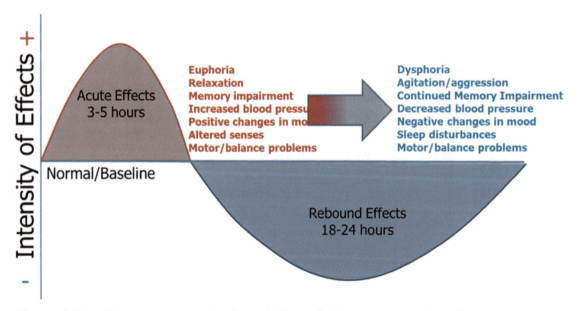

Figure 2.7 ⌐This is an acute and rebound effect of a drug that lasts about 3 to 5 hours. This shows that such a drug would likely produce a rebound effect lasting 18 to 24 hours and during that time the opposite effect would take place.⌐

Source: Brian Kelley

the drug wears off and is, generally, lasts longer and is worse than it was before the drug was taken. Sleep aids provide a good example. Obviously, the reason people take sleep aids is to help them sleep. However, if a person discontinues use after several days, they will often experience several nights of insomnia. During the rebound phase, even more drug will be required to achieve an effect because the drug now has to bring the behavior back to normal before it can begin to produce the desired effect. This is why the rebound effect plays a significant role in maintaining compulsive drug use.⌟

Nicotine

Nicotine is one of the most addicting stimulants. Not surprisingly, it is one of the most commonly used drugs in the world. People with a crippling addiction to nicotine generally resort to smoking as their primary route of administration. When a person smokes a cigarette, they feel the effects about as quickly and powerfully as heroin or cocaine. Unfortunately, this may be all it takes for one to get addicted, and attempts to quit within the first week of smoking often fail (DiFranza, 2008).

Nicotine acts on many different neurotransmitters to elicit its addicting properties. Two neurotransmitters involved with nicotine use are norepinephrine and dopamine. Nicotine acts on norepinephrine to enhance mental efficiency and increase one's wakefulness, while also acting on dopamine, providing those crucial calming and reinforcing effects (Nowak, 1994).

Cocaine

Cocaine is another popular stimulant that influences dopamine levels in the brain. Cocaine produces reinforcing and addictive effects in its users by blocking the reuptake mechanisms of dopamine, serotonin, and norepinephrine (Ray & Ksir, 1990), resulting in more of these neurotransmitters left in the synapse, and the "feel good" feeling that follows. Cocaine is usually snorted in its powdered form, or smoked in its freebase form, known as crack cocaine, which results in a much stronger "high" in its users.

Alcohol

Alcohol is one of most commonly abused depressants. It slows neural processing and can disrupt memory formation if consumed in large quantities. Alcohol can also increase the chances of disinhibiting its users, or slowing the brain activity involved in judgment and decision making. For example, both men and women are more likely to participate in casual or unprotected sex and experience unwanted sexual encounters while under the influence of alcohol (Presley et al., 1997).

Alcohol's ability to disrupt judgment and decision making makes alcohol even more dangerous when someone has used alcohol and gets behind the wheel of a car. Coupled with the effect of blurred vision that alcohol can cause, we can see why drunk driving is such a serious problem.

What Kind of Drug Is Alcohol?

⌞Is it a stimulant?
Conventionally, it is classified as a depressant. However, alcohol also acts as a stimulant in some situations, increasing the frequency, duration, and intensities of many behaviors.

Is it a depressant?

Yes. Alcohol suppresses breathing, heart rate, and overall brain function.

Is it a hallucinogen?

Yes, alcohol can cause hallucinations. Severe withdrawal from alcohol results in delirium tremens, a condition marked by significant hallucinations.

Is it an antianxiety agent?

Yes. Alcohol is the world's most commonly employed antianxiety agent, and people will often drink to reduce social and/or situational anxiety.

Is it an epileptic?

© Maria Fomina/Shutterstock.com

Yes. Alcohol is both an epileptic and an antiepileptic. Acute use will prevent seizures, but severe withdrawal from alcohol can result in seizures, which can be fatal.

Is it a solvent?

Yes. Alcohol, at high concentrations, can damage and dissolve cell membranes.

In all of the scenarios noted above, the active ingredient is unchanged. It doesn't matter what type of alcohol is consumed, it is the exact same drug in every case—it is only the concentration or dose that changes.

Opiates

Opiates, specifically morphine and heroin, are two commonly abused depressants (psychoactive drugs that depress neural functioning). Morphine or heroin use leads to decreased respiratory function, slowed breathing, relaxation, and care-free pleasure as pain and anxiety subside.

Research done by Siegel (2001) has shown that opiate use and *tolerance* to opiate use is closely tied to environmental cues. For example, when researchers give repeated doses of heroin to rats in a specific environment, they eventually develop *tolerance* and need more of the drug to reach the same effects as before. This isn't surprising; however, if the researchers take the rat out of the environment that was usually paired with the opiate, and then give the rats the same dose of heroin as before, the rats overdose from the drug. What does this tell us? It tells us that these rats have *conditioned responses* that are elicited by the environment, which in a way "prepare" them for the drug. Without the environmental cues prior to drug taking, the rats are not expecting to the get the drug, their biological mechanisms used to fight the drug's effects are not there, and the likelihood of overdosing therefore increases.

The review of neuronal communication above addressed the key parts of the synapse. Of course, the synapse is considerably more complex, but a basic overview of key processes and features is provided in this book. Understanding what different neurotransmitters are responsible for, provides the most effective way to understand how drugs work because all drugs work by modifying existing neurotransmitters. A list of neurotransmitters, their effect, location, and functions, as well as which drugs interact with them, is noted in the following table.

Neurotransmitter	Effect	Location	Functions	Affected by
Acetylcholine	Excitatory	Cortex, spinal cord, neuromuscular junctions, organs activated by peripheral nervous system (PNS)	Excites or inhibits organs; learning, memory, and movement	Nicotine, some hallucinogens
Adenosine	Inhibitory	Brain, PNS	Sleep, wakefulness, and vasodilation	Caffeine
Anandamide	Inhibitory	Brain, spinal cord, PNS	Regulates the release of other neurotransmitters	Marijuana
Dopamine	Inhibitory	Limbic system, basal ganglia, cerebellum	Movement, emotional behavior, attention, learning, memory, and reward	Cocaine, amphetamine, methamphetamine, Ritalin, Adderall
Endorphins	Inhibitory	Brain, spinal cord	Pain reduction, emotional behavior, eating, learning	Heroin, Oxycodone, morphine
Epinephrine	Excitatory	Spinal cord, limbic system, cortex, organs activated by sympathetic nervous	Attention, hunger, energy, arousal, and fight or flight response	Cocaine, ephedrine, pseudoephedrine, amphetamines
Gamma-amino butyric acid (GABA)	Inhibitory	Brain, spinal cord	Primary inhibitory neurotransmitter in the brain. General inhibition, affects arousal and anxiety	Alcohol, barbiturates, benzodiazepines
Glutamate	Excitatory	Brain, spinal cord	Long-term memory, cognitive functioning	Alcohol, PCP, ketamine
Glycine	Inhibitory	Brain, spinal cord	General inhibitory effects	Antiepileptic drugs, some sedatives
Norepinephrine	Both	Spinal cord, cortex, limbic system,	Arousal, eating, emotional behavior, learning, and memory	Cocaine, ephedrine, amphetamines
Serotonin	Inhibitory	Brain, brainstem	Emotional behavior, arousal, sleep	MDMA (Ecstasy), LSD, mescaline, other hallucinogens

Connecting this to substance use disorder, what drug is someone most likely to abuse, becoming dependent or addicted? The answer is not universal; instead, the answer is the readily available drug that is the most rewarding to that particular person at that particular time. Both of these factors are significantly enhanced by biology but equally so by environment and social factors. To be succinct, **the most dangerous abused substance is the one *you* find most rewarding**. The behaviors that lead up to substance use, abuse, and dependence include a wide variety of biological, psychological, and sociological factors—just like any other complex behavior. Nearly all human behavior has biological, psychological, and sociological factors driving it. So, to fully understand what drives people to do just about anything, one must employ a form of analysis that includes all relevant factors.

What Does the Bible Say?

The Bible has a lot to say about using drugs to alter behavior and mental processes mainly because it puts people at risk for a host of serious problems. The Bible speaks more about alcohol than other drugs but the statements on alcohol can be generalized to any drug that alters behavior or causes health concerns.

Ephesians 5:15–21 ESV

"Look carefully then how you walk, not as unwise but as wise, making the best use of the time, because the days are evil. Therefore do not be foolish, but understand what the will of the Lord is. And do not get drunk with wine, for that is debauchery, but be filled with the Spirit, addressing one another in psalms and hymns and spiritual songs, singing and making melody to the Lord with your heart, giving thanks always and for everything to God the Father in the name of our Lord Jesus Christ, submitting to one another out of reverence for Christ."

Proverbs 20:1 ESV

"Wine is a mocker, strong drink a brawler, and whoever is led astray by it is not wise."

Proverbs 21:17 ESV

"Whoever loves pleasure will be a poor man; he who loves wine and oil will not be rich."

Proverbs 23:30–35 ESV

"Those who tarry long over wine; those who go to try mixed wine. Do not look at wine when it is red, when it sparkles in the cup and goes down smoothly. In the end it bites like a serpent and stings like an adder. Your eyes will see strange things, and your heart utter perverse things. You will be like one who lies down in the midst of the sea, like one who lies on the top of a mast. 'They struck me,' you will say, 'but I was not hurt; they beat me, but I did not feel it. When shall I awake? I must have another drink.'"

ORGANIZATION OF THE NERVOUS SYSTEM

While neurons are the building blocks for brain function, they clearly don't work in isolation—in fact, the exact opposite is true. Neurons work by interacting with other cells, especially other neurons, sensory and muscle cells. In the brain, neurons work together in groups to serve a common function. Generally, groups of neurons working together are referred to as **nuclei**. Nuclei are grouped together to form **structures**, and many structures working together are called **systems**. While the brain is often discussed in terms of

Nuclei: Groups of neurons working together.

Structures: Formed when nuclei are grouped.

Systems: Many structures working together.

structures and systems, in order for any given structure to have use, it must be able to communicate with other structures. So even well-defined structures derive their function by having connections: one *receives* information from other cells or structures (often called afferent projections) and at least one connection that *sends* information to other cells or structures (often called efferent projections). The brain derives its complex function by interacting and sharing information across structures and systems (e.g., similar to the Internet). The arrangement of these structures and systems is highly organizational and purposeful. It would have to be, considering that the brain may well be the most complex thing in the universe, and it only weighs about 3.5 pounds!

© SciePro/Shutterstock.com

⌐It helps to understand that sensory information enters the back (posterior) of the spine while movement information exits the front (anterior) of the spine. Much of the brain is dedicated to the integration of sensory-motor function, and this organization is maintained until information reaches the central relay structure (i.e., thalamus) located at the center of the brain. As information enters the brain, from a sensory system like touch, it travels upwards and eventually outward, terminating at some predetermined cortical area. Generally, the opposite is true for movement. Conscious movement starts at the front of the brain and works its way toward the center, down toward the spine, and eventually out to specific muscle groups.

The **central nervous system** (i.e., the brain and spinal cord) becomes more complex as information moves upward and outward. Related, the way in which the brain analyzes information also becomes more sophisticated as information travels to higher brain regions. At the base of the brain, function centers on vital reflexes. In the center of the brain, purpose centers on immediate and long-term survival functions. The surface, and most complex part of the brain, focuses on perceptions and maintaining our consciousness.⌐

The central nervous system (CNS) consists of the brain and **spinal cord**. It is via the spinal cord that most of the major neural pathways conduct impulses between brain centers and various glandular, muscular, and sensory systems.

The system of neural networks that fan out from the CNS into various parts of the body is the **peripheral nervous system** (**PNS**; Figure 2.8). The peripheral nervous system is linked to all sensory organs and to the muscles and glands; it is also involved in physiological activities such as respiration, heart action, sweating, and crying.

Therefore, in a way, the CNS consists of the brain and spinal cord, while the PNS consists of everything else in the nervous system.

The peripheral nervous system has two divisions. The **somatic system** transmits impulses relating to sensations of heat, cold, pain, and pressure to the CNS. It also transmits impulses in the opposite direction, from the CNS to muscles involved in voluntary movement.

Central nervous system (CNS): The human nervous system, which includes the brain and the spinal cord.

Spinal cord: Main link between the brain and sensory and motor systems, closely involved in reflexes such as the knee-jerk reflex.

Peripheral nervous system (PNS): The neural networks that fan out from the central nervous system to various parts of the body.

Somatic system: Part of the peripheral nervous system concerned with bodily sensations and muscular movement.

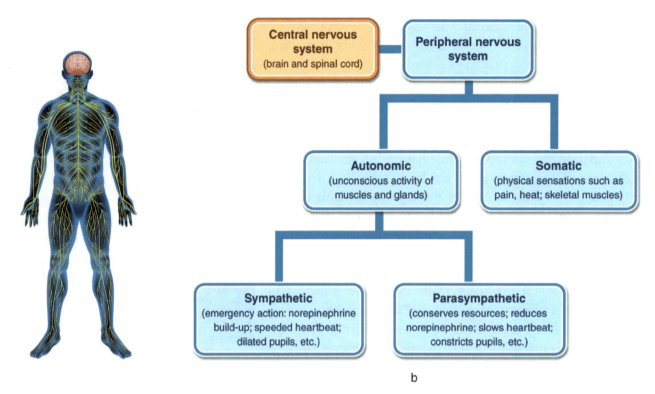

Figure 2.8 The human nervous system. Part (a) depicts the two major divisions of the nervous system: the central nervous system (bright orange) and the peripheral nervous system (darker). The organization and functions of each are described in (b).

Left image: © BlueRingMedia/Shutterstock.com

The **autonomic nervous system**, the other part of the peripheral nervous system, is directly involved in the action of muscles and glands that are automatic and involuntary. It includes the **sympathetic nervous system**, which is responsible for mobilizing the body's resources, particularly in emergency situations. It is your sympathetic nervous system that causes **adrenaline** to be pumped into your system. The result is that your heart beats faster, more blood rushes through your blood vessels, and you might tremble in anxiety, blush in shame, or respond with any of the other physiological changes that accompany intense emotion.

Most of us have little control over our physiological reactions, a fact that led to the invention of the common lie-detector. This instrument is capable of detecting changes that result from activity of the autonomic nervous system. If you become anxious when you lie (as most people do), your sympathetic nervous system reacts accordingly. As a result, your palms start to sweat, your breathing changes, and your heart rate increases.

But your heart rate does not accelerate indefinitely, nor do you tremble more and more violently. The **parasympathetic nervous system**, the other part of the autonomic nervous system, slows your heart rate, steadies your trembling, increases your control over bowel and bladder functioning, and in other ways opposes some of the functions of the sympathetic nervous system. It is as though the parasympathetic nervous system serves to conserve bodily resources.

Autonomic nervous system: That part of the peripheral nervous system that is not ordinarily under conscious control. It regulates physiological functions such as respiration, heart rate, temperature, and digestion and includes the sympathetic and parasympathetic systems.

Sympathetic nervous system: Part of the autonomic nervous system that instigates the physiological responses that accompany emotional behavior.

Adrenaline: Also called *epinephrine*. A substance produced by the adrenal glands, released in response to stress.

Parasympathetic nervous system: Part of the autonomic nervous system that regulates physiological reactions that accommodate emotional reactions.

Simply put the sympathetic nervous system serves a "flight-or-fight-or-freeze" purpose, while the parasympathetic nervous system serves a "rest-and-digest" purpose. Considering the general function of the autonomic nervous system and its impact on every organ and organ system (e.g., heart and cardiovascular system), it should not be surprising to learn that most side effects from drugs tend to occur across this system. People like to reduce discomfort, so when cold and flu season hits, it is common for people to use medication to alleviate such symptoms. A popular medication for nasal congestion is pseudoephedrine. Pseudoephedrine is generally taken to reduce nasal and sinus congestion, or congestion of the tubes that drain fluid from your inner ears. The drug goes throughout your entire body but the target area for symptom relief is comparatively very

When we're anxious, as might happen when we lie to a police investigator, our sympathetic nervous system kicks up our heart rate, our palms start to sweat, and our breathing changes. We can't control these reactions, they are automatic, and the "lie-detector"—a polygraph machine that measures these changes—reveals our lie.

© pefostudio5/Shutterstock.com

Preganglionic axons
Postganglionic axons
Pupil
Salivary glands
Heart
Vagus nerve
Cranial nerves (12 pairs)
Cervical nerves (8 pairs)
Lungs
Stomach
Celiac ganglion
Pancreas
Liver
Thoracic nerves (12 pairs)
Muscles that erect hairs
Adrenal gland
Sweat gland
Kidney
Small intestine
Large intestine
Lumbar nerves (5 pairs)
(Most ganglia near spinal cord)
Bladder
Pelvic nerve
Sacral nerves (5 pairs)
Uterus
Coccygeal nerve (1 pair)
Sympathetic outflow
Parasympathetic outflow
Genitals

Figure 2.9 The autonomic nervous system impacts every organ of the body with the sympathetic preparing the body for fight or flight while the parasympathetic preparing the body for rest and digest. Many drug side effects exert their influence on one of these systems.

© Emre Terim/Shutterstock.com

small. Because this drug impacts the sympathetic nervous system (i.e., fight or flight or freeze), it results in general increased activity of this system—not just in the nasal passages but everywhere. As such, it causes a variety of problems including nervousness, restlessness, dizziness, anxiety, loss of appetite, sleep difficulty, constipation, elevated heart rate, and increased blood pressure. These effects all occur through increased activity of epinephrine in the central nervous system but mostly in the autonomic nervous system.⌐

What Does the Bible Say?

⌐Anxiety and stress can result in a number of health problems as well as distractions in daily living and function. To a certain degree, we can learn to control our fight or flight or freeze response so that we don't feel as overwhelmed. Focusing and dwelling on what makes one anxious is a maladaptive pattern of living. Sometimes this could occur because of specific experiences or developmental trauma but it is clear that living this way is not ideal.

Philippians 4:6–8 ESV

"Do not be anxious about anything, but in everything by prayer and supplication with thanksgiving let your requests be made known to God. And the peace of God, which surpasses all understanding, will guard your hearts and your minds in Christ Jesus. Finally, brothers, whatever is true, whatever is honorable, whatever is just, whatever is pure, whatever is lovely, whatever is commendable, if there is any excellence, if there is anything worthy of praise, think about these things."

Matthew 6:25–34 ESV

"Therefore I tell you, do not be anxious about your life, what you will eat or what you will drink, nor about your body, what you will put on. Is not life more than food, and the body more than clothing? Look at the birds of the air: they neither sow nor reap nor gather into barns, and yet your heavenly Father feeds them. Are you not of more value than they? And which of you by being anxious can add a single hour to his span of life? And why are you anxious about clothing? Consider the lilies of the field, how they grow: they neither toil nor spin, yet I tell you, even Solomon in all his glory was not arrayed like one of these."⌐

The Endocrine System

The **endocrine system** is separate from the CNS, but it influences most of the organs, cells, and functions of the body. It includes glands that secrete **hormones** directly into the bloodstream and are therefore known as the ductless glands. Chief among them are the **pituitary gland**, which is frequently termed the "master" gland because of its role in regulating activity of other glands. The ductless glands also include the **adrenal glands** and the **gonads**.

The adrenal glands, which sit on top of the kidneys, are mainly responsible for releasing the hormone *adrenaline* in response to stress. The gonads include the testes, which produce male sex hormones such as *testosterone,* and the ovaries, which produce *estrogen* in females.

Endocrine system: A system of glands that secrete hormones whose functioning affects things such as growth, maturation, behavior, and emotion. Includes the pituitary, the adrenal glands, and the gonads.

Hormones: Chemicals that have a pronounced effect on growth, maturation, behavior, and emotions and that are produced by endocrine glands and secreted directly into the bloodstream.

⌐What are some similarities and differences between hormones and neurotransmitters? Each has several features in common. For example, both hormones and neurotransmitters are chemical messengers. Both are released from cells and activate receptors, and both are capable of eliciting physiological changes within the body. Although neurotransmitters tend to excerpt only local changes, hormones are capable of triggering whole body responses. Neurotransmitters are released from neurons into a synapse, whereas hormones are released from glands into the blood stream.⌐

> **Pituitary gland:** A small endocrine gland found as a protrusion off the hypothalamus. The *master gland* involved in controlling functioning of other endocrine glands.
>
> **Adrenal glands:** Endocrine glands situated at the top of the kidneys, involved in releasing hormones at times of stress.
>
> **Gonads:** Hormone-producing sex glands. Testes in the male; ovaries in the female.

THE BRAIN

The most important part of our CNS is our brain, which is arguably the single most complex structure in the entire known universe. We have known for some time this unimpressive-looking lump of grayish tissue is the very center of our ability to learn, feel, and think—it determines and defines our very essence. But we did not always know this. In fact, the ancient Egyptians considered the brain so unimportant that they did not bother to preserve it in their mummies, removing it instead through the left nostril (Blakemore, 1977). Only recently have modern discoveries revealed some secrets of the structures and functions of our brains, providing additional pieces to our human puzzle.

Studying Brain Functions

September 13, 1848 was an unlucky day for Phineas Gage, a railway worker on a rail line in Vermont. On that day, a tamping rod measuring 3 feet, 7 inches, shot out of a blasting hole and went through the left side of his face, through his brain, and out the top of his head! The blow hurled him to the ground. Most people would not survive such an extensive and serious blow to the head, but he quickly picked himself up, made his way to a cart, and went home.

Phineas' physical recovery was rapid and apparently complete. Friends, family, and anyone who knew Phineas before his accident said that he became moody and selfish and prone to outbursts of violent temper—behaviors very uncharacteristic of him. His physician, Dr. John Harlow, and a Harvard surgeon named Dr. Henry Bigelow concluded that the damaged part of his brain was responsible for controlling various aspects of emotions and personality (Macmillan, 2000). In fact, prior to the development of modern brain scanning technology, performing case studies of individuals with brain injuries was one of the first ways that scientists discovered different functions of the brain, also called localization of function.

Based on the structure and cracks in Phineas Gage's skull, which is now housed at Warren's Anatomical Museum within Harvard Medical School's Countway Library of Medicine, it is believed that the tamping rod primarily damaged Phineas Gage's *frontal lobe*. However, as Macmillan (2008) points out, no one ever examined Phineas Gage's brain directly, so there really is no certainty about what structures were damaged as a result of his injury. Also, there seems to have been some exaggeration and contradiction in reports of his case: There is a strong likelihood he did not change as dramatically as has sometimes been reported. The fact that he later began to suffer seizures and eventually died as a result might indicate his recovery was far from complete.

Brain Ablations

The problem with studying the brain using injuries such as those caused by tumors or by accidents is that these injuries don't usually have very specific effects. They often affect large parts of the brain, and investigators certainly cannot control who will have an accident—which makes for poor research.

Another approach is to deliberately cut out small portions of the brain and then see what the effects might be, also known as brain lesions. Understandably, this kind of research finds very few volunteers with healthy brains. Except where surgical procedures are required in cases of brain damage, epilepsy, tumors, or for other medical reasons, most of this research has been and has to be done with animals, primarily rats and mice.

A pioneer researcher in this area, Karl Lashley (1924), taught some rats how to run through a maze. He was convinced that different memories leave a trace in a tiny part of the brain, and he thought that if he cut out just the right part, the rat would no longer remember how to get through the maze. But Lashley never did find this memory trace (called an *engram*). It did not seem to matter what part of the brain he removed, or how much; the rat continued to run through the maze—although sometimes much more slowly. We now know that the kind of memories Lashley was studying were likely stored in parts of the brain he did not remove.

Brain Stimulation

Another way of studying the brain is to stimulate different parts of it with electrodes or with chemicals. For example, Olds (1956) implanted electrodes in the brains of rats and accidentally discovered that stimulating part of the *hypothalamus*—now labeled the "pleasure center"—seemed to be extremely pleasurable for the rat. When the electrodes were connected to a lever so that rats could stimulate their own brain, many would pass up food to do so. One rat stimulated himself more than 2,000 times an hour for 24 consecutive hours! Even more telling is that Olds (1958) found out that these rats would also be willing to cross a painful electrified grid to get the opportunity to press a lever to stimulate their pleasure centers.

Stimulating the brain with electrodes is an invasive and difficult undertaking; chemical stimulation is much simpler. It is possible to administer different drugs (chemicals) and to observe their effects on the participant's behavior and their effects on the brain. For example, chemical stimulation of the brain reveals that the neurotransmitter dopamine is involved in neural activity associated with pleasure. Dopamine, as we previously learned, is a naturally occurring neurotransmitter. Normally, when it is released as a result of neural stimulation, it is quickly recaptured by affected neurons (Kalat, 2009). But certain drugs such as amphetamines and cocaine act as *agonists* by preventing the immediate reuptake of the dopamine so that *dopaminergic neurons* (neurons that use dopamine for neural transmission) stay active longer. Because dopamine is associated with neural activity in one of the brain's "pleasure" centers, the ultimate effect of cocaine is intensely pleasurable (Morcom et al., 2010).

The prolonged use of agonists such as cocaine, however, leads the brain to synthesize less dopamine naturally as it adapts to the drug. In a way, drugs that act on dopamine, such as cocaine, can trick the brain into thinking there is plenty of dopamine available, and that the dopamine systems are functioning just fine. But the brain is mistaken. After the artificial source of dopamine activity (the drug) is gone, the brain is left with a depleted amount of the neurotransmitter. As a result, the chronic drug user often experiences depression and other negative moods rather than pleasure when the effects of the drug begin to wear off (termed *withdrawal*). Also, dopamine receptor activity decreases with repeated drug use (termed drug *tolerance*) so that ever-increasing amounts of the drug are required to reach the same effect of the drug as before (Slomski, 2006). Tolerance and the presence of withdrawal symptoms are important indicators of addiction.

Electrical stimulation of the brain's pleasure centers, as well as natural reinforcers such as food, water, and sex, and substances such as nicotine and alcohol, all lead to the release of dopamine (Lajtha & Sershen, 2010). And all of these substances and activities are potentially addictive.

Brain Imaging

The effect of chemicals on the brain is usually detected by means of one or more of the various sophisticated brain-imaging techniques researchers now have at their disposal ⌐as seen in the following table.⌐

⌐**Electroencephalogram (EEG)**  © Daniela Sachsenheimer/Shutterstock.com	An instrument used to measure and provide recordings of electrical activity in the brain.
Positron Emission Tomography (PET) 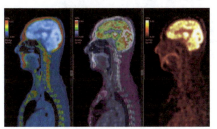 © springsky/Shutterstock.com	An imaging technique used extensively in medicine and in physiological and neurological research. Records changes in blood flow by detecting the distribution of radioactive particles injected in the bloodstream.
Functional Magnetic Resonance Imaging (fMRI)  © Levent Konuk/Shutterstock.com	A diagnostic imaging technique that detects extremely subtle changes in magnetic fields in the human body (related to the blood oxygen level), allowing technicians to view real-time, computer-enhanced images of soft tissue. Used extensively to diagnose disease as well as to study neural activity in the brain.
Magnetoencephalography (MEG) 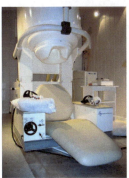 © Steve Shoup/Shutterstock.com	A recording of magnetic fields that correspond to electrical activity of the brain. MEG recordings are obtained at the scalp by means of a magnetoencephalograph to yield event-related fields (ERFs).⌐

⌐These⌐ brain-imaging methods are used not only to study the effects of drugs, but also to look at brain activity during specific tasks. They are highly useful in studies of the brain's role in intellectual activities.

Structures of the Brain

Physical examination of the brain reveals a grayish mass inside the skull (Figure 2.10). Some of its various structures are identifiable through this type of examination. But determining the functions of these structures is not so simple: The structures themselves present few clues to their functions.

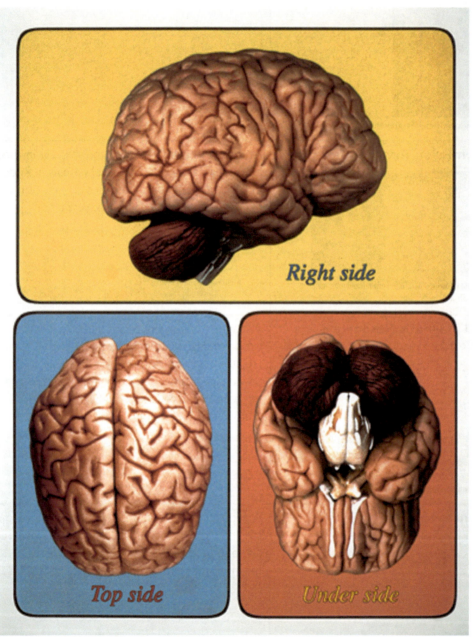

Figure 2.10 Top, right side, and under side view of the human brain. The outer covering of the brain is called the cerebral cortex.

Photolibrary/Imagestate Pictor

Hindbrain

As shown in Figure 2.11, the human brain is normally divided into three basic parts: hindbrain, midbrain, and forebrain. These parts are thought to have evolved in that order, with the hindbrain being the oldest structure and the forebrain the most recent. Structures of the hindbrain and of the midbrain make up the **brain stem**—that part of the CNS that connects the spinal cord with higher brain structures.

The hindbrain is the lowest part of the brain in a person standing upright. It consists mainly of the **cerebellum** (the word means *small brain*), the **medulla**, and the **pons**.

The medulla is involved in physiological functions such as breathing, heart functioning, and digestion. And the pons, which takes the form of a bulge at the front of the medulla, serves as a link between the medulla and higher brain centers (*pons* means bridge). ⌊The pons plays an important role in arousal. Unfamiliar or unanticipated sensory information is usually interpreted as important, along with information that is particularly intense such as loud noises or bright lights. Often, individuals have trouble sleeping in a new environment, especially if the person is exposed to unfamiliar sounds, lighting conditions, or even the unfamiliar feel of a different mattress. As people try to fall asleep, they often become focused on this sensory

> **Brain stem:** Part of the brain that connects the spinal cord with the higher brain centers. Includes the hindbrain (medulla, pons, cerebellum) and the midbrain (reticular formation).

> **Cerebellum:** A major brain structure attached to the rear of the brain stem, the principal functions of which appear to be coordinating motor activity and maintaining balance.
>
> **Medulla:** The lowest part of the brain, found at the very top of the spinal cord and containing nerve centers involved in regulating physiological activity such as breathing, digestion, and heart functioning.
>
> **Pons:** A small brain structure that appears as a bulge at the front of medulla. Part of the brain stem involved in breathing and arousal.

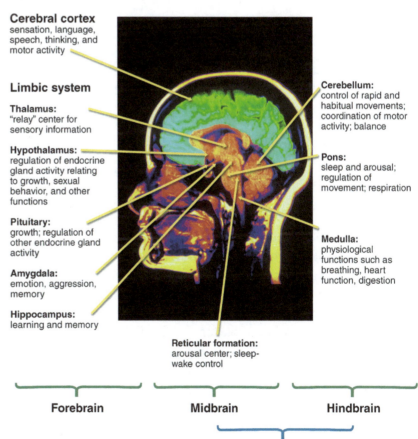

Figure 2.11 A sagittal (bisected front to back) view of the human brain showing major structures and some of their principal functions ⌊and an illustration of the neurological cells and sections of the brain.⌋

Photolibrary/Oxford Scientific (OSF)/Scott Camazine

Cerebral cortex
sensation, language, speech, thinking, and motor activity

Limbic system

Thalamus:
"relay" center for sensory information

Hypothalamus:
regulation of endocrine gland activity relating to growth, sexual behavior, and other functions

Pituitary:
growth; regulation of other endocrine gland activity

Amygdala:
emotion, aggression, memory

Hippocampus:
learning and memory

Cerebellum:
control of rapid and habitual movements; coordination of motor activity; balance

Pons:
sleep and arousal; regulation of movement; respiration

Medulla:
physiological functions such as breathing, heart function, digestion

Reticular formation:
arousal center; sleep-wake control

Forebrain   Midbrain   Hindbrain

Brainstem

HUMAN BRAIN

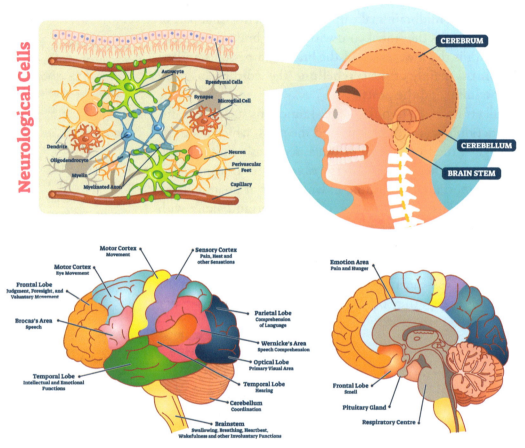

Figure 2.11   (Continued)

© VectorMine/Shutterstock.com

information and experience anxiety as a result of their inability to sleep. In such cases, the pons is allowing unfamiliar sensory information to reach a person's attention. However, after being repeatedly exposed to the same information, the pons can habituate to these stimuli and prevent them from passing into higher brain circuits. The pons' ability to discriminate is illustrated by a spouse who can sleep through a husband's massive snoring but can wake at the first whimper of a child.

The cerebellum is responsible for coordinating the brain's outgoing motor signals. It is a finely tuned, precise structure that also plays an important role in balance and coordination. While people often take it for granted, muscle movement is an incredibly complex process. Even the act of smiling requires the coordination of 47 muscles and the cerebellum facilitates such processes.

It's important to understand that it takes time for a neural impulse exiting the brain to reach the appropriate muscle. This latency is so small that humans simply don't notice it. However, the amount of time that it takes for any given signal to reach a specific muscle is unique, depending on the length of the nerve and the type of cells that make up the nerve. Therefore, it takes longer for the brain to send an impulse to a person's foot then it does to send an impulse to a person's shoulders because the neural impulse has to travel a longer distance.

₋Athletes provide an excellent illustration of the role of the cerebellum. When a basketball player attempts a jump shot, the athlete's muscles must contract with the proper amount of force. Those muscles must also contract in the proper sequence. The athlete's arms might contract at the same time as his legs, but wrist motion follows later. However, since it takes longer for a neural impulse to reach different parts of the body, the brain simply cannot send out all of the impulses at the same time. If it did, perhaps the athlete's arm muscles would contract too quickly. Conversely, the athlete's leg muscles might contract too slowly. The result would be an uncoordinated stumble.

₋Instead, the cerebellum staggers the outgoing impulses so that they reach the appropriate muscle groups in perfect harmony. The cerebellum accounts for the various timing delays in different nerves and helps to turn the cognitive intention into a coordinated movement. The cerebellum is remarkably precise, calibrating outgoing impulses down to one ten-thousandth of a second. Since this structure is functioning at such a high level of precision, it doesn't take much to disrupt it.₋

© Aspen Photo/Shutterstock.com

When substances, such as alcohol, cross through what is called the blood–brain barrier, they can interrupt normal functioning of the hindbrain. This is what police are indirectly measuring when they administer field sobriety tests for suspected drunk drivers; they are seeing if the subject has ingested enough alcohol to the point of affecting their cerebellum (involved in walking and balancing). Furthermore, if the subject ingested so much alcohol to the point of unconsciousness, then the alcohol may have affected their medulla or pons (involved in breathing and heart rate), leading to life-threatening circumstances.

The Midbrain

₋The term "midbrain" refers to a group of subcortical structures that emerge from the brainstem. It is involved in the coordination of movement and the integration of sensory information. The midbrain is also responsible for many of the involuntary aspects of vision. For example, it controls how much light enters into the eye, dilating and constricting the pupils. Consequently, drugs that affect the midbrain will often cause a person's pupils to dilate or constrict abnormally. Additionally, damage to different parts of the midbrain can result in motor impairment. The substantia nigra is a structure within the midbrain. It is involved in motor coordination and movement. Parkinson's disease is caused by severe damage and cell loss in the substantia nigra. This severely impairs a person's ability to move consciously. Uncontrollable tremors and shaking are also characteristic of Parkinson's disease. Normally, cells in the substantia nigra gradually die off in people with Parkinson's disease.₋

The midbrain includes the **reticular formation**, found on the upper part of the brain stem. This structure is involved in maintaining

> **Reticular formation:** (Reticular activating system; RAS) That portion of the brain stem assumed to be responsible for the physiological arousal of the cortex as well as for the control of sleeping and waking.

arousal, or degree of alertness and motivation. It also contains nerve fibers associated with physical movement. Associated nerves are *dopaminergic,* meaning that the main neurotransmitter involved in their activation is dopamine.

The Forebrain

The largest and most complex brain structure is the forebrain. It is also the most important structure for understanding human thought, behavior, and emotion. It includes the hypothalamus, the thalamus, and other structures of the limbic system, as well as the cerebrum and cerebral cortex.

The **hypothalamus** is a bean-sized structure near the top of the brain stem. It is mainly involved in regulating activity of the autonomic nervous system. One of the primary jobs of the hypothalamus is to maintain **homeostasis**, which is the body's way of maintaining stability in changing conditions. In many ways, it is similar to the cruise control systems installed in many cars. If you set your cruise control to 60 miles per hour, the cruise control system can't perfectly keep the car running at that speed, so often the car will cruise at speeds varying from about 57 to about 63. As the car begins to go above the predetermined speed, it slows down. If it begins to go too slow, it speeds up. The car can't anticipate hills, turns, or other obstacles that affect the car's performance. Rather, it reacts to the environment, adjusting the car's speed to keep the car running at the optimal pace you selected. In a very similar manner, the hypothalamus regulates various functions, making adjustments when necessary, to maintain optimal performance. The hypothalamus plays a large role in regulating hunger and thirst as well as in the regulation of arousal, sleep, body temperature, and sexual function. It is often conceptualized as a "drive center," since our biological drives originate there. If a person's body needs more water or food, they will become thirsty or hungry. As a person eats, the feeling of hunger begins to subside. Thus, the hypothalamus regulates many drive-based behaviors such as eating, drinking, and sleeping.

> **Hypothalamus:** A small structure at the base of the brain involved in the functioning of the autonomic nervous system and in temperature regulation.
>
> **Homeostasis:** The body's ability to maintain a relatively stable physiological equilibrium under chancing circumstances.

A wide variety of drugs are known to affect the hypothalamus, including marijuana, alcohol, scopolamine, cocaine, and antidepressants. They hinder its ability to maintain homeostasis, essentially changing the settings of the "cruise control" of a person's body. Alterations in hunger, thirst, and sexual function are acute side effects of drugs that affect the hypothalamus. Long-term use of some of these drugs can significantly alter a person's hormone levels. Weight gain or weight loss is also an indication of a drug's long-term effects on the hypothalamus. Within the hypothalamus is a small but important structure called the suprachiasmatic nucleus. This structure is very important for setting our biological clock and maintaining the body's 24-hour day and night cycle as well as increasing and decreasing arousal to accommodate both wakefulness and drowsiness. This nucleus is principally activated by light. For example, blue light alone is able to suppress melatonin production and alter circadian rhythm shifts. Interestingly, recent research has demonstrated that blue light, in addition to altering melatonin and circadian rhythms, is capable of altering alertness, thermoregulation, sleep architecture, and heart rate in normal subjects (Cajochen et al., 2005; Munch et al., 2006). This finding was a major driving force in creating blue light reducing apps for smartphones and tablets as well as blue light blocking films for reading glasses.

The **thalamus** is found between the midbrain and the cerebral cortex. Its main function is to act as a relay station for transmitting sensory signals to the cerebral cortex. All sensations, except those having to do with smell, go through the thalamus. It is also involved in regulating sleep and consciousness.

> **Thalamus:** A small brain structure that serves as a major relay center for incoming sensory signals.

The **limbic system** includes parts of the hypothalamus and various other structures such as the **amygdala** and the **hippocampus**. Generally speaking, these are structures involved in emotions ⌐and reward.⌐ The hippocampus also plays an important role ⌐in supporting memory; more specifically, converting short-term experiences into long-term memories.⌐ Alzheimer's disease and amnesia are both associated with damage to the hippocampus (American Academy of Neurology, 2009). ⌐Additionally, it is responsible for encoding the emotional and temporal aspects of a memory. The hippocampus is a particularly unique structure compared to other structures within the brain. Scientists long believed that the brain was incapable of growing new neurons after birth. However, newer evidence has shown that the hippocampus does grow new neurons. In fact, one effect of antidepressant medication is the growth of new neurons in this structure (Anacker et al., 2011; Taupin, 2006).

⌐The amygdala is another critical part of the limbic system. The amygdala consists of two teardrop-shaped structures, one on each side of the brain. These teardrops are attached directly to the hippocampus and form many direct connections with it. The amygdala has long been associated with the production of "fear." It plays an important role in mood regulation; although, it is not the only structure that contributes to this process. Many substances can affect amygdala functioning, and humans often use drugs to self-medicate their unpleasant emotions.

> **Limbic system:** A grouping of brain structures located beneath the cerebral cortex, associated mainly with emotion, memory, and reinforcement and punishment.
>
> **Amygdala:** A small structure in the limbic system (part of the forebrain) that is involved in emotion and aggression and that plays an important role in the processing and storage of memories that have to do with emotion.
>
> **Hippocampus:** A limbic system structure in the forebrain, which is primarily involved in learning and memory.

What Does the Bible Say?

⌐You may have heard the phrase practice makes perfect. What that phrase might really mean is the more we do something the easier it becomes to do it again. If we practice anger, we become better at it. The learning networks in our brain and their underlying synapses improve with increasing use; they become more easily activated. So, being angry and, in essence, practicing that behavior results in more anger and for that anger to be more easily elicited. Anger has a whole host of negative health and relationship outcomes. This is why the Bible speaks so clearly about living a life free from anger. This is why when the Bible speaks about all sorts of unfavorable and even sordid behavior, anger is often included in those lists. This is distinct from short periods of legitimate anger that we all experience from time to time.

Ecclesiastes 7:9 ESV

"Be not quick in your spirit to become angry, for anger lodges in the heart of fools."

Ephesians 4:17–32 ESV

"Now this I say and testify in the Lord, that you must no longer walk as the Gentiles do, in the futility of their minds. They are darkened in their understanding, alienated from the life of God because of the ignorance that is in them, due to their hardness of heart. They have become callous and have given themselves up to sensuality, greedy to practice every kind of impurity. But that is not the way you learned Christ!—assuming that you have heard about him and were taught in him, as the truth is in Jesus, to put off your old self, which belongs to your former manner of life and is corrupt through deceitful desires, and to be renewed in the spirit of your minds, and to put on the new self, created after the likeness of God in true righteousness and holiness. Therefore, having put away falsehood, let each one of you speak the truth with his neighbor, for we are members one of another. Be angry and do not sin; do not let the sun go down on your anger, and give no opportunity to the devil. Let the thief no longer steal, but rather let him labor, doing honest work with his own hands, so that he may have something to share with anyone in need. Let no corrupting talk come out of your mouths, but only such as is good for building up, as fits the occasion, that it may give grace to those who hear. And do not grieve the Holy Spirit of God, by whom you were sealed for the day of redemption. Let all bitterness and wrath and anger and clamor and slander be put away from you, along with all malice. Be kind to one another, tenderhearted, forgiving one another, as God in Christ forgave you."

2 Peter 1:5–11 ESV

"For this very reason, make every effort to supplement your faith with virtue, and virtue with knowledge, and knowledge with self-control, and self-control with steadfastness, and steadfastness with godliness, and godliness with brotherly affection, and brotherly affection with love. For if these qualities are yours and are increasing, they keep you from being ineffective or unfruitful in the knowledge of our Lord Jesus Christ. For whoever lacks these qualities is so nearsighted that he is blind, having forgotten that he was cleansed from his former sins. Therefore, brothers, be all the more diligent to confirm your calling and election, for if you practice these qualities you will never fall. For in this way there will be richly provided for you an entrance into the eternal kingdom of our Lord and Savior Jesus Christ."

The structures in the limbic system play an important role in supporting learning. The greater role the limbic system has in memory processing, the easier it will be for the brain to attend, encode, and retrieve information. Another way to say this is the greater the emotional value of the information—good or bad—the easier it will be to remember. This is why people can remember songs, sport facts, and movie quotes but can't recall terms from a psychology book. One important strategy is to take the relatively emotionless content from the book and work to make it not only emotional but also personal. For example, if you are studying a disorder, try imagine what it would be like to live with that disorder for a day. The emotional and personal connection to that disorder will make it easier to remember.

The largest and most complex of our brain structures is the **cerebrum**, which divides naturally into two halves, the left and right *cerebral hemispheres*. Its outer covering, the **cerebral cortex**, is centrally involved in higher mental functioning. This covering is highly convoluted and deeply fissured, the fissures resulting in four natural divisions (*lobes*) in each of the hemispheres. These lobes have been separated by scientists based on the actual structure and function of these brain areas and what traits and behaviors they have been implicated in. These four lobes include the frontal lobe, parietal lobe, occipital lobe, and temporal lobe. There is also a right and a left hemisphere of each of these lobes (Figure 2.12).

At the front of the cerebral cortex are the **frontal lobes**, which are involved in motor activity as well as in higher thought processes. On either side are the **temporal lobes**, involved in language, speech, and hearing. The *auditory* cortex is the part of the temporal lobe concerned with hearing.

Cerebrum: The main part of the human brain, consisting of the two cerebral hemispheres and covered by the cerebral cortex.

Cerebral cortex: The convoluted outer covering of the cerebrum, the main functions of which have to do with higher mental processes like thinking and imagining.

Frontal lobes: Frontal part of the cerebral cortex, centrally involved in higher thought processes.

Temporal lobes: Cerebral structure located on either side of the cerebrum, associated primarily with speech, language, and hearing.

Just behind the temporal lobes are the **parietal lobes**, implicated in physical movement and in sensation and physical orientation. At the very back are the **occipital lobes**, involved in vision. The part of the occipital lobes involved in vision is referred to as the *visual cortex*.

It is important to note that the main tasks and responsibilities of each of these cerebral divisions are not very simple or clear. Most functions are carried out by more than one part of the brain. Note, too, that areas of these four lobes that are not involved directly in motor activity or sensation are nevertheless involved in higher mental processes such as thinking, remembering, learning, and speaking. These are referred to as **association areas of the brain**.

Parietal lobes: Cerebral lobes located just above the temporal lobes, between the frontal and occipital lobes. The parietal lobes are involved in sensation.

Occipital lobes: Part of the cerebral cortex located at the rear of the brain, involved in vision.

Association areas of the brain: Parts of the four cerebral lobes involved in higher mental processes like thinking, learning, and remembering.

The Hemispheres

Phineas Gage's accident provided some of the first crude evidence that the brain might be differentiated into separate functions, and since then, there has been other historical evidence as well. Paul Broca, a neurologist, was sent a patient suffering from aphasia, a language disorder that we now know is linked to brain damage. The patient died within a few days and Broca performed an autopsy, discovering lesions in the left temporal lobe. The area of the lobe that was affected by these lesions is now known as Broca's region. Subsequent research has established that aphasia may be linked to lesions that are almost always on the left side of the brain. Lesions in the right half of the brain rarely disturb either *receptive* or *expressive* language functions, particularly in right-handed individuals, leading researchers to believe that language functions reside primarily in the left half of the brain in right-handed individuals and in most left-handed individuals (Holland et al., 2007).

Parts of the Human Brain

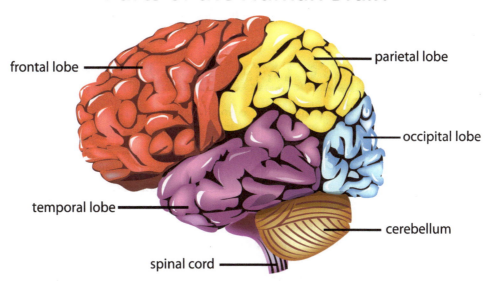

frontal lobe

parietal lobe

occipital lobe

temporal lobe

cerebellum

spinal cord

Figure 2.12   A left-side view of the cerebral cortex with the four right lobes labeled." Although each lobe is associated with certain functions, the lobes are highly integrated in terms of structure and function. The *corpus callosum* (not pictured) is primarily responsible for this integration.

© Matthew Cole/Shutterstock.com

There is evidence as well that the right hemisphere might be more involved with emotions as well as with music and art (Workman et al., 2006). These findings have led some to speculate that there are "right-brained" and "left-brained" individuals, distinguishable in terms of their major preoccupations and abilities. Thus, the "left-brained" would be expected to excel at verbal and logical tasks; the "right-brained" would be more artistic and more musical. This sort of speculation has led to the view that conventional education neglects the "right" brain because it emphasizes highly verbal, logical, scientific content and neglects more artistic and musical content. **Holistic education**, designed to educate both sides of the brain, is sometimes advocated as a remedy for this situation.

> **Holistic education:** A label for educational approaches that attempt to remedy what is seen as the failure of traditional education to educate the whole brain—especially the right hemisphere, which is speculatively linked with music, art, and emotion.

Unfortunately, much of what passes for information in this area is speculation and exaggeration rather than fact (Bruer, 2006). There is enormous overlap in the functions of the cerebral hemispheres. Nor are the hemispheres highly exclusive in their specializations. For example, although the left hemisphere is somewhat more involved in language production functions than is the right hemisphere, when the left hemisphere is injured, especially if the injury occurs early in life, the right hemisphere frequently takes over left hemisphere functions—a striking example of an important characteristic of the human brain: *plasticity.*

Brain plasticity is also evident in patients who suffer motor and language problems after brain damage resulting from a stroke. These patients often recover much of their previous functioning as other parts of the brain take over (Lazar et al., 2010). In extreme cases, *hemispherectomies* may need to be performed on individuals with life-threatening diseases or disorders. If these procedures are performed on a young child, their chances of recovering and maintaining their previous functioning are actually quite good. *Plasticity* makes it all possible.

Recovery of lost brain function may also result from **neurogenesis**—the formation of new neurons. Although most neurogenesis occurs during the prenatal period, it also continues into adulthood (Reynolds & Weiss, 1992). The finding of adult neurogenesis contradicts a long-held belief that we are born with a set number of neurons, and that we gradually lose them as we live our lives.

> **Neurogenesis:** The active production of new neurons. Most prevalent during the prenatal period but also occurs in adulthood.

LIMBIC VERSUS FRONTAL LOBE

Development is no easy task; perhaps, this is the reason we only experience these crucial time periods once. While no one can remember being born, who can really forget going through puberty? Puberty, more generally referred to as adolescence, is marked by significant and often dramatic transitions in social, emotional, and intellectual ability. Underlying these new abilities are even more impressive changes in neural (brain), hormonal, and bodily processes. As a result of these changes, teens, compared to other age groups, too often exercise poor judgment, especially in terms of evaluating and appreciating the risks and long-term consequences associated with their behaviors (Greene et al., 2000). The culmination of these abilities and behaviors is now thought to place teenagers at an elevated risk for drug abuse problems. Combine the elevated risk with the enormous variety of drugs available today and it becomes increasingly difficult to mount effective education, prevention, and treatment efforts, even though such efforts are necessary. Changes in brain development are responsible for physical growth, social networking, emotional maturation, and gains in cognitive abilities. Teens tend to seek new, exciting experiences during this period, but often lack the maturity to weigh the consequences of their decision-making (Steinberg, 2008). Therefore, drug experimentation, which is almost universally initiated during adolescence, often results in a number of primary and secondary adverse events.

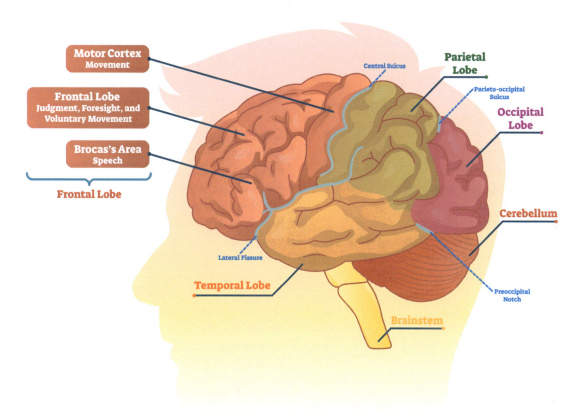

Frontal Lobe

Motor Cortex
Movement

Frontal Lobe
Judgment, Foresight, and
Voluntary Movement

Brocas's Area
Speech

Frontal Lobe

Central Sulcus

Parietal Lobe

Parieto-occipital Sulcus

Occipital Lobe

Cerebellum

Lateral Fissure

Temporal Lobe

Preoccipital Notch

Brainstem

Figure 2.13 ⌐The diagram shows the frontal lobe that is located just behind the eyes and is responsible for complex aspects of cognition like attention, movement, and planning.⌐
© VectorMine/Shutterstock.com

⌐During adolescence, the brain grows/matures unevenly. Parts of the brain responsible for reward and pleasure develop first, often during early adolescence, while parts of the brain responsible for reasoning and problem-solving develop later, often during late adolescence. To this end, if one defines adolescence based on maturation of their brain systems, then adolescence generally begins during the very early teen years and isn't complete until around age 21 to 25. This is a rather long period of time, especially compared to prenatal development. However, life is very complicated, so it is not surprising that it takes the brain over 10 years to transition from childhood to adulthood. This disparity in development is the likely reason why the adolescent period is associated with the highest levels of death and disability. It is during this phase of development that the brain is beginning to understand pleasure and reward in new ways. For example, what age were you when you first decided there was a particular genre of music you enjoyed more so than others? Similarly, how old were you when you first asked to go to the mall with your friends—without your parents. It is likely that nearly all of these behaviors occurred during early adolescence.

⌐These behaviors are all driven by the onset of limbic system development usually between 11 and 13 years of age. Although the limbic system is responsible for attaching meaning/value to things that are rewarding and pleasurable, it is not the structure involved in evaluating the overall risk associated with decision-making. The frontal lobe is involved in this behavior and is the very last part of the brain to develop across adolescence. This is the quintessential problem of adolescent development. Parts of the brain involved in pleasure seeking develop before parts of the brain involved in reasoning and judgment. Historically, adolescence was a time of mentorship and apprenticeship. Teens were often surrounded by adults who helped to manage the challenges of adolescence. Today, many teens spend large amounts of their teen years almost devoid of meaningful parental or adult supervision or intervention.

Functions of The Limbic System (Reward System)	Functions of the Frontal Lobe (Executive System)
Energy Appetite and eating behaviors Certain aspects of smell Water balance/thirst Temperature regulation Hormones (*and all that goes with it*) Sexual behavior Emotional processing and behavior Social processing, especially emotions of faces Reward/reinforcement/pleasure—Addiction Certain aspects of learning and memory Anger Aggression Certain aspects of pain Sleep and dreams Motivation (*the why*)	Seat of personality Planning Judgment Reasoning Problem-solving Rational decision-making Impulse control Regulates aggression Organizes thoughts Seat of working memory Controls conscious movement Contributes to the storage of new memories Connects actions with consequences Attention Cognitive flexibility (multitasking) Goal persistence/motivation (*the how*)
Examples of Limbic Processes	**Examples of Frontal Lobe Processes**
I want it now	Waiting would be better
More is better	Probably should limit myself
I am scared so I won't do it	I need to do this even though I am scared
I am tired, so I am going to skip that class	I am tired but I don't want to risk missing class
I am angry and you're going to know it	I am mad but will wait until I am calm
You bet I will have another drink (alcohol)	I better not drink anymore; I have class tomorrow
I have no idea why I did that	I have planned for days to do this

What Does the Bible Say?

One of the Bible's overarching messages is about denying our own needs and instead putting God's needs and that of our neighbor above our own. This has to be an intentional mindset and has to be practiced. It is a continuous struggle as our body drives many immediate needs but not all of these needs are healthy for us. For example, not denying some of our bodily drives can result in obesity, laziness, and ignorance. We have to work against those behaviors otherwise they will likely occur, bringing negative consequences. Take a moment to think about what you have been learning about the brain and the body's drives in light of the following verses.

James 1:16–25 ESV

"Do not be deceived, my beloved brethren. Every good gift and every perfect gift is from above, and comes down from the Father of lights, with whom there is no variation or shadow of turning. Of His own will He brought us forth by the word of truth, that we might be a kind of first fruits of His creatures. So then, my beloved brethren, let every man be swift to hear, slow to speak, slow to wrath; for the wrath of man does not produce the righteousness of God. Therefore lay aside all filthiness and overflow of wickedness, and receive with meekness the implanted word, which is able to save your souls. But be doers of the word, and not hearers only, deceiving yourselves. For if anyone is a hearer of the word and not a doer, he is like a man observing his natural face in a mirror; for he observes himself, goes away, and immediately forgets what kind of man he was. But he who looks into the perfect law of liberty and continues in it, and is not a forgetful hearer but a doer of the work, this one will be blessed in what he does."

Romans 8:1–8 ESV

"There is therefore now no condemnation for those who are in Christ Jesus. For the law of the Spirit of life has set you free in Christ Jesus from the law of sin and death. For God has done what the law, weakened by the flesh, could not do. By sending his own Son in the likeness of sinful flesh and for sin, he condemned sin in the flesh, in order that the righteous requirement of the law might be fulfilled in us, who walk not according to the flesh but according to the Spirit. For those who live according to the flesh set their minds on the things of the flesh, but those who live according to the Spirit set their minds on the things of the Spirit. For to set the mind on the flesh is death, but to set the mind on the Spirit is life and peace. For the mind that is set on the flesh is hostile to God, for it does not submit to God's law; indeed, it cannot. Those who are in the flesh cannot please God."

BIOLOGY OF CONSCIOUSNESS

We humans are conscious of our awareness, and we can communicate this consciousness to others—as you and I are doing at this very moment.

We have a **mind** made possible by our brain.

> **Mind:** A term referring primarily to human consciousness. Often defined as originating from or resulting in processes of the brain associated with activities like thinking, imagining, and perceiving.

Consciousness

If a neurosurgeon were to crack open the thick bony casing that protects your brain, would he uncover your mind? Perhaps, although he would not really *see* it; all he would see is a grayish lump of matter. But he might well presume that your *mind,* your *self-awareness,* resides in complex patterns of billions of interconnections that have formed among the neurons in your brain. And he might speculate, as he looks at this chunk of tissue, that at this very moment chemical and electrical changes and impulses swarm through many of the intricate patterns of neural networks. And some of these impulses will be associated with thoughts and feelings that you are now having: They will define your own private state of **consciousness**.

Consciousness, like *mind,* is a term with many meanings. The two terms are very closely related. *Mind* refers primarily to activities of

> **Consciousness:** Awareness of one's personal identity. Self-awareness. Awareness of mental processes like thinking, imagining, and feeling.

the brain such as thinking and feeling that result in a sense of self; *consciousness* refers to an awareness of self and the environment.

In effect, there are two broad states of consciousness: sleeping and waking. In addition, there are *altered* states of consciousness that might result from certain drugs or perhaps from hypnosis.

SLEEP

Sleep, as you well know, is the state that ensues when you close your eyes and eventually lose immediate contact with your environment. It ends when you regain awareness of external events. But that does not mean you are completely unaware of your physical environment as you sleep. As you lie precariously on your bed, a few feet above your floor, you have little fear of falling. You casually assume that your body has some control over its movements during sleep and that it is responsive to signals indicating dangerous proximity to the edge of your sleeping platform. And if your baby cries in the middle of the night, you instantly awaken—strong evidence that you are not totally unconscious while you sleep; part of your brain remains alert.

▶ **WHAT IS A BEHAVIORAL NEUROSCIENTIS**

Circadian Rhythms

We seem to be biologically prepared to sleep at night and to be active during the day—a phenomenon labeled a **circadian rhythm**. Circadian rhythms are daily cycles in biological and behavioral processes such as sleeping, temperature change, and the production of **melatonin**. Melatonin is a hormone closely tied to the regulation of sleep. It increases in the evening and during the night and decreases during the day. Melatonin is sometimes used to treat sleep disorders (Zee, 2010). ⌐As noted previously, increased light exposure, especially in the evening generally due to screen use, can result in decreased

> **Circadian rhythm:** A biological/behavioral cycle that is approximately 1 day long. It describes our sleep/wake and temperature cycles.
>
> **Melatonin:** A natural hormone closely tied to sleep/wake cycles. Also called the sleep hormone.

melatonin production and simultaneous increase in activity of the hypothalamus. This often results in difficulty falling asleep. It is now recommended that one eliminate any screen exposure at least one hour before going to bed. This of course is challenging because the last thing most people do before going to bed is look at their screen. It is also interesting to note that there has been a major uptick in sale and use of melatonin supplements especially in children. It seems that increased screen exposure, especially in the late evening is suppressing melatonin production and people are buying melatonin supplements to replace the naturally occurring melatonin. Perhaps, a better solution is decreased screen time.⌐

Although our sleep–wake cycles seem to be closely tied to the rising and setting of the sun, our ability to generate our own cycles becomes evident when we find ourselves in latitudes that have more or fewer hours of daylight. Other things being equal, we continue to sleep for approximately the same length of time and at about the same time each day. Even when participants are kept in surroundings that provide no clues about day and night, circadian rhythms tend to adjust to periods very close to 24 hours (Gronfier et al., 2007).

Stages of Sleep

When early sleep researchers observed sleeping subjects, they saw that sleep involves eye closure, reduction of muscle tension, reduction of heart rate, lowering of blood pressure, slowing of respiration rate, and a marked decrease in body temperature. They also noticed people, and animals, don't seem to sleep uniformly and consistently. Sometimes sleepers breathe rapidly, moving and fidgeting as they sleep; at other times, breathing is regular and there is little twitching and jerking. Dogs, too, jerk and fidget and moan and even bark as they sleep. Based on these changes, researchers concluded that there are distinct stages in depth of sleep (Neubauer, 2009).

EEG recordings and observations of eye movements below closed eyelids have led researchers to describe four stages of sleep based on changes in brain activity. These four stages are followed by a period of rapid eye movements (REM; Figure 2.14). EEG recordings indicate that when awake, the brain typically produces small, fast waves called **beta waves** (13 to 30 cycles per second), but these become slower, changing to **alpha waves** (8 to 12 cycles per second) as the individual relaxes. During Stage 1 sleep, different waves called **theta waves** (4 to 7 cycles per second) become evident, interspersed with spikes of rapid brain activity. Perhaps 10 minutes later, if not awakened first, the sleeper enters Stage 2 sleep, also marked by bursts of rapid brain activity called *sleep spindles*. Note that Stages 1 and 2 are very brief.

In Stage 3, body temperature and heart rate continue to decrease and **delta waves** (up to 4 cycles per second) begin to appear. These slow, deep waves are characteristic of Stage 4 sleep, often described as the *deepest* stage of sleep.

> **Beta waves:** Typical shallow and rapid brain waves of person who is awake, having a frequency of 13 to 30 cycles per minute.
>
> **Alpha waves:** Slower, deeper brain waves characteristic of deep relaxation, having a frequency of 8 to 13 cycles per second.
>
> **Theta waves:** Slow brain waves (4 to 7 per second) characteristic of the early stages of sleep.

> **Delta waves:** Very slow brain waves (frequency of up to 4 per second) characteristic of deep sleep.

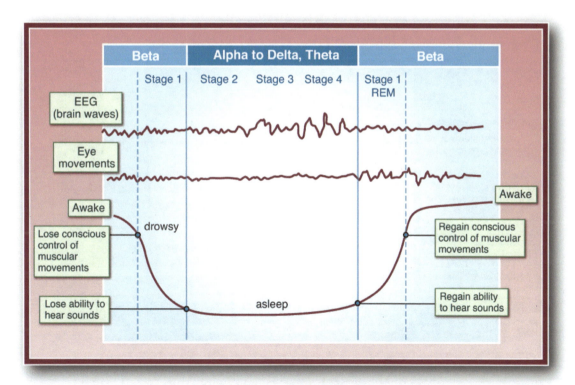

Figure 2.14 Physiological changes during sleep." Stage 1 REM sleep is sometimes labeled Stage 5 sleep, although brain waves during this stage are identical to those of Stage 1 sleep. The difference is that during this stage the rapid eye movements that typically accompany periods of dreaming are observed.

Interestingly, following Stage 4 sleep, a person will return to Stage 3, 2, and 1 (respectively) *before* entering the stage of **rapid eye movement sleep (REM sleep)**. It is during this stage that most of our dreaming takes place.

Between 20% and 25% of our normal sleep is spent in REM sleep, and the remaining 75% to 80% is spent in non-REM sleep (Stages 1–4).) There are some marked differences between these two sleep states, apart from their typical duration and the presence or absence of rapid eye movements. During REM sleep, physiological functions are very similar to those expected in a normal, awake person (hence this stage of sleep is often labeled **paradoxical sleep**): Heart rate ranges between 45 and 100 beats per minute, breathing is irregular, and EEG patterns are similar to those seen in quiet resting states with the eyes closed (alpha). However, voluntary muscle groups are typically in a state of paralysis during REM sleep. There is speculation this muscular paralysis is meant to keep the body from acting out violent dreams and possibly hurting itself or others.

In adults, REM sleep occurs fairly regularly at approximately 90-minute intervals and lasts for 25 minutes or more. It does not begin for 30 or more minutes following onset of sleep. If a person is awakened from non-REM sleep and kept awake for a few minutes, REM sleep will not begin for at least 30 minutes, even if the person had been in non-REM sleep for the last hour or more (Figure 2.15). Thus, it is possible to deprive subjects of REM sleep simply by waking them whenever rapid eye movements begin. Interestingly, if one is deprived of REM sleep, they will advance more quickly into REM stage sleep the next time they fall asleep compared to someone not deprived of REM. Similarly, it is possible

> **Rapid eye movement (REM) sleep:** Sometimes referred to as the Stage 5 of sleep, the stage during which most of our dreaming occurs.

> **Paradoxical sleep:** Another label for REM sleep, so called because during this stage of sleep physiological functions such as heart and respiration rate are very similar to those of a waking state.

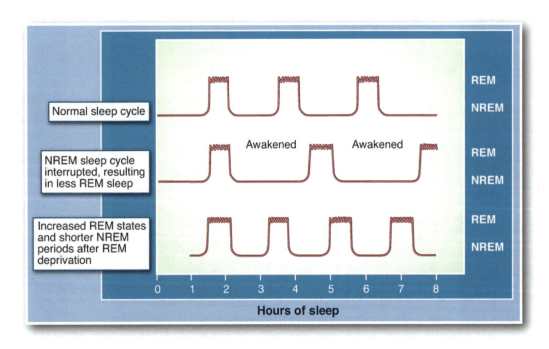

Figure 2.15 Cycles of REM/non-REM sleep." During a normal sleep cycle, REM sleep occurs fairly regularly at about 90-minute intervals and lasts for 25 minutes or more. If we are awakened from non-REM sleep, REM sleep will not begin for 30 minutes or more after the onset of sleep. If we are awakened during REM sleep (as in a dream-recording experiment), the result is shorter non-REM periods between REM states during the subsequent night.

to deprive subjects of non-REM sleep. One of the results of this procedure is that subjects who are deprived of one type of sleep tend to make up for it during subsequent nights. A second effect of REM or non-REM deprivation is that subjects who are allowed only one type of sleep frequently feel and function as if they had not slept at all. It seems clear that we have a need for both types of sleep and that neither is more restful than the other in spite of the apparently greater reduction in rate of physiological functioning during non-REM sleep.

There is an interesting paradox when it comes to sleep aids. The vast majority of medications used to produce what is often called sleep, instead produces sedation or unconsciousness. To be clear, neither sedation nor unconsciousness resembles sleep. In fact, sleeping pills generally interfere with the most restorative stages of sleep but especially REM sleep. This can leave the use more tired in the morning and throughout the early afternoon. Worse yet, after several days of taking such pills, people experience rebound effects in that they now have increased arousal in the absence of the pills making it harder to fall asleep. It often becomes a vicious cycle—can't sleep without them but also feeling bad and lethargic with them.

Why We Sleep

We still don't know for sure why we must sleep (*The Science of Sleep*, 2010). What we do know is that following prolonged periods of sleep deprivation our behavior becomes very bizarre, we suffer from hallucinations, our ability to respond appropriately to the environment is severely impeded, and we might eventually experience serious health problems, the most severe of which is death (Buysse et al., 2008). No experiments have been conducted with human subjects that directly substantiate this last bit of speculation, although sleep deprivation of animals sometimes leads to their deaths (Newman et al., 2009).

There are a number of theoretical explanations for sleep. One theory maintains it is necessary to repair physiological damage and maintain the body and mind in good working order. Evolutionary theory speculates sleep is an evolved mechanism, the usefulness of which lies in the fact that hidden sleeping animals are less likely to be preyed upon, particularly if their sleep cycles correspond with predation cycles. It also appears reasonable to suppose sleep might have evolved as a system for conserving energy (a hibernating bear may come to mind). Some researchers also suggest a select few stages of sleep, especially REM sleep, are important for consolidating memories and perhaps for resting important neural systems.

Research suggests that sleeping gives resting neurons the opportunity to repair the damage done to them throughout the day. Furthermore, there is evidence to suggest that sleep gives the body the opportunity to get rid of any damaged and irreparable the neurons that are beyond repair (Gilestro et al., 2009; Siegel, 2003; Vyazovskiy et al., 2008).

Dreams

Contrary to some beliefs, everybody dreams, but not everyone remembers dreams with equal clarity. In fact, most people remember only a small portion of what they dream, with women remembering their dreams more often than men (Schredl, 2010). Nor, as is popularly believed, and stated in Christopher Nolan's 2010 film, *Inception,* is a dream a condensed version of real-time events. Indications are that the amount of time that might have elapsed had dream events been real is very similar to the amount of time during which the dream occurred. Evidence that this is so is derived from tracings of eye movements, from verbalizations, or from movements corresponding to an event in a dream. Interestingly, in many cases, eye movements during dreams appear to actually scan dream objects. It is as though dreamers are actually looking at the dream scene or at the object for which they're reaching (Leclair-Visonneau et al., 2010).

Why We Dream

Psychologists are not certain why we dream. Nor can we easily investigate the effects of not dreaming because doing so requires the interruption of sleep and any observed effect could as well be due to sleep deprivation as to dream deprivation. Still, we have a number of dream theories.

1. *Dreams as symbols for disguised impulses.* Perhaps the best-known dream theory is one proposed by Sigmund Freud—sadly, a theory generally unsupported by any scientific research. Freud believed dreams represent disguised manifestations of unconscious impulses. He thought most of these impulses are linked to sexual desires, aggression, or other socially taboo inclinations. Hence they're disguised, even in dreams, as a form of self-protection or, more precisely, as a form of sleep protection. Were they not disguised, we would continually awaken horrified at our vile and base cravings. If the father we want to murder appears in a dream as a spider, we can step on that creature with no fear of self-reprisal. Only Freud and other gifted psychoanalysts would be expected to uncover what the spider represents.

2. *The threat-simulation theory of dreams.* Another dream theory suggests our dreams provide us with an opportunity to practice responding to threats. This might be why, as Revonsuo (2000) suggests, so many of our dreams and nightmares have to do with chasing or being chased. Revonsuo's *Threat Simulation Theory* argues that, even though our legs and arms might not be moving while we dream, we might still be practicing a variety of "fight and flight" responses. In support of this theory, there is evidence suggesting when we dream our brains often fire in ways highly similar to the way they might fire if we were awake and actually threatened.

3. *Dreams as cognitive tools.* There is also the possibility that dreaming may have a beneficial effect on cognitive functioning and attention (Cartwright, 2010). This is suggested by studies of partial and temporary dream deprivation, accomplished by waking individuals at the onset of REM periods. In the absence of dreams, explains Cartwright, the individual finds it difficult to attend to reality upon awakening.

    Additional evidence that dreams might provide a cognitive benefit is found in the observation that when rats are placed in mazes during the day, their patterns of brain activity that night closely parallel their brain activity while they were in the maze (Ego-Stengel & Wilson, 2010). These authors suggest dreams provide us with an opportunity to sort our memories into those worth remembering and those we can afford to forget.

4. *Dreams as therapy.* Another current dream theory, somewhat reminiscent of Freud's, suggests that dreams are a form of therapy. Hartmann (2007) notes dreams are often laden with emotion. As such, they provide an opportunity to confront difficult and surprising emotions and perhaps learn how to deal with them. Dreams allow us to think through our emotions.

What Does the Bible Say?

In the Bible, we see evidence of a fifth theory on the function of dreams. Throughout the Bible, we see that God uses dreams as a form of communication with his people and to further His work on earth, both on an individual level and for the collective of His people, the nation of Israel and the broader Church, and followers of Jesus Christ.

In the Old Testament, God communicated with Joseph directly regarding his own future (Gen. 37:1-10) and also used Joseph to interpret Pharaoh's dreams so that many people could be saved through preparations for the coming famine (Gen. 41:1-36).

In the New Testament, God came to another Joseph, the earthly step-father of Jesus, via an angel in a dream to warn him of the death plots against the child, Jesus.

Matthew 2:13 ESV

"Now when they had departed, behold, an angel of the Lord appeared to Joseph in a dream and said, 'Rise, take the child and his mother, and flee to Egypt, and remain there until I tell you, for Herod is about to search for the child, to destroy him.'"

The Bible even describes how God's spirit will be manifested in the Last Days, and one of those ways is through dreams.

Acts 2:17 ESV

"And in the last days it shall be, God declares, that I will pour out my Spirit on all flesh, and your sons and your daughters shall prophesy, and your young men shall see visions, and your old men shall dream dreams."

While there is debate among theologians about the use and frequency of God communicating through dreams today, the Bible does present an additional perspective for a fifth theory on the function of dreams in human lives.

In this connection, Cartwright (2010) notes the various dreams collected from a single individual on the same night typically present such a coherent pattern that it is impossible to believe dreams represent random happenings. She argues dreams may well have a therapeutic purpose, since they often appear to be directed toward the resolution of conflict-laden situations.

And, of course, there are those who believe dreams serve none of these functions—that they are simply the result of random brain activity, or what is referred to as *cortical noise*.

What Does the Bible Say?

Sleep and dreams are discussed throughout the Bible. A good night sleep is often hard to come by especially when worry and stress permeate our busy lives. The Bible, especially the Old Testament, speaks about the power and importance of dreams.

Proverbs 3:24 ESV

"If you lie down, you will not be afraid; when you lie down, your sleep will be sweet."

Psalm 4:8 ESV

"In peace I will both lie down and sleep; for you alone, O Lord, make me dwell in safety."

Proverbs 3:21–24 ESV

"My son, do not lose sight of these— keep sound wisdom and discretion, and they will be life for your soul and adornment for your neck. Then you will walk on your way securely, and your foot will not stumble. If you lie down, you will not be afraid; when you lie down, your sleep will be sweet."

Joel 2:28 ESV

"And it shall come to pass afterward, that I will pour out my Spirit on all flesh; your sons and your daughters shall prophesy, your old men shall dream dreams, and your young men shall see visions."

Genesis 40:8 ESV

"They said to him, 'We have had dreams, and there is no one to interpret them.' And Joseph said to them, 'Do not interpretations belong to God? Please tell them to me.'"

Daniel 7:1 ESV

"In the first year of Belshazzar king of Babylon, Daniel saw a dream and visions of his head as he lay in his bed. Then he wrote down the dream and told the sum of the matter."⌟

HYPNOSIS

Sleep—and the dreams that might then come—are one state of consciousness; being awake is the other. Does hypnosis represent a third, altered type of consciousness?

The answer is: perhaps. However, the final verdict is not yet in. We are not quite certain about **hypnosis**—not even certain whether or not we should investigate it: There has long been a faint odor of mysticism, magic, and pseudoscience about hypnosis. And, as scientists, we often fear and distrust such mysterious phenomena.

> **Hypnosis:** A state characterized by heightened suggestibility (willingness to do and to believe what is suggested by the hypnotist).

Some Facts

Contrary to some popular misconceptions, hypnosis does not involve some powerful personality putting subjects into a state where, zombie-like, they have to obey. As defined by the American Psychological Association, hypnosis is ⌐"a state of consciousness involving focused attention and reduced peripheral awareness characterized by an enhanced capacity for response to suggestion" (*The Official Division 30 Definition and Description of Hypnosis*, 2014).⌟

Basically, what happens in hypnosis is this: The hypnotist uses some form of what is termed *hypnotic induction* to heighten the **suggestibility** of the subject (Gafner, 2010). A common hypnotic induction technique, the *eye-fixation method,* uses an object to focus the subject's attention while the hypnotist speaks. Pocket watches were used extensively in 19th-century France and Germany and are often shown in graphic portrayals of hypnotists plying their trades. Of course, it is not an object that induces hypnosis, but the hypnotist's words. A very common induction technique does not ask subjects to fix their gaze on an object; it simply uses verbal directions to increase the subject's relaxation and suggestibility.

> **Suggestibility:** A characteristic of a hypnotic state wherein subjects become exceedingly ready to believe whatever is suggested by the hypnotist and willing to perform whatever activities are asked of them.

A rather surprising discovery is that, in terms of physiological functioning, a hypnotic state is much closer to a waking state than to a sleep state. EEG waves are typically alpha, and respiration and heart rates may range from deep relaxation to strenuous physical activity. The single most striking feature of a hypnotic state is the willingness of subjects to do what is asked and the matter-of-factness that accompanies even the most bizarre behaviors requested of them.

Is Hypnosis a Different State of Consciousness?

Whether hypnosis is a different mental state or whether it simply involves imaginative role-playing remains uncertain and controversial (Revonsuo et al., 2009). Much of the research examining this question has compared the performance of hypnotized subjects with that of others pretending to be hypnotized. Those who believe hypnosis represents a different state of consciousness try to find differences between the psychological processes of hypnotized and non-hypnotized persons; those who think hypnosis involves imaginative role-playing look for similarities.

Among other things, this research has sometimes found that *simulators* (participants who fake being hypnotized in hypnotism research studies) are often capable of many of the same impressive feats and deceptions as are hypnotized subjects, including total-body catalepsy (rigidity), apparent amnesia, age regression, hallucinations, and the ability to tolerate pain (anesthesia; Orne, 2009). These findings would seem to support the notion that hypnosis does not represent an altered state of consciousness.

Other psychologists believe that hypnosis can be partially explained as a social phenomenon. Specifically speaking, hypnotized subjects speak and behave as a good hypnotizable subject *ought* to behave. Furthermore, the authoritative presence of the hypnotist is believed to play an important role in influencing the behavior of the subject under hypnosis.

Nonetheless, there are interesting studies indicating that brain activity changes during hypnosis (Naish, 2010); simulators are not ordinarily able to alter their brain activity deliberately to please an investigator. For example, when hypnotized subjects are instructed to imagine black-and-white objects being brilliantly colored, activity in the part of the brain associated with color vision increases; this is not the case for nonhypnotized participants asked to imagine the same thing (Oakley & Halligan, 2010).

Applications of Hypnosis

There is evidence the use of hypnosis can be effective for a variety of medical procedures, including childbirth and even surgery. It has also been used successfully in dentistry (Brown, 2009).

A variety of psychotherapies also make use of hypnosis (Barber & Westland, 2011). For example, Almas and Landmark (2010) reviewed a large number of studies in which the use of hypnosis was effective in treating sexual problems.

Hypnosis has also been used in courtrooms in an attempt to help witnesses, and sometimes victims, recall details of a crime. However, because it is difficult to establish the veracity of what hypnotized individuals appear to remember, the use of hypnosis in court remains highly controversial (Lynn et al., 2009).

The results of research that has attempted to determine whether hypnosis can be beneficial in the teaching–learning process remain somewhat uncertain. Some studies claim to have demonstrated that learning, motivation, and retention can sometimes be improved as a result of posthypnotic suggestion (Vernon, 2009). But other studies have failed to find differences between experimental groups and control groups, particularly when control groups are highly motivated. The most valid conclusion to be derived from a large number of related studies appears to be that hypnosis can be very effective in increasing motivation, but it does not increase intelligence or memory. There is also virtually no evidence it has any harmful effects, other than any indirect harm that may arise as a result of believing in hypnosis' sometimes grandiose and false claims of effectiveness.

SUMMARY

Our species, *Homo sapien,* has certain physical limitations but with a remarkable brain and nervous system ⌐as well as complex language.⌐ The basic unit of our nervous system is the neuron. Neurons, through chemical and electrical activity, compose our communication systems, the intricate arrangements of which define our very essence.

The brain and spinal cord make up the central nervous system; the *peripheral* system includes the *somatic* system (concerned with bodily sensations) and the *autonomic* system (the *sympathetic* and *parasympathetic* systems concerned with unconscious physiological responses). The brain coordinates activity in these diverse systems. Its major divisions are the hindbrain (the *medulla, pons,* and *cerebellum,* involved in balance and locomotion, respiration, sleep, and arousal), the midbrain (the *reticular formation,* involved in arousal and motivation), and the forebrain (the *hypothalamus,* concerned with temperature regulation and circadian rhythms; the *thalamus,* a relay center; the *limbic system,* implicated in emotions; and the *cerebrum,* divided into the four cerebral lobes, which include the *visual* and *auditory cortices* and the *association areas of the brain*). The *brain stem* includes structures of both the hindbrain and the midbrain.

Biology prepares the human animal to learn and do certain things easily (learning languages; learning taste aversions) but makes other behaviors difficult (restraining our cravings for fat and sugar). Our consciousness seems to reside in patterns of activity in our brains. These patterns can change drastically while an organism is asleep or under hypnosis.

Sleep, of which there are two states, REM sleep (during which we do most of our dreaming) and non-REM sleep, is not a completely *unconscious* state. Stages of sleep are distinguishable by the nature of accompanying brain waves, ranging from small fast *beta* waves when awake, through *alpha, theta,* and *delta* waves (progressively slower and deeper). We don't know clearly why we sleep or why we dream, but we do know that deprivation has negative consequences.

Hypnosis is a procedure in which subjects are given suggestions for "imaginative experiences" that lead to "alterations in perception, sensation, emotion, thought, or behavior." Its hallmark is the desire of participants to obey the hypnotist's instructions. It is not clear whether hypnosis represents a different state of consciousness, but it has important implications in medicine and psychotherapy.

⌐We are fearfully and wonderfully made, and the complexity of our brain is amazing evidence of God's creation. Also, the complexity of our brain uniquely positions humans to be able to have a relationship with God.⌐

© Alissala/Shutterstock.com

Chapter 3

Sensation and Perception

LEARNING OBJECTIVES

- ⌐Explore⌐ the differences between sensation and perception.
- Explain the process from sensation to perception for each of the senses.
- Identify the sensory receptors for each sense.
- ⌐Explain the process of sensation to perception within the visual system.
- Apply visual information to the development of computer vision syndrome.
- Review⌐ the differences between top-down and bottom-up processing.
- Explain how humans use different cues to infer visual depth.
- Identify how perceptual illusions can tell us something about how perception works.

THE BASICS OF SENSATION AND PERCEPTION

The vast majority of information acquired throughout life often begins as environmental energy. Our ability to detect environmental energy, however, is very limited with respect to the immense amount and tremendous diversity of energy available. The distinction between energy that is detectable *versus* energy that is not (both in type and intensity) is the defining feature of a **stimulus**. In order for something to be called a stimulus, it must have the capacity to interact with and stimulate specialized cells located within our body. These specialized cells form the basis for what most people understand as sensations, and it is these sensory experiences that produce our perception of the world. In fact, much of consciousness, even in the absence of sensory input, seems to involve sensory imagery. For the most part, thinking and the conceptualization of things requires or at least involves some form of imagery (e.g., visual, auditory, and kinesthetic imagery). Aside from providing the basis for consciousness, sensory systems provide important information used to control movement (e.g., balance) as well as maintain arousal (e.g., attention).

> **CHAPTER 3 OVERVIEW**

> **Stimulus**: A quantifiable pattern of physical energy, which is able to interact with an organism and produce a change in the condition of the organism. That is, a stimulus is a type of environmental energy, like light, that we are capable of detecting and responding to.

The interaction between an organism and the external world is not mutually exclusive, but a dynamic process (hence, ever changing). In order to function purposefully in an ever-changing environment, it is necessary to detect the energies around us. With regard to humans, it has been argued the external world is represented within each individual due to the patterns of activity occurring within the brain. The persistence of these neural patterns of activity within the brain, independent of the physical medium or specific environmental energy involved, is the essential notion for what most people refer to as memory, thought, consciousness, or the "mind." Although this information sounds both technical and rather advanced, Protagoras, a Greek philosopher in 450 BC, stated that "Man is nothing but a bundle of sensations." Additionally, it is interesting to note that the progress of science emerges from and is completely contingent upon what one is able to observe or sense. In essence, we are what we sense and perceive.

What Does the Bible Say?

We take so much for granted. We are blessed with much and often forget because so many of our most fundamental blessings are effortless, spontaneous, and instantaneous. What blessings meet these defining characteristics? The answer is our sensations and perceptions. Our ability to see, hear, balance, feel, smell, and taste occur without any training and work. Just consider how different your life would be if you were missing one of your senses, like sight. The Bible has a lot to say about what we expose our senses to. While Jesus healed many sensory problems like blindness, he also warned that it would be better to be blind than to let your eyes lead you to sin. In contrast, God created the world for people to enjoy and appreciate. Its beauty and evidence of God's creation continuously surrounds us. We should also not take God's wondrous creation for granted.

Mathew 5: 29 ESV

"If your right eye causes you to sin, tear it out and throw it away. For it is better that you lose one of your members than that your whole body be thrown into hell."

Luke 11:33–36 ESV

"No one after lighting a lamp puts it in a cellar or under a basket, but on a stand, so that those who enter may see the light. Your eye is the lamp of your body. When your eye is healthy, your whole body is full of light, but when it is bad, your body is full of darkness. Therefore, be careful lest the light in you be darkness. If then your whole body is full of light, having no part dark, it will be wholly bright, as when a lamp with its rays gives you light."

Psalm 96: 11–13

"Let the heavens be glad, and let the earth rejoice; let the sea roar, and all that fills it; let the field exult, and everything in it! Then shall all the trees of the forest sing for joy before the LORD, for he comes, for he comes to judge the earth. He will judge the world in righteousness, and the peoples in his faithfulness."

In just these three verses we have the sound, sight, and smell of the sea and the forest. The Bible often uses our senses and imagery to explain complex phenomenon.

SENSATION VS. PERCEPTION

Sensation is best defined as the detection of some physical stimulus in the environment by one of your sensory organs. Do not be "thrown off" by the use of the word "stimulus." A stimulus is simply a scientific term for anything that acts on your own behavior or mental processes. A stimulus can be a shape on a computer screen, the smell of pizza, or even the words on the page you are currently reading. Stimuli (the plural of stimulus) lead to changes in your behavior (also called responses, as you will also learn in this book). Simply put, sensations refer to your body's ability to interact with specific types of energy from the environment like light, sounds, tastes, and so on. Once this information reaches the brain, meaning is attached to it, which is the defining feature of a perception.

So more specifically, **perception**, on the other hand, is your brain *making sense* of the physical stimulus from the world by organizing the stimulus into a representation of something useful. For example, the sensations of certain wavelengths of light, and a certain combination of smells may lead to the perception of an apple.

Sensation and perception are both important for what you might consider a normal, everyday experience. Perception is not generally possible without sensation because the machinery used to gather physical stimuli from the environment is a crucial requirement. Imagine trying to estimate how much rain your hometown received without having a rain gauge. You could guess about the amount of rainfall, but you would probably not be very accurate. Similarly, you cannot make meaningful, predictable, and useful interactions with the world around you without being able to connect stimuli to perceptions.

Sensation: The detection of physical stimuli in the environment such as light waves, sound waves, pressure, or chemical molecules.

Perception: The detailed process of interpreting and making sense of a combination of sensations.

© BMJ/Shutterstock.com

Consider individuals dealing with schizophrenia. The most significant and debilitating symptom of schizophrenia is hallucination. Hallucinations are perceptual experiences not connected to reality. This is especially problematic because individuals with schizophrenia generally don't realize these hallucinations are not real and act on them. This creates a whole host of problems as can be imagined. How can one function purposefully in a world that is not entirely real?

> ⌐**Hallucinations:** Perceptions of experiences without corresponding external stimuli together with a compelling feeling that these are real.⌐

Similarly, this is also one of the reasons why hallucinogens are so dangerous. People take these drugs and experience sensory events that are not real and by acting on them, they put themselves at serious risk for harming themselves or others. It is extremely important to have a continuous system to connect us to the environment so we can respond quickly to changes.

⌐There are many different types of hallucinations; the most common include:

- **Auditory hallucinations**: When someone *hears* something that is not there, such as a voice or TV.
- **Visual hallucinations**: When someone sees something that is not real, such as a person or creature.
- **Olfactory hallucinations**: When someone *smells* something that is not there, such as smoke or coffee.
- **Gustatory hallucinations**: When someone *tastes* something they did not eat, like metal or spoiled milk.
- **Tactile hallucinations**: When someone *feels* like something or someone touched them, like being grabbed or pulled.
- **Somatic hallucinations**: When someone *feels* something within their body, such as that of bugs crawling under the skin or like an object trapped in their abdomen.⌐

⌐Another⌐ great real-world example of this is the controversial topic of extrasensory perception, otherwise known as ESP. Extrasensory perception is the alleged ability to perceive something through the mind alone, but without reception of physical stimuli through any of the known senses. A classic example of ESP in practice includes psychics, whose claims to fame are centered on the ability to "know" things about a person that seem "unknowable." Professional skeptics, such as James Randi, have made careers out of debunking claims of ESP. There is no known sense organ or mechanism that could pick up on someone else's thoughts. Thus, until evidence suggests otherwise, ESP is not scientifically supported (Moulton & Kosslyn, 2008).

⌐Term	Definition and Description
Sensation	Sensations refer to certain, immediate, and directly qualitative experiences or attributes such as hard, warm, sweet, red, or bright, produced by simple isolated physical stimuli. These specialized cells form the basis for what most people understand as sensations, and it is these sensory experiences that ultimately give rise to our perceptions. Sensations always travel in an ascending fashion, starting from a particular sensory receptor and terminating in the brain. Sensations are produced by stimuli.
Stimulus	A stimulus is defined as a quantifiable pattern of physical energy, which is able to interact with an organism and produce a change in the condition of the organism. That is, a stimulus is a type of environmental energy, like light, that we are capable of detecting and responding to.

Term	Definition and Description
Potential stimuli	Potential stimuli are physical energies that have yet to be detected, but are in fact detectable, like a distant sound. Therefore, if the physical energy from the environment does not cause a change in the organism, it would not be considered as a stimulus. For example, certain animals can detect ultraviolet (UV) light, magnetic energy, or very high-pitch sounds, while humans can't, so such patterns of energy would not be stimuli to humans.
Perceptions	Perceptions refer to the psychological processes whereby meaning, past experience or memory, and judgments are used to evaluate the significance of particular stimuli. For example, how is it that we are able to, in a crowded and loud room, attend to our name being said but not to other names? Obviously, our names have greater significance and history than other names. In addition, perceptions are associated with the organization and integration of sensory attributes. For example, flavor is a perception and is the culmination of taste, smell, and texture.

Once we have a way of detecting the physical stimuli from the environment (sensation), we will need a way to interpret those stimuli. For instance, even with a rain gauge, you will need some way to make sense of what a certain amount of water in a cylinder actually means. This illustrates the problem of sensation *without* perception. Although sensation is necessary, it is not by itself sufficient to account for a normal day's experiences. Due to the complexity of converting sensations to perceptions and the variety of sensations and perceptions available, in order to fully grasp the process, asking the right questions is important.

Questions for the Study of Sensations and Perceptions…

In order to understand exactly how we sense and perceive the world around us, a number of questions must be addressed for each sensory system.

1. What is the nature of the stimulus? What type of energy is involved? What are the defining properties of the stimulus?
2. How is the physical energy transformed into electrochemical energy? How does our body absorb energy? What is the energy range necessary to activate each system?
3. Where precisely does the transduction process take place? Where exactly are the receptor mechanisms located?
4. How are signals carried from the peripheral sites (sensory organs) to more central sites (brain)?
5. Where do signals from each sensory modality terminate (where in the brain do we perceive)?
6. What area of the cortex is involved in decoding and perceiving stimuli?
7. How are the signals and patterns decoded by higher brain regions? How does our brain know what signals are related to which stimuli?
8. Can previous knowledge influence our perceptions?
9. Can learning influence our ability to detect a stimulus?
10. What are the limitations of each sensory system? How fast can information be processed in each system? Does the process of aging influence our sensory systems?

The Process

To this point we have discussed the importance of both sensation and perception. However, getting from sensation to perception is also a fascinating and important ⌞process.⌟ The physical energy (stimulus) must be modified into a form the brain can use. This modification process is called **transduction**. Try this thought experiment: Below is the chemical structure for theobromine, a chemical contained in chocolate. What is appealing about the picture? If you are like most people, your answer is probably "nothing." There is nothing appealing about the chemical structure for theobromine. However, when consumed in combination with other chemicals included in chocolate, your sensory receptors for taste analyze this exact chemical structure. So, how is it that a seemingly arbitrary chemical structure can result in such a pleasant experience as eating a piece of your favorite chocolate? The answer to this question is where transduction fits. Transduction changes the physical stimulus of chocolate—your taste buds recognizing that you are eating a sugary, high-calorie item—into a pleasurable experience you would very much like to repeat (the perception).

> **Transduction:** The process of converting a physical stimulus into a meaningful and useful neural signal capable of being interpreted by the brain.

⌞All sensory receptors have the ability to take information from the world around us and convert it into neural codes that are able to generate neural activity that our brain is able to interpret. This process takes place in the following order: stimulation, reception, transduction, transmission, and perception. It is interesting to note, at this time, that some of our sensory systems are near their maximal sensitivity. If these systems were any

© Zerbor/Shutterstock.com

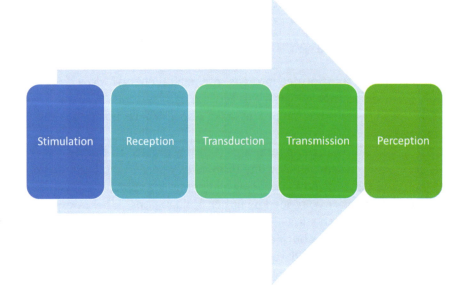

Figure 3.1   The process of sensation to perception.

Source: Brian Kelley

more efficient, then our sensory systems would actually fail to work effectively (e.g., they would be detecting thermal noise). For example, a single photon can activate a photoreceptor, and if our ears were any more sensitive, we would actually be able to hear the sound of blood traveling through the vessels around our eardrum. Another important characteristic of sensory cells is that they are often spontaneously active, that is, they demonstrate some baseline level of activity even in the absence of stimulation. This is extremely important because it allows for differential activation by very subtle stimuli, which can serve to increase or decrease that sensory cell's firing rate. Hence, receptor activation is bidirectional, causing either stimulation or inhibition. It is this bidirectional process that allows us to accurately discriminate between two similar stimuli. Another way of stating this is that our sensory systems are particularly skillful in detecting contrasts or changes in the environment and are particularly poor at detecting constant stimulus energy. Lastly, when stimulus energy is transduced by the sensory receptor into neural energy, specific features of the stimulus, such as intensity and duration, are represented in the resultant pattern of action potentials.

ᒪ**Modality**: Different forms of energy are transformed by the nervous system into different sensations or sensory modalities. Five major sensory modalities have been recognized since the history of man: vision, hearing, taste, touch, and smell; however, there are actually more. Furthermore, each modality has submodalities (i.e., taste: sweet, sour, bitter, or salty). Each nerve fiber is activated by certain stimuli and serves one modality, although under unusual circumstances a blending of effects can be observed (i.e., a punch to the eye can produce a bright flash of light even when no light enters the eye). Finally, each modality has a target (terminal) cortical area that maximally responds to only one sense modality.

ᒪ**Intensity**: Intensity or the amount of a sensation depends on the strength of the stimulus. At the receptor level, stimulus intensity is influenced by two factors: the first relates to the total number of receptors activated (spatial coding), whereas the second relates to the output generated by a single receptor or a group of receptors (temporal coding). The lowest stimulus intensity a subject can detect is defined as the sensory threshold. Interestingly, sensory thresholds are not stable across time nor are they similar across different people. Psychological factors like practice, fatigue, and the context in which the stimuli are presented can influence sensory thresholds. (This is the area where psychophysics really became a science, particularly in psychology.)

ᒪ**Duration:** The duration of a sensation is defined by the relationship between the stimulus intensity and the perceived intensity. Essentially, if a stimulus persists for a sustained period of time, its intensity decreases over time. This phenomenon is known as adaptation. For example, if a person decides to go swimming and jumps into a swimming pool, the water may feel cold at first. However, this sensation tends to fade over time. The one place this sensation will not fade, however, is the area of skin that is interfacing with both the water and the air. This emphasizes another perceptual phenomenon—perception is greatest at the regions of greatest contrast. Sensory systems are able to detect change the best, not constant stimulation.

ᒪ**Location:** There are two important measurements of a person's ability to detect spatial aspects of a sensory experience: (1) the ability to locate the source/site of stimulation, and (2) the ability to distinguish between two closely spaced stimuli. Since drugs directly activate the brain, there's no way information about location could be encoded. The user is not concerned with the stimulus' location anyway, except perhaps concerning the route of administration, which does have a definitive location.

The Common Pathway of the Sensory Systems: From Receptor to Awareness

ᒪDespite their diversity, all sensory systems and subsystems extract the same basic information from stimuli, including modality, intensity, duration, and location. These events are transformed from environmental energy to awareness through very similar biochemical and neural mechanisms. Once the energy is transduced (i.e., transformed from environmental energy to biochemical energy), it is carried by certain pathways to a number of brain structures. Each sensory system has a peripheral area of maximal sensitivity and an area of the brain dedicated solely to processing that information. Collectively, the sensory systems are very similar with regard to how they work and the manner by which they convey, distribute, and examine information. For example, most of the sensory systems include the following features (each of these topics will be discussed in detail):

1. Environmental energy
2. Detection of environmental energy
3. Activation of sensory receptors
4. Transduction of energy
5. Neural encoding
6. Mapped organization
7. Neural pathways
8. Neural relays
9. Sensory subsystems
10. Central or multisensory integration

Understanding the sensory systems and their corresponding perceptual attributes is and has been a multidisciplinary field of study. Our knowledge concerning our sensory systems includes contributions from a variety of fields like physics, computer science, chemistry, anatomy, physiology, genetics, medicine, and psychology. Despite the vast amount of information gained from scientists within these fields, it is not how energy is collected and sent to more central structures that has eluded scientists; instead, it is how the brain takes this information and creates what we call our consciousness that continues to perplex scientists. For example, much is known about how the eye collects and converts light energy into neural impulses and how and where that information is sent within the brain, yet almost nothing is known about how one is able to perceive a stimulus as one object versus another. We take for granted the fact that we can walk into a room and instantaneously comprehend what is going on. In addition to occurring immediately, this process generally requires no input from us; no computer could even come close to performing such a task.

Sensory receptors are sensitive to a specific form of physical energy (e.g., light, sound, pressure, or movement). Despite their apparent diversity, sensory receptors can be broadly classified into three categories: (1) exteroceptors, (2) proprioceptors, and (3) interoceptors. **Exteroceptors** respond to environmental energy or stimuli that are occurring from the outside of one's body, such elements include light, sound, touch, and chemical agents (extero-: external). **Proprioceptors** are sensory receptors that are activated by muscular movement or passive displacement of body parts (proprio-: position). While our conscious awareness of internal and external changes only includes information obtained from exteroceptors and proprioceptors, there is yet another category of receptors that are essential for survival. The last group of receptors are called **interoceptors** (intero-: internal), and they are able to respond to materials inhaled, ingested, or passed, and to changes in chemical surroundings, mechanical pressure, or shearing force (i.e., stretching). It is these types of receptors that trigger the release of insulin after we eat or increase respiration

Exteroceptors: Receptors that respond to environmental energy or stimuli that are occurring from the outside of one's body, such elements include light, sound, touch, and chemical agents.

Proprioceptors: These are sensory receptors that are activated by muscular movement or passive displacement of body parts.

Interoceptors: These receptors that are able to respond to materials inhaled, ingested, or passed, and to changes in chemical surroundings, mechanical pressure or shearing force.

during period of increased oxygen demand. Interoceptors are located within the mucus lining and smooth muscle walls of the respiratory, digestive, and urinary tracts.

⌐Another way to categorize sensory receptors is based on the type of energy they transduce or are activated by, and this breakdown includes the following: photoreceptors, mechanoreceptors, chemoreceptors, thermoreceptors, and nociceptors. **Photoreceptors** are sensitive to radiant electromagnetic energy (light). **Mechanoreceptors** sense deformations and motion of solids, liquids, and gases. Mechanical forces are those that tend to deform or accelerate objects possessing mass. **Chemoreceptors** detect chemicals, although not every chemical is detectable. A chemical must be water soluble, lipid soluble, and made up of organic material (i.e., in most cases). **Thermoreceptors** are sensitive to changes in temperature. Finally, **nociceptors** respond to painful stimuli or stimuli that are capable of causing tissue damage. All sensory receptors are made up of one of these five types of receptors. While it is helpful to consider each of the senses separately, our perceptions depend largely on multisensory inputs the combination or culmination of a number of senses, often including motors systems.⌐

Photoreceptors: ⌐Receptors that are sensitive to radiant electromagnetic energy (light).⌐

⌐**Mechanoreceptors:** Receptors that sense deformations and motion of solids, liquids, and gases. Mechanical forces are those that tend to deform or accelerate objects possessing mass.⌐

⌐**Chemoreceptors:** A class of receptors that detect water and lipid soluble chemicals.⌐

⌐**Thermoreceptors:** Receptors that are sensitive to changes in temperature.⌐

⌐**Nociceptors:** A type of receptor that responds to painful stimuli or stimuli that are capable of causing tissue damage.⌐

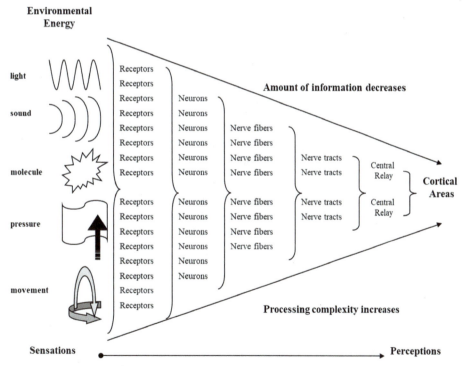

Figure 3.2   ⌐As the body transforms environmental energy to perceptions, the amount and complexity of the information changes. The nervous system systematically decreases the information but at each step, it also increase the information's complexity.⌐

Source: Brian Kelley

METHODS

▶ RESEARCH
SENSATION AN[D]
PERCEPTION

Now that you know something about sensation and perception, we should clarify how modern psychological scientists study sensation and perception in participants. There are two basic methods of studying the sensation and perception of individuals, both involving measuring sensation's limits otherwise known as thresholds. Those methods are absolute threshold and difference threshold.

A person's **absolute threshold** is measured by taking the smallest amount of a stimulus and gradually increasing its strength until a person correctly guesses the stimulus's presence 50% of the time. For example, imagine we are measuring someone's absolute threshold for vision. As psychologists, we would begin by presenting the faintest possible light to a participant. At first the participant will probably not perceive the light; it is below the person's threshold. However, the psychologist will gradually increase the intensity of the light until the person correctly indicates that the light is present.

> **Absolute threshold:** A method used to study the limits of sensation; the smallest amount of a physical stimulus that can be correctly detected 50% of the time.

This minimum amount of a stimulus's intensity that can be detected is known as the absolute threshold. Each of the senses we discuss in subsequent sections of this chapter has its own absolute threshold, which is directly related to our own sensitivity to different types of physical stimuli in the environment; for instance, human olfaction is far less sensitive than that of canines.

A **difference threshold** is estimated by comparing the intensity of two stimuli, and gradually increasing the difference between their intensities until a difference can be detected by the person. For instance, imagine holding two pieces of fruit of approximately the same weight. You will probably not be able to tell a difference in their weights because of the similarity. However, if we begin increasing the weight of one piece of fruit, the difference will also increase. Due to this increased difference between the two pieces of fruit, there will be a point at which you can accurately detect the difference. This point is called the difference threshold, also known as the just noticeable difference (JND).

> **Difference threshold:** A method used to study the sensitivity of sensation; the smallest difference between two stimuli that can be correctly detected 50% of the time; this is also called the just-noticeable difference.

A fascinating aspect of the difference threshold is that it is not fixed, but relative. For example, if a researcher places a 10-pound weight in your left hand and a 5-pound weight in your right hand, you will probably be able to accurately indicate there is a difference in weight. However, if we put 50 pounds in your left hand and 45 pounds in your right hand, you will have a much more difficult task of accurately indicating the difference in weight. Why would this happen? The difference in both examples is 5 pounds. **Weber's law**—derived by Ernst Weber—suggests the difference threshold between two stimuli is relative to the size of the original stimulus. In the weight example described previously, Weber's law would predict that the 5 pound difference is easier to detect in the first example because 5 pounds is 50% of the weight in your left hand as opposed to being only 10% of the weight in your left hand when carrying 50 pounds. Give this a try the next time you are at the gym!

> **Weber's law:** A principle in sensation that suggests that the size of the difference threshold is relative to the strength of the original stimulus.

There are also a number of nonsensory factors that can affect the observer's performance in a signal/sensory detection task.

1. Motivation
2. Attention
3. Experience
4. Fatigue
5. Expectation

⌐All of the previous factors also play a role in biasing the response to a stimulus. For example, of the previous, which is most important for a radiologist (i.e., a physician that looks at medical images) compared to a person who has never looked at an x-ray? Considering equal visual ability, what makes the difference between one person seeing a bone fracture and one person not? If both can see equally well, the biggest difference would be training and experience. Training plays a significant role in people's ability to detect a stimulus. Expectation also plays a critical role in noticing a stimulus. If you have driven the same route every day for work, day after day, and year after year, and one day a new stop sign was installed, there is a good chance that on that first day, you would drive right through it. But, a person who was driving that road for the first time

© ANN PATCHANAN/Shutterstock.com

would likely not miss it. Expecting or not expecting something has a significant impact on behavior. So, while it would seem that the most important aspect of detecting a sensory signal would be the sensory signal itself, often the psychological variables can overshadow an obviously detectable or obviously not detectable stimulus. For example, if the signal is present on nearly every trial, a person will adopt a pattern of responding in which "yes" responses are overestimated and the number of false alarms increases. If the signal is rarely present, the result might be many more "no" responses, when in fact the signal was present.⌐

Adaptation

The sensitivity of sensory receptors can also be affected by the duration of a stimulus. For example, imagine walking across a ⌐movie theater parking lot⌐ on a sunny day. While walking, you have been in constant sunlight for the duration of ⌐just⌐ a few minutes. When you arrive ⌐in the theater⌐ a few minutes late, the ⌐theater⌐ appears pitch black and you stumble over ⌐feet, purses,⌐ and empty chairs before you find your seat. After sitting in ⌐the theater⌐ a few minutes, everything seems to be more visible. You ⌐can laugh a bit⌐ as another ⌐person⌐ stumbles to his or her seat. ⌐The exact opposite process plays out when leaving the theater. Having sat in the dark for about two hours, when you leave the light seems especially bright and even blinding for a couple of minutes until you adjust.⌐ This example illustrates something called **sensory adaptation**. Our sensory receptors become less sensitive when exposed to a constant stimulus for a certain amount of time. For example, our sensory receptors for vision become less sensitive after prolonged, constant exposure to sunlight. When the

> **Sensory adaption:** A decline in a sensation's sensitivity resulting from the presence of a constant stimulus.

sunlight is removed by walking into a dark classroom, our sensory receptors are much less sensitive to the minimal amount of light, thus making the room appear very dark.

THE SENSES

Vision

ᴸ"It is a terrible thing to see and have no vision."
"Of all the senses, sight must be the most delightful."

Helen Keller

ᴸWhile anecdotal, the power of light and color has become an integral component of our everyday language. Clearly, we connect how we feel with light, such as feeling "bright" or "dark" and even more specifically we associate and explain how we feel with color. So much so that contemporary languages describe internal states, such as mood, energy, and behavior, based upon color. For example, we often say we feel "blue" when we are sad, "red hot" when we are angry or aroused, "green" when we are jealous, new at something, or sick, "black" when we are feeling morbid or powerful, and we also say that we feel "white" as a ghost when scared or angelic or "yellow" when sick or cautious. Also, as a general rule, pink is associated with feminine and blue with masculine traits.

Color Summary

- ᴸBlue: sad, depressed, melancholy
- Red: angry, aroused
- Green: jealous, sick, a beginner
- Black: morbid, powerful
- White: scarred, angelic
- Yellow: sick or cautious
- Grey: mature
- Feminine: pinks
- Masculine: blues

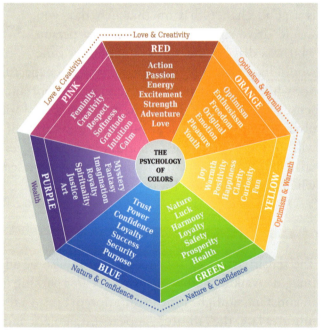

© artellia/Shutterstock.com

ᴸWhy study vision in a course about psychology? Our senses impact our behavior in many unexpected ways. Often the small, subtle changes in our behavior can result in significant and cumulative changes in behavior over time. Consider the issue around screen time. Estimates suggest more than 14% of optometry visits are related to eye or vision problems resulting from computer, tablet, or smartphone use. Considering that there are over 70 million optometry visits each year, as many as 10 million people are visiting the doctor to help alleviate their computer vision problems. More specifically, the National Institute for Occupational Health and Safety (Gupta et al., 2013) has found that 50% to 90% of individuals working at some sort of video display have visuals symptoms (e.g., burning eyes or blurred vision) with 22% showing musculoskeletal problems (e.g., neck or back pain). Not only does this condition impact millions of individuals but it also creates an enormous financial burden. Estimates for just diagnosing and treating computer vision syndrome are said to be over $2 billion annually and, this amount does not include lost wages and decreased workplace productivity (Abelson & Ousler, 1999). While the syndrome is unlikely to result in any permanent damage, it can increase one's risk for eye-related problems as well as be acutely debilitating and very costly.

One of the most significant causes of Computer Vision Syndrome is decreased **ocular lubrication**, also known as tears. Decreased ocular lubrication is caused primarily by decreased blink rate. Blinking is very important because each blink works to coat the eye with tears. Several studies have shown (Meadows, 2005; Sheedy et al., 2005) that people typically blink about 12 times per minute; however, blink rate is typically reduced by half for computer users. Even worse, studies on computer gamers have found that blink rates can drop to as low as only one or two blinks in three minutes (Meadows, 2005). When you consider

© tuaindeed/Shutterstock.com

how much time children spend playing video games, watching television, using the Internet, and text messaging, these findings make one ponder the possible long-term consequences of such prolonged developmental exposure to video displays.

First, most people work in offices designed prior to the advent of modern, desktop computers. Thus, when the computer is placed

Ocular lubrication: Our visual system is able to make its own surface liquid which serves to keep the eye moist; natural tears are the mechanism for this process.

on the desk, people typically have to focus their gaze upwards in order to effectively view the computer monitor. Besides placing stress on the neck and back, people compensate by elevating their eyelids above normal levels, thus, exposing more of the **cornea** (e.g., the surface of the eye). Now, an already reduced number of tears have to cover an even larger ocular surface; however, the problem is made even worse because a larger ocular surface also allows for more rapid rate of tear evaporation. As if this isn't bad enough, air conditioning, static buildup, airborne paper dust, photocopy toner, ventilation fans, and overall poor indoor air quality increase the rate of

© vesna cvorovic/Shutterstock.com

tear evaporation and eye irritation, therefore, further increasing dry eye problems. This is no trivial matter as decreased tear production alone can result in eye inflammation, corneal infection, and scarring.

Cornea: The surface of the eye

Dry eye problems associated with Computer Vision Syndrome increase with increasing age, in people with contact lenses, people who have had LASIK surgery, and occurs slightly more often in females compared with males (Blehm et al., 2005). Frequently used medications, including antihistamines (e.g., drug used for allergies), tricyclic antidepressants, birth control, nasal decongestants (e.g., drug used for colds), and Accutane (e.g., drug used for acne), are also known to decrease tear production, thereby, intensify Computer Vision Syndrome. Lastly, while it may seem contradictory, over-the-counter eye drops for "red eyes" can actually increase dry eye problems. Primarily because such drops don't match a tear's natural lubricating ability and dry eye and red eye are different problems. So, natural tears or ocular lubrication are one of the keys to good eye health.

⌐Inappropriate computer monitor distance and angle are additional causes of eye strain and Computer Vision Syndrome. Computer workstations should follow a more ergonomic design (Figure 3.3), thus, allowing people to work more comfortably and efficiently. Briefly, ergonomics is the applied science of equipment design intended to maximize productivity by reducing operator fatigue and discomfort (also referred to as human engineering, the physical side, and human factors psychology, the behavioral side). Focusing on close objects, compared to distant objects, requires more ocular muscles and those muscles have to work harder. For example, in order to view a close object, the lens has to be stretched by the ciliary muscles, so the image is focused on the light sensitive tissue in the back of the eye, the retina. The **lens** is a biconvex crystalline structure that is actually quite stiff and difficult to stretch, so it

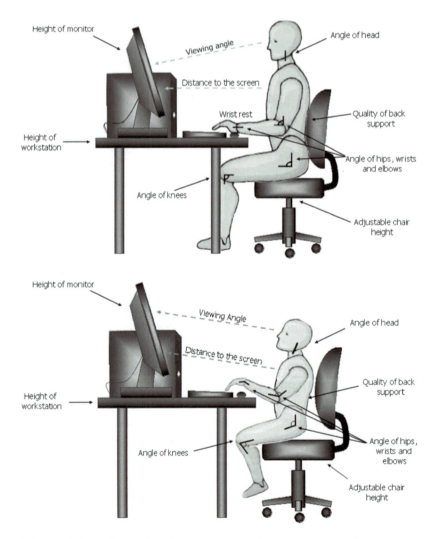

Figure 3.3   ⌐Example of computer workspace ergonomics.⌐
Source: Brian Kelley

shouldn't be surprising to learn that eye fatigue occurs quickly after constant near viewing. Not only do the **ciliary muscles** have to work hard, but so do the ocular muscles. Close viewing requires the eyes to **converge** (i.e., move toward one another), much like what you see when someone "crosses" their eyes, perhaps not quite as dramatic. If you don't think this sounds like a difficult task, try crossing your eyes and holding that "converged" focus for a couple of minutes (despite what you may have heard previously, they will not get stuck like that). The muscles involved in close-viewing fatigue and the consequence of such fatigue is the muscles "locking-up" in that squeezed position, thereby making it difficult to see distant objects. Once the muscles finally relax, it may be difficult to see close objects.

The problem is often further magnified when children use phones and tablets because they generally don't sit appropriately creating further strain on their neck and back.

People have been reading for thousands of years now, so why are we just now noting so many reading problems in computer users? Is reading from paper compared to a computer really different enough to account for all of these visual and musculoskeletal problems? The answer is an emphatic yes! There are significant differences between computer reading and paper reading. First, even the highest quality computer screens have lower **pixilation** compared with paper. Pixilation is a physical measure of resolution (the sensory component; what we see), which is described in psychological terms as **acuity** (the perceptual component; how we see it) or described in everyday language as detail. For example, average printed material has 600+ dpi (i.e., dots per inch), which is considerably higher than most computer monitors and higher still compared to mobile phones. Also, computer screens have a lower contrast compared with printed material; that is, the difference between the black letters on paper and the white background is more pronounced compared with computers. Additionally, the black ink on paper is blacker than the black emitted from a computer screen. Virtually no **glare** occurs from paper, while it can be considerable with computer monitors. It is also important to note that computer monitors flicker (i.e., the screen refreshes about 60 times per second), while printed text does not; worse yet, may people work in offices or classrooms with fluorescent lights which also have a

> **Lens:** A biconvex crystalline structure that helps focus the visual image onto the retina in the back of the eye.
>
> **Ciliary muscles:** The muscles within the eye that stretch or compress the lens for the purpose of focusing the visual image.
>
> **Converge:** The ability of the two eyes to move, rotate inward toward the nose; this is often referred to as being cross-eyed.

> **Pixilation:** A physical measure of resolution on a screen.
>
> **Acuity:** The level of detail in a picture or the sharpness of an image.
>
> **Glare:** An uncomfortable level of brightness

© robuart/Shutterstock.com

© Veja/Shutterstock.com

blink rate multiplying the computer monitor problem. Lastly, it is easy to adjust the distance of paper as we read and readjust it as the muscle get tired of being in one location; however, this is not the case with computer monitors. Generally, computer monitors are too far away and angled too high for comfortable reading. In conclusion, spending a lot of time in front of a computer monitor or screen, compared to printed material, can results in considerable eye strain.

Table 3.1   Comparison of Computer Monitors vs. Printed Material

Variable	Computer	Print
Resolution	Generally low	Generally high
Contrast	Typically low	Typically high
Text color/Blackness	Poor	Rich
Glare	Moderate to high	Very low
Flicker	Moderate to high	None
Ergonomics	Hard to manipulate	Very easy to manipulate

Table 3.2   Adopted from Sheedy's Five Categories of CVS Symptoms

Symptoms	Examples	Causes
Visual	Near objects are blurred, hyperopia Distant objects are blurred, myopia Double vision, diplopia Color distortions	Refractive error (focus) Accommodation problems Binocular difficulties
Ocular surface (cornea)	Dry and burning eyes Irritated eyes Water eyes CL intolerance	Low blink rate Incomplete blink Tear film abnormalities Corneal drying
Asthenopia (near work and/ or focusing difficulties due to uncorrected vision problem)	Headaches Eye strain Eye fatigue General Fatigue	Refractive errors Accommodative problems Convergence difficulties Work space ergonomics
Photophobia (intolerance or sensitivity to light)	Glare Computer screen flicker Computer screen to bright Overhead lights to bright	Poor room lighting Reflections Low refresh rate for screen
Musculoskeletal	Neck pain Shoulder pain Back pain	Poor work-station ergonomics Incorrect viewing height Inappropriate glasses (bifocals specifically)

Fixing the Problem

Considering how much time we *have* to spend at a computer, here are some basic recommendations that you can follow to protect your visual system (American Optometric Association, 2020). First, take frequent breaks; specifically, every 20 minutes take a 20 second break and look at least 20 feet away. This will help exercise your eye muscles. Next, blink often! This is harder than its sounds. So, if you are like me, you might need to place a sticky note on your monitor to remind you to blink. If you find that your eyes hurt, because you are not blinking enough, try using some artificial tears (but not red-eye reduction drops). It is important to have your eyes examined by an optometrist, because many people have uncorrected visual problems that are exacerbated by computer use. Another simple thing to do is adjust your computer monitor so that it is 18 to 30 inches from your eyes. Additionally, the top of the monitor should be just below your eye height; that is, you should be looking down at the monitor. Similarly, adjust the monitor's brightness and contrast so that the monitor is not the brightest light source in the room, and minimize glare, especially from nearby windows, and excessive overhead lighting. Finally, clean your monitor regularly. Ever notice how much dust accumulates on your television or computer monitor? Static electricity, which builds up on monitors, attracts dust which can reduce monitor clarity.

In summary, frequent computer use can produce a variety of adverse effects and even a number of health concerns; however, subtle changes in workplace behavior and workstation ergonomics can go a long way in preventing these problems.

Isn't it rather astounding how a little knowledge can change your life? We too often take something as simple as blinking or workstation designs for granted, yet it can have an escalating impact on one's behavior and physical health. Considering you are likely reading this right now on a screen, it would be important to give consideration to the advice below. So, when it comes to sensory systems and psychology, this is just one example of how understanding a little about vision can have many downstream influences on behavior.

10 Simple Steps to Protecting Yourself from Computer Vision Syndrome

1. Take a break every 20 min for 20 seconds and focus 20 feet away.
2. Blink! Blink! Blink!
3. Use artificial tears if necessary
4. Visit eye doctor regularly
5. Adjust monitor distance and height
6. Adjust monitor brightness and contrast
7. Minimize glare
8. Control excessive overhead light
9. Clean monitor frequently
10. For longer projects, read from paper if possible

Let There Be Light

Light, also known as electromagnetic radiation, is the fundamental energy source for our visual system and is the first and necessary step in an amazingly complicated process whereby environmental energy is transformed into private, personal experiences. In order to appreciate the nature of what we see, we have to *look* into, at least at some basic level, the natural phenomenon that initiates this process—light.

Simply stated the human eye is capable of collecting, detecting, transducing, and encoding electromagnetic radiation. Although this is, in and of itself, an astounding capability, there are many devices that can accomplish the same basic task, such as a camera. Like the eye, even a camera has a lens, light filter, an aperture control, and an image sensory; however, neither cameras nor any similar device has the ability to add the perceptual depth that we so readily can. Our ability to see, for all practical purposes, is effortless, spontaneous, and instantaneous. It is not like we really have to work to *see*. Unlike cameras, images from the eye are sent to the brain, which is uniquely capable of taking these images and transforming them into an integral part of our very consciousness. So, while the eye is an essential component in the pathway to visual perception, it is simply

© denniro/Shutterstock.com

a means to an end. With that being said, please understand the eye is the single most complex sensory organ. Nearly the entire weight of the eye is derived from extremely sophisticated accessory structures, that is, support structures.

Only a very, very small part of the eye is actually dedicated to converting patterns of light energy into neural codes. In order to fully appreciate the inner workings of the eye and their related perceptions, one must first understand how the eye manipulates light.

Our ability to "accurately" see the world around us is perhaps one of the most important abilities humans possess; the word *accurately* is placed in quotes for reasons you will discover later in this chapter when we discuss the topic of perception.

Light Waves

The electromagnetic spectrum most available to us starts as nuclear fusion within the sun. The natural consequence of the sun's nuclear fusion is the production of massive amounts of heat (try 27,000,000°F at the sun's core) followed by an equally impressive flow of electromagnetic radiation into space. The sun converts 8 million tons of matter into energy every single second (Lawton, 1981). Because light travels at 186,282 miles per second in a vacuum, and the earth is 93 million miles from the sun, the sun's light

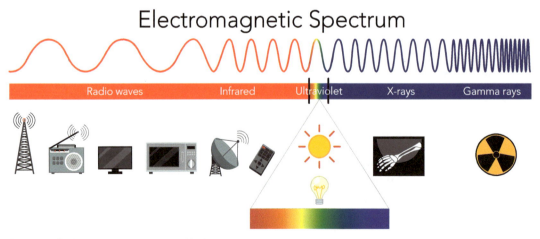

Figure 3.4   The spectrum of light.
© brgfx/Shutterstock.com

reaches the earth in a mere 8.4 minutes. While it is true that light from the sun is ultimately responsible for sustaining all life on earth as well as providing the stimulus necessary for sight, such positive news is tempered by the fact that the same sunlight can also cause widespread damage to the very life it is simultaneously supporting. The reason behind this apparent contradiction is the sun generates not only a massive amount of energy but also a large range of energy. Simply referred to as light, electromagnetic radiation includes radio waves, microwaves, infrared, visible light, ultraviolet, x-rays, and gamma rays. While we use different names to describe light, there is no fundamental difference between light at one end of the spectrum versus light at the other end aside from wavelength dependent properties such as frequency and energy. For example, gamma rays, visible light, and radio waves are all electromagnetic radiation just with decreasing wavelengths, respectively; thus, each moves at the same speed and are governed by the same principles.

While all light follows the same basic laws, light does not affect all objects equally. I imagine when asked to consider the nature of light, the visible spectrum immediately comes to mind. Intuitively, we generally consider information most available to us and what is more readily available to us than what we see? However, there is so much more to light than what we see. Our visual system is only capable of transducing a very small fraction of the entire range of electromagnetic radiation. This is not to say nonvisible light isn't useful, though. Scientists have learned to exploit and utilize the large range of nonvisible light to enhance our lives. For example, your mobile phone, television, radio, CD/DVD player, remote control, microwave oven, and a variety of medical devices operate by means of light energy.

If all light follows the same laws, this sort of begs the question, why can't we see microwaves or x-rays? Much of light's purpose is determined by its relationship with the objects with it comes in to contact. The interaction of light with matter is dependent upon both the specific wavelength of light and unique composition of the matter. Thus, our eyes (matter) are only capable of interacting with a small range of light energy. Radio waves, in contrast, have low energy and such a long wavelength our eyes cannot detect them; as a matter of fact, radio waves pass right through our eyes. It takes a specialized device (again, matter) to capture this type of light energy, like an antenna. Lastly, on a hot summer day, consider the sensation that would result from touching a black, steel handrail versus a white, vinyl or plastic one. This difference is due to objects ability to absorb infrared light (heat).

In order to fully appreciate how light impacts our visual system a more in-depth analysis of light is necessary. Light, such as a lamp or rays from the sun, is actually composed of waves. These waves are analogous to waves in an ocean and may have a similar pattern if we view them from a side profile. Waves of light can be very different, and these differences correspond to our perceptions of different colors and their intensity. Also, humans are only capable of registering a certain amount of the possible spectrum of light. Going back to the rain gauge metaphor, the rain gauge is wonderful at catching rain. However, other forms of precipitation may not be as accurately registered. For example, thick snow may not be as easily measured in a narrow rain gauge, and hail may not fit into the opening at the top of the rain gauge. Of course, this does not mean heavy snow and hail are nonexistent in the world. We know from experience those forms of precipitation

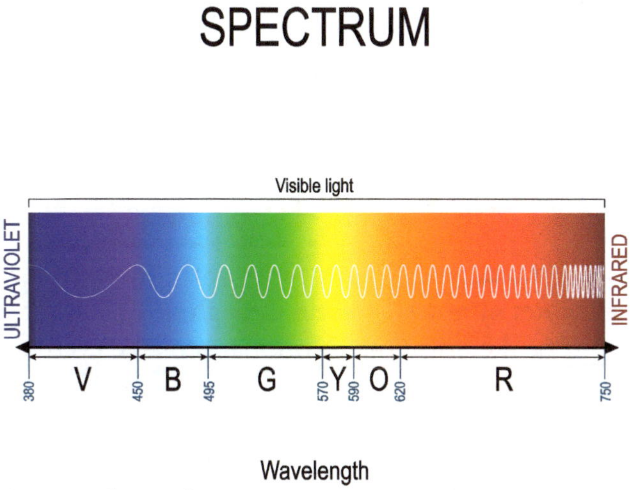

© Designua/Shutterstock.com

occur. Similarly, there are many forms of visible light (e.g., ultraviolet, infrared) that cannot be sensed by the human eye, but may be sensed by other species (e.g., bees, snakes).

The wavelength of a light wave—the distance from peak to peak—is the physical property of the light wave stimulus that we would perceive as color. Red has a longer wavelength than blue. The amplitude of a light wave—the vertical distance from peak to trough (the low point)—is the physical property of a light wave that corresponds to the brightness, or intensity, of a color.

Average Luz Levels Table

Cloudy dark night	0.0001 Lux
Moonlight	0.1 Lux
Street lighting	10 Lux
Room with only TV on	50 Lux
Flash from cell phone	80 Lux
Average living room	100 Lux
Bathrooms	150 Lux
Entrance hall/Foyer	160 Lux
Sunrise or sunset	400 Lux
Brightly lit office	500 Lux
Cloudy winter day	4,000 Lux
Light therapy	10,000 Lux
Average sunny day	32,000 Lux
Very bright sunny day	100,000 Lux

(Based in part from Lam, 1998; http://www.weblightmeter.com/; http://www.ndlight.comau/lix_levels.html)

The particular wavelength of light is dictated by the object that the light is bouncing off; a wavelength of light associated with the perception of red is reflected off an apple and a fire truck.

From the World to the Eye

Light waves bounce off objects in the physical world and enter our mental world through small holes at the front of the eyes. The colorful area of the eye that is documented on your driver's license is called the iris, and it is the fibrous muscular structure that contains these small holes. These holes are called pupils and are the black circles that expand and contract depending

© Gladskikh Tatiana/Shutterstock.com

on whether you are inside or outside in the sun. In addition, law enforcement officers sometimes use pupil dilation to check for consumption of drugs; pupils will dilate or constrict differently depending on the specific type of drug induced (Richman et al., 2004). ⌐Pupil diameter is also influenced by stress and arousal (like lying). Pupil diameter is controlled by the autonomic nervous system. The autonomic nervous system regulates many important physiological processes in response to changes in activity or emotional arousal. Parasympathetic (e.g., "the rest and digest" system) activation allows for pupil constriction, whereas sympathetic (e.g., the "fight or flight" system) activation allows for pupil dilation.

⌐Like a seesaw, these two opposing processes must work together to affect pupil diameter, and the constriction response is more powerful compared to the dilation response as too much light could result in damage, while too little might moderately impair vision. Across many behaviors, changes in arousal level, from relaxation to fear, are accompanied by changes in pupil diameter. Rest and emotional arousal that is pleasing are accompanied by pupil dilation (termed mydriasis; sympathetic control). Thus, if you are happy to see someone, the likely response is pupil dilation. In contrast, if you are angry, frustrated, or scared, your pupils will constrict (termed miosis; sympathetic control). While the pupil plays a direct role in controlling the amount of light entering the eye, it can also play an indirect role in shedding some light onto one's internal emotional state.⌐

© sruilk/Shutterstock.com

Keep in mind that these black circles are not structures at all. In fact, they are literally just holes in the structure of your eye, but they fall directly behind a covering called the cornea. The pupils appear black because there is no reflected light inside of the eye.

Good Pupils Don't Lie

⌐The relationship between pupil diameter and emotional feeling has many practical applications. For example, scientists have exploited this reflexive change as a measure of the discomfort (i.e., emotional arousal) associated with lying (Dionisio et al., 2001). In the future, perhaps a simple eye scan will be able to determine if someone is telling the truth or lying. Furthermore, scientists have been working on a computer workstation that will be able to quantify the emotional state of the user, via pupil diameter, and adjust certain software features in response to user frustration or anger (Barreto et al., 2007).

A recent study demonstrated that empathy for negative emotions has an autonomic component. Specifically, this study showed that pupil diameter increases when people are sad, which is not surprising; however, what the scientists also noted was that an observer's pupil diameter mirrors that of the sad person they are interacting with, all without their explicit knowledge. While ancient philosophers considered the pupil the window into the soul, they may not have been too far off. Today's scientists continue to connect and elaborate on the relationship between the pupil and the inner workings of our private thoughts.

Besides providing a window into one's emotional state or recent drug use, examination of pupil diameter has another very important, practical application. The diameter of the pupil is ultimately controlled by **pupilloconstrictor zone** located within the pretectal area of the midbrain (to be covered in more detail in the following chapter). This region is located near the third ventricle and is especially sensitive to insult. Brain damage, even minor, can result an increase in intracranial pressure (e.g., swelling). Therefore, a sluggish or reduced pupilloconstrictor response to light is one of the most important vital signs to monitor after a head injury. As intracranial pressure builds, the pupils become more fixed and dilated thus less responsive to incident light. Further, if, after an accident, the pupils appear normal at one point in time and show a rapid deterioration in function, it is indicative of rapid swelling and likely serious trauma. Measuring pupil diameter is used extensively in amateur and professional sports as an indicator of possible concussion and brain damage. The incidence of sports related concussions is increasing in frequency and covering a larger, ever younger age group. Concussions are noted frequently in boxing, soccer, football, motocross, hockey, wrestling, field hockey, basketball, softball, and volleyball and present greater risks in younger athletes (Guskiewicz et al., 2004; Kirkwood et al., 2006; Oliaro et al., 2001).

> **Pupilloconstrictor zone:** The part of the midbrain responsible for controlling the diameter of the pupil.

© Margaret Kite/Shutterstock.com

Light waves travel through the opening in the front of the eye (the pupil) and are processed on a structure at the back of the eye. This structure is crucial for human vision. Its name: the retina. As you learned earlier in this chapter, each of the senses requires a specific type of sensory receptor, designed to process a specific type of physical stimulus from the environment. The sensory receptor for vision is called a **photoreceptor** and many of these photoreceptors rest on the structure called the **retina**.

> **Photoreceptor:** A type of sensory receptor specifically for vision, which is located on the retina at the back of the eye.
>
> **Retina:** A light-sensitive membrane at the back of the eye that contains the sensory receptors for vision.

Rods and Cones

The photoreceptors are not created equal, however. Different types of photoreceptors may process light waves in different ways and with different clarity. There are two basic types of photoreceptors in the human eye: rods and cones. **Rods** are rod shaped and better at processing dim light, which may be experienced at dusk or at night. The acuity—or HD-ness—of rod-based vision is fairly low, though. If we could somehow watch a movie made entirely with rods it would be blurry and black and white. This does not mean that rods are useless. Rods require less light to function, and therefore they are wonderful assets when we are trying to see something (a tiger, perhaps) in the failing light at the end of the day.

Cones are cone shaped and are specialized to process colorful images in very high detail. Keep in mind that there is a tradeoff, though. Cones also require substantial light in order to properly

> **Rods:** A specific group of photoreceptors that are specialized to process dim light and are useful for night vision and peripheral vision.

> **Cones:** A specific group of photoreceptors that are specialized to process color and are useful for daylight vision and high visual acuity.

work. For example, do you find it difficult to determine the colors of objects and read fine print in a dimly lit classroom? If so, it is because your cones—which are necessary for achieving color vision and high acuity—require large amounts of light in order to properly function.

Cones and rods are also distributed on the surface of the retina in very different ways. Suppose we took the retina out of the eye and flattened it on a table. We could then look at the number of cones and rods in different locations on the retina. What we would find is that cones are mostly located in

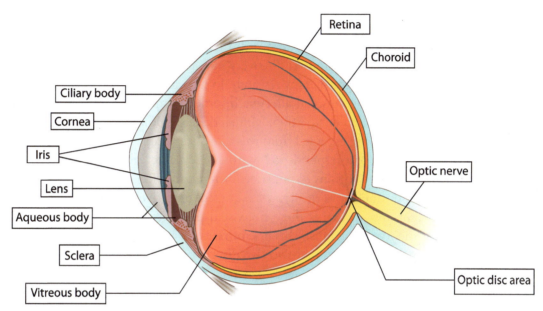

Figure 3.5   ⌐Diagram of the human eye.⌐

© Miro Kovacevic/Shutterstock.com

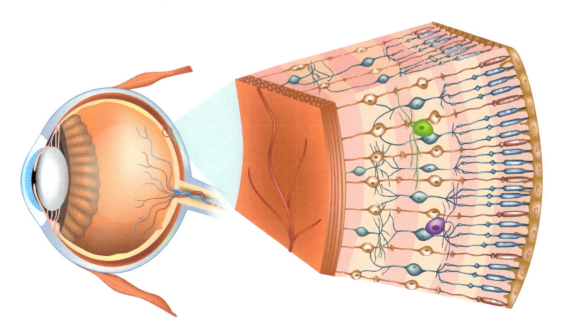

Figure 3.6   Photoreceptor cells in retina of human eye.

© Sakurra/Shutterstock.com

the **fovea**, an area on the retina associated with the center of vision. When we look at an object, the center of that object is located in the fovea on our retina. The number of cones significantly decreases as we move from the fovea toward the edges of the retina. These edges of the retina contain far more rods than cones.

> **Fovea:** An area at the center of the retina that contains the highest density of cones; visual acuity is highest in this region.

Not only has recent research on light exposure and arousal noted the importance of both intensity and time of day (morning exposure is better than evening exposure), it has actually demonstrated the importance of wavelength (color) as a contributing factor in the overall efficacy of light and arousal. For example, recent research has found that light closest to the blue region of the spectrum induces an antidepressant effect in people with seasonal affective disorder. The finding that blue light has unique physiological properties was somewhat of a serendipitous discovery in that low-intensity blue and red lights were used as placebo control conditions in light therapy research. In fact, low-intensity blue light was superior to low-intensity red light in alleviating seasonal affective disorder symptoms and comparable to bright white light (full spectra light) (Cajochen et al., 2005; Munch et al., 2006).

A remarkable new scientific finding emerged from this line of research. The human visual system has a nonvisual photosensitive receptor that responds to low-frequency blue light and this nonvisual photoreceptor connects to important brain regions responsible for manipulation of hormones, daily rhythms, and mood—the suprachiasmatic nucleus of the hypothalamus. It tentatively appears that the underlying mechanism of action for light and arousal is these nonvisual photoreceptors and their projections to specific "arousing" areas of the hypothalamus. This line of research is important because it helps establish why bright light therapy works for seasonal effective disorder as well as helping people adjust to jet lag. Despite overwhelming evidence, many professionals remain in the dark about the benefits of light therapy. Current research demonstrates a positive effect of light therapy across a number of conditions

Figure 3.7 Color vision test images. Find the hidden number in each circle (answers from left to right: 23, 36, 9, 4, 48, and 15).

including, traumatic brain injury (Vlessides, 2020), schizophrenia (Naifeh, 2011), dementia, addiction, anorexia (Bellavite et al., 2005), obesity (Gur, 2002), antepartum, postpartum depression (Corral et al., 2000), premenstrual depression and premenstrual dysphoric disorder, bulimia nervosa (Blouin et al., 1996), shift work and jet lag adjustment (Horowitz et al., 2001), adult attention-deficit disorder, and a variety of sleep disorders (Horowitz et al., 2001; Terman & Terman, 2005).

Tentative Conditions That Respond to Light Therapy

- Traumatic brain injury
- Schizophrenia
- Dementia
- Addiction
- Anorexia
- Obesity
- Bulimia
- Antepartum
- Postpartum depression
- Premenstrual depression
- Premenstrual dysphoric disorder
- Shift work
- Jet lag
- Adult attention deficit disorder
- Sleep abnormalities

From the Eye to the Brain

There is also an interesting quirk about the retina that is a result of the specific way the human eye is constructed. Notice in the figure that there is a hole in the retina where the **optic nerve** must exit the inside of the eye. In this location there are zero rods *or* cones. Therefore, the point at which the optic nerve leaves the eye—the **blind spot**—is quite literally not sensitive to light waves because there are no photoreceptors on that part of the retina. However, amazingly, you do not walk around with the perception of blind spots in your visual field. Instead, neighboring photoreceptors help fill in the empty areas in perception. To illustrate the blind spot, close your left eye and stare at the star in Figure 3.8. Gradually move forward or backward and you will notice something amazing. The red circle to the right will seem to disappear! This is because that image has moved into the blind spot in your right eye.

After leaving the eye, the optic nerves meet in the brain at a point called the **optic chiasm**. Here, the optic nerve from each eye splits into two smaller bundles of axons—one for the right and left visual fields of each eye—and is sent to different regions of the brain for higher-order perception.

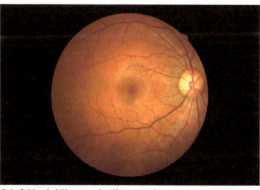

© Left Handed Photography/Shutterstock.com

Optic nerve: A large bundle of axons that leave the back of the eye and carries visual information to the visual cortex of the brain.

Blind spot: A gap in the retina due to the exit of the optic nerve where no photoreceptors are located; this causes a blind spot in the visual field during sensation.

Optic chiasm: The point in the brain at which the optic nerves from each eye meet and partly cross over to the other side of the brain.

Figure 3.8   Blind spot example.

AUDITION (HEARING)

Hearing, or audition, is an important sensation used in creating the perceptual experience we call reality. While sitting through a college lecture, most people are able to discern the different sounds being projected from the professor and interpret them as words, sentences, and coherent thoughts. However, the initial process of detecting, amplifying, and processing sound is what we must first discuss.

Sound Waves

Similar to vision, the physical stimulus for audition comes in the form of a wave: a sound wave. Sound waves are produced by vibrating molecules in the air or water. The vibrating molecules are the result of something else in the environment vibrating at a certain frequency (e.g., a guitar string, vocal chords). Sounds are produced by vibrations (sound can only take place in a medium—gas, solid, or liquid), and these vibrations radiate outward from the source, such as a speaker, vocal cords, or piano strings, with alternating peaks and valleys of pressure. Otherwise stated, sound is a result of cycles of compressions and rarefactions. The frequency of the wave or the number of peaks that occur during a defined unit of time determines the pitch. Sound waves are analyzed by the number of cycles that occur per second, termed a Hertz. Pitch is a psychological attribute that is made up by variations in the frequency of the auditory stimulus and can be defined as the highness of lowness of the sound (i.e., a bass guitar would be low, while a siren would be high). Humans can usually hear sound waves that cycle between 20 and

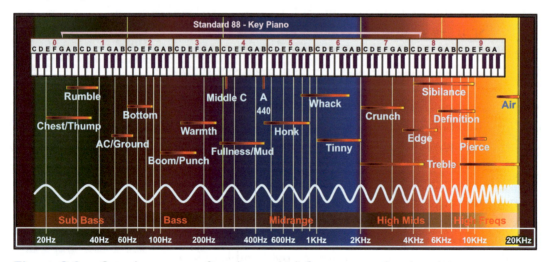

Figure 3.9   Sounds can range from low to high frequency and a piano is a great example of these sounds with the left side being low-frequency sound and the right side being high-frequency sound.

© Fouad A. Saad/Shutterstock.com

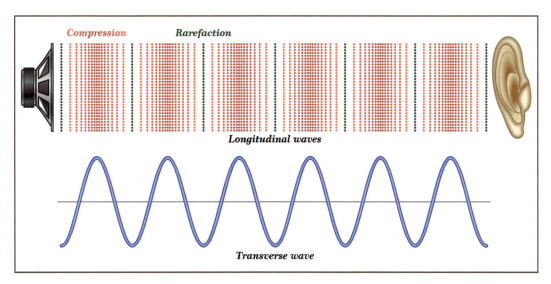

Figure 3.10 ˩Sounds occur as compressions and refractions in the air much like a wave goes up and down.˩

© Fouad A. Saad/Shutterstock.com

20,000 Hertz. **Wavelengths** and frequencies are inversely related (a wavelength equals the distance traveled divided by the number of cycles in a second). A higher frequency means more pressure changes occur in a given second and occur closer to each other in space, thus producing a shorter wavelength.˩

> ˩**Wavelength:** The linear distance between two successive compressions or peaks in light waves.˩

The properties of sound waves dictate our perceptions of sounds in the environment. Properties of waves we have already discussed—wavelength and amplitude—can be used to describe certain qualities of sound. Amplitude for sound waves corresponds to the perception of loudness, with higher amplitudes of sound waves indicating louder noises. Wavelength in sound waves corresponds to pitch, the relative highness or lowness of a sound. So, a tug boat horn may have a high amplitude value but a low wavelength value. The sound of fingernails softly being raked across a chalkboard may have a low amplitude value but a high wavelength value.

˩The **amplitude** of the wave is the maximum change in air pressure (i.e., the extent to which vibrating particles displace the medium—usually air). Amplitude is correlated with the psychological attribute loudness. Loudness is related to intensity and intensity is related to

> ˩**Amplitude:** The amount of vibration or pressure in a sound wave often referred to as loudness.˩

pressure. For example, the psychological attribute loudness depends on the amplitude of the sound waves, which correspond to the intensity of the vibration, which is directly proportional to the pressure variation (pressure is defined as force per unit area). The intensity or loudness of a sound is usually measured in decibels (dB), which can range from 0 to approximately 160. Alexander Graham Bell developed this logarithmic scale. The sound pressure for a tone of a given frequency is specified relative to the threshold pressure for that frequency (we are able to hear sounds of a given frequency better than sounds of other frequencies). Because the threshold sound pressure varies as a function of the frequency, a different reference pressure is necessary for each frequency. When the threshold for each frequency is used as its own reference, the sound pressure ratio in decibels is referred to as the sensation level (a reference pressure is always necessary in order for decibels to have precise meaning). The range of sounds over which the ear responds is about 120 dB, so that the loudest sound that can be heard without discomfort has a million times greater pressure than the faintest sound the ear can detect (auditory stimuli that occur at greater than 100 dB can damage the sensory apparatus in the ears).˩

The scientific measurement used to describe the loudness of a particular sound is called a **decibel**. The decibel level is set to have a minimum of 0, which is the lowest sound audible to the human ear. You can also think of the 0 decibel level as the absolute threshold for audition. ⌞Fans⌟ of the National Football League's ⌞Kansas City Chiefs⌟ set the world record for decibel level at a sporting event in ⌞2014⌟ by collectively creating a sound wave registering at ⌞142.2⌟ decibels, a level just below that of a jet engine ⌞(Guinness World Records, 2020).⌟ This level of loudness would be dangerous even for short durations.

> **Decibel:** The scientific unit of measurement for loudness.

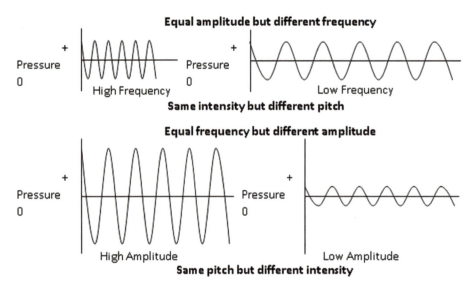

Figure 3.11   ⌞The top image shows sounds of equal loudness but difference pitches while the bottom shows the same pitch at difference loudness levels.⌟

Source: Brian Kelley

Figure 3.12   Various events and their associated levels of loudness.

Decibals	Event	Danger
0	Lowest audible sound	
30	Whispering in a library	
65	Normal conversation	
85	City traffic inside a car	Danger with prolonged exposure
105	Lawnmower	Danger after 2 hours of exposure
125	Balloon popping	Sounds become painful
⌞142	Jet engine at 100 feet⌟	Short-term exposure may cause permanent hearing loss
140	⌞Loudest sporting event recorded⌟	
160	Shotgun blast	Instant perforation of eardrum

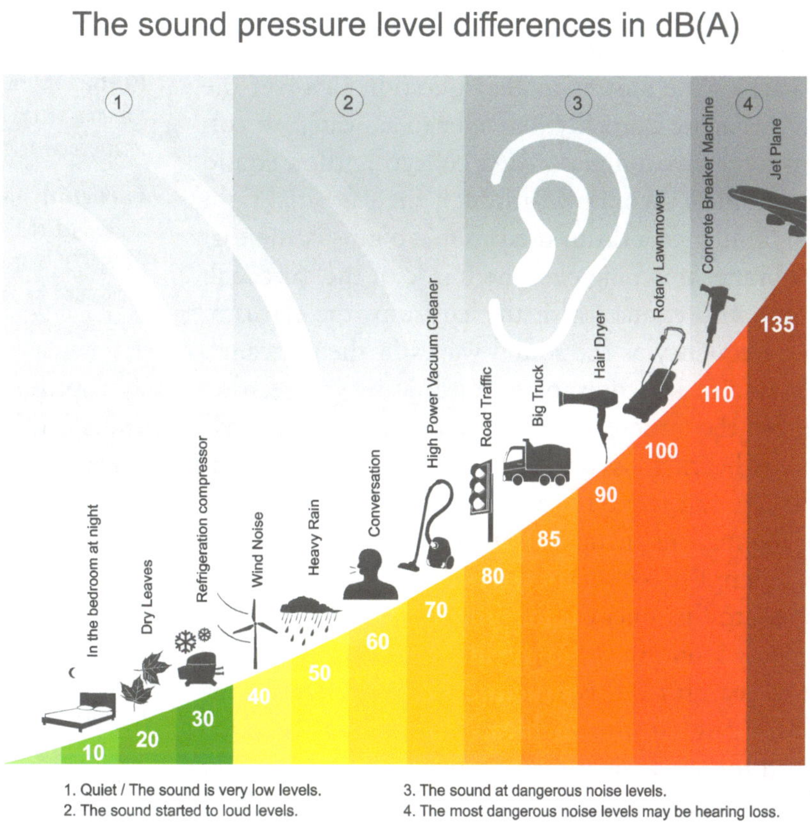

The sound pressure level differences in dB(A)

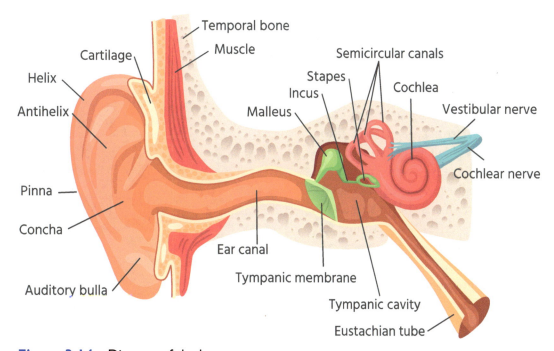

① Concrete Breaker Machine — Jet Plane

1. Quiet / The sound is very low levels.
2. The sound started to loud levels.
3. The sound at dangerous noise levels.
4. The most dangerous noise levels may be hearing loss.

Figure 3.13 ⌐The image demonstrates the energy requirements for increasing sound intensities.⌐

© Studio BKK/Shutterstock.com

Temporal bone
Muscle
Cartilage
Helix
Antihelix
Semicircular canals
Stapes
Incus
Cochlea
Malleus
Vestibular nerve
Pinna
Cochlear nerve
Concha
Ear canal
Tympanic membrane
Auditory bulla
Tympanic cavity
Eustachian tube

Figure 3.14   Diagram of the human ear.

© Tartila/Shutterstock.com

From the World to the Ear

Have you ever wondered why we have these "satellite dishes" on each side of our head? Part of the answer to that question involves the ability of the **pinna**, what we normally just refer to as "ears," to collect sound waves from the environment. After collecting these sound waves, the outer ear funnels them down through the ear canal right up to the **eardrum**. Similar to a drum used to make music, the eardrum is a thin membrane stretching over the inside of the ear canal. As sound waves come into contact with the eardrum, the eardrum vibrates at the same frequency as the sound waves in the ear canal.

> **Pinna:** The outer funnel-shaped structure of the ear; normally, this is what people refer to as their ear.
>
> **Eardrum:** The thin membrane at the end of the ear canal that vibrates at a specific frequency when bombarded by sound waves.

Occasionally, either due to infection, or to loud noises, the eardrum may rupture. This is typically a painful experience, but the outlook is normally very good; ruptured eardrums usually heal within only a few months, and any hearing loss due to the rupture is most often short-lived.

Sound waves are then transferred from the eardrum to three tiny bones that constitute the middle ear. The tiny bones are the malleus (hammer), incus (anvil), and stapes (stirrup). Together, the function of these tiny bones is to amplify the sound waves coming into contact with the eardrum, and to send the amplified sound waves to the inner ear for processing.

The middle ear sends sound waves to the inner ear through a tiny structure similar to the eardrum. This structure is called the oval window and is the "front gate" to the **cochlea**. The cochlea—derived from the Greek word for snail—is the location where transduction of sound waves finally begins to occur. The cochlea is essentially a fluid-filled tube that is coiled inside the inner ear. As amplified sound waves travel through the fluid in the cochlea, a structure called the basilar membrane begins to ripple as well. Attached to the basilar membrane are the sensory receptors for sound. These sensory receptors are called **hair cells**. As the basilar membrane bends due to

> **Cochlea:** The spiral structure in the inner ear that contains both fluid and the basilar membrane; the latter houses sensory receptors for audition.
>
> **Hair cells:** Thin, hair-like structures that are the sensory receptors for audition; these are located on the basilar membrane inside the cochlea.

sound waves, so too do the hair cells. As these hair cells bend with the sound waves, the physical energy is transduced into neural impulses sent from the auditory nerve to the appropriate parts of the brain for higher-order processing. Thus, the stimuli (sound waves) are finally converted to information the brain can use through the process of transduction in the cochlea.

With a better understanding of auditory biomechanics and physiology it is now possible to implant an artificial apparatus into the ear of deaf individuals so certain sounds can be heard. Specifically, a surgeon working with an audiologist have actually created and installed a device that is able to stimulate the auditory nerve electrically in response to external sounds. The device is able to analyze the frequency composition of sounds into ranges of stimulus frequencies. The implant involves inserting microelectrodes along specific regions of the basilar membrane. The basilar membrane is the part of the inner ear

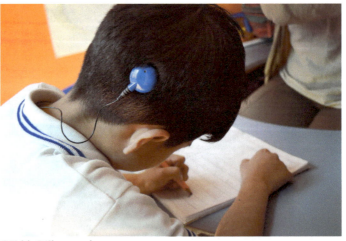

© Kalah_R/Shutterstock.com

that holds the sensory cells of the auditory system. Thus, the device is able to provide information about the traveling wave along the basilar membrane. With such a device, deaf individuals are able to hear and understand music and even human speech sounds.

⌐Sitting above the inner ear is the vestibular system that is responsible for equilibrium or balance. This sense of spatial orientation is essential for the coordination of motor responses, eye movements, and posture. An intact vestibular system is essential in such activities as gymnastics, figure skating, and scuba diving (or any activity that requires knowledge of our body in three-dimensional space). Although one's sense of balance is not the most prominent sensory system in our consciousness (i.e., like vision, auditory, or tactile), damage to this system can lead to a disruption of the sense of balance, dizziness, and nausea. So, the irony is that when this system is working, people are generally unaware of it; but when it is not working, it almost always captures our immediate attention as it generally is hard to move around when feeling dizzy or disoriented. The sensory receptor cells of the vestibular system (i.e., saccule, utricle, and semicircular canals) respond to accelerated movements of the head or to changes in the rate of acceleration (i.e., rate of acceleration resulting from an altered position of the head). The entire vestibular system works with the eye muscles and certain cells (nuclei) in the cerebellum and brainstem in order to reflexively maintain posture.⌐

OLFACTION (SMELLING)

As you know by this point in the chapter, every sense must detect a specific physical stimulus from the environment. For vision and audition, this physical stimulus came in the form of a wave of physical energy. For olfaction, the stimulus comes in the form of chemical molecules in the air, which are released by the substance we are smelling (e.g., chemical molecules released by a bar of chocolate).

These chemical molecules enter the nostrils and stimulate the olfactory receptors that are located at the top of the nasal cavity. Once these olfactory receptors are stimulated, the neural signals are sent through the porous part of the skull at the top of the nasal cavity and on to the olfactory bulb. The olfactory bulb, which resides inside the skull, sends messages to other parts of the brain for higher-order processing and perception of the specific odor. ⌐The olfactory system has one feature that sets it apart from any other sensory system, and that difference is appearing to be of great scientific importance. The olfactory receptor cells are actual neurons; they have a dendritic rod, an axon, and the conduct nerve impulses (action potentials) into the central nervous system. The olfactory receptor cells undergo continuous neurogenesis (reproduction) about once every 25 to 30 days; the neurons in the olfactory system are the only neurons known to reproduce. It has been suggested, because the olfactory nerve fibers provide a direct means for foreign particles (such as viruses, bacteria, or toxins) to enter the brain, that Alzheimer's or Parkinson's disease may be caused, in part, by certain harmful elements traveling along the olfactory system into the brain.⌐

At this point in time, hundreds of specific olfactory receptors have been identified, each responsible for responding to certain chemical molecules (Gottfried, 2010). However, the seemingly large number of olfactory receptors is far fewer than the many thousands of distinct smells humans are capable of detecting. So, there does not seem to be a one-to-one correspondence between olfactory receptor types and specific smells. Instead, research has shown that the thousands of distinct smells we are capable of detecting are actually the result of a specific combination of activation for several types of olfactory receptors (Shepherd, 2006). For example, when we smell chocolate, the "chocolate" olfactory receptors are not activated; there are no "chocolate" receptors. Instead, several different receptors are activated, and this specific combination of receptor activation leads to the perception of the smell of chocolate.

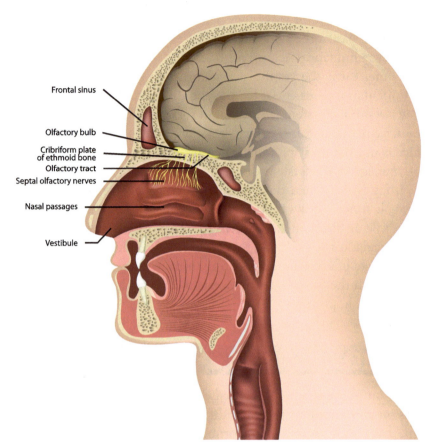

© medicalstocks/Shutterstock.com

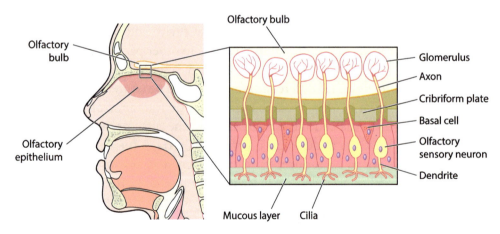

Figure 3.15   Diagrams of the human olfactory bulb.

© Blamb/Shutterstock.com

As humans, our olfactory sensitivity is directly related to the number of total olfactory receptor cells in the nasal cavity. Although humans have approximately 10 million olfactory receptor cells, and a very good sense of smell, many dogs have approximately 200 million olfactory receptor cells, and a much better sense of smell (Sela & Sobel, 2010). Dog owners realize this discrepancy in sense of smell any time they are taking their pet for a walk; dogs tend to smell things that humans are not capable of sensing, which can lead to incredibly long walks! However, some research suggests that humans may be better at olfaction ⌊than⌋ previously thought (Porter et al., 2007).

GUSTATION (TASTE)

The sensation of taste—scientifically known as *gustation*—is the focus of our next section. The stimuli ⌊for taste⌋ are various chemicals contained in food we consume. Saliva in the mouth ⌊helps⌋ breaks down food and releases these chemicals, which are then free to be processed by the sensory receptors for gustation. The sensory receptors for gustation are located on your **taste buds**.

> **Taste buds:** The sensory receptors for gustation that are located deep within porous structures on the tongue; there are five basic types of taste buds.

The human tongue contains many thousands of bumps and grooves. Inside these grooves are taste buds, and each taste bud contains several gustation receptors. The gustation receptors are slightly specialized for certain types of taste; each receptor is *most* sensitive to one particular taste and *less* sensitive to the other types of taste. When these receptors are activated by certain chemicals in the saliva, the receptors send signals to the thalamus, and then to various parts of the brain for higher-order processing.

There are five basic types of taste: sweet, salty, sour, bitter, and umami. We can think of each type of taste serving a particular function. Things that are sweet tend to be sugar- and calorie-rich foods that are desirable to eat. Salty foods are high in sodium, which was a scarce resource in ancestral environments. Sour and bitter tastes may have served as a cue that something is undesirable about the food, thus making the person not want to eat that particular food item. Umami, a relatively newly discovered taste, is associated with foods high in protein such as meat.[1]

One interesting aspect of our sensation for taste is that it can also illustrate the occasional mismatch between the present day and the environments our senses were design to navigate. For example, humans desire sweet and salty foods because sugar and salt are highly useful in small amounts ⌊and are rewarding.⌋ This insatiable appetite for items that are easily available ⌊and have high reward value⌋ may contribute to modern problems such as obesity and type 2 diabetes.

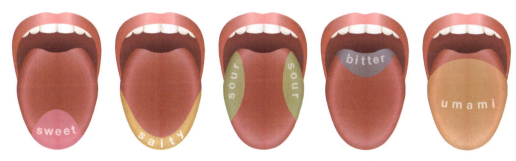

© Peter Hermes Furian/Shutterstock.com

TOUCH AND PAIN

⌊Most of our sense of touch is located in our skin. In fact, the skin is the largest organ of the body and typically covers around 3,000 inches. Also, receptors for this sensory system are the only nonlocalized sensory receptors. From a developmental perspective, it is interesting to note that cutaneous reflex activity can occur as early as the late embryo stage, when the baby is only 1 inch from head to rump. Similarly, at three months, a fetus (3.5 inches in length) is able to demonstrate localized cutaneous reflexes of the eyes, mouth, and face when touched. Our sense of touch is very important because it gives our brain information about environmental stimuli that are directly in contact with the skin. If something is touching our skin, we definitely want to know about it!

Major Functions of the Skin

1. **Maintenance of body temperature:** In response to an increase in ambient temperature or strenuous exercise, the production of perspiration by sweat glands helps lower core body temperature and skin temperature (see next chapter).

2. **Protection:** The skin covers the body and provides a formidable physical barrier that protects underlying tissues from physical abrasion, bacteria, dehydration, and ultraviolet radiation. An individual can actually survive for some time without skin as long as body temperature and infections are contained.

3. **Excretion:** The skin is able to expel dangerous waste material through perspiration (i.e., excretion of salts, organic materials, and some drugs). By the way, perspiration doesn't necessarily smell bad; it is the bacteria that quickly reproduce on your skin that omit the unpleasant odor.

4. **Synthesis of vitamin D:** Upon exposure of the skin to ultraviolet light, the skin is able to produce vitamin D (chemical name is 1,25 dihydroxycalciferol), which acts as a hormone.

5. **Immunity:** Certain cells of the epidermis play a role in increasing the immune response.

6. **Blood reservoir:** The skin and underlying vascular supply provide a substantial supply of blood that can quickly be shifted to muscles in times of increased activity.

7. **Detection of stimuli:** The skin has a number of receptors that provide information about touch, pain, temperature, and deep pressure. This aspect of the skin is the focus of this section.

> **Somesthesis:** Bodily sensations.
>
> **Kinesthetic sensitivity:** Kinesthetic sense refers to knowledge about spatial position and movement information occurring from mechanical stimulation of mobile joints, muscles, and tendons.
>
> **Cutaneous sensitivity:** Cutaneous senses (skin sense) refers touch, pressure, temperature, and pain (nociception).

There are two types of sensory experiences that make-up **somesthesis,** which is what we collectively refer to as out bodily sensations: (1) **kinesthetic sensitivity** and (2) **cutaneous sensitivity.** Kinesthetic sense refers to knowledge about spatial position and movement information occurring from mechanical stimulation of mobile joints, muscles, and tendons. Cutaneous senses (skin sense) refers touch, pressure, temperature, and pain (nociception).

> **Pacinian corpuscles:** The sensory receptors for touch located under the skin; these sensory receptors respond to pressure applied to the surface of the skin.

The physical stimulus for touch comes in the form of any force enacting pressure on the surface of the skin. The sensory receptors for touch are called **Pacinian corpuscles,** which are located just below the surface of the skin. These Pacinian corpuscles sense pressure being exerted on the surface of the skin and send neural messages to the appropriate parts of the brain for processing.

Interestingly, Pacinian corpuscles are distributed with different frequencies throughout the body. This difference in distribution is reflected through the different levels of sensitivity for different parts of your body. For example, our faces, hands, and feet are highly sensitive to touch. This is partly due to the fact that there are many more Pacinian corpuscles in these areas. In contrast, our elbows and knees are less sensitive because they have fewer Pacinian corpuscles just below the surface of the skin. There are more receptors than just the Pacinian corpuscles.

SENSORY RECEPTORS IN SKIN

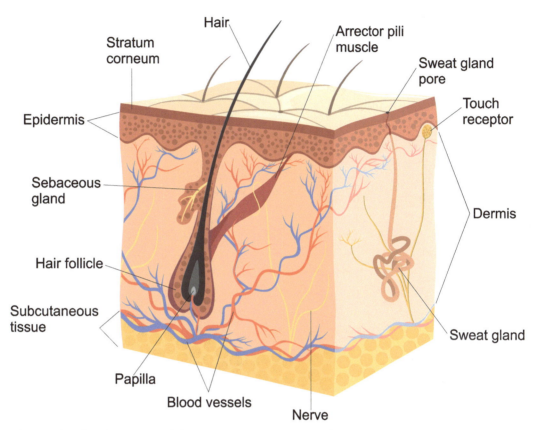

Figure 3.16 ⌐Diagram of the sensory receptors in skin.⌐
© logika600/Shutterstock.com

Cutaneous Receptors Table

⌐There are a number of receptors involved in cutaneous sense and these receptors are usually divided into where they are located (superficial vs. deep) and the type of environmental energy in which they respond to (slowly adapting vs. rapidly adapting). All receptors involved in somesthesis are mechanoreceptors, those involved in touch include the following.

1. **Meissner's corpuscles** are sensitive to flutter and are located in the superficial region of glabrous skin (hairless skin) also known as the epidermis. These receptors are rapidly adapting, and have very fine areas of sensitivity (as small a 2–4 mm) or one could say their receptive field is small.
2. **Merkel receptors** are activated by steady skin indentations and are also located in the epidermis of the skin. They are slow adapting receptors and their receptive field is larger than those of the meissner corpuscles.
3. **Pacinian corpuscles** are activated by vibrations and are rapidly adapting. They are located in the dermis (deep skin) and have large receptive fields (many mm's).
4. **Ruffini receptors** are activated by steady skin indentation and are slowly adapting. These receptors are also located in dermis. Their receptive field is also large.⌐

The touch area of the brain (i.e., primary somatosensory cortex) is somatotopically organized. Each area of skin has a receptive field (the area from which a stimulus can activate a sensory receptor). This receptive field is maintained as the information is carried to the brain, so that as one activates a particular receptive field, and then activates an adjacent receptive field the corresponding sensory areas in the brain would also be adjacent. Receptors are denser in areas that require better touch discrimination such as the finger tips and are less dense in areas where tactile information is less pertinent to overall function such as the back of the arm.

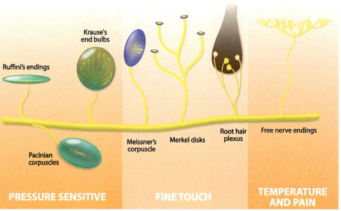

Cutaneous Receptors

© Designua/Shutterstock.com

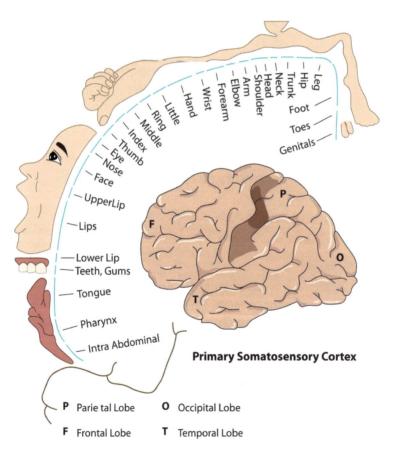

Figure 3.17 The diagram demonstrates that the brain has dedicated greater cortical space to areas of the body that have greater density of sensory receptors.

© Vasilisa Tsoy/Shutterstock.com

In addition, the size of the corresponding sensory region of the cortex is inversely proportional to the receptive field (indicating that the brain dedicates more cortical space to areas of the body with the greatest density of receptors). Most of our sense of touch is dedicated to the face and hand.

It was once thought that pain is simply explained by overstimulation of various proprioceptive and cutaneous receptors. We now know pain is an extremely variable and difficult system to both explore and make definitive statements about. Pain is a complex perceptual phenomenon influenced by a number of physiological, cognitive, and emotional factors. Although most people prefer to avoid painful stimuli whenever possible, the failure to perceive pain is extremely problematic and always results in premature death to those affected by this pathology.

Our awareness of pain is said to be due to a specialized receptor known as a nociceptor. These receptors work to make one aware of potential or ongoing damage to tissue. These receptors are the most widely distributed receptors in the body, meaning they are almost everywhere. They are located everywhere from the skin to most bodily organs and connective tissue and are thought to be made up of free nerve endings. Pain information is mediated by several classes of nociceptors. **Thermal** or **mechanical nociceptors** are associated with sensations of sharp, stinging pain, and tend to be well localized. **Polymodal nociceptors** are activated by a variety of high-intensity mechanical, chemical, and very hot or very cold stimuli. Activation of these nociceptors, which tend to be nonlocalized, produces the sensations of dull, throbbing pain. In the case of deep or visceral pain (which tends to be of the throbbing, nonlocalized type), there is a phenomenon called referred pain, which is characterized by pain in a part of the body other than the area that was actually injury. Referred pain usually originates in one of the visceral organs but is felt in the skin or sometimes in another area deep within the body. Because some somatosensory information and nociceptive information travel along the same peripheral nerves and neural pathways, the brain can make mistakes interpreting the exact location of the pain.

> **Thermal or mechanical nociceptors:** Nociceptors associated with sensations of sharp, stinging pain.
>
> **Polymodal nociceptors:** Nociceptors activated by a variety of high-intensity mechanical, chemical, and very hot or very cold stimuli.

The perception of pain is highly complex and individualized. It is affected by a variety of external and internal influences. The cerebral cortex is concerned with the appreciation of pain, its quality, location, and intensity; thus, an intact sensory cortex is essential to the perception of pain (just as an intact somatosensory cortex is necessary for the sense of touch). In addition to neural influences that transmit and modulate sensory input, the perception of pain is affected by psychological and cultural responses to pain-related stimuli. A person can be unaware of an acute injury at the time the injury occurred or when under very stressful conditions, when in a state of depression, or when experiencing an emotional crisis. Cultural influences also precondition the perception of and response to painful stimuli. The reaction

Table 3.3   Comparison between Thermal/Mechanical and Polymodal Pain Receptors

Thermal/Mechanical	Polymodal
1. Small diameter axons	1. Small diameter axons
2. Axons are thinly myelinated	2. Axons have no myelin
3. 30 meters/second conduction speed	3. 2 meters/second conduction speed
4. Sharp, stinging pain	4. Dull, throbbing pain
5. Immediate onset, quickly dissipates	5. Delayed onset, long lasting
6. Well localized	6. Nonlocalized
7. Not associated with referred pain	7. Associated with referred pain

to similar circumstances can range from a profound absence of pain to hysterical behavior. This is very interesting because no other sense is impacted by so many factors. Our mood, cultural background, for example, don't impact our hearing or seeing.

What Does the Bible Say?

Pain has a very important function. It drives us away from things that are harmful to us and keeps us from using parts of the body that are healing. However, sometimes pain can occur in the absence of a stimulus or chronic pain can occur as a result of an injury. Obviously, no one wants to live in pain. There are many negatives to living with pain besides just the obvious discomfort. It causes irritability, disability, and distractibility as well as limits daily living. The Bible actually has a lot to say about pain and discomfort.

Romans 5:3–5 ESV

"More than that, we rejoice in our sufferings, knowing that suffering produces endurance, and endurance produces character, and character produces hope, and hope does not put us to shame, because God's love has been poured into our hearts through the Holy Spirit who has been given to us."

Isaiah 53:4–12 ESV

"Surely he has borne our griefs and carried our sorrows; yet we esteemed him stricken, smitten by God, and afflicted. But he was wounded for our transgressions; he was crushed for our iniquities; upon him was the chastisement that brought us peace, and with his stripes we are healed. All we like sheep have gone astray; we have turned—every one—to his own way; and the Lord has laid on him the iniquity of us all. He was oppressed, and he was afflicted, yet he opened not his mouth; like a lamb that is led to the slaughter, and like a sheep that before its shearers is silent, so he opened not his mouth. By oppression and judgment he was taken away; and as for his generation, who considered that he was cut off out of the land of the living, stricken for the transgression of my people?"

PERCEPTION

Earlier in this chapter we learned about the basic transduction process for different sensory systems. Our contact with the world typically starts with information reception from our sensory receptors (e.g., rods and cones for the visual information) and ends with meaningful interpretation of the environment based on a higher level of information integration at the brain level (e.g., occipital lobe for visual information). Perception is what enables us to effectively interact with the environment. It is "the acquisition and processing of sensory information in order to see, hear, taste, or feel objects in the world; also guides an organism's actions with respect to those objects" (Sekuler & Blake, 2002, p. 621).

In an effort to efficiently gather meaningful and useful information, perception allows us to be selective and even occasionally ignore unimportant information. In this restructuring process, you will see the world guided by your perception, which may be different from your friend's view. For

Figure 3.18   Figures vs. background.
© Ye Liew/Shutterstock.com

example, take a look at Figure 3.18. What do you see? You might see two human heads, in profile, facing each other. Conversely, you might see a single vase. It is possible to see both features as well. The process of sensation does not tell us whether to focus on the background or on the front figure. It is perception that enables us to evaluate the visual stimulus and produce a meaningful answer for this illustration. On a side note, it is a quite common *misbelief* that what you see (the figure or the ground) says something about you (the viewer). These ambiguous figures are designed to be interpreted in two different ways simultaneously; your first focal point will shape the outline of the figure and allow you to see either a face or a vase.

THE WHOLE IS GREATER THAN THE SUM OF ITS PARTS

Our awareness of the visual world around us is an amazingly complex and puzzling process, starting with a two-dimensional, inverted image on the retina of the eyes, which is then processed by a number of parallel neural pathways. In the end, we are able to perceive a sophisticated series of three-dimensional structures with varying depths, colors, and shadowing effects. As you will soon appreciate from the evidence below, the neuronal mechanisms of attention and conscious awareness are beginning to emerge as one of the prominent unresolved problems in perception and neuroscience as a whole.

The process of visual perception can be simplified into three basic tasks:

1. Detection
2. Discrimination
3. Identification

The three tasks grow more complex and require more information as one moves from simply detecting to identifying. The important questions for these behaviors include what features are important for each of these processes? How much detail is necessary for detection or discrimination or identification? How long does it take to accomplish each task above? For detection, in many cases, only a small change in the visual field is necessary, yet how much more do we need to discriminate and is it based on shape, color, or movement? Identification requires previous learning and may require the processing of much information. While the answers to these questions are still being sought after, it is important to understand the tremendous complexity involved in simply being aware of what we see.

The ambient illumination, size, shapes, and brightness of the images that are projected upon the retina of the eye change as one moves about. Under normal conditions, the objects themselves do not appear to be changing. For example, as an object or person moves toward you, you perceive the object as getting closer and closer; you do not perceive the object as getting bigger and bigger, even though the image on the retina does enlarge. Similarly, as we move from a brightly lit park into a dimly lit room, the intensity can vary 1,000 fold, yet in the dim room, as in the bright light of the sun, we see a white shirt as white and a red pair of shorts as red. The visual system does not simply record images passively, like a camera; instead, the visual system transforms transient light stimuli on the retina into mental constructs of a stable three-dimensional world.

The degree to which visual perception is transformational and therefore creative has only recently been appreciated within the scientific world. The view that perception is not simply a reduction of complex forms but a holistic, creative process was first introduced by a school of thought termed Gestalt psychology. The Gestalt psychologists argued that the brain creates three-dimensional images by organizing sensations into stable patterns, or perceptual consistencies. The visual system accomplishes this organization by following certain rational principles of shape, color, distance, and movement of objects in the visual field. Simply stated, the brain makes certain assumptions about what is to be seen in the world, and these expectations seem to be derived in part from experience and also from innate neuronal wiring.

⌐Gestalt grouping may enhance our ability to process complex visual phenomenon by decreasing the time required to understand the individual elements of a particular object. For example, elements that are closer together tend to be organized or grouped together, and objects that are similar tend to be grouped together, which are termed by the Gestalt school as proximity (or nearness) and similarity, respectively. The term good continuation refers to elements that appear to follow in the same direction. Closure is a term used to denote groupings that occur in a way that favors the perception of the more enclosed figure. Priority is given to objects that favor a more symmetrical configuration. This process of organization is continuous and dynamic (ever changing), as evident in the well-known alternation of figures on a background (i.e., either a vase or two figures can be seen in Figure 3.18). The figure-ground example illustrates one principle of visual perception termed a winner-take-all strategy (also termed singleness of action), because only part of the image can be selected as the focus of attention; the rest must become part of the background.⌐

TOP-DOWN PROCESSING VS. BOTTOM-UP PROCESSING

Given that perception is a way of processing information, we have to think about commonly mentioned information processing approaches: top-down and bottom-up processing. **Top-down processing** emphasized the importance of the context and cognitive structures we have. It is "processing influenced by the individual's knowledge and expectations rather than simply by the stimulus itself" (Eysenck & Keane, 2005, p. 2). Different from the objective transduction of neuronal impulses (sensation), more often our perception is filtered by (organized by) our past experience and expectation and top-down processing will be relevant.

Bottom-up processing, on the other hand, is more focused on gathering information from individual stimuli. For example, if we are only using bottom-up processing, we might have a difficult time figuring out that "A" and "a" are the same letter in the alphabet. The letter "A" is composed with three lines in the first example (see Figure 3.19), but the second example "a" looks quite different from the prototype.

> **Top-down processing:** An information-gathering process starting from an individual's knowledge, expectations, and prior experiences.

> **Bottom-up processing:** An information-gathering process starting from each individual stimulus.

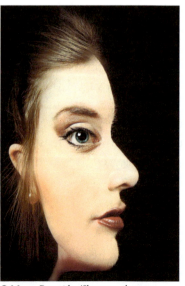

© kovalto1/Shutterstock.com   © Christos Georghiou/Shutterstock.com   © Megan Betteridge/Shutterstock.com

However, in both cases, most of us will be able to interpret both letters as the alphabet "A" based on our previous experience and knowledge.

Figure 3.19   Composition of the alphabet A.

The same principle applies when interpreting Figure 3.20. If we only rely on bottom-up processing, we will not be able to see the whole picture since you are only focused on individual stimulus. Luckily, most of us use top-down processing as well and are able to see either a rabbit or a duck in Figure 3.20. Figure 3.21 demonstrates the same idea in a slightly different way. To your naked eye, which of the two circles looks bigger to you? Is it the inner circle on the left side, or the inner circle on the right side? If the inner circle to your right seems bigger to you, you are relying on top-down processing. The two inner circles, which are exactly the same size, have different context (surrounding) information. The inner circle on the right is surrounded

Figure 3.20   Duck vs. rabbit.

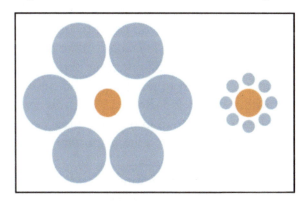

Figure 3.21   Ebbinghaus illusion.

by much smaller circles and thus appears much larger than the inner circle on the left, which is surrounded by much larger circles. If you only use bottom-up processing, you will not experience this optical illusion.

Which do you think is a better way of understanding and making sense of the world? Should bottom-up processing be a superior way than top-down processing (or vice versa)? Or do you think both are equally valuable ways of organizing events occurring around us? Keep this in mind as we go through the rest of the perception process. ⌐In reality, though, both of these processes tend to co-occur.⌐

IMPORTANCE OF ATTENTION IN THE PERCEPTUAL PROCESS

When you are looking for your blue sedan at a shopping mall parking lot, you will first focus on all the blue cars and narrow down your search. You will ignore all the SUVs for the same reason. Likewise, we often get help from attention to recognize and locate particular objects. In a way, object perception is a goal-driven process. There is a plethora of information around us and it is neither practical nor meaningful to process all of the sensory input. That is why we need a selective filter known as **attention**. The term attention refers to "a large set of selective mechanisms that enable us to focus on some stimulus at the expense of others" (Wolfe et al., 2012, p. 217).

> **Attention:** A concentrated mental effort that functions as a filter to ignore unimportant events and focus on important events.

Attention, or concentrated mental effort, is crucial in the beginning of perception. Imagine driving on a highway. If you decide to text your friend while driving, you might be too engaged in the conversation and might not see a road construction warning sign.

Simons and Chabris (1999) devised a very simple, yet powerful, experiment to test this phenomenon in a more controlled environment. Participants watched a short video and were given a specific instruction to count the number of passes that individuals wearing white shirts made in the video. In the middle of the video, a confederate in a gorilla suit walks across people passing the ball. At the end of the study, participants were asked if they saw a gorilla. Results showed half of the respondents were not aware the presence of the

© Andrey_Popov/Shutterstock.com

gorilla! (You can visit Simons and Chabris's website at http://www.theinvisiblegorilla.com/videos.html to check out the video and test it yourself.) Similar to what might happen to you while texting and driving, this study clearly shows the importance of attention as a precursor of perception. When you do not (or fail to) allocate attention, you can miss quite obvious scene changes or a big gorilla. The unpredictability of an event or diverted attention will result in failure of accurate scene detection (as if we are blind to that event) for a short time. This phenomenon is known as **inattentional blindness** (Mack & Rock, 1998). This concept clearly shows the importance of attention in our perceptual process.

> **Inattentional blindness:** Diverted attention resulting in failure of accurate scene detection as if we are blind to that event.

So far, we have walked through a few important concepts related to our perceptual processes and fundamental differences between perception and sensation. Unlike sensational process, the context surrounding individual stimulus as well as your personal expectations and experience will shape your perceptual process. We will continue to examine how these neuronal signals (sensory input) are assembled in the higher level of brain.

What Does the Bible Say?

Perception is often a product of training and attention. We can decide what to pay attention to as well as what and how we perceive things, and further upon what we reflect. I have often heard people listen to music that contains words and phrases that are generally in opposition to their values. Oftentimes, when challenged on the issue, the phrase, "I am only listening to the beat not the words" is stated. However, our brain perceives all of the information and over repeated exposure that message has a lasting impact. I wonder how many song lyrics people have memorized that are in totally opposition to their belief systems. As noted earlier, we are what we are exposed to and much of what we are exposed to is a choice. We should be very cautious about the types of words and messages that we allow to influence us. In fact, there is a specific description for the phenomenon of not being able to let go of the last song you listened to and it is called last song syndrome because it is so common and pervasive. It would be wise for the last song syndrome to be related to something uplifting and positive. To that end, we are to be light to those around us and to use music to praise God and lift one another up.

Romans 12:1–8 ESV

"I appeal to you therefore, brothers, by the mercies of God, to present your bodies as a living sacrifice, holy and acceptable to God, which is your spiritual worship. Do not be conformed to this world, but be transformed by the renewal of your mind, that by testing you may discern what is the will of God, what is good and acceptable and perfect. For by the grace given to me I say to everyone among you not to think of himself more highly than he ought to think, but to think with sober judgment, each according to the measure of faith that God has assigned. For as in one body we have many members, and the members do not all have the same function, so we, though many, are one body in Christ, and individually members one of another. Having gifts that differ according to the grace given to us, let us use them: if prophecy, in proportion to our faith; if service, in our serving; the one who teaches, in his teaching; the one who exhorts, in his exhortation; the one who contributes, in generosity; the one who leads with zeal; the one who does acts of mercy, with cheerfulness."

Ephesians 5: 11–21 ESV

"Take no part in the unfruitful works of darkness, but instead expose them. For it is shameful even to speak of the things that they do in secret. But when anything is exposed by the light, it becomes visible, for anything that becomes visible is light. Therefore it says,

'Awake, O sleeper,

and arise from the dead,

and Christ will shine on you.'

Look carefully then how you walk, not as unwise but as wise, making the best use of the time, because the days are evil. Therefore do not be foolish, but understand what the will of the Lord is. And do not get drunk with wine, for that is debauchery, but be filled with the Spirit, addressing one another in psalms and hymns and spiritual songs, singing and making melody to the Lord with your heart, giving thanks always and for everything to God the Father in the name of our Lord Jesus Christ, submitting to one another out of reverence for Christ."

PERCEPTUAL PROCEDURE AT THE BRAIN LEVEL

The first steps in sensation will allow us to objectively register sensory inputs. If the input were visual information, these neural signals have to be carried to the visual cortex in our brain before we can see things meaningfully. In this chapter, we take a closer look at how visual and auditory neural signals are projected in our brain.

Visual Cortex

The information processed through rods and cones will eventually be projected to the back of our brain known as the **occipital lobe** (Wolfe et al., 2012). This is where all the visual information will first be processed in our brain (Figure 3.22).

Occipital lobe: The part of our brain responsible for processing the visual information.

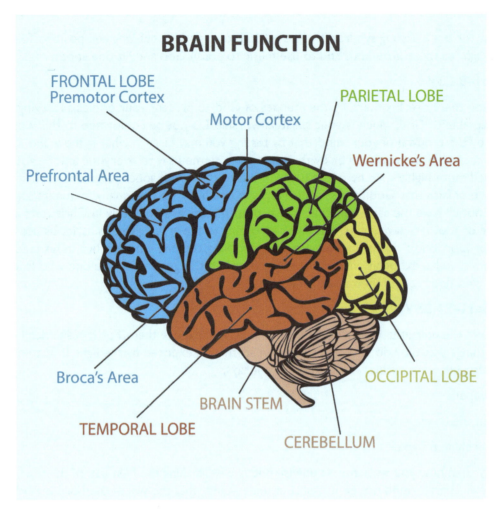

Figure 3.22   Human brain areas.
© okili77/Shutterstock.com

The occipital lobe is further localized based on the types of visual information we receive. For example, when you see a red apple flying across a gym, you are processing three types of visual information: a color (red), an object (apple), and a movement (flying across). The primary visual cortex can be subdivided into five different sections depending on its primary function (Coren et al., 2004). Going back to our apple example, the area in the brain known as V4 will concentrate on processing the color information, and V1 on the object's form, whereas another area—V5—will be better equipped to interpret and gather the visual information about global movements. We will not go into too much detail about the segregation of the visual cortex but will take a look at how visual stimuli are processed in our visual cortex.

The primary visual cortex also processes retinal images in a very specialized way through M and P pathways. The **magnocellular pathway** (or M pathway) receives information from M ganglion cells about peripheral vision and therefore low spatial resolution images from the retina (Palmer, 1999; Zeki, 1993). The **parvocellular pathway** (or P pathway) receives information from P ganglion cells about central vision and therefore high spatial resolution images. These separate pathways serve as the anatomical basis for more localized visual information processing even at an earlier stage (Chaudhuri, 2011; Wolfe et al., 2012).

Magnocellular pathway: A visual pathway for peripheral vision and low spatial resolution images from the retina.

Parvocellular pathway: A visual pathway for central vision and high spatial resolution images.

In the primary visual cortex, retinal images that crossed over the optic chiasm will once again be separated. Ultimately, retinal images from the left visual field are transmitted to the right hemisphere and images from the right visual field are transmitted to the left hemisphere (Figure 3.23). This is known as the contralerality of visual processing and shows that each side of the brain hemisphere processes the images from the opposite side of the visual field (e.g., Rodieck, 1998; Rosenzweig et al., 1999).

We have seen how the initial stage of visual information processing is done somewhat separately through different pathways. However, later in the perceptual process it is combined again to provide a meaningful and wholesome picture. There are two main streams of processing that start from the occipital lobe (V1, to be specific). The pathway going into the temporal lobe is known as the **"what" pathway** and responds to and integrates information about the size, color, and/or the identity of the object (Husain & Jackson, 2001; Posner, 1980). The other pathway, which goes into the parietal lobe, is called the **"where" pathway**. As you can presume from the name, the parietal pathway helps you find the location of an object. Visual cortex areas are localized based on their primary responsibilities in the earlier stage of processing. In the higher level of processing, these local areas communicate with each other to convey the appropriate meaning to the visual images and allow us to respond effectively.

> **"what" pathway:** A visual pathway projected into the temporal lobe that responds to and integrates information about the size, color, and/or the identity of an object.
>
> **"where" pathway:** A visual pathway projected into the parietal lobe that integrates information about the location of an object.

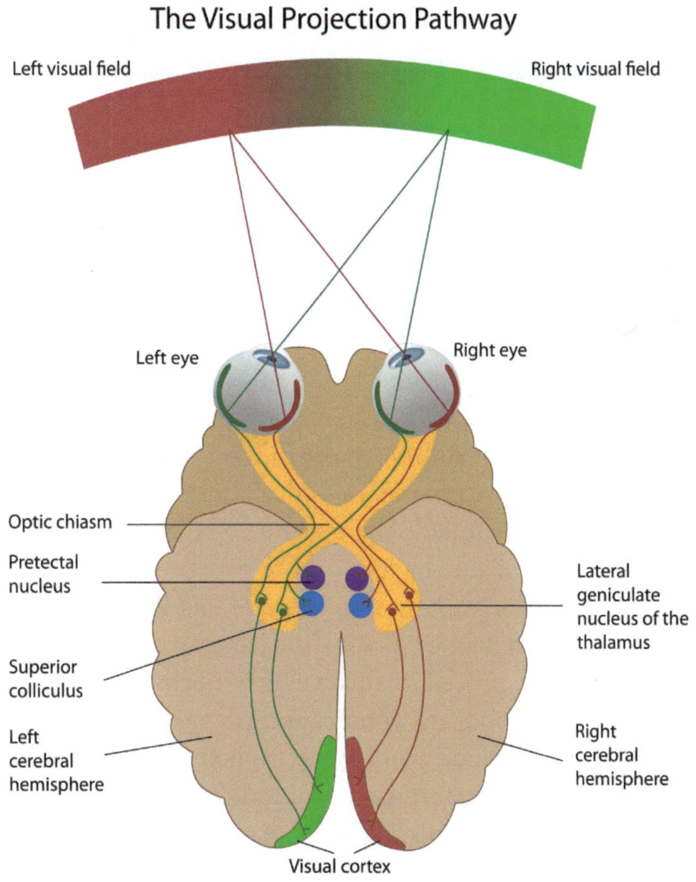

Figure 3.23   The visual projection pathway.
© Alila Medical Media/Shutterstock.com

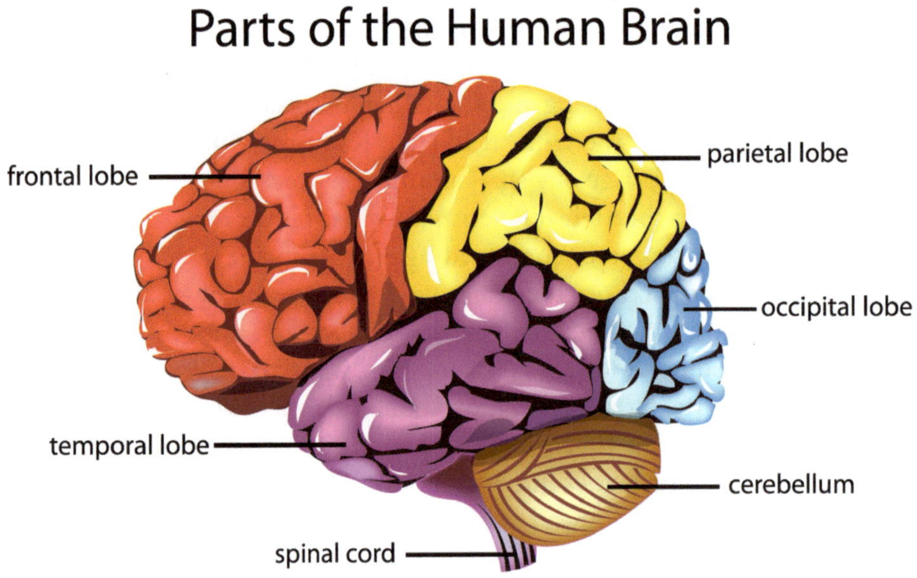

Parts of the Human Brain

Figure 3.24   "Where" vs. "what" visual pathways.
© Matthew Cole/Shutterstock.com

PERCEPTUAL ASPECTS OF VISION

Visual Illusion

Perception of the visual information involves your conscious awareness. Nonetheless, we are not sensitive enough to acknowledge the neuronal connections continuously made in our brain during the process. This process is a highly efficient and organized process to help us provide meanings to the scenes around us and to allow us to make appropriate judgment based on the sources of the information. For example, if you see a friendly face, you might decide to approach the person to say hello or, conversely, an unfriendly face may make you decide to avoid another person. During this delicate process, our brain makes a great deal of assumptions based on our expectations and past experiences. Perception attempts to find useful ways to make the most of our surroundings, sometimes even at the cost of misrepresentation of the visual stimulus (Blake & Sekuler, 2005). This is why we experience optical illusions. Take a look at Figure 3.25. There are five black horizontal blocks and in the middle there seems to be two gray blocks occluding some parts of the black blocks. Take a closer look at the shades of those two gray blocks. Would you believe that those gray blocks are the same luminance (brightness or in this case, shade)? Due to the surroundings—black for the left gray block and white for the right gray block—the left gray block seems to be much lighter than the right gray block. Though the sensory procedure involves an objective processing of the visual information, our brain is making an assumption about the context and changes the overall perception of the shades or the colors. In other words, the information you receive from your eyes about left and right gray blocks is exactly the same. However, the context information around the stimuli will make your brain "think" and come to a conclusion that these two blocks do not have the same luminance. ⌐The next image, snakes, gives the impression of movement in the absence of any actual movement.⌐

A different optical illusion founded in a similar principle is shown in Figure 3.26. In Figure 3.26, three individuals are the same height. However, the vanishing point (where the straight lines are converging in one corner) allows you to experience a sense of distance between these individuals and perceive the individual closer to the vanishing point as being further away from you compared to the individual to the far left. This is why the individual standing to the far right seems taller than the other two, although all three are the same height.

Gestalt psychologists proposed that people tend to follow a simple rule to organize objects (i.e., Law of Pragnanz). The members of the Gestalt school articulated the importance of context and holistic understanding of the world rather than dissecting the environment by an individual stimulus (Wolfe et al., 2012). Though they did not explicitly emphasize the role of the assumptions the brain makes, Gestalt principles delineate how we identify and group visual elements. During this perceptual procedure, our brain will find the most efficient way to interpret the visual input and may trick us to believe a phantom existence of a stimulus. To see illusory contours, go to http://perceptualstuff.org/illuscont.html.

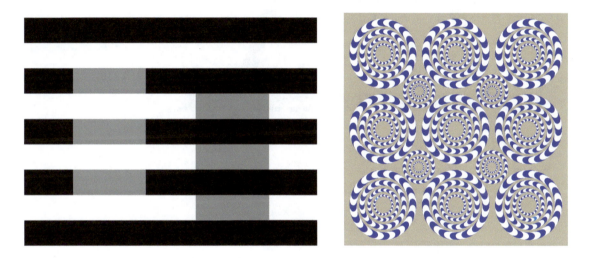

Figure 3.25 Examples of relative luminance and the impact of that phenomenon on an illusion.

Image on left: © diskoVisnja/Shutterstock.com, right: © lotan/Shutterstock.com

Figure 3.26 Linear perspective and relative height.

© Darq/Shutterstock.com

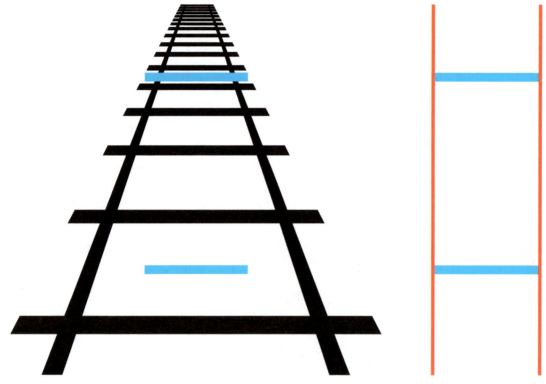

Figure 3.26   (Continued)
© Peter Hermes Furian/Shutterstock.com

DEPTH PERCEPTION

Depth perception can also be the evidence for another level of information integration process. If you recall the sensory procedure of vision, humans should see the world as two-dimensional images from the retinal images. However, we all see the world as three-dimensions. In other words, we use diverse depth cues around us to access the depth information (Blake & Sekuler, 2005). In Figure 3.27, we perceive the dog as being closer to us because it appears to be similar in size compared to the trees behind it (when in real life a tree should be bigger than a dog). Furthermore, the dog is obscuring some parts of the grass and trees. We make the assumption that an object blocking something is closer to us than the object being blocked and extract depth information from those cues. This concept is known as **occlusion**. Occlusion is just one example of monocular depth cues. We can also estimate depth by using multiple cues and sometimes experience visual illusion because of this practice (Figure 3.28).

> **Occlusion:** A phenomenon in which an object closer to a viewer appears to block another object that is farther away from the viewer.

Though we can receive plenty of depth information by using one eye (monocular cues), we get more sophisticated information by using both of our eyes (binocular cues). Because your left and right eyes cover slightly different visual fields, the images from the left and right eyes are slightly different (binocular disparity) and provide the information for depth perception.

Figure 3.27   Monocular depth cue: Occlusion.

© Podlesnyak Nina/Shutterstock.com

Figure 3.28   Three-dimensional chalk drawing illusion.

© hipproductions/Shutterstock.com

AUDITORY CORTEX

Sound waves or sound information is useful for locating, identifying, and reacting to objects around us. The transduction process in the auditory sensory receptors (e.g., hair cells) codes and transmits the basic sound inputs to the brain. The **auditory cortex** then assembles these neural signals into meaningful sounds, such as your friend's voice or a siren from an ambulance. Similar to our visual information processing, perception of sound information involves a higher-order acoustic information processing. In sum, once the basic auditory input (sound wave) is registered by the hair cells, it is transmitted to the primary auditory cortex, which is the temporal lobe (Figure 3.29).

> **Auditory cortex:** The part of our brain that is primarily responsible for processing the auditory information.

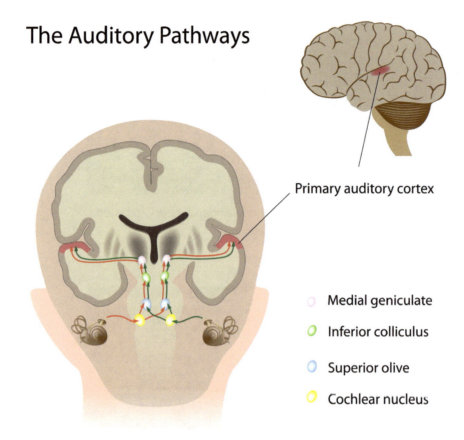

The Auditory Pathways

Primary auditory cortex

○ Medial geniculate

○ Inferior colliculus

○ Superior olive

○ Cochlear nucleus

Figure 3.29   The auditory pathways.
© Alila Medical Media/Shutterstock.com

The neuronal signals from our hair cells in the cochlea reach both the left and right side of the temporal lobe earlier in the process and this early integration of sound input is useful to locate the sound source (Wolfe et al., 2012). Similar to the localization of the visual cortex, the auditory cortex processes sound waves in a segregated manner based on the types of auditory information before the information reaches the higher order integration center. From a certain distance, you can trace the direction of an aircraft judging by the sound of its engine. In this example, the two pieces of sound information are about the object (aircraft) and about its trajectory (direction). The auditory cortex then combines information about "what" and "where" separately and uses two pathways for each function similar to the visual "what" and "where" pathways (Rauschecker & Tian, 2000). Two main processing streams start from the primary auditory cortex and send one projection to the temporal lobe (what pathway) to concentrate on identification of objects. The other projection is sent to the parietal lobe (where pathway) to process the locations of sounds more in depth.

In addition, the auditory cortex has areas specializing in speech language input such as voice. Speech sounds are given extensive attention in our auditory cortex, such as the left auditory cortex areas (Belin et al., 2000; Zatorre et al., 2002). Interesting facts are shown with stroke patients. Patients with brain damages in certain areas have shown distinct deficits in speech language production and comprehension. These two brain areas are known as Broca's and Wernicke's areas, named after the surgeons who first discovered these areas (Coren et al., 2004).

PERCEPTUAL ASPECTS OF AUDITION

Early psychophysists such as Ernst Weber (1795–1878) and Gustav Fehner (1801–1887) argued that there is a difference between the objective intensity of physical stimulus and people's subjective experience of this stimulus. For example, when you listen to music through a headphone you can either increase or decrease the sound volume. However, if the music is too loud you might not notice the difference in volume when you increase the intensity of the volume. You will have a similar perception of sounds at the opposite extreme end. Weber explained this perceptual experience in relation to a difference threshold. Because the physical intensity of a stimulus has a logarithmic function with our experience, a greater sound intensity will be needed at the higher end of the sound wave spectrum for us to notice a difference (production of JND). This notion is captured in the **equal loudness contours**.

> **Equal loudness contours:** Lines measuring the function of loudness and frequencies of sound waves.

Equal loudness contours show the function of loudness and frequencies. Let's say you are comparing the two frequencies of 100 Hz and 1,000 Hz. According to the equal loudness contours, to reach 40 phons (or equal loudness level), an 100-Hz stimulus requires an intensity (loudness) setting of 60 dB_{SPL} whereas a 1,000 Hz only requires an intensity of 40 dB_{SPL} to reach the same loudness perception. This represents how frequency and loudness are both collectively used to perceive the sound waves and experience physical stimulus (Fletcher & Munson, 1933; Gulick et al., 1989). When interpreting sound waves and to detect an increase or decrease in sounds, we must use both frequency (pitch) and amplitude (loudness) information.

The auditory system is able to distinguish the location/direction—analogous to depth in vision—of a sound source as well as the relative distance of sound-emitting stimuli. This is accomplished by the use of **monaural** and **binaural cues** (again, just like monocular and binocular visual cues). There are a number of important factors involved in deciphering spatial properties of sounds from monaural cues. Individuals utilize the intensity of a stimulus to judge the distance of a sound source. If two sounds are presented simultaneously, the louder one is perceived to be closer. Also, we can determine that an ambulance is approaching based on the intensity and the pitch of the siren (particular if the observer is stationary). The change in pitch emitted by an object moving horizontally in space, in relation

> **Monaural cues:** Auditory depth perception that occurs with just one ear.
>
> **Binaural cues:** Auditory depth perception that occurs with the use of both ears.
>
> **Doppler shift:** The change in pitch emitted by an object moving horizontally in space, in relation to a stationary observe.

to a stationary observe, is termed the **Doppler shift**. The basis for this shift in pitch is that as a sound producing body moves toward you, each of its successive sound waves is emitted slightly farther ahead in its path. The sound waves tend to be more compressed (or bunch-up) and there is an increase in the frequency. On the other hand, the sound waves following the object tend to be more stretched-out, and the frequency of that sound is perceived as lower.

Although it is possible, albeit difficult, to determine the relative location of a sound source in space with one ear (monaural), accurate location of a sound-emitting object is only possible with binaural cues. The auditory system utilizes the physical/quantitative differences in stimulation that occur between the two ears. One of the important methods used to locate auditory stimuli is by means of **interaural time differences**, the time differences produced when a sound reaches one ear before the other. Amazingly, research has shown that sounds whose time of arrival differ by as little as 0.0001 seconds

> **Interaural time differences:** The slight difference in time sound arrives at one ear before the other ear.

(even less in some cases) are sufficient to allow for accurate localization. The process of locating an audible stimulus in space is accomplished through neural mechanisms. Activation of one ear and its respective cortical region prior to activation of the other inhibits activity on the opposing side of the brain. Simply stated, if the left ear receives a sound first, the right auditory cortex becomes more active, while simultaneously deactivating the left auditory cortex.

In the end, the probability of locating the source of the sound is enhanced because downsizing the stimulus arriving later in time at the opposing audi-

Doppler Effect

Low Frequency

High Frequency

© Vecton/Shutterstock.com

tory cortex enhances the cortex that responds first. For example, place a set of headphones over your ear; set the stereo on mono, as opposed to stereo; adjust the balance so there is slightly more music stimulating one ear. Within a couple of seconds, you will be unable to hear any music from the side of lesser intensity. This observation provides support for the notion that the auditory system weighs the first sounds more heavily and tends to suppress later arriving sounds.

Another binaural process by which the brain can determine the location of a sound in space is called the **interaural intensity difference**, which results from the minuscule intensity difference between the sounds reaching each ear. A sound not only strikes the nearer ear first but also delivers a slightly more intense sound to that ear. This should make intuitive sense, because the head serves as a major source of impedance and the sound must travel around the head before it can be detected. Interestingly, if two sounds approach the ears simultaneously, yet one is slightly more intense than the other is, the person will perceive the source of the sound to be coming from the direction of the louder sound. Another source of information

Interaural intensity difference: The slight difference in sound volume at it reaches one ear compared to the other.

Phase difference: The slight difference in the degree the sound wave is moving through its wave when it reaches one ear compared to the other.

the brain can use to localize sound is the **phase difference** between the sounds reaching the two ears. For example, sounds of low frequencies have wavelengths that exceed the diameter of the head. Because these sounds are defracted (or bent) around the head, they reach each ear at slightly different phases. That is, the waveform of the sound reaching one ear may be in a different part its compression-rarefaction cycle than the waveform of the sound arriving at the other ear. This method of sound localization only works for sound waves that are lower than about 1,000 Hz.

The **dual or two-process theory** of sound localization suggests that we localize low-frequency sounds by using time or phase differences, or both, at the two ears, and that we localize high frequency sounds by using the intensity differences caused by the **sound shadow** (simply defined as difference in sound intensity due to head blocking/deflecting some of the sound waves) produced by the head and differences in their distance from the sound source.

Dual or two-process theory: The idea that we localize low-frequency sounds by using time or phase differences, or both.

Sound shadow: The difference in sound intensity due to head blocking/deflecting some of the sound waves.

SUMMARY

We opened this chapter by asking you to imagine a very simple activity: listening to a lecture and going to the student union following class. However, as we have described throughout this chapter, the underlying psychological processes that are occurring during these seemingly simple events are far from simple. Many years of scientific research conducted by psychologists have helped us understand that our experience of a continuous world is driven by two processes: sensation and perception.

Sensation is a process of registering environmental stimuli from the external world, and perception is the process of making sense of those environmental stimuli. Our sensation and perception processes have evolved to help us navigate the world very well. However, as we have discussed in the sections about illusions, sometimes our brains misinterpret physical stimuli.

These illusions should not lead us to the conclusion that humans are flawed, but they should point to the fact that the world is an unimaginably complex place, and that through the processes of sensation and perception, our minds do a very good job of guiding us through the world unscathed … with only a few mistakes here and there. We hope you take a moment to reflect on the amazing complexity of human sensation and perception the next time you do something mundanely uninteresting, such as sitting and reflecting about the grandeur of the human mind.

⌐The Bible speaks to our ability to understand God's creation through our senses. The wonder of the world is available to us through our ability to interact with it and in our ability to recall those interactions as well as share them with others. We are to make a joyful noise as we praise God and that noise, music, should audible to those around us. This chapter speaks to some of the most complex aspects of all human physiology—our senses—yet they work so well, so fast, and with such little effort we seldom even consider them unless they are not working.⌐

Chapter 4

Learning, Memory, and Intelligence

LEARNING OBJECTIVES

- ❏ Define learning.
- ❏ Explain the key concepts of behaviorism.
- ❏ Differentiate between classical and operant conditioning.
- ❏ Identify various schedules of reinforcement and impact on behavior.
- ❏ Analyze limitations of behavioristic explanations.
- ❏ List the key principles of cognitive psychology.
- ❏ Define the term, reciprocal determinism.
- ❏ ˻Explain˼ the different types of memory and their hierarchical organization.
- ❏ ˻Review˼ the process by which information to goes from sensory to long-term memory (LTM).
- ❏ Explain the process of encoding, storage, and retrieval.
- ❏ Identify some applications and problems of LTM.
- ❏ ˻Explore˼ how to improve memory.
- ❏ ˻Explore˼ the historical beginning of intelligence tests ˻and their underlying theories.
- ❏ Demonstrate˼ how to calculate IQ.
- ❏ Identify some cultural, ˻environmental, and biological determinants to intelligence and IQ testing.˼

WHAT IS LEARNING?

Learning, psychology tells us, consists of changes in behavior. But not all changes in behavior are examples of learning. Some changes are temporary; they might result from fatigue or from the use of drugs. Other changes appear to be mainly due to physical maturation; still others might result from injury or disease of the brain or other parts of the nervous system.

> **Learning:** ⌊A process resulting in a relatively consistent change in behavior or behavioral potential and is based on experience.⌋

▶ **CHAPTER OVERVIEW**

Learning is defined as *relatively permanent changes in behavior that result from experience but are not caused by fatigue, maturation, drugs, injury, or disease* (Figure 4.1). Strictly speaking, however, it is not the changes in behavior themselves that define learning; the changes are simply evidence that learning has occurred. Learning is what happens to the organism as a result of experience. ⌊If all learning were only temporary, ultimately what benefit would it have? In order to function purposefully and adaptively, there has to be a mechanism for the long-term storage of information. So, learning is viewed as a process resulting in a relatively consistent change in behavior or behavioral potential and is based on experience.⌋ In many cases there will be no evidence of learning until an opportunity to display a behavior is presented; and in some cases, that opportunity may never occur. It might forever remain latent (meaning potential but not apparent).

⌊Learning is difficult to assess because it cannot be observed directly; instead, inferences are made about learning based on changes in performance. This is evidenced when learning how to play a sport or drive a car in that the more you do it the better you get at the task. Another difficulty is that performance doesn't always accurately reflect learning. For example, to say that you earned a 72% on a psychology exam doesn't necessarily mean that you only know 72% of the information. It is quite possible that an individual's behaviors were changed as a consequence of a lecture or the contents in the text that would otherwise be impossible to assess with an exam, such as attitudes or beliefs. This problem is often referred to as the learning-performance distinction—the difference between what has been learned and what is expressed, or performed, in overt behaviors.⌋

© Chinnapong/Shutterstock.com

Approaches to Learning

Learning is not easily separated from other major topics in psychology. Changes in behavior are centrally involved in many aspects of psychology, including motivation, personality, perception, development, and even mental disorders. We are not simple, highly predictable organisms with static and unchanging patterns of behavior. We profit from experience—and that defines learning. ⌊This is further complicated by the fact that much of our learning occurs below our conscious awareness.⌋

Not surprisingly, most of the first psychologists devoted considerable effort to discovering the laws and principles of learning. As we saw in Chapter 1, these early efforts, especially in the United States, rejected the more philosophical and intuitive approach of an earlier age. Instead, they embraced a

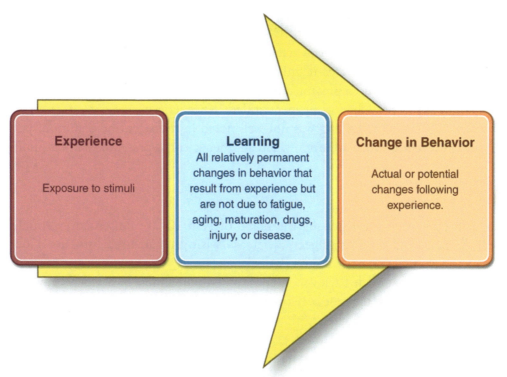

Figure 4.1 Evidence of learning is found in actual or potential changes in behavior as a result of experience. But learning itself is an invisible, internal neurological process.

scientific approach—an approach concerned mainly with the objective and observable aspects of human functioning. The most important pieces of the puzzle, these early psychologists thought, would have to do with the rules that govern relationships between stimuli (observable conditions that can give rise to behavior) and responses (actual, observable behavior). ⌊In the most brief explanation, learning⌋ is a change in behavior (or the potential for behavior) as a result of experience.

Because they deal with observable *behaviors,* the theories that resulted from early psychologists are labeled **behavioristic theories**. Sometimes they're also referred to as *S-R* or associationistic theories because they deal mainly with associations between **stimuli** and **responses**. And although the early psychologists have sometimes been accused of leading to a mechanistic and incomplete description of human learning, they have contributed a great deal to our understanding that continues to be both valid and valuable.

A second major group of learning theories are **cognitive theories**. They are concerned less with the objective aspects of behavior than with more *mental* processes such as thinking, imagining, anticipating, problem solving, decision making, and perceiving.

Behavioristic theories: Theories concerned with objective evidence of behavior rather than with consciousness and mind.

Stimulus (*pl.* stimuli): A physical stimulus is any change in the physical environment capable of exciting a sense organ. Stimuli can also be internal events such as glandular secretions or even thoughts.

Response: A muscular, glandular, or mental reaction to a stimulus.

Cognitive theories: Theories that look at intellectual processes such as those involved in thinking, problem solving, imagining, and anticipating.

BEHAVIORISTIC APPROACHES

An American ⌐named⌐ Edwin Twitmyer was actually the first person known to have reported the principle of *classical conditioning*. He discovered it while doing research for his doctoral dissertation, publishing his findings in 1902. In 1904, he even presented these findings to the American Psychological Association (when William James was its president) as a paper entitled "Knee Jerks without Stimulation of the Patellar Tendon" (Twitmyer, 1905). ⌐The finding was not well noted in the scientific community as that time; however, the concept received much attention when another scientist presented similar findings.⌐

Classical Conditioning

And then about a year later, a Russian by the name of Ivan Pavlov presented essentially the same findings—only he had used dogs as subjects whereas Twitmyer had used humans. Nobody knows Twitmyer's name today, but everybody knows Pavlov's.

Ironically, the discovery that made Pavlov so famous came about almost by accident. Pavlov was a physiologist, not a psychologist, and at the time of his lucky discovery, he was busily investigating and measuring secretions related to digestion. That's when he noticed that some of his more experienced dogs began to salivate whenever they saw their handlers. The less experienced dogs also salivated, but only when given food.

Pavlov rightly guessed that his older dogs had learned something that the more naive dogs had yet to learn: The older dogs learned to associate the sight of a handler (stimulus) with food (Figure 4.2). But only one of these stimuli, food, would normally lead to salivation. So, in a sense, what the dogs had learned was to substitute one stimulus (handler) for another (food). Not surprisingly, this kind of learning is sometimes called *learning through stimulus substitution;* its more common label is **classical conditioning**.

> **Classical conditioning:** Learning through stimulus substitution as a result of repeated pairings of an unconditioned stimulus with a conditioned stimulus.

That the dog has *learned* something is clear: there has been a change in behavior (specifically, in the response to the handler) as a result of experience (repeated pairing of the handler and food). That is, a previously neutral stimulus (sight of handler) now leads to a response ordinarily associated with another stimulus (food). This defines *classical conditioning*.

⌐This brings us back to the importance of being able to think critically and creatively as well as to combine ideas together as a means to systematically work toward wisdom. Pavlov was able to combine his knowledge of physiology with new and competing observations, which ultimately resulted in him making a profound discovery.⌐

Pavlov's Experiments

To clarify the laws of classical conditioning, Pavlov devised a series of experiments (Pavlov, 1927). In the best known of these, a dog is placed in a harness-like contraption similar to the one shown in Figure 4.3. The apparatus allows food powder to be inserted directly into the dog's mouth or to be dropped into a dish in front of the dog. The salivation that occurs when food powder is placed in the dog's mouth is an unlearned response and is therefore an **unconditioned response (UR)**. The stimulus of food powder that gives rise to the UR is an **unconditioned stimulus (US)**.

> **Unconditioned response (UR):** The automatic, unlearned response an organism gives when the US is presented.
>
> **Unconditioned stimulus (US):** A stimulus that elicits an automatic, unlearned response from an organism.

Figure 4.2   What Pavlov first noticed was that the sight of the handler was enough to cause experienced dogs to salivate. He later paired other stimuli, such as bells and buzzers, with the presentation of food to study the details of classical conditioning.

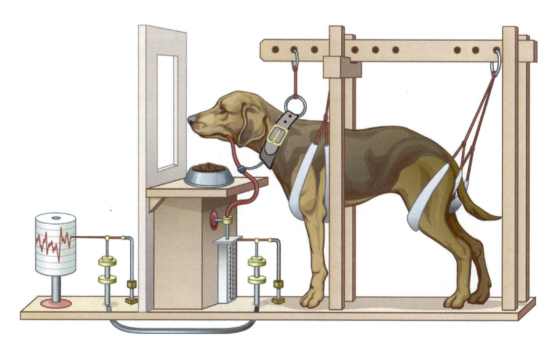

Figure 4.3   Pavlov's dogs were placed in harnesses such as the one shown. Saliva dropping through the tube activates the balancing mechanism so that the amount of salivation is recorded on the revolving drum. In this demonstration, presentation of food is paired with a light that shines through the window.

Most animals, including humans, are born with a number of these simple, prewired (meaning they don't have to be learned) stimulus–response associations called **reflexes**. More complex behaviors that are also unlearned are **instincts**. That we blink when something brushes our eye is a reflex—as is our tendency to salivate in response to food, to withdraw from painful stimulation, and to jerk the knee in response to a sharp blow below the kneecap.

In Pavlov's conditioning demonstration, the trainer arranged for a buzzer to sound as food powder was inserted into the dog's mouth. This procedure was repeated a number of times. After a while, the trainer simply sounded the buzzer without providing any food powder. And the dog still salivated. The animal was been conditioned to respond to a buzzer, termed a **conditioned stimulus (CS)**, by salivating, a **conditioned response (CR)** (Figure 4.4).

Although the concept of classical conditioning might seem abstract or not applicable to important human behavior, it is one of the more important factors in maintaining dependence on abused drugs. For example, when people take drugs, the drug (UCS) elicits a cascade of physiological responses. The body reflexively fights these drug-induced changes (e.g., cocaine causes a rapid increase in heart rate and blood pressure) by producing the exact opposite type of effect in order to reestablish homeostasis. The body's natural, reflexive response to the drug is the unconditioned response (UR). Over repeated administration of the drug, this compensatory response also becomes the conditioned response (CR). That is, in settings or contexts typically paired with drug use (the CS), the body physiologically prepares itself (the CR) for the drug's predictable effects. Increases in drug use occur because the user must now administer enough of the drug to counter these conditioned, counter effects prior to the "high." As drug use increases, so do the compensatory responses. Conditioned stimuli multiply quickly as drug use increases in frequency and duration.

Each injection, inhalation, or drink serves as a conditioning session. Self-administering a drug produces rewarding effects—operant conditioning. The biological changes produced by the drug get paired with stimuli in the environment—classical conditioning. Since a drug user might self-administer a drug several times a day, for many years, an enormous amount of conditioning can take place. The longer a drug is used, the greater the conditioning, and, therefore, the more resistant the user is to forgetting about the use of the drug or, really, unlearning the associations. Since a conditioned stimulus serves to predict subsequent drug effects, the body responds reflexively. For example, heroin produces euphoria while decreasing heart rate and blood pressure; therefore, conditioned stimuli produce dysphoria while increasing heart rate and blood pressure. As a result, after the drug is administered, biological functions are less disrupted than they would be without the conditioned stimuli.

What would happen if familiar stimuli were absent during drug administration? Consider this: what would happen if a person used drugs in an unfamiliar location? The different location would play a principal role in potential overdose. The drug would produce a greater effect on a person's body because the body did not have a chance to reflexively adapt to the impending drug effects. The absence of conditioned stimuli prevented a person's body from reflexively preparing itself for the impending drug effects. The euphoria experienced would be more pronounced; however, decreases in vital reflexes, such as the heart rate, blood pressure, and respiration, would also be more pronounced. The adaptive responses produced by classical conditioning would have elevated these vital reflexes prior to the drug administration. Since this would not happen, a person's vital reflexes would decrease drastically after injecting heroin.

Reflexes: Stimulus–response associations.

Instincts: Complex unlearned, behaviors.

Conditioned stimulus: A once neutral stimulus that becomes conditioned after repeated pairings with the US.

Conditioned response: Previously the UR that is now given in response to the CS.

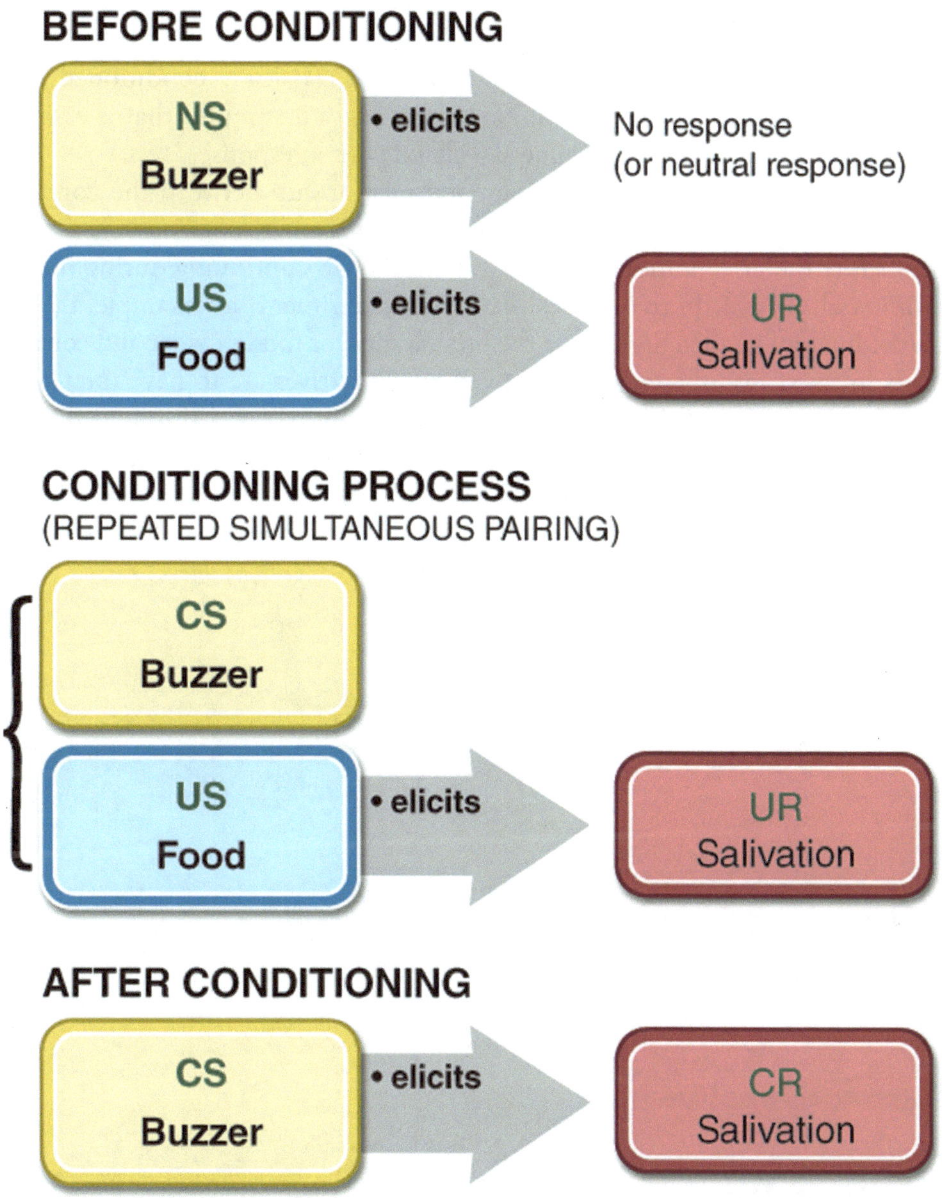

BEFORE CONDITIONING

NS
Buzzer   • elicits   No response
(or neutral response)

US
Food   • elicits   UR
Salivation

CONDITIONING PROCESS
(REPEATED SIMULTANEOUS PAIRING)

CS
Buzzer

US
Food   • elicits   UR
Salivation

AFTER CONDITIONING

CS
Buzzer   • elicits   CR
Salivation

Figure 4.4   Classical conditioning. Initially, the stimulus (buzzer) does not elicit salivation. After repeated pairings of this stimulus with the unconditioned stimulus (food), the buzzer has become a conditioned stimulus that now elicits a conditioned response (salivation).

This difference would be significant enough to result in an overdose and death. It's important to remember that almost anything can serve as a conditioned stimulus. Drug users often show biological reactions to even the sight of a picture of a house associated with drug use. Drug dealers, other drug users, and drug paraphernalia are common conditioned stimuli. Therefore, even when a user decides to quit using drugs, familiar environmental stimuli still trigger biological and psychological responses equivalent to withdrawal symptoms (O'Brien, 2001; O'Brien & Mclellan, 1996). Despite efforts to the contrary, this leads to self-administration of the drug, resulting in more classical conditioning, further reinforcing the cycle of drug abuse.

Acquisition

Several factors are directly related to the ease with which a classically conditioned response can be acquired. One is the distinctiveness of the CS. Not surprisingly, a stimulus that is easily discriminated from other stimulation will more easily become associated with a response.

A second critically important factor is the temporal relationship between the conditioned and the unconditioned stimuli. The ideal situation, *delayed* (or *forward-order*) *conditioning,* presents the conditioned stimulus before the unconditioned stimulus, with the CS continuing during the presentation of the US (Hussaini et al., 2007). In the classical Pavlovian experiment, for example, the fastest learning occurred when the buzzer sounded just before the presentation of food powder and continued while the food powder was injected into the dog's mouth. Other alternatives are to have the CS begin and end before the US, termed *trace conditioning;* to present the US and the CS simultaneously (*simultaneous conditioning*); or to present the US prior to the CS (*backward conditioning*). Figure 4.5 summarizes the relationship of these temporal factors to classical conditioning.

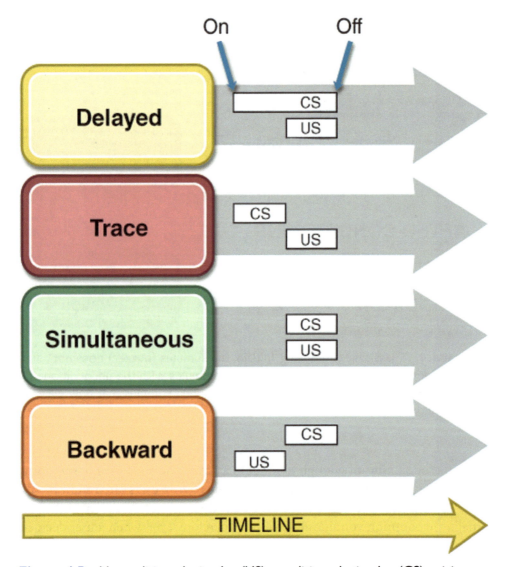

Figure 4.5   Unconditioned stimulus (US)–conditioned stimulus (CS) pairing sequences are shown here in the order of effectiveness. Conditioning takes place most quickly in the delayed sequence where the CS (buzzer) precedes the US (food powder) and continues throughout the time the US is presented.

As noted, fastest learning typically occurs when the conditioned stimulus precedes the unconditioned stimulus (forward-order conditioning). The opposite situation, backward conditioning, in which the conditioned stimulus follows the unconditioned stimulus, has generally not resulted in learning except under very specific circumstances. For example, presenting a dog with food and then later ringing a bell does not normally lead the dog to salivate in response to the bell.

Backward conditioning can sometimes be effective, however. For example, Minnier et al. (2007) successfully conditioned taste aversions in rats by injecting them with lithium chloride (which makes them sick—a US) either 15 or 45 minutes *before* they were allowed to drink sweetened water (the CS). Most rats who experienced the 15-minute delay later avoided the sweetened water.

Keith-Lucas and Guttman (1975) conditioned rats to avoid a plastic toy by shocking them electrically and then placing a plastic hedgehog-like toy in their cages. A significant number of rats exposed to the hedgehog 1, 5, or 10 seconds after receiving the electric shock displayed avoidance behavior the following day. Backward conditioning had been established after a single trial—unlike Pavlov's dog, who required many trials before learning.

The significance of these results is not simply that they illustrate that backward conditioning can be accomplished. More important, they illustrate that many organisms have biological predispositions to learn behaviors that have survival value. Rats are prepared to learn to avoid strange objects such as plastic hedgehogs, ˪and˩ many preyed-upon animals, as Griffin and Galef (2005) point out, are highly prepared to learn about predators. ˪Humans˩ seem to be prepared to learn strong taste aversions—which is useful when the tastes you learn to avoid belong to objects that might kill you if you ate them. Similarly, many people acquire fear of snakes, insects, and other potentially dangerous creatures relatively easily (Öhman et al., 2007). ˪In summary, there are four factors that can significantly impact the acquisition of learning in a classical conditioning paradigm. These factors include timing, predictability, signal strength, and attention.˩

Generalization and Discrimination

A dog trained to salivate in response to a buzzer may also salivate in response to a bell, a gong, or a human imitation of a buzzer. This phenomenon is called **stimulus generalization**. It involves making the same responses to different but related stimuli. An opposite phenomenon, **stimulus discrimination**, involves making different responses to highly similar stimuli.

> **Stimulus generalization:** Involves making the same responses to different but related stimuli.
>
> **Stimulus discrimination:** Involves making different responses to highly similar stimuli.

Watanabe (2010) conditioned a group of pigeons by reinforcing them when they pecked at paintings that human judges had labeled "good" and not reinforcing them when they pecked at others judged "bad." When these pigeons were later shown new paintings, they *generalized* what they had learned, pecking the "good" paintings far more often than the "bad." As Watanabe puts it, "the results showed that pigeons could discriminate novel 'good' and 'bad' paintings" (2010, p. 75).

Extinction and Recovery

Many classically conditioned responses are remarkably durable. A dog conditioned to salivate in response to a tone and then left to do nothing but dog things for many months will immediately salivate when he is brought back into the laboratory and he hears the bell.

But classically conditioned responses can be eliminated—a process called **extinction**. Extinction requires that the experimenter present

> **Extinction:** Process by which classically conditioned responses are eliminated.

the conditioned stimulus repeatedly without the unconditioned stimulus. For example, if Pavlov's well-conditioned dog heard the tone repeatedly but it was never again paired with food, it would soon stop salivating in response to the tone. ⌐During extinction, the paired association (e.g., the bell and the food) is slowly weakened until the bell can no longer consistently elicit a food-like response (i.e., salivation). Thus, it is the conditioned response that is being extinguished.⌐

Once a classically conditioned response has been extinguished, it can be reacquired much more easily than was initially the case. A dog who has learned to salivate in response to a tone and whose conditioned response is later extinguished, will learn to salivate again after only one or two pairings of tone and food powder. In fact, an extinguished response sometimes recurs in the absence of any training. This phenomenon, termed **spontaneous recovery**, illustrates that behaviors that are apparently extinguished are not necessarily completely forgotten. ⌐Spontaneous recovery has a big impact on relapse with substance abuse. For example, a person may have smoked for 10 years and then quit for 3 years; however, just one full day of cigarette smoking would be sufficient to activate the previously learned process and play a profound role in the subsequent reinitiation of daily smoking.⌐

Classical conditioning is sometimes a good explanation for unconscious emotional learning—like acquiring a fear (or a love) of dogs.

© Rob Hainer/Shutterstock.com

> **⌐Spontaneous recovery:** Is a classical conditioning-related behavior referring to the rapid reemergence of a previously extinguished behavior.⌐

Contiguity

Why does an emotional (or other) response such as fear become conditioned to a particular stimulus (or class of stimuli)? Pavlov's explanation is that the simultaneous or near-simultaneous presentation of a stimulus and a response leads to the formation of a neural link between the two. In this view, what is most important in the conditioning situation is the **contiguity** (closeness in time) of the stimulus and response. A contiguity explanation of classical conditioning maintains that the stimuli associated with "dog" (appearance, smell, sound, movement) were also associated with my initial fear response. Thus, the sight, sound, or smell of a dog continues to plague me in my otherwise peaceful adult life. ⌐Again, this is really important when it comes to substance abuse as the time between drug administration and drug effect is a powerful predictor of the abuse potential of that drug such that drugs that work fast have the highest abuse potential. This is why most drugs of abuse ultimately make their way to either being smoked or injected—the two fastest ways to get a drug into your system.⌐

> **Contiguity:** Closeness in time of the stimulus and response.

Blocking

Although contiguity might appear to be an adequate explanation for what happened to Pavlov's dogs, there are some relatively simple experimental situations that it does not explain. For example, Kamin (1969) paired a noise and a light (two unconditioned stimuli) with electric shock (a conditioned stimulus) administered to the feet of a group of rats (we'll call them the A group). In this study, the light and noise were turned on, and immediately afterward the rats were shocked. Classical conditioning theory would clearly predict that after the light and noise are paired often enough with the shock, either the light or the noise alone would cause an avoidance reaction in the rat. The prediction is correct.

But now Kamin threw a twist into the procedure. First he conditioned a group of rats by pairing only noise and electric shock (this is the B group). Then, once these rats showed a well-conditioned fear response to the noise, he conditioned them exactly as he had the A group, this time pairing both light and noise.

Recall that the A-group rats responded with fear to both the light and the noise. The B group rats also responded with fear to the noise. Strikingly, however, they showed no fear in response to the light in spite of the fact that they were conditioned in exactly the same way as the A group—but only after they had already been conditioned to the noise alone. It seems that for the B-group rats, learning that noise means shock *blocked* them from learning that light might also mean shock—a phenomenon appropriately labeled **blocking** (Figure 4.6).

> **Blocking:** A phenomenon in classical conditioning in which conditioning to a specific stimulus becomes difficult or impossible because of prior conditioning to another stimulus.

Contiguity does not explain blocking. Clearly, if conditioning depends only on the simultaneous presentation of stimulus and response, there is no reason why both groups of animals should not have learned the same things. One explanation for blocking is this: Whenever something new happens to an animal, it immediately searches its memory to see what events could have been used to predict it. So when a rat receives a mild foot shock, it scans its memory to see what just preceded the event. The A-group rat notes that both light and noise always come before the shock, and so it freezes whenever it hears the noise or sees the light. ⌐The⌐ B-group rat, who already knows that noise means shock, learns absolutely nothing new when later exposed to both noise and light followed by shock. Once the rat has learned that noise means shock, it no longer needs to pay attention to other stimuli.

Consequences

Learning is a fundamentally adaptive process: changes in behavior are what allow organisms to survive. Clearly, we, like any other animal, need to remember what is edible and where to find it; we need to recognize potential enemies; we need to stay away from electric shocks. Put another way, we have to learn what goes with what—what the most likely outcomes of our behavior are.

One explanation for classical conditioning says, in effect, that what is learned is not a simple pairing of stimulus and response as a function of contiguity, but the establishment of relationships between stimuli. This explanation holds that what is important in a conditioning situation is the information a stimulus provides about the probability of other events. When a dog salivates in response to a tone, it is because the tone now predicts food. In the blocking experiments, animals who have learned that stimulus A means shock find it difficult to learn that B also means shock. That's because when A and B are subsequently paired, there is no new information provided by stimulus B.

Operant Conditioning

Classical conditioning theorists were not especially concerned with consequences; they studied relationships among stimuli and responses. But a second form of conditioning, **operant conditioning**, is built around the importance of behavior's consequences. Operant conditioning is closely associated with B. F. Skinner (1953, 1969,

> **Operant conditioning:** (Skinner) describes changes in the probability of a response as a function of its consequences.

1971, 1989), one of the most influential psychologists of this age. He dealt with a large and important piece of the puzzle.

Skinner noted that although classical conditioning explains some simple forms of learning where responses are associated with observable stimuli (termed **respondent** behavior), most of our behaviors are of a different kind. Behaviors such as walking, jumping, listening to music, writing a letter, and so on are more deliberate; they are seldom associated with a specific stimulus the way salivation might be. These behaviors appear more voluntary. Skinner calls them **operants** because they are operations that are performed on the environment rather than in response to it. Classical conditioning does not provide an easy explanation for behaviors such as deciding to go for a walk or, at a simpler level, a dog learning to sit or roll over.

> **Respondent:** A response elicited by a known, specific stimulus. An unconditioned response.
>
> **Operant:** An apparently voluntary response emitted by an organism.

The Skinner Box

In his investigations, Skinner used a highly innovative piece of equipment now known as a **Skinner box**. Typically, this *experimental chamber* is a small, cage-like structure with a metal grid for a floor. At one end is a lever; above it, a light; below it, a small tray. Outside the structure are various mechanical or electronic devices designed so that if the lever inside the cage is pushed down, the light will go on, a click will be heard (if someone is listening), and a food pellet will drop into the tray.

> **Skinner box:** An experimental chamber used in operant conditioning experiments.

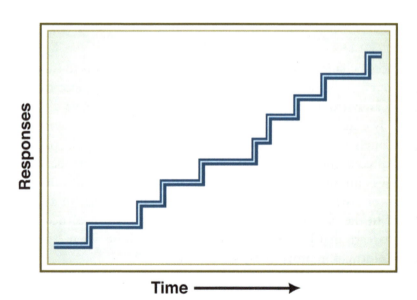

Figure 4.6 The photo shows B. F. Skinner with a rat in a Skinner box. The graph is a typical learning curve recorded on a revolving drum. The drum revolves at a constant speed, and each depression of the lever causes the recording pen to move up a notch. Steepness of the curve reveals response rate.

Photo on right: © Nina Leen/Contributor/Getty Images

When a naive rat is placed in this box, it does not respond as predictably as a dog in Pavlov's harness. Its behaviors are more deliberate, perhaps more accidental. It does not know about Skinner boxes and food trays. It needs to be magazine trained. In a typical magazine training session, the experimenter depresses a button that releases a food pellet into the tray. At the same time, there is an audible clicking sound. Eventually the rat is drawn to the tray, perhaps by the smell of the pellet, perhaps only out of curiosity. Now the experimenter releases another food pellet, the rat hears the click, eats the pellet, hears another click, runs over to eat another pellet … In a very short period of time, the rat has been magazine trained.

Now the experimenter stops rewarding the rat unless it depresses the lever near the food tray. Most rats will eventually do so in the course of sniffing around and exploring. And when they do, they hear the tell-tale click and immediately rush over to the food tray. Very shortly, the rat will have learned to depress the lever. ⌐Whether⌐ a light is paired with the presentation of food, the rat may eventually learn to depress the lever simply to see the light go on.

The Basic Operant Conditioning Model

All of the basic elements of Skinner's theory of operant conditioning are found in the rat-in-Skinner-box demonstration. The bar pressing is an operant—an emitted behavior. The food is a **reinforcer**; **reinforcement** is its effect. Any stimulus (condition or consequence) that increases the probability of a response is said to be reinforcing. In the Skinner box the light, too, may be a reinforcer.

> **Reinforcer:** Any stimulus condition or consequence that increases the probability of a response.
>
> **Reinforcement:** The effect of a reinforcer.

What happens to a rat in the Skinner box may be described simply: A naive rat placed in this situation eventually emits a specific operant (bar pressing); the operant is reinforced; the probability of the operant occurring again increases with each reinforced repetition. When placed in the same situation on another occasion, the rat may begin to emit the operant immediately. The rat has learned associations not only between the operant and reinforcement, but also between the operant and specific aspects of the situation—called **discriminative stimuli (S^D)**. These discriminative stimuli might include things such as the sight and smell of the inside of the cage. They are stimuli that allow the rat to discriminate between this situation and others where the operant is impossible or will not be reinforced. To some extent, the operant is now controlled by discriminative stimuli as well as by its consequences.

> **Discriminative stimulus (S^D):** Skinner's term for the features of a situation that an organism can discriminate to distinguish between occasions that might be reinforced or not reinforced.

In brief, Skinner's explanation of learning is based not on associations that might be formed between stimuli as a function of their co-occurrence (classical conditioning), but on associations that are established between a behavior and its consequences. Any other distinctive stimulus that happens to be present at the time of those consequences may also come to be associated with the operant.

The basic law of operant conditioning is the **law of effect**, first proposed by Edward Thorndike (1898). This law states that behaviors that are followed by reinforcement (Thorndike called them "satisfying states of affairs") are more likely to be repeated. Conversely, behaviors that are not followed by reinforcement (that lead to "annoyers," in Thorndike's words) are less likely to recur.

> **Law of effect:** Behaviors followed by reinforcement are more likely to be repeated and behaviors not followed by reinforcement are less likely to recur.

Shaping

But operant conditioning does suggest a way of teaching animals ⌐or humans⌐ very complex behaviors. This is done by reinforcing small sequential steps in a chain of behaviors that will ultimately lead to the desired final behavior—a process called **shaping**. The animal (or person) does not learn a complete final response at once, but is reinforced

> **Shaping:** Reinforcing small sequential steps in a chain of behaviors, leading to the desired final behavior.

instead for behaviors that come progressively closer to that response—hence the phrase *differential reinforcement of successive approximations.* Using *shaping* techniques, pigeons have been taught to bowl, chickens to play baseball, mules to dive into shallow waters from precarious heights, and pigs to point pheasants.

Shaping can be a useful technique for toilet-training infants. For example, in the first phase of a potty-training study described by Smeets et al. (1985), whenever infants "strained" as though they were about to soil their diapers, mothers or research assistants tapped on a nearby potty and called or touched the infant. This first phase of the *shaping* procedure was designed to draw the child's attention to the potty and to reinforce the infant for paying attention to it—after which the infant was placed on that piece of equipment.

In the second phase, the potty was kept within reach of the child so that when signs of imminent defecation or urination appeared, the infant could be guided to grab the potty before being placed on it. And in the third phase, the potty was placed further away so that self-initiated movement toward the potty could be reinforced. By then, many of the infants had learned to crawl toward the potty.

Throughout all three phases, mothers and attendants reinforced the infants, primarily through smiling, verbal praise, and other gestures of approval. And all were toilet trained before they had learned to walk.

Schedules of Reinforcement

Skinner's primary interest had been discovering the relationships between behavior and its consequences. His investigations with rats and pigeons quickly revealed that the way in which reinforcement is given (the *schedule of reinforcement*) is an important factor in determining responses.

Table 4.1 ⌐Types of Reinforcement Schedules

Fixed Ratio (FR): This schedule provides reinforcement after a specific/defined number of responses are made. For example, if you were to tell your child that they could have a piece of candy after they pick up 10 toys, that child would be on a FR 10 schedule.
Variable Ratio (VR): This schedule provides reinforcement after a certain yet changing number of responses are emitted. For example, if you were to tell your child that they could have a piece of candy after they pick up about 20 toys, they would be on a VR 20 schedule. The difference between this schedule and a FR schedule is that they could be rewarded after picking up 15, 17, 18, 21, 24, or 25 toys.
Fixed Interval (FI): This schedule provides reinforcement for the first response made after a certain time period has elapsed since the last reward, regardless of how many responses have been made during the interval. For example, you tell your child to eat his or her dinner and, to ensure that your child is eating, you tell him or her that you will check on him or her every 3 minutes. If they are eating when you check on them, you tell them that they can have a piece of candy.
Variable Interval (VI): This schedule provides a reinforcement after the first response is made after some period of time has elapsed, but the time changes or varies from reinforcer to reinforcer. For example, if you were to tell your child to do his homework and to ensure that it was actually being done you check on him at 2, 4, 8, 10, 12, 16, and 18 minutes, that child would be on a VI 8 minute schedule.⌐

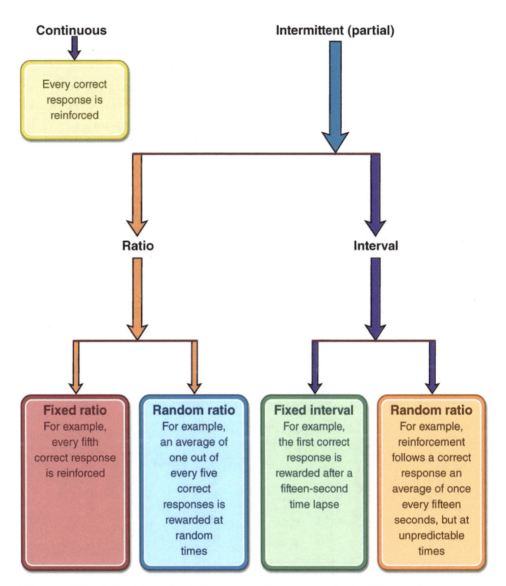

Figure 4.7 Schedules of reinforcement. Each type of schedule tends to generate a predictable pattern of responding.

The experimenter has several alternatives: Every correct response (called a "trial") might be reinforced (*continuous reinforcement*) or only some responses might be rewarded (*partial* or *intermittent reinforcement*). In turn, partial reinforcement can be based on a proportion of trials (*ratio reinforcement*) or on the passage of time (*interval reinforcement*). Furthermore, reinforcement can be regular (fixed), or irregular (random or variable).

Effects of Different Schedules

The effects of different schedules of reinforcement are evident in three different *dependent* variables: rate of learning (*acquisition rate*); rate of responding; and rate of forgetting (*extinction rate*). The *independent* variable in studies of operant conditioning is the experimenter's control of reinforcement (the schedule of reinforcement).

Initial learning—that is, rate of acquisition—is usually more rapid when every correct response is reinforced (a continuous schedule). If only some responses are reinforced (intermittent schedule), learning tends to be slower and more haphazard.

If, after initial learning, the experimenter continues to reinforce every correct response with food, the animal may respond at a high rate for a while, but will eventually become satiated and stop responding. Hence, the best training combination for an animal is usually a continuous schedule initially, followed by an intermittent schedule.

With intermittent schedules, rate of responding seems to be closely tied to expectations the animal might develop about how and when it will receive reinforcement. For example, under variable schedules, when it is difficult to predict when the reward will occur, rate of responding tends to be high and relatively unvarying. But under a fixed-interval schedule, when reinforcement occurs after the first correct responses following a predetermined time lapse, rate of responding tends to drop off dramatically immediately after reinforcement and picks up again just before the end of the time interval (Figure 4.8).

Rate of extinction, which is the cessation of a response following withdrawal of reinforcement, is also a function of schedule of reinforcement. Extinction is typically more rapid with a continuous schedule than with intermittent schedules. And of the intermittent schedules, variable ratio schedules typically result in the longest extinction times—a fact that has not escaped the attention of slot-machine programmers ⌐or video game developers.⌐ Skinner reports the case of one pigeon that, after complete withdrawal of reinforcement, emitted more than 10,000 pecks before extinction was complete.

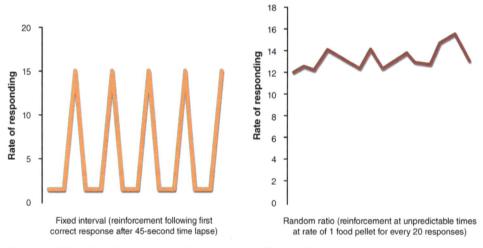

Figure 4.8   Idealized graphs showing the effects of two reinforcement schedules on rate of responding.

Types of Reinforcement

The fact that a pigeon would wear its beak to a frazzle before giving up an apparently unreinforced behavior may be evidence that reinforcement is not nearly as simple or as obvious as these few pages might suggest. We really have no basis for concluding that pecking itself is not a rewarding activity for the pigeon and that it requires no extrinsic reinforcement to be maintained. ⌐As noted earlier,⌐ pigeons are biologically programmed to peck—as pigs are to root and humans are to explore. These activities don't necessarily require **extrinsic reinforcement**.

> **Extrinsic reinforcement:** Reinforcement to increase a behavior in the future that comes from an external source (e.g., reading to earn a reward).

Extrinsic reinforcement includes the variety of external stimuli that might increase the probability of a behavior. In contrast, **intrinsic reinforcement** may be loosely defined as satisfaction, pleasure, or reward that is inherent in a behavior and that is therefore independent of external rewards. The satisfaction that people sometimes derive from their work is a form of intrinsic reinforcement; the money and the praise that might also result are forms of extrinsic reinforcement.

Skinner distinguishes between two broad classes of reinforcers. **Primary reinforcers** are stimuli that are rewarding for most people, most of the time, without anybody having had to learn that they are rewarding. They include food, drink, sleep, comfort, and sex.

Secondary reinforcers include the wide range of stimuli that may not be reinforcing initially but that eventually become reinforcing as a function of having been associated with other reinforcers. Thus, secondary reinforcers are learned; primary reinforcers are not. Social prestige, praise, money, and applause are very powerful secondary reinforcers.

In general, reinforcement is any stimulus (situation) that increases the probability of a response occurring. If the stimulus increases the probability of a behavior it follows, it is a **positive reinforcer**. Food pellets in the rat's cage are examples of positive reinforcers. So is the applause a performer receives, the money a worker gets paid, and the satisfaction a student gets from learning.

But some reinforcers are effective not when they are *added* to a situation, but rather when they are *removed*. For example, if a mild electric current is turned on in the rat's cage and then is turned off when the rat depresses the lever, the result might be an increase in the probability that the rat will subsequently press the lever. In this case,

> **Intrinsic reinforcement:** Reinforcement to increase a behavior in the future that comes from an internal source (e.g., reading because one loves to read).

> **Primary reinforcers:** Stimuli that are naturally rewarding for an organism.

> **Secondary reinforcers:** Stimuli that may not be reinforcing initially but that eventually become reinforcing as a function of having been associated with other reinforcers.

> **Positive reinforcer:** Pleasing or positive stimulus is given and consequently, the probability that the behavior will be repeated is increased.

Operant conditioning is based on the consequences of behavior. They can be positive and reinforcing, as when this young lad is given his medal. Or they can be negative, as this driver is discovering.

Photo on left: © StockImageFactory.com/Shutterstock.com, right: © Lisa F. Young/Shutterstock.com turning off the electric current is an example of a **negative reinforcer**. In much the same way, the removal of pain might be a negative reinforcer for taking some medication, even as the alleviation of withdrawal symptoms might be a negative reinforcer for continued drug use.

> **Negative reinforcer:**
> Unwanted or painful stimulus is removed and consequently, the probability that the behavior will be repeated is increased.

The important point is that reinforcement is defined in terms of its *effects* rather than in terms of the characteristics of the reinforcing stimuli used. And the effect of reinforcement, by definition, is to *increase* the probability of a behavior. A positive reinforcer does so when it *follows* a behavior; a negative reinforcer does so when it is *removed* following a behavior.

Again, going back to an important example with drug abuse. Positive reinforcement occurs when a behavior allows a person to experience something that is pleasurable—like getting high or onset of euphoria/reward. In turn, this increases the probability that the person will engage in that behavior in the future—smoking, drinking, or injecting drugs. The reinforcing properties of abused drugs and chemicals can lead to powerful operant conditioning, making drug-seeking behavior difficult to control—especially when the time between the administration and the high is very short like with smoking or injecting drugs.

However, there are other reasons people keep using drugs even when they wish to quit. For example, when people have negative feelings, "getting high" helps to reduce these negative, unwanted emotions. In short, using abused drugs can take away something that is undesirable. The learning that occurs in this type of situation is negative reinforcement. Negative reinforcement occurs whenever a behavior gets rid of something undesirable, and the person becomes more likely to engage in that behavior in the future, so the experience is positive because a bad thing is taken away. Another example of this is how pain medication can lead to abuse in older adults. The majority of older adults do not want to use pain medication to get high. If they develop an addiction to a painkiller, it is usually because they were trying to get rid of their pain, often from some sort of chronic injury. Pain, depression, and anxiety are all undesirable experiences, and people will often use drugs to remove them from their consciousness and when this pattern is repeated, it can lead to dependence and abuse.

Remember that although people are sometimes aware of the implications of operant conditioning, the learning is more often subconscious (i.e., taking place whether they realize it or not). For example, drinkers may claim they drink because they "have a better time" when they do. In reality, they might drink because they have subconsciously learned that drinking alleviates their social anxiety, and they "have a better time" as a result. Nevertheless, there are also conscious elements to operant conditioning. The original choice to use pain medication to alleviate back pain is both logical and conscious. Drug administration is also a voluntary action. However, repeated use becomes more than just a conscious choice. The environment heavily influences these actions. Recall that in operant conditioning, behaviors are preceded by stimuli that signal a consequence is available. The connections between these stimuli and the urge to behave in certain ways are always subconscious. Thus, suffice to say, operant conditioning is a process that always has subconscious and sometimes conscious, elements to it. Drug administration is a complex behavior governed by many factors, most of which occur outside of our conscious awareness.

Punishment

Negative reinforcement is often confused with punishment, although the two are quite different. Negative reinforcement increases the probability of a response; the intended effect of punishment is precisely the opposite.

In essence, the consequences of behavior can involve the removal or presentation of stimuli that are pleasant or unpleasant (noxious). This presents the four distinct possibilities that are relevant to operant learning: positive reinforcement, negative reinforcement, and two types of punishment (Figure 4.9).

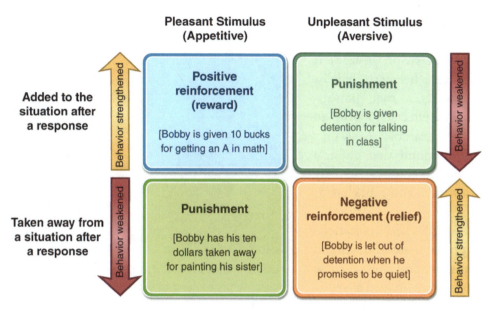

Figure 4.9   Reinforcement and punishment.

Table 4.2   ˪Comparing Punishment and Reinforcement Types

Positive Reinforcement	Positive Punishment
Increases the probability of a behavior's occurrence. Involves giving the person a desired stimulus	Decreases the probability of a behavior's occurrence. Involves giving the person an undesired stimulus
Negative Reinforcement	Negative Punishment
Increases the probability of a behavior's occurrence. Involves the removal of an undesired stimulus	Decreases the probability of a behavior's occurrence. Involves the removal of a desired stimulus ˩

There are countless illustrations of each of these possibilities in human behavior: Josephine is complimented on a new hairstyle (the addition of a pleasant stimulus; positive reinforcement); a pill relieves Norbert's headache (removal of an unpleasant stimulus: negative reinforcement); Arnaldo is reprimanded for losing his homework (addition of an unpleasant stimulus: punishment); Ronald has his jelly beans confiscated for throwing one in the goldfish bowl (removal of a pleasant stimulus; punishment).

The Ethics of Punishment

Is punishment ethical? Is it even effective? Or does it just teach us to be sneakier? Psychology offers some tentative answers.

First, punishment is not always effective in eliminating undesirable behavior. Certainly, it is not nearly as effective as reinforcement in bringing about more desirable behavior. Second, punishment often leads to undesirable emotional side effects sometimes associated with the punisher rather than with the punished behavior. For example, punishment might lead a child to dislike and fear the punisher, and might result in efforts to avoid punishment rather than efforts to avoid the transgressions for which the punishment was administered. Third, punishment does not present a guide for desirable behavior; instead, it emphasizes undesirable behavior. Finally, some research indicates that punishment sometimes has effects opposite to those intended. For example, Mulvaney and Mebert (2007) found that physical punishment of young children actually increased maladjustment and misbehavior later in life.

Note that most of these objections apply mainly to physical punishment and not to other forms of punishment. These other forms of punishment (verbal reprimands, loss of privileges) have long been considered legitimate and effective means

Verbal reprimands and loss of privileges are legitimate and effective forms of punishment not subject to the same objections as physical punishment.
© Evgeny Atamanenko/Shutterstock.com

of controlling behavior; ⌐however, it can be argued that taking these forms of punishment to the extreme is also harmful to development.⌐ There are instances when punishment appears to be effective in suppressing destructive, aggressive, and dangerous behavior in children (and sometimes in adults as well).

⌐If punishment is to be used, here are six evidence-based guidelines:

1. The punishment or aversive stimulus must be swift and brief.
2. It should be administered right after the inappropriate response occurs.
3. The punishment should be of limited intensity.
4. The punishment should be aimed at reducing unwanted behavior not at humiliating the person or attacking their character.
5. The punishment should be limited to the situation in which the response occurs.
6. It should consist of penalties instead of physical pain.

Of course, keep in mind that just as there are inappropriate ways to administer punishment there are also inappropriate ways to administer reinforcement.

⌐While there may appear to be tremendous controversy surrounding punishment, even to the extent that in some circumstances it is entirely discouraged, there is just as much controversy with using reward as a means of controlling behavior, especially in children. One of the most significant issues around reward is that by rewarding a behavioral that should be occurring naturally and/or intrinsically motivated, the reward will eventually result in that behavior decreasing, especially in the absence of reward. Consider this example, a teacher or parent desires for a child to read more. The adult offers the child $10 for reading for 30 minutes. The child quickly complies. Over time though the child only reads when offered money but the value of the exchange goes down. Now the child won't read unless he receives $20. If this process can play out, how long would it take before the cost of paying a child to read is prohibitive? What happens if the child is told he will no longer receive any money for reading? Through reward, it is now almost certain that reading will stop. Furthermore, consider how to handle a child that likes to run out in the road or parking lot. This is really scary as a parent. What do you think would happen if you offered the child a small piece of candy for not running into the road—because you are against punishment? If determining how much punishment is too much, how do you similarly determine how much reward is too much? If the child doesn't comply with a small reward, would it be ok to give the child a much larger reward like 10, 50, or 100 pieces of candy? In this scenario, the child learns the best way to receive a reward is to disobey and with increasing frequency of disobedience comes increasing frequency of reward. But, what is the practical significance of this reward problem? The child will quickly learn the best way to receive a reward is to run into the street or parking lot. Just like the controversy around punishment, reward can result in the behavior going away over time instead of increasing and it can shift behavior away from self-control to the control of others through reward.

Perhaps, it would be better to reconceptualize punishment from strictly discipline to discipleship. What is the difference between the two? One simply desires to decrease an unwanted behavior, discipline, while one desires to develop the person primarily through appropriate mentorship and modeling, discipleship.

What Does the Bible Say?

Have you ever participated in a sport, musical, or dance/theater? Often, we want these activities to be fun, but generally before that can happen, a lot of hard work and practice is involved. That hard work and practice is often managed by a coach, teacher, or instructor—that is, an expert who can guide us so we can improve over time. It is often the case with a coach that we don't like the methods but sure enjoy the winning, but can you have one without the other? A good coach is one who corrects you and makes sure you are doing it right while following the rules. If this is true of sports, music, dance/theater, then why do we generally get so upset when corrected by others in matters that are so much more important? One of the most important responsibilities of parents is to raise up healthy, happy, successful, and self-disciplined children. Unfortunately, you cannot have the healthy, happy, and successful without discipline.

The Bible has a great deal to say about the subject of discipline, but in the simplest way, it can be viewed as discipleship; that is, a form of teaching (i.e., coaching). Regardless of how you define and prioritize discipline, it works best when it occurs within the framework of a loving relationship. Furthermore, it works best when both the behaviors that are being asked to decrease and the behaviors that are being asked to increase are modeled by the one administering the discipline.

In the Bible, discipline includes all the ways we guide our children toward discipleship with our words and actions (i.e., modeling). On the proactive side, discipline involves modeling, teaching, encouraging, training, and setting clear expectations. On the reactive side, it involves praising, correcting, rebuking, and letting children experience the consequences of their actions. In much of the Bible the phrase "spare the rod" is not necessarily synonymous with physical punishment but discipline in general. In all relationships, we disciple those we care about. We are wise to be disciplined as well. There is a warning, though, when it comes to discipline and that it should not be too harsh or so often that the child has no other relationship with the parent other than one of punishment. Taking it to that extreme can often produce the exact opposite results as intended. Nonetheless, we should be quick to listen and respond to discipline.

Proverbs 12:1 ESV

"Whoever loves discipline loves knowledge, but he who hates reproof is stupid."

Proverbs 13:24 ESV

"Whoever spares the rod hates his son, but he who loves him is diligent to discipline him."

Hebrews 12:5-11 ESV

"And have you forgotten the exhortation that addresses you as sons? 'My son, do not regard lightly the discipline of the Lord, nor be weary when reproved by him. For the Lord disciplines the one he loves, and chastises every son whom he receives.' It is for discipline that you have to endure. God is treating you as sons. For what son is there whom his father does not discipline? If you are left without discipline, in which all have participated, then you are illegitimate children and not sons. Besides this, we have had earthly fathers who disciplined us and we respected them. Shall we not much more be subject to the Father of spirits and live?"

Hebrews 13:17 ESV

"Obey your leaders and submit to them, for they are keeping watch over your souls, as those who will have to give an account. Let them do this with joy and not with groaning, for that would be of no advantage to you."

James 5:19-20 ESV

"My brothers, if anyone among you wanders from the truth and someone brings him back, let him know that whoever brings back a sinner from his wandering will save his soul from death and will cover a multitude of sins."

Ephesians 6:4 ESV

"Fathers, do not provoke your children to anger, but bring them up in the discipline and instruction of the Lord."

Colossians 3:21 ESV

"Fathers, do not provoke your children, lest they become discouraged."

Operant Conditioning and Human Behavior

Human behavior is seldom as simple as the pecking of a pigeon or bar pressing of a rat. Still, many of the results of investigations with these animals generalize easily to our behavior. There is no denying the effectiveness of rewards and punishments in our lives. The persistence with which people play slot machines, where reinforcement is on a random ratio schedule, is one example.

But in some ways, we are quite unlike the caged rat or pigeon. Neither of these animals has much choice: to peck or not to peck; to press or not to press. We, on the other hand, have a stunning array of choices: to study or not to study, to go to a movie, to go to the gym, to text a friend, to listen to music, and on and on. And each of these behaviors might be associated with a very different type and schedule of reinforcement. In short, our lives illustrate what are called **concurrent schedules of reinforcement**—a variety of options, each linked with different kinds and schedules of possible reinforcement.

> **Concurrent schedule of reinforcement:** A situation in which two or more different reinforcement schedules, each typically related to a different behavior, are presented at the same time.

Studies of the effects of concurrent schedules on animal behavior typically present the animal with the choice of two behaviors (two levers to press; two keys to peck), each of which is linked to a different type or schedule of reinforcement. In a study of a new drug treatment for cocaine addiction, for example, rats had a choice of lever A, which would lead to a small dose of intravenously administered cocaine, or lever B, which would provide a highly palatable food as a reinforcer (Thomsen et al., 2008). The rat preferred the drug.

Other studies indicate that, when given choices, rats and pigeons typically match their responses to maximize the likelihood of reward (Herrnstein, 1997). Not surprisingly, studies with humans lead to much the same conclusion. In experimental situations where participants can choose between different behaviors with different probabilities of reward, they try to maximize the payout (Borrero et al., 2009).

There are six important variables in determining which models will be most likely to influence behavior:

1. A model's observed behavior will be most influential when it is seen as having reinforcing consequences.
2. The model is perceived positively, liked, and respected.
3. There are perceived similarities between features and traits of the model and the observer.
4. Observational learning is also impacted by the degree to which the observer is rewarded for paying attention to the model's behavior.
5. The model's behavior must be visible and must stand out in comparison to other models.
6. The observer must be capable of reproducing the behavior that is being observed.

A TRANSITION TO COGNITIVISM

OVERVIEW BEHAVIORISM

Historically, behavioristic theory has recognized two general classes of behaviors, respondent and operant (elicited or emitted) and two general sets of rules and principles to account for each of these. One set relates to classical conditioning; the other, to operant conditioning.

Classical conditioning theory has been found most useful for explaining learning involving autonomic and reflexive reactions, such as those associated with emotional responses, over which we ordinarily have no conscious control.

Operant conditioning had generally been thought to apply to all behaviors that were not respondent—that is, to all behaviors that were not elicited by specific, identifiable stimuli but that simply occurred and could then presumably be brought under the control of reinforcement. Whereas classical conditioning appealed to principles of contiguity, operant conditioning invoked the law of effect: The consequences of behavior determine the probability of future occurrence or of change.

Problems for Traditional Behaviorism

Early behaviorists had hoped to discover laws of learning that would prove sufficiently general to explain most human behaviors. Unfortunately, behavior did not prove to be as simple as behavioristic theory might have indicated. Even animals sometimes behave in ways that are troublesome for traditional conceptions of behaviorism. The Brelands, two of Skinner's students, trained some 6,000 animals to perform a bunch of stunning animal tricks. But then many of these animals began to "misbehave," reverting to their more natural inclinations—a phenomenon called instinctive drift.

Instinctive drift presents a problem for traditional operant theory. It is now apparent that not all behaviors can be conditioned and maintained by schedules of reinforcement, that there is some degree of competition between unlearned, biologically based tendencies and the conditioning of related behaviors.

There are other examples of what are labeled biological constraints that have a clear effect on what an organism learns. Behaviors that are highly probable and relatively easy are typically those that have high adaptive value. Among humans, these might include behaviors such as avoiding bitter-tasting substances so that we don't poison ourselves, or learning a language so we can communicate. Among animals, behaviors such as pecking in birds and nosing around levers in rats are examples of highly probable, biologically based learning.

Organisms are prepared to learn certain things and contraprepared to learn others. Thus, it is almost impossible to teach a rat to depress a lever to escape an electric shock (Bolles, 1970). A rat's natural response to danger is to fight, flee, freeze, or become frantic; it is not to approach a lever and depress it. Therefore, a rat can be trained to jump to escape shock. The ease with which this is accomplished demonstrates preparedness. That the rat cannot be trained to depress a lever to escape a shock illustrates contrapreparedness. As Guthrie (1935) put it, "We cannot teach cows to retrieve a stick because this is one of the things that cows do not do" (p. 45).

Insight

Bertrand Russell (1927) made the interesting observation that U.S. and German rats must be quite different. "Animals studied by Americans rush about frantically, with an incredible display of hustle and pep, and at last achieve the desired result by chance," he wrote, adding, "Animals observed by Germans sit still and think, and at last evolve the solution out of their inner consciousness" (p. 33).

He was referring to the fact that U.S. psychology was then largely dominated by the behavioristic notion that responses are learned as a result of the reinforcement of a "correct" response that occurs through trial and error (i.e., by chance). At the same time, some German psychologists were working on different parts of the human puzzle.

One of these psychologists, Wolfgang Köhler, spent 4 years in the Canary Islands during World War I trying to frustrate apes with a pair of problems: the "stick" problem and the "box" problem. Both problems are essentially the same; only the solutions differ. In both, an ape finds itself unable to reach a tantalizing piece of fruit, either because it is too high or because it is outside the cage beyond reach. In the "stick" problem, the solution involves inserting a small stick inside a larger one to reach the fruit. In the "box" problem, the ape has to place boxes one on top of the other (Figure 4.10).

Figure 4.10   In the box problem, the chimp piles boxes to reach some fruit—a process involving insight, claimed Köhler. Playing chess, too, requires insight.

Photo on left: © Lilo Hess/Contributor/Getty Images, right: © Everett Collection/Shutterstock.com

The solution, insists Köhler (1927), does not involve trial and error, although some of that type of behavior might be displayed in the early stages. When the ape realizes that none of its customary behaviors is likely to obtain the bananas, it may sit for a while, apparently pondering the problem. And then, bingo, it leaps up, quickly joins the sticks or piles the boxes, and reaches for the prize.

That, according to Köhler, is **insight**, the sudden recognition of relationships among elements of a problem. It is a complex, largely unconscious process, not easily amenable to scientific examination.

> **Insight:** The sudden recognition of relationships among elements of a problem.

The behaviorists were hard-pressed to explain the behavior of Köhler's apes. Many were tempted to assume that the apes simply tried a number of apelike actions, eventually resorting to combinations of these when none of the simple behaviors was rewarded. Staunch behaviorists would assume that the ape's recognition of the solution would not occur until the fruit was in hand.

Many psychologists, however, were reluctant to accept behavioristic explanations for insight, a phenomenon that is common enough among our species that its existence is difficult to deny. And in time, the lowly rat was allowed to contribute in a small way to the study of insight.

In a pioneering study, Tolman and Honzik (1930) allowed a rat to become totally familiar with a maze in which there were several routes to the goal. Once the rat has learned the maze, barriers were placed so that the rat had to choose one of the alternatives. Typically, a rat will always select the shortest route—and the next shortest if that one is later blocked. The behaviorist assumption is that the rats developed a preference for the shortest routes as a result of receiving reinforcement more quickly when they follow these routes than when they stupidly meander through lengthy detours.

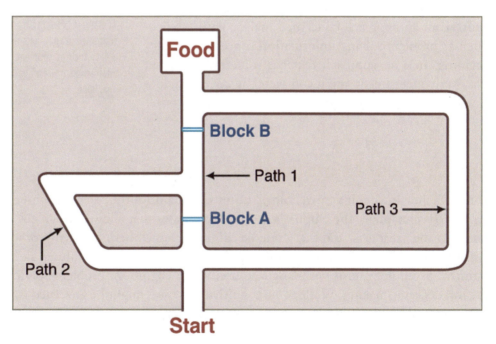

Figure 4.11 In the Tolman and Honzik (1930) blocked-path study, rats that had learned this maze almost invariably selected path 3 when path 1 was blocked at B. It seemed they somehow knew that the barrier at B also blocked the much shorter path 2.

The maze, shown in Figure 4.11, has three alternatives. Path 1 is the most direct and is almost invariably chosen when there are no barriers. When there is a barrier at A, the rat would be expected to choose alternative 2. This is, in fact, the case some 93% of the time. When the barrier is at B, rats might again be expected to select path 2 since its opening is not blocked. They don't. These clever rats now run all the way around path 3, despite the fact that they should still have a higher preference for path 2. One explanation is simply that they have developed a *cognitive map*—a mental representation—of the entire maze, and that they understand that a barrier at B also blocks route 2.

Other studies have shown that a rat will learn a maze even without any tangible reinforcement. Rats who are allowed to explore a maze without food learn the maze considerably more quickly than naive rats when food is later introduced. Such observations indicate that rats, too, have some understanding of their environments that goes beyond the formation of simple associations among stimuli, responses, and rewards.

And we humans, too, form *cognitive* maps that allow us to navigate in our environment. In doing so, report Foo et al. (2005), we tend to rely heavily on our recollection of landmarks and their positions relative to each other and to our preferred paths. Forming mental representations of our worlds is a uniquely *cognitive* activity.

COGNITIVE APPROACHES

⌐If⌐ behaviorism does not explain the simpler behaviors of animals, then the presumably more complex behaviors of humans might be even less well explained. If even animals have concepts and apparent thought processes, psychology should perhaps concern itself with these as well as with more easily observed and described behaviors.

Enter **cognitivism**, an approach concerned mainly with intellectual events such as problem solving, information processing, thinking, and imagining. It is an approach that has sometimes rejected behaviorism as overly mechanistic and incomplete. Behaviorism does not deal well with thinking—with *cognition*. For that, we need other approaches.

> **Cognitivism:** An approach concerned mainly with intellectual events such as problem solving, information processing, thinking, and imagining.

The Main Beliefs of Cognitive Psychology

The dominant metaphor in cognitive psychology, notes Garnham (2009), is a computer-based, *information processing (IP)* metaphor. The emphasis is on the processes that allow the perceiver to perceive, that determine how the actor acts, and that underlie thinking, remembering, solving problems, and so on. Not surprisingly, experimental participants in cognitive research tend to be human rather than non-human. ⌐Cognitive psychology deals with language use, visual cognition, problem-solving, reasoning, and judgment and decision-making. While some cognitive processes might be governed by unconscious mental process, they would not be grouped together with the general concept of reflexes.⌐

Learning Involves Mental Representation

Cognitive approaches to learning presuppose mental representation and information processing. The behaviorist view, as we saw, tends to describe learning as a largely unconscious process where factors such as repetition, contiguity, and reinforcement push the organism this way and that. In contrast, the cognitive view describes an organism that is more *thoughtful,* that can mentally imagine and anticipate the consequences of behavior. In this view, the learner is not a passive receiver of information, pushed and prodded by stimuli and their consequences. Instead, the learner actively participates in the learning process, discovering, organizing, and using strategies to maximize learning and reward.

Learners Are Not Identical

Behaviorism sees all learners as relatively equal in terms of their susceptibility to the effects of reward and punishment. In contrast, cognitivism emphasizes that learners are different. Individuals come with different background information, different inclinations and motives, different genetic characteristics, and different cultural origins. As a result, even in the same situation, individuals often learn very different things.

New Learning Builds on Previous Learning

The importance of individual differences among learners rests partly on the fact that new learning is often highly dependent upon previously acquired knowledge and skills. Take 100 naive rats; most of them can easily be *conditioned* to depress a small lever. But take 100 15-year-olds, and perhaps only a handful will be ready to understand the mysteries of quantum theory.

As we see in later chapters, for most important topics in human psychology (such as memory, motivation, and social learning), the continuing search for pieces of the puzzle has taken a largely cognitive turn.

Bandura's Social Cognitive Theory

You cannot, in any simple sense, *condition* someone to learn quantum physics. Still, explains Albert Bandura (1997), we learn many things through conditioning. It is clear that we are highly responsive to reinforcement—and perhaps to punishment as well. What is not so clear in most accounts of human learning through operant conditioning is just how operants come about in the first place.

Imitation is a powerful teacher among children. And sometimes among animals, too.

Photo on left: © Jacob Lund/Shutterstock.com, right: © P.Burghardt/Shutterstock.com

Bar pressing and key pecking are simple behaviors that are highly likely to occur in a given situation. A complex human behavior such as driving a car is not likely to appear fully formed, ready to be reinforced. And *shaping* such a complex behavior by reinforcing behaviors that slowly approximate the complete sequence of required behaviors would be a highly ineffective way of learning.

Nor do we learn complex behaviors such as how to drive a car through trial and error. We learn many of these complex behaviors, explains Bandura, through **observational learning**—that is, by observing and imitating **models**. And, in a sense, learning through **imitation** is a form of operant learning in that the imitative behavior is like an operant that is learned as a result of being reinforced.

A large number of studies indicate that social imitation is a powerful teacher among humans: Even children as young as 2 or 3 imitate and learn from each other. Moreover, a number of investigations show that monkeys, dogs, birds, and dolphins can learn a variety of relatively complex behaviors by observing their trained fellow animals (Ferrari et al., 2009; Miller et al., 2009).

> **Observational learning:** Bandura's theory involving learning through observing and imitating models.
>
> **Model:** A pattern for behavior that can be copied by someone. Also refers to descriptions of objects or phenomena. In science, models often serve as a sort of mental guide.
>
> **Imitation:** Copying behavior. To imitate a person's behavior is simply to use that person's behavior as a pattern.

What Does the Bible Say?

The Bible has a lot to say about self-control especially in the context of contributing to the behavior of others. Much of our own behavior is learned by observing others. This can be good or bad. The Bible warns we should not model behavior that could ultimately be harmful to someone else—even if that same behavior is not bad for us. Better to not do it at all than to do it and cause someone else to stumble or sin.

Romans 14:21

"It is good not to eat meat or drink wine or do anything that causes your brother to stumble."

1 Corinthians 15:33-34

"Do not be deceived: 'Bad company ruins good morals. Wake up from your drunken stupor, as is right, and do not go on sinning. For some have no knowledge of God. I say this to your shame."

1 Corinthians 10:23-24 ESV

" 'All things are lawful,' but not all things are helpful. 'All things are lawful,' but not all things build up. Let no one seek his own good, but the good of his neighbor."

Models

In Bandura's **social cognitive theory**, models are not limited to people who might be imitated by others; they include **symbolic models** as well. Symbolic models are any representation or pattern that can copied, such as oral or written instructions, pictures, book characters, mental images, cartoon or film characters, and television actors.

Models provide the imitator with two kinds of information: how to perform an act, and what the likely consequences of doing so are. And if the observer now imitates the behavior, there is a possibility of

> **Social cognitive theory:** An explanation of learning and behavior that emphasizes the role of social reinforcement and imitation as well as the importance of the cognitive processes that allow people to imagine and to anticipate.
>
> **Symbolic model:** A model other than a real-life person. For example, books, television, and written instructions are important symbolic models.

two different kinds of reinforcement. **Direct reinforcement** results from the consequences of the act itself. If 10-month-old Norbert is given a glass of milk when, in trying to imitate his sister, he says, "mwuff" (Norbert's best attempt at "milk"), he may soon learn to say "mwuff" whenever he is thirsty.

> **Direct reinforcement:** Results from the consequences of the act itself.

The other source of reinforcement is *secondhand,* labeled **vicarious reinforcement**. When you see someone doing something repeatedly, you unconsciously assume that the behavior must be reinforcing for that person. You might now imitate this behavior and continue to produce it even in the absence of any direct reinforcement.

> **Vicarious reinforcement:** When you see someone doing something repeatedly, you unconsciously assume that the behavior must be reinforcing for that person.

Reciprocal Determinism

There is little doubt that we engage in many behaviors because of the reinforcing consequences of so doing. But reinforcement does not control us blindly, explains Bandura (1997); its effects depend largely on our *awareness* of the relationship between our behavior and its outcomes. What is fundamentally important is our ability to figure out cause-and-effect relationships and to anticipate the outcomes of our behaviors.

Not only can we anticipate and imagine the consequences of our behavior and therefore govern ourselves accordingly, but we can also deliberately select and arrange our environments. That we are both products and producers of our environment is the basis of Bandura's concept of **triadic reciprocal determinism**.

> **Triadic reciprocal determinism:** Describes the three principal features of our social cognitive realities: our personal factors (our personalities, our intentions, what we know and feel); our actions (our actual behaviors); and our environments (both the social and physical aspects of our world).

In this view, there are three principal features of our social cognitive realities: our personal factors (our personalities, our intentions, what we know and feel); our actions (our actual behaviors); and our environments (both the social and physical aspects of our world). These three factors affect each other reciprocally. For example, a harsh, demanding environment might alter Joe's personality, making him bitter and cynical. This might change his behavior, driving him to more selfish acts. These actions might destroy friendships, thus changing important aspects of his social environment. And the changing social environment, in turn, might further affect his personality and his behavior.

On the other hand, instead of making him bitter and cynical, a tough environment might lead Joe to rally his friends that they might struggle together to ease their lot. The reciprocal influence of person, action, and environment might be no less in this case, but the outcomes might be vastly different (Figure 4.12).

Effects of Imitation

Through observational learning, we learn three different classes of behaviors, explain Bandura and Walters (1963): We learn brand new behaviors (**modeling effect**); we learn to suppress or stop suppressing deviant behaviors (**inhibitory/disinhibitory effect**); and we learn to engage in behaviors similar but not identical to the model's behavior (**eliciting effect**; Table 4.3).

> **Modeling effect:** The type of imitative behavior that involves learning a novel response.
>
> **Inhibitory/disinhibitory effect:** The type of imitative behavior that results either in the suppression (inhibition) or appearance (disinhibition) of previously acquired deviant behavior.
>
> **Eliciting effect:** Imitative behavior in which the observer does not copy the model's responses but simply behaves in a related manner.

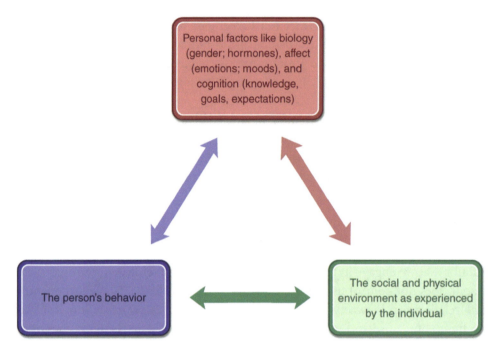

Figure 4.12   Bandura's notion of triadic reciprocal determinism. Behavior, the person, and the environment all mutually influence and change each other

Table 4.3   Three Effects of Imitation: Bandura's Theory

Type of Effect	Description	Illustration
Modeling Effect	Acquiring a new behavior as a result of observing a model.	After watching a mixed martial arts program, Jenna tries out a few novel moves on her young brother, Liam.
Inhibitory-Disinhibitory Effect	Stopping or starting some deviant behavior after seeing a model punished or rewarded for similar behavior.	After watching Jenna, Nora, who already knew all of Jenna's moves but hadn't used them in a long time, now tries a few of them on her sister (disinhibitory effect). Nora abandons her pummeling of her sister when Liam's mother responds to his wailing and takes Jenna's smartphone away (inhibitory effect).
Eliciting Effect	Engaging in behavior related to that of a model.	Robin tries to learn to play the guitar after her cousin is applauded for singing at the family reunion.

Humans as Agents of Their Own Behaviors

Some of our behaviors, such as our classically conditioned fears, are under the control of stimuli. Others, like our highly reinforced imitations, are controlled more by their consequences. ⌞A⌟ third group of behaviors are controlled by cognitive activities such as thinking and imagining. Bandura labels these three behavior control systems *stimulus control, outcome control*, and *symbolic control*.

In the end, although stimuli and outcomes might affect our behaviors, it is the symbolic control system that is most important in Bandura's description. We are not simply pawns pushed hither and yon by rewards and punishments and classically conditioned reflexes. We are in charge, Bandura (2001) insists: We are agents of our own actions.

Being agents of our own actions requires three things: First, it requires *intentionality.* If someone bumps into you, causing you to spill your latte on your friend, you would not be considered an agent of *that* action. But if you deliberately threw your coffee at said friend, you would be the agent of *that* action. Second, intentionality implies *forethought.* It is the ability to symbolize that allows you to foresee the consequences of the actions you intend. You could not intend to amuse your friend with your behavior unless you could foresee the effects of tossing your coffee. Finally, being agents of our actions implies being able to reflect on them and to reflect on ourselves and especially on our own effectiveness—on our **self-efficacy**. Self-efficacy is a very important concept in human motivation. Our estimates of our personal effectiveness, of our likelihood of success, have a lot to do with what we choose to do and how much effort we are willing to expend doing it.

> **Self-efficacy:** Judgments we make about how effective we are in given situations.

What Does the Bible Say?

⌐God created humans in his image (Genesis 1:26). Unlike animals, which act mainly on instinct, we resemble our Creator in our capacity to display such qualities as planning and reasoning as well as love and justice. And like our Creator, we have free will. We have the capacity to make choices and have those choices direct our path. While we have free will, we are also impacted by how we spend our time and with whom we spend it. When we make choices to engage in unhealthy behaviors, broadly defined, those behaviors can impact our unconscious learning through operant and classical conditioning. While one can argue that those behaviors are often reflexive and perhaps outside or our conscious control, too often it was a conscious decision to put ourselves in the position to be influenced by those variables. For example, if you were on a diet and making an effort to eat healthy and then went to an all-you-can-eat buffet and ended up overeating, and overeating especially unhealthy food, you couldn't argue that it was simply a reflexive response to powerful stimuli. Part of our free will is acknowledging the limitations around our self-control and, as such, staying far away from temptation.

1 Corinthians 10:13 ESV

"No temptation has overtaken you that is not common to man. God is faithful, and he will not let you be tempted beyond your ability, but with the temptation he will also provide the way of escape, that you may be able to endure it."

Romans 12:2 ESV

"Do not be conformed to this world, but be transformed by the renewal of your mind, that by testing you may discern what is the will of God, what is good and acceptable and perfect."

Romans 8:5-6 ESV

"For those who live according to the flesh set their minds on the things of the flesh, but those who live according to the Spirit set their minds on the things of the Spirit. For to set the mind on the flesh is death, but to set the mind on the Spirit is life and peace."

Colossians 3:2 ESV

"Set your minds on things that are above, not on things that are on earth."⌐

PRACTICAL APPLICATIONS OF LEARNING PRINCIPLES

There are countless, every day, intuitive applications of classical and operant conditioning principles and of Bandura's social-cognitive theory. People are controlled and manipulated by organizations and by other people, sometimes quite unconsciously—although often consciously as well. Performers' behaviors are shaped by the responses of their audience; the behavior of teachers is shaped by the responses of their students; consumers' behaviors are affected by advertising media; models are used to influence consumers; drug addicts are reinforced by the effects of the drugs they take. Even criminals are reinforced by the outcomes of their behaviors.

Applications of Behaviorism

Findings in behaviorism have led to the development of a variety of practical applications in fields such as education and psychotherapy. For example, many teachers use systematic reinforcement programs to foster learning or to prevent or correct deviant behavior.

General instructional recommendations that derive from conditioning principles suggest that teachers should:

1. Try to maximize pleasant unconditioned stimuli in their classrooms. This might involve making sure learners are comfortable, that surroundings are colorful and upbeat, and that no individual is faced with overwhelming demands. At the same time, teachers need to minimize the unpleasant aspects of being a student to reduce the number and potency of negative unconditioned stimuli in the classroom.
2. Use punishment—especially corporal punishment—sparingly as it is not very effective for eliminating undesirable behavior and even less effective for teaching desirable behavior.
3. Be aware of what is being paired with what in the classroom, so as not to inadvertently condition undesirable behaviors. If the teacher smiles when Johnny does something outrageous—or if his classmates all laugh—doing outrageous things may well be what Johnny learns.
4. Limit the use of repetition without reinforcement; it does little to improve learning.
5. Emphasize positive rather than aversive methods of control.

The systematic application of learning principles to change behavior is labeled **behavior modification**. Behavior modification is widely used in schools and institutions for children with behavioral and emotional problems, as well as in the treatment of mental disorders. Essentially, it involves the deliberate and systematic use of reinforcement, and sometimes punishment, to modify behavior.

> **Behavior modification:**
> Systematic application of learning principles to change behavior.

Applications of Cognitivism

Cognitivism typically views the learner as an active, information-processing being, capable of imagining and anticipating the consequences of behavior, and essentially responsible for his or her own actions, as well as for *constructing* his or her own view of the world. This orientation lends itself especially well to **discovery learning**. This is a learner-centered approach where content is not organized by the teacher and presented in a relatively final form. Instead, learners are

> **Discovery learning:**
> A learner-centered approach to teaching in which the acquisition of new knowledge comes about largely through the learner's own efforts.

expected to investigate and discover for themselves, and to *construct* their own mental representations—hence the current expression for discovery and other related approaches, widely used in educational circles: **constructivism**.

A cognitive view of the learner also supports approaches designed not so much to teach students specific content, but more to teach them *how* to learn—to make self-regulated learners of them. To this end, cognitively oriented educational psychologists suggest that teachers should develop problem-solving skills in students—for example, by giving them practice with the five-step strategy for general problem solving suggested by Bransford and Stein (1993). The five steps are easily remembered with the acronym IDEAL:

> **Constructivism:** A general term for student-centered approaches to teaching, such as discovery-oriented approaches, reciprocal learning, or cooperative instruction—so called because of their assumption that learners should build (construct) knowledge for themselves.

1. Identify problems and opportunities.
2. Define goals and represent the problem.
3. Explore possible strategies.
4. Anticipate outcomes and act.
5. Look back and learn.

There are a wide variety of specific, cognitively based approaches to teaching, including **reciprocal teaching**, a method designed to improve reading comprehension, and **cognitive apprenticeship**, where novice learners are paired with older learners, teachers, or parents who serve as mentors and guides. There are also various programs designed to develop cognitive strategies, as well as to help learners become aware of their own use of cognitive strategies, to reflect on them, to evaluate their effectiveness, and to change them as needed.

> **Reciprocal teaching:** A method designed to improve reading comprehension.
>
> **Cognitive apprenticeship:** Novice learners are paired with older learners, teachers, or parents who serve as mentors and guides.

MEMORY AND INTELLIGENCE

Of all the mental processing abilities covered in cognitive psychology, perhaps the single most important processing ability is attention. Information is thought to move from the environment or from the deep recesses of our memory to our current consciousness by means of attention. Thus, attention is thought to be an early process in the stepwise progression of information processing. However, how can attention be an early decision-making process if the factors that influence what we decide to attend to reside in our memory (i.e., a subsequent mental process). This is the fundamental paradox of attention. Intelligence tests rely on attention as a key index of cognitive ability.

ATTENTION

Despite our difficulties in fully understanding or even defining attention, research shows that people with well-developed attention tend to be more successful (with all other factors being equal); in contrast, a lack of attention is considered to be the single most significant predictor of academic difficulty. Some scientists suggest that video games and modern television shows negatively impact the development of attention. It is thought that because these activities place such limited demands on attention that this cognitive skill fails to mature and improve. If there is a high level of playing or viewing across development, it may permanently impair attention.

Attention is the somewhat illusive process that enables people to actively select certain information for further (i.e., more elaborate) processing. Generally, attention has been conceptualized as a state of concentrating on something (focalization of consciousness) or as a finite processing capacity that can be allocated in a variety of ways. Contemporary models of attention tend to fall into two general categories:

> **Attention**: A concentrated mental effort that functions as a filter to ignore unimportant events and focus on important events.

- Theories that view attention as a causal mechanism, which distinguish between automatic and controlled processes.
- Theories that see attention as a consequence of other processes, like priming activities for some memory.

Attention can also be divided based upon the task performed. For example, divided attention or multitasking occurs when two or more separate tasks or mental operations are performed simultaneously. On the other hand, focused attention or selective attention occurs in situations when one information source must be attended to at the exclusion of others; that is, paying attention to one stimulus while simultaneously ignoring others. Considering how busy and complex our lives are and because of technology's near constant infringement on our attention resources, we rarely have the opportunity to selectively attend to a particular activity, even despite our best efforts. Even when we do attempt to focus our attention, we are almost always functioning at the very line that separates focused from divided attention.

Cognitive overload is an old problem with a new name. Cognitive overload occurs when excessive demands are placed on particular cognitive processes, especially attention and memory. As people try to multitask, their cognitive resources get "stretched" to their maximum ability, which interferes with performance as well as results in more rapid fatigue. Multitasking also requires cognitive shifts from one source or activity to another. With each shift in attention, there is a loss of attention and cognitive momentum (i.e., time and energy). Repeated shifts can result in slowed processing time and increased error rates.

> **Cognitive overload**: The amount of working memory resources dedicated to a specific task with the idea that there is a limit to the amount of processing load the brain can manage.

Of course, multitasking is not always bad. It would be impossible to safely drive a car without being able to rapidly shift one's attention from one view to another (e.g., front view and side and rearview mirrors) or from one activity to another (e.g., like moving one's foot from the gas to the break while simultaneously depressing the clutch and switching gears). Lastly, multitasking allows us to constantly monitor our environment and switch our attention from less important to more important stimuli and tasks.

Factors Influencing Attention

Selective attention is influenced by a variety of factors. That is, our attention is more easily divided by the following:

1. **The number of sources:** As the number of sources increase, focused attention becomes more difficult to maintain. For example, having email, instant messenger, a photo editor, a music player, and an Internet browser open and active on a computer desktop simultaneously will certainly decrease your ability to effectively and efficiently carry out any single activity. The most effective way to work is to focus on one activity at a time (e.g., only reading/responding to email twice a day).

2. **The similarity of sources:** Attention is impacted significantly by competition, and the more similar the stimuli are the more divided one's attention will be. For example, listening to the news while washing dishes is certainly a lot easier than trying to listen to the news while talking on the phone. Similarly, trying to study/read is negatively impacted by music with high lyrical content but not by instrumental music. Further, trying to write a paper or report is negatively impacted by such activities as watching a movie or talking with a friend. It is impossible to carry out both activities successfully.

3. **The complexity of the tasks:** As the task becomes increasingly more complex, it demands more and more attention. These more demanding tasks also cause attention governing resources to fatigue faster. For example, when driving in a new location during bad road conditions, as is the case during a terrible rain storm, people tend to sit up straighter in their seats, turn off any music, and ask passengers to be quite. Clearly, those other activities aren't going to change the weather or make the directions any clearer. However, they enable a conscientious driver to pay more attention to the road. Further, activities like talking on the phone while driving are particularly bad as both talking and driving are complex tasks. Having an in-depth phone conversation negatively impacts attention (and reaction time).

4. **Automaticity:** As procedural tasks, like riding a bike, playing an instrument, or throwing a baseball, become more and more practiced, they require less and less attention. While complex procedural tasks may demand all of one's attention initially, over time, highly rehearsed tasks become easier and easier to do until such tasks require virtually no attention. This is why we can play the guitar or piano and sing at the same time or even perform complex surgical procedures while listening to music or talking with a nurse.

MEMORY

The Basics of Memory

Everything we are, in our conscious experience, is dependent upon memory. Without memory we would live in a constant state of rediscovery, whereby every instance would be newly learned, even if the instance had occurred several hundred times. And thus, the question of who we are could plausibly be answered differently each day. **Memory** is simply a process of encoding, storing, and retrieving pieces of information. Each stage in the memory process in important for the accuracy and the ability to retrieve the information later. Colloquially, we refer to the information itself as a "memory." The ability to bring that particular memory into my cognitive awareness depends on encoding, storage, and retrieval.

> **Memory:** The process of encoding, storage, and retrieval of any piece of information obtained through conscious experience; a memory can also be an individual instance of encoded, stored, and retrieved information.

To illustrate the process of memory, imagine that you are a scientist conducting interviews for your research on the long-term effects of watching too much reality television. As a scientist, you need a lot of data! Another name for data is simply *information*. As participants come to your experiment they are handed a questionnaire that asks various questions about how often they watch reality television. Now, the questions on the questionnaire are very important for real scientists, but the limiting of questions also draws a nice parallel with the process of encoding.

There is a finite but unimaginably large amount of information that can be gathered and stored in the human mind, just as there are an almost infinite number of questions a scientist can ask about reality television. However, as humans, and as scientists, we must pick the most important information and change it to a form we can use. For example, if I ask a question such as, "Do you enjoy reality television?" participants may write things such as "absolutely!," or "No, it is the bane of human existence." These are informative, but I need numbers in order to analyze the data. So, we must transform the information into a useful form that can be stored. The process of **encoding** changes information into a form that can be used later, perhaps during some important task.

© Andrey_Popov/Shutterstock.com

After encoding occurs, the information must then be stored in the mind. This component of the memory process is titled **storage**. For the psychologists studying reality television, these data may be stored on a flash drive, or as copies in a ⌊computer.⌋ The organization of how these files (memories) are stored is important for the last step: retrieval.

Retrieval occurs when we pull some of the information stored in memory back to conscious awareness. For the psychologists this would be like taking data from ⌊an Internet/cloud-based storage system, analyzing that information, and then writing a report based on that data.⌋ For example, if someone asks you about your third grade teacher, the memories for this period of your life are most likely not active in conscious awareness. Rather, they must be retrieved from storage.

> **Encoding:** The process of transforming experienced information into a form that can be later stored and used by the brain.

> **Storage:** The process of storing.

> **Retrieval:** The process of recognizing and then correctly recalling a piece of information from storage in long-term memory.

> **Sensory memory:** A form of memory that holds large amounts of sensory information such as sights and sounds for a very brief amount of time, normally only a few seconds.

Memory Structures (STM- WM and LTM)

So far, we have discussed the process of encoding → storage → retrieval to illustrate how information gets to conscious awareness. However, this process is a little more complicated. To begin, there are three basic types of memory, not just one as we have discussed thus far. The stage model of memory suggests the process of encoding → storage → retrieval is integrated into these three different levels of memory. These levels are sensory memory, short-term memory, and long-term memory.

Sensory memory is a very short duration type of memory that helps construct a continuous perceptual world rather than thousands of isolated segments. We have different types of sensory memory for the different senses humans possess. For example, sensory memory for vision is also called iconic memory,

© issaro prakalung/Shutterstock.com

F	T	C	Q
G	B	O	J
W	K	R	S

Figure 4.13   Example stimulus shown to participants in Sperling's classic 1960 study.

whereas sensory memory for audition is sometimes called echoic memory. The duration and capacity of sensory memory were partly discovered by a series of interesting experiments conducted by George Sperling (Sperling, 1960).

In his experiments, Sperling briefly presented participants with a display consisting of rows of letters similar to Figure 4.13. Each display was visible for 1/20 of 1 second, and was followed by a short duration of time—no more than 1 second. After this short duration, the participants would hear a low-, medium-, or high-pitched tone indicating that they should try to recall their visual memory for either the bottom, medium, or top row of letters.

In his classic experiment, Sperling discovered after about 1/3 of 1 second, participants were unable to recall letters in the rows. This demonstrated sensory memory may have a large capacity, but its duration is quite limited (e.g., 1/3 second). Years of research after Sperling's study have demonstrated sensory memory's capacity is quite large, but its duration ranges from 1/4 to only a few seconds.

Unlike other types of memory we discuss in the sections to follow, sensory memory cannot be retained for a longer duration through the process of rehearsal (e.g., studying). Instead, sensory memory seems to happen automatically, without awareness, and is very difficult to manipulate through psychological techniques. Further, sensory memory captures a very large amount of information. This information must be selected and sent to conscious awareness. In order to send certain pieces of sensory information to conscious awareness, we must focus—pay attention to—that specific information. Thus, attention is the gateway from sensory memory to conscious awareness.

The conscious awareness we have been discussing to this point is more formally termed **short-term memory**, at least for those of us who study human memory processes. Another term for short-term memory is "**working memory**." The name "working memory" illustrates qualities of this memory stage by point to its global function, rather than simply its duration relative to long-term memory.

Short-term, or working, memory can be imagined as a desktop on which you do homework. A desk is only a certain size; therefore, the capacity of books, papers, pencils, and so forth that can be held on

Short-term memory: A type of temporary memory used to hold information long enough for an individual to process it, and make sense of it; also called *working memory*.

Working memory: The Baddeley model describing how information is processed in short-term memory by means of a control system (central executive system) and systems that maintain verbal material (phonological loop) and visual material (visual-spatial sketch pad).

Row 1	1 6 7 9 7 1
Row 2	2 7 7 2 4 2 5
Row 3	3 7 4 2 9 7 8 3
Row 4	4 2 7 9 4 6 3 5 9

Figure 4.14   Sample stimulus used to test a person's short-term memory capacity.

the desk is quite certainly limited. ⌊Short-term⌋ memory has a limited capacity. For example, try this on your friend or roommate: Take a look at Figure 4.14 containing various numbers of digits. Beginning at Row 1 and, moving from left to right, read aloud one digit per second until you reach the end of the row. After stating the digits, ask your "participant" to repeat back that number of digits. This is a simple test of short-term memory.

Research conducted by George Miller (1956) demonstrated the same pattern your participant will probably demonstrate: that accuracy of recalling the string of digits decreases as more digits are added (going from Row 1 to Row 4). To be specific, Miller discovered humans have a short-term memory capacity of approximately seven plus or minus two items. So, we seem to be capable of holding five to nine different items for a short amount of time. Contemporary research has examined this "magic number seven" idea more carefully. The results of highly controlled studies seem to suggest that short-term memory actually has a smaller capacity: four plus or minus one (Cowan, 2001, 2010).

Short-term memory also has a limited duration, as does sensory memory. However, the duration for short-term memory is much longer ⌊but still surprisingly short.⌋ On average, the amount of time a piece of information will remain in short-term memory—without rehearsal—is 20 seconds. The "without rehearsal" piece of this statement is very important. By using different rehearsal techniques people can retain information in short-term memory for much longer.

Until this point in the chapter, we have discussed short-term memory as though it is a singular unit. However, research by Alan Baddeley led to the formulation of the Baddeley working memory model of short-term memory (Figure 4.15). According to Baddeley, short-term memory is divided into three components: the visuospatial sketchpad, the phonological loop, and the central executive. The **visuospatial sketchpad** is specialized to process visual and spatial information, as the name implies. For example, if you ask a veteran student where a certain building is located on campus, the student may provide verbal instructions on where to go. As you hear the verbal instructions, you may be creating a mental map of where to go. This spatial organization of a campus's layout on your small mental "desktop" is performed, according to Baddeley, using the visuospatial sketchpad.

The verbal instructions provided by the veteran student are processed by the **phonological loop**, which is specialized for auditory and verbal information. This is also the part of short-term memory assumed to be used during most traditional memory tasks, such as remembering word lists. The **central executive** of short-term memory acts as a type of CEO. It organizes and integrates the specialized processing of the visuospatial sketchpad and phonological loop prior to encoding the information into long-term memory. The central executive also plays a key role in dictating when retrieval from long-term memory will occur, and which information will be retrieved.

Once information is in short-term memory after leaving sensory memory, it has the potential to become stored in long-term memory. Encoding, as mentioned earlier, helps move information from its temporary state in short-term memory to a much longer lasting state in long-term memory. This process is also sometimes called **rehearsal**. There are two main types of rehearsal that can be used to get information into long-term memory—they are called maintenance rehearsal

Visuospatial sketchpad: A part of Alan Baddeley's working memory model specialized to process visual and spatial information.

Phonological loop: A part of Alan Baddeley's working memory model specialized to process verbal and auditory information.

Central executive: A part of Alan Baddeley's working memory model responsible for coordinating the input and output of information to working memory, as well as to integrate the separate pieces of information from the visuospatial sketchpad and phonological loop; the "CEO" of working memory.

Rehearsal: The process of repeatedly introducing new information in order to retain the information in short-term memory, or to introduce into long-term memory.

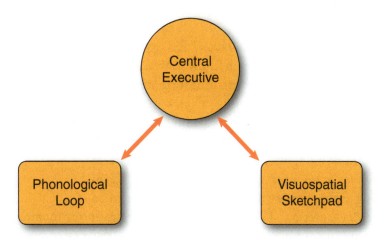

Figure 4.15   Baddeley's working memory model.

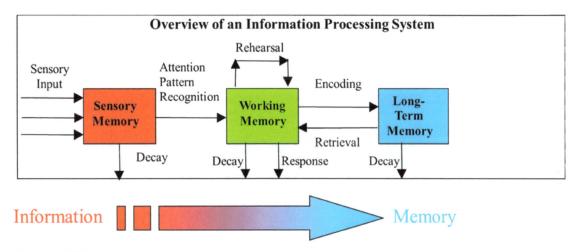

Figure 4.16

Source: Brian Kelley

and elaborative rehearsal. **Maintenance rehearsal** is a very shallow level of processing. A good example of maintenance rehearsal is simply rote memorization, or saying a phone number over and over again to yourself.

Elaborative rehearsal is a much deeper level of processing that is more effective at storing information into long-term memory. Elaborative processing works by trying to create connections between the newly acquired information and existing information already present in long-term memory. For example, if you were using elaborative rehearsal to try and remember classical conditioning, you might think about the temporal layout of the process of classical conditioning. You might also think of several examples of classical conditioning from your own life, and you might try to imagine new situations to which classical conditioning could be applied. All of these events use already-existing information in long-term memory in order to more efficiently encode new information into long-term memory.

Maintenance rehearsal: A relatively shallow level of rehearsal typically characterized by repeating something many times (e.g., repeating a phone number in your head).

Elaborative rehearsal: A type of rehearsal in which a person actively tries to tie new information to pre-existing information already in long-term memory. The net effect is to increase the likelihood that the new information is retained in long-term memory.

Long-Term Memory (And Application)

Who is your favorite childhood cartoon character? Do you remember what classical conditioning is? What happened at your 16th birthday? Do you know how to ride a bicycle? If you can answer these questions, you are successfully retrieving appropriate information from your **long-term memory system.** Later in this chapter we see how these questions require you to find sources from different types of long-term memory. Successfully encoded memories, partly through rehearsals, transition from working memory to a much longer-term storage capacity known as long-term memory. Unlike short-term (working) memory, long-term memory allows the information to be

> **Long-term memory:** One of the human memory systems that can store information for a long-period of time.

retrieved at longer delays (Anderson, 1990). Thus, in theory, long-term memory can store an infinite amount of information as long as we want. Then, we can retrieve the content any time we want. In reality, however, our long-term memory system is not perfect.

Likewise, long-term memories seem to have several subtypes. Atkinson and Shiffrin (1968) were among the first researchers to argue for diverse long-term memory types. Later, numerous lab studies (e.g., Jacoby et al., 1993; Schacter & Tulving, 1994) successfully differentiated between at least 3 and 4 long-term memory systems (Figure 4.17).

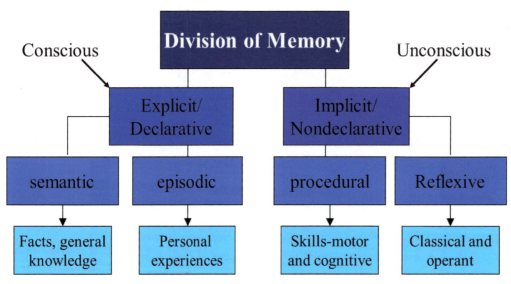

Figure 4.17 ⌊Different types of long-term memory.⌋

Source: Brian Kelley

EXPLICIT MEMORY

Explicit memory is conscious recollection of facts or experiences (Graf & Schacter, 1985). It requires you to consciously think about general knowledge about this world and specific concepts (semantic memory), or may involve your conscious access to your personal

> **Explicit memory:** A type of long-term memory; conscious memory about facts or experiences.

experiences that took place at a specific time in a certain place (episodic memory). It is possible for you to have semantic memory of camping (e.g., an outdoor activity in the forest) by learning its definition but if you have never camped, you will not have episodic memory. For some of you, it is possible to have experienced camping before reading it in a book. You might remember one summer night when you were sitting by a bonfire making s'mores with your cousins at a camping site. In this case, you have built your episodic memory first and have gained knowledge about what camping is (semantic memory) based on that experience (Figure 4.18).

Semantic memory is similar to a reservoir of facts and knowledge about this world. It shows how words, concepts, languages (e.g., verbal symbols), and their relations are woven together to provide an understanding of facts (Tulving, 1972). **Episodic memory** enables us to remember, "a specific moment in one's personal past and consciously recollects some prior episode or state" (Wheeler et al., 1997, p. 333). Semantic and episodic memories are conceptually distinct, and recent brain-damaged patients are providing more vivid evidence supporting the differences between the two memory systems. Episodic memory seems to be more vulnerable to neuronal deterioration and showed a greater severity in anterograde amnesia (failure to form new memories since the onset of the damage-inducing event) than semantic memory (Tulving, 2002). In addition, these two memory systems seem to be processed in different brain areas. Episodic memory depends on the hippocampal area, whereas semantic memory is primarily concentrated in the underlying cortices (Vargha-Khadem et al., 1997).

> **Semantic memory:** A type of long-term memory (explicit memory, to be exact); it is one's general knowledge about the world and specific concepts.
>
> **Episodic memory:** A type of long-term memory (explicit memory, to be exact); conscious recollection of one's personal experiences that took place at a specific time in a certain place.

Figure 4.18   ⌐An example of an episodic memory about camping.⌐
© Olesia Bilkei/Shutterstock.com

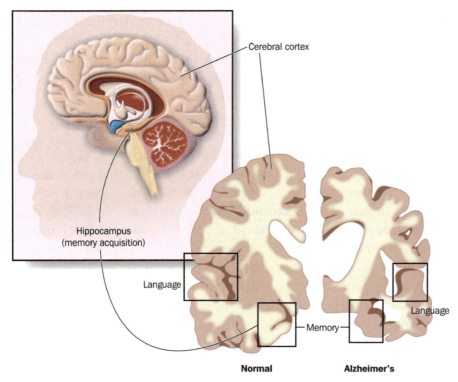

Figure 4.19   Hippocampus area.

© Blamb/Shutterstock.com

Figure 4.20   Semantic (left) vs. procedural (right) memory.

Image on left: © studioVin/Shutterstock.com, right: © Tribalium/Shutterstock.com

IMPLICIT MEMORY

Unlike explicit memory, **implicit memory** is unconsciously accessible, and it is generally easier to demonstrate or perform this memory than to explain it. Imagine you have to teach someone how to tie a knot only by words. It will be much easier to teach someone by showing your performance. In other words, implicit memory is shown when "performance on a task is facilitated in the absence of conscious recollection" (Graf & Schacter, 1985, p. 501). One type of implicit memory is known as procedural memory, which involves learning of motor and cognitive skills (Schacter et al., 2000). In the next section, we discuss procedural memory and some evidence that supports the difference between procedural and semantic memory systems.

> **Implicit memory:** A type of long-term memory; memory about how to perform a task (usually accessed unconsciously).

What Memory Researchers Learned from H. M.

"Right now I'm wondering, have I done or said anything amiss? You see, at this moment everything looks unclear to me, but what happened just before? That's what worries me. It's like waking from a dream; I just don't remember. Every day is alone in itself, whatever enjoyment I've had, and whatever sorrow I've had."

—Henry Gustav Molaison, aka H. M. (1926–2008)

Amnesia patient H. M. is one of the most famous patients in memory research. At the age of 10 H. M. started having minor seizures and by 16 he was having so many epileptic seizures that they began to seriously debilitate him. H. M. ended up receiving brain surgery that included bilateral removal of the hippocampus and part of the temporal lobes in treatment of seizures (Corkin, 1984).

After the surgery, H. M. maintained a normal I.Q. score and digit span, and was able to carry out a normal conversation (Scoville & Milner, 1957). However, just a few minutes after speaking with someone, he had no memory of having a conversation. H. M. seemed to have lost the ability to transfer information into long-term memory. Despite serious anterograde amnesia (lack of ability to remember after the amnesia-inducing events such as brain surgery or brain damage) related to explicit memory, H. M. still preserved the ability to learn procedural memory. For example, H. M. was given instructions to learn a star-tracing task (tracing an outline of a star) only by using a reflection in the mirror. He showed a typical normal learning curve (getting better after 3–4 sessions) and therefore demonstrated his procedural memory. However, he had no conscious recollection of having ever learned the task before (Milner, 1970). Case studies with H. M. greatly advanced our understanding of the difference between short-term and long-term memory, as well as the difference between explicit and implicit (procedural, to be exact) memory systems. We now know, and we owe this to H. M., the importance of the hippocampal area and the medial temporal lobe as long-term memory consolidation places.

As shown by H. M., amnesia patients and other brain-damaged patients suffer from different kinds of memory loss. However, memory loss is not always a neurological concern but a truly natural event that occurs to healthy normal people.

Forgetting

One can argue that we have limited storage and when we learn new things, old things have to be deleted (forgotten) to make room for the new materials. Others might think (e.g., Freud) we forget things because certain memories are too big of a threat to our reality identity. Though there are many different ways to argue why we forget, here we will look at the interference theory.

INTERFERENCE THEORY

Interference theory is currently the dominating theory to explain forgetting (Eysenck & Keane, 2005). First, interference can happen because new materials are competing with something you used to know and interferes with the old information. This is known as **retroactive interference**, a "disruption of memory by learning other material during the retention interval" (Eysenck & Keane, 2005, p. 563). You can think of this as an overwriting model. New information writes over what you had known previously and interferes with old materials.

Interference can happen in an opposite way. Old materials can compete with new things we are trying to learn. This type of interference is known as **proactive interference**, a "disruption of memory by previous learning, often of similar materials" (Eysenck & Keane, 2005, p.564). We can understand this as a force-of-habit model. For example, your email portal regularly requests you change your password for security purposes. Next time you log on to your email you might type in your old password and make an error. Old information has become a habit and interferes with the new material.

> **Interference theory:** A theory of forgetting which suggests most forgetting is the result of an interaction between new and previously learned information, leading either to a failure to learn new material, or a forgetting of past material.
>
> **Retroactive interference:** A theory of forgetting in which more recent information gets in the way of trying to recall older information.
>
> **Proactive interference:** This is when old information prevents the formation or recall of newer information.

Why does it happen? One possible explanation is retrieval cue competition between target words (the words that you are asked to remember) and similar nontarget words (distractor words that are similar to the target words, but that you are not asked to remember; Lustig & Hasher, 2001). When target information is not consolidated, seemingly similar targets can compete and result in interference at a retrieval cue. In this context, (memory) consolidation is "the process lasting for several hours or possible even days which fixes information in long-term memory" (Eysenck & Keane, 2005, p. 225).

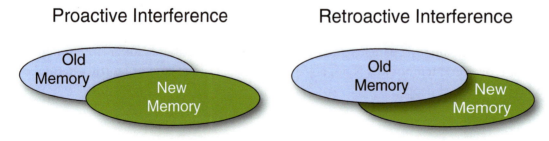

Figure 4.21   Proactive (left) and retroactive (right) interference.

In our lives, however, interference is not the only obstacle for accurate memory recall. Think about a penny. Most of us have used a penny and would show a high confidence in our ability to accurately recall (or recognize) a penny. Contrary to our expectation, in Nickerson and Adams's (1979) study, most participants failed to identify the correct penny among 15 different versions of U.S. penny. This surprising result suggests there is little correlation between your confidence level and memory accuracy. If the accuracy of long-term memories does not measure up to our expectation, what makes us forget things so easily? There is no one absolute answer to this question, but we will review a few characteristics of our long-term memory.

Seven Deadly Sins of Memory

Schacter (1999) discussed the forgetful nature of our long-term memory with following seven characteristics.

1. **Absent-mindedness:** This refers to the breakage between your memory and your attention. Attention is required to encode the information accurately, and inattention will lead to a failure of proper encoding. This can sometimes happen due to distractions, and if it happens, you may have to repeat the same task. For example, let's think about our absent-minded professor Dr. Jones. While talking to a friend on her cellphone, Dr. Jones complains how her memory has gotten worse lately. Dr. Jones then says, "For example, at this very moment, I can't even remember where I put my cell phone!" forgetting she was using the exact device she "misplaced." This illustrates the concept of absent-mindedness.

2. **Transience:** Despite our effort, memory tends to diminish quickly. It describes the temporal nature of our memory. Rehearsal or repeat can be useful in overcoming transience.

3. **Blocking:** Blocking is also known as the tip-of-the-tongue phenomenon—when you feel and try to remember things but cannot articulate it. It happens because of the inaccessibility of stored information. If you want to try this yourself, pull out a piece of paper and write down the names of the seven dwarves from the story of Snow White. Can you remember all of their names? If you can picture their faces and feel you know their names but just can't articulate them, you are experiencing the tip-of-the-tongue phenomenon!

4. **Misattribution:** This refers to the confusion of the original source of information. You might have a general scheme of an event, but have difficulty remembering when and where it had happened. You might remember Tim as the person who borrowed a book from you a year ago, when in fact it was Paul.

5. **Suggestibility:** Due to the constructive nature of our memory system, leading words or suggestions from others can alter and bias our memory. See the section on memory reconstruction for further information on suggestibility.

6. **Bias:** Current personal experiences or events can cloud how we remember similar events that happened in the past.

7. **Persistence:** According to Schacter, negative events tend to linger longer than neutral or positive memories. Other studies have shown better memory for emotionally (any emotions) intense information (Ashcraft & Radvansky, 2010).

Memory Reconstruction

Human memory is a fascinating construct though it has several limitations such as the seven weaknesses we have just reviewed. Long-term memory is malleable; it can be surprisingly easy to implant a new memory or alter one's existing memory. In a series of studies, Loftus and colleagues provided strong evidence that the human memory system does not work as a recording device but rather is susceptible

Figure 4.22   Car accidents and estimated speed. How fast were the cars going when they bumped (smashed) into each other ... ?

© Photo Spirit/Shutterstock.com

to changes. In one study, Loftus and Palmer (1974) showed a short video describing a car accident to participants. Later she asked the participants to estimate the speed of the cars by using leading verbs such as, "How fast were the cars going when they contacted (in other conditions, the word "contacted" was replaced by *hit, bumped into, collided with, smashed into* each other?" The results showed that participants' memory about the speed of cars systematically increased in relation to the severity of the leading verb. For example, if the lead word was "smashed," the estimated speed was a little over 40 mph. On the other hand, when "contacted" was used as the lead word, the estimated speed was around 31 mph.

Additionally, Loftus (1975) found implanting a new false memory was not as difficult as one might think. She used a similar paradigm as in her previous study and showed another short video involving a car accident. Later Loftus asked one group of participants, "How fast was the white sports car going when it passed the barn while traveling along the country road?" There was no barn shown in the film. The other group received the same question without the leading word ("How fast was the white sports car going while traveling along the country road?"). Participants were brought back to the lab a week later and were asked whether they remember seeing a barn in the film. Surprisingly, 17% of the participants in the leading-word condition answered that they saw a barn. These results show the long-term memory system may not be as accurate as we wish and can be changed by a simple leading question.

What would happen if we apply memory reconstruction to eyewitness testimony? Since eyewitness testimonies are so critical in legal procedures (either false or true), would witnesses' long-term memory be free from this reconstructive nature? Unfortunately, study results imply the answer is no. This bias worsened when there was a weapon involved in the crime scene (Loftus, 1979). The unexpectedness of the crime and the brevity of the scene with the combination of a life-threatening weapon seemed to consume most of the victim's attention. As a result, victims showed poorer memory recall (or recognition) for other important details.

Long-Lasting Memories

As we have seen so far, long-term memories are not perfect. However, there seem to be special events immune from forgetting. For example, people still vividly recall the 9/11 terrorist attack, the Sandy Hook elementary shooting, ⌐the Paris attacks, Paul Walker's car accident, and Kobe Bryant helicopter crash, because all ⌐ were very emotional and had an impact in our lives to a certain degree. Memories formed by "very important, dramatic, and surprising public or personal events" are known as **flashbulb memories** (Eysenck & Keane, 2005, p. 272). For example, people tend to remember clearly when they heard the news, where they were, how they felt at the time, and whom they were with. In addition, due to the nature of the events, flashbulb memories are frequently rehearsed and have personal importance (Conway et al., 1994).

> **Flashbulb memories:** A type of long-term memory. Memories formed by dramatic and surprising public or personal events; typically known to be immune from forgetting.

Flashbulb memories are typically long lasting, precise, and accurate (Brown & Kulik, 1977). It seems people have surprisingly accurate time-stamped memory for certain events. It is therefore quite natural to be curious why flashbulb memories are exceptionally resistant to forgetting. To examine the mechanism behind flashbulb memory, Conway et al. (1994) asked U.K. and non-U.K. groups their memory about Margaret Thatcher's (a former Prime Minister of the United Kingdom from 1979 to 1990) resignation. At the time of the study, her resignation was quite unexpected and considered historic by most British people. Both U.K. and non-U.K. groups were tested three to four times (within 10 days of the resignation, 14 days, around 350 days; a small group was tested again after 26 months of the resignation) for the flashbulb memory formation. If flashbulb memories are similar to any other types of long-term memory, people should show a typical forgetting curve and not be able to retain many concrete details about the event. Contrary, Conway's result showed that 86% of U.K. group showed very detailed memories about Thatcher's resignation even after 26 months; only 29% of the non-U.K. group showed the similar level of flashbulb memories.

The differences between U.K. and non-U.K. groups hint at the critical role of prior knowledge and rehearsal in flashbulb memory. U.K. participants who would have had more interest about Thatcher would be more likely to talk about the resignation frequently with their colleagues or family in their daily lives. In addition, her resignation received great media exposure, which made it easier for people to follow media reports (Conway et al., 1994) and give a greater chance for repeated encoding of the information.

Improving Memory

Based on what we have learned, what can we do to make the results benefit our own memory? Particularly, there are a few useful strategies for successful studying habits. Repeat the materials. As several studies showed, proper encoding and repetition help maintain the information for a longer period of time. In addition, when you repeat the materials, leave some space between your study sessions. New materials are more vulnerable to forgetting, so repeat the process to consolidate that information. Next, make the

© Ken Tannenbaum/Shutterstock.com

© Petr Kovalenkov/Shutterstock.com

© Ovidiu Hrubaru/Shutterstock.com

© Gina Jacobs/Shutterstock.com

Figure 4.23 ⌞9/11 attack (top left), Paris attacks (top right), Kobe Bryant (bottom left), and massacre at Sandy Hook Elementary School (bottom right).⌟

materials meaningful. Information that goes through elaborative rehearsal is processed deeply and more deeply processed information is typically remembered better (Craik & Lockhart, 1972). Lastly, minimize interference if possible. If you are studying two similar contents, leave ⌞sometime⌟ between the two rather than working on them back to back. Devising your own memory aid (mnemonic device) can be useful to retain the information for a long time.

INTELLIGENCE

Intelligence and intelligence testing has been one of the most studied and controversial constructs in the history of psychology (Wasserman, 2012). On the one hand, it has been extremely useful in identifying individual strengths and weaknesses by providing additional information on how to best teach struggling students. On the other hand, it has been used to segregate and label individuals that, in turn, has produced devastating effects. Because of this, many professionals have debated intelligence tests in relation to their use and misuse, which has led to an ongoing debate about their appropriateness. To make matters even more difficult, psychologists have not been able to agree on an operational definition of intelligence.

© metamorworks/Shutterstock.com

> **Intelligence:** The overall capacity to think and act logically and rationally within one's environment.

History and Development

To gain a better perspective on intelligence, it is important to understand its historical underpinnings. Although the concept of intelligence can be traced back thousands of years to ancient philosophers, it was not until the late 19th to early 20th centuries that intelligence was quantifiably measured. Moreover, there were different events that sparked an interest into the need for intelligence testing. The first event was the advent of compulsory schools (Fagan & Wise, 2007). Simply put, compulsory schools meant children were mandated to attend school. By having compulsory school laws, schools were flooded with both students with and without disabilities. For the first time, educational systems were responsible for educating all children. This mandate presented an opportunity to utilize intelligence testing to identify whether students needed special education services (Wasserman, 2012).

Due to the demand to educate all students, Alfred Binet designed a test to measure intelligence among children. Because of this, he is often referred to as the "father" of the intelligence tests (Foschi & Cicciola, 2006). Binet collaborated with Theodore Simon and created a scale for intelligence in 1905. Although Binet used his scale to delve deeper into his understanding of intelligence, the test was primarily used to identify and treat individuals who were experiencing difficulties within the educational system (Nicolas & Levine, 2012). That is, Binet and Simon's first test was used to identify whether children could be educated within the traditional confines of a school building. To better understand how such results were achieved, it is important to gain a better understanding of the construct of the test.

The Binet–Simon Scale was designed so that test items increased in level of difficulty related to age. As you can expect, a 10-year-old should be capable of completing more complex tasks than a

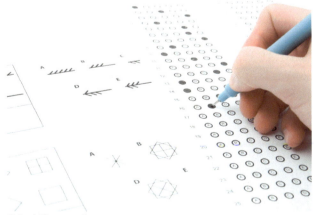

© Jirsak/Shutterstock.com

7-year-old. This is the genesis of the concept of mental age. A child's overall intelligence was calculated by dividing the child's mental age by chronological age and multiplying the results by 100. Here would be the mathematical calculation for the child:

$$7 \text{ (mental age)}/10 \text{ (chronological age)} \times 100 = 70 \text{ (IQ)}$$

Therefore, if students were demonstrating problem-solving abilities consistent with their chronological ages, they would be thought of as average intellect. Conversely, if a child was performing problem-solving abilities much lower than his or her chronological age (per the example above), they would have been thought of as intellectually inferior. Thus, the results of the test were used to give each student a classification describing the student's abilities and for making a determination as to the best placement for education. Currently, an IQ of 100 is considered average.

After the design of the Binet–Simon Scale, the popularity of intelligence tests began to rise due to the practicality of their use (Gottfredson & Saklofske, 2009). In 1910 Henry Goddard revised the Binet–Simon Scale for use within the United States. Also, in 1916 Lewis Terman (of Stanford University) revised and extended the work of Binet and Simon into adulthood to create the Stanford–Binet Intelligence Scale (Boake, 2002). One of the major changes made to the Binet–Simon Scale was that Terman introduced the term **intelligence quotient** (IQ) rather than using **mental age**. Within a few years, the Stanford–Binet Intelligence Scale was widely used throughout the United States. Currently, the Stanford-Binet Intelligence Scale is on its fifth revision and is viewed as one of the top intelligence tests used by practicing psychologists today. As mentioned, the

> **Intelligence quotient:** The global score derived from standardized intelligence tests.
>
> **Mental age:** The age given at which a child is currently performing intellectually.

practicality and popularity of intelligence tests created a lot of interest within the psychological field. This became particularly evident around the commencement of World War I.

Prior to World War I, the United States' military lacked preparedness (Wasserman, 2012). Thus, Robert Yerkes created a taskforce to extend the use of intelligence testing from strictly education into the military (Boake, 2002). Yerkes and colleagues created two group-administered intelligence tests: **Army Alpha** and **Army Beta**. Both intelligence tests were used to assess incoming soldiers on their ability to serve the military and move into leadership positions. The two tests differed, however, in that Army Beta was administered to those who were illiterate or had language-based deficiencies. The Army Alpha was administered to those that were literate. In sum, over 2,000,000 soldiers were evaluated; during this time, intelligence testing grew largely in popularity within educational and noneducational settings (Sattler, 2008).

> **Army Alpha:** The test given to literate military personnel to determine rank.
>
> **Army Beta:** The nonverbal test given to illiterate military personnel to determine rank.

In 1939, David Wechsler introduced the Wechsler–Bellevue Intelligence Scale. Approximately 20 years prior, Wechsler received training as a psychological examiner and worked extensively with Army personnel that had failed both the Alpha and Beta intelligence tests (Boake, 2002). Therefore, it is no coincidence that the Wechsler–Bellevue Intelligence Scale was largely derived from the Army Alpha and Army Beta subtests (Sattler, 2008). That is, Wechsler did not design subtests from scratch, but rather utilized and modified a number of subtests that were currently in use on other measures of intelligence. Furthermore, Wechsler wanted to extend intelligence testing to adult populations that currently could not be assessed using the Stanford–Binet. Currently, there are four different Wechsler intelligence tests (Wechsler Preschool and Primary Scale of Intelligence–Fourth Edition, Wechsler Intelligence Scale for Children–Fifth Edition, Wechsler Adult Intelligence Scale–Fourth Edition, and Wechsler Nonverbal

Ability Scales) widely used for intellectual assessment. Although the Stanford–Binet–Fifth Edition and the Wechsler scales are the more popular intelligence tests, it is important to note that a number of other intelligence tests exist and have demonstrated utility.

Right now, you may be wondering why there are so many intelligence tests. Remember at the beginning of this chapter when we said that psychologists have not been able to operationally define intelligence? Hence, a number of theories have been proposed throughout the previous century in an attempt to answer that question. One of the largest contributions to the overall understanding of intellectual theories is the use of statistics utilizing factor analysis. Further, factor analysis assists in identifying the number of factors that exist within a data set. Although the following is not an exhaustive list of contemporary theories, you will no doubt have a better understanding about how particular theorists would describe intelligence.

Table 4.4   Contemporary Theories on Intelligence

Theorist and Theory Highlights	Abilities/Categories of Intelligence
CHARLES SPEARMAN This is one of the first theories of intelligence. Using statistical analysis, Spearman noticed there were large positive correlations among different test scores, leading him to argue that all the individual test scores were measuring one similar construct which he described as **Psychometric g**, or general intelligence. **Psychometric g:** A term coined by Spearmen regarding a person's general or overall intelligence.	**Psychometric g** is a global measure of an individual's overall ability and is highly predictive of intellectual performance. Psychometric g is widely accepted by many psychologists in the field today. Spearman contended that there was one factor related to overall intelligence; other psychologists disagreed.
LEWIS THURSTONE In contrast to Spearman's view on intelligence, Thurstone contended that intelligence is not derived from a single factor (g) but rather seven equally weighted abilities.	1. **Word fluency**—the ability to generate as many words as possible about a given topic, either semantic or phonemic. 2. **Verbal comprehension**—the ability to understand verbal and written language in the form of questions, reading analogies, verbal fluency, similarities, and word usage and retrieval. 3. **Spatial visualization**—the ability to mentally manipulate and analyze both two- and three-dimensional visual information. 4. **Number facility**—the ability to carry out mathematical operations quickly, accurately, and internally and being able to use numbers in mathematical problems. 5. **Associative memory**—the ability to learn new information through repetition and the relationship between unrelated situations. 6. **Reasoning**—ability in all three types: inductive, deductive, and arithmetic. 7. **Perceptual speed**—the capacity to quickly and accurately compare letters, symbols, or pictures, in two similar visual spaces.

(Continued)

Table 4.4 ⌐Contemporary Theories on Intelligence *(Continued)*

Theorist and Theory Highlights	Abilities/Categories of Intelligence
ROBERT STERNBERG ⌐Sternberg proposed that⌐ intelligence is best understood/defined by those who adapt successfully within their environment ⌐and⌐ believed individuals could use their intelligence to adapt and shape their external environment to achieve success. ⌐His⌐ triarchic theory of successful intelligence ⌐suggests individuals are not limited to just strength or one of the three areas. Rather, individuals need to identify their strengths and use those to overcome their weaknesses to succeed and adapt within the context of their environment.⌐	1. **Analytical intelligence**—used while analyzing, evaluating, criticizing, reasoning, and judging 2. **Practical intelligence**—used when implying, implementing, and using the intelligence 3. **Creative intelligence**—used when discovering, inventing, and creating
HOWARD GARDNER ⌐Howard Gardner's Multiple Intelligence Theory is more recent.⌐ Gardner believed intelligence is much more broadly defined than through a single IQ score or psychometric g. It can Consequently, ⌐he⌐ proposed a theory of **multiple intelligences** ⌐because he believed intelligence could be best described and understood through multiple abilities (at least eight different types).⌐ **Multiple intelligences:** A theory suggesting that intelligence is a product of a number of abilities rather than one ability.	1. **Logical-mathematical intelligence**—the ability to detect patterns, think logically, reason deductively, and carry out mathematical operations 2. **Linguistic intelligence**—involves the mastery of spoken and written language to express oneself or remember things 3. **Spatial intelligence**—involves the potential for recognizing and manipulating patterns of both wide spaces and confined spaces 4. **Musical intelligence**—the capacity to recognize and compose musical pitches, tones, rhythms, and patterns and to use them for performance or composition 5. **Bodily–kinesthetic intelligence**—involves the use of parts of the body or the whole body to solve problems or create products 6. **Interpersonal intelligence**—the ability to recognize the intentions, feelings, and motivations of others 7. **Intrapersonal intelligence**—the ability to understand oneself and use that information to regulate one's own life 8. **Naturalistic intelligence**—the ability to discriminate patterns in nature

Table 4.4   Contemporary Theories on Intelligence *(Continued)*

Theorist and Theory Highlights	Abilities/Categories of Intelligence
CATTELL–HORN–CARROLL (CHC) This is one of the most researched and widely accepted theories of intelligence. The **CHC Theory of Intelligence** is actually an integration of Cattell and Horn's and Carroll's models of intelligence. Originally, Cattell determined psychometric g could be broken down into a combination of two different broad abilities Gc (crystallized intelligence) and Gf (fluid intelligence). Horn expanded on Cattell's model and discovered, through factor analysis (advanced statistics), that there were many more broad abilities that could be aggregated to ascertain psychometric g. The combination of Cattell and Horn's work led Carroll to further investigate the statistical structure of intelligence. Carroll added to their work through additional factor analytic studies. He concluded that intelligence can be thought of, and supported, as a three-stratum model. • Stratum III: an overall general ability (psychometric g). • Stratum II: a number of broad abilities uncovered by Cattell and Horn. Today, most commonly administered intelligence tests measure approximately seven broad abilities. • Stratum I: narrow abilities that comprise the broad abilities. Approximately 90 narrow abilities have been identified. Carroll's work at identifying a three-stratum model of intelligence has been extremely influential for psychologists and scholars alike. It has provided a foundation for the understanding of what intelligence is and is not. It has also provided a common language to aid in the design and interpretation of intelligence tests, meaning, most intelligence tests use factor analysis to determine whether the test has items that represent many of the broad abilities proposed by the contemporary CHC theory.	1. **Crystalized intelligence (Gc)**—depth and breadth of knowledge and skills that are valued by one's culture 2. **Fluid intelligence (Gf)**—the deliberate but flexible control of attention to solve novel problems that cannot be performed by relying exclusively on previously learned information 3. **Short-term memory (Gsm)**—the ability to encode, maintain, and manipulate information in one's immediate awareness 4. **Long-term storage and retrieval (Glr)**—the ability to store information and fluently retrieve it later through association 5. **Processing speed (Gs)**—the ability to quickly perform automatic, routine cognitive tasks, particularly when pressured to maintain focused concentration 6. **Visual processing (Gv)**—the ability to analyze and synthesize visual stimuli 7. **Auditory processing (Ga)**—the ability to analyze and synthesize auditory stimuli **CHC Theory of Intelligence:** The most researched and widely supported theory of intelligence.

Genetic and Environmental Influences

Across decades, researchers have attempted to identify the exact influence of genetics and environment on intelligence (Sattler, 2008). Some of the questions have been answered, yet many other questions remain. For the purpose of this text, it is important to know you are not born with a level of intelligence. That is, intelligence is *not* innately given to each individual and can change throughout one's lifetime. Rather, you are born with a genetic predisposition or genotype that is expressed through interactions with your environment or your phenotype. One way in which psychological researchers have examined the relationship between intelligence and genetic/environmental influences is through twin studies. Specifically, researchers have measured intellectual ability of both monozygotic and dizygotic twins to identify the similarities and differences.

© iQoncept/Shutterstock.com

A ⌐large volume⌐ of research has been conducted to identify whether monozygotic twins (100% same genetics) have higher correlational coefficients than dizygotic twins (50% same genetics). There has been a convergence of data suggesting monozygotic twins have more similar IQs than dizygotic twins (Bartels et al., 2002). This suggests that, in fact, genetic predispositions do affect IQ test scores. If genetic predispositions, however, accounted for 100% of the similarity in monozygotic twins, one would expect IQ scores to remain stable and similar across time. On the contrary, research shows the correlational coefficients between monozygotic twins decreases over time (Sundet et al., 2008). This provides evidence as to the effects of the environment on IQ test scores. Nobody truly knows the exact percentage genetics or environment play in overall IQ scores; however, it is widely agreed that both do influence IQ test scores. Therefore, intelligence is not a fixed number. Rather, it is a manifestation of your genotype as it interacts with your phenotype throughout development.

Cultural Differences

As you can see from the history of intelligence testing and lack of an operational definition of intelligence, scrutiny can and does exist within the psychology profession. That is, intelligence and intelligence testing are ripe with controversy. If, as a psychologist, one cannot define intelligence, the floodgate is open for those who disagree with the results. This has never been as evident as it is in the field of education where multiple levels of litigation have ensued. Dating back to the second half of the 20th century, multiple landmark court cases have attempted to answer the question, "Are intelligence tests **culturally biased**?" This question arose because children from ethnic minorities were being classified for special education at a rate much higher than their overall percentage within the United State population. Judges have ruled in such cases yielding different interpretations. In *Larry P. v. Riles,* the judge concluded intelligence tests are racially and culturally biased. Conversely, in *Parents in Action on Special Education v. Joseph P. Hannon,* the federal court ruled intelligence tests

> **Culturally biased:** A term used when an intelligence test gives an unfair advantage to White, affluent, male test takers.

are not culturally biased. These conflicting views have made it difficult to answer the question "Are intelligence tests culturally biased?" Rather, they have sparked a call for those familiar with intelligence testing to make judgments about their application with different ethnic groups (Sattler, 2008).

These seminal cases have created a political "hot potato" resulting in polarizing viewpoints as to the use of intellectual tests for ethnic minorities. The aforementioned litigation have presented the opportunity for psychologists to dissect intelligence tests specifically looking at their psychometric properties. An effective test,

© Gina Smith/Shutterstock.com

for example, must consistently yield the same results (reliability) and also must accurately measure what it purports to measure (validity). Advancement in statistical methods and analyses has allowed researchers to answer these questions as well as identify a hierarchical model (another statistical analysis) of intelligence. Results of such analyses should be able to identify whether intelligence tests are culturally biased. That is, if intelligence tests are consistent in their measurement across ethnic groups, they are not assumed to be culturally biased. The consensus is that intelligence tests are psychometrically fair (Gottfredson & Saklofske, 2009). The question remains, "Why are there group differences in IQ scores across racial/ethnic groups?"

To this point, we have touched on sensitive issues as to whether current intelligence tests are culturally biased. Current psychologists would often argue "no"; however, others might argue "yes." It is important to differentiate between culturally biased and culturally loaded. In fact, intelligence tests are culturally loaded (Sattler, 2008). Therefore, all intelligence tests have some degree of relationship with the culture in which they were designed. Tests that are largely language based can be considered to have high cultural loadings, whereas tests that require visual–spatial processing may be less **culturally loaded**. Moreover, it would be virtually impossible to eliminate any influence of culture that exists within an intelligence test. Therefore, it is entirely possible that different levels of cultural exposure could result in group differences in IQ scores. This, along with many other expla-

> **Culturally loaded:** A term used when many of the items on the intelligence test are derived from the mainstream culture.

nations, must be taken into account through interpretation by a psychologist. For example, we would never recommend giving a largely language-based intelligence test to somebody who just moved to the United States from a non-English speaking country. Thus, intelligence test scores must be interpreted within the context that they are achieved.

Intelligence Conclusions

To this point, you have learned much more about the psychological construct of intelligence and current theories attempting to explain what intelligence is and is not. You also have learned about some of the controversy surrounding intelligence, specifically intelligence tests. What we would like you to understand is that all current theories are essentially inaccurate (Horn & Blankson, 2012). Theories are designed to be picked apart and put together to make a better theory. This is the basic nature of science. This has and will continue to occur as our understanding of intelligence evolves. In the past century, we have seen many benefits of using intelligence tests to predict successes, but we have also seen some of their drawbacks as well. If the continued use of intelligence tests is to label and segregate individuals, the same negative outcomes that have had detrimental effects on the profession will continue to exist. If, however, results of the tests are used to identify individual strengths and weaknesses, intelligence tests will continue to be a valuable asset to society. Our hopes would be that we continue to have these difficult discussions about their utility and how to make more accurate predictions using their results. ⌞Regardless of the difficulty of this issue, the value of each human is always independent of their intelligence. God created each of us in his image and as such we have infinite worth.⌟

SUMMARY

Learning is a relatively permanent change in behavior resulting from experience but not including the effects of fatigue, maturation, drugs, injury, or disease. Two behavioristic approaches to learning are classical and operant conditioning. Classical conditioning (Pavlov) describes learning through stimulus substitution as a result of repeated pairings of an unconditioned stimulus with a conditioned stimulus; whereas, operant conditioning (Skinner) describes changes in the probability of a response as a function of its consequences. Behaviorism, however, was not able to explain and predict many aspects of behavior. Thus, a cognitive approach to psychology soon developed. This approach focused on an individual's ability to be self-aware, anticipate the consequences of behavior, and guide actions accordingly. Some principles of the behavioristic approach such as behavior modification are still used today.

In this chapter we ⌞covered the importance of attention and strategies to improve your attentional resources. In this chapter, we also⌟ discussed the complicated and fascinating processes involved in memory, as well as the interesting work that has occurred over the past century in order to fully understand human intelligence. These two psychological topics—memory and intelligence—are closely intertwined. Together they have helped us inhabit every corner of the planet. What does the future hold? It is difficult to tell, but any major accomplishments of our species, whether good or bad, will undoubtedly also be due to the both our ability to encode, store, and retrieve information (memory), and our ability to rationally engage and navigate the environment (intelligence).

⌞Attention, learning, and memory are amazing capabilities that allow us to engage our world in ways other living things cannot and this includes the ability to read, memorize, and react to Scripture. Our cognitive abilities separate humans from all other living things and allow us to have a relationship with God as well as understand abstract concepts like sin, forgiveness, and redemption.⌟

© AntonioDiaz/Shutterstock.com

Chapter 5

Motivation and Emotion

LEARNING OBJECTIVES

- Define motivation.
- Differentiate between instincts and reflexes.
- Explain the relationship between needs and drives.
- Describe Maslow's hierarchy of human needs.
- Define cognitive dissonance theory.
- Assess the relationship between achievement motivation and attribution theory.
- Recognize the importance of self-efficacy.
- Recall the main theories of emotion.
- Explain how arousal relates to behavior.
- List common eating disorders.
- ⌐Evaluate control of emotions from a biblical worldview.
- Examine instincts and behavioral influences on behavior from a perspective of biblical free will.⌐

WHAT IS MOTIVATION?

▶ CHAPTER 5
OVERVIEW

A Definition

The term, **motivation**, is derived from the Latin verb *movere*, which means "to move." Hence, motivation deals with the force—conscious or otherwise—that prompt us to action. Furthermore, motivation theorists seek to understand why people do certain things and what initiates or stops behaviors. Motives are closely tied to emotions. Complex combinations of feelings such as hate, fear, love, disgust, anger, and so on, are the reasons for much of what people do. As a biological organism, you have complex internal mechanisms that regulate your bodily functioning and help your survival. Internal states of deprivation trigger bodily responses that motivate you to take action to restore your body's balance. Also, psychologists use motivational explanations when the variations in people's performance in a constant situation cannot be traced to differences in ability, skill, practice, or chance. So, motivation is used to account for behavioral variability. Also, motivation is used to infer private states from public acts. Psychologists and laypersons are alike in typically moving from observing some behavior to inferring some internal cause for it. People are continually interpreting behavior in terms of likely reasons why it occurred as it did. Motivation is used to assign responsibility for actions. Personal responsibility presupposes inner motivation and the ability to control your actions. Finally, motivation is used to explain perseverance despite adversity. Related to this concept is that motivation is used to explain why organisms perform behaviors when it might be easier not to perform them (e.g., practicing piano). People are judged less responsible for their actions when (1) they did not intend negative consequences to occur, (2) external forces were powerful enough to provoke the behaviors, or (3) the actions were influenced by drugs, alcohol, or intense emotion.

> **Motivation:** Conscious and unconscious forces that initiate and direct behavior.

▶ APPLICATIO
OF MOTIVATIO
AND EMOTION

PHYSIOLOGICAL AND BEHAVIORISTIC APPROACHES

Early theorists looked at biology and behaviorism for explanations of motivation. Some basic instincts and drives that people inherit might account for much of their behavior. And, other behaviors can be explained through behaviorism and learning.

Instincts

Some theorists have reasoned that people, like animals, have some automatic, biologically based behaviors. For example, migration for birds and butterflies, spawning and nesting for fish and fowl, and mating for mouse and man are all examples of biologically-determined behaviors. Theoretically, behaviors labeled **instincts**, are common to all members of a species, are apparently unlearned, and not often affected by experience (Figure 5.1).

> **Instincts:** An innate, consistent response to stimuli.

Many theorists, including William James (1890–1950), listed an enormous number of human instincts, among which were jealousy, cleanliness, clasping, biting, sucking, and even kleptomania. At one point, Bernard (1924) counted more than 6,000 human instincts. The problem with Bernard's figure was that many of these tendencies might not be instincts at all. That is, they are not common

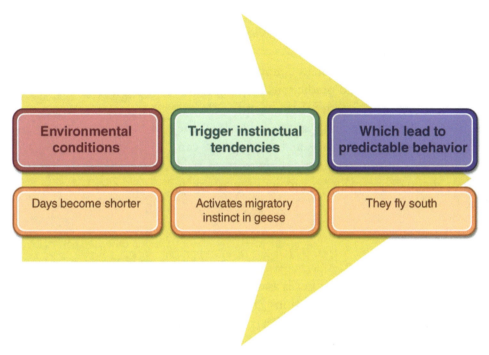

Figure 5.1   The ⌊traditional⌋ instinct model.

to all members of ⌊humanity,⌋ and ⌊can be changed⌋ by experience. Furthermore, lists of instincts ⌊are merely superficial.⌋ To say ⌊people⌋ are jealous because ⌊they⌋ have a jealousy instinct does ⌊not provide the impetus for their jealousy; it⌋ merely labels it. This is called the **nominal fallacy**—the ⌊faulty⌋ assumption that naming something explains it.

Nominal fallacy: The ⌊faulty⌋ assumption that naming something explains it.

The nominal fallacy is not uncommon in psychology. ⌊For⌋ example, Robert ⌊setting⌋ fires because he ⌊is a pyromaniac;⌋ Sandra ⌊having⌋ trouble learning because she ⌊has attention-deficit/hyperactivity disorder (ADHD);⌋ or Nora ⌊not eating⌋ because she has anorexia do not explain these behaviors. ⌊Although people may fight because of aggression instincts, there may be other forces at play.

⌊Currently, the trend is to study⌋ instincts in relation to animal rather than human behavior. ⌊Many⌋ psychologists contend that inherited biological tendencies play an important role in human behavior. As we saw in Chapter 2, for example, evolutionary psychologists point out that biology "prepares" ⌊people⌋ to learn language or ⌊develop⌋ aversions to bitter-tasting and possibly poisonous foods, or ⌊adopt a fear of⌋ snakes. Other ⌊scholars⌋ suggest that our tendencies toward aggressiveness ⌊or toward overeating⌋ may also have a biological basis (van Honk et al., 2010).

Psychological Hedonism

⌊In addition to instincts motivating behavior, one historical⌋ explanation of motivation is ⌊that people⌋ behave so as to achieve pleasure and to avoid pain. This notion, labeled **psychological hedonism** (or the pain–pleasure principle), seems to be a ⌊reasonable⌋ explanation for ⌊some⌋ human behavior, supported by science and by anecdotal evidence (Riediger et al., 2009). For instance, ⌊one⌋ can think of

Psychological hedonism: ⌊A psychological⌋ approach suggesting that humans ⌊are ultimately motivated by a desire for pleasure and the avoidance of pain.⌋

countless examples in which a person performed a behavior for the sheer pleasure of it or avoided other behaviors because of the unpleasant results.

The problem with the aforementioned definition of hedonism is that it does not lead to valid predictions or explanations unless pain and pleasure are defined beforehand. Pleasure and pain are subjective states and not rigidly defined. If the "Great Magician Mammoon" eats broken bottles, one can assume that he is driven toward pleasure and away from pain, but that does not adequately explain or predict his glass-eating behavior in the first place.

Needs and Drives

In addition to instincts and hedonism, needs and human drives motivate behavior. As we saw in a previous chapter, food, drink, praise, and money are positive reinforcers and increase the probability of performing a particular behavior. These are stimuli that satisfy our various needs. Hence, they are motivating and provide a behavioristic explanation for our actions.

PHYSIOLOGICAL NEEDS

One way of looking at needs is that they are foundational; they drive behavior. **Physiological needs** can be defined as basic needs to satisfy internal functions of an organism. They are central to survival and when they are lacking, a **drive** is created in the organism to obtain satisfaction of the need. Thus, the need for food gives rise to a hunger drive (or for drink, to a thirst drive; and for sex, to a sex drive, etc.). From a hedonistic point of view, satisfaction of a basic need may be described as pleasurable and the failure to satisfy a need as unpleasant.

It is clear that physiological drives are related to actual needs with respect to hunger and thirst. Deprivation of food and water leads to detectable physiological changes that are responsible for our awareness of these needs. Drinking or eating leads to a reduction in the drive—hence, the label, **drive reduction**, but there is more to hunger and thirst than simple physiology. Homeostasis is a state of equilibrium that an organism works to maintain. Drives are aroused when deprivation creates disequilibrium or tension. These drives activate the organism toward tension reduction; when the drives are satisfied or reduced—when homeostasis is restored—the organism ceases the act. A host of external stimuli, as well as cognitive and emotional states, contribute to our eating and drinking behaviors (Figure 5.2).

In regard to sex, deprivation does have the same physiological risks as dehydration or starvation, but physiological urges are still

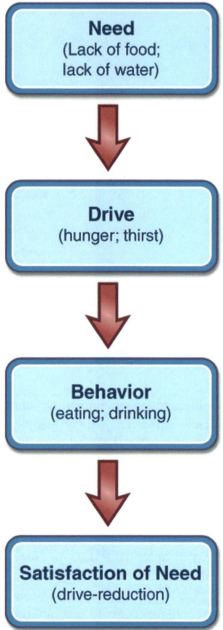

Figure 5.2   The drive-reduction model of motivation.

Physiological needs: Basic needs to satisfy internal functions of an organism.

Drive: A state of motivation to act in a particular way to satisfy a need.

Drive reduction: Behaviors that reduce an individual's drive state.

an influential factor. Perhaps much more important for humans, however, are the cognitive, emotional, perceptual, and cultural forces that are inextricably linked with sexual behavior.

One of the weaknesses of the drive-reduction explanation of behavior is that the drive-reduction explanation suggests that a person engages in a behavior to satisfy an inner need and when the need is met, the behavior will reduce. However, even with physical drives like hunger, it appears that eating behavior can be motivated by more than just the reduction of hunger. If eating was only engaged in when someone was hungry, people would always eat just as much as required to activate the physiological mechanism that says, "Whoa, you've had enough." Of course, many people continue to eat far more if the food looks and tastes especially good.

© luchschen/Shutterstock.com

Additionally, some people eat more if they are given a small appetizer first, even though the appetizer should reduce the hunger drive. Still, even rats will run a little faster toward the goal box when given a taste of food beforehand (Zeaman, 1949; Figure 5.3). They do so because the food has incentive value and it provides the rat (and people) with **incentive motivation**. Basically, incentive relates to the subjective value of a goal or reward; the higher the value, the greater is the incentive. Incentive motivation is external stimuli or rewards that do not relate directly to biological needs, so watching a movie, reading a book, or having a conversation with a friend would all be examples of incentive motivation.

Incentive motivation: The greater the subjective value of an item or reward, the more someone is motivated to achieve the item or reward.

Different goals have different incentive value. For example, monkeys typically work harder to obtain a banana than a piece of lettuce (Harlow, 1953)—and humans willingly pay more for a steak or a lobster than for a bowl of soup, having more incentive value. People can anticipate the consequences of their behavior, which are powerful influences in directing their activities. People's anticipation underlines the importance of the cognitive aspects of motivation.

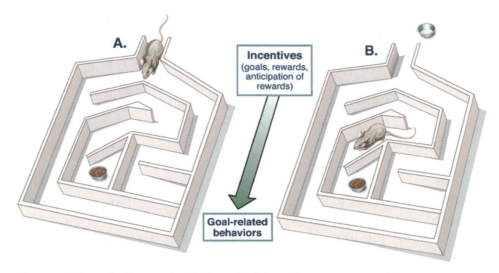

Figure 5.3   In Zeaman's 1949 study, drives alone cannot explain some behaviors.

Hunger Drive

Subjectively, hunger may be described as the bodily sensations that result from not eating for a period of time. Such sensations range from mild discomfort (the gentle growling of a hollow belly) to severe pain (the tortured pangs of intense hunger). Normally, death by starvation is preceded by cessation of hunger pains. Hunger is a function of certain physiological mechanisms related to survival. It is also a function of taste, smell, appearance, and learning, and it does not always relate to nutrition.

© ElenaGaak/Shutterstock.com

Stomach Contractions

For many years, most psychologists and physiologists believed hunger results directly from the actions of an empty or nearly empty stomach. ⌐Early theorists thought that people eat because the stomach is empty and it begins to contract.⌐ Cannon and Washburn (1912) developed an ingenious test ⌐for this hypothesis.⌐ Washburn swallowed a balloon that was then inflated inside his stomach. The balloon was connected to a recorder so that stomach contractions could be measured. Whenever he felt a hunger pang, Washburn ⌐recorded⌐ the event.

⌐Eventually, Washburn's stomach contracted and simultaneously he thought he felt hunger (Cannon & Washburn, 1912). Yet,⌐ even people with no stomachs get hungry and hunger persists even when neural pathways from the stomach to the brain are ⌐severed.⌐ There have now been many experiments with "gastric" balloons (Schachter, 1971). Contractions may sometimes be involved in sensations of hunger, but sometimes not, and it is likely that the duodenum (upper part of the small intestine) is even more involved.

The Role of the Brain

The brain plays a key role in hunger motivation. Satisfying hunger is highly rewarding. It leads to a pleasant state that can easily become conditioned to various situations—to the taste and smell of food, to its appearance, and to other situational factors. In fact, ⌐Panksepp (2010) argues that⌐ the positive emotional states that accompany eating, ⌐like⌐ those that accompany drug use, may be very important in explaining addictions.

Using magnetic resonance imaging (MRI) recordings, Martin et al. (2010) found significantly increased brain activity in the limbic systems (medial prefrontal cortex) of participants when they simply looked at images of food. Interestingly, obese participants displayed more brain activity than normal participants—both before and after a meal. This activity, ⌐Martin et al. (2010)⌐ suggest, is closely related to food motivation.

It has been known for some time that certain parts of the hypothalamus are involved in eating behavior. Patients with tumors or other injury of the hypothalamus sometimes overeat and consequently become obese (Rowell & Faruqui, 2010). ⌐Furthermore,⌐ MRI studies now indicate that the cerebellum, too, is closely involved in controlling hunger, perhaps via its connections with the hypothalamus (Zhu & Wang, 2008).

Taste and Smell

Taste and smell clearly contribute to food motivation, as is dramatically illustrated in studies using the black blowfly. When this fly is given a choice between a totally nonnutritive sugar substitute and a more nutritious alternative, it insists on eating the sweeter substance. In fact, it will continue to do so until it starves to death (Dethier, 1976).

⌐Much like the blowfly, people often prefer tastier food,⌐ regardless of nutritional value; ⌐however,⌐ when ⌐people⌐ are really hungry, taste becomes less important than the immediate availability of food (Hoefling & Strack, 2010). The evidence suggests as ⌐people⌐ become hungrier, they pay more attention to food cues. When par-

© victoriaKh/Shutterstock.com

ticipants are asked to detect specific ⌐visual targets rapidly presented⌐ that are randomly inserted among other images, hungry participants are easily distracted by food-related images (Piech et al., 2010).

Metabolic Factors

Hunger is a complex motive, tied not only to the body's need for food and to brain activity, but also to various metabolic factors. ⌐For instance,⌐ as levels of glucose (a form of sugar) in the blood drop, hunger increases; as blood glucose levels rise, there is a decline in hunger. ⌐Actually,⌐ the relationship between blood sugar level and hunger is not quite so simple because participants who are given sugar substitutes such as aspartame do not subsequently eat more than participants given sucrose, although their measured blood-glucose levels are significantly lower (Anton et al., 2010).

Many hormones and chemicals alter hunger. For example, fat cells produce *leptin,* a hormone that signals the hypothalamus to reduce appetite. Mice that lack the gene for leptin typically become obese. When they examined children's metabolic profiles, Eriksson et al. (2010) found that leptin was the best predictor of being overweight among 8-year-old children.

Another chemical related to hunger control is cannabinoid (THC or *tetrahydrocannabinoid*), the active ingredient in marijuana. There is considerable ⌐research,⌐ both with rats and humans, that THC increases hunger and leads to overeating, even in satiated organisms. There is also evidence of differences in cannabinoid sensitivity between some obese people and others of normal weight. Drugs that counter the effects of cannabinoids are ⌐infrequently⌐ successful in combating obesity, ⌐with many of these drugs also having⌐ negative side effects ⌐(Bermudez-Silva et al., 2010).

⌐You have been provided with a variety of mechanisms that contribute to your physical sense of hunger or satiety (i.e., feeling full). To regulate food intake effectively, organisms must be equipped with mechanisms that accomplish four tasks. First, organisms must be able to detect internal food need. Second, they must be able to initiate and organize eating behavior. Third, organisms must be capable of monitoring the quantity and quality of food eaten. Finally, they must be able to detect when enough food has been consumed to stop eating. Scientists have tried to understand these processes by relating them to peripheral mechanisms in different parts of the body, like stomach contractions, or to central brain mechanisms, like the functioning of the hypothalamus. If one or more of these processes is not functioning correctly, it can result in under- or overeating.⌐

Obesity

Unfortunately, hunger control systems do not always work perfectly. Overeating, termed **hyperphagia**, is one possibility that may result in obesity. **Obesity** is a global problem ⌐with⌐ about 15% of the world's population—slightly more than 1 billion people—and more than one third of the adult U.S. population ⌐being⌐ obese (Figure 5.3). Americans now spend about $60 billion a year in efforts to lose weight, mostly on drugs, physicians, weight-reducing programs, weight-reducing medications, and weight-reducing literature

> **Hyperphagia:** Overeating ⌐caused by intense sensations and hunger drives.⌐
>
> ⌐**Obesity:** A disorder involving excessive body fat that can lead to significant health issues.⌐

(*Worldometers,* 2010). An impressive 30% of all those who seriously attempt to lose weight will be substantially successful. Sadly, only 6% of these—hence, fewer than 2% of all who try to lose weight—will maintain their reduced weights for any length of time.

A variety of factors may be at play in obesity. Metabolic factors, such as a malfunctioning pituitary gland or hypothalamus, account for a small number of cases. Genetic tendencies are also involved, and a handful of gene defects have now been identified as causing severe obesity (Farooqi, 2010). ⌐The⌐ incidence of obesity among children in the United States has ⌐more than tripled since the 1970s, suggesting⌐ that environmental factors may be more important ⌐than genetic or metabolic factors (CDC, 2019).⌐ This may be due to situational factors such as socioeconomic status, cost of healthy foods, or even lack of time needed to cook meals. ⌐This reality is easily seen at a local grocery store where foods rich in nutritional value are more expensive than foods low in nutritional value.⌐

⌐Recently, researchers have discovered some of the actual genetic mechanisms that may predispose some individuals to obesity. For example, a gene has been isolated that appears to control the signals to the brain that enough fat has been stored in the body in the course of the meal—so the individual should stop eating (Choquet & Meyre, 2011). If this gene, called leptin, is inactive, the individual will continue to eat, with obesity as a potential result. In fact, researchers have discovered small populations of obese people with mutations in this gene; the mutation appears to explain their obesity (Mark, 2013). Because these mutations are extremely rare, they cannot account for the vast majority of cases of obesity. Even

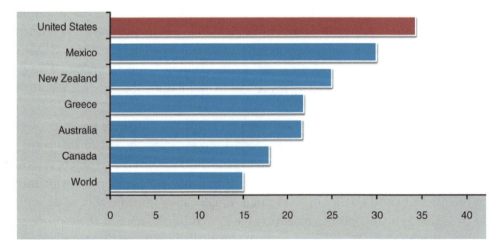

Figure 5.3   Percentage of adult population with a body mass index over 30 ⌐(obesity),⌐ based on health estimates rather than self-reported data. Based on U.S. Bureau of the Census, 2010, Table 1306. Retrieved August 20, 2010, from http://www.census.gov/compendia/statab/2010/tables/10s1306.pdf

so, the conformation that leptin plays a role in weight regulation has encouraged researchers' efforts to identify and understand other weight-related genes.

The most important factors that underlie obesity include the overwhelming popularity and availability of calorie-dense, high-sugar, and high-fat foods, coupled with an increasingly sedentary lifestyle among children. As Must and Anderson (2010) point out, by the time children have reached adolescence, detrimental eating and exercise habits have been repeated and reinforced so often that they are very difficult to change.

Body mass index is a measure of body fat based on height and weight that applies to adult men and women. Body mass index is a person's weight in kilograms/pounds divided by the square of height in meters/inches. Body mass index does not measure body fat directly, but research has shown that body mass index is moderately correlated with more direct measures of body fat obtained from skinfold thickness measurements, bioelectrical impedance, densitometry (underwater weighing), dual energy x-ray absorptiometry (DXA) and other methods. Also, body mass index appears to be as strongly correlated with various metabolic and disease outcomes, as are these more direct measures of body fatness. In general, body mass index is an inexpensive and easy-to-perform method of screening for weight category, for example: underweight, normal or healthy weight, overweight, and obesity. However, certain healthy athletes like body builders can have high body mass index yet be in excellent health. So, although it is not a universal index of being overweight, it is very quick and easy to calculate. The following chart applies to adults and not to children. Children would follow a different calculation given their rapid growth and variability across growth.

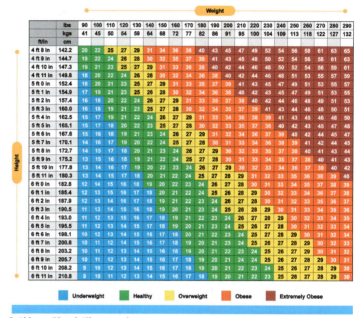

© Abhijeet Bhosale/Shutterstock.com

Anorexia, Bulimia, and Binge Eating Disorder

Malfunctions of our hunger control systems may be evident in overeating (hyperphagia); they may also be manifested in undereating (termed aphagia). Clinically, they may lead to one of three eating disorders: anorexia nervosa, commonly shortened to *anorexia;* bulimia nervosa; and binge-eating disorder.

Anorexia is classified as an eating disorder. Anorexia nervosa is diagnosed when an individual weighs less than 85% of her or his expected weight. Its symptoms include unwillingness or inability to eat and eventual emaciation. It is often characterized by a significantly distorted body image and is sometimes fatal. Its possible causes include cultural standards that glamorize thinness, family and peer pressure, and occasionally genetic factors and psychological issues such as low self-esteem or depression. It is most common among

Aphagia: Undereating.

Anorexia nervosa: Psychological disorder characterized by being significantly underweight.

Bulimia nervosa: Psychological disorder characterized by binging and purging.

Binge-eating disorder: Psychological disorder characterized by excessive binging; however, the individual does not engage in purging behaviors.

adolescent girls (Keel et al., 2010). Moreover, individuals with anorexia often experience fear associated with gaining weight. Therefore, to regulate their emotions, they will engage in minimal amounts of food intake.

Bulimia nervosa, on the other hand, is characterized by patterns of intense, out-of-control overeating, followed by measures aimed at eliminating the excessive caloric intake. The main characteristics of bulimia are recurrent episodes of often secretive and guilt-ridden binge eating, followed by purging behavior to eliminate the food consumed. An individual is diagnosed with bulimia when this pattern of behavior occurs at least once a week over a period of 3 months. Purging behaviors include self-induced vomiting (purging) and sometimes the use of laxatives or diuretics to combat weight gain. Purging can have damaging effects. For example, quickly purging after eating a meal may not provide the nutritional value that a body needs. Additionally, frequent vomiting may rot teeth. Bulimia is most common among adolescent girls.

Binge-eating disorder is also marked by episodes of excessive compulsive eating but, unlike bulimia, does not involve purging or other attempts to get rid of excess calories. As a result, whereas individuals with bulimia are often very thin or of normal weight, those with binge eating disorder are often obese. For example, in one binge, an individual may consume thousands of calories.

Interestingly, these three eating disorders often manifest at different ages. Anorexia appears earliest, peaking at around age 14, and then again around age 18. Bulimia peaks somewhat later, at around age 19, and often occurs among girls who were previously anorexic. Binge eating disorder appears even later, at around age 25 (Keel et al., 2010). Various factors are related to greater risk of eating disorders, including genetic background, emotional disorders, brain injury and disease, and metabolic malfunction. Perhaps, more important than any of these factors are cultural pressures stemming from what Saguy and Gruys (2010) described as the American media's glorification of excessive thinness.

The aforementioned are a taste of the many problems of hyperphagia and aphagia. Unfortunately, scientists are still searching for the factors that cause these malfunctions of our hunger control systems and effective treatments. There are a variety of possible therapies for anorexia, bulimia, and binge-eating disorder, including cognitive therapies (Murphy et al., 2010), behavior therapies (Kroger et al., 2010), drug therapies, and sometimes even hospitalization.

Sex Drive

Psychologists still do not completely understand sexual motivation, another powerful biological motive. Unlike hunger and thirst, sex is not necessary for the individual's survival, but it is clearly essential for the survival of the species—nor is it a simple motive, easily explained by a lack or deficiency. If one does not eat, he or she will eventually become very hungry. In contrast, the relationship between the sex drive and lack of sex is not quite so clear. Hormones contribute to two aspects of sexual behavior, which include organizational and activating effects. Organizational effects are permanent changes in the brain, which alter the way an individual responds to hormones. The activating effects are reversible changes in behavior, which remain as long as certain hormones levels are elevated.

The important hormones for females are estrogens and progestins, and the most important ones are estradiol and progesterone. The important male hormones are androgens, and the most important one is testosterone. Each of these hormone groups is found in both males and females but shows dramatically different levels in each sex. Scientific research affirms that hormonal factors are closely linked to sexual urges. At puberty, when the body begins to produce the sex hormones—mainly estrogen among females and androgens (mainly testosterone) among

Estrogen: Female sex hormone.

Androgens: Male sex hormone.

males—sexual drive increases dramatically. ⌞Indirectly supporting this is that⌟ injections of sex hormones are known to increase sexual drive (Meletis & Wood, 2009).

⌞Yet,⌟ hormones are only part of the story. In fact, when the organs that produce sex hormones–the ovaries in women and the testes in men–are removed, sex drive does not necessarily disappear. Even nonhuman primates display sexual motivation that seems to be independent of hormones. Giles (2008) summarizes a number of studies that have shown that nonhuman primates that have been castrated continue to display both sexual interest and activity. Similarly, women who have had their ovaries removed typically experience little change in sex drive. ⌞So, like many other human behaviors, sex is influenced by biological, psychological, sociological, and developmental factors.⌟

Sex hormone

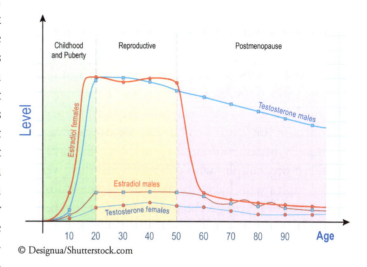

© Designua/Shutterstock.com

Sexual motivation has a number of cultural and learned components as well, as is clear from looking at the sometimes dramatically different sexual behaviors of different cultures. Hence, some aspects of sexual motivation are clearly ⌞socialized.⌟ Cultural standards play an important role in determining what we find sexually arousing, even as they define sexual behaviors that are acceptable. ⌞In fact, every major religion across the globe has rules and recommendations around sexual behavior. And, this is for good reason as there are often lifelong consequences associated with sexual behavior that are quite distinct from other drive-based, motivational behaviors. Some of these consequences include dramatic changes in relationships, pregnancy, abortion, sexually transmitted disease, guilt/shame, and intimacy issues (Vasilenko et al., 2012). There are obviously benefits to sex especially when occurring in the confines of a trusting, loving, and affirming marriage. Some of these include improved intimacy in your marriage, enhanced immune response, longer life span, lower blood pressure, better sleep, lower heart attack risk, reductions in certain types of cancer, stress relief, and improved mental health (Anderson, 2013).

⌞There are multiple factors that interact in attraction. First, proximity plays a significant role in attraction. Typically, the more one is exposed to something new, the more comfortable he or she will be with it. Consider your college friends, who do you tend to spend the most time with? It is probably the people in your dorm and those with whom you have class that prove to be your best friends. That is, the people you see the most become your friends, rather than the other way around. People tend to become attracted to others with whom they are in close proximity. It is important that there is a general tendency for people to like objects and people just by virtue of more exposure. The more you are exposed to something or someone, the more you like it. Think about this in terms of the type of concert you attend. You likely attend concerts for which you know most of the songs. Additionally, physical attractiveness often plays a role in the kindling of friendship. There is a strong stereotype in Western culture that physically attractive people are also good in other ways, like being more sociable and extraverted. People tend to befriend others who are similar to them in terms of beliefs, attitudes, and values. Finally, you tend to like people whom you believe like you. Furthermore, because of the way your beliefs can affect your behaviors, believing that someone likes or dislikes you can help bring that relationship about.

Passion, intimacy, and commitment are thought to be the three dimensions that define the experience of love. However, keep in mind the difference between having a loving relationship and being in love. While one may love many people, most people are only in love with one person.

The phases of human sexual response in males and females have similar patterns (e.g., excitement, plateau, orgasm, and resolution). The primary differences are in the time it takes for males and females to reach each phase and in the greater likelihood that females will achieve multiple orgasms. Because sex is not simply a biological response, psychosocial factors can weigh heavily in the process and enjoyment from it. Interestingly, the National Health and Social Life Survey (Laumann et al., 1992), conducted in 1992, found that the most enjoyable and most frequent sex occurring among married people, those who attended church weekly—any church, whether Catholic or not—and people who had the least sexual partners. Similarly and more recently, a new study demonstrates that while it may be common for couples to have sex before marriage, couples who wait until marriage are happier with the quality of sex compared to couples who have intercourse before their vows (Busby et al., 2010). Furthermore, couples who delay sex until their wedding night have more stable and happier marriages than couples who have premarital sex. The study involved 2,035 married participants in an online assessment of marriage. According to the study, people who waited until marriage: rated sexual quality 15% higher than people who had premarital sex, rated relationship stability as 22% higher, and rated satisfaction with their relationships 20% higher. While there are many possible explanations as to why this is the case, the research seems to suggest that focusing on the quality of the relationship, instead of focusing on the frequency of sex, while building trust, was critical to long-term relationship success.

There are often a lot of mixed messages when it comes to sex, including different messages for males versus females, different messages for young adults compared to older adults, and different messages for not married versus married. Commonly in more religious settings, there is limited discussion on sex and often a sense of shame is associated with sex. However, after marriage, couples from religious backgrounds are implicitly told to have sex. Lack of consistency and secrecy about sex can leave young people, especially, confused on the subject. Often adults, like parents, don't discuss it but people of all ages are exposed to sexual messaging across every media. So, better to be open and honest about it and answer questions than to create shame and confusion around such an important topic and behavior.

What Does the Bible Say?

The Bible actually has a lot to say about sex because it is important. If it wasn't important, then it wouldn't be exploited in ads, television, and movies.

Genesis 2:18–25 ESV

"Then the Lord God said, 'It is not good that the man should be alone; I will make him a helper fit for[e] him.' Now out of the ground the Lord God had formed every beast of the field and every bird of the heavens and brought them to the man to see what he would call them. And whatever the man called every living creature, that was its name. The man gave names to all livestock and to the birds of the heavens and to every beast of the field. But for Adam[g] there was not found a helper fit for him. So the Lord God caused a deep sleep to fall upon the man, and while he slept took one of his ribs and closed up its place with flesh. And the rib that the Lord God had taken from the man he made[h] into a woman and brought her to the man. Then the man said,

'This at last is bone of my bones
and flesh of my flesh;
she shall be called Woman,
because she was taken out of Man.'

Therefore a man shall leave his father and his mother and hold fast to his wife, and they shall become one flesh. And the man and his wife were both naked and were not ashamed."

I Corinthians 6:18–20 ESV

"Flee from sexual immorality. Every other sin a person commits is outside the body, but the sexually immoral person sins against his own body. Or do you not know that your body is a temple of the Holy Spirit within you, whom you have from God? You are not your own, for you were bought with a price. So glorify God in your body."

I Corinthians 7:2 ESV

"But because of the temptation to sexual immorality, each man should have his own wife and each woman her own husband."

PSYCHOLOGICAL NEEDS

In addition to physiological needs, human behavior is also motivated by psychological needs. Although the basic physiological needs seem clear, there is less agreement about what our **psychological needs** are. Some psychological needs that have been identified are the need for affection, belonging, achievement, independence, social recognition, and self-esteem.

> **Psychological needs:** Needs such as affection, belonging, achievement, independence, social recognition, and self-esteem that drive behavior.

Research supports the notion that outcomes such as emotional well-being and academic achievement are linked with satisfied psychological needs (Faye & Sharpe, 2008). However, unlike physiological drives that can be assumed to be common for most individuals, it is not clear whether everyone has the same psychological needs. Consequently, some people seem to have a higher need for acceptance, achievement, or love than others.

Physiological needs can be entirely satisfied, at least temporarily. One can eat or drink until he or she does not want any more food. Psychological needs, on the other hand, are not so easily satisfied. Few people are ever totally content with the love, achievement, or affection they receive.

Maslow's Hierarchy

A dominant theory of motivation that includes both physiological and psychological needs is Abraham Maslow's Hierarchy of Needs. In his theory, Maslow (1970) suggests human actions may be accounted for by two systems of needs: basic needs and **meta needs**. Basic needs are also called "deficiency needs" because when they are unsatisfied, they lead to behaviors designed to satisfy them. They include both physiological needs (food, drink) and psychological needs (security, love, and self-esteem).

> **Meta needs:** Higher-level needs related to an organism's tendency toward psychological growth.

Meta needs are higher-level needs; they include cognitive needs, aesthetic needs, and the need for self-fulfillment. They are called *growth needs* because activities relating to them do not result from deficiencies, but from the organism's tendency toward growth.

According to Maslow, needs are hierarchically arranged as shown in Figure 5.4. Lower-level needs must be satisfied first before higher-level needs are attended to by the person. Thus, it is unlikely that

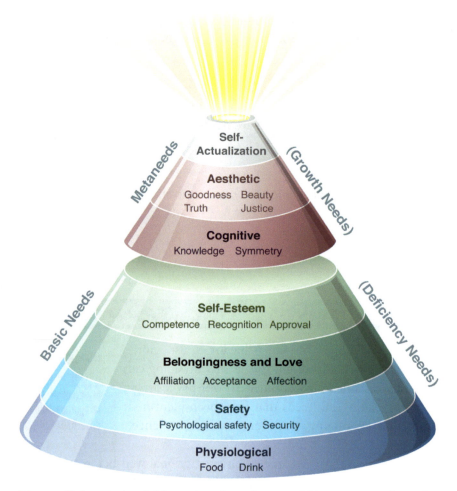

Figure 5.4 Maslow's hierarchy of needs pyramid is open ⌐to show the never-ending process of⌐ self-actualization.

a starving person would be attending to ⌐self-esteem⌐ needs rather than the basic physiological need for ⌐sustenance⌐ (Harper & Guilbault, 2008). Once the basic needs are met, however, that same individual ⌐will likely⌐ begin to focus on the ⌐cognitive⌐ growth needs.

To better understand Maslow's hierarchy of needs, consider the example of being stranded on a deserted island. What would be your first priority? How about your second priority? ⌐Likely,⌐ your first priority would align with ⌐your⌐ physiological needs ⌐for⌐ food, water, warmth, and rest—⌐only then followed with more serious attempts for self-rescue.⌐ This is precisely what Maslow was describing when he created the hierarchy of needs.

Maslow ⌐(1970)⌐ was concerned with developing a theory that would encompass the more "human" qualities of behavior that define our "higher nature." ⌐People⌐ have an overpowering tendency toward growth ⌐which⌐ defines ⌐people's⌐ very essence and is absolutely fundamental to mental health and happiness. The highest and most important of growth needs is the need for **self-actualization**.

⌐Unlike the more basic needs (satisfied through appropriate activities such as eating), self-actualization is never satisfied, is rarely an achieved state; it is more of an ongoing process. According to Rowan (1998), the depiction of Maslow's theory as a triangle is misleading because it implies an end point to personal growth.

> **Self-actualization:** An ongoing process in which an organism attempts to reach its ⌐full⌐ potential.

Maslow's hierarchy of needs is one of the most recognizable theories in psychology and Abraham Maslow is often listed as one of the most influential theorists in modern psychology (Compton, 2018). However, as reviewed by Compton (2018), Maslow's work on needs has received quite a bit of criticism due to the lack of strong empirical support for this structure of needs and the ideas presented within his theory. Some have questioned whether the order of the needs is correct (i.e., do physiological needs always take precedence over safety needs?) or whether others like cognitive needs or creativity needs should be included. Furthermore, what self-actualization is and whether it is truly related to happiness/satisfaction has been debated. However, despite the questions surrounding Maslow's hierarchy of needs, his theory remains important to our discussion of how needs are fulfilled and possibly ordered and what motives drive humans in life. More research is always needed. This should be viewed as an initial theory on needs which included more than just basic, physical needs; it introduced the concept that psychological or higher needs may also be important when considering what drives human behavior.

Cognitive Views of Motivation

Some early biological and behavioristic positions tended to view people as passive victims of forces over which they have little control. Personal motives were seen as internal or external catalysts that pushed people to and from certain behaviors based on internal or external needs/demands.

Cognitive views of motivation present a more active view of human beings. They take into account the wealth of human thinking and emotions involved in behavior. Cognitive views of motivation pay attention to thoughts and emotions—not as forces over which people have no control—but as mental experiences they actively and sometimes consciously manipulate. Thus, cognitive theorists try to understand the process of ongoing human behavior as it is mediated and controlled by ongoing cognitive activity of which one's affect (emotion) is a central component.

What Does the Bible Say?

While biological or behavioral theories of motivation may suggest that our behaviors are mere reactions to internal and external states, thus subtly removing control from the individual, the Bible presents a different view. In fact, when we read Scripture, we see very clearly that God has given us more active responsibility for behaviors. Free will is a foundational principle given to us by God. Human will is seen throughout Scripture as God gives us choices and then allows us to reap the consequences of our choices. We see the first instance of it in Genesis when God told Adam that he must not eat of the tree of the knowledge of good and evil. In Genesis 2:17 (ESV), God says, "but of the tree of the knowledge of good and evil you shall not eat, for in the day that you eat of it you shall surely die." As seen here, God gave man choice and He also created consequences for our choices. Furthermore, God does not remove responsibility for our actions simply because some other force "made us do it." When Adam passes blame to Eve and Eve attempts to blame the serpent for her sinful actions, both were still seen as culpable and reaped consequences for their behaviors (Genesis 3:12-13). Additionally, in Galatians 5:13 (ESV), we read, "For you were called to freedom, brothers. Only do not use your freedom as an opportunity for the flesh, but through love serve one another."

Therefore, when we evaluate the reasons for our behaviors and how our behaviors are motivated, it is important to recognize that multiple biological and/or social forces may lead us toward certain behaviors. But, God has given us responsibility for our behaviors. We are commanded to walk in the Spirit and not the flesh thus pointing further to the multiple causes of behaviors and our choice to allow the Holy Spirit to help us overcome fleshly motivations for behavior.

Note, however, not all behaviorists view the organism as totally passive and reactive. Even Skinner's rat is an active organism exploring the environment and responding to it rather than simply reacting blindly to external forces. The main contrast between behavioristic and cognitive approaches to motivation is that the cognitive theorist looks at the role of rewards and punishments in terms of the individual's evaluation and anticipation. In so doing, cognitive theories take into account what might be one of the

© Fabio Berti/Shutterstock.com

most powerful concepts in human motivation—our ability to delay gratification. Moreover, the ability to delay gratification is something that separates human beings from many other animal species. For example, most workers understand that if they put in the hours, they will eventually be paid (even 2 weeks later), providing sufficient motivation for them to complete their duties. Now, imagine telling a dog if he does not chew on the couch, he will be rewarded with a steak in 2 weeks. The difference is that while humans can employ forward thinking, self-restraint, and advanced planning, animals (mostly) live shortsightedly in the moment, limited by their cognitive abilities.

Cognitive Dissonance Theory

One theory that shows the importance of cognitions in the motivation of behavior is cognitive dissonance theory. This theory is based on a series of studies conducted by Festinger and Carlsmith (1959) in which they asked college students to perform an extremely boring and apparently pointless task as part of an experiment. The students were divided into three groups—one of which did nothing else besides the task, serving as a control group—the other two groups were asked to help the experimenter by lying to new participants, proclaiming that the experiment was exciting and worthwhile. All agreeing, one group of participants was paid $20; the other group, ignorant of how much the others had been paid, was given a single dollar.

After members of these two groups had each spoken to the "new" participants (actually confederates [actors] of the researchers), they were interviewed about their true feelings regarding the experiment. Not surprisingly, the control group still found the experiment boring and useless. The $20 group had not changed their minds and still found it boring. Interestingly, the group who had been paid a single dollar now thought the experiment was useful and quite interesting (Figure 5.5).

Why did one group change their minds but the other group did not? Festinger (1957), concluded that the answer lies in the theory of **cognitive dissonance**, which predicts that whenever there is conflict between cognitions (e.g., conflicting information about behavior, beliefs, values, and desires), people will try to reduce the conflict. Cognitive dissonance (cognitive conflict) may arise when people do things contrary to their beliefs, when they compromise principles, or when they observe people doing unexpected things.

> **Cognitive dissonance:** A conflict between cognitions regarding behaviors, beliefs, values, desires, and so on.

In the Festinger and Carlsmith (1959) experiment, participants experienced dissonance when they told a lie. Yet, if they were well-paid, they felt justified for their deception, experiencing little dissonance. Those who were paid very little money had less justification for lying and experienced more dissonance. Thus, the experiment established that volitionally changing one's attitude is one of the easiest ways to reduce dissonance.

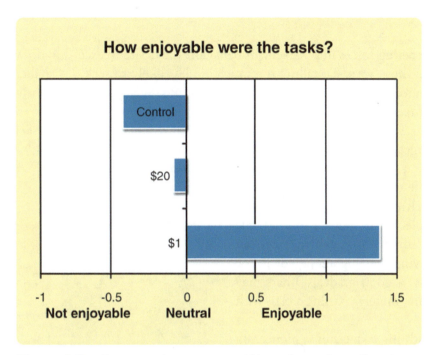

Figure 5.5   Cognitive dissonance and "forced compliance" in the Festinger and Carlsmith study.

Cognitive dissonance theory contradicts the ⌐notion that,⌐ "[T]he grass is greener on the other side of the fence." When participants are given a choice between two relatively equal options, they select the one they ⌐that is⌐ most desirable. Cognitive dissonance theory provides an easy explanation ⌐because whatever⌐ conflict results from having had to make an uncertain choice is quickly reduced when participants become convinced they've made the best choice. ⌐Not surprisingly,⌐ people who buy houses, cars, and other objects that require major decisions immediately begin to exaggerate the positive aspects of their choices. They are simply reducing dissonance or guarding against its ⌐presence.⌐

There are several ways of reducing dissonance, depending on the behavior from which dissonance originated. Changing attitudes is one common method, illustrated in the ⌐aforementioned experiment.⌐ A second method ⌐for reducing dissonance⌐ involves changing behavior. ⌐For example, individuals experience dissonance regarding the negative health consequences from⌐ smoking. ⌐One very simple way to⌐ reduce ⌐such⌐ dissonance ⌐is to "simply" quit smoking.⌐

Distorting information or perceptions can also reduce dissonance. When Gibbons et al. (1997) interviewed individuals who had stopped smoking but later started again, they found that ⌐the participants⌐ had significantly distorted their perception of the risks associated with smoking. ⌐Thus, people rationalized negative behaviors so they could reduce cognitive dissonance.⌐

Cognitive dissonance theory has become a relatively common approach to therapy. Changes in the attitudes of patients with eating disorders or addictions can sometimes be brought about by creating cognitive dissonance to stimulate change in attitudes or behavior. For example, Smith-Machin (2009) created cognitive dissonance among groups of female undergraduates with eating disorders using discussion, exercises, and homework assignments aimed primarily at countering cultural pressures and beliefs about women's bodies. She found significant reductions in dieting behaviors and *bulimic* symptoms among these women.

Achievement Motivation

There are two competing forces in achievement behavior: the desire to excel and do well, and an opposing fear of failure. Those who fear failure too much are less likely to seek out challenging and difficult undertakings. Failure, as ˌmany people discover, is often uncomfortable and demotivational.

ˌUrgesˌ that propel us toward achievement are complex and not easily defined or measured, although their influence can be extremely powerful. Those urges can vary widely from one individual to another. Some people have a ˌhigh personal standard of excellence driving them to excel while others may not have that same highˌ **need for achievement (nAch).**

> **Need for achievement:** A strong desire to excel, meet some inner standard of excellence, and do well.

© Lucky Business/Shutterstock.com

A classic example can be related to academic performance. For some, the desire to excel can only be met by having the ˌhighestˌ grade in the class, ˌand not just a good grade.ˌ Others may be perfectly content ˌmerelyˌ passing a class with ˌlow grade.ˌ

McClelland and his associates' ˌpioneering research onˌ the need for achievement revealed several ˌprovocativeˌ findings (McClelland et al., 1953). First, those with ˌa higher need for achievement normally do so at a higher level. Still, justˌ having a burning drive to achieve and succeed brings no ˌguarantee. In fact, sometimesˌ those ˌwho areˌ more intelligent, more talented, more persistent, or ˌmore fortunate, are most successful.ˌ

Another ˌsignificantˌ finding from this research is that children with high nAch scores tend to be ˌmore cautious in risk taking whileˌ those with lower scores tend to be either very low risk or very high risk takers. McClelland (1958) had young children play a ring-toss game where they could stand as close to the target as they wanted, ˌwinningˌ prizes for accurate tosses. High-need achievers tended to stand a moderate distance away, ˌbutˌ low-need achievers ensured success by standing very close to the target or ˌensuredˌ failure by standing ˌtooˌ far away. ˌThus, whenˌ there is very little probability of success, failure carries little stigma.

ˌMcClelland (1958) asserts that thereˌ are two competing forces involved in achievement behavior. One is the desire to achieve success; the other is a fear of failure. ˌAchievement-orientedˌ behavior is a combined function of approach tendencies (resulting from a desire to achieve) and avoidance tendencies (resulting from fear of failure). ˌFor instance, a piano student must balance his or her goal of attending Julliard with a realistic appraisal of personal abilities.

Attribution Theory

ˌMany people fear failure because it might present them as someone they do not want to be. Weiner (2008) suggests that all people do not theˌ same way to successes and failures. Some of us believe we do well or poorly because we are intelligent or not so intelligent; others think they are just lucky or unlucky. **Attribution theory** looks at the ˌcauses that we attribute to behaviors and is important in the motivation of behaviors.

> **Attribution theory:** ˌThe causes that peopleˌ attach to ˌthe behaviors of themselvesˌ or others.

Locus of Control

According to Weiner (2008), our attributions depend on our **locus of control**— that is, on whether we are internally oriented or externally oriented. If one has an internal locus of control, he tends to take responsibility for the consequences of his own actions, attributing them either to ability or to effort, both of which are under his control. If one has an external locus of control, however, he

> **Locus of control:** When people attribute their successes or failures to internal or external factors.

attributes success or failure to factors not under his control, such as the difficulty of the tasks that he faces or due to pure chance. With these factors not under his personal control, he is not required to accept responsibility for either success or failure. For example, an externally oriented individual attributes a good test score to the fact that the teacher made the test easier rather than him studying more, with the reverse being true for the internally oriented individual. So, in summary, a locus of control orientation is a belief about whether the outcomes of your actions are contingent on what you do or on environmental factors (internal vs. external). Another way to examine this mindset is to see if such an outlook occurs across a number of situations or only under very specific conditions (unstable vs. stable).

Weiner (2008) also differentiates between stable and unstable causes of behavior. Ability and task difficulty are stable factors; that is, they do not vary for a given task or a given individual. Unstable factors, in contrast, can include effort, which can be high or low, or luck, which can be present or absent (Figure 5.6).

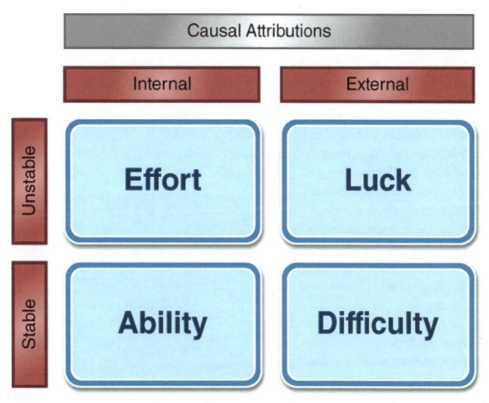

Figure 5.6 Four important possible causal attributions for success and failure.

Attributions and Need for Achievement

One of the striking and consistent findings from attribution studies is that people who are high in need achievement are much more likely to attribute outcomes to internal factors for which they have personal responsibility. They are likely to think that ability and effort—or lack thereof—are responsible for their successes and failures.

When they are successful, individuals low in measured need for achievement may attribute success to any of the four causal factors. That is, they might conclude that they succeeded because of hard work (effort), high intelligence (ability), an easy task (difficulty), or good fortunate (luck). However, when those individuals who are low in need for achievement are not successful, they are more likely to attribute the outcome to their lack of ability. According Dweck (2006), this is because they naively believe the myth that intelligence is fixed and unchanging. Still, even if a myth, this belief (the **entity theory**) shapes one's goals and efforts. Those who are convinced that intelligence is fixed often go to great lengths to convince people that they have much of it (or strive to hide their inadequacies). In either case, the individual avoids challenges that might expose his or her weaknesses.

> **Entity theory:** The belief that intelligence is fixed and unchanging.

On the other hand, if one believes that intelligence is not fixed and can be improved with effort (the **incremental theory**), she will develop what Dweck (2006) labels a growth mindset. One can actually develop astonishing skills and talents with work at it, ultimately accepting challenges that others would fear (Dweck & Grant, 2008).

> **Incremental theory:** The belief that intelligence is not is fixed and can be improved upon with effort.

Self-Efficacy

Attribution theory presents an active view of people. People do not simply behave; they actively evaluate behaviors and try to make sense of them. When people fail or succeed, they try to understand the reasons why. Depending upon predispositions, personality characteristics, and previous histories, people ascribe causes to specific factors. Similarly, personal opinions of how competent one is in different situations (**self-efficacy**) is important in determining which tasks are chosen and how much effort is put into them.

> **Self-efficacy:** Judgments and personal evaluations of one's own competence.

Personal competence and self-efficacy judgments are foundational to attribution theory (Bandura, 1997). These evaluations are made regarding personal effectiveness in different circumstances. Thus, those with high self-efficacy see themselves as more than capable and effective in most situations.

Judgments of self-efficacy are instrumental in determining what people do; hence, they are important, motivationally. In most circumstances, people do not engage in activities in which they expect to perform badly. In other words, the level of difficulty for the

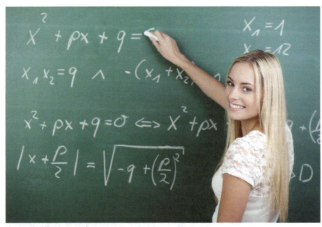
© racorn/Shutterstock.com

task determines whether people engage in them or not. In contrast, those with high judgments of self-efficacy are more likely to accept challenges that might help validate their judgments. Slanger and Rudestam (1997) found that level of self-efficacy judgments was one of the variables that most clearly differentiated between high and low risk takers in sports such as sky-diving, kayaking, rock climbing, and skiing.

Self-efficacy judgments determine not only what tasks people will choose, but also how much time and effort they are willing to put into their efforts. For example, if one is a great mechanic, he or she would be more willing to put in the time and effort needed to fix a car. Those who do not see themselves as very capable are far more likely to give up rather than persist when they encounter difficulties. That is one of the reasons why self-efficacy judgments are so important in schools. For example, in a study that looked at students in 33 different schools, Williams and Williams (2010) found a significant relationship between math achievement and self-efficacy. Those who had higher levels of self-efficacy were more likely to work through difficult problems.

Based on the aforementioned study, potentially, self-efficacy is critical for success in education. A school system is designed to continually challenge students through the presentation of new, more difficult information. If a student has low self-efficacy, the very purpose of school might not be accomplished if the student gives up and does not learn new material.

Additionally, certain parenting styles are associated with children who score high on achievement motivation tests. The parents of these children tend to:

1. Encourage the child to attempt difficult tasks, especially new ones.
2. Offer praise and other rewards for successful attempts and perseverance.
3. Encourage the child to find new ways to succeed instead of complaining about failure.
4. Prompt the child to go on to a more challenging task.

Each of these areas of parenting encourages children's sense of self-efficacy, which contributes to the children doing well on achievement motivation tests. Building resilient learners who see learning as valuable, fun, and beneficial to problem solving will have lasting impacts on their personal and professional successes.

Sources of Self-Efficacy Judgments

Not only does high self-efficacy contribute to high achievement, it also contributes to a heightened sense of competence. In fact, direct experiences of success or failure (termed enactive because they result from personal actions) are probably the most important sources of information people have about their competence. Thus, enactive learning occurs through completing a task by oneself. For self-efficacy to remain strong, one must complete tasks over and over making minimal mistakes. By doing so, minor mistakes often are of little impact to one's judgments of self-efficacy.

Second, people learn about their effectiveness from vicarious (secondhand) sources—that is, through the observations of others. For example, when learning math in school, the teacher may do multiple problems on the board. She may intentionally make mistakes and demonstrate how to correct those mistakes. Thus, vicarious learning is very important in that it allows a novice to learn many nuances of the task through the observation of an expert. Many individuals feel more confident completing a task after they have seen it performed. A third source of influence is *persuasion*. If others express faith in a person's abilities, if they continually urge, "Why don't you try? I know you can do it," a person might, in the end, come to believe just a little more in his or her effectiveness and competence.

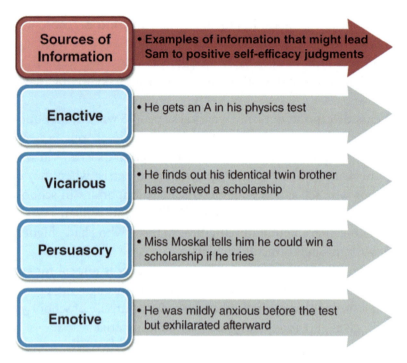

Figure 5.7 Sources of information that influence our judgment of personal effectiveness and competence.

Finally, Bandura (1997) ⌐explains that⌐ emotions can have a direct impact on estimates of capability. Under conditions of extreme arousal, for example, ⌐one⌐ might decide that ⌐he or she⌐ is capable of outrunning a threatening ⌐grizzly bear⌐ or swimming across a river to save a baby. ⌐Plus,⌐ if an activity makes ⌐people⌐ feel especially good, ⌐they are⌐ more likely to conclude that ⌐they are⌐ good at it than if it ⌐made them⌐ feel frustrated and unhappy (Figure 5.7).

Efficacy and Expectancy-Value Theory

⌐People⌐ are not simple creatures. No matter how overwhelmingly positive ⌐personal⌐ judgments of self-efficacy ⌐are⌐ and how high ⌐personal⌐ expectations of success, there are other factors at play. ⌐According to⌐ Eccles and Wigfield (2002), ⌐choices,⌐ persistence, and performance are profoundly influenced by the value of the outcome ⌐one expects. The⌐ cost of the activity, in terms of amount of effort required, sacrifices entailed, and other opportunities given up, also has to be taken into account. ⌐This is the⌐ basis of Eccles's **expectancy-value theory** (Wigfield et al., 2009).

> **Expectancy-value theory:** The belief that motivation is determined by the expectancy of success and the value of the reward.

⌐In⌐ this theory, ⌐expectancy⌐ is similar to a judgment of self-efficacy. ⌐It⌐ is defined by the individual's belief about how well he or she will do on a task. Value is a combined function of four factors: the personal importance of the task in terms of how it fits into the individual's plans and self-image (attainment value); its intrinsic value based on the personal satisfaction the person gets from doing the task; its utility value, which has to do with what the task contributes to short- and long-term goals; and its cost in terms of the amount of effort required, the probability of failure, associated stress, conflicting options, and so on.

What Does the Bible Say?

When we look at the expectancy-value theory, it is clear that personal benefit and individual reward are central to an individual's choice to engage in a behavior. While that may be true for human motives, God teaches us how to reframe what would be considered "value" or "worth it." In the following verses, we can see how God teaches to look beyond the rewards on this earth and beyond our own personal gain when deciding to engage in behaviors, and, through this biblical lens, we can see how He is teaching us to place our value on others' gain and eternal reward.

Matthew 6:19–21 ESV

"Do not lay up for yourselves treasures on earth, where moth and rust destroy and where thieves break in and steal, but lay up for yourselves treasures in heaven, where neither moth nor rust destroys and where thieves do not break in and steal. For where your treasure is, there your heart will be also."

Philippians 2:4 ESV

"Let each of you look not only to his own interests, but also to the interests of others."

2 Corinthians 4:18 ESV

"…as we look not to the things that are seen but to the things that are unseen. For the things that are seen are transient, but the things that are unseen are eternal."

People make choices based on a sort of mental calculus. If either the expectancy (one's ability to successfully perform a task), or the value (what one gets out of performing a task), are inconsistent with expectations, one will not engage in a task. For some, the motivation of money is extremely appealing. If a man was told that he would be given a million dollars for completing a task, he would be highly motivated to engage in the task. If he was tasked with learning to speak Japanese fluently within 10 minutes, he would probably dismiss the task (assuming that all people fluent in Japanese previously were excluded from participating). The important factors in this calculation include one's expectations of success, judgments of effectiveness and competence (self-efficacy), and the values and costs associated with each of the various options (Figure 5.8).

EMOTION

There is another side to human motivation. As Turner and Goodin (2008) explain, when people succeed in attaining a goal, they feel positive emotions. In contrast, people's failure can lead to negative emotions. Everyone has memories related to extreme happiness or sorrow. Examples may include graduating from high school, the death of a family pet, getting a job, the birth of a child, a car being stolen, and so on. All of these examples have emotions associated with them and all also relate to why we engage in certain behaviors. Hence, emotions are a fundamental part of human motivation.

What Is Emotion?

Emotions have presented a great deal of difficulty for psychologists. They cannot easily be defined or described; they are difficult to measure; their physiological bases do not clearly differentiate among them.

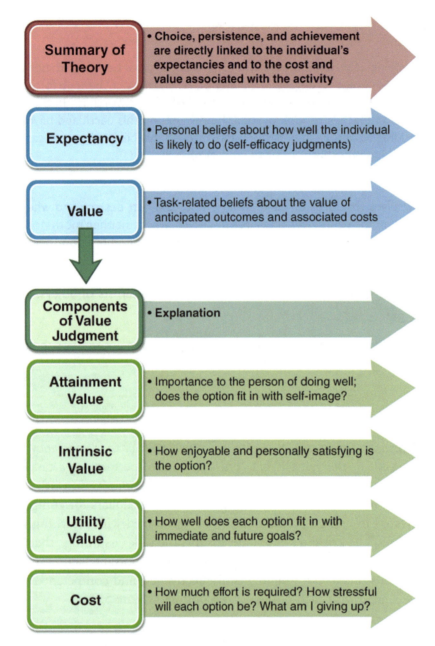

Figure 5.8 Eccles's expectancy-value theory of motivation ⌐is used⌐ to guide our choices and our efforts.

Yet, they are a fundamental part of being human. In fact, it is difficult to imagine any human experience that does not involve emotions.

⌐Emotions⌐ (also known as one's ⌐affect⌐) have two broad dimensions. The first is intensity, which, for most emotions, can range from low to high. Thus, anger might range from annoyance to rage; disgust, from mild aversion to utter revulsion; and joy, from contentment to absolute ecstasy. Emotions vary not only in intensity, but also in ⌐the second broad dimension,⌐ whether they are positive or negative. Joy, love, happiness, and interest are generally positive feelings; fear, anger, rage, and disgust are generally negative feelings.

> ⌐**Emotions:** Complex feeling states that include predictable physiological arousal, cognitions, and behaviors.⌐

What Does the Bible Say?

ᴸWhen we look at the range of emotions that humans can experience (both good and bad), we may find ourselves asking, "Are emotions biblical?" It is easy to see how emotions like joy or happiness may be biblical, but what about anger or sadness?

A quick search through the Bible reveals that a vast array of emotions are definitely a part of the human experience. Take a look at the following verses:

Psalms 42:3 ESV

"My tears have been my food day and night, while they say to me all the day long, 'Where is your God?'"

Galatians 5:22–23 ESV

"But the fruit of the Spirit is love, joy, peace, patience, kindness, goodness, faithfulness, gentleness, self-control; against such things there is no law."

John 11:35 ESV

"Jesus wept."

Furthermore, other verses instruct us on what we are to do with our emotions:

Ephesians 4:13 ESV

"Let all bitterness and wrath and anger and clamor and slander be put away from you, along with all malice."

Ephesians 4:26–27 ESV

"Be angry and do not sin; do not let the sun go down on your anger and give no opportunity to the devil."

Psalm 56:3 ESV

"When I am afraid, I put my trust in you."

Psalm 42:5–6a ESV

"Why are you cast down, O my soul, and why are you in turmoil within me? Hope in God; for I shall again praise him, my salvation and my God."

Proverbs 29:11 NIV

"Fools give full vent to their rage, but the wise bring calm in the end."

So, are emotions biblical? When we look at emotions through the lens of Scripture, it seems that emotions are part of the human experience and we are called to act on them in godly ways. Life will come; we will have troubles (John 16:33), and those troubles will cause emotions. However, understanding how to biblically respond when emotions arise is part of becoming more like Christ and perfecting in His image. In the words of David in Psalm 73 (ESV):

"When my soul was embittered,
when I was pricked in heart,
I was brutish and ignorant;
I was like a beast toward you.

Nevertheless, I am continually with you;
you hold my right hand.
You guide me with your counsel,
and afterward you will receive me to glory.
Whom have I in heaven but you?
And there is nothing on earth that I desire besides you.
My flesh and my heart may fail,
but God is the strength my heart and my portion forever.
For behold, those who are far from you shall perish;
you put an end to everyone who is unfaithful to you.
But for me it is good to be near God;
I have made the Lord God my refuge,
that I may tell of all your works."⌋

⌊Psychologists believe, however, that emotions are more than just our affect, or feelings, in a given situation, but are actually complex feeling states include three distinct components: physiological arousal, cognition, and behaviors. The *physiological arousal* component of emotion is the predictable bodily arousal and changes that we see in emotion. The *cognitive* component of emotion includes the way we think and appraise a feeling in a situation, as well as the judgments we make about the feeling and/or arousal. And, the *behavioral* component of emotion includes all of the ways we express emotion (i.e., facial gestures), as well as our behavioral responses to emotion (i.e., our tendency to run away or approach something). While emotions are fairly difficult to measure and study, we do know that emotions are accompanied by predictable physiological responses, cognitions, and behaviors.⌋ For example, imagine a time when ⌊a person⌋ became extremely angry. Think about what was happening from a physiological and behavioral perspective. ⌊No doubt, the person's⌋ anger was generally accompanied by increased heart and respiration rates as well as other physiological changes, and it may also be evident in changes in facial expressions, voice, and body language.

There are several thousand words referring to emotion in the English language, so it is very difficult to agree on the precise number of different emotions of which we are capable. Many psychologists have tried to summarize our emotions with lists of basic emotions. For example, Izard (2009) suggests we can easily distinguish among six distinct emotions: sadness, anger, disgust, fear, interest, and joy/happiness. Others, such as Parrott (2004), divide basic emotions into related secondary and tertiary emotions. For example, secondary emotions related to joy include cheerfulness, zest, contentment, pride, optimism, enthrallment, and relief. ⌊Each⌋ of these secondary emotions might be described more precisely in terms of a tertiary emotion. For example, cheerfulness brings with it the possibility of many other emotions, including amusement, bliss, ⌊conviviality,⌋ glee, jolliness, joviality, delight, satisfaction, and ecstasy.

Not only ⌊is the number of emotions debated, scholars and scientists⌋ cannot always agree about whether a given emotion is positive or negative. Consider the element of surprise. On one hand, ⌊all people⌋ have been pleasantly surprised ⌊at one time in their life, such as receiving a birthday card⌋ or present. On the other hand, ⌊all people have also⌋ been surprised/⌊shocked⌋ when somebody jumped around a corner and scared ⌐them.⌐ Therefore, ⌐one⌐ may wonder ⌐whether⌐ surprise ⌐is⌐ pleasant or unpleasant? In fact, ⌐this is indeterminable because emotion is not⌐ a property of stimulation, but a property of ⌐one's⌐ subjective reaction to stimulation—⌐with "subjective" referring⌐ to the individual's interpretation ⌐of his or her reaction to the stimulation.

⌐The subjective experience of emotion has six characteristics:

1. Emotions are transitory
2. Emotions show valence, meaning they are positive or negative
3. Cognitive appraisals evaluate the emotional stimuli
4. Emotions elicit an action tendency or provide motivation to act
5. Emotions alter thought processes
6. Emotions invoke passions, which are behaviors that you don't directly initiate

⌐Some people, for example, rape and incest victims, survivors of plane and serious automobile crashes, combat veterans, and others who have personally experienced traumatic events may react emotionally with posttraumatic stress disorder (PTSD). PTSD is a stress reaction in which individuals suffer from persistent reexperiences of the traumatic event in the form, for example, of flashbacks or nightmares. Sufferers experience an emotional numbing in relation to everyday events and feelings of alienation from other people. Finally, the emotional pain of this reaction can result in an increase in various symptoms, such as sleep problems, guilt about surviving, difficulty in concentrating, and an exaggerated startle response. So, emotional responses to events can a long-lasting impact on one's life trajectory.⌐

© Oleg Zabielin/Shutterstock.com

Physiologial Arousal Component

The physiological changes that accompany ⌐emotion that can be detected and measured are called **arousal**.⌐ In situations of high arousal, the body's physiological systems prepare the individual to respond. If arousal becomes too high, panic may result and the effectiveness of behavior may drop. For example, some studies indicate that many soldiers under attack fail to fire their rifles ⌐due to extremely high arousal; some⌐ may even run away.

> ⌐**Arousal:** The physiological aspects of emotion that can be detected and measured.⌐

The term, arousal, has both physiological and psychological meanings. As a physiological term, it refers to activity of the sympathetic nervous system. ⌐The⌐ sympathetic nervous system is activated for your "fight, flight, ⌐or freeze⌐," response. Physiological arousal ranges from states of very low activity such as those characteristic of sleep or deep comas (alpha, theta, or

> **Electrodermal response:** Electrical conductivity of the skin.

delta waves; low **electrodermal response**, or electrical conductivity of the skin; ⌐and⌐ low respiration and heart rates), to very high activity such as might be characteristic of extreme anger, fear, or panic.

As a psychological term, *arousal* refers to the alertness or vigilance of the organism and to the emotions accompanying physiological arousal. Thus, an individual at a very low level of arousal might be asleep; a moderately aroused individual is alert and attentive; ⌐and⌐ one who is extremely aroused may be in a state of extreme emotion. Given these three states, it seems that the moderately aroused individual would perform the best on a variety of tasks.

The Yerkes–Dodson Law

The effectiveness of ⌐one's⌐ behavior is closely tied to arousal level. At very low levels of arousal, such as when asleep or almost asleep, ⌐one⌐ might have trouble responding to the simplest ⌐of questions. Likewise, at very high levels of arousal, such as if⌐ a house is on fire, ⌐one may have similar difficulty performing easy tasks.⌐

© Azret Ayubov/Shutterstock.com

▶ **DISCUSSIO ON RESEARCH IN MOTIVATIO AND EMOTION**

High arousal, evident in increasing anxiety and sometimes even fear or panic, explains why some highly competent students do poorly in oral or written examinations. ⌐Most people have⌐ probably experienced arousal ⌐that is⌐ virtually nonexistent, or arousal ⌐at an amplified level that has hindered their ability to perform⌐ tasks to the best of ⌐their⌐ ability. ⌐According to Chen (2009),⌐ considerable research ⌐supports the notion that⌐ anxiety ⌐negatively impacts⌐ school performance ⌐at all levels.⌐

⌐More than a century ago,⌐ Yerkes and Dodson (1908), ⌐explained⌐ that there is a level of arousal at which behavior is most effective. A lower or higher level of arousal is associated with increasingly ineffective behavior. ⌐As arousal increases, performance becomes more effective until an optimal level is reached. Increases in arousal beyond this level lead to decreasingly effective behavior.⌐ This observation, ⌐is⌐ known as the **Yerkes–Dodson Law**, ⌐and is⌐ widely accepted in psychology (Landers, 2007).

> ⌐**Yerkes–Dodson Law:** An optimal level of arousal exists for different behaviors and this level varies both for different individuals and for different behaviors.⌐

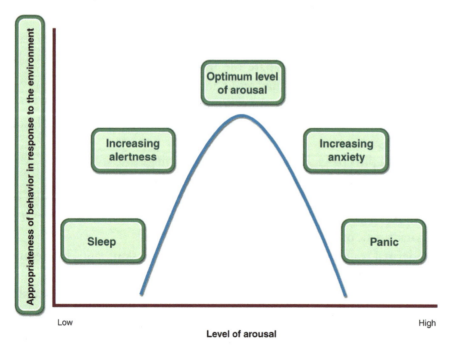

Figure 5.9   ⌐The Yerkes–Dodson law.⌐

The general adaptation syndrome includes three stages: an alarm reaction, a stage of resistance, and a stage of exhaustion. One could view a typical semester as a series of alarm reactions, brief periods of bodily arousal that prepares the body for vigorous activity, followed by periods of resistance. Resistance is a state of moderate arousal in which the body fights against the debilitating effects of the prolonged stressor. Finally, when the body has used all of its reserves it begins to fail.

Need for Stimulation

In a classic experiment on sensory deprivation, Hebb and his colleagues (Hebb, 1972; Heron, 1957) paid college students 20 dollars a day to do "absolutely nothing." Students laid in a cot with a U-shaped pillow over their ears with a white noise machine to dampen their sense of hearing, a translucent visor over their eyes to restrict their vision, and cardboard tubes over their hands and arms to limit their sense of touch. In this greatly restricted sensory environment, they only got up to use the bathroom or eat.

This was the first of a large number of studies on sensory deprivation. For example, in a more recent demonstration, the BBC arranged for six volunteers to spend 48 hours alone in totally darkened nuclear bunkers (Total Isolation, 2008). The outcome in this demonstration was highly consistent with previous studies, most of which found that participants typically cannot endure such isolation for very long. In the Hebb (1972) experiment, most people only lasted 2–3 days before asking for the experiment to be ended and to be released. In other more extreme deprivation experiments—where, for example, participants floated unattended in a brine solution while in complete darkness and silence—their length of stay was considerably reduced.

Among the findings from these studies is the poignant observation that most participants eventually experience some impairment of perceptual and intellectual functioning. Tasks that are very simple before isolation become extremely difficult and sometimes impossible after prolonged sensory deprivation. In the BBC demonstration, one participant's performance on simple memory tasks had dropped by 36%. In addition, many isolation participants experienced emotional changes and rapidly fluctuating moods ranging from nervousness and irritability to anger or fear. Three of the six participants in the BBC study reported having hallucinations involving objects such as snakes, zebras, and oysters; and a fourth became convinced that her sheets were soaking wet. Other deprivation experiments have had similar outcomes (Mason & Brady, 2009).

Sensory deprivation research strongly suggests humans have a need for variety of sensory stimulation. If true, perhaps some of otherwise unexplainable behaviors might be accounted for—behaviors such as curiosity and exploration. This need for stimulation is the basis for an **arousal theory** of motivation.

> **Arousal theory:** A theory stating that individuals behave in a way to maintain an optimal level of arousal.

Arousal Theory

Arousal theory rests upon two assumptions (Hebb, 1972). The first, already mentioned, is the *Yerkes–Dodson Law*—the belief that there is an optimal level of arousal for different behaviors and that this level varies both for different individuals and for different behaviors. For example, playing well in an intense, physical sporting activity such as football may require that players be "psyched up" (highly aroused). The same level of arousal, though, may be a detriment in a highly cognitive task like writing an examination or following a recipe when baking.

The second assumption is individuals behave so as to maintain an optimal level of arousal. This is evident in highly arousing situations where an intensely frightened individual tries to escape or change the situation. The consequences of escaping from an angry mob will surely be a reduction of arousal. The assumption is double edged, however: It predicts not only that people behave so as to reduce arousal when it is too high, but also that they will attempt to increase arousal when it is inappropriately low.

Evidence of this is clear in sensory deprivation studies, ⌊when⌋ participants whistle, sing, talk to themselves, try desperately to engage the experimenter in conversation when food is brought in, and otherwise try to increase the amount of stimulation ⌊that⌋ they are receiving. This ⌊explains⌋ why, ⌊when⌋ alone in a quiet place, ⌊people⌋ instinctively feel the need to turn on the television or listen to the radio. Doing so increases your level of arousal to an optimal state. One of the effects of sensory stimulation is to increase arousal.

Sources of Arousal

The physiological changes that accompany arousal are brought about by activity of the autonomic nervous system, which is not ordinarily under the individual's conscious control. We cannot easily "will" our skins to become more conductive to electricity, our hearts to beat faster, ⌊or induce⌋ brain-wave activity ⌊changes.⌋

Still, there are ways ⌊that one can influ⌋ence the autonomic nervous system.⌋ For example, simply imagining highly arousing scenes, or seeing them depicted in pictures, films, or words, can clearly increase ⌊one's⌋ physiological arousal. Hence, one source of arousal is internal, cognitive activity.

© Halfpoint/Shutterstock.com

A second obvious source of arousal is external stimulation. The sheer amount of stimulation, however, may not be especially important. In the original ⌊Hebb (1972)⌋ isolation experiments, there was considerable sensory stimulation, including the ⌊white noise machine sounds,⌋ the pressure of the cardboard ⌊tubes,⌋ sensations relating to clothing and diffuse light, and perhaps even tastes inside the mouth and vague odors in the environment. ⌊Yet,⌋ this stimulation was constant and unchanging, and consequently, ⌊the arousal level dropped⌋ dramatically. Recordings of participants during isolation indicate that their brain-wave functioning was more like that of the deeper stages of sleep than like that of participants who are awake (Zubek, 1973).

The types of stimulation that appear to cause the greatest arousal are those associated with emotion. At one extreme, emotion-laden experiences can increase arousal dramatically, as is evident in panic situations. In general, the most arousing stimuli are those capturing interest and attention—that is, stimuli that are surprising, novel, meaningful, ambiguous, or complex (Berlyne, 1960). These qualities of stimuli are linked with emotions such as interest and excitement; their opposites are associated with boredom and apathy. All these emotions are closely linked with motivation ⌊and the physiological component of emotion is very important to mobilizing us to act based on the emotions we feel in a situation. As you will see later, the physiological arousal inherent in emotion is a key component to various theories of emotion.

Cognitive Component of Emotion

In addition to experiencing physiological arousal during emotion, individuals will have thoughts associated with the emotion. Is this experience threatening or challenging? Is it relevant or irrelevant? Is it real or not real for me? There are many thoughts we have as we experience an emotion and as you will see in the theories of emotion, how we appraise an emotional experience greatly affects our reactions to it and our behaviors in response to it.

Behavioral Component of Emotion

In addition to the physiological arousal associated with an emotion and the thoughts we have when experiencing emotion, when an individual experiences an emotion, there is also a behavioral component to it. Emotions can be expressed in behavior, as, for example, when you run from an angry competitor or chase after something you want. In these examples, the motivational component of the emotion is clear in that emotions include a behavioral action in response to the experience of the emotion.

Most emotions may be seen as having approach or avoidance tendencies, although these will not always be overtly expressed. Emotions may also be expressed verbally. Much of the richness of human conversation derives from the expression and interpretation of emotion. So, too, do books, movies, and art forms influence or manipulate human emotions.

Emotions are expressed nonverbally as well, and they have been extensively studied as manifestations of facial expression. Ekman (2005) and others have noted that there appear to be a number of emotional expressions that are innate and common to all members of our species. Raising the eyebrows is a quasi-universal expression of greeting or acknowledgment while smiling is a universal gesture of approval and friendliness.

Many emotional expressions, however, are learned and culturally specific. Klineberg (1938) examined some Chinese novels to discover how their authors describe emotional expression. It might seem strange in western society that sticking out the tongue means surprise, clapping the hands indicates anxiety or disappointment, and scratching the ears shows happiness. The Chinese might be equally surprised to find westerners frowning when puzzled, chewing lips in concentration, pounding fist in palm to signal determination or anger, and wetting one's lips in anticipation.

Theories of Emotion

Several theories of emotion exist that attempt to make sense of our emotional experiences and to explain how our physiological arousal, cognitions, and behaviors fit together in an emotional experience. Among the leading theories of emotion are the James–Lange theory, the Cannon–Bard theory, and Schachter's Two-Factor theory.

The James–Lange Theory

Early theorists made much of physiological changes due to emotion. William James (1890/1950) went so far as to say that emotion results from physiological changes, an idea developed simultaneously by a Danish psychologist, Lange. As a result, the theory came to be known as the *James–Lange theory*. In essence, it maintains that an emotion-related stimulus gives rise to certain physiological changes and that the individual perceives these physiological changes and then interprets them as an emotion. As James (1890/1950) concludes, "We feel sorry because we cry . . . afraid because we tremble"

(p. 1006). ⌐The key principle of this theory is that our physiological responses occur in a situation and then, because we are physically responding, that tells us we are experiencing some emotion.⌐

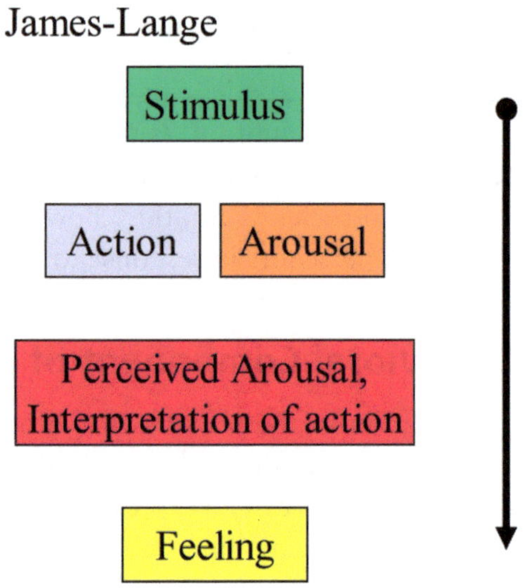

The Cannon–Bard Theory

Two other researchers, Cannon and Bard ⌐(1929, 1939),⌐ objected to the James–Lange theory. They thought ⌐human⌐ awareness of physiological changes is too slow to explain how ⌐people⌐ can instantly react to emotion-laden situations. Besides, physiological changes such as increased heart rate that accompany different emotions, do not appear to differentiate among them. ⌐Increased⌐ heart rate may occur when an individual is happy or when fearful, ⌐so how do we know what we are feeling just from physiological arousal?⌐ Also, Cannon demonstrated ⌐with⌐ cats ⌐that cutting the nerves linking their⌐ brain to parts of the body involved in emotional reactions still behaved as though they "felt" emotion, ⌐leading to the⌐ Cannon–Bard theory.

The Cannon–Bard theory suggests ⌐that⌐ when an individual perceives an emotion-related situation or object, the hypothalamus sends messages both to the cortex, where the emotion is felt, and to the body, where physiological reactions take place. As a result, awareness of emotion and awareness of physiological changes are independent, although they result from the same source of stimulation. It is the organism's awareness of the emotional significance of an experience that gives rise to an emotion ⌐and the physiological arousal and psychological experience of emotion happen at the same time (not one before the other as in the James–Lange theory).⌐

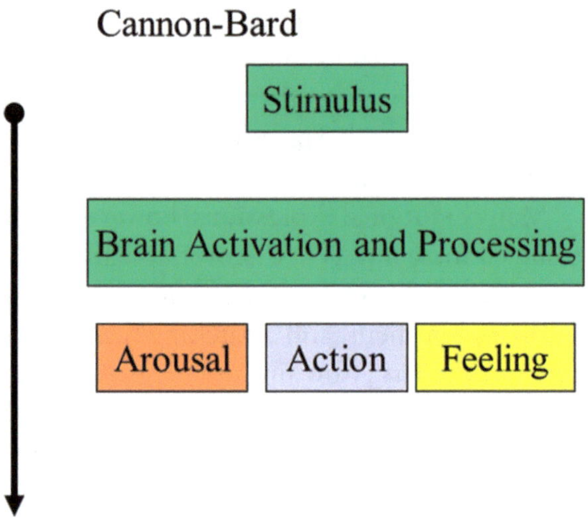

Schachter's Two-Factor Theory

James-Lange

Figure 5.10 ⌐Model of the James–Lange theory of arousal.⌐
Source: Brian Kelley

Cannon-Bard

Figure 5.11 ⌐Model of the Cannon–Bard theory of arousal.⌐
Source: Brian Kelley

It turns out that both the James–Lange and the Cannon–Bard theories are probably at least partly right. In an early study, Maranon (1924) injected human participants with epinephrine, a compound very similar to noradrenaline, and found that while they experienced physiological reactions similar to those that accompany intense emotion, they did not feel any specific emotion.

Schachter ⌐and Singer (1962)⌐ later replicated the Maranon ⌐(1924)⌐ studies to try to clarify the relationship between physiological changes and cognitions in producing emotional states. Participants in an experiment were told they would receive injections of a new drug that would improve their performance on a test of visual perception. Some participants received injections of epinephrine; the others received a placebo. After the injections, they were given one of three types of information about the effects of the drug. The informed group was told what the actual effects of the drug might be and how long these effects normally last; the ignorant group was told that the drug would have absolutely no side effects; and the misinformed group was told that a slight numbness and itchiness might result.

Members of each group were then assigned to one of two experimental conditions, or to a control group. The control group waited quietly for a period of time, and members were then questioned about their emotional reactions. Not surprisingly, they reported no particular emotion, as had been the case in the earlier Maranon ⌐(1924)⌐ studies.

In ⌐the⌐ experimental ⌐euphoria⌐ group, participants were left to wait in a room with another individual who was introduced to them as a fellow participant. In fact, this person was a confederate of the experimenters who had been instructed to perform a standardized "euphoric-manic" routine—dancing, playing basketball with crumpled pieces of paper, making little projectiles and launching them with rubber bands, playing with a hula hoop, and otherwise trying to convey the impression that this was really a lot of fun.

In the second experimental ⌐anger⌐ group, participants were left with a confederate and were asked to fill out a long and intensely personal questionnaire while waiting. It asked about the personal hygiene of every member of the subject's family—how often they took a bath and brushed their teeth, and who had the most disagreeable body odor; participants weren't allowed to answer "no" or "none." One question read: "With how many men (other than your father) has your mother had extramarital relationships? The confederate, acting according to precise directions, became progressively angrier while completing the questionnaire, finally crumpling it up and leaving the room.

Following this, all participants were individually interviewed to uncover their emotional reactions. Results were as follows: participants who were uninformed or misinformed (and who had received epinephrine) exhibited and felt anger or euphoria, depending on the experimental condition; informed participants and those individuals who had received placebos typically did not ⌐respond emotionally.⌐

Schachter ⌐and Singer's (1962)⌐ explanation for these findings is the basis of ⌐Schachter's⌐ two-factor theory of emotion: One factor is an undifferentiated state of physiological arousal that underlies all emotions—as James had argued. The second factor is the individual's interpretation of arousal in light of what caused it. Thus, participants who had a logical explanation for their physiological states (the informed group) experienced no emotion. They simply labeled their physiological states according to the explanations given by the experimenter. Those who had been misinformed or not informed attributed their physiological states to emotions ⌐that⌐ they thought they should be feeling, ⌐labeling⌐ these emotions according to the confederate's behavior. In short, although physiological changes are clearly involved in emotional reaction, ⌐an⌐ individual's cognitive label for the change determines the nature of the emotion. ⌐Therefore, Schachter's Two-Factor theory advanced what we thought about emotions by adding a cognitive appraisal component to the physiological arousal that accompanies emotional experiences. It is this cognitive appraisal component that helps us label what we are feeling (both physiologically and psychologically) in a situation.⌐

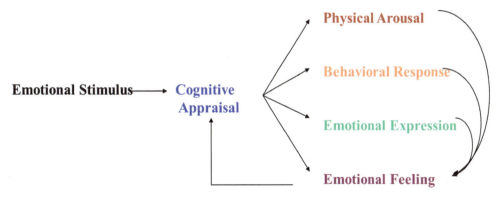

Figure 5.12 ⌐Model of Schachter's theory of arousal.⌐

Source: Brian Kelley

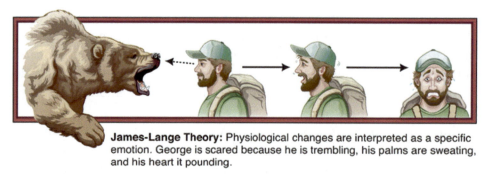

James-Lange Theory: Physiological changes are interpreted as a specific emotion. George is scared because he is trembling, his palms are sweating, and his heart it pounding.

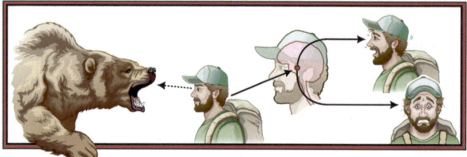

Cannon-Bard Theory: George's fear results from his understanding, mediated through the hypothalamus which has sent messages to his cortex as well as his autonomic nervous system, that this is a dangerous bear.

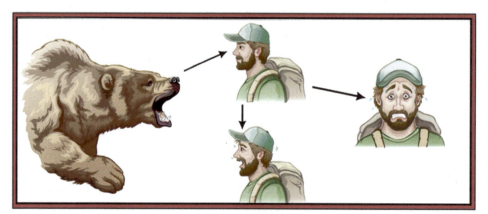

Schacter Two-Factor Theory: George is scared because he is aroused and he interprets his arousal as being caused by the danger in this situation.

Figure 5.13 Three historical explanations of emotion.

Recent Theories

Both the Cannon–Bard theory and Schachter's two-factor theory hold that the nature and intensity of an emotion depend largely on the individual's conscious understanding of the emotional significance of an event. These are attribution theories of motivation, ⌊both emphasizing⌋ that it is the individual's conscious understanding of the meaning of a situation (or of the reasons for physiological arousal) that determines the emotion (Moors, 2009).

Some theorists point out, however, that not all emotional reactions require a conscious understanding of a situation. Scherer (2005) argues emotional responses can also result from unconscious cognitive activity. Someone experiencing a classically conditioned fear response, for example, might not always have a clear, conscious explanation for the accompanying emotion.

Other theorists have proposed ⌊that⌋ emotional responses are represented in the brain in complex, linked networks that can be activated by a wide range of related stimuli (Lewis, 2005). These emotional responses may well have been classically conditioned in the first place. The behaviorist John Watson (1930) suggested that infants are born with three basic emotional reactions: fear, rage, and love. Each of these is elicited by specific stimuli as an unlearned reflex. ⌊Thus,⌋ stroking the infant evokes emotions related to love; confining the infant might elicit rage; and fear can be brought about

© Flashon Studio/Shutterstock.com

by loud noises. Over time, these emotions become classically conditioned to a wide range of other stimuli. ⌊Whenever⌋ an individual has an emotional experience, information about the situation (the individual's behavior and a variety of other related details) is stored in memory and linked with other related emotions. As a result, previously neutral stimuli can come to have emotional significance for an individual.

The Dual-Pathway Model for Fear

The notion that there are unconscious as well as conscious processes involved in emotional reactions has led to an important model of emotional processing of fear-related stimuli—the dual-pathway model. What this model says, in effect, is that there are two systems involved in fear reactions: one is unconscious and faster; the other is conscious and slower (LeDoux, 2010).

When ⌊one sees⌋ an avalanche come barreling down, visual and auditory stimuli race to ⌊the⌋ thalamus. From there, the information forks out into the two paths of this dual-pathway system. One path ⌊leads⌋ to the amygdala—that part of the brain directly involved with fear and danger—⌊giving rise to immediate physiological and muscular reactions.⌋ Meanwhile, the other path carries information to the ⌊visual⌋ cortex, allowing ⌊a person⌋ to interpret the situation more thoroughly (Figure 5.14). A fraction of a second later, ⌊one⌋ might decide ⌊his⌋ initial reaction was unwarranted, that this looked like an avalanche but was just a few snowflakes on the periphery of ⌊his⌋ vision and ⌊he⌋ can relax.

Gender Differences for Displaying Emotions

⌊Think back to your childhood and how you displayed emotions. Some studies have shown that there are significant differences between how boys and girls display their emotions (Chaplin & Aldao, 2013). In a recent meta-analysis of 166 studies examining emotional expression in boys and girls across development, Chaplin and Aldao (2013) found significant, although very small, gender differences in the expression of emotion. Most notably, they found that boys were more likely to express externalizing emotions like anger or rage, while girls were more likely to express positive emotions and internalizing emotions like sadness, empathy, and anxiety. Also, they noted that age moderated the gender differences in emotional expression, as well as situation (with some situations yielding greater gender differences in

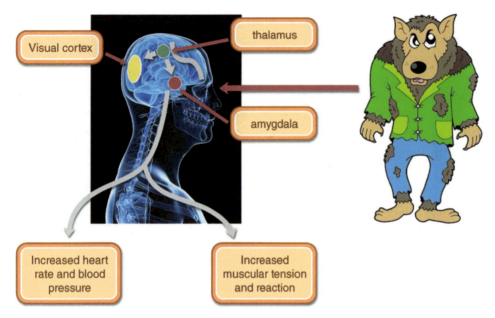

Figure 5.14   The dual-pathway fear system.

Photo on left: Thinkstock/iStockphoto, illustration on right: Thinkstock/Hemera

emotional expression than other situations). It is likely that biology and socialization contribute to some gender differences in expressing emotions. The combination of hormone differences (i.e., testosterone/estrogen levels), paired with culturally constructed conventions (i.e., boys don't cry) may lead to differences in emotional expression.

└When considering the culture of the United States, it is no surprise that emotions are expressed differently between genders. "Big boys don't cry" and "Sugar and spice and everything nice" have traditionally been taught to children, thus suggesting how boys and girls should be. Gender differences in toys are also evident and have been proposed as another way that appropriate gender behavior, to include emotional expression, is taught (Li & Wong, 2016). While some research suggest that children are nurtured to display certain differences between the genders (see review in Liben & Bigler, 2002), much controversy still remains on whether which influence (nature vs. nurture) is more significant.┘

The Brain and Emotions

Research with humans also indicates that certain parts of the brain, especially of the limbic system, are closely involved in emotional reactions. For example, Koelsch (2010) showed that music, which can evoke very strong emotions, └regularly┘ leads to activation of virtually all limbic structures.

Odors, which often evoke strong emotions, also lead to activation of the limbic system. Schredl et al. (2009) stimulated 15 sleeping participants during rapid-eye-movement

LIMBIC SYSTEM STRUCTURES

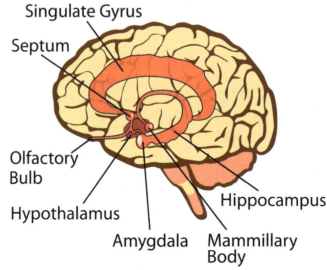

© Athanasia Nomikou/Shutterstock.com

(REM) sleep with one of two smells—hydrogen sulphide (a rotten egg smell) or phenylethyl alcohol (the smell of roses). Not only did these smells lead to activation of the limbic system, but they also affected the content of the participants' dreams. ⌐Schredl et al. (2009)⌐ suggest it might be valuable to study the effect that olfactory stimuli conditioned to pleasant reactions might have on nightmares.

Among limbic system structures that are involved in interpreting emotions and in guiding behavior in appropriate directions, the amygdala is especially important in processing fear reactions (Bush et al., 2009). There is some suggestion that impairment of amygdala functioning in individuals may be linked to psychopathology and, consequently, to criminal behavior. Such individuals may be unemotional, callous, and fearless, and more prone to committing acts of violence without fear of consequences (DeLisi et al., 2009).

The amygdala and other structures of the limbic system, such as the hypothalamus, are involved not only in fear reactions but also in the recognition of emotional expression (Batista & Freitas-Magalhaes, 2009). Individuals with impaired limbic system functioning—as sometimes happens as a result of diseases such as ⌐Parkinson's⌐ or alcoholism—may have difficulty interpreting the meaning of facial expressions (Marinkovic et al., 2009).

Not surprisingly, brain surgery can also be used to control emotional reactions. It has sometimes been used with mentally disturbed people for whom all other forms of therapy have been unsuccessful. The practice of removing parts of the cortex (for example, ⌐a⌐ prefrontal lobotomy or eucotomy), once relatively common, has largely been abandoned since the discovery that very small lesions have many of the same positive effects without the same side effects. Rosemary Kennedy, sister of President John F. Kennedy, was left permanently incapacitated after a eucotomy (Feldman, 2001).

Cognitive Control of Emotions

It is possible that, at least to some degree, ⌐people⌐ are masters of ⌐their⌐ emotions and not ⌐just⌐ prisoners. In an experiment conducted by Lazarus and his associates, participants were exposed to films of woodshop accidents (Koriat et al., 1972). In the films, one man lacerates the tips of his fingers, another cuts off a finger, and a third is skewered through the midsection by a plank propelled from a circular saw.

Some participants were asked to detach themselves from events in the film; others were asked to involve themselves. In neither case were they told how to do this. Heart rate changes were recorded for every individual during ⌐the⌐ presentation of the film, and reports were obtained of subjective emotional states. Significantly, participants who were asked to detach themselves from the film had much lower emotional reaction in terms of both their heart rates and self-reports. Those who were told to involve themselves experienced ⌐physiological changes and⌐ profound emotional reactions.

When questioned about their strategies, a majority of the involvement group said they imagined they were the person ⌐(empathy)⌐ to whom the accidents were happening, or they attempted to relate the accidents to other accidents they might have witnessed or in which friends or relatives ⌐(sympathy)⌐ had been involved. Members of the detachment group pretended that the events had been "staged" for the filming or paid particular attention to the technical details of the film.

The cognitive control of emotions is an important coping mechanism, explains Lazarus (1974, 1999). For example, a study of patients before and after surgery revealed that those who adopted detachment strategies (not wanting to know details of their surgery, recovery, or ⌐potential⌐ complications) experienced ⌐quicker and easier⌐ recoveries than patients who were more involved. Lazarus ⌐(1974, 1999)⌐ speculates that paying undue attention to possible signs of complications, or even to signs of recovery, is probably associated with more anxiety (stress) and is negatively associated with recovery. In Lazarus's view, ⌐a person's⌐ cognitive activity ⌐greatly impacts⌐ emotional states.

Emotion is seldom a single, identifiable response to a given situation; more often, it is a complex ∟response.⌟ Moreover, ∟it is a⌟ complex ∟of responses, shifting⌟ continually. Anger turns into despair, grief into elation, rage into apathy, joy into sorrow, anxiety into relief, ∟and so on.⌟ Emotions ebb and flow as ∟people⌟ appraise ∟their⌟ situations, relationships with people and things, ∟and the⌟ probabilities of attaining or not attaining goals. The fundamental point is that we are the ones doing the appraising; the emotion resides not in the situation but in our appraisal of it. Furthermore, ∟people⌟ exercise control over ∟their⌟ appraisals, sometimes deliberately reducing emotional reaction, as may be the case with anger or fear, sometimes purposely enhancing it, as with love or joy.

∟The appraisal of emotion and our cognitive control of emotions is actually something that the Apostle Paul spoke of often in his letters. In fact, in Philippians, Paul gives us concrete guidance for how to manage our emotions and keep our focus positive. In Philippians 4, Paul tells us how to experience peace when he writes:

> *"Do not be anxious about anything, but in everything by prayer and supplication with thanksgiving let your requests be made known to God. And the peace of God, which surpasses all understanding, will guard your hearts and your minds in Christ Jesus.*
>
> *Finally, brothers, whatever is true, whatever is honorable, whatever is just, whatever is pure, whatever is lovely, whatever is commendable, if there is any excellence, if there is anything worthy of praise, think about these things. What you have learned and received and heard and seen in me—practice these things, and the God of peace will be with you."*

∟As stated by Lazarus (1974, 1999), cognitive control of emotions is an important coping mechanism and through the Bible (like this passage in Philippians), we see guidance on how to have this cognitive control. As stated by Paul and as shown in research, prayer (Ai et al., 2005; Whittington & Scher, 2010), gratitude (Emmons & Mishra, 2011), and thinking of positive things (Naseem & Khalid, 2010) can reduce negative emotions and help us cope effectively in life.

∟Bower's model proposes that when a person experiences a given emotion in a particular situation, that emotion is stored in memory along with the ongoing events, as part of the same context. This pattern of memory representation gives rise to mood-congruent processing and mood-dependent memory (Gilligan & Bower, 2013). Mood-congruent processing occurs when people are selectively sensitized to processing and retrieval information that agrees with their current mood state. Material that is congruent with one's prevailing mood is more likely to be noticed, attended to, and processed more deeply and with greater elaborative associations. Mood-dependent memory refers to circumstances in which people find it easier to recall information when their mood at retrieval matches their mood when they first committed the information to memory. This is one of the reasons why stress and anxiety can lead to more stress and anxiety. As you begin to ruminate on the stressors in your life, it triggers memory systems related to those memories making it easier to recall similar memories. Your body responds by matching your cognitive and emotional state with behavioral and physiological responses. This creates a positive feedback loop and over time this cycle can contribute to heightened stress and eventually burnout.

∟Understanding emotions can be surprisingly difficult and humans are especially bad at it. Many factors can negatively impact our ability to appraise our emotional state. Knowing these factors can be really helpful in gaining better control and understanding of your emotions, but also understanding the emotions of the people around you. Once you consider this list, you will realize that many of the emotional responses that trigger you, such as from a loved one, friend, or colleague, are a response to their being stressed and often has little to do with you. So, once you can remove the emotional response from your own reaction to their stress, it will be easier to offer a compassionate and timely response to their ongoing stress. This will help to deescalate everyone's stress. According to Gagné and Deci (2005), the top 10 factors that tend to impact our emotional state for which we don't give enough credit to include:

1. Being worn-out physically
2. Totally frustrated
3. Exhausted or sleep deprived
4. Sick or just not feeling well
5. Distracted or preoccupied
6. Physical arousal (of any kind)
7. Nothing left (just ran out of emotions)
8. Hormonal changes
9. Mood-dependent memories
10. Emotional intelligence (high or low)

© Monkey Business Images/Shutterstock.com

ₗA stressor is a stimulus event that places a demand on an organism for some kind of adaptive response. Furthermore, a stressor can be of three types: environmental, psycholog-

© arka38/Shutterstock.com

ical, and social. Finally, the four dimensions are intensity, duration, rate, and predictability. It is difficult to find a single definition for "stress," because stress can be both a positive experience, which can act as a motivator, or a negative experience, which can act as a deterrent. Also, people react to stressors very differently. For example, a stressor for one person may act as an energizer, while the same stressor may be problematic for others. Stress in college can be particularly high because so many rapid changes have occurred, which include geographic mobility, new school, new job, new lifestyle, new friends and time pressures, competition, financial problems, noise, disappointments, failure, and crowding.

© Stokkete/Shutterstock.com

Signs of Being Stressed-Out			
Emotional	**Cognitive**	**Behavioral**	**Physiological**
Anxious Scared Irritable Moody	Low self-esteem Fear of failure Can't concentrate embarrass easily Worry Preoccupied Forgetfulness	Stutter Cry without cause impulsively Tremble, ticks nervous laughter Grind teeth Smoke Drug/alcohol use Accident prone Under-eat/overeat	Perspiration Increased heart rate Eating problems Dry mouth Tire easily Frequent urination Sleep problems Diarrhea (gastrointestinal [GI] problems) Headaches/neck and back pain Increased illness

THE STRESS ARC
maintaining motivation without burnout

motivation and healthy pressure

PEAK PERFORMANCE

energetic
creative
motivated
interested
too comfortable
bored
unaware

tired
indecisive
fuzzy mind
exhausted
irritable
anxious
burnout

stress and over-pressured

Stress occurs when perceived pressure on an individual exceeds ability to maintain resilience

© desdemona72/Shutterstock.com

SUMMARY

This chapter discusses the topic of motivation, which deals with the conscious and unconscious forces that instigate, direct, and control our behavior. This chapter explained motivation from both the physiological and behavioristic approaches. The hedonistic principle (people seek pleasure and try to avoid pain) and need-drive theory support the behavioristic notion that satisfying needs is reinforcing. Most important is the *incentive* value of goals, linked with the ability to imagine and anticipate the consequences of personal actions. Next, Maslow's hierarchy of needs was discussed. Maslow suggests people are driven by low-level basic (deficiency) needs and higher-level (growth) needs, hierarchically arranged so that higher-level needs are not attended to until lower-level needs have been satisfied. The highest human need is the need for self-actualization. Finally, in the area of motivation, cognitive views and important terms were examined including cognitive dissonance theory, achievement motivation theory, attribution theory, and expectancy-value theory.

This chapter also covered the topic of emotions. Emotions are motives; people are driven toward positive emotions and away from negative emotions. Intensity of emotions is reflected in physiological arousal. The human need for stimulation and the efforts to combat boredom reflect the principle (Yerkes–Dodson Law) that there is an optimal level of arousal for most tasks. Intensity of emotions is reflected in arousal level; the nature of the emotion has to do with cognitive interpretation. This chapter covered three theories on emotion including the James–Lang theory, the Cannon–Bard theory, and Schachter's two-factor theory. The James–Lange theory of emotion says people feel an emotion because of their physiological reactions. The Cannon–Bard theory says that emotion and physiological reaction are separate; a person feels an emotion because of his or her cognitive interpretation. Schachter's two-factor theory says the physiological reaction is basic to the emotion, but its nature is determined by the cognitive attribution the individual makes. The limbic system is closely involved in emotions.

Finally, this chapter discussed hunger and sex drives. Hunger control has to do with stomach sensations, changes in blood sugar level, hormonal and chemical signals (many of which affect the limbic system and especially the thalamus), and a host of learned factors associated with the taste, smell, and appearance of food and with cultural values associated with food and with body appearance. Malfunctions of hunger control systems can result in obesity. Sex drive is related to hormonal, cultural, and other factors, sometimes including love.

As can be seen by this chapter, the field of psychology has largely explained the motivation of behavior in terms of physiological or psychological drives and through cognitive and emotional processes. While this may be a fair representation of how our human selves respond to stimuli and behaviorally respond, we know from the Bible that there is more to our behaviors. We know that we are called to be more than just physical responders to our internal or external motivating drives/needs. Because we are spiritual beings as well, we are called to be motivated by a desire to please God and glorify Him. We have not only been called to glorify God in our bodies and with our behaviors, but we have also been equipped to do so by the Holy Spirit (2 Peter 1:3). Galatians 5:16-18 instructs us to "walk by the Spirit, and you will not gratify the desires of the flesh. For the desires of the flesh are against the Spirit, and the desires of the Spirit are against the flesh, for these are opposed to each other, to keep you from doing the things you want to do" (ESV). We know, however, from the writings of Paul in Romans 7 that controlling our behaviors is not easy and the fleshly desires that we all have can lead us to behave in ways that we don't always want to do. But, as Paul says as he concludes Chapter 7, it is only through the power of Jesus that we can serve God and do what glorifies Him.

"So I find it to be a law that when I want to do right, evil lies close at hand. For I delight in the law of God, in my inner being, but I see in my members another law waging war against the law of my mind and

making me captive to the law of sin that dwells in my members. Wretched man that I am! Who will deliver me from this body of death? Thanks be to God through Jesus Christ our Lord! So then, I myself serve the law of God with my mind, but with my flesh I serve the law of sin" (ESV).

⌊In conclusion, our behaviors are motivated by a number of physiological, social, cognitive, and emotional factors. And, we are also motivated by our relationship with God and our desire to honor Him with our behaviors. Each behavior should be seen in terms of all of these factors which make us uniquely and intricately human. A complete view of human behavior and motivation includes our spiritual side and how God's Spirit works in us to behave in ways that glorify Him.⌋

Chapter 6

Developmental Psychology

LEARNING OBJECTIVES

- ❑ Recall the major areas of study within developmental psychology
- ❑ Explain how research conducted by developmental psychologists changes across the lifespan
- ❑ Describe how prenatal development progresses
- ❑ Identify possible negative outcomes due to environmental exposure to hazardous substances
- ❑ State the changes in cognitive functioning that occur in childhood and adolescence
- ❑ Assess how attachment in early life affects later development
- ❑ ⌐Discuss how attachment research can be applied to attachment to God.⌐
- ❑ Describe the outcomes of different parenting styles
- ❑ Analyze how families have changed across the last century
- ❑ Explain how the sense of morality develops according to Kohlberg
- ❑ Based on Erikson's theory of psychosocial development, differentiate between how life crises are successfully and unsuccessfully resolved.
- ❑ ⌐Explain developmental changes in adolescence.⌐
- ❑ Describe key issues facing older adults.
- ❑ Explain how the Bible describes free will and behavior.
- ❑ Discuss how to view motivation from a biblical worldview.⌐

Period of Development	Age Range
Prenatal	Conception–birth
Infancy	Birth–2 years
Toddlerhood	2–4 years
Preschool	4–6 years
Early Childhood	6–8 or 9 years
Middle Childhood	8 or 9 years–puberty
Adolescence	Puberty–18 years ⌐(perhaps up to 21)⌐
Early Adulthood	18–35 or 40 years
Middle Adulthood	35 or 40 years to 60 or 65 years
Late Adulthood	60 or 65 years+

© Annasunny24/Shutterstock.com

WHAT IS DEVELOPMENTAL PSYCHOLOGY?

Developmental psychology can be defined as the study of ⌐physical, emotional, cognitive, and social⌐ change across the life span. Changes in skills and behaviors come in many forms including increases, decreases, and changes in type. ⌐Although many people might believe developmental psychologists only study children, this is not at all the case. Development

> **Developmental psychology:**
> The study of change across the life span.

includes conception to birth and birth through death as well as everything in between. Additionally, developmental psychologists study a variety of domains including physical, cognitive, language, and social changes across the life span. Technology has played a tremendous role in changing the way we engage with the world and has opened up important new areas of research across development including social media, virtual reality, smartphones, distance/virtual learning, and many others. Often people conceptualize the life span as mostly gains—changes for the better—in childhood and mostly losses—changes for the worse—over the course of adulthood. However, the perspective on development that fits best is one that emphasizes options; and therefore, gains and losses—trade-offs—are features of all development. Understanding change across development is challenging as it is different for different people but also different across cultures. Therefore, to document change, a good first step is to determine what an average person is like—in physical appearance, cognitive abilities, and so on—at a particular age. This provides a good starting point by which to compare individuals and determine whether their development is occurring along a normal continuum.

- Nature versus Nurture
- Stability versus Change
- Continuity versus Stages
- Conditioning versus Modeling
- Passive versus Active Processes

Developmental psychology is divided into three main domains of study: biological, cognitive, and social and emotional development. Biological development pertains to changes in body, brain, perception, motor capabilities, and health, while cognitive development pertains to changes in thought processes, intellectual abilities, and learning styles. Social and emotional development relate to the development of emotions, self-understanding, interpersonal skills, relationships, and moral reasoning.

Studying change across time requires different research approaches that include different goals and methodologies. To collect information from people, researchers rely on observation, reports from others, and physiological assessments like movement tracking, eye scans, and brain waves. If possible, data collection from interviews and self-reports can be used in complex methodological designs.

Developmental psychologists compare physical, cognitive, and social statuses of people at different stages and circumstances throughout human life spans. They do this through **cross-sectional design** where researchers collect pertinent information from different groups of people at different stages of development while utilizing the same methodological design. For example, researchers may interview a group of 8-year-old children, a different group of 16-year-old adolescents, and a different group of 32-year-old adults. In comparison, a **longitudinal design** collects data by following the same person or group of people over time—for example, at 5-years old, again at 18 years old, then at 45 years old, and so on. Although the longitudinal design provides relevant data about developmental changes in a person's lifetime, a cross-sectional design gathers snap shots of different developmental periods, using different groups of people.

> **Cross-sectional design:** Research design that collects information from different groups of people of different ages.
>
> **Longitudinal design:** Research design that collects information from the same group of people across time.

Developmental psychologists use several types of research designs to understand possible mechanisms of change. In a longitudinal design, the same individuals are repeatedly observed and tested over time, often for many years. By isolating the moment of change, researchers can gain a better understanding of what circumstances preceded the change. Researchers also often use longitudinal designs to study individual differences. To understand the life outcomes of different people, researchers may assess a range of potential causal factors early in life and see how those factors influence each individual's life course (e.g., prenatal drug exposure, childhood stress, divorce, and so on). A general advantage of longitudinal research is that, because the participants have lived through the same socioeconomic period, age-related changes cannot be confused with variations in differing societal circumstances. A disadvantage, however, is that some types of generalizations can be made only to the same cohort, the group of individuals born in the same time period. Also, longitudinal studies are costly, and participants are very hard to keep track of. For these reasons, most research on development uses a cross-sectional design, in which groups of participants, of different chronological ages, are observed and compared at the same time. A researcher can then draw conclusions about behavioral differences that may be related to age changes. A disadvantage of cross-sectional designs comes from comparing individuals who differ by year of birth as well as chronological age. Age-related changes are confounded by differences in social or political conditions experienced by birth cohorts.

⌐As one would expect, developmental psychology encompasses the whole of a person's life span, including⌐ biological, cognitive, and social/emotional development. ⌐In sections to follow, prenatal and physical⌐ development ⌐will be addressed, as well as⌐ Piaget's theory of cognitive development, ⌐Erikson's theory of psychosocial development, and other⌐ key ideas related to social/emotional development, ⌐such as⌐ attachment, temperament, parenting, morality. ⌐Furthermore, this chapter will address the different stages of adolescent and early adulthood as well as aging and geriatric development.⌐

▶ **SPEAKING WITH A DEVELOPMENTA PSYCHOLOGIST**

PRENATAL DEVELOPMENT

Prenatal development begins with conception and ends with the birth. The process of prenatal development is best understood in three stages: germinal period, embryonic period, and fetal period. The **germinal period** begins with conception, when sperm fertilize eggs, and ends when the zygote implants in the uterine wall about 2 weeks later. ⌐During the next 6 weeks of prenatal development, the embryonic period, the most rapid development occurs. The foundations of all the major structures of the body are formed making this the most critical period of development. Although not all systems are functioning, the cells are differentiating and migrating to form the bases for all the major organ systems. Scientifically, sexual differentiation begins at the end of the embryonic period with the development of external genitalia; however, the programming for these changes is founded in the genetic material. The genetic material, DNA, is formed shortly after conception. The fetal period is the longest stage of prenatal development, lasting from week 8 of pregnancy until birth, and is a time of continued growth and preparation of the fetus for birth. The organ systems are more organized, and, across the entire 7-month period, the organ systems begin to function.⌐ The **process of delivery** begins with contractions and ends with the birth of the baby.

> **Prenatal development:** Period of development from conception to birth.
>
> **Germinal period:** First period of prenatal development from conception to implantation.
>
> **Process of delivery:** The three-stage process of giving birth.
>
> **Delivery:** The second stage of the process of delivery in which the fetus passes through the birth canal.

What Does the Bible Say?

⌐What does the Bible say about prenatal development? When we look through Scripture, it is clear that prenatal development is important and that even before birth, a person is important to God. Psalm 139:13-16 (ESV) reads:

> "For you formed my inward parts;
>
> you knitted me together in my mother's womb.
>
> I praise you, for I am fearfully and wonderfully made.
>
> Wonderful are your works;
>
> my soul knows it very well.
>
> My frame was not hidden from you,

when I was being made in secret,

intricately woven in the depths of the earth.

Your eyes saw my unformed substance;

in your book were written, every one of them,

the days that were formed for me,

when as yet there was none of them."

In the book of Jeremiah, we read that Jeremiah was called to be a prophet while still in his mother's womb. Jeremiah 1:5 says, "Before I formed you in the womb, I knew you, and before you were born I consecrated you; I appointed you a prophet to the nations" (ESV). Similarly, Isaiah was appointed by God while he was being formed in his mother's womb. Isaiah 49:1 says, "Listen to me, O coastlands, and give attention, you peoples from afar. The LORD called me from the womb, from the body of my mother he named my name" (ESV).

There is much debate in the world about when an individual is "human" and has rights to life. But, God's Word is very clear. Within the womb, and even before conception, God has known each person and has planned his or her days.

A lot has been learned about prenatal development in recent years because of advancements in imaging technology, especially ultrasounds. An ultrasound is the procedure and technology while the resultant image is called a sonogram. Ultrasounds allow for rather detailed images of fetal development and often help to determine normal from abnormal development. There are even three-dimensional (3-D) and four-dimensional (4-D) sonograms that allow detailed images and videos of fetal development and movement.

Human Embryonic and Foetal Development

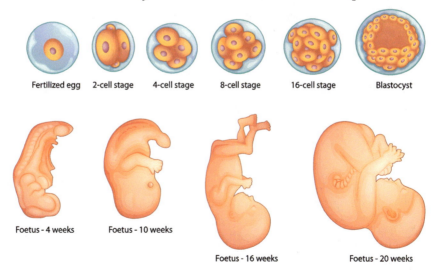

Figure 6.1   Early stages of human embryonic and fetal development.

© BlueRingMedia/Shutterstock.com

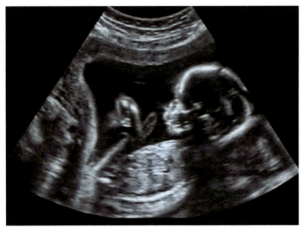

© GagliardiPhotography/Shutterstock.com

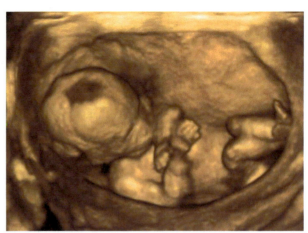

© whitetherock photo/Shutterstock.com

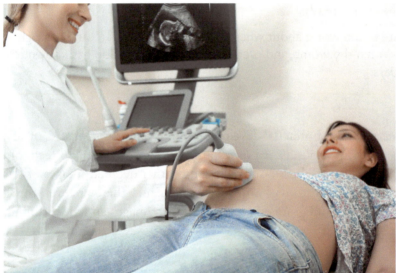

© Africa Studio/Shutterstock.com

Once in the world, babies are assessed using the APGAR Scale (Bregman, 2005) at 1 minute and then again at 5 minutes after birth on the following five items: activity level, pulse, grimace (reflex response), appearance, and respiration. Babies can receive 0 to 2 points for each item or 10 points total. Scores between 7 and 10 are within the normal range. Babies in the normal range will be cleaned and kept warm; it is unlikely that medical intervention will be needed. Scores between 4 and 6 indicate some medical intervention may be needed, such as suction and oxygen. Scores below 4 mean babies are in need of immediate medical interventions to save their lives. ⌐The primary reason for carrying out this quick and easy assessment is to provide the necessary support if the baby is experience any sort of crises especially around cardiac (i.e., heart) or pulmonary (i.e., breathing) issues (American College of Obstetricians and Gynecologists, 2015).⌐ Prenatal development can be negatively ⌐affected⌐ by external agents called **teratogens**. Teratogens are any substances ingested, consumed, or experienced by the mother that can cross the placental barrier and damage the developing organism during pregnancy. These substances

> ⌐**Teratogens:** Any substances ingested, consumed, or experienced by the mother that can cross the placental barrier and damage the developing organism during pregnancy.⌐

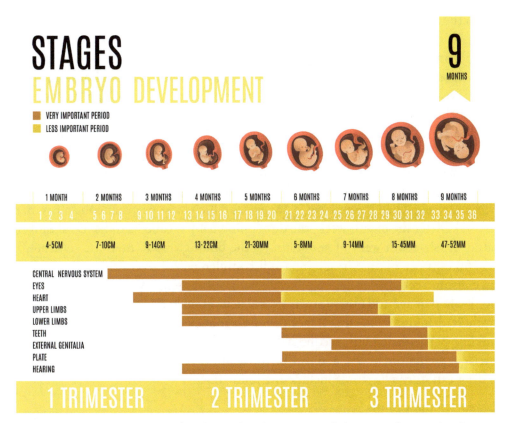

Figure 6.2 ⌐The stages of embryo development and the critical periods of development of major organs, parts, and systems.⌐

© Sabelskaya/Shutterstock.com

can be: (a) environmental influences like mercury, radiation, and lead; (b) legal drugs such as alcohol, ⌐smoking and vaping (and⌐ second-hand smoke) and prescription or over-the-counter drugs; (c) illegal drugs such as marijuana, cocaine, methamphetamines, ⌐and opioids;⌐ and (d) maternal factors like ⌐genetics,⌐ disease, stress, ⌐aging, and malnutrition. The impact of teratogens on prenatal development depends on the timing of exposure. Teratogens cause the most negative outcomes when they are ingested during the sensitive period when the major systems are still being formed and are most vulnerable to damage.⌐

The negative consequences of teratogens can range in severity and type and can be expressed in a variety of developmental issues from physical changes, cognitive delays, emotional and behavioral problems, and medical issues. For example, fetal alcohol spectrum disorder (FASD) is a result of women drinking alcohol during pregnancy. Symptoms of FASD include changes in facial features resulting in smaller eyes, an absent or flattened groove above the lip (philturm), and a thin upper lip, as well as varying degrees of intellectual disabilities, attentional problems, and hyperactivity (Sokol et al., 2003).

Despite the possible negative outcomes of teratogens, most prenatal development occurs without incident because developing organisms are resilient. For optimal prenatal development, it is recommended that parents are aware of possible teratogens and take steps to reduce to eliminate their impact. For more information on how to remain healthy during pregnancy (or to learn more about possible teratogens) visit the National Institutes of Health's website at ⌐http://www.nlm.nih.gov/medlineplus/pregnancy.html.

⌐Of all the drugs that are abused during pregnancy, alcohol produces some of the worst outcomes. Drinking during pregnancy is the single most preventable cause of mental retardation in the United

States. Although the relationship between alcohol and adverse birth outcomes has been known since our earliest histories, as noted from the Bible in the book of Judges (13:7), it wasn't until about 1973 that fetal alcohol syndrome was a formal postnatal diagnosis. In addition to the host of physical problems due to alcohol exposure (i.e., fetal alcohol spectrum disorders and fetal alcohol effects/alcohol-related birth defects), the psychological issues are often the most debilitating. Although it is not a complete list, there are several behavioral or psychological issues associated with prenatal alcohol use listed below. In the following lists, perinatal refers to the period of weeks directly before and after birth. Neonatal refers to newborn children.

The earliest behavior of any kind is the heartbeat. It begins in the prenatal period, when the embryo is about 3 weeks old and only a sixth of an inch long. Response to physical stimulation has been observed as early as the sixth week, when the embryo is not even an inch long. Spontaneous movements are noted by the eighth week. After the eighth week, the developing baby is called a fetus. Fetal movements can be detected around the sixteenth week of gestation. As the brain grows in utero, it generates new neurons at the rate of 250,000 per minute, reaching a full complement of over 100 billion neurons by birth. Mothers who consume certain substances, like alcohol, during sensitive periods put their unborn children at risk for brain damage and other impairment. Facial abnormalities, for example, are most likely to arise from mothers' drinking in the first 2 months of pregnancy. Pregnant women also put their children at risk by smoking, particularly in the second half of pregnancy. Smoking during pregnancy increases the risk of miscarriage, premature births, and low birth weight babies.

Perinatal drug exposure symptoms include the following:

- Pregnancy complications
- Prematurity
- Decreased weight and length
- Decreased head circumference
- Small gestation age
- Intraventricular hemorrhage (i.e., bleeding in the brain)
- Fetal abstinence syndrome
- Still birth
- Sudden infant death syndrome (SIDS)
- Increased infant mortality (i.e., death)

(Jansson et al., 2009; Minnes et al., 2011)

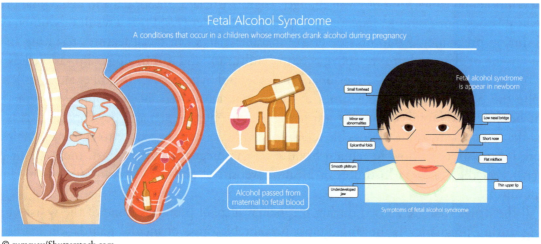

© rumruay/Shutterstock.com

Table 6.1   Neonatal Abstinence Syndrome Symptoms

Central Nervous System	Gastrointestinal System	Metabolic, Vasomotor, and Respiratory
• Unusual irritability, fussiness • High-pitched crying • Hypersensitivity to stimuli • Tremors • Seizures • Skin irritation on knees, elbows, and face from hyperactivity/squirming • Changes in muscle tone • Sleep disturbances	• Dehydration • Poor feeding • Regurgitation/throwing up • Diarrhea • Skin irritation on buttocks • Excessive sucking activity	• Nasal stuffiness, sneezing • Frequent yawning • Fever • Sweating • Tachypnea/rapid breathing • Apnea/suspension of breathing

(Jansson et al., 2009; Minnes et al., 2011; Pediatrics, 1998)

Sadly, alcohol is not the only drug that impacts prenatal and postnatal development. There has been a national crisis surrounding use of opioids. This crisis has created a tremendous problem of babies born dependent upon opioids. The term for this phenomenon is neonatal abstinence syndrome. Babies born exposed to such drugs have a very difficult time and show a variety of withdrawal symptoms.

These symptoms often occur between the first 2 to 7 days after birth. Peak symptoms manifest themselves around days 10 through about 21. However, they may last up to 6 months. Sadly, these at risk, high-need babies often go home to an environment that increases risk due to poor maternal/paternal

support. These babies are harder to take care of because of their continued substance exposure symptoms and are often being taking care of, or not taken care of, by parents still dealing with their own substance use problems. The combination of biological risk combined with an often chaotic and stressful environment makes healthy early growth and maturation nearly impossible. This is effectively the nature versus nurture problem.

Drug abuse during pregnancy has serious and often lifelong consequences. The following list is just a partial list and as research continues on this topic, it is highly likely the list will get longer.

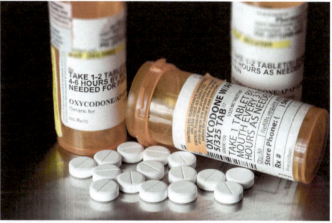

© Steve Heap/Shutterstock.com

Lifelong symptoms include the following:

- Mental retardation
- Attention deficits
- Memory deficits
- Hyperactivity
- Difficulty with abstract concepts
- Inability to manage money
- Poor problem-solving skills

- Difficulty learning from consequences
- Immature social behavior
- Inappropriately friendly to strangers
- Lack of control over emotions
- Poor impulse control
- Poor judgment (Burger et al., 2011; Foltran et al., 2011; Larkby & Day, 1997; Paintner et al., 2012; Popova et al., 2011; Sood et al., 2001).

Of course, assigning a poor birth or developmental outcome to prenatal drug exposure is very hard to do as there are a near infinite number of variables that impact early development. The most significant problems are the co-occurrence of risk factors such as the following (nonexhaustive list):

- More than one drug used/abused during pregnancy (polysubstance use)
- No accurate way to measure amount or frequency of substance use
- Poor maternal health
- Lack of prenatal care
- Poor nutrition
- High levels of stress
- Preexisting health or behavioral problems
- Genetic predisposition to certain problems or diseases
- Low educational attainment
- Low social economic status
- Lack of social support
- Birth problems
- Poor neonatal environment
- Inadequate child-rearing environment
- Observational bias
- Poor accuracy of diagnostic tests
- Lack of long-term follow-up
- Child abuse and neglect

It is often hard to distinguish prenatal drug exposure from a poor child-rearing environment. Often the two problems co-occur. Although substance use often decreases during pregnancy, the rate of postpartum relapse is alarmingly high (80%) (Forray et al., 2015). A mother who abuses or abstains from drug use during pregnancy overwhelmingly continues to use drugs across much of the newborn and infant's formative years causing a cascade of developmental issues that set the child up for similar patterns of maladaptive behavior. When the relationship between the different types of child maltreatment and substance abuse has been examined, neglect clearly demonstrates the strongest association with substance abuse (Famularo et al., 1992). Substances that are most often abused by perpetrators of child abuse and neglect include cocaine, opiates, heroin, and alcohol, with more than 24% of parents abusing multiple drugs (Chance & Scannapieco, 2002). The Drug Abuse Treatment Outcome Study (DATOS) examined both men and women who entered a community-based drug and alcohol treatment program and in a sample of mothers, cocaine was the drug of choice for 58%, heroine for 24%, alcohol/marijuana for 8%, and nonspecified for 9% (Cash & Wilke, 2003). Mothers who were using cocaine or heroin were twice as likely to abuse and neglect their children compared to mothers who used other substances. Parental drug abuse has been shown to predict recurrence of child abuse and neglect (Bays, 1990). Similarly, substance use of any type, either in the past or presently occurring, appears to increase the likelihood of being reported for child maltreatment (Kelly et al., 2002). Parental substance abuse has also been found to influence re-referrals to child protective services (English et al., 1999), suggesting substance abuse continues to occur in these parents after child protective service involvement is initially discontinued.

PHYSICAL DEVELOPMENT

⌞Newborns⌟ come into the world with an array of reflexes ⌞that⌟ disappear within the first 6 months of life. ⌞These reflexes help newborns adapt to and engage with the world around them until their⌟ motor skills ⌞adequately develop.⌟ Several reflexes are dominant in those first few months (see Table 6.2).

Newborns also use their senses to manipulate the world around them. At birth, the senses of smell, taste, hearing, and touch are fully developed. However, vision still has much development to become similar to adult visual abilities. When born, infants' visual acuity is about 20/400, which means they can see clearly at 20 feet what adult vision can normally see at 400 feet (Balaban & Reisenauer, 2005). Visual acuity levels similar to adults are not developed until about 6 months to 3 years (Slater et al., 2007), with visual development continuing into adolescence. Therefore, for the first few months of life, infants can see basic colors and shapes but lack the details of objects.

© mikumistock/Shutterstock.com

Table 6.2 Dominant Reflexes in Newborns

Reflex	Description	When Reflex Disappears
Sucking Reflex	When something touches the roof of his mouth, his lips close and he sucks.	About 2 Months
⌞Moro Reflex	The Moro reflex is often called a startle reflex. That's because it usually occurs when a baby is startled by a loud sound or movement. In response to the sound, the baby throws back his or her head, extends out his or her arms and legs, cries, then pulls the arms and legs back in.	About 2 Months⌟
Crawling Reflex	When placed on her stomach, she will make crawling motions.	About 2 Months
Babinski Reflex	When the sides of her feet are stroked, she points her big toe and curls up other toes.	About 4 Months
Stepping Reflex	When supporting his weight and his feet touch the ground, he will make a walking motion.	About 3 Months
Rooting Reflex	When her cheek is stroked, she will turn her head toward the touch and open her mouth.	About 4 Months
Gag Reflex	Gag response to prevent choking.	Never Disappears

Infants' visual attention centers on contrasting elements (and faces) to understand the world around them. In general, infants prefer moderately complex color contrast patterns, but lack the visual acuity to fully comprehend or differentiate between patterns. They prefer to look at bold, moderately complex patterns (Banks & Ginsburg, 1985) and naturally arranged faces rather than faces that have been rearranged or are upside-down (Cassia et al., 2004). Furthermore, they use motion to help detect object size and color (Spelke & Hermer, 1996). These concepts may help explain why infants become so fascinated with brightly colored mobiles.

Hearing is fully developed in the womb, so infants are very familiar with the sound of their mothers' voices and remember their voices later as infants (DeCasper & Fifer, 1987). Infants are also able to recognize their mothers' smell within the first few days of life (MacFarlane, 2008), prefer the sweet taste of their mothers' breast milk (Mennella et al., 2004), and are soothed by the soft touch of skin-to-skin contact (Gray et al., 2000).

At birth, infants have comparatively large heads, large eyes, small noses, small mouths, and fluffy cheeks to that of older children and adults. These proportions make infants especially attractive to adults and promote nurturing. Most early physical development occurs from head to toe, using the **cephalocaudal** (from the Greek for "head to tail") pattern of development. For example, infants will gain the ability to hold their heads up before they can sit up without support and will sit up without support before they can walk.

> **Cephalocaudal:** Pattern of development from head to toe.

The other pattern of development is the **proximodistal** pattern, which refers to the development of motor abilities that develop from the center outward to appendages. In reference to motor skills, infants are able to use their core muscles to roll over before they can accurately grasp at items and before they have the digital dexterity to pick up small items (like Cheerios®).

> **Proximodistal:** Pattern of development from core out to appendages.

These two patterns of development (cephalocaudal and proximodistal) are consistent across all stages of development, except an awkward period in adolescence. In the adolescent period of physical development, bodies grow opposite to the proximodistal pattern resulting in teenagers with large feet and hands in comparison to the rest of their bodies. Growing opposite to the proximodistal pattern leads to teens appearing out of proportion with small trunks and long arms and legs.

COGNITIVE DEVELOPMENT

The domain of cognitive development includes the study of the changes in the way our brains make sense of the world around us. Children are not only different from adults in the amount of knowledge they have but also in the way that they think. Children rely on different strategies than adults to organize information that they encounter in the world. Children often think and learn in different ways across their development. Young children are limited in their logic and rationalizations, but as they develop into adolescents, their skills in logic and rational thinking increase.

Jean Piaget is thought to have completely changed the study of how children think (Flavell et al., 2002), and his theory of cognitive development has influenced school curricula and teaching styles. Over the years, researchers have criticized and expanded upon Piaget's initial work by supplementing his theory with empirical evidence supporting his claims. Still, current theorists and researchers still use Piaget's ideas as a foundational guide their thinking and scientific studies.

Piaget's theory is widely accepted because it ⌐highlights⌐ the general abilities and limitations of children at stages across their lives and because of its breadth and applicability to a variety of ⌐developmental⌐ contexts. Central to Piaget's theory is the concept that children are mentally and physically ⌐active⌐ in their own cognitive ⌐processes⌐ (Piaget, 1969, 1973). Children ⌐have a self-interest⌐ to organize and understand their world. Therefore, children ⌐are not passive⌐ while their cognitive abilities change; instead, children are like "little scientists" ⌐undertaking breaching⌐ experiments to test out their ideas

© wavebreakmedia/Shutterstock.com

and drawing conclusions ⌐by actively engaging⌐ their social and physical environments. Children discover many⌐ important ⌐life lessons⌐ without the assistance of others.

Information is organized into **cognitive schemas**, or frameworks, placing information into classifications and groups (Piaget, 1963). ⌐All people⌐ have a general understanding of what a cookie is, ⌐providing⌐ a cookie schema. ⌐Most everyone knows⌐ that cookies are often brown, sweet, and delicious; ⌐people⌐ organize ⌐their⌐ experiences with cookies using this general schema for cookies. When experiences and information ⌐do not⌐ match the current structure of the schemas, children ⌐enter a⌐ state of ⌐disequilibrium, or imbalance.⌐ Children in a state of disequilibrium must resolve these discrepancies to reestablish cognitive balance. ⌐Schemas are mental structures that enable individuals to interpret the world and Piaget believed schemas to be the building blocks of developmental change. Both assimilation and accommodation are thought to play a critical role in the child development by giving the child a means to analyze the world.⌐

> ⌐**Cognitive schemas:** Pattern of thought, based on experience, which organizes information about objects, events, and things in the world.⌐

Children use two basic processes, assimilation and accommodation, to help organize experiences into cognitive schemas (Piaget, 1999). **Assimilation** is the process ⌐of integrating⌐ new information in a form to match current schemas. For example, children may have a schema for goats. They understand goats, ⌐who⌐ are furry, brown, medium-sized farm animals that produce milk ⌐(the goats that is).⌐ If children are exposed to goats that are black and white, this new experience does not match their current schema of goats. ⌐Thereafter, children⌐ assimilate this ⌐new⌐ information into their ⌐goat⌐ schema ⌐which now includes different colors of fur.⌐

> ⌐**Assimilation:** The process of integrating new information in a form to match the current schemas.⌐

The second process of organizing schemas is **accommodation**, which is ⌐the⌐ adapting ⌐of⌐ current schemas to match the new information or experience. ⌐Utilizing the previous⌐ example, children exposed to llamas (which may have characteristics similar to goats) will need to accommodate their goat schema because the new information cannot be easily included in the goat schema. Children must develop an entirely new schema to describe llamas. The llama schema would describe llamas as furry, brown, larger farm animals with long necks. Children have accommodated the new information by developing new schemas.

> **Accommodation:** The process of adapting the current schemas to match the new information or experiences.

Piaget's Stages and Ages

Piaget's theory of cognitive development suggested that children progress through their cognitive development in a series of stages (Piaget, 1969, 1973). Like all stage theories, children ⌐move⌐ through the stages in the same order and each new stage marks ⌐the advent of⌐ qualitatively different skills and abilities than ⌐in⌐ the previous stages. According to Piaget, from birth through adolescence, children's cognitive skills are changed and altered across four ⌐main⌐ stages of cognitive development: sensorimotor, preoperational, concrete operational, and formal operational.

Stage of Cognitive Development	Age Range
Sensorimotor	Birth to 2 years
Preoperational	2–7 years
Concrete Operational	7–12 years
Formal Operational	12+ years

During the **sensorimotor stage** (from birth to about 2 years of age) infants rely on their senses and motor abilities to help them understand ⌐their surroundings. They⌐ will place ⌐keys⌐ in their mouths, grasp ⌐their parents fingers,⌐ throw ⌐pacifiers,⌐ and shake ⌐their formula bottles. It is through this exploration and manipulation that infants learn about the world around them⌐—shape, texture, ⌐taste,⌐ temperature, ⌐odor, sound, and so on—marking the beginning of their learning personal preferences and parameters. With each experiment in their new life, infants begin to make connections and come to understand cause and effect,⌐ consequences of behaviors, and much more. ⌐Despite what appear to be very simplistic activities, infants are actually expanding⌐ and altering their cognitive schemas.

⌐According to Piaget, the⌐ major achievement of the sensorimotor stage is **object permanence** — the understanding that objects exist even when out of sight (Piaget, 1954). ⌐This⌐ permanence occurs slowly over the first 2 years, ⌐starting with⌐ infants ⌐only recognizing or showing⌐ interest in objects when in plain view. ⌐When that object is⌐ removed, ⌐they will not seek it out; it as if it has just disappeared. At 8–12 months though, infants begin to understand that a hidden object, although out of sight, still exists and will search for it. At this stage, they are able to follow one move, but not cognitively able to follow multiple moves with their limited object permanence abilities.⌐

© leungchopan/Shutterstock.com

Watch the A-not-B Error Experiment
⌐https://www.youtube.com/watch?v=4jW668F7HdA⌐

The **preoperational stage** of cognitive development (ages 2–7 years) builds on the skills and schemas developed ⌐earlier in⌐ the sensorimotor period. ⌐In this stage, children have object permanence and⌐ begin to expand their understanding and use ⌐of⌐ objects, but ⌐they still have⌐ limited cognitive ability. ⌐Perhaps, the⌐ greatest achievement of the preoperational stage is the development of **symbolic thought**, ⌐wherein⌐ children are able to ⌐substitute⌐ one object to for another, ⌐mentally. This manifest itself in creative play, when sticks becomes swords and playground structures become "castles." Their⌐ understanding of objects ⌐transforms⌐ beyond simple reality ⌐to⌐ complex personal ⌐symbolism.⌐

Even with their new complex understanding of objects and schemas, in the preoperational stage ⌐children⌐ are severely limited in their thought processes. ⌐They are egocentric, lacking⌐ the ability to see the world from another person's point of view. **Egocentrism** can be demonstrated in both spatial abilities and speech. Children sitting on one side of a table ⌐viewing⌐ mountain scenery are unable to describe what another person may see from the opposite side of the table (Piaget & Inhelder, 1977). Additionally, ⌐their⌐ conversations demonstrate this ⌐self-centered⌐ perspective. ⌐They focus mainly on their own private matter, ignoring the⌐ other side of the conversation.

⌐For example, one could hear an exchange between children as follows: "I like pizza," says Elliot. "I have a TV in my room," replies James. "With pepperoni and cheese!" says Elliot. "Yeah, but I like to watch cartoons on it," James concludes.⌐ The conversation between the two preschool boys above shows the egocentric focus. ⌐Fortunately, as⌐ children progress through the preoperational stage, ⌐egocentrism decreases.⌐

Related to the limitations of egocentrism, children in the preoperational stage also become fixated on one characteristic of an object at the exclusion of other characteristics. This **centration** on the most noticeable characteristic of objects limits their ability to accurately assess changes in size, volume, mass, and distance. This limitation

> **Centration:** The fixation on one characteristic of an object at the exclusion of other characteristics.

in cognitive ability is tested using the classic conservation task (Piaget, 1954). First, children are shown two identical short glasses of juice and are asked if the two glasses have the same amount of juice or a different amount of juice. ⌐They⌐ demonstrate an understanding that the two glasses are identical and have the same amount of juice. Next, one glass of juice is poured from the short glass into a tall, skinny glass of juice and asked again if the tall, skinny glass and the short glass have the same amount of juice. Preoperational children will respond that the tall, skinny glass of juice has more in it because it is taller, even though they just watched the liquid from the short glass being poured into the taller glass. ⌐They⌐ are so focused on the height of the liquid in the glass that the children overlook that the volume of juice has remained the same.

⌐Moving forward, during the⌐ **concrete operational stage** (ages 7–12 years), children overcome ⌐their previous cognitive limitation and begin the development of⌐ logical thought. Around age 7, children begin ⌐to use observation and⌐ reason to ⌐investigate and judge various life situations that they encounter (and their associated problems). They⌐ now ⌐can⌐ successfully complete the conservation task (Figure 6.3) by reporting the short glass and the tall, skinny glass have the same amount of liq-

uid because the contents of one glass was just poured into the tall, skinny glass. They are no longer focused on the most obvious characteristics and can now consider multiple aspects of objects. However, this logical reasoning does not extend to hypothetical situations. Concrete-operational children still engage in trial-and-error when problem solving. Because they are unable to generate hypothetical scenarios, elementary school children will actually need to physically manipulate their world

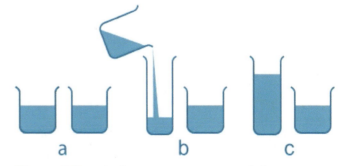

Figure 6.3 ⌐A classic conservation task for testing centration in children.⌐

to test out their problem-solving skills. For example, when asked to mix paints to form a new color, children will not be able to think about hypothetical situations in which they have mixed colors and their outcomes, but instead, children will need to mix real paints to test out their ideas.

In the final stage of Piaget's theory of cognitive development, ⌐known as the⌐ **formal operational stage,** the limitations in reasoning from the previous stage are overcome. For Piaget, the formal operational stage is the considered the final stage. Adolescents are able to reason about situations and problems using hypothetical thought. When faced with ⌐a⌐ new problem or situation, adolescents are able to generate possible outcomes and strategies without having to physically test them. In the ⌐aforementioned⌐ paint-mixing problem, adolescents are able to reason about what would happen if they mixed colors without actually having to mix the paints. ⌐According to⌐ Piaget, not all adolescents or adults will obtain hypothetical thought. ⌐Although most will obtain it, Piaget believed that not all adolescents or adults with fully developed hypothetical thought abilities.⌐ Cognitive skills obtained in the formal operational stage allow adolescents and adults to think about alternate realities and complex social constructs like justice and fairness.

© Ollyy/Shutterstock.com

Piaget's theory of cognitive development has many criticisms (Miller, 2011). First, the stage model of development implies thinking within the stage is consistently demonstrated across domains. For example, children's mastery of the liquid conservation task (mastering the concept of volume) does not mean ⌐that⌐ children will be able to master changes in space or mass. Additionally, ⌐he⌐ underestimated the cognitive abilities of infants and preschoolers. Piaget developed rather challenging tasks (like the conservation task) to test his concepts that were ⌐often too⌐ complex for infant and preschoolers to understand and master. Finally, Piaget understated the role of social interactions in cognitive development by focusing too much on the role of children actively manipulating their world. In addition to actively engaging their world, children also learn from their environment by observation and interactions with adults and peers (Bandura, 1977; Vygotsky, 1962).

SOCIAL AND EMOTIONAL DEVELOPMENT

⌐People⌐ spend quite of bit of time interacting with others in social settings. Social and emotional development ⌐includes⌐ areas such as ⌐the bond⌐ between the caregiver and child, temperament, child rearing, morality, and ⌐other⌐ social hurdles ⌐experienced in⌐ life. Developmental psychologists who investigate social and emotional ⌐issues⌐ try to understand the influence people and social constructs have on our developmental ⌐process.

Attachment

⌐Attachment⌐ is the emotional bond that connects two people together. The first important⌐ relationship children have is with their primary caregiver. This can be with the father, ⌐grandparents, or other relatives (or nonrelatives), but most contemporary research⌐ has focused on the relationship between mother and child.

> ⌐**Attachment:** The emotional bond that connects two people together.⌐

Scientific interest in attachment-bonds increased during the 1930s and 1940s after people noticed children—who were orphaned or otherwise separated from their parents—often struggled later in social environments, with other relationships, and in parenting their own children (Spitz, 1949). These early observations led to experimental research with rhesus monkeys (Harlow & Harlow, 1965; Harlow et al., 1971; Harlow & Zimmerman, 1959). In a series of studies, Harry Harlow and his associates demonstrated the negative effects of being orphaned and isolated from birth. The rhesus monkeys were well cared for and healthy but were not exposed to other monkeys. The developmental patterns of the rhesus monkeys raised in isolation were later compared to the developmental patterns of other monkeys reared by their mothers.

© tratong/Shutterstock.com

In analyzing the two monkey groups, striking differences were observed. First, the isolated monkeys' social skills were greatly lacking when placed with other monkeys to socialize. Often acting fearful, the monkeys also spent time soothing themselves by rocking back and forth. Second, the isolated monkeys showed little interest in relationships with other monkeys, including mating behaviors. Finally, after impregnation and delivery, the new mothers frequently rejected or ignored their offspring's needs, sometimes even attacking them. This initial research by Harlow and associates demonstrated the importance of early attachment between parent and child for social development. Additional studies have examined the specific aspects of parental care that were quintessential for the development of attachment.

One question to consider is whether the bond between mother and child forms because of a physical attachment (food and protection) or an emotional one (nurturing, warmth, and affection). To investigate this question, Harlow and colleagues reared rhesus monkeys with two "mothers": one a wire mother providing food and nourishment and one cloth mother providing warmth and support. The baby rhesus monkeys preferred the warm cloth monkey to the wire monkey that provided food. The baby rhesus monkeys would nurse from the wire mothers while clinging to the cloth mothers. When frightened or needing emotional support, the monkeys relied on the cloth mothers for soothing. Although food and nourishment are important to survival, Harlow et al.'s research showed that the emotional bonds between mother and child were also key for the child's surviving and thriving.

Based on the pivotal ideas from Harlow, as well as ideas from evolutionary theorist Konrad Lorenz (Lorenz, 1952), John Bowlby proposed attachment theory, which was later extended by Mary Ainsworth (Ainsworth, 1973). Bowlby postulated that infants were not simply dependent on their mothers for survival, but were innately motivated to investigate the world around them (Bowlby, 1953, 1969). Infants need to have, what Bowlby termed, a **secure base**: a safe supporting relationship from which to explore their world. Infants rely upon this safe haven for encouragement in times of stress while learning on their own.

> **Secure base:** A safe, supportive relationship that infants use to explore and understand their world.

The quality and process of the development of attachment shapes how infants and children view their world. If the initial attachment to caregivers is nurturing and supportive (and the developmental process is smooth) infants and children will view the world positively. However, if the initial attachment to caregivers is unreliable and harsh (and the developmental process is difficult) infants and children will have a negative view of the world.

⌐Bowlby proposed a process for infants as they develop their initial attachments, observable in a series of four phases. The first phase (birth to about 6 weeks) has infants utilizing their natural responses and reflexes to signal to and connect with their caregivers that they needed attention. In the second phase (6 weeks to 6 months), infants begin to show preference for one particular person among others around them. In the third phase (6–18 months), infants

© Oksana Kuzmina/Shutterstock.com

overtly choose and depend upon a person with whom they identify with security and comfort. In the final phase (18–24 months), infants develop a more reciprocal relationship with this sole caregiver who has invested in their care and development (although infants also begin simultaneously developing attachments to their fathers, grandparents, and siblings).⌐

These attachments to caregivers help infants and children develop **internal working models** setting the foundation for future relationships, as well as the development of self-identity, emotions, and self-worth. Internal working models are shaped by the dependability and quality of care received. Infants and children who receive reliable, quality care tend to develop a positive view of the world, themselves, and relationships. Infants who receive unreliable and/or lower quality care tend to develop a negative view of the world, themselves, and relationships.

⌐The model in Figure 6.4 is really important because how an infant interacts with a parent or caregiver is generalized to other people. Infants quickly learn how to engage and extract positive reinforcement

> **Internal working model:**
> The expectations and understanding of the world formulated by the first attachment with caregivers.

Table 6.3   Bowlby's Model of Phases of Attachment

Name	Time	Description
⌐Preattachment	Birth to about 2 months	Infant does not discriminate one individual from another—no fear of strangers.
Attachment in process	2 to about 6 months	Infant directs behavior (cues) to a specific individual. Infant is able to recognize parents but shows limited protest when separated.
Well-defined attachment	6 months to about 3–4 years	Infant shows separation anxiety from specific individual(s), often mother and father.
Goal-directed relationship	3–4 years and beyond	Separation protests decrease as child begins to understand caregiving schedule as well as develop skills for self-entertainment.⌐

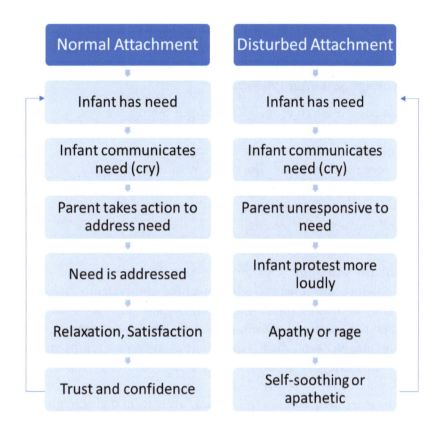

Normal Attachment	Disturbed Attachment
Infant has need	Infant has need
Infant communicates need (cry)	Infant communicates need (cry)
Parent takes action to address need	Parent unresponsive to need
Need is addressed	Infant protest more loudly
Relaxation, Satisfaction	Apathy or rage
Trust and confidence	Self-soothing or apathetic

Figure 6.4 ⌐Figure shows the cycle of positive attachment and cycle of disturbed attachment.⌐

Source: Brian Kelley

from their environment. Because of their lack of abilities, all of their needs are met by someone else. The infant learns to cry, laugh, smile, and maintain eye contact to create engagement and have that engagement drive their immediate needs. Sadly, with the advent of smartphones, many parents are now multitasking when spending time with their infant. Face-to-face interaction is replaced with the baby looking at a caregiver's face while the caregiver stares into a screen.⌐

Ainsworth ⌐(1973) expanded upon the ideas⌐ of Bowlby by providing empirical support ⌐for⌐ the different types of attachments ⌐that⌐ infants and children can have with caregivers. Based on her **strange situation** technique (Ainsworth et al., 1978), Ainsworth developed descriptions for secure and insecure attachments. During the strange situation procedure, securely attached infants will use their caregivers as a secure base to explore the room, will play with the available toys, will often bring toys to the caregivers, will show some distress when the caregiver leaves the room, and will be comforted by their caregiver's return. ⌐Most middle-class

© AntonioDiaz/Shutterstock.com

Strange situation: The procedure developed by Ainsworth to assess different attachment styles.

infants, about 60%–65%, will be securely attached to at least one caregiver. However, the rate is lower, about 50%, for infants who live below the poverty line (Thompson, 1998; van Ijzendoorn et al., 1999).

Events During the Strange Situation Procedure

- Mother and infant enter research room with stranger. Stranger leaves.
- Infant plays with available toys and mother responds naturally.
- Stranger enters and after a few minutes mother leaves.
- Infant is alone in room with stranger. The two may interact naturally.
- Mother returns and stranger leaves. After a few minutes, mother leaves.
- Infant is alone in room for a few minutes.
- Stranger enters and interacts with infant.
- Mother returns.

Insecurely-attached infants will show a variety of ⌞negative⌟ reactions to the strange situation procedure. Infants labeled "insecure resistant" ⌞(often called ambivalent)⌟ are typically very clingy during the procedure. They will not explore the room or play with toys and become very upset when the caregiver leaves the room. However, upon the caregiver's return, "insecure resistant" infants will seek out their caregiver but ⌞then⌟ resist their caregiver's attempt at ⌞comforting them.⌟ For middle-class infants, this category accounts for roughly 10% of attachments (van Ijzendoorn et al., 1999).

Infants determined to be insecure/avoidant typically stay away from their caregiver during the strange situation and upon the caregiver's return do not acknowledge his or her presence. About 15% of middle-class infants will be classified as insecure/avoidant (van Ijzendoorn et al., 1999).

That leaves about 10% to 15% of infants unclassified by Ainsworth's system because either the infants' behavior did not clearly match one category, or their behavior was too disorganized for classification. Disorganized/disoriented infants typically want the support and attention from their caregivers but are often unsure or fearful of that attention (Main & Solomon, 1990). These infants may lack the skills to properly signal their needs, may be fearful of their caregiver, or may lack the social skills to properly interact with their caregiver.

Overall, children who were securely attached as infants tend to have better social skills (Lucas-Thompson & Clarke-Stewart, 2007), better control over their emotions (Cassidy, 1994), are more well-adjusted (Brumariu & Kerns, 2010), and have better relations with peers in adolescence (Carlson et al., 2004). The positive outcomes associated with being securely attached as infants could be due to the quality of parental care, the consistency of the environment, or both. Although children's attachments are relatively stable across time (Fraley, 2002), attachments can change with the environment (Lewis et al., 2000). For example, children who are insecurely attached to their caregivers can become securely attached to a different caregiver in a different environment.

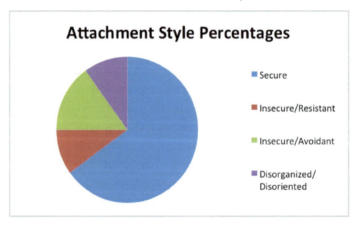

Attachment Style Percentages

- Secure
- Insecure/Resistant
- Insecure/Avoidant
- Disorganized/Disoriented

Table 6.4   Relationship between Types of Attachment across Stages

Relationship between Types of Attachment across Stages				
	Stage 1: Attachment	**Stage 2: Independence**	**Stage 3: Achievement**	**Stage 4: Altruism**
Secure	Friendship, cooperation, respect, trust, affection, and love	Self-controlled, self-assured, self-sufficient, responsible, and independent	Accomplished, problem solver, creative, determined, and motivated	Caring, considerate, compassionate, and empathetic
Resistant	Attention-seeking, thrives on attention, and often clingy	Rebellious, intimidates, manipulative, hasty, and passive aggressive	Competitive, sensation seeking, recognition focused, conniving, and troublemaker	Selfish, codependent, overindulgent, and degrading
Avoidant	Withdrawn, rejected, lonely, overly suspicious, and alienating	Learned helplessness, unconstrained, false confidence, more easily misguided, and irresponsible	Under-achiever, failure-focused, apathetic, immature, doesn't like change, and unmotivated	Focused on self, reward, and pleasure; immediate needs outweigh long-term benefits

What about Attachment to God?

There is much about attachment research that can be useful in understanding our attachment to God. In the original conceptualization of attachment, Bowlby termed a secure base as a safe supporting relationship, from which to explore their world. And, in reading the overview of research on attachment, you can see how having a secure attachment to one's caregiver gives someone confidence, independence, and courage to do new things and reach out in compassion and empathy.

Similarly, if we view our attachment to God, we can see how we can have that same security in Him to endure uncertain times, explore our world, or step out in new ways for Him. In fact, in a recent study by Leman et al. (2018) secure attachment to God was related with psychological health and well-being. Furthermore, Beck (2006) found that viewing God as a secure base was related to willingness to theologically explore, and participants with a secure attachment to God reported greater peace and less distress on their spiritual journeys.

This seems consistent with Scriptures like the Psalmist describing God as "our refuge and strength, a very present help in trouble" (Ps. 46:1, ESV) or Paul writing how "neither death nor life, nor angels nor rulers, nor things present nor things to come, nor powers, nor height nor depth, nor anything else in all creation, will be able to separate us from the love of God in Christ Jesus our Lord" (Rom. 8:38 ESV). Secure attachment is certainly evident in Philippians 4:13, "I can do all things through him who strengthens me" (ESV).

© Rawpixel.com/Shutterstock.com

Parenting and Family

Parenting is a complex and ever-changing concept. Quality, consistency, and type of parenting affect attachments (and their long-term outcomes). As children age, their needs change, which requires parents to adapt their parenting styles. For children, parents instruct and model manners, rules, norms, taboos, relationships, social skills, activities, and values.

Each parent has a different style that guides the way they interact with their children. Four different **parenting styles** have been established by researchers (Baumrind, 1973): authoritative, authoritarian, permissive, and rejecting–neglecting. These parenting styles are based on the amount of responsiveness, demands, and control placed upon children by their parents. Parents high on responsiveness (the degree of warmth and support parents provide their children) are attentive to their children's needs and often respond in supportive, caring ways. Alternatively, low responsiveness indicates parents are less or inconsistently attentive and are less caring or supportive. Parents high on demandingness (the degree of governance and strict expectations parents have over their children) are often controlling and expect their children to comply with strict demands; parents low on demandingness have little control over their children with fewer demand upon them.

Authoritative parents are high in responsiveness and high in demandingness. They have clear, firm expectations and rules for their children and respond to their children's needs in attentive, supporting ways. Often children of authoritative parents are given some degree of autonomy and have the freedom to discuss and negotiate rules; however, the parents make the final decision. Punishment for breaking the rules is typically fair and matches in severity to the degree of rule-breaking. Children and adolescents of authoritative parents are socially competent, self-secure, accepted by their peers, and demonstrate more healthy and prosocial behaviors (Baumrind, 1991a).

> **Authoritative parenting style:** Parenting characterized by high warmth and high demands.

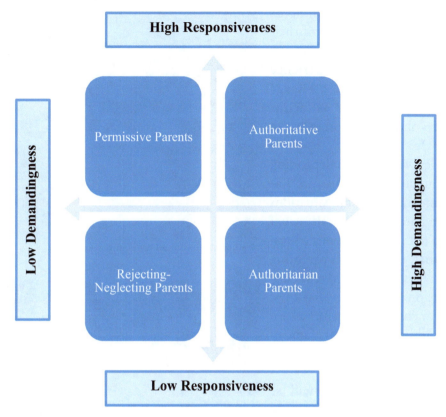

High Responsiveness

Low Demandingness

Permissive Parents

Authoritative Parents

Rejecting-Neglecting Parents

Authoritarian Parents

High Demandingness

Low Responsiveness

Figure 6.5 ⌞The four different parenting styles.⌟

Authoritarian parents are low on responsiveness and high on demandingness. They can be overly controlling and can be cold when responding to their children's needs. Punishment is often harsh, and intimidation tactics are a common way to control their children—⌞for example, utilizing threats and psychological manipulation. These children⌟ have higher rates of depression, anxiety, lower self-esteem, ⌞and⌟ display more negative behaviors ⌞such as⌟ aggression and delinquency (Baumrind, 1991b).

Permissive parents are highly responsive to (but not demanding) of their children. They are warm, attentive, and supportive of their children's needs but place ⌞few⌟ expectations on their children. Often too lenient with the rules, ⌞permissive parents⌟ are unable to enforce the few rules they do ⌞assert. These⌟ parents ⌞are not lacking⌟ rules because they do not care for their children; ⌞rather, they are more concerned that⌟ their children ⌞are⌟ unhappy or hindered by rules. ⌞Consequently, children⌟ of permissive parents tend to lack self-control, to have lower academic achievement, and more negative behaviors, ⌞such as⌟ impulsiveness and school misconduct (Baumrind, 1991a).

Rejecting–neglecting parents are low on demandingness and responsiveness. They are often ⌞inattentive⌟ to the needs of their children and place ⌞few⌟ demands or limits on their behavior. These

Authoritarian parenting style: Parenting characterized by ⌞low⌟ warmth and high demands.

Permissive parenting style: Parenting characterized by high warmth and low demands.

Rejecting/neglectful parenting style: Parenting characterized by low warmth and low demand.

parents ⌐are⌐ so focused on their own needs that they neglect or reject the needs of their children. Children ⌐of⌐ rejecting–neglecting parents ⌐are more likely to⌐ experience ⌐negative relationships and often engage in risk-taking behaviors such as delinquency, substance abuse, and promiscuity (Baumrind, 1991a).

⌐Parenting styles vary greatly depending upon culture, ethnicity, socioeconomic status, and environment. Stressful situations such as economic hardship, physical/mental health issues, and marital conflict place pressures on parents that, in turn, alter parenting styles. Parents can be so focused on reducing the stressful event on their family that they do so at the detriment of responsiveness or demandingness. Additionally, temperament (and personality type) also can affect the parent–child relationship.

⌐Although research is ongoing, it will be many years before the full impact of modern technology, like smartphones, tablets, and laptops, have on attachment and parenting. It seems that families, even at very young ages, spend a tremendous amount of time engaged with devices instead of each other.⌐

© pixelheadphoto digitalskillet/Shutterstock.com

© ESB Professional/Shutterstock.com

What Does the Bible Say?

⌐What does the Bible say about parenting? What style of parenting does God command? A search of verses on parenting yields the following:

Colossians 3:20-21 ESV

"Children, obey your parents in everything, for this pleases the Lord. Fathers, do not provoke your children, lest they become discouraged."

Ephesians 6:1-4 ESV

"Children, obey your parents in the Lord, for this is right. 'Honor your father and mother' (this is the first commandment with a promise), 'that it may go well with you and that you may live long in the land.' Fathers, do not provoke your children to anger, but bring them up in the discipline and instruction of the Lord."

Proverbs 13:24 ESV

"Whoever spares the rod hates his son, but he who loves him is diligent to discipline him."

Proverbs 22: 6 ESV

"Train up a child in the way he should go; even when he is old he will not depart from it."

Deuteronomy 6:6-9 ESV

"These commandments that I give you today are to be on your hearts. Impress them on your children. Talk about them when you sit at home and when you walk along the road, when you lie down and when you get up. Tie them as symbols on your hands and bind them on your foreheads. Write them on the doorframes of your houses and on your gates."

When we look at the Bible verses on parenting, we see a call to parents to be active in their children's lives, as well as to teach them the principles of God, and to not provoke their children, but rather to bring them up in the "discipline and instruction of the Lord" (Ephesians 6:4). When we examine how the Lord disciplines and instructs us, we get a good model for how we are to parent our children. In 2 Peter 3:9, we see that God is patient with us. In Lamentations 3:22-23, we see that God has everlasting love for us and offers us fresh mercies each morning. In Hebrews 12:3-11, we see that God corrects us lovingly and in John 1:14, He is full of grace and truth.

Therefore, when examining parenting methods and styles, looking to how God lovingly parents us with a mixture of grace and discipline, will give us good guidance on how to best parent our children with love and intentionality.

Temperament

Family dynamics and parental influence can also be affected by the **temperament** of children. Temperament is defined as the biological predisposition to respond to the world in predictable ways. Temperament in children is considered to be foundational for later development of personality. Unlike personality, temperament does not include aspects of attitude and opinions but instead is an innate pattern, or a basic reaction to stimuli and experience.

Temperament associated with reactions to experiences and emotions can later develop into the different dimensions of the Big Five personality types: openness, conscientiousness, extraversion, agreeableness, and neuroticism (see Chapter 8 for a more comprehensive discussion on personality). Thomas and Chess (1977) suggest three general temperamental characteristics to describe most infants. "Easy babies," as they are labeled, have easygoing temperament. They are quick to adjust to new experiences, establish predictable routines, are generally happy, and typically remain calm. In contrast, "difficult babies" tend to react negatively to new experiences, show high levels of fear and distress, and have irregular routines. "Slow-to-warm-up babies" start out somewhat difficult but over time become easier to manage over time.

> **Temperament:** Infants' and children's biological predisposition to respond to the world in predictable ways.

© Sergiy Bykhunenko/Shutterstock.com

More contemporary researchers, like Mary Rothbart (2011), use empirically based dimensions. Although the names of the dimensions may vary, the six basic concepts included in the dimensions remain the same. The temperament dimension of fearful/distress/inhibition measures the amount, duration withdrawal, and fear expressed when infants are presented with new stimuli (loud noises, large dogs, and changes in environment). Next, the dimension of irritable distress assesses infants' displays of fussiness, anger, or frustration when not allowed to do what they want. Infants who are able to look at objects and events for prolonged periods of time are high in attention span and persistence. Positive affect and approach refer to the amount and intensity of positive emotions like laughing and smiling, as well as seeking out new experiences and events. Infants high in this dimension smile and laugh often and approach new toys with positivity. How much infants move around ⌊(squirming, kicking, and waving arms)⌋ is captured by the dimension of activity level. Finally, rhythmicity reflects infants' preferences for routines and predictability, especially in bodily functions such as eating and sleeping.

© mathom/Shutterstock.com

© Egyptian Studio/Shutterstock.com

Temperament is relatively stable over time (Roberts & DelVecchio, 2000). ⌊Children⌋ who are high on positive dimensions of temperament and low on negative dimensions of temperament show better social and emotional adjustment later in life (Coplan & Bullock, 2012). Temperament also affects parenting style and parent–child interactions. For example, children who are high in negative temperament dimensions tend to have parents that use strict punishment found in the authoritarian parenting style (Eisenberg et al., 1999). The complex relationship among parenting, attachment, and temperament has sparked many lines of research and even more questions.

Erikson's Theory of Psychosocial Development

Erik Erikson proposed a social development theory describing the different challenges faced across the life span (Erikson, 1950, 1959). In each of the eight stages of Erikson's theory, a ⌊unique⌋ crisis must be resolved before ⌊moving to⌋ the next stage ⌊(and its crisis)⌋ or people will struggle to resolve this issue across the life span. The crises are specific to the challenges and hurdles of development within that age range. The first five stages cover birth through the end of adolescence, with the final three stages covering adulthood.

Erikson's first stage, **basic trust versus mistrust**, should be successfully resolved by the end of the first year of life. The critical issue or crisis that must be resolved is infants' trust in caregiver support and their ability to cope with the world versus the general sense of mistrust of the world and the infants' abilities. If successfully resolved, infants will learn that the world (mainly their parents) is nurturing and supportive and can be relied on in times of need. With this trust in others comes infants' confidence in their ⌊own⌋ abilities to appropriately interact and cope with changes. When not successfully resolved, infants develop a sense of skepticism about the world and doubt their abilities to cope with life's changes. Consistent and warm caregiving should lead to the successful resolutions of trust, whereas cold and/or inconsistent caregiving ⌊could lead to⌋ the unsuccessful resolution of mistrust.

From ages 1 to 3.5 years, toddlers must learn a sense of independence and self-control to successfully resolve Erikson's next stage, **autonomy versus shame and doubt**. Toddlers now have increased motor skills, language abilities, and social interactions. With new skills come the challenges that require toddlers to make appropriate choices and have confidence in their abilities to enact those choices. Toddlers want to start doing things on their own like pouring their own juice and dressing themselves. Supportive caregiving ˌthat allowsˌ toddlers to learn these important skills without fear of reprisal helps to successfully resolve this crisis, ˌwhich leadsˌ to autonomous, confident toddlers. In contrast, harsh or unsupportive caregiving during this crisis leads to toddlers who have high levels of shame and ˌwhoˌ doubt their abilities to act independently ˌinˌ their world.

Table 6.5   Erikson's Stages, Age Range, and Crisis Information

Stage	Crisis to Resolve	Age Range
Basic Trust vs. Mistrust	Trusting in caregiver and own ability to cope with challenges	Infancy
Autonomy vs. Shame and Doubt	Making appropriate choices and having confidence in skills	Toddlerhood
Initiative vs. Guilt	Setting and attaining goals	Preschool
Industry vs. Inferiority	Learning the rules and customs of the culture	Childhood
Identity vs. Role Confusion	Developing a coherent identity	Adolescence–Early Adulthood
Intimacy vs. Isolation	Forming close, intimate relationship bonds	Early Adulthood
Generativity vs. Stagnation	Considering the legacy left behind	Middle Adulthood
Ego Integrity vs. Despair	Reflecting back on life	Late Adulthood

What Does the Bible Say?

ˌErik Erikson in his theory of Psychosocial Development puts identity development in adolescence and early adulthood. In his theory, identity is formed through interactions with others and through success in various activities from sports to occupational choice. Successful resolution of this stage involves an individual having a strong sense of who they are.

When we examine the Bible, we see that God has much to say about our identity. Genesis 1:27 says that we have been created in the image of God and Ephesians 2:10 tells us that as believers, we are "his workmanship, created in Christ Jesus for good works, which God prepared beforehand, that we should walk in them" (ESV). Once we receive Jesus as our Savior, God tells us we are friends of His (John 15:15), heirs (Ephesians 2:19), and children of God (John 1:12). Furthermore, Ephesians 1:4 tells us that God chose us before the foundation of the world.

While we have been given gifts and talents to use for His glory, our identity rests primarily in being His child and not in what we achieve, the jobs we have, or the labels we carry in the world. The world may lead us to identify with things of this world, but identity in Jesus means much more and has eternal significance.

> Much like Erikson sees adolescence and early adulthood as a period of understanding our identity, we should teach our teenagers and young adults to seek their identity in Christ over things of this world. In fact, one of the richest passages of Scripture about our identity can be found in Ephesians 1 where we are described as having a new identity when we accept Jesus. According to Ephesians 1, we have been given every spiritual blessing; we are chosen, adopted, redeemed, purposed, forgiven, lavished with grace, and unconditionally loved and accepted. We have been given the promise of spending eternity with God, no matter what we do. Once our identity is in Christ, we cannot alter this identity, no matter what we do.
>
> When you think about psychological security and the psychological health that theoretically comes from successfully navigating Erikson's stages, one can see how a biblical identity of unconditional and eternal acceptance can lead to much more psychological health and security.

The crisis of the next stage in Erikson's theory is **initiative versus guilt** (ages 4–6 years). Erikson believed that during the preschool years, children must learn to set goals and how to achieve ⌐them.⌐ Setting and attaining goals require the ability to take action and have self-control. Caregivers teach their children these skills through behavioral examples and setting rules and standards for behaviors. ⌐Parenting where children are helped to⌐ set and attain reasonable goals leads to children who successfully resolve the stage and who develop solid internal motivators and abilities. However, parents who are overly controlling or critical will have children who do not successfully resolve the crisis, ⌐lacking⌐ self-control or ⌐becoming⌐ overly controlling, ⌐themselves.⌐

⌐Some⌐ children are exposed to more people within their culture, such as teachers and friends. ⌐The⌐ responsibility of successful resolution of future crises extends beyond the parents to all people with whom children have contact. Erikson's fourth stage—**industry versus inferiority** (6 years to puberty)—involves children successfully learning the rules and customs of their culture. To resolve this crisis, children must accept and ⌐embrace⌐ the standards of their culture into their cognitive and social skills, which ⌐allows⌐ them to appropriately interact with peers. Also, these cultural skills help children to become productive members of their culture or become industrious. Children who do not gain the appropriate cultural knowledge tend to have feelings of social and personal inadequacy or inferiority.

Erikson's fifth stage of psychosocial development is **identity versus role confusion** (adolescence through early adulthood). After puberty, adolescents have new internal/external pressures to form romantic relationships and set career/educational goals. ⌐During adolescence they are transitioning⌐ in identity to be the adults that they wish to become. The crisis of this stage is the need to develop a coherent, fully considered identity. If successfully resolved, adolescents will be secure in their identity and career choices, leading to complex adult identities. If not successfully resolved, adolescents may be confused about whom they are and lack educational and career goals to become secure adults.

During early adulthood, people must resolve the crisis of **intimacy versus isolation**. Successfully overcoming this crisis requires people to form close, intimate relationship bonds with others by becoming spouses, parents, and friends. People who do not overcome this crisis typically have a fear of losing their identity in those relationships and think about themselves first, leading to isolation from others.

Erikson's seventh stage, **generativity versus stagnation**, spans middle adulthood. During this time, people begin to think about their legacy to the world and their contribution to the next generation. People who are able to help support and guide the next generation through their experiences have successfully resolved this stage's crisis by contributing positively to society. ⌐Self-focused people⌐ who do not foster the next generation have not successfully resolved this crisis or have become stagnant in their phase in life.

The eighth and final stage of Erikson's theory is **ego integrity versus despair**. In late adulthood, people have the ability to reflect back over their lives and take stock of their accomplishments. When people are able to achieve a sense of purpose and meaning in life, ⌐have a solid sense of integrity,⌐ and take pride in their ⌐accomplishments,⌐ they have successfully resolved the final crisis of life. People who fear death and who do not find a sense of meaning in life will face despair in the final stages of life.

MORAL DEVELOPMENT

Morality, according to Lawrence Kohlberg (1969, 1976, 1978), reflects people's sense of fairness and justice. Moral development is the process of learning what is right/wrong, fair/unfair, or just/unjust. Kohlberg was most interested in the development of the thought processes behind moral decision-making rather than the acquisition of "correct" moral choices. Children move from self-centered reasoning to a social-based reasoning to a flexible reasoning style.

© Belinda Pretorius/Shutterstock.com

⌐Based on Piaget's theory,⌐ Kohlberg ⌐(1969, 1976, 1978),⌐ created a theory of moral development to examine the cognitive processes associated with moral decisions. To gain information about how people make ⌐choices,⌐ Kohlberg developed an interview procedure ⌐offering⌐ a series of ambiguous moral dilemmas. The Heinz Dilemma involves a man, Heinz, whose wife is dying of cancer. Heinz must choose to steal the lifesaving drugs from the local pharmacy or to allow his wife to die. ⌐To be clear,⌐ Kohlberg was not concerned with whether ⌐or not⌐ people felt Heinz should steal the drugs; he was more concerned with their reasoning behind their decisions.

Full Heinz Dilemma

> *A woman was near death from a special kind of cancer. There was one drug that the doctor thought might save her. It was a form of radium that a druggist in the same town had recently discovered. The drug was expensive to make, but the druggist was charging ten times what the drug cost him to produce. He paid $200 for the radium and charged $2,000 for a small dose of the drug. The sick woman's husband, Heinz, went to everyone he knew to borrow the money, but he could only get together about $1,000, which is half of what the drug cost. He told the druggist that his wife was dying and asked him to sell it cheaper or let him pay later. But the druggist said: "No, I discovered the drug and I'm going to make money from it." So, Heinz got desperate and broke into the man's store to steal the drug for his wife. Should Heinz have broken into the laboratory to steal the drug for his wife? Why or why not? (Adapted from Kohlberg, 1981).*

Based on ⌐the rationale for their⌐ moral decisions, people ⌐are⌐ classified into one of three general stages of moral development: preconventional, conventional, and postconventional. Cognitive reasoning in the **preconventional** stage, typical during the preschool and early elementary school years, reflects thinking ⌐that seeks⌐ reward or ⌐the avoidance⌐ punishment. In this stage, thinking is very self-focused,

> **Preconventional moral reasoning:** Kohlberg's first stage of moral development when children focus on receiving rewards or avoiding punishments.

reflecting the egocentrism dominant in this level of cognitive development. Children will make moral decisions to gain positive outcomes (e.g., favor from others or tangible benefits) or will make moral decisions to avoid negative outcomes (e.g., punishment or loss of admiration). For the Heinz dilemma, preconventional moral thinkers will answer in the affirmative that Heinz should steal the drug because his wife will love him for saving her life (reward) or because if she dies, Heinz will be lonely and sad (punishment). Conversely, examples of negative answers that Heinz should not steal the drug would be because Heinz would get sympathy from his friends if his wife died (reward) or because Heinz would get in trouble for stealing (punishment). Preconventional moral thinking is commonly overcome when egocentrism is replaced with logical thought.

Conventional moral reasoning is Kohlberg's next stage of moral development and is the most common level of moral thinking. Most adults reason using the conventional moral thinking approach, which is focused on maintaining social order and laws. Through logical thought and hypothetical reasoning, people are able to move past self-centered cognitions and are better able to consider the good of society overall. Examples of affirmative responses to the Heinz dilemma reflect reasoning about the need to maintain social order, suggesting that Heinz should steal the drug because the pharmacist is abusing his position and patients by overcharging. Moreover, Heinz could potentially help others suffering from cancer by sharing those drugs with them. The rationale behind the negative response rests upon the premise that Heinz should not steal the drug because theft is morally and socially wrong, and unhealthy. Plus, in a free market, the pharmacist has the right to charge whatever he or she wants, and still be moral.

> **Conventional moral reasoning:** Kohlberg's second stage of moral development when people focus on maintaining social order.

Postconventional moral reasoning, the final stage of Kohlberg's theory, is only achieved by a small group of adults. Interestingly, Kohlberg never officially interviewed a person who could be classified at this level. Theoretically, postconventional thinkers have a flexible cognitive style allowing them to understand universal truths and the need to strive for a universal justice that transcends oppressive civil codes. The great reformer, Martin Luther vocally and publicly resisted the selling of indulgences by the Roman catholic church in the 16th century; Mother Teresa actively and systematically rescued, cared for, and nurtured the rejected untouchable class in Kolkata, India; and the British humanitarian Nicholas Winton who covertly saved 669 Jewish children from Nazi-occupied Czechoslovakia during World War II (WWII) are all examples of those who could be said to have reached this level. Similarly, in the Heinz dilemma, one could argue that all people should have access to the life-saving treatment regardless of its cost or availability. In contrast, negative responses suggest that Heinz should not steal the drug because he would be impinging on the pharmacist's freedoms in an open society or because the needs of one person should not outweigh the needs of all people.

> **Postconventional moral reasoning:** Kohlberg's third stage of moral development when people focus on equality and the greater good.

Kohlberg's theory has received much scholarly criticism. First, people who often make life and death decisions (such as doctors and judges) tend to score higher on Kohlberg's stages (Miller, 2011). Most people do not have to decide whether to steal drugs to save a life, but doctors and judges have more experience with these types of moral dilemmas, leading to deeper consideration of the moral situations. People with less experience with complex moral dilemmas may not be lower in moral reasoning but may have not had the time or the opportunity to reflect on the situation, causing their thinking to appear to be more self-focused or shallow.

Also, Kohlberg's theory has been criticized because the final stage, postconventional reasoning is unobtainable for most people (Miller, 2011). Even though people may be able to cognitively understand this level of reasoning, very few people are able to achieve this level of thinking as their dominant form of moral reasoning. By setting this as the highest level of thinking, Kohlberg may have been setting unrealistic expectations of people and series of stages that do not reflect the true complexity of moral reasoning.

TEENS AND YOUNG ADULTS

Adolescence is a time of transition between childhood and adulthood. Historically, the delineation between childhood and adulthood was clearer. In more tribal cultures, there was often a specific age that had to be reached or task an individual had to accomplish and that would signify the transition between these two periods; this was really advantageous in many ways because it significantly reduced the ambiguity that tends to capture so much of adolescent development today. Changes in responsibilities around work and relationships would follow. Of course, this model didn't mean that young people were not mentored or supported.

© Aleksandar Todorovic/Shutterstock.com

In fact, just the opposite was often the case as tribal elders would place a premium on raising the next generation of community members and leaders.

More modern cultures, especially with a focus on extended formal education, have contributed to this in-between period as well as expanding the length of the period. This can create a lot of confusion. For example, at the age of 18 in the United States, you are legally defined as an adult and can enter a legal contract and be held to that contract. At this age you can also vote. Yet at this same age, if in high school, you still have to raise your hand and get permission from a teacher to use the restroom. However, at that same age they still require input from their parents to apply to college and receive financial aid yet those some adults could forgo college and enter the military with no parental support required. Additionally, while defined as an adult at 18 and even if that adult is in the military, that person would be unable to purchase tobacco or alcohol until the age of 21. Similarly, legal adults are often unable to even rent a car until the age of 25. Often adults, even if they are living on their own and married, can stay on their parents' medical insurance through the age of 26. Many individuals in the United States over the age of 18 are still being supported by their parents financially, including staying on their parent's health and car insurance as well as staying on their cell phone plan. Similarly, most adults cannot rent an apartment without their parents cosigning the lease.

On the other side of this scenario, there are also situations in which children, individuals below the age of 18, who have committed crimes and have been tried as adults. In fact, the youngest person to have been sentenced to life in prison without the possibility of parole, was 13 years of age at the time of trial and sentencing. You can get a job around the age of 14 in most states as well as get a license to operate a car independently by 16 years of age. Also, if you go to a middle or high school nurse and request an aspirin, you will be denied such medication unless the nurse has written parental consent; however, in many states (e.g., California, Connecticut, Hawaii, Maine, and others), that same child can legally get an abortion without any parental consent. In many states, a child age 11 or older can provide input as to which parent they want to live with if the parents are divorced and custody cannot be decided by the parents. The ultimate decision is up to the judge, because individuals under 18 cannot engage in a legal contract; however, children can still provide compelling input and that input is often given great weight in the decision-making process.

This begs the question, what is an adult? It seems that defining an adult in the United States is surprisingly difficult. So, how do we communicate to children how to become adults if we cannot effectively define it?

The teen years are full of a whole host of incongruities. For example, during our teen years our bodies are likely to be more resilient, flexible, and tireless.

© DisobeyArt/Shutterstock.com

We are often in our very best physical shape, have the best reaction time, and are the most resistant to all sorts of pathogens and diseases. Reasoning power increases. The size of one's social network expands. While stress may increase during these years, so does a teen's capacity to intellectually and emotionally manage such challenges. Yet, it is also during these years that death and disability are the highest—car accidents, suicide, and homicide, for example. Understanding adolescent and young adult development can help explain the seemingly contradictory findings often noted across this period of development.

© Syrota Vadym/Shutterstock.com

© frantic00/Shutterstock.com

Stages of Adolescence

Adolescence can be subdivided into three stages: early adolescence (ages 10–13), middle adolescence (ages 14–17), and late adolescence (ages 18–21 and older). Early adolescence can be characterized by rapid changes in physical characteristics including hair growth under the arms and around the genitals, breast development in females, and enlargement of the testicles in males. Females usually start a year or 2 earlier than males, and it can be normal for some changes to start as early as age 8 for females and age 9 for males. Many girls may start their period around age 12, on average 2–3 years after the onset of breast development. During this time, adolescents tend to have more concrete/black-and-white thinking, often noting in the communication that some things are absolutely right or absolutely wrong. There is also a general focus on themselves where they often overestimate the amount of attention garnered by others. This can be difficult because at this age teens tend to feel self-conscious about their looks and behavior because they think they are being observed and judged by their peers. Often this is the age in which increased need for privacy occurs. That privacy will be seen in who they talk with and what they say, and this is made more complicated with technology as parents have little means to monitor potentially unhealthy activities.

 Middle adolescence is characterized in males with continued and rapid growth, often in spurts and can be uneven. They may have some voice cracking, for example, as their voices lower. Some develop acne. Physical changes may be nearly complete for females, and most girls now have regular periods. This is often the age that interest in romantic relationships occurs. This is also the age in which adolescents tend to argue with their parents more as they try to juggle independence, parental expectation, and need for parental support in their activities, like meeting friends at the movies, mall, or restaurant. This is also the age in which adolescents become good thinkers and can use reason to solve and understand problems, but they tend to not be able to apply those skills as effectively in managing their own behavior and understanding risk. This is one of the most quintessential aspects of adolescents. It is the reason that individuals at this age can score perfectly on an informational quiz on the adverse effects of smoking cigarettes yet still smoke. The difference is that while they understand the seriousness of the issue, like smoking, they often overestimate their ability to control the behavior or its negative impact on them. For example, many cigarette smokers believe they can quit at any time and often say they will quit smoking after they finish high school, but these young people often see their smoking increase after graduation not decrease. During this stage, adolescent thinking becomes more complicated. It is at this age most adolescents can imagine what their future will be like, but they have a hard time applying those thoughts to their decision-making process and managing their day-to-day activities to reach these goals. They also question things a lot more with a special focus on fairness. So, while they have increased cognitive capabilities, they often use these new skills to rationalize their own maladaptive behaviors. This thinking process is often called the personal fable: they see themselves as special and unique. It is for these reasons that adolescents are more likely to: be impulsive, misunderstand emotions and social cues, have more accidents, arguments, and fights, and take greater risks and make dangerous choices.

 In late adolescence, teens begin to think outside themselves in a new way. They may think more about what's happening in the world and the major challenges facing society. They may also become concerned with career choices and what to do after they leave home. There is an increased desire to have an impact and feel important as well as build recognition. In late adolescence, teens generally have completed physical development and grown to their full adult height. They usually have more impulse control and are likely to be better able to gauge risks and rewards accurately and establish methods to achieve those rewards (e.g., requirements for high school graduation, saving money for a car, and applying to college or vocational programs). Teens in late adolescents who are transitioning to early adulthood have a stronger sense of their own individuality now and can identify their own values. They may become more focused on the future and base decisions on their hopes and ideals. Friendships and romantic relationships become more stable and often begin to shrink as quality becomes more important than quantity. This can also lead to a lot of stress as their decisions can have weighty and lasting impacts—like borrowing large amounts of money to pay for college. They become more emotionally and physically separated from their family. However, in a more positive way, many reestablish an "adult" relationship with their parents, considering them more an equal from whom to ask advice and discuss mature topics with, rather than an authority figure.

There are many examples that can be used to explain the differences in adolescent development including thinking and emotional responses. However, one that seems especially pertinent centers around texting and driving. Driving is an especially challenging and risky endeavor, especially for teens. It is often quite challenging to communicate to young people the gravity of driving, particularly since most have been in cars their entire life with little reason for concern. It only takes a second of distraction for a crash to occur and that crash can result in life-changing consequences. More specifically, in a study of more than 101,000 teenagers, researchers found that nearly 40% had texted or sent an e-mail while driving at least once in the past 30 days, and that the older the driver, the more likely he or she was to text while driving—all despite the fact that laws in most states ban young drivers from engaging in these activities (Li et al., 2015). Texting while driving appeared to be associated with other risky behaviors, such as not regularly wearing a seat belt and drinking alcohol while driving. Cell phone use behind the wheel reduces the amount of brain activity associated with driving by 37%. According to the National Highway Traffic Safety Administration (Distracted Driving, 2017), 3,166 people were killed in 2,935 distraction-affected crashes in 2016, accounting for 9% of all fatal crashes in the United States. Crash rates ending in fatalities are three times greater for teens than for drivers aged 20 and over. Texting while driving makes a crash up to 23 times more likely. Teens make up the largest age group reported as distracted in fatal crashes. More than 58% of teen crashes are due to driver distraction. Though 97% of teens marked "agree" that texting while driving is dangerous, 43% do it anyway (2017). This goes back to the issues of the personal fable in which they know the risk but don't think it will apply to them.

© Oranzy Photography/Shutterstock.com

© Gorgev/Shutterstock.com

Physical Growth and Development

Years ago, much of the stress and trauma of adolescence was blamed on "raging hormones." Upon more careful examination and research, it appears the major organ responsible for managing the transition from childhood to adulthood is the brain. New developments in neuroscience have provided insight into adolescent development. G. Stanley Hall was the first psychologist of the modern era to write at length about adolescent development. He, as well as others, believed that extreme turmoil is a normal part of adolescent development, but more recent findings note that the vast majority of adolescents do not experience extreme turmoil. In fact, according to the long running Youth Risk Behavior Surveillance System, most teens today are engaged in a lot less risky behavior than decades ago. Reduction in risks includes such behaviors as injury and violence, sexual behavior/teen pregnancy, alcohol and other drug use, tobacco use, and bringing a gun or weapon to school (CDC, 2018b). Although outcomes are looking positive across a number of measures, there are still a number of factors negatively impacting young people today.

Undoubtedly, the most obvious features of adolescent development are the dramatic gains in physical stature; however, the brain is the driving force for all these recognizable changes. Thus, physical development during adolescence is characterized by the following:

- Rapid physical growth
- Changes in sleep patterns
- Change in appetite
- Changes in hormones
- Sexual maturation
- Secondary sexual characteristics
- Changes in body shape
- Increases in strength and endurance
- Menstruation in females
- Changes in vocal sounds

In addition to overt physical changes, there are a number of central nervous system (i.e., brain) changes take place. While these changes are necessary for the transition from childhood to adulthood, sometimes the dramatic shift in psychological development can produce unintended consequences. These challenges are especially difficult for adolescents with less than ideal circumstances or for those with genetic predispositions or early developmental trauma (Blakemore et al., 2010; Masten et al., 2008; Pfeifer & Blakemore, 2012; Sawyer et al., 2012; Viner et al., 2012). Biologically based characteristics that distinguish males and females are referred to as sex differences. These characteristics include different reproductive functions and differences in hormones and anatomy. These differences are universal, biologically determined, and unchanged by social influence. Sex differences may also explain the finding that, after infancy, boys are more physically active and aggressive than girls. In contrast, gender is a psychological phenomenon referring to learned, sex-related behaviors and attitudes. Cultures vary in how strongly gender is linked to daily activities and in the amount of tolerance for what is perceived as cross-gender behavior. Gender identity is an individual's sense of maleness or femaleness; it includes awareness and acceptance of one's sex. Gender roles are patterns of behavior regarded as appropriate for males and females in a particular society. They provide the basic definitions of masculinity and femininity. Sadly, potential differences between males and females have often been popularized as an "us versus them" approach—rooted in conflict. Instead, it should focus more on a complimentary approach for which differences, albeit often small, should be celebrated not criticized.

© koya979/Shutterstock.com

Substance Use and Abuse

Changes in brain development are responsible for physical growth, social networking, emotional maturation, and gains in cognitive abilities. Teens tend to seek new, exciting experiences during this period, but often lack the maturity to weigh the consequences of their decision-making (Steinberg, 2007). Therefore, drug experimentation, which is almost universally initiated during adolescence, often results in a plethora of primary and secondary adverse events. These events impact the substance user, their family, and their community, in addition to the involvement of local, state, and federal agencies. While the personal costs associated with substance abuse problems are immeasurable, in 2017, the National Institute on Drug Abuse estimated that substance use and addiction cost Americans more than $740 billion annually. The numbers continue to rise. The nearly trillion dollars spent per year includes only healthcare expenditures, lost earnings, and costs associated with crime and accidents; it does not reflect the high economic burden substance abuse places on the family (e.g., divorce, child abuse, parental absence, reduced academic support, etc.) (Cartwright, 2008). Drug abuse related costs greatly exceed those associated with chronic conditions such as cancer and diabetes. Substance abuse is considered our nation's number one public health problem. It is also the single most problematic financial issue facing American society. Any reduction in the number and/or severity of substance abuse problems would yield enormous economic and other less tangible benefits for our nation.

Given that substance abuse is such a widespread problem, the United States spending for treatment of substance use disorders (SUDs) is predicted to reach $42.1 billion in 2020 (SAMHSA, 2014a). There are a number of private- and community-based programs that contribute countless dollars and hours toward prevention. While prevention efforts are costly, they frequently produce a positive impact. Current studies show a reduction in use across most categories of abused drugs, with the principle exceptions including inhalants and prescription drugs. According to Substance Abuse and Mental Health Services Administration's (SAMHSA) National Survey on Drug Use and Health (2018), among youths aged 12–17, the types of drugs used in the past month varied. With respect to alcohol, a little more than half of Americans aged 12 or older reported current alcohol use; almost one fourth (24.5%) participated in binge drinking at least once in the 30 days prior to the survey; and heavy drinking was reported by 6.1% of the population sampled (SAMHSA, 2018). Lastly, in this same survey, an estimated 58.8 million Americans aged 12 or older were current (past month) tobacco users. In addition, 47 million persons (17.2%of the population) were current cigarette smokers; 12.2 million smoked cigars; 8 million (3.5%) used smokeless tobacco; and 2.1 million smoked tobacco in pipes. Initiation of drug use is the highest among people age 12–18. The average age for first use of an abused substance in 2016 was about 18.2 for inhalants, 17.4 for alcohol, 18 for nicotine, and about 19 for illicit drugs (Lipari et al., 2017). Initiating substance use during childhood or adolescence increases the risk of developing dependence or SUD's in the future (SAMHSA, 2014b). The pattern of use noted in this survey and other similar studies (Kandel et al., 1992) offer direct evidence that substance abuse is a pediatric/developmental disease. Furthermore, such evidence provides convincing evidence of the "gateway model of drug abuse," which suggests the typical pattern of substance use is to start with more conventional, legal, and readily available substances (e.g., nicotine, alcohol, and inhalants) followed by a systematic elevation in the type of drug abused, like illicit drugs (e.g., marijuana, cocaine, methamphetamine, heroin, and ecstasy).

This phenomenon, termed the "gateway drug effect," has been well documented (Johnston & O'Malley, 1986; Johnston et al., 1991; Kandel et al., 1992; O'Donnell & Clayton, 1979; Torabi et al., 1993). One study noted a dose-dependent relationship between smoking, binge drinking, and illicit drug use. In particular, pack-a-day smokers were three times more likely to drink alcohol, seven times more likely to use smokeless tobacco, and 10 to 30 times more likely to use illicit drugs compared to nonsmokers (Torabi et al., 1993). The culmination of these and similar findings have serious implications. Initiating substance use during adolescence is correlated with an increase in severity of dependence, greater addiction liability, higher daily consumption, and reduced probability of quitting (Breslau

& Peterson, 1996; Chambers et al., 2003; Chen & Millar, 1998; Spear, 2000; Taioli & Wynder, 1991). Also, escalation of drug use is more rapid, and the risk of dependence is greater in adolescents compared to adults (Chen et al., 1997; Clark et al., 1998; Estroff et al., 1989; Robins & Przybeck, 1985). The escalation from tobacco, inhalants, alcohol, or prescription drugs to illicit drug use, abuse, and dependence may include factors beyond the obvious sociocultural factors (e.g., peer pressure, advertising, media, etc.). The majority of young people report using drugs for the first time because of sociocultural factors such as the following:

- Peer pressure
- Curiosity
- Advertising
- Movies, television, and music
- Parental use
- Sibling use
- Cost
- Access
- Not perceived of as a drug
- Seen as a grown-up behavior

⌐They continue to use drugs because of the addictive properties of drugs. Teens especially (and adults) routinely downplay the significance of the social forces that act upon them. Even though social factors provide a strong initiating force for drug use, it is possible, even probable, that the "gateway" effect may be due, in part, to neurochemical alterations in reward systems. It is possible that adolescent substance use could serve as a neurochemical "gateway" for subsequent drug abuse and dependence, and normal developmental processes could elevate the risk for drug use, misuse, abuse, and dependence.

⌐The elevation in substance use, abuse, and dependence noted during adolescence has increasingly been shown to be associated with rather remarkable changes in brain processes. For example, across adolescent development, the central nervous system is subject to dramatic changes in hormone levels, synaptic pruning, apoptosis, cell replication and migration, as well as the functional programming of behavioral responses (Altman & Bayer, 1990; Bayer et al., 1982; Huttenlocher, 1990; McWilliams & Lynch, 1983; Rezvani & Levin, 2004; Spear & Brake, 1983). Similarly, changes in brain processes are associated with a unique pattern of behavior including increased rates of novelty seeking, risk taking, exploration, impulsivity, social behavior, and aggression (Spear, 2000). Markedly, these processes are impacted by a broad spectrum of pharmacological agents that can disrupt and impair development (Slotkin, 2004; Spear, 2000). To this end and in support of the "neurochemical gateway effect," previous research has shown that adolescent substance abuse exposure permanently alters reward systems, placing substance-exposed subjects at greater risk for drug abuse problems throughout life (Kelley & Middaugh, 1999; Kelley & Rowan, 2004; Nolley & Kelley, 2007). Contrary to the customary observation that adolescence is part of a continuum of change (i.e., from childhood to adulthood), evidence now suggests that adolescence is instead a unique developmental period that is particularly vulnerable to substance use initiation and drug insults.

Emotions and Mental Health

⌐The rapid neurobiological changes that transpire during adolescence not only elevate the risk for substance abuse problems, such changes also increase the risk for mood disorders. As a matter of fact, adolescence is the period of highest risk for the onset of depression (Burke et al., 1990). According to a nationally representative survey of adolescents (age 13–18 years) in the United States, the most common mental disorders by lifetime prevalence are anxiety (31.9%), behavior (19.1%), and mood (14.3%) (Merikangas et al., 2010). Specifically, elevated risk for depression begins in the early teens and continues to rise in a linear fashion throughout adolescence. More specifically, population-based studies show the prevalence rate to be approximately 0.5% in children age 3–5, 2% in children age 6–11, and 13.3% for ages 12–17 (Perou et al., 2013). Unfortunately, too many adolescents deal with negative affective states by using a variety of readily available substances.

While such chemicals may offer immediate, short-term relief for their bad feelings (e.g., depression, anxiety, and/or stress), the long-term problems associated with such use far exceed the very short-term perceived gains. In fact, it is most likely that the use of such chemicals will result in a deterioration of the exact problem they are trying to self-medicate away due to rebound effects. This pattern often results in the teen quickly self-administering more of the drug, which may provide some minimal relief from their problems, but will exacerbate the issue they are trying to suppress, often resulting in a terrible cycle of abuse. While self-medicating is a common reason for teen drug use, it is also likely that teen drug use results in the development of psychological problems. Drugs directly impact important brain centers involved in emotional arousal and control of emotions, so damage to these brain centers alone can result in the development of psychological problems, which are then further medicated with abused drugs, thus, drastically accelerating the problem.

The majority of people who experience mental health issues will first experience them during adolescence. Changes in mood combined with drastic shifts in emotional and cognitive development which is then paired with a life-stressor can serve as a trigger for mental health problems. Some of the most profound life stressors are now referred to as adverse childhood events. If these problems are ignored or masked by drug and alcohol use, more than likely, the problems will accelerate and possibly result in significant problems or serious disability. Despite the allure and quick fix associated with abused drugs, they have no medicinal value and always make the problems worse.

How serious is the problem? According to Friedman (2006), there is an epidemic of mental illness among youth and teenagers in the United States. Recent surveys suggest that between 13% and 20% of children have a mental, behavioral, or emotional disorder. According to the recent National Comorbidity Survey (Kessler et al., 2005), 50% of lifetime serious adult psychiatric illnesses, including depression, anxiety, and substance abuse, started by age 14. Furthermore, 75% of such disorders present by age 25.

Lifetime prevalence estimates are as follows:

- Anxiety, 31%
- Mood disorders, 21.4%
- Impulse control disorders, 24.8%
- Substance abuse disorders, 14.6%
- Any disorder, 46.4%
- Median age of onset surrounds the adolescent period
- Half of lifetime cases begin by age 14
  (Statistics taken from Kessler et al., 2005; DSM IV)

The above disorders are due in part to alterations in certain neurotransmitters and brain structures that are known to expand and develop rapidly during adolescence. Difficulty managing these new thoughts, feelings, and behaviors is known to precede drug use in some teens. Such drug use is aimed at mitigating the developmental changes in these brain chemicals. That is to say, unwanted emotional states are ultimately a consequence of changes in neurotransmitter activity. People try to readjust these neurotransmitters through the use of abused drugs. Different affective states are brought about through different neurotransmitters. People select the abused drugs that are perceived to help make the adverse feelings go away. Although short-term relief of such problems may occur, over time, the exact conditions that are being suppressed with medications get amplified due to the drug exposure. Compounding the initial problem, there are often enormous delays in diagnosis and treatment. This delay likely skews the data toward a higher age range, meaning the age is likely younger than reported.

Selective social interaction theory suggests that, as people age, they become more selective in choosing social partners who satisfy their emotional needs. Generativity describes a person's ability to look beyond his or her own needs.

 THE PSYCHOLOGY OF LONELINESS

MIDDLE ADULTHOOD

Upon successful completion of adolescent and early adult development, there is often a period of stability and continuity. Early adulthood takes place generally between the ages of 21 and 35. In early adulthood, individuals may continue to add a bit of height and weight. Hormonal changes also continue to occur, often showing a gradual drop-off, but the effects are less pronounced than they were during adolescence. In terms of physical development, this period is the least dramatic. Middle adulthood takes place between the ages of 35 and 65. In middle adulthood, individuals often start to experience more noticeable changes again but often in terms of decline. There is great variability during this time and in many ways determined by biological, social, and psychological factors. For example, a healthy 50-year-old could be enjoying all of the benefits of their many years of hard work (e.g., consider Jenifer Aniston, age 51, or Paul Rudd, age 50); however, around the same age someone could begin to experience significant declines in health, which would have cascading impacts on career, relationships, and hobbies/interests (e.g., Michael J. Fox, age 58, who has suffered from Parkinson's disease for many years). Because we start to see and feel the physical changes in our bodies, we may begin to think about our physical development once more. One of the most noticeable outward changes is the loss of skin elasticity, but internally there are gradual changes in organ system function with a general decrease in function. There are also declines in sensory system function with seeing and hearing being the notable as glasses and hearing aids become more common.

© Jaguar PS/Shutterstock.com

© DFree/Shutterstock.com

The top causes of death for individuals in middle adulthood include the following:

- Accidents
- Cancer
- Heart disease
- Suicide
- Homicide
- Chronic liver disease and cirrhosis
- Chronic obstructive pulmonary disease (COPD)
- Diabetes mellitus
- Cerebrovascular disease (CDC, 2010)

The major development tasks that take place during middle-adult include the following:

- Death of one or more parents and experiencing associated grief.
- Launching children into their own lives.
- Adjusting to home life without children (often referred to as the empty nest).
- Dealing with adult children who return to live at home (known as boomerang children in the United States).
- Becoming grandparents.
- Preparing for late adulthood including changes in career, income, and retirement.
- Redefining hobbies and interest given changes in physical abilities.
- Dealing with changing health status and potential chronic illness.
- Acting as caregivers for aging parents or spouses (Lachman, 2004).

In summary, making the transition from young adulthood to middle adulthood to older adulthood can be difficult for many individuals. There are many changes affecting areas of a person's biology, their psychology, their social life, and their spiritual relationship. For some, it can be a period of reflection associated with pride and for others a time of disappointment. As there are more drastic changes in later adulthood, we will focus more on that stage for the remainder of the chapter.

AGING AND OLDER ADULTHOOD

According to the U.S. Census Bureau, the number of older adults is growing in the United States and is projected to be the largest segment of the population by the year 2030. Defined as people 65 years of age and older, older adults are projected to make up 21% of the population by 2030 (see Figure 6.6). The driving force behind this trend is the fact that Baby Boomers (individuals born after WWII between 1946 and 1964) are aging and living longer than previous generations due to improved healthcare. Named the "Graying of America," this aging of the Baby Boomer cohort will mean that older adults will soon outnumber children for the first time in our country's history (see Figure 6.7), and with it will come important developmental considerations that will require research, resources, and attention.

In addition to the additional healthcare and economic resources that will be required to care for an aging population, there are several psychological and social implications of aging for developmental psychologists to consider. Among these areas of research and concern are coping with chronic illnesses, quality of life, and cognitive decline.

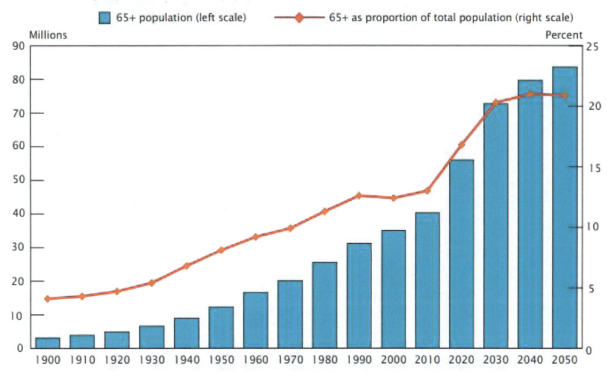

Population Aged 65 and Over: 1900 to 2050
(For information on confidentiality protection, nonsampling error, and definitions, see www.census.gov/prod/cen2010/doc/sf1.pdf)

Figure 6.6 ⌐The population aged 65 and over from 1900 to 2050.⌐
Source: U.S. Census Bureau, 2014

Chronic Illness

⌐According to the National Council on Aging, approximately 80% of older adults have at least one chronic illness and 68% have at least two. As seen in Figure 6.8, the most common chronic illnesses are hypertension, high cholesterol, arthritis, heart disease, and diabetes. Also notable, are depression and dementia which are seen in 14% and 11% of the older adult population (Healthy Aging Team, 2017).

⌐Managing chronic illness is an important part of older adulthood. In addition to the physical management of chronic illness which often includes dietary changes and adherence to prescribed medication, managing one's chronic illness often involves attention to quality of life and depression. Patients with chronic illnesses are shown to have a high prevalence of comorbid depression (Katon, 2003). Furthermore, individuals with chronic illnesses report lower quality of life overall than those without chronic illnesses. The chronic illnesses that are most associated with decreased quality of life are cancer, hypertension, osteoporosis, and diabetes (Fortin et al., 2006; Li et al., 2009).

⌐Quality of life has been a popular concept in research as our population has aged and medical treatments have kept patients alive longer. It was first introduced in the medical literature in the 1960s and has grown to be an important outcome measure in studies of older adults. One of the earliest

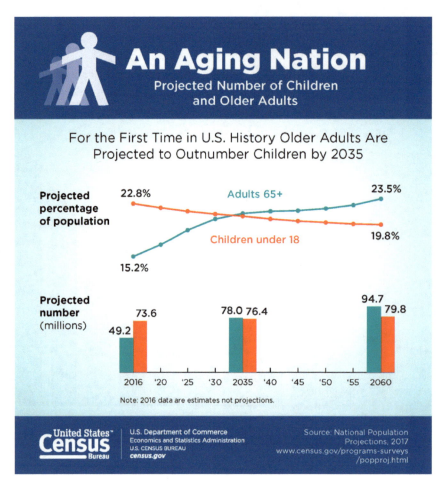

Figure 6.7 ⌐The projected number of children and older adults in the United States.⌐

Source: U.S. Census Bureau, 2017

publications discussing quality of life was an editorial in the *Annals of Internal Medicine*. In this editorial, Elkington (1966) discussed a new ethical issue of balancing effective medical treatments with patients experiencing decreased well-being due to adverse effects of those treatments. In his article, Elkington wrote:

> *What every physician wants for every one of his patients old or young, is not just the absence of death but life with a vibrant quality that we associate with a vigorous youth. This is nothing less than a humanistic biology that is concerned, not with material mechanisms alone, but with the wholeness of human life, with the spiritual quality of life that is unique to man. Just what constitutes this quality of life for a particular patient and the therapeutic pathway to it often is extremely difficult to judge and must lie with the consciousness of the physician (p. 714).*

⌐While the 1960s and 1970s saw few articles related to quality of life, recent decades have seen thousands of articles per year addressing older adults' quality of life and ways to improve it while dealing with chronic illness. Since 1949, the World Health Organization (WHO, 2006) has defined health as "a state of complete physical, mental, and social well-being and not merely an absence of disease and infirmity." In 2005, WHO emphasized the importance of improving older adult's quality of life (WHO, 2005). Because people are living longer than ever before, researchers have changed the way they view health, looking beyond just physical markers of health and to the quality of an individual life.

In older adulthood, researchers have shown the following factors to be related to quality of life: physical and mental ailments, social connection, exercise and physical activity, and sense of purpose. Older adults with more physical and mental ailments report lower quality of life, while those who are socially connected, regularly exercise, and have a sense of purpose reported higher quality of life. Furthermore, spirituality and regular church attendance has also been shown to be related to quality of life in older adults (Abdala et al., 2015). When investigating why this association exists, it appears that spirituality and regular church attendance leads to greater social connectedness, better coping with stressors and loss, and a greater sense of meaning and purpose in life, all of which lead to improved quality of life for older adults (Abdala et al., 2015).

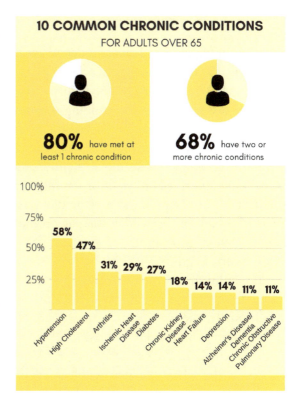

Figure 6.8 The 10 common chronic conditions for adults over 65 years of age.
Source: Bailee Robinson. Data from ncoa.org.

What Does the Bible Say?

Purpose in life and quality of life are important psychological constructs in the aging research literature. But, what does the Bible say about older adults? And, how does the Bible describe meaning and purpose among older adults?

Proverbs 23:22 tells us to "listen to your father who gave you life, and do not despise your mother when she is old" (ESV). Furthermore, Job 12:12 says that "Wisdom is with the aged, and understanding in length of days" (ESV). In addition, God instructs older men and women on how to act in the Apostle Paul's letter to Titus in which he writes, "Older men are to be sober-minded, dignified, self-controlled, sound in faith, in love, and in steadfastness. Older women likewise are to be reverent in behavior, not slanderers or slaves to much wine. They are to teach what is good, and so train the young women to love their husbands and children, to be self-controlled, pure, working at home, kind, and submissive to their own husbands, that the word of God may not be reviled" (Titus 2:2-5, ESV).

God is clear that we are to respect older adults and to learn from them. In Leviticus 19:32a, God says, "You shall stand up before the gray head and honor the face of an old man" (ESV). As can be seen throughout the Bible, one's purpose as he or she ages is to mentor young believers and teach them from their wisdom. Psalm 145:4 tells us that "one generation shall commend your works to another, and shall declare your mighty acts." This aligns well with Erikson's life stage for older adults to focus on generativity, giving back to other with the wisdom and lessons they have learned.

It is clear from the Bible that there is much purpose in older adulthood and among that purpose is to share God's truth with younger people to help them grow in their faith. Additionally, it champions that older adults are to be honored for their age and wisdom.

Cognitive Decline in Older Adulthood

ˌAs seen in Figure 6.8, 11% of older adults have been treated for Alzheimer's disease or another form of dementia. While some cognitive decline is normal in older adulthood (to include slight memory loss or slower cognitive processing), Alzheimer's disease and other forms of dementia are conditions marked by memory loss and difficulty thinking or problem-solving that is usually progressive and interferes with everyday activities. Dementia is caused by changes in the brain as an individual ages and is not considered a normal part of aging.

ˌResearch on dementia and Alzheimer's disease has identified that the main risk factors for these conditions are age and family history, things that largely cannot be controlled. However, researchers have identified other factors that may predict onset and progression of dementia. Diet, cholesterol, exercise, and sleep have all been identified as promoting brain health and related to dementia. It appears that staying active, getting proper amounts of sleep (at least 7 hours per night), and diet are important to maintaining cognitive health.

ˌIn addition to understanding the predictors of Alzheimer's disease and dementia, psychological researchers are also interested in promoting wellness and coping in individuals with dementia. Additionally, the well-being of caregivers of dementia patients has garnered much research attention. According to the Alzheimer's Association, about 15.7 million adult family caregivers care for someone with dementia or Alzheimer's disease (Alzheimer's Association, 2015). Research on caregivers reveals that it can be related to increased burden and stress. Termed caregiver burden, caregivers often experience negative psychological, behavioral, and physiological effects (Gouin et al., 2008; Lee et al., 2003). It should be noted, however, that research has also revealed positive effects of caregiving. A survey by the National Research Opinion Center (2014) revealed that 83% of caregivers viewed caregiving as a positive experience. Caregivers have reported that caring for another gave them a sense of purpose, was an opportunity to give back to someone who had given or cared for them, led to personal growth, and gave them a sense of satisfaction that their loved one was getting excellent care (Beach et al., 2000; Haley et al., 2003; Harmell et al., 2011). Therefore, research shows that caregiving can lead to strain, but also can be a positive experience involving growth and meaning, two outcomes that appear to coexist in the caregiving experience.ˌ

SUMMARY

Developmental psychology is a complex field that uses unique data-collection methods and research designs to study ˌchangesˌ across time in the physical, cognitive, and social/emotional domains. Within the biological domain of development, we learned that prenatal development occurs in three periods: germinal, embryonic, and fetal. The germinal period is the shortest period lasting from conception to implantation in the uterine lining. During the embryonic period, the major foundations of all organ structures are developed causing embryos to be especially vulnerable to teratogens. The fetal period is marked by the most growth. The fetus puts on weight and gains inches preparing for birth.

We also learned about the biological domain of development and that infants are born with important reflexes, like the sucking reflex, that promote survival in the first few months of life. These reflexes often disappear before the end of first year. The four of the five senses are fully developed at birth with the fifth sense, vision, being fully developed by 6 months to 1 year of age.

ˌWe explored cognitive and social development through childhood.ˌ One theory of cognitive development outlined in the chapter was Piaget's theory of cognitive development, which explains development in a series of four stages: sensorimotor, preoperational, concrete operational, and formal operational.

Each stage builds on the previous stage and is marked by unique achievements and limitations. Piaget's theory has spurred much research and application. ˌAdditionally, severalˌ aspects of social/emotional development were addressed. Attachment ˌconcernsˌ the bonds that tie two people together. The first attachments to develop are with caregivers and provide the foundation for infants' views of the world and relationships. Secure attachments have been linked to positive outcomes in childhood, adolescence, and adulthood.

Parenting styles are different from parent to parent but follow four general trends in warmth and strictness. The authoritative parenting style is associated with the most positive outcomes for children and adolescents. The other three parenting ˌstylesˌ—authoritarian, permissive, and rejecting/neglecting—are associated with some positive and negative outcomes for children and adolescents. ˌIn addition to parenting styles, temperament,ˌ the predictable way that infants and children respond to the world, ˌvaryingˌ from infant to infant, ˌplays a vital role in children.ˌ Several theories of temperament have been developed to describe the characteristics of infants and patterns of response. Temperament, in infancy, has been linked to both positive and negative outcomes later in life.

Kohlberg's theory of moral development is a series of stages that explains the cognitive processes behind moral decisions. People move from a self-focused reasoning to universal truths based reasoning. Kohlberg established his stage theory using interviews about ambiguous moral dilemmas.

Erikson's theory of psychosocial development emphasized the psychosocial influences on development. According to Erikson, people progress through a series of eight stages in which a central conflict must be resolved. If unsuccessfully resolved, people will continue to struggle with that conflict throughout life until the conflict is successfully resolved.

ˌThis chapter also presented development across adolescence and early adulthood, as well as during older adulthood. During adolescences and early adulthood, some of the primary challenges of these ages include rapid physical changes and development, substance use and abuse, cognitive and emotional development, and mental health. The ongoing research and challenges concerning the growing population of older adults, particularly related to dementia and quality of life, were also discussed.

ˌThroughout this chapter, the Christian perspective on human development was introduced with emphasis in building strong Christian foundations in raising up children and making wise decisions through adulthood.ˌ

© Anna Maltseva/Shutterstock.com

Chapter 7

Personality and Social Psychology

LEARNING OBJECTIVES

- ❏ Define and describe personality.
- ❏ Know the trait-type approaches to personality and understand the difference between trait and type.
- ❏ Identify and describe the Big Five personality characteristics.
- ❏ Outline main beliefs of biological approaches to personality.
- ❏ Understand how Freud describes normal and abnormal personality development.
- ❏ ⌐Discuss learning theories of personality.
- ❏ Discuss Humanistic theories of personality.
- ❏ Explain personality assessment.
- ❏ Articulate a biblical perspective on personality.⌐
- ❏ Define social psychology.
- ❏ Differentiate ⌐between⌐ the terms *compliance* and *conformity*.
- ❏ Differentiate among the terms *attitudes*, *beliefs*, *opinions*, and *stereotypes*.
- ❏ ⌐Identify⌐ key factors related to attitude change.

- ❑ Define aggression.
- ❑ Describe the causes and manifestations of antisocial and prosocial behavior.
- ❑ Describe the concept of love ⌐scientifically and biblically.⌐

⌐The study of personality and social psychology often go together as we try to understand human behavior. One of the leading journals in the field of social psychology is called the *Journal of Personality and Social Psychology* and as you will see throughout this chapter, one's personality and one's social environment are often discussed and studied together as predictors of behavior. This chapter explores both personality and social psychology as we continue to explore research and biblical perspectives on human behavior.

⌐We will begin our chapter with a discussion of personality and the ways that various theorists have explained and studied personality. We will also discuss biblical perspectives as we go along.⌐ Personality can be defined in a number of ways; however, most would agree that, generally, personality is a set of characteristics that shape how an individual thinks, behaves, and reacts. Personality is complex and influenced by genetics, learning history, and social experiences. ⌐And personality is one of the ways that God has created you uniquely you.⌐ This chapter discusses the major approaches to personality theory ⌐in Psychology,⌐ including⌐ common ways to measure or assess personality ⌐and challenges you to think about a biblical perspective on personality.⌐

▶ CHAPTER 7 OVERVIEW

Traits, Types, and Concepts of Personality.
© kentoh/Shutterstock.com

PERSONALITY

The fact is, we are all different. We all have a **personality**—a collection of characteristics that define who we are. In a general sense, personality can be defined as stable characteristics, including abilities, talents, habits, preferences, weaknesses, moral attributes, and predominant moods that vary from one person to another.

The word *personality* comes from the Latin word *persona,* which referred to the masks worn by Roman actors. Using these masks, an actor could play many different roles in a single play. A persona was, in a very literal sense, a way of changing one's personality, a way of becoming somebody else.

In one sense we all make use of *personae* (masks or roles): We appear to become different people in different situations. The type of behavior expected of us in formal situations is often quite different from what we display in less formal circumstances. ⌐But overall, we have a fairly stable set of characteristics that we would call our personality. Everyone has a personality. Even Jesus had a

Personality: The set of attributes that characterize an individual, including temperamental, emotional, mental, and behavioral tendencies, influenced by genetics, learning, and social experiences.

▶ WHAT IS PERSONALITY?

personality. If you are human, you have a personality and a big part of the field of psychology is understanding your personality and how it has been formed by, as well as affects, various aspects of your life.⌟

Approaches to Understanding Personality

Psychology offers a variety of approaches and theories to explain personality and individual differences, none of which is exclusively correct or categorically wrong. Each approach or theory simply represents a different orientation and a different emphasis.

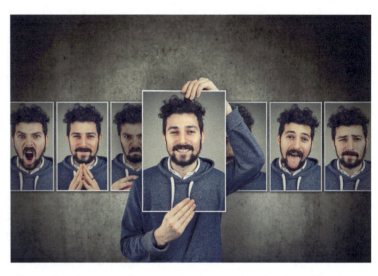

⌞Personality theorists tell us we⌟ all make use of masks: ⌞In⌟ different situations, we have different behaviors.

© pathdoc/Shutterstock.com

Because personality is a function of many different forces, it is not surprising that various theories focus on distinct aspects. Much of what you are is a function of your genetic composition; biological factors are therefore important in determining manifested personality. Similarly, private experience, social situations, cognitive factors, and psychodynamic forces may all be involved in personality. This suggests at least ⌞five⌟ approaches to personality theory: trait-type, biological, psychodynamic, learning-based, and humanistic (Table 7.1).

TABLE 7.1   Approaches to Understanding Personality

Approach	Major Points	Representative Theorists
Trait-Type	Discovering and verifying the existence of related clusters of traits composing personality types	The Greeks Jung Costa and McCrae
Biological	Looking at genes (genomics) and at brain structures and functions (neuropsychology) to identify processes and structures underlying personality	Eysenck Researchers in genomics and neuropsychology
Psychodynamic	Clarifying the interplay of unconscious forces; understanding the conflict between basic inclinations and social/environmental constraints	Freud Jung
Learning-Based	Personality as learned habits, predispositions, attitudes; also looks at rational contributions to behavior and emotions, decision making, attributions	Watson Skinner Bandura Rotter
Humanistic	The self; worth, dignity, individuality	Maslow Rogers

Note some of the theories and principles discussed in relation to each of these approaches include aspects of other approaches. The decision to categorize a single position as a trait-type approach rather than social, or biological rather than psychodynamic, is based on the main characteristics of the position, but not on all its characteristics; some approaches represent more than one orientation.

The Trait-Type Approach

The thousands of adjectives, nouns, and phrases used to describe people are all examples of trait names. A **trait** is any distinct, consistent quality in which one person can be different from another. There are physical traits (blonde, big, buxom), behavioral traits (quick, quiet, quarrelsome), moral traits (bad, base, benign), and many more, totaling to approximately 17,000 possible traits used to describe a person (Allport & Odbert, 1936).

> **Trait:** Any distinct, consistent characteristic that can vary from one person to another.

One approach to personality has been to attempt to reduce the total number of possible traits to a few highly representative adjectives. The most useful would be those most often displayed in human behavior, most variable from one person to another, and most distinct. Typically, all synonyms or near-synonyms are excluded from such lists, and an effort is made to pair the words as opposites. Thus, a person can be emotional or stable, humble or assertive, outgoing or withdrawn.

Another way of looking at a trait is to say it implies a prediction about behavior. To say an individual is bold is to predict the person is more likely to act boldly than are less bold people in similar circumstances. This, however, is quite different from saying a bold individual will always act boldly. Psychology mostly deals with *average* behavior, and thus the knowledge of predominant personality traits simply allows for predictions of behavioral tendencies. Predictions made using this method are more likely to be accurate than those based solely on intuition.

Among the best known of the trait approaches is that proposed by Cattell (1946), who reduced Allport and Odbert's list of more than 17,000 adjectives by eliminating all synonyms, obscure and infrequent words, and apparently irrelevant terms. After extensive analysis of individuals who had been rated by close friends using Cattell's adjectives, he further reduced the list to 16 traits by combining separate but closely related traits using a statistical process called **factor analysis**. This statistical procedure analyzes correlations among variables and combines those found to be closely related. It is commonly used to reduce large numbers of related variables—such as traits—to a smaller number of meaningful categories. Some of the 16 personality traits resulted from Cattell's work are shown in Figure

> **Factor analysis:** A statistical procedure for reducing correlational data to a smaller number of dimensions by grouping closely related variables.

7.1. The traits are based on popular adjectives used to describe people in meaningful ways. The traits are arranged in pairs of opposites.

Cattell is now widely recognized as the founder of current personality and trait measurement (Denis, 2009). His approach to identifying and measuring personality traits continues to be widely used.

Personality **type** is a more inclusive term than *trait*. Whereas a trait is inferred from a tendency to behave in a given way in certain situations, a type describes a group of related traits. For example, *Type A* personality defines individuals who are characterized by *traits*

> **Type:** A related grouping of personality traits.

such as aggressiveness, competitiveness, high need for achievement, and perhaps other traits such as low frustration tolerance, impatience, and rudeness.

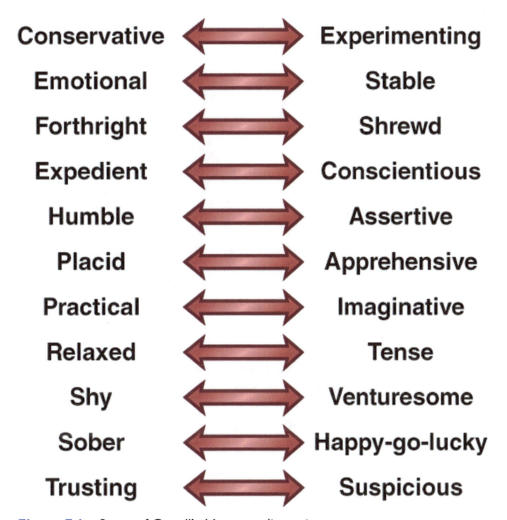

Figure 7.1   Some of Cattell's 16 personality traits.

It is important to note traits and types are not the causes of behavior, but indicate certain identifiable consistencies in behavior. Thus, people do not fight because they are hostile; but because they fight, we may describe them as hostile. If causes can be identified, it may be due to as much the situation as the person.

Early Trait-Type Approaches

An ancient approach to personality types was suggested by Greek philosophers, who described four distinct types of individuals: the *sanguine* (optimistic and happy); the *melancholic* (unhappy, depressed); the *choleric* (of violent temper); and the *phlegmatic* (apathetic, not easily moved to excesses of emotion; see Figure 7.2). They thought each of these personality types depended on fluids in the body—then called "humors." The sanguine individual had a preponderance of blood; the melancholic, of black bile; the choleric, of ordinary bile; and the phlegmatic, of phlegm. Unfortunately, science has revealed us not to be so simple; this information is now only of historical interest.

A widely accepted typology was originated by Carl Jung (1923), whose theory, like Sigmund Freud's, was a **psychodynamic theory**.

> **Psychodynamic theory:**
> The elaborate theory developed by Freud, based on his notion that behavior and personality are developed by unconscious urges and motivations.

TEMPERAMENTS

Figure 7.2 Personality types according to Greek philosophers.
© Inspiring/Shutterstock.com

Psychodynamic theories are based on the belief behavior is motivated by unconscious forces. These theories emphasize the interplay between unconscious and conscious motives. He believed many of our unconscious motives stem from **archetypes**. Archetypes are a sort of unconscious, shared historical memory—part of what he labeled the *collective unconscious.*

> **Archetypes:** Literally, the first or original model. In Jung's theory, a universal thought or shared historical memory which is largely unconscious.

Among the most common archetypes, explains Jung, are the man/woman dichotomy (his labels are *anima/animus*). In a sense, these archetypes serve as motives impelling us to accept masculine and feminine characteristics. Similarly, there is an archetype relating to God, and this, he suggests, accounts for the existence of religions.

In his personality theory, Jung proposed two main *types,* which include great clusters of traits: extraversion (also spelled *extroversion*) and introversion. These represent the two possible attitudes with which all people approach life, Jung explained. On the one hand, there are extroverts—those who run toward life, are adventurous, bold, eager to live and to experience, are concerned with others, with sports, with all the external world. Extroverts are fun-loving, outgoing, friendly, and active.

Introverts, on the other hand, are those who turn inward and away from the world (*intro* meaning inward). They are concerned more with subjective than objective reality. Introverts are described as timid and quiet. According to Jung, they avoid social interaction and dislike adventure and physical risk.

Typically, when we think of introversion and extraversion, we think of it in terms of sociability. However, according to Jung's original conception, it is less about sociability and more about where an individual is energized. The extravert is energized by the external world and the introvert is energized by time alone and internal states. This is demonstrated, of course, in how social and outgoing someone appears and how much time they spend in social situations or alone. It should be noted that no one is completely introverted or completely extraverted, but we typically connect better with one of the attitudes.

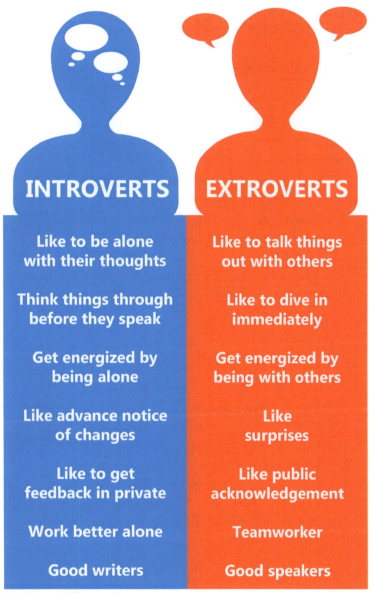

© desdemona72/Shutterstock.com

The Big Five

Jung's ancient typology is a theory of personality that has withstood the test of time: today's personality theorists agree overwhelmingly that extraversion and introversion represent a consistent and important dimension of human personality. They also agree these two labels represent only one of five personality types—commonly labeled the **Big Five factors** (or the *Five Factor Model*).

> **Big Five factors:** A widely accepted personality typology that includes extraversion, openness, conscientiousness, agreeableness, and neuroticism.

The five factors were discovered independently by different researchers and have been extensively investigated over the years (Digman, 1990). Much of this research uses factor analysis to look at how different traits tend to co-occur. This has allowed personality theorists to reduce a very large number of traits to five *big* factors, each of which is one extreme of a pair of opposite types. Thus, *extraversion* is one of the five factors, but *introversion* is not: It is simply the opposite of extraversion.

The Big Five factors, which are thought to include most of the traits describing personality, are **c**onscientiousness, **a**greeableness, **n**euroticism, **o**penness, and **e**xtraversion. As a memory aid, note the first five letters spell the acronyms CANOE or OCEAN.

Extraversion

Those who have high levels of **extraversion** tend to be outgoing, to seek stimulation, and want to be in the company of others. They are engaged in the world, highly sociable, and energetic. At the other extreme are the introverts—those who shy away from social interaction. Whereas, extraverts tend to be gregarious, assertive, and bold,

> **Extraversion:** A "Big Five" personality factor that includes the traits outgoing, energetic, and positive.

introverts tend to be solitary, withdrawn, and more timid. This does not mean introverts are necessarily shy and have no friends; however, research indicates they are likely to have fewer friends, and are more socially reserved (Selfhout et al., 2010).

Openness

Openness is characterized by a high degree of inventiveness, adventurousness, and curiosity. Those who are highly open seek out new experiences; they want to know, to discover, to find out things. Openness implies an appreciation for different, unusual things, for art, and imagination. The opposite dimension is characterized by a

> **Openness:** A "Big Five" personality factor consisting of the traits inventive, curious, and unconventional.

more rigid, conventional, traditional approach to life. Those who are *closed* rather than open prefer things be straightforward and obvious rather than complex and ambiguous. Highly creative individuals tend to score high on the openness factor (Sung & Choi, 2009).

Neuroticism

Neuroticism is marked by fluctuating emotions, high anxiety, and a tendency toward negative moods such as anger and depression. Those who score high on this factor are sometimes described as *emotionally unstable*. They tend to be more vulnerable to the effects of stress and are more often in a bad mood. In

> **Neuroticism:** This "Big Five" personality factor includes the traits nervous, sensitive, and moody.

contrast, those who score low on the neuroticism scale tend to be emotionally stable and calm when faced with stressful events. They are generally characterized by positive rather than negative moods. ⌐Interestingly, recent research has shown that those high in neuroticism tend to engage in less prosocial behavior (Guo et al., 2018; Habashi et al., 2016).⌐

Conscientiousness

Those who are careful and highly responsible score high on the **conscientiousness** scale. They tend to exhibit a high degree of organization, self-discipline, thoroughness, and a need to achieve. Such

> **Conscientiousness:** A "Big Five" personality trait, it includes awareness of one's personal identity and mental processes like thinking, imagining, and feeling.

individuals are often described as perfectionists or workaholics. They tend to be highly diligent, well-prepared workers (Woodman et al., 2010). In contrast, those who score low on conscientiousness display a lower need for achievement. They are more laid back, less disciplined, and less compulsive.

Agreeableness

Agreeable people are those who are friendly and easygoing. They strive to be pleasant and cooperative. They are polite and compassionate, they value friendships, and they tend to have an optimistic view of people. In contrast, those low on the **agreeableness** factor are more suspicious of people, have a lower opinion of human nature, and are less likely to try to be accommodating and friendly. Research suggests anger and hostility may be associated with low agreeableness scores (Sanz et al., 2010). (See Figure 7.3 for a visual of the Big Five approach to personality types.)

> **Agreeableness:** A "Big Five" personality factor comprised of the traits friendly, compassionate, and cooperative.

Individuals scoring high in Openness exhibit characteristics of being adventurous, daring, and tend to try new things.

© Photobac/Shutterstock.com

Figure 7.3 The Big Five factor model. A typology of human personality.

© John T Takai/Shutterstock.com

Contemporary Trait Theory

Although the Big Five factors are widely researched and widely accepted in personality theory, the approach has its critics. Some suggest there are other important factors not included in the model—factors such as honesty, sense of humor, masculinity–femininity, and conservativeness (Block, 1995). In response to these critics, some have proposed broader inventories; however, to measure the Big Five traits with 15 subfacets in order to enhance the breadth of description of personality (Soto & John, 2017). Other criticisms include the argument that the factors do not predict individual behaviors well (Mischel, 2004). There is also question about the stability of traits over time or whether traits can change. Still, others point out the five factors are based solely on statistical analyses of personality tests but lack a theoretical basis.

These criticisms have fueled much continued research in trait theory to address these concerns and issues. In a recent special issue of *Journal of Personality*, a series of articles discussed some key questions in personality research that trait theorists must answer to more fully contribute to personality theory. Fajkowska and Kreitler (2018) offered six burning questions that still remain to be answered by trait theorists and that are currently being researched and discussed:

1. What is the nature of traits? Are they real?
2. What is the relationship between traits and behaviors?
3. Are personality traits stable or changeable?
4. What is the relationship between trait and state?
5. What are the descriptive and explanatory powers of traits?
6. What is the function of personality traits (i.e., their practical utility or influence on function)?

In closing, it is important to note the trait-type approaches to personality are primarily *descriptive;* their main concern is to describe and label the dimensions of personality rather than to explain how personality develops. The above questions are valid questions to consider, however, when thinking about personality as a whole and its function, origin, and utility. In contrast to the trait theories that focus on describing personality, learning-based and biological approaches are more concerned with the *causes* of personality.

BIOLOGICAL APPROACHES

Biologically oriented theories of personality look at genetics as an important *cause* of our relatively stable behavioral tendencies, such as our tendency to seek or avoid social situations. **Genomics** is the discipline in genetics attempting to map the human **genome** and establish its relationship to human characteristics.

> **Genomics:** The discipline studying genomes in an attempt to establish relationships between genes and characteristics.
>
> **Genome:** The complete set of chromosomes of an organism. All of an organism's inheritable traits.

Whether genomics will find a demonstrable link between genes and personality has been widely debated. Research with identical and fraternal twins strongly suggests genetics does play a role. For example, in their study of 250 pairs of twins, Jang et al. (1996) found high positive correlations for identical twins on each of the Big Five personality factors. This finding has also been demonstrated in different cultures, suggesting that it is not only a side effect of Western culture (Yamagata et al., 2006). Genetic research continues to explore whether there is a link between genes and personality and while molecular genetic research has failed to find a consistent link between specific genes and personality, behavioral genetics research has shown consistent results that personality may be 40% to 50% heritable (Jarnecke & South, 2017).

Research in neuropsychology also looks for the biological bases of personality characteristics, and some personality-related psychological disorders. For example, some research indicates high impulsivity may be linked with deficits in frontal and temporal lobe functioning—deficits may be due to injury, disease, or genetics (Seres et al., 2009). In its extreme forms the trait of impulsivity may be an important characteristic of *borderline personality disorder* (discussed later ⌐in this⌐ chapter).

Although the links among genes, neurological functioning, and personality are still not very clear, this should not be taken as an indictment of the field. Instead, the study of the genetic causes of personality is exciting and presents a fertile field for future scientific discoveries that may unlock some of the mysteries of why we behave the way we do.

Eysenck's Biological Theory

Social expectations, explains Hans Eysenck (1947, 1967), must be congruent with biological expectations and explainable at the biological level. One of Eysenck's basic premises is we are born with tendencies to behave in certain ways. He initially thought only two dimensions (types) were needed to describe human personality: extraversion and neuroticism (as opposed to introversion and emotional stability). Later, in collaboration with his wife, he added a third dimension: psychoticism (as opposed to self-control; Eysenck & Eysenck, 1976).

Eysenck uses the terms *extraversion* and *introversion* in much the same way as they are used in the Five Factor model. *Neuroticism* refers to a personality dimension ranging from emotional instability to stability. *Psychoticism* denotes high aggression, antisocial tendencies, and high egocentrism—contrasted with high self-control and respect for authority, rules, and laws.

Analysis of numerous personality tests led Eysenck to the conclusion that these dimensions of personality are essentially independent. An individual can be high on one without being high on the other, or can be high or low on all three. Although the tendency to be neurotic or extroverted (or their opposites) is largely genetically based, Eysenck does not rule out the influence of the environment. What he says, essentially, is individuals who score high on the neurotic factor have less stable (more labile) types of nervous systems and are more likely to acquire conditioned anxieties. This is principally because they react too strongly to situations evoking less intense emotional responses from individuals lower on a neuroticism scale (Figure 7.4).

Research Evidence

Much of Eysenck's experimental work has been directed toward establishing the validity of these personality dimensions and their biological bases. A basic assumption underlying the theory is that the nervous systems of *extroverts* and introverts differ, as do those of neurotics or psychotics and so-called "normal" people. Accordingly, he predicted extroverts should have lower levels of cortical excitation (low arousal levels) than introverts. Pavlov had already demonstrated conditioning is closely related to the level of cortical activity with animals whose brains were most active. The high cortical–activity animals were conditioned more rapidly than others whose brains were typically at lower levels of arousal.

To test his biological theory of personality, Eysenck used the research procedure of Pavlov. If Eysenck's theory was correct, then certain hypotheses derived from the theory should also be supported in an experiment. Specifically, if extroverts have more inhibited cortexes (lower arousal levels at resting states), they should condition more slowly than introverts. And, behold, this hypothesis was supported by research (Eysenck, 1967), which supported Eysenck's biological theory of personality.

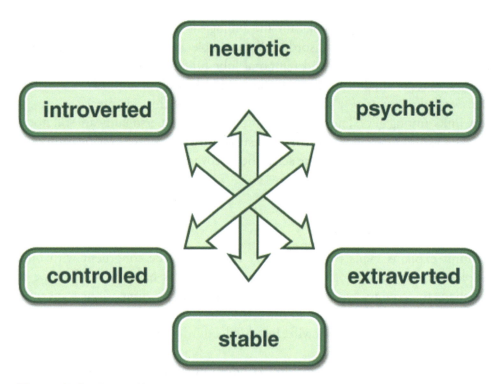

Figure 7.4 Eysenck's three dimensions of personality. Each dimension is independent of the others, so one individual might be high on two different factors and low on the third; another might be high on one and low on the other two.

Other indirect tests of Eysenck's theorizing come from studies of personality disorders and in countless practical applications of the personality test he developed (Revised Eysenck Personality Questionnaire). Using this test, researchers have found strong relationships between high introversion and suicide attempts (Li & Lei, 2010). Others have reported a relationship between happiness and low neuroticism (Robbins et al., 2010). The test has been found to be generally useful for identifying individuals at risk of mental disorders in a wide variety of different settings and cultures (Kokkinos et al., 2010).

Eysenck's Organization of Personality

Eysenck's view of the structure of personality may be summarized as follows: Our nervous systems differ in important ways from those of people who have fundamentally different personality characteristics than us. Basically, we inherit greater or lesser tendencies toward introversion–extroversion, neuroticism–stability, or psychoticism–self-control. These tendencies are evident in the functioning of our nervous systems. In sum, the tendencies give rise to behavioral predispositions, labeled traits. The traits themselves are translated into habits – consistent patterns of responding. Specific habits manifest themselves in our actual responses. Thus, personality is hierarchically structured.

As an example of the hierarchical nature of personality, consider Nathan, who finds himself telling jokes to a group of strangers on a commuter train out of New York. There is a high probability he would score near the top on an extroversion scale; hence his type is *high extrovert–low introvert;* the trait he is manifesting might be labeled *sociability;* the relevant habit is entertaining strangers; and the specific behavior is telling this story at this time, in this situation.

Had we known beforehand the extent of Nathan's extroversion, we might have predicted a behavior not unlike what was observed. Theorists who have been more concerned with the identification and measurement of specific traits, however, would point out, had we been aware of the extent of his trait of sociability, the same prediction could have been made. If we had known of his habit of telling jokes to strangers, our prediction would have been even more accurate. Consider, however, how much simpler and more economical it is to be able to classify traits or types than to classify habits. In addition, habits change; traits and types are more enduring.

A PSYCHODYNAMIC APPROACH: FREUD

Deep-seated psychological forces, sometimes instinctive, often unconscious, interacting with the environment produce personality and guide behavior, claimed Freud. This is a *psychodynamic* approach to personality—so called because it emphasizes the interaction of unconscious emotional and mental processes and their influence on personality and behavior.

Freud's Basic Ideas

Among the most basic of Freudian notions is the belief that powerful instinctual tendencies account for human behavior and development (Freud, 2003; Lear, 2005; Roazen, 1975). Most important among these are the urge to survive and to procreate (labeled eros after the Greek word for love). Because survival is not ordinarily threatened by reality, it is of secondary importance. Far more important in Freud's theory is the urge to procreate, which meets with considerable social resistance. Sexual urges are so important in this theory they warrant a separate label: **libido**.

> **Libido:** A Freudian term for sexual urges.

A second important instinctual urge in Freud's system is the death wish (labeled **thanatos** after the Greek word for death). Freud thought this instinct is sometimes manifested in high-risk behaviors (such as car racing, skydiving, and related sports) and, more importantly, in aggressive behaviors. As a result, he gives sexuality and aggression a central position in his theory. These two forces are the main motivators of our behaviors, Freud explained, but their influence is largely unconscious: We are not ordinarily aware that many of our behaviors have sexual or aggressive significance.

> **Thanatos:** A Freudian term denoting the death wish or death instinct.

Three Components of Personality

There are three broad, sequential stages of personality development, says Freud. These are manifested in the development of id, ego, and superego.

- **Id** The Freudian infant is all primitive instincts, a bundle of unbridled psychic energy seeking almost desperately to satisfy urges based on the drive to survive and to procreate. These urges, labeled **id**, are a lifetime source of energy; they are the basic, underlying motives for all we do.

> **Id:** In Freudian theory, all the instinctual urges that humans inherit, including eros and thanatos.

Unlike older children and adults, the infant has no idea of what is possible or impossible, no sense of reality, no sense of right and wrong, no internal moral rules governing conduct. As a result, says Freud, the infant is driven by an almost overwhelming urge to obtain immediate satisfaction of impulses. An infant who is hungry does not wait; right now is the time for the nipple and the sucking!

The infant is all id, according to Freud—desperate to satisfy immediate urges, with no idea of what is possible or realistic. Feed me now! Or, of course, I'll cry.

© leungchopan/Shutterstock.com

- **Ego**   But life is harsh, and almost from birth, there is an abrupt clash between these powerful libidinal urges and reality. Even hunger, the most powerful of the survival-linked drives, cannot always be satisfied immediately. The reality is the infant's satisfaction has to be delayed or denied. Even defecation cannot always occur at will. This constant conflict between id impulses and reality results in the development of the second aspect of personality, the **ego**.

This rational component of human personality grows out of a realization of what is possible and what is not. It develops as a result of a child's experiences leading to the realization that delaying gratification is often a desirable thing, long-term goals sometimes require the denial of short-term goals. Although the id wants immediate gratification, the ego channels these desires in the most profitable direction.

> **Ego:** In Freud's theory, the rational, reality-oriented level of human personality, developing as the child becomes aware of what the environment makes possible and impossible.

- **Superego**   The id and the ego work together. Both have the same goals: satisfying the needs and urges of the individual. But the third component of personality—the **superego**—has a different agenda.

The superego (or conscience) begins to develop in early childhood, says Freud, and results mainly from the child's identifying with parents. **Identification** involves attempting to become like others—adopting their values and beliefs as well as their behaviors. By identifying with their parents, children learn the religious and cultural rules governing their parents' behaviors; these rules become part of the superego. Because many religious, social, and cultural rules oppose the urges of the id, the superego and the id are often in conflict. Freud believed this conflict underlies many mental disorders and accounts for much deviant behavior (Figure 7.5).

> **Superego:** The personality structure that defines the moral or ethical aspects of personality.

> **Identification:** Refers to the process of assuming the goals, ambitions, mannerisms, and so on of another person.

Psychosexual Stages

Parallel to the development of the three aspects of personality is the child's progression through what Freud labels the *psychosexual* stages. A psychosexual stage is a developmental stage characterized by identifiable sources of sexual gratification and by behaviors related to these sources of gratification. Through the course of development, these sources of gratification change; with each major change, a new developmental phase appears.

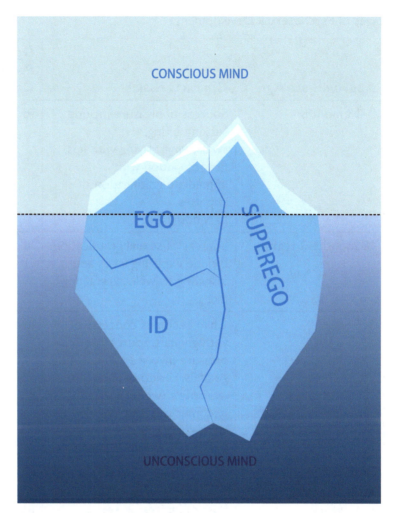

Figure 7.5   Freud's three components of personality.
© T and Z/Shutterstock.com

To make matters simple, the stages are labeled according to the area or activity providing the greatest source of sexual gratification. In chronological order, they are oral, anal, phallic, latency, and genital. The ages corresponding to each of these stages, their major characteristics, and the dominant personality component are summarized in Table 7.2.

Normal and Abnormal Personality

There are three main routes the individual may take in the course of development. One is shown in Table 7.2. It is the route presumably resulting in a normal personality. A second possibility is **fixation**, the cessation of development at a given stage, sometimes because of trauma (severe emotional shock) and sometimes because of excessive sexual gratification at the stage. The third possibility is **regression**, which involves reverting to a previous development stage, again sometimes because of trauma, or perhaps because of insufficient sexual gratification at a later stage.

Fixation: A developmental delay due to unsuccessfully developing through a stage, sometimes manifested in personality characteristics and emotional disorders relating to the earlier stage.

Regression: A Freudian expression for the phenomenon of reverting to some of the activities and preoccupations of earlier developmental stages.

Table 7.2   Freud's Stages of Psychosexual Development

Stage	Approximate Age	Characteristics	Dominant Personality Component
Oral	0–18 months	Sources of pleasure include sucking, biting, swallowing, playing with lips. Preoccupation with immediate gratification of impulses. Id is dominant.	Id
Anal	18 months–3 years	Sources of sexual gratification include expelling feces and urinating, as well as retaining feces.	Id and Ego
Phallic	3–6 years	Child becomes concerned with genitals. Source of sexual pleasure involves manipulating genitals. Period of **Oedipus complex** (where the father becomes the male child's rival—unconsciously) or **Electra complex** (a female version of the Oedipus complex).	Id, Ego, and Superego
Latency	6–11 years	Loss of interest in sexual gratification. Identification with like-sexed parent.	Id, Ego, and Superego
Genital	11+	Concern with adult modes of sexual pleasure, barring fixations or regressions.	Id, Ego, and Superego

The behavior of adults who are fixated at a certain stage, or who have regressed to that stage, is related to the forms of sexual gratification characteristic of the stage. Thus, *oral characters* (fixated or regressed at the oral stage) are those who chew their nails, bite their lips, smoke, chew gum, and otherwise exercise their mouths. *Anal characters* are compulsive, orderly, stingy, and perhaps aggressive—these characteristics presumably being related to the pleasure (sexual gratification) associated with the retention and expulsion of feces during the anal stage. *Phallic characters* are concerned with the immediate satisfaction of their sexual urges without regard for the object of their satisfaction; they are sadists and rapists (according to Freudian theory).

Oedipus complex: A Freudian concept denoting the developmental stage (around 4 years) when a boy's increasing awareness of the sexual meaning of his genitals leads him to desire his mother and envy his father.

Electra complex: A Freudian stage (around 4 years) when a girl's awareness of her genital area leads her to desire her father and to become jealous of her mother.

Defense Mechanisms

In both normal and abnormal development, explains Freud, the id constantly strives for gratification. Meanwhile, the superego battles against the id, raising moral and cultural objections to unbridled gratification. Through all this, the ego struggles to find some way of finding the gratification the id craves, but within the constraints imposed by the superego.

In trying to compensate for not being able to satisfy all of the id's urges, the ego often resorts to **defense mechanisms**. Defense mechanisms are ways of channeling urges and of reinterpreting (and often distorting) reality. The ego is successful, explains Freud, when it eliminates or reduces the anxiety accompanying the continual struggle between the id and the superego. In a sense, these mechanisms are the ego's attempt to establish peace between the id and the superego so the personality can continue to operate in an apparently healthy manner. Thus, at one level, defense mechanisms are normal, healthy reactions to the world. What sometimes happens, however, is the individual comes to rely on them too much. The result may be a dramatically distorted view of self, of others, and of reality, and may be evident in various personality disturbances.

Several dozen distinct defense mechanisms have been described by Freud and his followers. The most common of these are summarized and illustrated in Table 7.3.

According to Freud, oral characters are fixated at the oral stage and chew their nails, smoke, chew on pens, and so on. Unfortunately, our personalities have proven more difficult to classify than Freud's typology would imply.

© Jeanette Dietl/Shutterstock.com

> **Defense mechanisms:** An unconscious mental strategy designed to avoid conflict and anxiety; examples include denial and repression.

Table 7.3   Some Freudian Defense Mechanisms

Mechanism	Example
Displacement: Undesirable emotions are directed toward a different object.	A man who is angry at his wife yells at his dog or drives his car unusually aggressively.
Reaction formation: Behavior is the opposite of the individual's actual feelings.	A woman loves an unobtainable man and behaves as though she dislikes him.
Intellectualization: Behavior motivated by anxiety-provoking emotions is stripped of its emotional meaning.	A football player who enjoys hurting opponents convinces himself he is moved by the desire to win and not by his desire to inflict pain.
Projection: Undesirable feelings or inclinations are attributed to others.	A student who is extremely jealous of another who has received a scholarship convinces himself it is the scholarship winner who is jealous of him.

(Continued)

Table 7.3 Some Freudian Defense Mechanism *(Continued)*

Mechanism	Example
Denial: Unpleasant, anxiety-provoking aspects of reality are distorted.	A heavy smoker, unable to give up the habit, concludes there is no substantial evidence linking nicotine with human diseases.
Repression: Unpleasant experiences are buried deep in the subconscious mind and become inaccessible to waking memory.	A person who was sexually abused as a child remembers nothing of the experience.

Review of Freudian Theory

Freud's theory is one of the most comprehensive and influential of all psychological theories. It continues to have an enormous impact on psychotherapy. Freudian theory has had a tremendous influence on our attitudes toward children and child rearing. More than anyone else, Freud was responsible for making parents realize how important early experiences can be.

Freudian theory has also had an enormous impact on the development of other theories. However, many of Freud's students and followers have rejected important aspects of the theory, and much of his theory has been criticized by other scholars. First, because Freud proposed that much of these conflicts occur beneath human awareness, it is impossible to study the validity of it. Good theories must be **falsifiable,** which means that they should be able to be tested through scientific methods and shown to be false or true. In the case of many of Freud's unconscious elements, falsifiability is impossible because they cannot be accessed and measured. For that reason, it is impossi-

> **Falsifiable:** The quality of being able to be tested through scientific methods and shown to be false or true.

ble to say if it is true or if it is false. Second, many have argued Freud placed much too much emphasis on sexual drive, and that his limited focus on two drives does not capture all of human motivation. Third, for many, Freud paints too dark and cynical a picture of human nature: In his view, primitive forces over which we have no control drive us relentlessly toward the satisfaction of instinctual urges and bring us into repeated conflict with reality.

In spite of these criticisms, Freud's work still stands as an immensely rich basis for thinking about and understanding human personality. And, for biblical scholars, Freud's position on man having a dark and selfish core that can put him in conflict with the world and others, may not be that far off. In fact, when biblical scholars talk about man, you will see the sin nature as being a driving force in us. In fact, Paul write about this sin nature within himself in Romans 7:

> *15 For I do not understand my own actions. For I do not do what I want, but I do the very thing I hate. 16 Now if I do what I do not want, I agree with the law, that it is good. 17 So now it is no longer I who do it, but sin that dwells within me. 18 For I know that nothing good dwells in me, that is, in my flesh. For I have the desire to do what is right, but not the ability to carry it out. 19 For I do not do the good I want, but the evil I do not want is what I keep on doing. 20 Now if I do what I do not want, it is no longer I who do it, but sin that dwells within me.*

> *21 So I find it to be a law that when I want to do right, evil lies close at hand. 22 For I delight in the law of God, in my inner being, 23 but I see in my members another law waging war against the law of my mind and making me captive to the law of sin that dwells in my members. 24 Wretched man that I am! Who will deliver me from this body of death? (v. 15-24, ESV).*

⌐In conclusion, many theorists disagree with Freud's conceptualization of the id and an inner force that drives us towards selfish desires, almost uncontrollably. And, while many want to claim that we have a more positive, good nature, this contradicts what we are taught in the Bible about the nature of man due to sin. There are many valid criticisms of Freud's theory, but he just may have been closer than the others in terms of the depravity of man.⌐

LEARNING-BASED APPROACHES

Biological approaches to understanding personality focus on the relationship between inherited predispositions and manifested behavior; psychodynamic approaches are concerned with interactions among competing or cooperating psychic (mental) impulses; learning-based approaches are more concerned with the role of the environment, of social interaction, and of cognitive processes. The unifying theme of learning-based approaches to personality is primarily acquired through experiences rather than genetically determined or influenced.

Behaviorism

As we saw in previous chapters, behaviorism provides one explanation for how personality traits might be learned. Some early behaviorists such as John Watson were absolutely convinced that the metaphor of the mind as a *blank slate* (*tabula rasa* in Latin) was correct. "Give me the child and my world to bring it up in," he wrote, "and I'll make it crawl or walk; I'll make it climb and use its hands in constructing buildings of stone or wood; I'll make it a thief, a gunman, or a dope fiend. The possibility of shaping in any direction is almost endless" (Watson, 1928, p. 35).

The clear assumption of behavioristic approaches to personality is we are born with few genetically determined personality characteristics; what we become is a function of the experiences we have. In other words, personality characteristics are *learned.*

Skinner, another behaviorist who wholeheartedly accepted the *tabula rasa* doctrine, believed the consequences of our actions shape our behaviors and ultimately determine what we are most likely to do. Our environments, not our inherited natures, shape our traits. It is the experiences we have that make us brave or fearful, outgoing or shy, altruistic or selfish.

Few personality theorists now believe personality is entirely determined by environmental experiences. As Robins (2005) notes, about half of the variability in personality traits seems to be related to genetics, the other half is clearly shaped by environmental influences. Especially important among these are early social experiences.

Bandura's Social Cognitive Theory

Bandura's social cognitive theory, the details of which are included in previous chapters, is one of the best-known and most useful learning-based theories examining the effects of social experiences.

Observational Learning

Much of our learning results from *observational learning,* explains Bandura—observing and imitating models. Learning to drive a car, for example, is not a question of classical conditioning, of trial and error, or of reinforcement of emitted behaviors. Instead, we instruct the learner in certain fundamentals, we show her the positions and purposes of various controls, we demonstrate their operation, and we allow her to attempt the task with verbal and sometimes physical guidance. In effect, what has happened is a number of models have been presented and imitated.

What Does the Bible Say?

⌐Bandura's social learning theory places great emphasis on observational learning and modeling. According to his theory, we do not have to have direct experience with every situation, but rather can learn by watching others and can pick up the behaviors of those who we observe and hang around. When we think about social relationships and the importance of them in our lives, one way they are important is in this observational learning and modeling of others' behaviors. We often do what we see people around us doing.

When we think about our susceptibility to others' in our environment, it is no wonder that God provides some guidance to us regarding our friendships. In I Corinthians 15:33, Paul writes, "Do not be deceived: "Bad company ruins good morals" (ESV). And, in Proverbs 13:20 we read, "Whoever walks with the wise becomes wise, but the companion of fools will suffer harm" (ESV). We also see God warning the Israelites in the Old Testament to not marry into groups that were not devoted to Him because of the danger of picking up the practices of pagan people (Deuteronomy 7:1-4). It seems we have always been vulnerable to the influences of others and likely to pick up what those around us are doing, much like Bandura suggests in his Social Cognitive Theory.

While God has warned us about the influence of others, He has also encouraged us to seek out others who can help us in our Christian walks. In Hebrews 10:25, we are told by God to "not neglect to meet together, as is the habit of some, but to encourage one another, and all the more as you see the Day drawing near" (ESV). Furthermore, Paul told followers in Philippians 4:9 to put into practice the things they "have learned and received and heard and seen in me" (ESV). And, consistent with the concept of modeling, in I Corinthians 11:1, Paul tells us to imitate him as he imitates Christ.

We can see by both research and God's Word that we are greatly influenced by our social groups. And, we should be encouraged to seek out groups that can build us up and help us grow. By participating in groups that encourage our faith (i.e., church, small groups, Bible studies), we will see examples of godly behavior, will be encouraged in them, and will be socially reinforced to engage in them as well. Like Bandura said in his Social Cognitive Theory, we will then be likely to model the behaviors we see and are reinforced in!⌐

A model is not simply a person doing something that can then be imitated by a learner; it includes all the patterns for behavior complex societies present to their members, including books, verbal directions, film and cartoon characters, and a variety of other real or symbolic objects. Their prevalence is highly evident, as is their effectiveness.

Western societies present a preponderance of achievement-oriented, assertive, outgoing models for men. Not surprisingly, many males in these societies are achievement-oriented, assertive, and outgoing. In contrast, the Zuni culture presents models of cooperation and self-effacement, and these are the primary characteristics of its members (Roscoe, 1991).

Manifested personality is highly influenced by context. We can't easily determine how naturally nurturing this mother is, by observing her interactions with her infant.
© Blend Images/Shutterstock.com

It seems clear, manifested personality characteristics are highly influenced by social context. This does not mean theories based on the notion that there are inherited predispositions toward specific personality traits are incorrect. What it does indicate is biological predispositions will not necessarily be dominant over social influences.

Reciprocal Determinism

A central belief of all learning-based approaches is that our behaviors are strongly influenced by their outcomes. Bandura explains what is most important is our understanding of the relationship between our behaviors and their consequences, and our ability to anticipate consequences. Because we can anticipate consequences, we not only direct our behaviors toward the most desirable ends, but we deliberately arrange our environments to maximize positive outcomes. So, in the end, we affect the environment and it affects us in what Bandura labels *triadic reciprocal determinism.* Our actions and the environment are two aspects of the triad; our personalities (what we know and feel; our wishes and desires; our inclinations) constitute the third.

Personal Agency

Unlike Freud, who described human behavior as moved by instinctive and often unconscious forces and warring factions, Bandura insists we are agents of our own actions. Being agents, he explains, requires intentionality (being able to do what we intend), forethought (foreseeing the consequences of our actions), and **self-efficacy** (having a notion of our likelihood of success).

What Does the Bible Say?

ᴸA key part of Bandura's theory is personal agency and the ability to think about and control our own actions. Bandura asserted that the environment does not just affect us, but we also affect our environment. And a big part of the way we affect our environment is through our *belief* that we can control our own actions and produce outcomes in the environment. This belief that we can exert the desired effect on our situations is based on past experiences with success. We learn that we are efficacious in producing outcomes when we have experienced success in producing outcomes in the past (or when we observe people we identify with as effectively producing outcomes). This confidence in our ability to produce outcomes is termed self-efficacy.

When you think of this concept of self-efficacy, do you think it is biblical? What do you think the Bible says about this concept of self-efficacy?

If we use the passage from Romans 7 used earlier and Paul's inability to produce the outcomes in himself that aligned with godly living, one may be tempted to think that self-efficacy is not a biblical concept and that we don't really have control over our own actions and outcomes in the environment. However, perhaps instead of throwing self-efficacy out entirely, it just needs to be refined a bit. When we look at how God interacts with His people throughout the Bible, it is clear that He wants us to live confident, brave, and empowered lives. He wants us to believe in favorable outcomes and our ability to walk in them. But, God is also clear that we do not walk alone and that we are not the only agents at play in the world. In fact, while God wants us to live confidently, He constantly reminds us that He is our strength and the source of our abilities to execute in this world. Right after Paul laments his ability to control his sinful nature in Romans 7, he goes on to praise God for being the Spirit within him that can execute godly behaviors (Romans 7:24-25). In other letters, He repeated talks of God's power within himself to do all sorts of hard things (Philippians 4:13). As can be seen throughout Scripture, a believers' confidence to walk in situations and produce outcomes comes from God's power within us (Ephesians 3:20; 2 Corinthians 9:8; Romans 8:11). Therefore, it seems that self-efficacy is a good concept, especially due to its association with resilience and positive coping during hardship, but Bandura's focus on self would be more biblical with a focus on our confidence in God within us in all things. You could say that our self-efficacy is because of the God-efficacy we have. ⌐

Relevance of Bandura's Theory

The importance of Bandura's social learning theory of personality is not that it contributes to the identification of personality traits or to their measurement; nor is it particularly useful for understanding the structure of personality or the biological and dynamic forces at play. ⌐What it does is⌐ facilitate an understanding of the manifestation of personality ⌐through social situations.⌐

Most of the personality traits identified are meaningful only in social interaction. Agreeableness, extroversion, sociability, dependency—these are all qualities of human interaction. They describe typical ways of relating to social realities. Furthermore, they are not characteristics individuals manifest regardless of their immediate social context. For example, highly aggressive individuals might well display their aggressive tendencies in athletics and other physical activities where aggression is socially approved; few are likely to display aggression in a church choir or university classroom.

In summary, social approaches to personality highlight the tremendous influence of social customs, traditions, expectations, and situations on the manifestation of personality characteristics. They argue that acceptable and unacceptable social behaviors are learned ⌐and they study how the social world influences the development of individual differences in personality.⌐

Rotter's Cognitive Approach

In the course of learning socially acceptable behaviors, we learn what to expect when we choose one behavior versus a different one. Expectations guide our behaviors ⌐and should be a part of any meaningful approach to personality according to Julian Rotter (1982).⌐

Externality–Internality

In effect, expectations are beliefs about sources of reinforcement. Basically, claims Rotter, we can have one of two different attitudes toward our behaviors and their outcomes. We can be *externally oriented* or *internally oriented*—a notion later borrowed and elaborated by Weiner (2008) in his theory of motivation.

As we saw in a previous chapter, those who are internally oriented tend to take responsibility for the consequences of their actions. They see themselves as being in control; they attribute success or failure to internal factors (ability or effort). Those who are externally oriented believe they have little control over what happens to them. They attribute success or failure to external factors (luck and task difficulty). Expectations of reward, and behaviors, will be affected accordingly (Figure 7.6).

Various studies have uncovered a large number of situations where expectations based on *locus of control* affect behavior. Not surprisingly, those who think they are in control of outcomes (the internally oriented) are less likely to be obese (Adolfsson et al., 2005); they are more likely to participate in and profit from treatments to counter various delinquent behaviors, including alcoholism

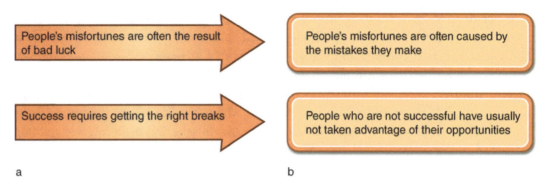

People's misfortunes are often the result of bad luck

People's misfortunes are often caused by the mistakes they make

Success requires getting the right breaks

People who are not successful have usually not taken advantage of their opportunities

a

b

Figure 7.6   Items similar to those used by Rotter to assess a person's locus of control."

(Cavaiola & Strohmetz, 2010); they are more likely to be successful at work and integrate more readily into new social environments (Vonthron & Lagabrielle, 2002); they are less likely to behave aggressively toward an intimate partner (Gallagher & Parrott, 2010); they are less likely to have eating disorders (Scoffier et al., 2010); and they tend to have generally more positive attitudes (Gianakos, 2002).

Personality theorists such as Bandura and Rotter look for regularities in individual decisions and beliefs, and they search for ways in which people can be identified on the basis of differences in their dominant modes of functioning. Their theories provide strong indications suggesting that important personality differences are evident in learned social interactions and they reflect our expectations.

HUMANISTIC APPROACHES

But surely, the humanists protest, there is more to human behavior and personality than inherited predispositions, basic instincts, warring psychic forces, and learned expectations and beliefs. We need to take into consideration what it means to be human. We need to emphasize the worth and dignity of every individual.

Abraham Maslow's Self-Actualized Person

Like most humanistically-oriented psychologists, Maslow's principal concerns have been with the development of the healthy person. Fundamental to his position is the notion we are moved by a hierarchy of needs, the lowest of which relate to physiological survival and the highest to the fullest and most desirable blossoming of the person. The process of growth is one of self-actualization—of *becoming* in the most abstract sense of the term. This involves a recognition of what one is, of what one can and should be, and a striving for fulfillment.

Maslow (1970) admits the concept of self-actualization is extremely difficult to define. It is characterized by the absence of "neurosis, psychopathic personality, psychosis, or strong tendencies in these directions" (p. 150). In addition, self-actualized people "may be loosely described as [making] full use and exploitation of talents, capacities, potentialities, etc." (p. 150).

Using these rather loose criteria, Maslow's search for self-actualized people among a group of 3,000 college students yielded only one actualized person and one or two dozen "potentials." Maslow concluded a fully actualized person is much more likely to be found among older people. He then selected a small number of cases (23) from among his contemporaries and historical figures. He interviewed them where possible (extremely informally), or read accounts of their lives. Maslow subsequently described some of their personality characteristics: autonomous and independent; highly accepting of themselves and others; tolerant; free of inhibitions; spontaneous and able to enjoy themselves; free of guilt.

Science might shudder to consider individuals were defined as being self-actualized by Maslow and were then interviewed by him to determine what self-actualized people were really like. The process is only slightly different from deciding authoritarian people are psychopaths, selecting a group of psychopathic authoritarian people, and interviewing them to determine whether authoritarian people are really psychopathic. The only surprises possible are those arising from errors in selection or in interviewer judgment.

Rogers's Phenomenology

Phenomenology is concerned with the world as it appears rather than as it actually might be. Humanistic positions are typically phenomenological; their main concern is with the individual at the center of realities, in essence, self-created. The argument is no two people see the world in exactly the same way, and understanding people requires understanding their notions of the world.

> **Phenomenology:** Concerned with the world of appearance—that is, the world as it appears to the individual.

Carl Rogers's theory of personality is well summarized by this abbreviated list of his theoretical beliefs (Rogers, 1951, Chap. 11):

1. Every individual exists in a continually changing world of which the person alone is the center. The person's world is thus private, unknown and unknowable by anyone else. As the existential philosophers have pointed out, existence is lonely; it is necessarily always alone.
2. My perception of the world is real. So is yours. We have our separate realities. If we are to understand each other, you must try to understand my world, and I yours.
3. We have one basic tendency—*actualization*. In short, we have an inner, directing need to develop ourselves in Maslow's sense of the word.
4. The structure of self—notions of I or me—develops as a result of interaction with the environment and, particularly, interaction with others.
5. Values attached to notions of self are obtained either as a result of direct experience or indirectly. Thus, I can learn I am good as a result of engaging in good behavior; or I can infer I am good as a result of having people tell me I am.
6. Most of our ways of behaving are consistent with our notions of self. We tend to engage in behaviors that do not violate our internalized conceptions of what we are like—our values and ideals.

Humanistic approaches do not present theories so much as a renewed emphasis on human worth and dignity. They look more to glorify the importance of the individual, the nature of being, and the sanctity of personal experience than to analyze and dissect in the sometimes impersonal laboratories of science. Their impact on approaches to mental health and counseling has been considerable. Carl Rogers's *person-centered therapy* continues to be widely applied in therapeutic settings (Cain, 2010).

MEASURING PERSONALITY VARIABLES

Many differences exist across the theories of personality. What each chooses to focus on, where each asserts personality comes from, and the way personality is structured are just a few of the ways that personality theorists differ in their approaches to studying personality. Another difference among theorists is how personality should be measured. There is little disagreement that personality exists, but how to measure it can be found at the center of many disagreements among personality theorists.

There are many ways we can determine what someone's personality is. First, we could simply observe someone's behavior. You have probably never given a personality test to your friends or family, but I bet you can describe their personality. You likely have a pretty good sense of what personality traits exist in your closest friends and family members simply because you have observed them in different situations and across time. Observation is one way psychologists can determine personality as well. But, as you can imagine, it takes several different situations over time to accurately deduce someone's personality and for many social and personality psychologists, there just isn't enough time to measure personality through observation. A more time efficient and widely used method is personality tests. Personality tests fall into one of two categories: projective tests and nonprojective tests.

Projective Tests

Projective tests of personality involve presenting an individual with an ambiguous stimulus or and then asking the individual to interact with the ambiguous stimulus in some way. Projective tests could include asking an individual to draw something or fill in the missing parts of a picture or sentence or to say what they think of when they see a particular picture or word. They could also be asked to describe what they see in an ambiguous picture. The

> **Projective tests:** Personality tests in which stimuli are ambiguous and testees' responses are interpreted as reflecting unconscious aspects of personality.

assumption underlying the use of projective tests is that unconscious fears, desires, and motivations, and personality traits may be projected in these ambiguous tasks. Proponents of projective tests claim that since these traits are unconscious, they would not ordinarily be revealed in conventional measures of personality. The ambiguous stimulus will elicit them in a way that a straightforward question on a personality test would not.

The Rorschach

Among the best known of the projective measures is the *Rorschach inkblot test,* so called because it presents the subject with ten stimulus cards with printed figures resembling elaborate inkblots (Figure 7.7). The scoring procedure is complicated, detailed, and not well validated, and interpretations of different experts vary a great deal. Furthermore, the relationships of scorer interpretations to the actual behavior of testees has been very difficult to establish, although there is evidence it can be used to discriminate between psychotic and nonpsychotic populations (Wood et al., 2010). It continues to be one of the most widely used personality measures in clinical practice (Sendin, 2010).

Figure 7.7   The Rorschach inkblot test.
© Kovalchuk Oleksandr/Shutterstock.com

The Thematic Apperception Test

Another well-known projective test is H. A. Murray's (1938, 1943) *thematic apperception test (TAT)*. It consists of 30 black-and-white pictures showing people in various situations and asks subjects to tell a story suggested to them by the pictures. Clinicians often use the TAT as a way of gaining insight into the subject's fantasies. Although the test does not measure specific personality characteristics, it may be highly suggestive of preoccupations, fears, unconscious needs and desires, personal relationships, and related themes. It is widely used in clinical practice as well as in research (Teglasi, 2010). For example, it has been the basis of many investigations of need achievement, with scorers looking for achievement-related themes in subjects' descriptions of the pictures. It has also been used to look at the concerns and interests of highly creative children (Garces-Bacsal, 2010).

Nonprojective Tests

While projective tests of personality use ambiguous tasks or stimuli to elicit unconscious traits, motives, or desires, **nonprojective tests** measure personality through straightforward questions or statements that individuals report on. There are hundreds of paper-and-pencil or computer-based personality tests, usually referred to as *scales* or *inventories*. Scales measure specific dimensions of personality (sociability, neuroticism, and so on); inventories are more inclusive. Typically, inventories consist of a number of different scales and yield a profile of personality characteristics.

> **Nonprojective tests:** Personality tests that measure personality through straightforward questions or statements on which individual's report.

The NEO-PI-R

The *Neuroticism Extraversion Openness Personality Inventory, Revised* (*NEO-PI-R;* Costa & McCrae, 1992) is an inventory designed specifically to assess the Big Five personality factors (**c**onscientiousness, **a**greeableness, **n**euroticism, **o**penness, and **e**xtraversion). It is available in a longer, 240-item format or in a shorter, 60-item inventory. Items are presented on what is called a Likert scale—a scale where the responder selects an option ranging from *strongly disagree* to *strongly agree.*

Research indicates this personality inventory has relatively high reliability (consistency) and validity in terms of its usefulness for predicting outcomes such as adjustment to career requirements. For example, scores on the NEO-PI-R correlate well with job success (Denis et al., 2010). It has been translated into many different languages and is reportedly useful across many cultures (Ortet et al., 2010; Plaisant et al., 2010).

The MMPI-2

One of the best-known, most rigorously developed, and most widely used of the personality inventories is the *Minnesota Multiphasic Personality Inventory-2 (MMPI-2).* There are various forms of this test, which is normally computer scored. Ordinarily, it yields measures on a wide number of dimensions. Ten of the original scales are *clinical scales.* Closely related to these are newer *restructured clinical (RC) scales.* These clinical scales provide scores on dimensions such as depression, hypochondriasis, hysteria, paranoia, schizophrenia, and social introversion. Some scales are *validity scales:* They provide indications of the extent to which an individual's responses may be considered reliable and valid. In addition, there are various *supplementary scales* measuring things such as proneness to substance abuse and anxiety.

MMPI-2 items were first developed with groups of individuals who had been clearly diagnosed with disorders such as hypochondriasis, depression, or psychopathy. Scores obtained by these groups were then compared to scores obtained by a normal "control" group, and items were selected on the basis of how well they discriminated between groups. If, for example, hypochondriacs always responded in one way to ten items, and controls always responded differently, these ten items would then make up the hypochondriasis scale. It would then be possible to identify people who respond in the same way as hypochondriacs by looking at their scores on the scale.

In many ways, the MMPI-2 is a masterpiece of objective test construction. Evidence suggests it is useful in making discriminations among groups of people and in preliminary diagnosis of abnormal behavior—which is the purpose for which it was designed. It appears to have impressive validity when used for this purpose. However, it is also often used for personnel assessment or as a screening tool with presumably normal individuals—purposes for which it has questionable validity. Indications are it remains an extremely powerful tool for identifying emotional and mental disorders (Caldwell, 2006). Few instruments have been used more widely in psychological diagnosis, and few have stimulated more research.

Some Cautions

Although personality inventories and other assessment devices have proven useful in a number of situations, both practical and theoretical, it cannot yet be argued any specific personality trait can be measured with unquestioned validity and reliability. Results obtained from different inventories for the same individual are sometimes different, and not all predictions made on the basis of diagnostic instruments have been entirely ⌞valid.⌟ For these reasons, interpretation of test scores requires both restraint and wisdom. Tests such as these can be dangerous in the hands of those who are not fully aware of their weaknesses. Users must constantly bear in mind that the stability of personality characteristics is still a matter of debate. A test revealing an individual to be tense does not establish anxiety is a pervasive and predominant personality characteristic in that person. Personality tests measure mood, fatigue, feelings of happiness or dejection, and a variety of other affective states. ⌞Also, while personality tests are useful to describe your tendencies, your preferences, your communication styles, and a host of other individual differences, it should be noted that for the Christian, personality tests do not give us license to behave in ways that do not glorify God. It is very tempting to look at a score on a personality test and say, "That's just how I am" and then not seek to grow in holiness. Your personality scores are not the end game, but rather should be used as information about yourself and a tool to continue growing in godliness. Furthermore, no personality measure is able to capture the full collection of traits, motives, and desires of an individual. There is no perfectly comprehensive personality measure out there. And even taken together, all of our personality measures still cannot fully capture the uniqueness of human personality. We are complex. We are wonderfully and fearfully made (Psalm 139: 14), our personalities included.⌟

SUMMARY

Personality is defined as stable characteristics including habits, preferences, weaknesses, strengths, moral attributes, and ways of thinking, feeling, and behaving. The major approaches to personality theory discussed in this chapter are types and traits, biological, psychodynamic, learning-based, and humanistic.

A personality trait is a specific quality that differentiates among different individuals (e.g., good-hearted or selfish); types are clusters of related traits. The Big Five personality factors are five independent personality dimensions, each of which can range from very high to very low: conscientiousness, agreeableness, neuroticism, openness, and extraversion.

Biological approaches emphasize the genetic underpinnings of personality. Eysenck's biological approach holds inherited differences in nervous system activity underlie the two main dimensions of personality, extraversion and introversion, as well as a third dimension, psychoticism. Recent approaches use genomics and neuropsychology to look for genetic and neurological structures and functioning underlying personality differences.

Psychodynamic approaches look at the interaction of basic inherited tendencies with physical and social reality to explain personality. In Freud's system, sexual and survival urges (id) often drive us in directions incompatible with social reality and conscience (superego). This leads to conflict that our conception of reality (ego) mediates and tries to resolve. Objects of sexual gratification progress from oral through anal, phallic, latent, and genital stages as we develop. Fixation and regression are two unhealthy possibilities, as is overreliance on defense mechanisms.

Learning-based approaches look at the role of the social and physical environment in determining personality. Behavioristic approaches describe how personality traits might be shaped and conditioned. Bandura's social cognitive theory describes personality development in terms of the effects of observation and the reciprocal determinism at play in person–behavior–environment interactions. It emphasizes the extent to which we are agents of our actions, anticipating and intending their outcomes, and estimating our likelihood of success in our endeavors (self-efficacy). Rotter's expectancy theory explains how locus of control (external and internal orientation) affects our personalities as reflected in our choice of behaviors.

Humanistic approaches focus on the development of self and the worth of the individual. Both Maslow and Rogers describe the development of human potential as the highest goal. They emphasize healthy human functioning and the uniqueness and worth of the individual.

Personality variables may be evident in life outcomes and observer ratings. They can also be measured with projective tests such as the Rorschach and TAT (where the individual reveals unconscious traits in responding to ambiguous stimuli), or with nonprojective written tests like the NEO-PI-R (which measures the Big Five personality types) and the MMPI-2 (which is designed mainly to measure personality disorders).

This ⌞section⌟ serves as an introduction into personality theory and approaches. Each approach emphasizes some part of personality theory and contains strengths and weaknesses. Personality can be influenced by many factors, including genetics, learning, social, ⌞and spiritual⌟ experiences. It is important to have a basic understanding of these approaches as well as personality assessment measures. ⌞Through it all, the study of personality should elicit in us wonder and amazement at the greatness of God and His creation. Much like David realized the greatness of God and His creation and expressed his praise throughout the Psalms, when we take time to examine the complexity of human personality, how to describe and measure it, we too should be reminded of the greatness and glory of God.⌟

SOCIAL PSYCHOLOGY

The 1960s were the stage for many changes in the United States, including the civil rights movement. As a recent college graduate, Eugenia "Skeeter" Phelan returns home to her high-society life in Jackson, Mississippi, with the desire to become a writer. Skeeter obtains a job with a local newspaper writing a column on household tips. Skeeter requests help on tips for the column from Aibileen Clark—a Black maid who works for a White family, the Holbrooks. Seeing the disparity between these families and their loyal maids, Skeeter decides to write about the maids, starting with Aibileen who has spent her entire life caring for others' children. Through

▶ **CONVERSAT WITH A SOCIAL PSYCHOLOGIST**

persuasion and with great reluctance, Aibileen agrees to provide her story to Skeeter. The fact that a White person is interacting on a personal level with a Black person violates the Jim Crow laws, which were still very much in effect in Mississippi during the first part of the 1960s. At the same time, Hilly Holbrook, Aibileen's employer and Skeeter's best friend, attempts to renew the community's waning respect for these laws. After several prominent civil rights workers are killed, more maids join Aibileen and tell their stories to Skeeter, who is finally able to publish her book using a pseudonym.

© nenetus/Shutterstock.com

The book and subsequent movie under the same name, *The Help*, provides a story of friendship and respect that transcends the (then) present societal status quos. This book also illustrates two of **social psychology's** most important concerns: human relationships—as illustrated in the friendship formed between Skeeter and Aibileen—and how stereotypes can be pervasive through communities—evident in how others in Mississippi respond to the changes brought on by the civil rights movement.

> **Social psychology:** Studies the relationships among individuals or between individuals and groups.

WHAT IS SOCIAL PSYCHOLOGY?

Social psychology is concerned with relationships among individuals or between individuals and groups. In Allport's (1968) terms, "Social psychologists regard their discipline as an attempt to understand how the *thought, feeling,* and *behavior* of individuals are influenced by the *actual, imagined,* or *implied* presence of others" (p. 3). Thus, social psychology says something about the opinions and stereotypes illustrated by Hilly and the Jim Crow laws, and also on how the relationship between Skeeter and Aibileen impacted the community's attempts to create positive civil rights changes (Stockett, 2009).

Social psychology's subject matter spans almost all facets of human behavior minus those that are clearly individual and not affected by the presence of others. Most of what we learn, think, feel, and do is influenced by others. Very few people have lives totally devoid of human relationships, and complete social isolation would require almost geographic remoteness or some form of mental disorder. Social psychology, however, tries to understand the socially influenced aspects of attitudes, relationships, and behaviors.

ATTITUDES AND ATTITUDE CHANGE

⌐Of the many areas of life that social psychologists study, the attitudes we hold and how they are formed and changed is one area of research within social psychology.⌐ Understanding social influence is paramount to understanding the formation and changing of attitudes, opinions, stereotypes, and prejudices.

An **attitude** is a prevailing and consistent tendency to think, feel, or act in a given way about the world around us. Psychologists have long asserted that attitudes have three components: affective (emotional), cognitive (thoughts), and behavioral (actions) components. These three components comprise how we feel about something, how we think about something, and how we act towards something. And as can be seen in Figure 7.8, affective, cognitive, and behavioral components of attitudes work together to determine

> **Attitude:** Prevailing and consistent tendency to react in a given way.
>
> **Opinion:** Evaluations, which lack the strong motivational consequences of attitudes.

one's attitude about something. Attitudes are either positive or negative; neutral reactions do not qualify as attitudes. Attitudes have strong motivational consequences, distinguishing them from **opinions**. Although opinions are also evaluations, they do not drive people to action like attitudes do (Figure 7.8). We have attitudes about just about everything. Most of our attitudes are focused on other people (either about individuals we know or about groups of people, such as the elderly), on social or political issues such as abortion or gun control, or on activities such as music or exercise. Attitudes are important to social psychologists because they generally direct our behaviors including how we treat other people, whether we exercise, how we vote, what we buy, and many other daily decisions.

One specific type of attitude that social psychology researchers examine is stereotypes. **Stereotypes** are widely held attitudes and opinions concerning identifiable groups. Stereotypes usually include value-laden beliefs and are often based on emotional reaction, illogical reasoning, and faulty generalization.

> **Stereotypes:** Widely held beliefs about groups based on illogical reasoning or faulty generalization.

Although stereotypes are often assumed to be negative, they can also be positive. Negative stereotypes have been shown to have detrimental effects on many kinds of interactions, including, for example, the perception of older drivers as more prone to accidents (Joanisse et al., 2013). In the Joanisse et al. study, older adults that were told about the negative stereotype of being more prone to accidents actually had more accidents than older adults not provided the stereotype. Current research also suggests that even positive stereotypes may have unintended negative effects (Markham, 2013).

As generalized beliefs about groups, stereotypes are virtually indispensable in daily interaction. They're like cognitive short-cuts telling us how to react without having to wait to see how other people are going to behave. For example, we may have a stereotype telling us panhandlers become aggressive if we look them in the eye but throw nothing in their hats. So either we don't look them in the eye or we toss a coin into their hats.

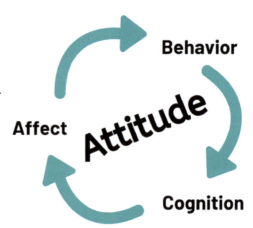

Figure 7.8   The three components of attitudes.

Source: Bailee Robinson

Not surprisingly, there is considerable research that some stereotypes agree remarkably well with more objective evaluations (Lee et al., 1995). This doesn't mean stereotypes are invariably accurate and useful; many are bigoted, inappropriate, and plain unjust.

Unlike stereotypes, which are widely held beliefs about groups, **prejudices** are personal rather than shared prejudgments. To be prejudiced implies having arrived at an opinion prior to obtaining relevant facts. Even today, many people still hold prejudices against others who they see as different.

> **Prejudices:** Personal beliefs about groups based on illogical reasoning or faulty generalization.

How attitudes, opinions, stereotypes, and prejudices are different is evident in a sample of most people's behaviors and beliefs. For example, a person's strong feeling that involvement in war is immoral and their attempt to persuade others they should protest illustrates an *attitude*—a personal, emotional, and clearly motivating belief. If this person were convinced military personnel are highly immoral even though he or she has had little exposure to them, that conviction would be a *prejudice*—a preconceived judgment. The individual's personal belief that seatbelt legislation is unnecessary and uneconomical is an opinion—a personal belief not necessarily shared by others and not directed toward an identifiable group. And their assumption that Americans are sufficiently resourceful and industrious that they will easily cope with global warming and other crises illustrates a *stereotype*—a belief about a specific group shared by a significant number of people.

Compliance and Conformity

Attitudes are powerful motives for behavior. Although attitudes tend to be stable and long lasting, they can change in response to various factors, including new information we acquire, social pressure, tendencies we have to obey or disobey, and the effects of persuasion. When we change our attitude, we usually also change our behavior. But, sometimes, our behaviors change due to environmental pressures and not because our attitudes have changed. When we talk about our behaviors being influenced by others, we are referring to another area of research conducted by social psychologists: social influence. Social influence on our behaviors includes many things, and among them are conformity, compliance, and obedience.

Conformity refers to changes in behavior due to unspoken group pressure. This group pressure can be real or imagined. You have probably conformed your behavior to group pressure in a number of social situations. For example, have you ever stood up and applauded at the end of a play or concert because everyone around you did even though you didn't think the performance was that good? Or, have you ever said you liked a movie that you really didn't like because everyone in the room was really excited about it? You have likely experienced conformity a lot over your life and quite simply, it is when you change your behaviors due to a silent, but influential pressure to go along with what other people are doing or saying. While conformity involves changing your behaviors due to an unspoken social pressure in a group, **compliance** occurs when you change your behavior because someone has explicitly asked. Requests to comply are often in the form of a clear and direct question (i.e., "Will you get me a glass of water?"), but can also be more subtle and communicated in a gesture, a look, or an unspoken request. However, regardless of whether it is actually verbalized or not, compliance involved changing our behaviors to a communicated request to do something.

In addition to the constructs of conformity and compliance, obedience is another construct in social influence that has been examined extensively. While compliance is a change in behavior due to a direct request from someone in your social group, **obedience** is defined as a change in behavior due to a direct request from someone in authority over you. Often referred to as a *demand*, the request comes from someone who has the legitimate authority to enact rewards or punishments and thus performing (or not performing) the requested behavior has consequences. Due to these consequences, people often

> **Conformity:** Changes in behavior due to unspoken group pressure.
>
> **Compliance:** Changing one's behaviors due to an explicit (verbal or nonverbal) request from a nonauthority figure.
>
> **Obedience:** Changing one's behavior due to a direct request from someone in authority.

report that obedience to an authority feels more like a requirement and less like you have a choice to perform the behavior.⌋

Research on Conformity, Compliance, and Obedience

Solomon Asch Conformity Study

Solomon Asch (1955) conducted one of the most classic studies of ⌊conformity.⌋ In a typical experiment, "participants" were placed in a semicircle facing an easel on which the experimenter placed two large cards. One of these cards had a single vertical line on it (the standard); the other had three vertical lines of different lengths, one of which is clearly equal in length to the standard (Figure 7.9). In a "test of perceptual accuracy," the "participants" were required to determine which of the three lines was equal to the standard.

The test was not of perceptual accuracy but of social pressure and its effects on ⌊conformity.⌋ Only one of the "participants" was actually a participant; the other "participants" were confederates. The confederates had been instructed to answer correctly for the first few trials and then to answer incorrectly but to agree on the incorrect answer. The actual participant had no reason to suspect the other individuals were not also participants. The true participant was the second to last to provide an answer.

In a series of studies carried out in three different institutions, over 120 participants answered incorrectly 36.8% of the time. A control group not exposed to social pressure answered correctly more than 99% of the time. Typically, participants were confronted with the conflicting opinions of as many as eight confederates. However, varying the number of confederates revealed that a majority of three was equally effective in eliciting ⌊conformity⌋ with the group (Asch, 1955). This observation is strikingly similar to the ancient Chinese proverb, *three men make a tiger*

The urge to conform, ⌊comply, and obey⌋ is a powerful social motive, ⌊driven largely by a desire to feel connected and liked by others. Our need to belong is a strong need and this can cause us to do things that we may not want to do, just so we can be accepted by those around us. While this can be a dangerous thing in the teenaged years or in other settings,⌋ this urge ⌊to belong and be accepted by others also⌋ does much to ensure that societies function smoothly.

© bikeriderlondon/Shutterstock.com

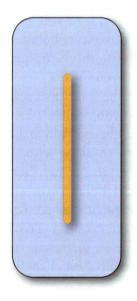

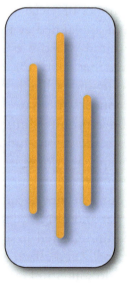

Figure 7.9 Asch (1955) used a simple visual perception test to determine the effects of social pressure. Both participants and the experimenter's confederates were asked which comparison line is the same length as the standard line. The confederates all chose an obviously incorrect line, but the confederate's solidarity pressured the participants to also choose an incorrect line.

(which is interpreted to mean that people will believe the most absurd things as long as enough other people seem to believe them).

When researchers questioned participants in the Asch experiment later, the participants indicated they knew all along their responses and those of the confederates were in error. But they still ⌞conformed⌟—later explaining their behavior in a variety of ways, such as "poor eyesight" or "misjudgment." Interestingly, not all the participants were equally susceptible to the effects of group pressure: one fourth of the participants continued to answer completely independently, never agreeing with the incorrect majority. In contrast, others nearly always agreed with the majority.

Many people interpret these experimental results as evidence of the gullibility of individuals and their susceptibility to group pressure. The implication is that these are undesirable qualities. However, it is precisely because we are susceptible to group pressures that complex social institutions such as governments, schools, and churches work. It is also because we are sensitive to the opinions and attitudes of others that we are able to interact effectively with them.

This should not be taken to mean compliance and conformity are always good; however, it does mean they are not always bad, in the same way that stereotypes aren't always totally wrong and useless.

Milgram Obedience Studies

Let's say your superior orders you to do something like hurt some innocent person: How likely are you to contradict the order? Or will you just do as you are told? Milgram (1963, 1965), in a remarkable series of controversial experiments, provided an answer to these questions. In Milgrim's studies, participants were duped into believing they were confederates of an experimenter studying the effects of punishment on learning. An alleged participant (actually a confederate, termed a *stooge* in this experiment) was to be presented with a series of learning tasks while attached to electrodes so he could be shocked whenever he made an error. The real participant's task was to depress the switch that would

Are you part of the crowd or do you try to be unique?

© iQoncept/Shutterstock.com

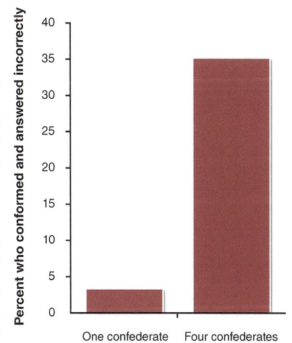

One confederate   Four confederates

Figure 7.10   When paired with a single confederate, participants in the Asch (1955) study were about as accurate as if they had been alone. But when paired with four, they complied with the majority more than one third of the time. Adding more confederates did not increase compliance significantly.

deliver the shock. Participants were first connected to the electrodes and administered a mild shock so they would have no reason to think that the shocks would not be real. They were then seated in front of an instrument panel containing a series of switches labeled from 15 to 450 volts, in 15-volt increments.

Verbal descriptions above the switches ranged from "Slight shock" to "Danger: severe shock" at 390 volts and "XXX" at 435 volts.

In Milgram's (1963) first experiment, "victims" (stooges who did not actually receive any shocks) were placed in a separate room and were instructed to make a predetermined number of errors. The participants controlling the switches were instructed to administer a shock for every error the victim made, beginning with the first switch and progressing as high as necessary, in one-step increments. If a participant hesitated or indicated any unwillingness to continue, the experimenter would employ a predetermined verbal "prod"; that prod failing, a second would be employed, then a third, and finally a fourth. In all cases, the prods were given in sequence:

- **Prod 1.** *Please continue, or please go on.*
- **Prod 2.** *The experiment requires that you continue.*
- **Prod 3.** *It is absolutely essential that you continue.*
- **Prod 4.** *You have no other choice. You must go on. (p. 374)*

Amazingly, none of the participants categorically refused to obey from the outset. In fact, of the 40 original participants, 26 obeyed the experimenter's instructions right to the very end ("victims" committed sufficient errors to ensure that participants would have an opportunity to administer the most severe shock—450 volts). The remaining 14 all obeyed until at least the 300-volt level (Figure 7.11).

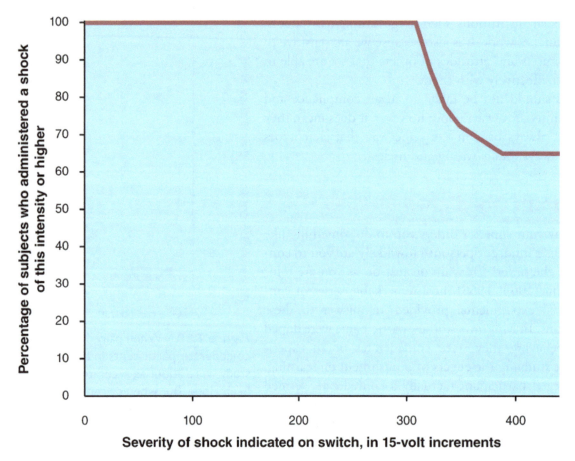

Figure 7.11   All participants in the Milgram study "obeyed" and administered shocks beginning at 15 volts and going to at least 300 volts. The next switch was labeled "extreme intensity shock." Five of 40 participants refused to go any further; 26 went all the way to 450 volts.

In related studies, Milgram (1965) looked at the effect of the distance between participant and victim using four different experimental conditions. In one, the participant could see, hear, and touch the victim, since both were in the same room. In a second, the participant could hear and see the stooge (typical a male confederate), but could not touch him. In a third condition, the participant could hear the stooge, but not see him, a curtain having been drawn between the two. In a final experimental condition, the participant could neither see nor hear the victim.

Again, participants complied with the experimenter's requests. But now, average intensity of shocks increased in direct proportion with the distance between the participant and the victim, with the highest shocks being administered when the participant could not see or hear the victim.

One finding that is sometimes overlooked when reporting the more sensational results of the Milgram obedience studies is that most participants, whether or not they obeyed, were disturbed by the procedure. Milgram (1963) writes:

> In a large number of cases the degree of tension reached extremes that are rarely seen in socio-psychological laboratory studies. [Participants] were observed to sweat, tremble, stutter, bite their lips, groan, and dig their fingernails into their flesh. These were characteristic rather than exceptional responses to the experiment. . . . On one occasion we observed a seizure so violently convulsive that it was necessary to call a halt to the experiment. (p. 375)

Studies such as these are disturbing for a number of reasons. They reveal aggressive aspects of humanity that many would prefer not to admit; they underline the power of authority and compliance in contrast to individual choice and freedom; and they present some serious moral issues with respect to deceiving participants into engaging in behaviors that potentially are psychologically damaging.

Given the fact that psychological investigations now typically require approval by an ethics committee and strict adherence to ethical guidelines, the Milgram studies have not often been replicated. Burger (2009) did replicate these studies with one significant variation: When participants reached the level of 150 volts (the point at which the "stooge" has been instructed to moan and protest), the experiment was discontinued.

Strikingly, Burger (2009) found obedience rates were only slightly lower 45 years after the original Milgram studies. Burger also found obedience rates for men and women did not differ significantly. Although, as Twenge (2009) noted, there has apparently been an increase in personality traits reflecting nonconformity (higher assertiveness and self-esteem), there continues to be a strong urge to comply with authority and to conform to the majority.

Zimbardo's Prison Experiment

Unquestioning ⌞obedience to⌟ authority has been dramatically demonstrated in concentration-camp atrocities performed under direct orders from powerful, potentially highly punitive or highly reinforcing superiors. More recently, it has been evident in the wanton acts of abuse and torture of prisoners at Abu Ghraib in Iraq (Bartone, 2010). Between 2003 and 2004, American personnel stationed at Abu Ghraib prison in Iraq tortured and abused enemy detainees. There may, however, be more to these atrocities than simple ⌞obedience to⌟ authority.

There is a culture among prisoners and guards, Zimbardo (2007) explains, that is the key to understanding how abuse and torture can occur under these circumstances ⌞that have an obedience component.⌟ In the classic 1971 experiment carried out at Stanford, 12 young men, who were among 75 who had answered an advertisement asking for volunteers for an experiment on prison life, were abruptly arrested by police, handcuffed, and brought into a prison (actually, a converted basement space in a Stanford building). There they were stripped, searched, deloused, fingerprinted, and in every way treated like real prisoners. Their guards were 12 other student volunteers instructed to do whatever was required to maintain order and command respect.

The results were sobering: Almost immediately, guards developed coercive, aggressive tactics, humiliating and dehumanizing prisoners. The guards forced the prisoners to do things like clean out toilet bowls with their bare hands, count aloud to reinforce their new numerical identities, and do physical exercise as "punishment" when they made errors. The conditions were so severe that 5 of the 12 prisoners had to be "released" before the experiment ended. The experiment was slated to run for 14 days, but it was abruptly terminated on the 6th day when one of the more than 50 outsiders who had seen the prison was shocked at what she saw and raised objections about the ethics of the experiment (Zimbardo, 2007).

The Stanford prison experiment suggests that we can quickly and easily adopt roles ⌐and perform behaviors thought to be appropriate to those roles⌐ even when they run counter to our values. The Milgram studies further underscored our willingness to obey those in authority.

© sakhorn/Shutterstock.com

The effects of the Stanford prison experiment were far greater than anticipated. Both the prisoners and the guards carried their roles to an unforeseen extreme. Fully one third of the guards exhibited what Zimbardo describes as genuinely sadistic tendencies. What the study illustrated was the power of institutions and of institutionalized roles. In contrast, the Milgram experiments were more about the power of individual authority.

The entire Stanford prison study was photographed and filmed and is available online (Stanford Prison Experiment, 2011).

Persuasion

⌐As seen in the previous studies, social⌐ influence is a powerful and pervasive force. We know people are influenced by norms expressed in the behaviors and attitudes of others, and we also know they respond to authority and to the roles they're called on to play. Research and common sense also suggest there are many subtle forms of social influence to which we are responsive.

Persuasion is a global term for some of these influences. It refers to deliberate, usually verbal, attempts to alter beliefs or behavior. Television commercials, religious and political propaganda, newspaper and magazine advertising, and political campaigning all represent attempts at persuasion.

> **Persuasion:** Deliberate attempts to alter behavior or beliefs.

The most powerful forms of persuasion are those that succeed in changing attitudes rather than simply behavior. Attitudes may change as a result of events within the person, a typically slow process. This change may result from rational decisions and occur very rapidly. Attitudes may also change as a result of external events that are accidental rather than deliberately persuasive. Thus, an individual who is rescued from death by a member of a minority group toward which they held highly negative attitudes may quite suddenly develop positive attitudes toward the group. Attitudes may also change as a result of persuasion.

Three characteristics of persuasion are important in determining its effectiveness: the nature of the message, its source, and some of the characteristics of the person being persuaded.

Importance of Message Characteristics

The nature of the message is important: It is much easier to persuade someone of something fitting with previous beliefs or with the individual's goals and wishes. For example, it is easier to believe a house is haunted if you already believe in ghosts or spirits. Conversely, it is difficult to change attitudes when the message runs counter to strongly entrenched prejudices and stereotypes.

Persuading someone to do something can be hard. Wouldn't it be nice if we all had this key on our computers?

© iQoncept/Shutterstock.com

Importance of Message Source

Belief in the importance of the *source* of persuasion is evident in the advertising media's use of powerful models in their attempts to persuade. Research in social psychology suggests the belief is warranted. Persuasion coming from a source marked by qualities such as expertise, liking, and high trust is most effective (Feng & MacGeorge, 2010). Similarly, people are more easily persuaded by opinions apparently shared by many, rather than by few. Horcajo et al. (2010) presented participants with strong or weak persuasive arguments, ascribing these either to a "majority" or to a "minority." Not surprisingly, whether they were strong or weak arguments, those arguments attributed to a majority source were more persuasive than those arguments thought to come from a minority.

The most powerful forms of persuasion are those that succeed in changing attitudes. That this will then result in a change in behavior is the hope of all politicians as they, like this man, try to persuade us.

© metamorworks/Shutterstock.com

The persuader's motives also play an important role (Ranganath et al., 2010). When persuaders were arguing in their own best interests, the persuasion was not nearly as effective as when the argument was opposed to the persuader's self-interest. When petroleum-linked interests suggest water and air contamination are not increasing as a result of oilfield activity, you are unlikely to believe them. The same argument presented by a radical "green" group is much more convincing.

Importance of Audience Characteristics

Finally, certain characteristics of the person being persuaded, such as intelligence and independence, are also important. In one study, Cacioppo et al. (1986) had participants read either a high-quality or a low-quality essay relating to why a university should institute comprehensive examinations. The more intelligent participants were more convinced by the high-quality essay. In contrast, other participants seemed less sensitive to the quality of the argument and were as easily convinced by the low-quality as by the high-quality essay.

In spite of these studies, attitudes are, by definition, pervasive predispositions to respond in given ways; as such, they resist change. Although it may be relatively simple for a skilled social psychologist to persuade individuals to vote for her, she may experience considerably more difficulty in getting them to love members of minority groups against whom they have highly negative prejudices. Persuasion is not likely to be at all effective in such endeavors, but prolonged face-to-face contact in a cooperative situation might be.

Cognitive Dissonance

In Chapter 6, we saw another source of attitude change: **cognitive dissonance**. Cognitive dissonance describes a situation where there is conflict among behavior, beliefs, or attitudes. The dissonance model predicts people will change their attitudes to conform to their behaviors when there is a conflict between the two, but only when there is insufficient justification for the behavior and when the behavior has been engaged in willingly. Experimentally, participants who were paid significant amounts for dissonant behavior, or who were forced to comply, showed little attitude change later.

> **Cognitive dissonance:** A situation where conflict exists among behavior, beliefs, or attitudes.

Cognitive dissonance is a theme in many movies and books. In Romeo and Juliet, the two Verona families, the Capulets and Montagues, are enemies. Yet, the movie is about the love between Juliet, a Capulet, and Romeo, a Montague. The cognitive dissonance is that Juliet and Romeo should be enemies but fall madly in love with each other instead.

Researchers have studied the effects of forc-

In Shakespeare's *Romeo and Juliet*, the two youth brave the rejection of their families for their love.

© Nando Machado/Shutterstock.com

ing participants to engage in dissonant behavior, theorizing that participants exposed to the most severe threats for engaging (or not engaging) in some dissonance-inducing behavior will experience the least amount of dissonance. In other words, the participants would be expected to change their attitudes—and their behaviors—less than those exposed to milder threats.

To study this prediction, Wan and Chiou (2010) selected 218 college students identified as having a strong inclination toward online gaming addiction. They had these students play a new and highly engaging online game and then asked them, individually, to convince a younger adolescent the game was not fun. They were instructed to continue until they had succeeded in convincing the "participant." In the "severe threat" manipulation, participants were told if they were unsuccessful in convincing the adolescent to agree with them, their parents would be informed of their addiction inclination. In the "mild threat" manipulation, participants were told their academic advisors would be notified if they gave up the persuasion task before completing it.

As expected, participants in the severe threat condition were far less likely to have changed their positive attitudes toward the online game. Because of the severity of the threat, their dissonant behavior was justified. In contrast, those exposed to mild threats would be expected to experience more dissonance because their behavior would not be so easily justified. As predicted, they were more likely to change their attitudes.

The bottom line is that if you resort to severe threats to coerce someone to do or not do something, you are less likely to get them to change their attitudes and subsequent behavior than if you can bring about the same behavior with less coercion—whether it be a reward or the threat of punishment.

In Wan and Chiou's 2010 study, participants were threatened into convincing younger adolescents that a video game was not fun. As predicted, participants in the severe threat condition were less likely to have changed their positive attitudes toward the online game at the end of the experiment.

© Witthaya lOvE/Shutterstock.com

Attribution and Attitude Change

As we saw in Chapter 6, one explanation for attitude change in dissonance situations has to do with the **attributions** we make for our behaviors and feelings and for the behavior and feelings of others (the reasons we ascribe to them). We are constantly observing our behavior, the behavior of others, and the circumstances surrounding behavior. As we observe, we make inferences about ourselves and others, attributing causes to the behaviors we observe. In some cases our attributions are **dispositional attributions** (they involve characteristics of the actor); in others they are **situational attributions** (they involve characteristics of the situation); and perhaps in many cases we arrive at mixed attributions.

> **Attributions:** Inferences regarding the causes of behavior.
>
> **Dispositional attributions:** Causes of behavior related to characteristics of an individual.
>
> **Situational attributions:** Causes of behavior related to characteristics of the situation.

We can further explain an attribution-based attitude change following dissonant behavior with the following: If I willingly do A without compulsion or reward and am then asked to express my attitudes about doing A, I will most likely attribute my behavior to the fact that I believe that doing A is right, good, and consistent with my attitudes. If, however, I am compelled to do A against my inclinations, I can attribute my behavior to causes within myself or to the situation. If the situation justifies my behavior (the reward is sufficient or the threat is compelling enough), I will likely invoke a situational attribution and I won't change my attitude. If the situation doesn't justify my behavior, I need to attribute it to a personal characteristic (a disposition). The result is that I may change my attitude toward the activity.

Overjustification

As described, attribution theories of attitude change in situations of forced compliance (dissonance-creating situations) maintain when there is low justification for engaging in dissonant behavior, people infer they did so because they wanted to. In contrast, when there is high justification, they attribute their behavior to external circumstances (e.g., compulsion or reward).

Lepper and Greene (1975, 1978) and others have also investigated the effects of justification on *consonant* behavior. These authors have proposed an **overjustification** hypothesis that says, in effect, large external rewards for behavior that are initially intrinsically motivated may undermine our attitudes toward the behavior. For example, if

> **Overjustification:** Large external rewards reduce the intrinsic value of a behavior.

you whistle because you like whistling (intrinsic motivation: positive attitudes toward whistling), and later someone promises you a high reward for whistling, you might in the end come to like whistling much less.

How does this hypothesis follow from attribution theory? Bright and Penrod (2009) describe the process as follows: Given our tendency to attribute our behaviors to intrinsic or extrinsic factors, following a behavior for which external justification is very salient (a behavior is externally *overjustified*), we are likely to attribute that behavior more to external causes than to internal causes. Having done so, we modify our attitudes (internal causes of behavior) and become less positively disposed toward the behavior.

This analysis might seem to contradict common sense. We have long assumed people like to do things that are highly rewarded, and have perhaps naively assumed if we increase rewards associated with a behavior, positive attitudes toward that behavior should also increase. But research on the overjustification hypothesis indicates these beliefs are wrong at least some of the time.

ANTISOCIAL BEHAVIORS

Another area of social behavior that is important to social psychologists is antisocial behavior, and more specifically aggression and violence. Researchers in social psychology have asked questions like: How do we justify our antisocial behaviors like aggression and violence? Do external rewards serve to *justify* and explain these behaviors? Is there something in our dispositions that explains them or does our environment cause them?

Aggression and Violence

A popular stereotype of North American males is that they are assertive, intrusive, domineering individuals bent on achieving their goals even at the expense of others. People base this view on the observation of **aggression** in males. Aggression is defined as an action delib-

> **Aggression:** Actions with the intent to harm others.

erately intended to do harm or undertaken with no consideration for the harm it might cause others. Aggressive behavior is basic to organized competitive sports such as football and hockey, is a key to success in the business and academic worlds, is one of the main themes of the entertainment media, and is characteristic of much human interaction.

Types of Behavior

terrorism

war

violence

domineering

intrusive

competitive

Figure 7.12   An aggression continuum. Aggression is defined as actions intended to harm others or to achieve one's goals without consideration of others. Thus, in a strict sense, assertive, competitive, intrusive, domineering, and even violent behaviors (such as might be evident in sports) are not examples of aggression unless they are intended to do harm. Terrorism, a form of violence perpetrated against civilian groups, is an extreme form of aggression.

Photo © ArtFamily/Shutterstock.com

Theories of Aggression

It is important to note at the outset that strong assertiveness and competitiveness are not instances of aggression when they are not intended to inflict harm on others; nor are they undesirable in all circumstances. Although aggression may involve violence—actual physical damage to persons or property—it might also be passive.

Frustration–Aggression   A number of beliefs have dominated social psychology's attempts to understand and explain aggression. Among them is Dollard and Miller's **frustration–aggression hypothesis**—the contention that aggression is the result of anger and the most important cause of anger is **frustration** (Dollard et al., 1939). To be frustrated is to be prevented from reaching a goal. The Dollard and Miller hypothesis argues that, following frustration, anger is experienced; but anger will result in aggression only if a suitable object or person releases the aggression (Figure 7.13).

> **Frustration–aggression hypothesis:** Hypothesis that frustration leads to anger, which will result in aggression if a suitable object or person releases the aggression.
>
> **Frustration:** Occurs when someone is prevented from achieving a goal.

This explanation of aggression has often been used to explain terrorism. Terrorism, an extreme form of aggression, may be linked to the frustration accompanying poverty, lack of opportunity, and repression (e.g., Zinchenko, 2009). In support of the frustration–aggression hypothesis, Hakulinen et al. (2013) report that higher unemployment is associated with higher hostility than among those employed.

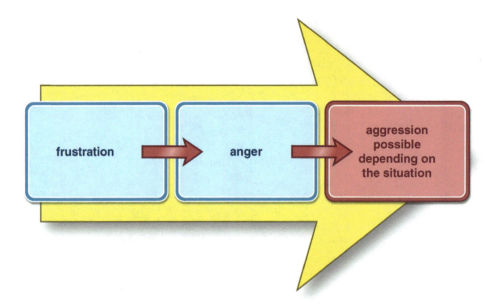

Figure 7.13   According to the Dollard and Miller frustration–aggression hypothesis, frustration leads to different degrees of anger, ranging from mild irritation to blind fury. Depending on the situation and the depth of emotion, frustration can also lead to aggressive behavior.

Territoriality   Another explanation, attributed to ethologists, is based on the assumption that we are aggressive by nature. Ethologists base this explanation on observations of aggression among nonhuman animals, and the assumption is that since aggression appears to be common among other animals, it must have a biological basis.

> **Territoriality:** Example of an innate or biological aggressive tendency.

According to this theory, certain stimuli in the environment serve as releasers for aggression. In some cases, the stimuli are highly specific and have clear survival or reproductive significance, as when bighorn sheep fight for the right to mate. In other cases, the stimuli are less specific, as in the case of **territoriality**. For example, male chimpanzees patrol defined geographic areas, intent on aggressively repelling any encroachment by males from other communities. Those who violate their boundaries risk death (Amsler, 2010). The survival value of many aggressive behaviors in nonhuman animals and their frequent instinct such as specificity (i.e., the fact that aggression usually occurs only in response to specific conditions) provide strong evidence that aggression in animals is at least partly genetically based.

The situation with humans, however, is not as clear. Although there is a possibility that we have (or had) instinctual tendencies toward aggressiveness, learning and environment affect so much of our behavior that "instinctual" tendencies like territoriality are difficult to isolate. For example,

© Kitch Bain/Shutterstock.com

some argue wars reflect territoriality (Fields, 2010) and others have suggested gang conflict might also be associated with territoriality (Deuchar & Holligan, 2010).

Still, the fact is that there are human societies where aggressive behavior is at an extreme minimum (e.g., the Zuni, the Hutterites, and the Amish); and there are others where it is at the opposite extreme (e.g., the Ik of Uganda, the Mundugumor of New Guinea, the Yanomamo of the Amazon). Although the existence of peace-loving societies does not prove we have no genetic tendencies toward aggression, it does indicate environmental and social factors are important.

Social Learning ⌞In addition to the frustration-aggression hypothesis and territoriality, the **social ⌟ learning theory** (see Chapter 4) is a widely supported theory ⌞to understand aggression. This theory⌟ argues that aggressive behavior is often learned as a result of observing aggressive models.

> **Social learning theory:** Argues aggression is a result of learning from models in our environment.

In a classic study looking at the effects of aggressive models on children, Bandura et al. (1961) exposed 3- to 6-year-old children to one of three experimental conditions. One group saw an adult being physically and verbally aggressive with a large, inflated "Bobo" doll (punching it, striking it with a mallet, kicking it, sitting on it, while making aggressive comments like "sock him in the nose. . . ," "throw him in the air. . . ," "knock him down"). A second group watched as the experimenter totally ignored the doll. And a control group saw the Bobo doll only in the testing part of the study, during which the children were observed as they interacted with the doll or played with other toys.

The results of this study clearly illustrate the effect of aggressive models. When left alone with the doll, children exposed to the aggressive model were significantly more aggressive than children exposed to nonaggressive models. And often, their aggression was precisely imitative: If the model punched the doll, that is what these children did; if the model kicked the doll instead, then that, too, is what they did. And, strikingly, those exposed to nonaggressive models engaged in far less aggressive behavior than those not exposed to any models at all (Figure 7.14).

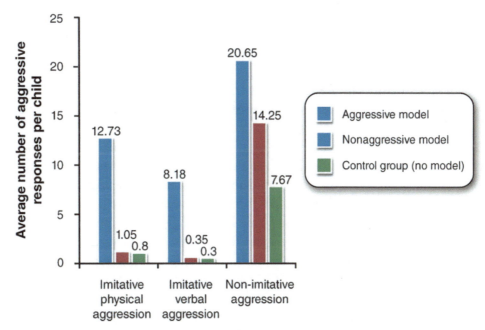

Figure 7.14 In the Bandura et al. (1961) study, children exposed to violent models consistently behaved more aggressively with the Bobo doll.

This study provides strong support for a social learning theory of aggression. And, in fact, many predictions based on social learning theory have been supported by research. For example, we would expect children who observe violence and aggression would themselves be more aggressive. In fact, that is often the case: Children who witness parental violence and abuse are more likely to be aggressive as adolescents (Ferguson et al., 2009). And there is evidence, as well, that violence in children's television programs tends to increase aggression among viewers (Linder & Gentile, 2009; Strasburger, 2009).

Physiology   We know that aggression, like all emotions, also has a physiological basis. For example, it appears aggression may be associated with hormones (injections of testosterone increase aggressiveness in monkeys); with olfaction (certain strains of mice respond aggressively to other mice who've been smeared with urine from mice that would ordinarily be aggressed upon); with brain damage or dysfunction or with stimulation of appropriate areas of the thalamus (rage can be produced in cats as a result of electrical stimulation); and with certain drugs (alcohol disinhibits aggression and is involved in a large number of violent crimes).

Research suggests at least five neurotransmitters and two hormones—the most important of which is testosterone—may be implicated in serious violent crimes (Beaver, 2010). But the fact that aggression has a physiological basis is not an adequate explanation for aggressive behavior because all aspects of human behavior have physiological bases. Nevertheless, knowledge of the physiological underpinnings of aggression, and of how these interact with the environment to produce aggression and violence, may prove useful in controlling extremes of violence (e.g., using psychosurgery and drugs; Figure 7.15).

Violence in Society

The most obvious instances of aggression in society are those involving overt acts of violence: rape, homicide, assault, and destruction of property. Interpersonal violence, which includes the first three of these, is committed primarily by males. The extent to which these acts can be attributed to frustration, deprivation, pain, or sex-related factors, and the extent to which character and personality disorders or other factors are involved, is not clear. There is little doubt, however, that each of these factors can play a significant role.

The incidence of violent crimes in Western industrialized societies appears to have declined somewhat during the last decades. Still, the incidence of violence is high, with a total of ⌊369⌋ violent crimes per 100,000 U.S. population in ⌊2018 (FBI, 2019).⌋

Violence in society is reflected not only in crime, but in international aggression as well. In the last century alone, well over half of all nations have been involved in war. Violence in the home is another example and one which is not always obvious. Child abuse presents one inexact index; the fact that 25% or more of all homicides and assaults involve members of the same family provides a second index. In fact, violence among intimate partners, surely a prime source of aggressive models for children, is alarmingly high. ⌊"About 1 in 4 women and nearly 1 in 10 men have experienced sexual violence, physical violence, and/or stalking by an intimate partner during their lifetime and reported some form of IPV-related impact" (CDC, 2019b). Additionally, "Over 43 million women and 38 million men experience psychological aggression by an intimate partner in their lifetime. Data from U.S. crime reports suggest that 16% (about 1 in 6) of homicide victims are killed by an intimate partner. The reports also found that nearly half of female homicide victims in the U.S. are killed by a current or former male intimate partner" (CDC, 2019b).

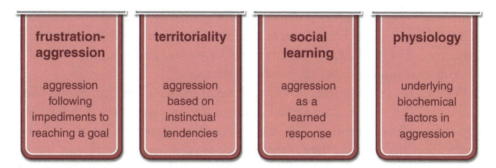

Figure 7.15 Four explanations for aggression. These aren't mutually exclusive, as aggression is often a function of several underlying factors.

Bystander Behavior

⌐One example of aggression that received a lot of press and spurred a lot of research in social psychology is the murder of Kitty Genovese. In the early hours of March 13, 1964, 28-year-old Kitty Genovese was stabbed to death outside of her apartment in New York City. While that alone may not be noteworthy, what was noteworthy is that an article published by the *New York Times* reported that 38 people claimed to have seen or heard the attack, but none of them came to her aid or even called the police (Gansberg, 1964; ⌐Latané & Darley, 1968). ⌐Even⌐ though her stalker took over half an hour to murder her, even leaving once and returning later to continue his attack, ⌐no one intervened to help and Kitty Genovese died.⌐

The Bystander Effect

This episode has been widely reported and has served as the basis for the conclusion that being part of a large group witnessing an act that requires intervention often serves to inhibit helping behavior. And although this appears to be true under some circumstances, unfortunately the Kitty Genovese case has often been exaggerated. Later investigation uncovered that there were considerably fewer than 38 eyewitnesses to the murder (some only heard the attack), that Kitty Genovese had been involved in loud altercations on other occasions, and that one witness did, in fact, call the police (Manning et al., 2007). Although this does not excuse the bystanders for not taking action, it is an explanation on why they didn't take action.

Still, there are other examples of what social psychologists call the **bystander effect**. Most of us would prefer to believe that the more

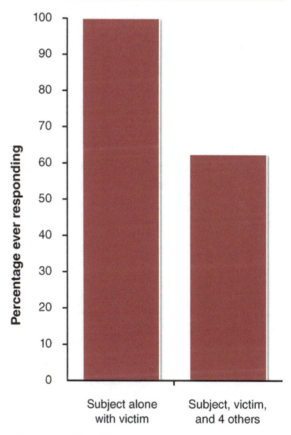

Figure 7.16 Effect of group size on the likelihood of responding in an emergency, based on Latané and Darley (1970).

Bystander effect: The more people who witness an event, the less likely they are to get help.

people who witness an event where someone desperately needs assistance, the more likely it is that one of them will help. Sadly, in some circumstances, the more witnesses there are, the less likely it is that someone will intervene. For instance, how many times have you just driven by a stalled car on the side of the road, thinking that someone else will provide assistance?

Latané and Darley (1970) conducted a series of experiments investigating the alleged apathy of bystanders. In one series of studies, participants alone in a room overheard an epileptic seizure apparently suffered by another "participant" (in fact, a tape-recorded "seizure"). Experimental conditions were such that participants either thought they're the only ones listening to the person having a seizure, or they believed there are other witnesses in different rooms. The dependent variable was whether or not the participant reported the seizure or otherwise tried to assist, and how long it took before helping behavior occurs.

As Figure 7.16 shows, all participants who thought they were alone with the victim responded by going to get help; in contrast, when participants thought there were four others besides the victim, only 62% responded.

In another experiment, participants were left in a room supposedly to wait for an interviewer (Latané & Darley, 1968). They were asked to fill out a questionnaire while waiting. Shortly thereafter, artificial smoke was blown into the room through a wall vent, continuing in irregular gusts, eventually filling the room, irritating the eyes, and making breathing difficult. If participants had not reported the smoke after 6 minutes, the experiment was discontinued and participants were debriefed. In one experimental condition, participants waited alone; in another, they waited with two other participants; and in a third, they were paired with two experimenter's confederates who had been instructed not to react to the smoke but to continue to fill out their questionnaires.

The results of these experiments were as expected: Participants alone reported the smoke 75% of the time; participants paired with two other participants reported it only 38% of the time and took longer before doing so. Most striking, only 1 of 10 participants paired with the confederates reported the smoke (Figure 7.17).

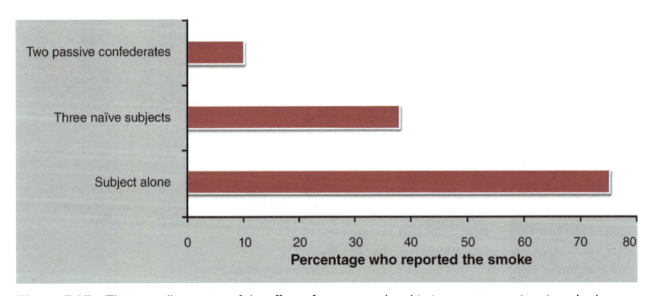

Figure 7.17 This is an illustration of the effect of group membership in emergency situations. In the Latané and Darley (1968) study, only 1 out of 10 participants reported the smoke when paired with two unalarmed confederates. Seventy-five percent reported it when left alone.

An Explanation

These studies indicate that individuals who have reason to believe themselves the only witnesses and hence the only immediate sources of intervention are more likely to involve themselves, either by reporting a potentially dangerous situation or by offering direct assistance. But when there are a number of apparent witnesses, people are more reluctant to become involved. However, this doesn't necessarily mean witnesses remain apathetic. In fact, there is considerable evidence they do care. Participants who did not report the "epileptic seizure" were often visibly shaken, their hands trembling, their faces pale and drawn.

A number of factors may be responsible for the greater reluctance of people to become involved when others could also be involved. They may not see themselves as the most competent; perhaps they simply assume someone else has already intervened; perhaps, too, there is a fear of making a wrong judgment and of appearing foolish.

Darley and Latané (1968) attribute the bystander effect to one of three sources (or a combination of these): (a) a process of diffusion of responsibility, where the presence of others reduces the cost of nonintervention; (b) a process of social influence, where the nonintervention of others leads the participant to misinterpret the seriousness of the situation; and, (c) a process of audience inhibition, where the presence of others brings about fear of making a wrong decision and acting unwisely.

In the example of the stalled car on the side of the road, we potentially have many reasons why we just drive by without calling for assistance. For example, we think that nearly every person has a mobile phone, and, therefore, we believe that if the person needed help, the person would call for help him- or herself. Or, perhaps we are misinterpreting the situation – the driver is taking a rest from driving. Finally, we worry about acting unwisely and if we put ourselves in danger by offering help.

How Common Is the Bystander Effect?

It is perhaps reassuring that many recent studies have not found a bystander effect, or have found a considerably less dramatic one than might have been expected. For example, McMahon and Farmer (2009) found a majority of student athletes would be willing to intervene in a case involving sexual violence. Reluctance to do so was often related to lack of skills required to intervene. Whether a person becomes a rescuer or remains a bystander may depend on level of moral development (DeZalia, 2009).

A person's willingness to help is often related to the seriousness of the situation. In their 2011 meta-analysis, Fischer et al. found reduced bystander inhibition (or increased helping behavior) in situations deemed as dangerous. There is one possible explanation for this phenomenon: Dangerous situations are often readily identified as such and contain less or no ambiguity.

As Latané and Darley (1970) noted, before bystanders intervene, they must notice an event, interpret it as an emergency, make a decision as to their personal responsibility, select a form of assistance, and implement that assistance. When Kitty Genovese was murdered, not all of the witnesses interpreted the situation as an emergency. Manning et al. (2007) reported three of the five witnesses who testified at the murder trial of the assailant reported they didn't immediately conclude a murder was taking place. And none of the court witnesses actually saw the stabbing. Nor is it likely that all who saw the situation as an emergency would then decide to take personal responsibility for bringing assistance—but one actually shouted and apparently frightened the attacker away, although he returned later. Others might have thought that someone else must have called the police—and apparently someone had! In the end, the incident, shocking though it might be given our implicit beliefs in the goodness of human nature, is not entirely surprising.

Choosing a form of assistance, other than calling on someone else (the police) for assistance, also presents a real problem. The man who was killing Kitty Genovese might not have hesitated to attack anyone else who might try to come to her assistance directly.

In summary, the Kitty Genovese case presents an extreme in which the possibility of intervening and the desirability of doing so are difficult and costly. It is not surprising that the likelihood of intervention is lessened by the presence of others who might also intervene.

Bystanders often ignore the plights of those who need help, especially if there are others around and if the cost of intervention is potentially high. Reassuringly, there are those, like this ⌐woman,⌐ who gladly help.

© i_am_zews/Shutterstock.com

PROSOCIAL BEHAVIORS

⌐In addition to the research that shows that the presence of bystanders can decrease helping behavior, there is also research that shows that real⌐ or imagined bystanders can have a powerful effect on ⌐engaging in⌐ prosocial behaviors such as helping and giving. For example, Potter et al. (2009) found that exposing students to models engaging in prosocial behavior—in this case, having to do with intervening in cases of sexual violence—increased the likelihood the students would later try to help if they witnessed similar episodes. ⌐Research on altruism, helping behavior, and giving to others has yielded much attention in recent years. Recent research has shown positive emotional and physical health effects of giving to others (Kahana et al., 2013; McClellan et al., 1993; Schwartz et al., 2003), as well as relationship and social benefits (Dew & Wilcox, 2013). The research is grounded in a long history of writings and research on altruism.

Altruism

⌐Altruistic behaviors are defined as any self-sacrificing behaviors that help another person. In its strictest sense, altruism is both *costly to the one performing the helping* and *helpful to the recipient*. Research in social psychology on altruism has focused largely on what would constitute altruistic behaviors and why people behave altruistically.

⌐Researchers who have studied supposed altruism⌐ among animals ⌐have developed⌐ a **sociobiological theory of altruism** championed by Richard Dawkins (1976/2006). According to this theory, altruism is nothing more than *genetic selfishness:* Genes can be thought of as having a selfish desire to ⌐continue to exist⌐ through reproduction

Altruistic behaviors: Self-sacrificing and helpful behaviors.

⌐Sociobiological⌐ altruism: An explanation for altruistic behavior that asserts organisms are helpful to others to ensure survival of the species.

and survival. As a result, they push organisms toward behaviors designed to ensure the survival of the genetic material of that species, though not necessarily of the individual that carries the genes. Thus, if an altruistic act increases the probability of reproduction of genes carried by the species, the survival needs of the species have been served. So, according to Dawkins's theory, an individual might take a risk in trying to save another if there is a chance that *both* will survive; however, there would be no net genetic advantage in being altruistic if one or the other will surely die.

ᒻWhile there is a tendency to risk one's life for those who share our genetic material, there is ample evidence that we also engage in altruistic behaviors for those we are not related to and for strangers. Therefore, biology (and the sociobiological theory of altruism)ᒻ clearly doesn't explain all altruism. Nor does it explain the fact that some people willingly help those in distress while others don't. In addition to biological altruism ᒻtheories,ᒻ there is what is labeled **reciprocal altruism**, in which an individual behaves altruistically with the expectation that others will reciprocate ᒻat some point. This can even be seen in animals.ᒻ For example, a monkey will willingly pick parasites off another's back—on the surface, a selfless, altruistic act. But later, the parasite-picking monkey will turn its back and expect the other to reciprocate.

> **Reciprocal altruism:** An explanation for altruistic behavior that asserts individuals are helpful to others because of the expectation this will be reciprocated.

ᒻSimilarly, we also sometimes do nice things for others with theᒻ expectation we might one day need them to reciprocate. ᒻOur motives for doing good for others is so that others will do good for us.ᒻ Some donate blood at least partly for that reason. ᒻAnother reason that has been shown for altruistic behaviors is that we do good things for others because it makes us feel good (Buchanan & Bardi, 2010). In these cases then, we can argue that doing altruistic thingsᒻ because it makes us feel good ᒻis not really altruism because it is not,ᒻ entirely selfless. ᒻSimilarly, otherᒻ studies of altruism indicate our altruistic behavior often depends on how altruistic we perceive others to be (Ellers & van der Pool, 2010). We are more likely to be altruistic if we think others are, or would be, under the same circumstances—a sort of positive bystander effect. These studies also reveal altruism is often related to the status of the actor, with higher-status individuals engaging in more altruistic behaviors (Liebe & Tutic, 2010). ᒻFrom these and other studies on altruism, we see that positive social behavior is not always as simply motivated or performed as we may think.ᒻ By definition, altruism goes beyond simple acts of warmth and kindness: it implies behavior where there is significant disadvantage to the doer or giver and clear potential advantage to the receiver.

What Does the Bible Say?

ᒻThere are many theories of altruistic behavior. From sociobiological to reciprocal theories, and arguments that we do good because it feels good have all been proposed and even moderately supported by research. But, none of the theories give us a complete picture of why altruistic behaviors exist. So, what does the Bible say? How would the Bible explain why altruism exists?

In a word, God.

The best example of a self-sacrificing act that was willingly done to benefit another can be seen in Jesus' death on the cross. As recorded in the New Testament, we see that Jesus willingly died a painful death on the cross so that our sins could be forgiven and we could go to heaven (something we could not do without payment for our sins). Jesus took our punishment so that we could live eternally in heaven.

Altruism is a construct that originates with God. And, it is a concept that we are instructed to model as we seek to model Jesus' behaviors and show Him to others. In many places throughout the Bible, God instructs to love others as ourselves and to do good for others with no concern of repayment, even if it costs us greatly (Leviticus 19:18; John 15:13; Philippians 2:3-4; Titus 3:14). Furthermore, He instructs us to do good for others quietly and to not brag about it (Luke 6:35). In fact, in Luke 6, Jesus rebuked the Pharisees for telling others of all the good they were doing for others. Helping others and giving to others, even at great personal cost, is something that God talks about a lot.

But, we also see in Scripture that the human heart is incapable of this type of pure altruism on it's own. Jeremiah 17:9 states that the human heart is "deceitful above all things, and desperately sick." Certainly not the place where unselfish love and care for another will originate. Scripture goes on to tell us that only through God Jesus and inviting Him into our hearts and behaviors can walk in the true altruism that He instructs (Galatians 2:20; Galatians 5:24; Colossians 1:9-10). Even Jesus Himself stated that "the Son can do nothing by himself; he can do only what he sees his Father doing, because whatever the Father does the Son also does" (John 5:19). Examination of the Bible shows us that altruism begins with God and is seen in us only when we reflect Him. And, while research on altruism gives us glimpses of pieces of this truth, it is only when we combine it with the Word of God that we get a complete understanding of what altruism is all about.

The Rules of Attraction

Another area of research that is important to social psychologists is research on interpersonal attraction, love, and relationships. **Interpersonal attraction** is generally considered "positive emotional evaluation of another person" (Montoya & Horton, 2014, p. 59). Interpersonal attraction can be thought of as the spectrum between liking and loving, and it appears to be strongly influenced by three things: proximity, similarity, and physical attraction.

Interpersonal attraction is strongly influenced by propinquity, similarity, and physical attraction.

© Syda Productions/Shutterstock.com

Propinquity

People in closer physical proximity (often referred to as **propinquity**) tend to have more in common and have much stronger ties than among those more physically distant (Hipp & Perrin, 2009). Propinquity, which is closely related to *similarity*, can describe stronger connection between people who attend the same churches, colleges, and clubs and go to the same beaches, bars, and bingos.

> **Interpersonal attraction:** Positive thoughts of another person that are strongly influenced by proximity, similarity, and physical attraction.

Similarity

In addition to propinquity, social psychologists have also researched whether liking is increased by similarity. For example, do birds of a feather flock together? Or, do opposites attract? Some early research speculated people are attracted to each other on the basis of their differences. Submissive people might be attracted to dominant people.

> **Propinquity:** Physical proximity; factor related to physical attraction.

Each might fulfill certain needs the other has. It is, however, not as logical to assume a highly aggressive individual will be attracted to a highly pacific individual or an extrovert will naturally gravitate toward an introvert, or, to carry the argument to its illogical extreme, the more dissimilar two individuals are, the more they will love each other.

In fact, research has found that similarity between people is ⌞more⌟ associated with attraction ⌞than dissimilarity.⌟ Newcomb (1961) provided a house for 17 male university students so he could study friendship patterns among them. Not surprisingly, roommates, regardless of similarity of interests and beliefs, tended to be attracted at the beginning. But as time passed and students got to know each other better, similarity gradually emerged as the most important factor in determining friendships.

Montoya and Horton (2013) conducted a meta-analytic review of 240 studies on similarity and attraction. The studies showed that attitude-similarity was important in interpersonal attraction, especially as it related to the degree of similarity and the awareness of attitude similarity. An older study of online attraction confirms these findings. Antheunis et al. (2010) looked at interaction patterns and social attraction among 704 members of a social networking site very similar to Facebook, MySpace, and Friendster. They found participants used three different strategies to reduce uncertainty about other members' attitudes, emotions, and behavior: *passive strategies* such as simply observing how the target person interacts with others; *active strategies* such as asking other people about the target person; and, most effective, *interactive strategies* where the two people interact directly. Interactive strategies often involve self-disclosure, which tends to elicit self-disclosure in the other person.

Results of this study indicate that in an online situation, knowing important things about the other person (reduction of uncertainty) is closely related to social attraction. Furthermore, degree of attraction is closely related to how similar each person thinks the other is. Montoya and Horton (2013) also found this was a consistent theme through other attitude-similarity studies.

People who are similar in important ways tend to like each other more than those who are less similar. For ⌞these,⌟ the beads, the headband, and the dress are loud signals of similarity.

© Nejron Photo/Shutterstock.com

Physical Attractiveness

Physical attractiveness is often ⌞another⌟ important variable ⌞in research on attraction.⌟ Walster et al. (1966) arranged for an elaborate "dating" experiment at the University of Minnesota involving 376 men and 376 women who were to attend a dance. Participants were unaware the dance had been arranged for experimental purposes. They were simply told they would be "computer matched" with a partner and were asked to fill out questionnaires for that purpose. Meanwhile, experimenters surreptitiously assigned them physical attractiveness ratings so as to divide them into three groups: ugly, average, and attractive. (In this age's more politically correct climate, it is unlikely that researchers would use the label *ugly* for those less physically attractive.)

Participants were then matched randomly except no woman was matched with a shorter partner. Of the 376 pairs thus formed, all but 40 actually attended the dance. During the intermission, some 2½ hours after the start of the dance, participants were asked to fill out an apparently anonymous questionnaire—which, of course, was not at all anonymous. It dealt with how much they liked their date, how attractive the date was, how comfortable the participant felt, how much the date seemed to like the participant, how similar the participant thought the date was in terms of attitudes and beliefs, how much effort each was putting into making sure that the other had a good time, and whether or not they were likely to date again. Actual frequency of subsequent dating was ascertained some 4 to 6 months later by contacting all participants directly.

The most important finding from this study was that of all the measures employed (intelligence, self-acceptance, extroversion, and a number of other scores in student files based on standardized tests such as the MMPI), physical attractiveness was the only significant variable in determining degree of social attraction. More attractive males and females were much less attracted to those classified as "ugly" or "average." Although members of the least attractive group would, in general, date anybody, they too said they preferred those more attractive.

That physical attractiveness is perceived as exceptionally important in interpersonal attraction is underlined in a study by Toma and Hancock (2010), which found online daters exaggerate their physical attractiveness in their self-descriptions. And the least attractive tend to exaggerate more than the more attractive.

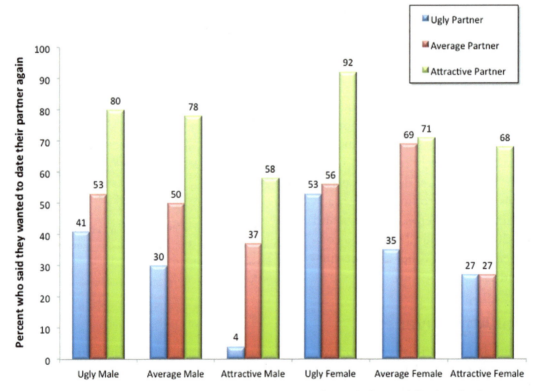

Figure 7.18 How important is physical attractiveness in dating behavior? Strikingly, the most attractive partners in a "random" dating study were those consistently more likely to be asked out again. Image courtesy of the author. Data from Walster et al. (1966). Importance of physical attractiveness in dating behavior. *Journal of Personality and Social Psychology, 4,* 508–516.

Graph courtesy of Darin Challacombe. Data Source: *Journal of Personality & Social Psychology.*

Seidman and Miller (2013) tracked eye movement across a Facebook page to determine what parts of the page participants focused on the most. Participants tended to pay more attention to personal information, such as likes or interests, on pages of males; conversely, participants focused more on the pictures and appearance of females' Facebook pages.

Physical attraction appears to be one of the most important factors at the beginning of a romantic relationship.

© pio3/Shutterstock.com

Liking and Loving

Freud (1914/1955) put it very simply: "[In] the last resort, we must begin to love in order not to fall ill, and we are bound to fall ill if, in consequence of frustration, we are unable to love" (p. 95).

How likely is it that we will fall ill if we cannot **love**? Science does not answer this question as confidently as have the poets. But then love was the province of the poet long before science claimed it. And even now, poets may know more about love than does science. Of the wonder and joy and all-consuming nature of love, the poets have had little doubt; however, about love's practical value, the poets remain

> **Love:** The province of poets rather than scientists. A strong, interpersonal attraction, says science: a combination of passion, intimacy, and commitment.

less certain. "True love," writes the poet Szymborska (1995), "Is it normal, is it serious, is it practical / What does the world get from two people who exist in a world of their own?" But we have little time for the poetry of love—here we deal only with its science.

Science provides us with ways of measuring, if not of completely understanding, love. For example, Rubin's (1970) *Loving and Liking Scales* provide a way of measuring interpersonal attraction. The scales are based on the assumption that those who like each other sense that they have things in common, evaluate each other positively, and appreciate each other's company. Items that indicate liking (but not loving) are items like *I think that _____ is unusually well adjusted,* or *I would highly recommend _____ for a responsible job.*

Loving implies deeper feelings, feelings of intense caring, strong attachment, and intimacy ⌐than liking.⌐ Love brings with it a degree of emotional interdependence, a quality of exclusiveness and absorption. If you simply like someone, that person doesn't dominate your thoughts and your dreams; nor are you concerned that someone else might also like the same person. Love, on the other hand, often brings with it a measure of fierce possessiveness and the possibility of jealousy and pain—perhaps the possibility of ecstasy as well. Rubin (1970) measures love with items such as *I feel that I can confide in _____ about virtually everything,* or *If I could never be with _____, I would feel miserable.*

A Model of Love

According to Sternberg (1986), interpersonal attraction ⌐and liking/love, specifically⌐ is no simple thing. There are at least eight varieties of ⌐love according to Sternberg (1986)⌐: nonlove, romantic love, liking, fatuous love, infatuation, companionship, empty love, and consummate love. What differentiates these states from one another is the combination of intimacy, passion, and commitment involved in each.

Accordingly, Sternberg has given us a **triangular theory of love**. But the triangle in this theory is not the classical male or male–female or female–female and male love triangle: It is the intimacy–passion–commitment triangle (Figure 7.19).

> **Triangular theory of love:** Sternberg's theory of loving involving commitment, passion, and intimacy.

In this model, *intimacy* refers to emotions that bring people closer together—emotions such as respect, affection, and support. Feelings of intimacy are what lead two people to want to share things, perhaps to disclose personal, private experiences and feelings. The more intimate you are with someone, the more likely you will be closer to them or spend time with them.

Passion is a strong, sometimes almost overwhelming, desire to be with another person. Passion is often, although not always, sexual. Sternberg suggests that passion is a feeling that builds rapidly but then gradually subsides. Sumter et al. (2013) showed higher passion in adults than in adolescents, with only a slight decline in passion for older adults. These findings contradict common thought that older adults have significantly less passion than younger adults.

Commitment implies a decision-making process and may involve either a short-term or a long-term decision. On a short-term basis, commitment requires making the decision that one is in love. From a long-term point of view, commitment involves deciding to cultivate and maintain the loving relationship. In practice, this often implies a decision to share living arrangements and sometimes the raising of a family, either in marriage or otherwise. In the Sumter et al. (2013) study, commitment increased proportionally in adolescents with age; however, the adult participants did not indicate any change in commitment as the adults aged.

Sternberg's (1986) theory of love holds that it is the particular combination of these three components—intimacy, passion, and commitment—that determines the nature of the relationship. As Figure 7.20 shows, for example, empty love involves commitment but is devoid of passion or of intimacy

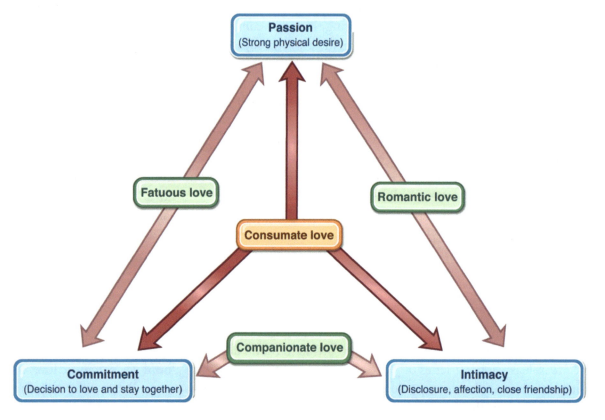

Figure 7.19   In Sternberg's triangle of love, different combinations of commitment, passion, and intimacy determine the nature of the love relationship.

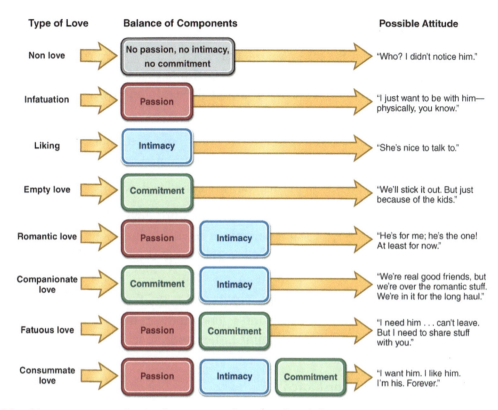

Type of Love	Balance of Components			Possible Attitude
Non love	No passion, no intimacy, no commitment			"Who? I didn't notice him."
Infatuation	Passion			"I just want to be with him— physically, you know."
Liking	Intimacy			"She's nice to talk to."
Empty love	Commitment			"We'll stick it out. But just because of the kids."
Romantic love	Passion	Intimacy		"He's for me; he's the one! At least for now."
Companionate love	Commitment	Intimacy		"We're real good friends, but we're over the romantic stuff. We're in it for the long haul."
Fatuous love	Passion	Commitment		"I need him . . . can't leave. But I need to share stuff with you."
Consummate love	Passion	Intimacy	Commitment	"I want him. I like him. I'm his. Forever."

Figure 7.20   How can you tell whether you really are in love? One way is to analyze your relationship in terms of the Sternberg model, looking at the balance among passion (physical attraction and desire), intimacy (affection, mutual disclosure), and commitment (conscious decision to love, to share, to be together).

("Okay, we'll stay together until the children are gone. Then goodbye!"). **Consummate love**, on the other hand, has all three components.

According to Sternberg, there is a pattern to the development of many relationships. Two individuals might begin with nonlove—no passion, commitment, or intimacy. In time, nonlove might give way to infatuation, which has passion but no commitment or intimacy—or perhaps to romantic love, which now adds intimacy but is still short of commitment. Eventually, consummate love might evolve as commitment is brought into the relationship. And perhaps the end result will be marriage or some other long-term commitment. You should remember this when you are sitting next to someone in class—that person may eventually become your spouse.

Even consummate love is not a static, unchanging thing. Sternberg (1986) points out that passion is usually very high early in a consummate relationship. But with the passage of time, it diminishes; at the same time, commitment and intimacy might increase. Research suggests that intimacy and commitment may be more important for a lasting love relationship than is passion (Madey & Rodgers, 2009).

> **Consummate love:** Love that has all three components from the triangular theory.

As Gibran says, the ways of love are hard and steep ... love carries no guarantees.

© Natali Glado/Shutterstock.com

POSITIVE PSYCHOLOGY

A Last Word to the Poets and Scientists

As we noted at the outset, while it is nice to believe that science has a grasp of love, it is possible that poets and sages know love better than science. ⌐And, it is definite that God knows love better than the poets, sages, and scientists. Nowhere can we find a clearer depiction and definition of love than in the Bible:

John 3:16: "For God so loved the world, that he gave his only Son, that whoever believes in him should not perish but have eternal life."

John 15:13: "Greater love has no one than this, that someone lay down his life for his friends."

I Corinthians 13:4-8a: "Love is patient and kind; love does not envy or boast; it is not arrogant or rude. It does not insist on its own way; it is not irritable or resentful; it does not rejoice at wrongdoing, but rejoices with the truth. Love bears all things, believes all things, hopes all things, endures all things. Love never ends."

I John 3:16-18: "By this we know love, that he laid down his life for us, and we ought to lay down our lives for the brothers. But if anyone has the world's goods and sees his brother in need, yet closes his heart against him, how does God's love abide in him? Little children, let us not love in word or talk but in deed and in truth."

I John 4:19: "We love because he first loved us."⌐

SUMMARY

The subject matter of social psychology deals with how thinking, feeling, and behavior are influenced by the real or imagined presence of others. In this chapter, we first looked at how attitudes ⌐are formed, changed, and how they⌐ influence behavior. We discussed the tendency to obey authority demonstrated in the Milgram studies and to assume socially accepted roles in the Stanford prison study. Next, the ⌐section⌐ examined human interactions, including those that are antisocial (aggression), prosocial (helping), and friendly. We concluded our discussion of social ⌐psychology⌐ with the topic of love, including various types and factors, and the impact of physical attraction. ⌐As you are beginning to see, the field of social psychology is full of research on how we relate to, interact with, and are affected by others. And, the Bible is equally full of instruction on how to interact with and love others well. Not included in this chapter is research on forgiveness, gratitude, and marriage. All are topics explored by social psychologists and all are topics discussed by God in His Word. There is much to be learned and explored about the social world through both research in social psychology and through the Bible.

⌐In conclusion, we are social creatures. We were created for relationship with God and with each other. In fact, God stated early in creation that it is not good for man to be alone (Genesis 2:18). And throughout human history we have repeatedly seen this to be true. Relationships are important to the wellness of mankind. And not only have relationships and the social world been created by God, but He has instructed us how to behave in them throughout His Word. And, science has also studied much of it and confirmed both the importance of relationships to human functioning as well as how best to operate in our relationship with others.⌐

Chapter 8

Psychological Disorders and Treatments

LEARNING OBJECTIVES

- ❏ Define mental illness.
- ❏ Differentiate between the terms *insanity* and *mental disorder*.
- ❏ Identify characteristics of the principal models used to understand mental disorders.
- ❏ List the neurodevelopmental disorders
- ❏ ⌐Review⌐ the symptoms of the principal *anxiety disorders*.
- ❏ Identify characteristics of *disruptive, impulse-control,* and *conduct disorders* in childhood.
- ❏ Identify the most common mood disorders.
- ❏ Differentiate between bipolar disorder and schizophrenia.
- ❏ Name the main sexual and gender identity disorders.
- ❏ Describe the characteristics of different personality disorders.
- ❏ List the main approaches to therapies for mental disorders.
- ❏ ⌐Explain Christian approaches to mental illness.⌐

Research and treatment of mental illness has improved significantly over the past 50 years. What was once a somewhat taboo topic in both society and in science has become a robust area of discourse with many advancements in the science and treatment of mental illness. Even in the church, where many used to fear discussions of mental illness, there has been much progress toward understanding and helping those who suffer.

In this chapter, we review different types of mental disorders, as well as review research in the etiology and treatment of mental illness. A discussion of Christian approaches to mental illness is also included as you get a taste of where we are today in the prevention, diagnosis, and treatment of mental disorders.

▶ CHAPTER 8 OVERVIEW

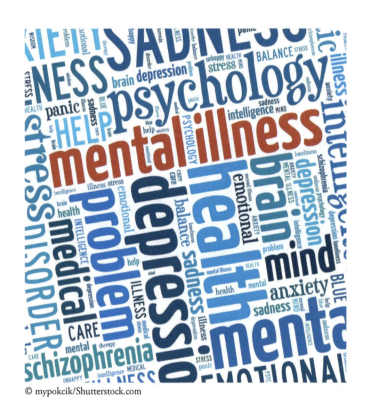

© mypokcik/Shutterstock.com

CURRENT DEFINITIONS AND MODELS

The American Psychiatric Association (2015) defines a **mental disorder** as a "major disturbance in an individual's thinking, feelings, or behavior that reflects a problem in mental function" (p. 1). Mental disorders often create problems in functioning at home, at work, at school, and in relationships.

> **Mental disorder:** A major disturbance in an individual's thinking, feelings, or behavior that reflects a problem in mental function.

It should be noted that it is normal to experience certain changes in mood or behavior due to loss, death of a loved one, or major life change. It is also normal to have moments of feeling sad, anxious, or angry in certain situations. These are not considered mental disorders. Mental disorders have a very clear and specific list of symptoms that define them and a clear classification provided by the American Psychiatric Association (not to be confused with the other APA, the American *Psychological* Association). In this chapter, we will discuss different classifications of mental disorders and the nature, onset, and implications of characteristic symptoms of each.

Before we begin our exploration of mental disorders, there is another term commonly used when we discuss mental health that we should define before we get started: insanity. It should be noted that **insanity** is a legal term, defined by law and determined by a court in consultation with mental health experts. Hence it is a legal issue that might determine whether a convicted person is *responsible* for a crime. Individuals found not guilty by reason of insanity are frequently provided with treatment rather than punishment. Although innocent by reason of insanity is a very popular theme in today's media, in reality it is rarely used in criminal cases.

The term *insanity* is seldom used in medicine and psychology, although it has been retained by the courts. The terms *abnormality, mental illness, personality disorders, psychological disorders, emotional disorders, mental disorders,* or other more specific descriptions are preferred.

How we look at and define mental disorders depends greatly on the **models** we use. In one sense, models are guides, or ways of looking at things. Models tell us what to look for when we're trying to understand, explain, and define what we mean by mental disorders. Among the various models used for this purpose are the *statistical*, the *medical/biological*, the *behavioral*, the *cognitive*, and the *psychodynamic*.

> **Insanity:** A legal term defined by law and determined by a court in consultation with mental health experts.

© Stuart Miles/Shutterstock.com

> **Models:** Guides or ways of looking at whether a behavior is abnormal or not.

The Statistical Model

One way of determining whether a behavior is abnormal is in relation to the prevalence of the behavior in the general population. According to this model, those whose behaviors or personality traits violate social norms and are therefore demonstrably different from the majority are abnormal in a statistical sense (Figure 8.1). Significant departure from normality with respect to emotional functioning, social behavior, perception, and so on may be directly related to mental health. Deviance is evident in behaviors and characteristics that have low frequency. To be afraid of red dirt is deviant because most people are not afraid of red dirt. But if you live where everybody knows red dirt is toxic, not being afraid of it might be abnormal.

The statistical model is useful in that it provides an objective method for identifying abnormal behavior. For example, **intellectual disabilities** are defined as a significant departure from average intellectual and adaptive functioning. Similarly, disorders such as autism spectrum disorder and **specific learning disabilities** are all defined in terms of behaviors that are not age-appropriate in a statistical sense.

> **Intellectual disabilities:** A significant departure from average intellectual and adaptive functioning.
>
> **Specific learning disabilities:** A developmental disorder marked by impairments in cognitive skills such as reading, writing, arithmetic, or mathematical skills.

Medical/Biological Models

Medicine deals with physical (organic) malfunctions due to injury, infection, chemical imbalances, genetics, or other causes, and can often be treated surgically or chemically. The medical view of

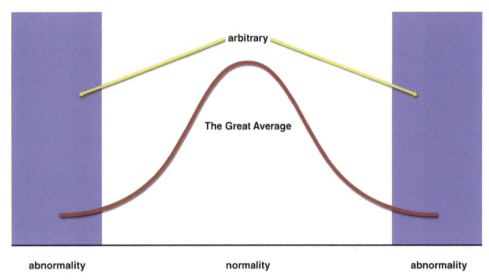

Figure 8.1   The statistical model of abnormality.

psychological malfunction is analogous. Accordingly, a psychological abnormality is sometimes seen as a disease or illness caused by internal factors (infection, system malfunction, or genetics) and open to the same sorts of treatment that might be employed for organic malfunctions. The finding of the high heritability of disorders such as bipolar disorder and schizophrenia suggests, at least for these diseases, there may often be an underlying genetic cause (Walsh et al., 2008). For example, there is evidence ⌊from both premolecular and molecular genetic studies that genetics is a strong risk factor for schizophrenia. While early, nonmolecular twin studies suggested⌋ as much as one third of the risk of acquiring schizophrenia is due to identifiable genetic variations, ⌊recent molecular genetic research suggests that the genetic contribution is clear, but complex, and more research is needed to identify it fully (Henriksen et al., 2017).⌋

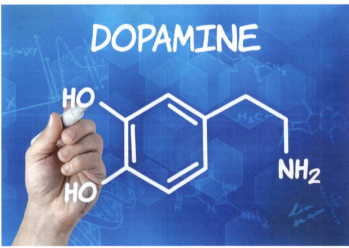

© Zerbor/Shutterstock.com

The most obvious advantage of the ⌊medical/biological⌋ models is that they encourage the search for specific organic causes of various disorders and suggest means of dealing with them. They look not only at genes as a possible cause, but also at neurological functioning and especially at the role various neurotransmitters play. The development of highly effective drug therapies for disorders such as depression is related directly to information that neuroscience provides about the role of neurotransmitters in areas of the brain involved in emotion.

Behavioral Models

The principal difference between ⌞medical/biological⌟ models of abnormality and the behavioral models lies in their explanations of causes. Whereas ⌞medical/biological⌟ models ascribe abnormality to internal causes such as disease, injury, or chemical imbalances, behavioral models claim abnormal behavior is learned, just as is any other behavior (Watson, 1916). Most behavioral models are premised on conditioning theories, or variations thereof, and concentrate principally on manifestations of abnormal behavior without paying much attention to supposed causes. Whereas ⌞medical/biological⌟ models lead to treatments designed to eliminate the causes of malfunctioning, behavioral models concentrate instead on "unlearning" unacceptable behavior and learning (or relearning) more "normal" forms of behavior.

Cognitive Models

The cognitive interpretation of psychological disorders revolves around the notion that these disorders involve cognitive problems that are often expressed in distortions of reality (Beck, 2008). Patients view themselves as worthless, unhealthy, and unhappy, have unrealistic appraisals of their future, and react inappropriately. Distorted views of reality are, in fact, one of the principal characteristics of the more serious mental disorders.

Contemporary cognitive models also take into account the interaction of genetic and neurological events with cognitive problems. For example, neuropsychological research provides a great deal of evidence indicating that an overactive amygdala may be associated with a higher risk of depression (Gaffrey et al., 2011). And genomics research (i.e., research on the contributions of genes) has discovered a variety of links between a genome (genetic complement) and a variety of disorders, including *bipolar* disorder (e.g., Choi et al., 2011).

Although the cognitive model considers these genetic and neurological causes, the emphasis is on the *cognitive* (intellectual) distortions underlying maladaptive behavior. For example, in this view, overreaction to stress may be genetically based, but it is mediated by cognitive distortions. Accordingly, therapies are directed toward altering individuals' perceptions of the world and of themselves—in other words, toward changing cognitions.

What Does the Bible Say?

⌞In much of his writings, the Apostle Paul talks about thinking. In many of his letters to churches, Paul discusses the importance of thinking patterns and urges his followers to have healthy mindsets.

Romans 12:2 ESV

"Do not copy the behavior and customs of this world, but let God transform you into a new person by changing the way you think. Then you will learn to know God's will for you, which is good and pleasing and perfect."

2 Corinthians 10:5 ESV

"We demolish arguments and every pretension that sets itself up against the knowledge of God, and we take captive every thought to make it obedient to Christ."

Philippians 4:8 ESV

"Whatever is noble, whatever is right, whatever is pure, whatever is lovely, whatever is admirable—if anything is excellent or praiseworthy—think about such things."

Even before neuroscience or social cognitive theory, God was instructing us, through His Word, to be mindful of how we think. Consistent with Cognitive Models of mental disorders, often times our mental problems are due to faulty thinking patterns and distortions of truth. Attention to our thinking patterns and changing faulty thinking patterns is the foundation of cognitive approaches to mental disorders. Just as Paul was aware of that and wrote about it in many of his letters, so also contemporary scholars recognize the importance of thinking patterns as contributors to some disorders and have developed methods to help change individual's cognitions.⌐

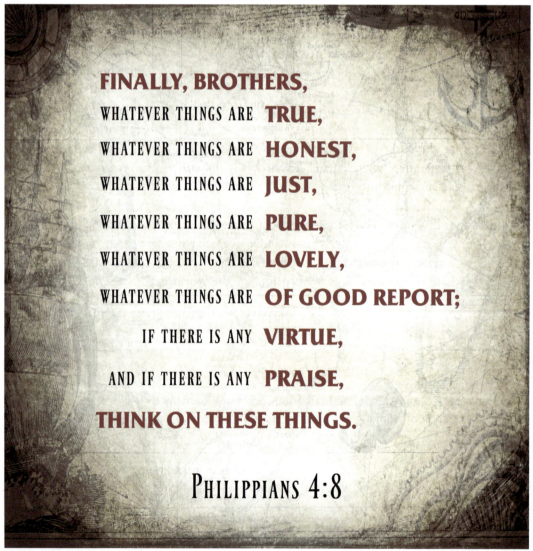

© TheBiblePeople/Shutterstock.com

Psychodynamic Models

The *psychodynamic* model describes how our basic libidinal urges (*id*) are continually being impeded by our immediate circumstances (*ego*) as well as by the fact that society does not permit unbridled expression of sexuality or aggression (*superego*). ⌐Based on the Psychodynamic theory (presented in Chapter 7), this model of mental disorders suggests that the conflict that exists among the id, ego, and superego produces anxiety in an individual, which then can manifest in different ways. Furthermore, defense mechanisms (i.e., denial, regression, sublimation, etc.) emerge to reduce this anxiety.⌐

If the anxiety is sufficiently severe, or if there is an overreliance on defense mechanisms, the result may be mental disorders of various kinds. Also, if the individual stays stuck in a developmental stage or regresses back to an earlier stage, development is said to be abnormal.

Which Model?

The ⌐existence of⌐ various models ⌐shows⌐ how complicated human behavior and thought can be. It is not possible to say one of the models is correct and the others not; nor is it possible to state categorically that one is more useful than any other. Each leads to a different view of mental disorders, and each leads to different forms of intervention or treatment.

The statistical model is useful in providing a relatively objective means of identifying bizarre, unconventional behavior, although its value in increasing our understanding of abnormal behavior or our ability to deal with it is clearly limited. The statistical model is primarily useful as a descriptive tool but does not help explain *why* an individual may display abnormal behavior.

Different models of mental disorders provide different explanations and different treatments. Most agree that

© light poet/Shutterstock.com

mental disorders involve problems in coping with the world and, as in the case of the girl shown here, significant distress and unhappiness. Medical models are valuable in providing methods for identifying and describing malfunctions, and often in providing specific treatments for them, as is clear in the widespread use of medications that are often highly effective treatments for a variety of mental disorders. The principal contribution of the behavioral and cognitive models has been the development of systematic learning-based therapies that have been highly effective in many situations. Psychodynamic approaches, despite their historical influence, tend to be imprecise and speculative. The various models of mental disorders are summarized in Table 8.1.

What Does the Bible Say?

Is there a Christian model to mental disorders?

⌐Table 8.1 details the major models of mental disorders within the field of Psychology today. As stated in the descriptions, each one focuses on different explanations, causes, or treatments. As can be seen in these models, there is reliance on statistics, genetics, and science to understand mental illness, and each model does help us understand mental disorders more so that we can help people who suffer from them.

There is something missing, however, in these leading models of mental disorders:

God.

As you learned in Chapter 1, there is brokenness that exists in the world because of sin. Although God created the world as perfect, Adam and Eve sinned and as a result, God's perfect creation became imperfect. Man became broken—that includes our minds, our bodies, and our mental health.

A Christian model of mental disorders understands that human behavior, mental illness, social relationships, cognitive processes, and a host of other things we've studied in this book are broken due to sin. Mental illness, like physical illness, is evidence of brokenness in the world. But, a Christian model also asserts that because of Jesus' death, burial, and resurrection, we are being restored and made whole; we will be made perfect again when we, as believers of Jesus Christ, are reunited with God when we die. But the hope of a Christian model does not only come after we leave this Earth. The hope is also found in the truth that we can seek guidance, hope, purpose, and healing from Jesus on this Earth, before we are reunited with Him in death. Christian counselors and psychologists can use the information from science about the causes and useful treatments of mental illness along with the hope and teachings of the Bible to help people with a variety of mental disorders. Mental illness, like physical illness, is evidence of brokenness in the world, but as Christians, we have been given hope to overcome that brokenness through Jesus Christ.

CLASSIFICATIONS OF DISORDERS

The *Diagnostic and Statistical Manual of Mental Disorders*, 5th Edition (*DSM-5*), of the American Psychiatric Association (2013) presents classifications of mental disorders in terms of categories, severity, and distinguishing characteristics (specifiers) of each disorder. The *DSM* is used extensively in psychiatric diagnosis.

The *DSM* is the handbook used by health care professionals in the United States and much of the world as the authoritative guide to the diagnosis of mental disorders. The *DSM* contains descriptions, symptoms, and other criteria for diagnosing mental disorders. It provides a common language for clinicians to communicate about their patients and establishes consistent and reliable diagnoses that can be used in the research of mental disorders. It also provides a common language for researchers to study the criteria for potential future revisions and to aid in the development of medications and other interventions.

The *DSM-5* presents 22 separate major categories. Since its first edition, the *DSM* has been revised regularly, often adding new disorders and removing or combining others as new scientific evidence emerges about the nature of mental disorders. The most recent revision restructured the format, emphasizing a more dimensional approach to mental disorders adopting the premise that most mental disorders present themselves along a continuum of symptoms and severity.

Diagnostic and Statistical Manual of Mental Disorders: A handbook used by health care professionals in the United States and much of the world as the authoritative guide to the diagnosis of mental disorders by classification in terms of categories, severity, and distinguishing characteristics of each disorder.

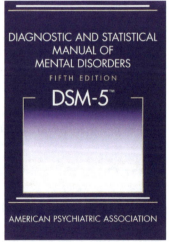

Reprinted with permission from the *Diagnostic and Statistical Manual of Mental Disorders*, Fifth Edition. Copyright © 2013. American Psychiatric Association. All Rights Reserved.

Table 8.1   Models of Mental Disorders

Model	Abnormality	What the Therapist Looks For	Treatment Approach
Statistical	A rare behavior	Uncommon behavior in a statistical sense	None. The statistical model identifies abnormal behavior but does not provide treatment.
Medical/ Biological	System malfunction	Organic, systemic, or genetic basis	Biological therapies treat abnormal behavior by looking for the biological cause of the behavior. A common example is drug therapy.
Behavioral	Learned behavior	Symptoms, not causes	Learning therapies that operate on the premise that bad behaviors can be eliminated and more appropriate and effective behaviors can be learned.
Cognitive	Inappropriate cognitions (beliefs, thoughts, perceptions)	Irrational or inappropriate beliefs about self or others	Cognitive therapies attempt to change how we think about and view our world, sometimes through learning more effective ways to view our problems.
Psychodynamic	Psychic conflicts, anxiety	History, relationships	Psychodynamic therapies may look for unconscious thoughts and urges and the resulting influence on behavior.

One of the important criteria for most *DSM-5* categories of mental disorders is the condition must present significant problems for the individual that cause a great deal of distress or impairment in their lives. The *DSM-5* classifications are summarized in Table 8.2.

The *DSM-5* presents well-defined criteria for diagnosing disorders. Clinicians do not need to rely on their interpretation of what is meant by a classification; they need only determine whether certain symptoms are present and apply relatively definite rules for making the diagnosis.

Today, the *DSM-5* is widely used by health care professionals. Such a detailed classification system is enormously useful in enabling researchers and clinicians to communicate and to understand what it is they are studying and treating. It provides a common language for describing mental disorders and a common set of criteria for identifying them.

TABLE 8.2   Major Categories of Mental Disorders According to the *DSM-5* of the American Psychiatric Association

Mental Disorder	DSM-5 Diagnostic Characteristics	Example
Neurodevelopmental Disorders	These disorders appear during childhood and are characterized by developmental problems that interfere with how we relate to others or perform in school or our jobs.	Intellectual Disabilities, Communication, Autism Spectrum, Attention-Deficit/ Hyperactivity, Specific Learning Disorders and Motor Disorders

(Continued)

Table 8.2 Major Categories of Mental Disorders According to the *DSM-5* of the American Psychiatric Association *(Continued)*

Mental Disorder	*DSM-5* Diagnostic Characteristics	Example
Schizophrenia Spectrum and Other Psychotic Disorders	These disorders are defined by problems in one or more of five areas: delusions, hallucinations, disorganized thinking, grossly disorganized or abnormal motor behaviors.	Delusional, Schizophrenia, Schizoaffective and Catatonic Disorders
Bipolar and Related Disorders	Disorders in this category are characterized by significant mood swings between periods of depressive and manic episodes.	Bipolar Disorders and Cyclothymic
Depressive Disorders	This disorder features long periods of sad, empty, or irritable mood, accompanied by changes in our feelings and thinking that significantly affect our ability to function.	Disruptive Mood Dysregulation, Depressive Disorders, and Premenstrual Dysphoric
Anxiety Disorders	These disorders center on long and very strong feelings of fear and dread. They go beyond normal reactions to danger or stress.	Anxiety Disorders, Phobias, Panic Disorders
Obsessive–Compulsive and Related Disorders	People with these disorders struggle with persistent thoughts, urges, or images that are experienced as intrusive and unwanted or repetitive behaviors or mental acts that an individual feels driven to perform.	Obsessive–Compulsive, Body Dysmorphic, Hoarding, Trichotillomania, and Excoriation
Trauma- and Stressor-Related Disorders	Individuals with this disorder experience abnormal amounts of distress following a traumatic or stressful event.	Posttraumatic Stress, Acute Stress, Adjustment and Reactive Attachment Disorders
Dissociative Disorder	Dissociative Disorders are characterized by a disruption of one's consciousness, memory, identity, emotion, perception, body representation, motor control, and behavior.	Dissociative Identity, Dissociative Amnesia, and Depersonalization/Derealizaton Disorders
Somatic Symptoms and Related Disorders	The common feature of these disorders is the prominence of physical symptoms associated with a great deal of distress and impairment. Bodily symptoms are the major focus of these disorders for which there is no real medical reason.	Somatic Symptom, Illness Anxiety, Fictitious Disorder and Conversion Disorder
Feeding and Eating Disorders	Feeding and Eating Disorders involve serious problems of eating-related behaviors resulting in the significant impairment of one's physical health or psychosocial functioning.	Pica, Rumination Disorder, Anorexia Nervosa, Bulimia Nervosa, and Binge Eating

Table 8.2 Major Categories of Mental Disorders According to the *DSM-5* of the American Psychiatric Association *(Continued)*

Mental Disorder	*DSM-5* Diagnostic Characteristics	Example
Elimination Disorders	Elimination Disorders involve the inappropriate elimination of urine or feces.	Enuresis and Encopresis
Sleep–Wake Disorders	Individuals with these disorders typically present with sleep–wake complaints regarding the quality, timing and amount of sleep resulting in problems with their daily functioning.	Insomnia, Narcolepsy, Apnea, Sleep Arousal or Behavior Disorders and Restless Legs Syndrome
Sexual Dysfunctions	This group of disorders is characterized by significant problems in a person's ability to respond sexually or to experience sexual pleasure, causing distress for the individual or problems in relationships.	Interest/Arousal Disorders, Orgasm Disorders, and Ejaculation Disorders
Gender Dysphoria	Gender Dysphoria is a condition where a person experiences discomfort or distress because there is a mismatch between their biological sex and gender identity. Individuals with this disorder feel that they are the wrong sex.	Gender Dysphoria
Disruptive, Impulse-Control, and Conduct Disorders	Disorders in this category involve problems in the self-control of emotions and behaviors. They show up in behaviors that violate the rights of others and/or bring the individual into significant conflict with social norms or authority figures.	Oppositional Defiant Disorder, Intermittent Explosive, Conduct Disorder, Pyromania, and Kleptomania
Substance-Related and Addictive Disorders	Substance-Related Disorders encompass ten different classes of drugs plus one nonsubstance related disorder—gambling. The essential feature of this disorder is that the individual continues using a substance despite significant physical, psychological or social problems or, with gambling, continues that behavior despite significant economic or personal problems.	Substance Use Disorders and Substance-Induced Disorders plus Gambling Disorder
Neurocognitive Disorders	This category of disorders includes the group of disorders in which the primary problem is a big and dramatic decline in the ability to think, problem solve, and remember.	Delirium, Alzheimer's, Traumatic Brain Injury

(Continued)

Table 8.2   Major Categories of Mental Disorders According to the *DSM-5* of the American Psychiatric Association *(Continued)*

Mental Disorder	*DSM-5* **Diagnostic Characteristics**	Example
Personality Disorders	These disorders represent a unique and long-lasting pattern of thoughts, feelings, and outward behaviors that are very different from what is usually expected from our culture.	Antisocial, Avoidant, Borderline, Narcissistic, Obsessive–Compulsive, Schizotypal
Paraphilic Disorders	These disorders involve strong and persistent sexual interests other than sexual interest in genital stimulation or what is considered normal sexual behavior between consenting adults.	Voyeurism, Exhibitionism, Sadism, Masochism, Pedophilic, Fetishism and Frotteurism

THE MOST COMMON DISORDERS

Mental disorders are common in all parts of the world. An estimated ⌐one in four⌐ Americans ages 18 and older suffer from a diagnosable mental disorder ⌐at some point in their lifetime (Johns Hopkins Medicine, 2020⌐; Kessler et al., 2005; Lopez-Duran, 2011). ⌐According to the National Institute of Mental Health (NIMH), approximately 46 million adults live with at least one mental illness (2017).⌐ According to a 2011 Centers for Disease Control and Prevention (CDC) report, mental illnesses account for a larger proportion of disability in developed countries than any other group of illnesses, including cancer and heart disease. Twenty percent of children in the United States will be diagnosed with a mental illness in a given year.

▶ **GET TO KNOW A CLINIC PSYCHOLOGIST**

Many people suffer from more than one mental disorder at a given time. Nearly half (45%) of those individuals with any mental disorder meet criteria for two or more disorders (Kessler et al., 2005). ⌐In the U.S. National Comorbidity Survey, 51% of patients with a diagnosis of major depression also had at least one anxiety disorder. Furthermore, when⌐ nicotine dependence is included among substance-abuse disorders, it becomes the most frequently diagnosed disorder, at 35% (National Comorbidity Survey Replication [NCS-R], 2010). ⌐There are many mental disorders that fall under several classification types. Oftentimes, they share common etiologies and research is ongoing to understand them all. There are far too many to review within this introductory text, so we will look at some of the most common classifications of disorders before looking at related therapies.⌐

NEURODEVELOPMENTAL DISORDERS

There are a number of disorders with onset in the developmental period, usually appearing early in childhood. The disorders are characterized by a range of developmental deficits in both specific and global areas of function. They produce impairments of personal, social, academic, or occupational functioning.

⌐Neurodevelopmental Disorders is a new classification section in the *DSM-5* and has replaced the *DSM-IV* TR section "Disorders usually first diagnosed in infancy, childhood, or adolescence." Within the Neurodevelopmental Disorders category are Intellectual Disabilities, Communication Disorders, Autism Spectrum Disorder, Attention-Deficit/Hyperactivity Disorder, Specified Learning Disorder, Motor Disorders, and other Neurodevelopmental Disorders. In this section, we discuss Intellectual Disorders, Autism Spectrum Disorder, and Attention Deficit/Hyperactivity Disorder.

Intellectual Disabilities

Within the classification heading Neurodevelopmental Disorders, there are several intellectual disabilities that are identified. Among them is **Intellectual Developmental Disorder (IDD)**. The term IDD is used because it has less of a negative connotation or stigma than the term used in previous classification manuals—retardation. The essential features of this disorder are below average intelligence or mental ability and impairment in everyday adaptive functioning when compared to individuals of similar age. Deficit in intellectual functions involve such things as reasoning, problem solving, abstract thinking, judgment, academic learning, and learning from experience. **Adaptive functioning** refers to an inability to meet developmental and sociocultural standards for personal independence and social responsibility in activities of daily life such as communication, social participation, and independent living. The deficits of those with IDD can range from mild, moderate, severe, to profound.

> **Intellectual Developmental Disorder (IDD):** A neurodevelopmental disorder characterized by deficits in general intellectual functioning, involving things such as reasoning, problem-solving, abstract thinking, judgment, academic learning, and learning from experience.
>
> **Adaptive functioning:** An inability to meet developmental and sociocultural standards for personal independence and social responsibility in activities of daily life such as communication, social participation, and independent living.

The cause of IDD typically involves something interfering with normal brain development. This can include genetic conditions, problems during pregnancy or childbirth, illness or injury, or other unidentified causes. In fact, in many cases, the cause of intellectual disability in children is unknown. There is no real cure for individuals with IDD. There is a wide variation of functioning and, depending on the degree of impairment, those individuals with mild IDD may be able to live independently with some help and supervision. Those individuals with profound IDD may have to be placed in special programs or institutions.

Autism Spectrum Disorder

One of the biggest changes to the Neurodevelopmental Disorders section in the *DSM-5* is how Autism Spectrum Disorder is classified and discussed. Previously, the diagnostic category for these disorders was "Pervasive Developmental Disorder" with subgroupings of autistic disorder, pervasive developmental disorder, Asperger's disorder, childhood disintegrative disorder, Rett's disorder, and pervasive developmental disorder not otherwise specified. Changes were made in the newest edition of the *DSM* due to research and discussion on the reliability and validity of the previous classification system. Neuroimaging research, genetic research, and case studies were all used to update the classification system and more clearly, in their minds, organize these disorders.

What Does the Bible Say?

Science is always changing. God's Word does not.

As you have seen so far in this chapter, the classification system of mental disorders has changed quite a bit over time. We are already on the fifth edition since its first publication in 1952. The *DSM* was originally developed out of a need for a common language and understanding of mental disorders so that clinicians could communicate well about them and ultimately treat people suffering from these disorders.

However, as science is conducted and technological advancements in research (and God) allow us to understand more about the brain and genetics, our views of disorders change as well. Also, as societal values and norms change, the classification of what is "abnormal" also has seen change. When human wisdom on mental disorders changes, the *DSM* changes as well.

You may be wondering, as Christians, what should we do with that?

Think back to the stair-step chart presented in Chapter 1. It is essential to put science and human logic/wisdom in its proper place. Although science has allowed us to uncover many truths about how God has ordered His creation, it is incomplete knowledge. Especially when studying humans (who are very complex) and mental disorders that affect us. It takes time to uncover all of the truths hidden in us. Sometimes we are wrong in how we collect the data, think about the data, or conclude things from the data. That is true in all research and it is particularly true as we attempt to understand mental disorders. Therefore, it is very important to remember that when you read research.

Additionally, not only is science incomplete in its understanding of human behavior and mental disorders, science also cannot tell us whether something is right or wrong. Understanding that a certain pattern of behaviors and causes exists within humans is not the same thing as deciding whether that pattern of behaviors is right. There are many things that we do that are not morally correct according to the Bible, and just because we can understand where they come from or how they manifest in human beings doesn't mean that the behavior is right.

So when you see classifications changing as we have seen in the *DSM* and as we see scientific knowledge changing over time, be reminded that science is incomplete and fallible. However, God's Word is infallible and never changes. Therefore, remember to keep God's unchanging Word as the authority over an ever-changing scientific community as you explore a variety of topics in Psychology.

The central features of **Autism Spectrum Disorder (ASD)** are persistent, pervasive, and sustained impairments in how an individual interacts with or communicates with others. It usually appears very early during childhood. Studies have shown that parents of children with ASD notice a problem before their child's first birthday and differences in social, communication, and fine motor skills are evident from 6 months of age (Bolton et al., 2012). Individuals with ASD may display repetitive patterns of behavior, interest, or activity. The problems in communication and interacting with others are big and lifelong. People with ASD just cannot get involved with others and share their thoughts and feelings. They make little eye contact, tend to look and listen less to people in their environment or fail to respond to other people, do not readily seek to share their enjoyment of toys or activities, and respond unusually when shown anger, distress, or affection.

> **Autism Spectrum Disorder (ASD):**
> A neurodevelopmental disorder of varying severity characterized by persistent, pervasive, and sustained impairments in how an individual interacts with or communicates with others, often accompanied by repetitive patterns of thought and behavior.

According to recent estimates from the CDC (2018), the incidence of ASD has increased dramatically in recent years and occurs in all racial, ethnic, and socioeconomic groups. Approximately 1 in 59 children has been identified with ASD. ASD is diagnosed four times more often in boys than girls (Baio et al., 2018).

Researchers are unclear of the causes of ASD but there may be genetic and environmental factors. In identical

© Ivelin Radkov/Shutterstock.com

twin studies, there is a 90% chance of having the disorder if a twin has it. If one sibling has ASD, the other siblings have ⌊10⌋ times the normal risk of also developing the disorder (⌊Sandin et al., 2014⌋).

Although there's no proven cure for ASD, treating ASD early, using school-based programs, and getting proper medical care can help the symptoms and increase the child's ability to function and learn. One type of widely accepted treatment is called *applied behavior analysis*. This form of intervention is designed to shape and establish new behaviors, such as learning to speak and play, and reduce undesirable ones. At this time, there are only a couple of antipsychotic medications approved by the Food and Drug Administration (FDA) to treat ASD. These medications can help reduce episodes of aggression, self-harm, or temper tantrums.

Attention-Deficit/Hyperactivity Disorder

The essential feature of **attention-deficit/hyperactivity disorder (ADHD)** is a persistent pattern of inattention and/or hyperactivity-impulsivity that interferes with functioning or development. Symptoms include difficulty staying focused and paying attention, difficulty controlling behavior, and hyperactivity (overactivity). This disorder must manifest itself in more than one setting, for example, in both the school and home. ADHD is one of the most common childhood disorders and can continue through adolescence and into adulthood. The ⌊current prevalence of ADHD in children is 11% of all children ages 4-17 (Visser et al., 2014). Approximately a third of children diagnosed with ADHD retain a diagnosis of ADHD in adulthood (Barbaresi et al., 2013).⌋

> **Attention deficit/ hyperactivity disorder:**
> A persistent pattern of inattention and/ or hyperactivity-impulsivity interfering with functioning or development.

Scientists are not sure what causes ADHD. It may be due to a combination of factors. Research suggests genes play a large role. Studies of twins show ADHD often runs in families. In addition to genetics, researchers are looking at possible environmental factors. For example, there may be a link between cigarette smoking and alcohol use during pregnancy and ADHD in children (Greenhill & Hechtman, 2009). Studies have also shown that preschoolers who are exposed to high levels of lead, sometimes found in the plumbing or paint of old buildings, may have a higher risk of developing ADHD (Froehlich et al., 2009). Some recent studies indicate there may be a link between food additives and hyperactivity. There is a popular belief that refined sugar may cause ADHD or make symptoms worse, but there is no real evidence to support this (NIMH, 2008).

ADHD is the most frequently diagnosed childhood mental disorder. In fact, many think it is grossly over diagnosed as a result of parents and teachers wanting explanations for child misbehaviors and pharmaceutical companies wanting to sell medication (Cohen, 2006). Another reason for over diagnosis may be as simple as the fact that many young boys are still relatively immature when they start kindergarten. As a result, their behaviors are marked by higher levels of activity and lower impulse control than is characteristic of older children. Following a study of some 12,000 kindergarten children, Elder (2010) reported younger children were 60% more likely than older children to be diagnosed with ADHD. By his estimates, as many as 1 million children in the United States may be wrongly diagnosed!

Although there is no cure for ADHD, symptoms can be helped. Treatment typically involves medications and behavioral interventions. Early diagnosis and treatment can make a big difference in outcome.

ANXIETY DISORDERS

Another classification of disorders in the *DSM-5* is Anxiety Disorders. The disorders included in this classification are Separation Anxiety Disorders, Selective Mutism, Specific Phobia, Social Anxiety Disorder, Panic Attack (Specifier) and Panic Disorder, Generalized Anxiety Disorders, among others. Anxiety is among the most devastating and the most baffling of human emotions. It can range from mild trepidation to acute terror and can occur in response to a wide variety of situations, or sometimes without any apparent provocation. In many cases it is both natural and normal and can be an asset for survival in potentially dangerous situations; however, in many situations it is maladaptive and irrational, and is the basis of a number of disorders collectively known as the *anxiety disorders,* the most commonly diagnosed mental disorders. In this section, we discuss Panic Attack (Specifier) and Panic Disorder, Generalized Anxiety Disorder, Specific Phobia, Agoraphobia, and Social Anxiety Disorder (Social Phobia).

Panic Attacks (Specifier) and Panic Disorder

A relatively common anxiety disorder involves recurring episodes of intense fear and anxiety, often accompanied by physical symptoms such as shortness of breath and heart palpitations. These episodes, known as **panic attacks**, occur for no apparent reason. Victims often feel they are having a heart attack or that they're in danger of fainting or even dying. The person could also experience severe sweating, lightheadedness, and a feeling of terror about their physical and emotional well-being. In some individuals, attacks occur only once or twice in their lifetime. Those who suffer from recurrent and persistent panic attacks are diagnosed as suffering from **panic disorder**. It is not uncommon for patients suffering from other mental disorders to also suffer from panic attacks (Ulas et al., 2010).

> **Panic attacks:** An episode occurring for no apparent reason involving intense fear and anxiety, often accompanied by physical symptoms such as shortness of breath and heart palpitations.
>
> **Panic disorder:** A disorder characterized by recurrent and persistent panic attacks.

Causes of panic disorder are linked to both biological and psychological causes. Biologically, panic disorder has genetic implications as it tends to run in families. Psychologically, people with panic disorder tend to misinterpret physical symptoms and view physical symptoms as more problematic than they are.

Panic attacks are relatively common, affecting an estimated 10% of the population (*Celebrities with Anxiety*, 2018; Panic Disorder, 2010). Among well-known people who have reportedly suffered panic attacks are Sigmund Freud, Tom Cruise, Princess Diana, Johnny Depp, Oprah Winfrey, Stephen Colbert, Kourtney Kardashian, Kristen Stewart, Adele, Missy Elliot, Kim Kardashian West, Kristen Bell, Ellie Goulding, Emma Stone, and Demi Lovato.

© Stuart Miles/Shutterstock.com

Generalized Anxiety Disorder

The most commonly diagnosed mental disorders are anxiety disorders. **Generalized anxiety disorder** is marked by excessive anxiety and worry, as a general state rather than episodic subjective sensation of anxiety, in the absence of specific situations or objects that might be associated with anxiety reactions. The hallmark of this disorder is worry in the absence of specific triggers. Individuals suffering from generalized anxiety, sometimes termed free-floating anxiety, recognize themselves as being predominantly tense, nervous, and fearful, and cannot associate their anxiety with any specific stressor. Although unpleasant, generalized anxiety is not marked by the same degree of terror and sensation of impending doom that is the hallmark of a panic attack.

> **Generalized anxiety disorder:** A disorder marked by excessive anxiety and worry, as a general state rather than episodic subjective sensation of anxiety, in the absence of specific situations or objects that might be associated with anxiety reactions.

Generalized anxiety disorder is often a debilitating disease that is present in 3% to 5% of the population (Wittchen, 2002). It appears to be clearly linked to increased susceptibility to a variety of physical diseases, including autoimmune disorders such as rheumatoid arthritis, lupus, celiac disease, and many others (Vieira et al., 2010). It is also highly predictive of other anxiety disorders (Katja et al., 2010).

Specific Phobia

Phobias are intense, irrational fears, recognized by the person as unreasonable, and often leading to avoidance of certain objects or situations. These disorders are typically chronic and can be distinguished in terms of the objects or situations that bring them about and an individual goes to great lengths to avoid the feared object or situation. It is thought individuals can be conditioned to develop a phobia or that we are biologically wired to be fearful of potentially harmful objects or situations and some individuals are more susceptible to extreme responses to a trigger. Some of the most common phobias are listed in Figure 8.2. The criterion for a phobia is simply that the fear be irrational, completely out of proportion to the potential danger of the feared object or situation, and not shared by a significant number of other people. It is interesting to note, however, that human phobias tend to be limited to a number of common situations, most of which imply some sort of danger. Thus, although very few people have furniture or vegetable phobias, a much larger number are afraid of open spaces, heights, closed spaces, insects, snakes, and darkness. Specific phobias include the variety of other specific fears that are not agoraphobic or social.

> **Phobias:** Intense, irrational fears, recognized by the person as unreasonable, and often leading to avoidance of certain objects or situations.

Agoraphobia

Literally, agoraphobia means fear of open or public places. This disorder manifests itself as severe anxiety related to places or situations from which departure or return home may be difficult, resulting in an active avoidance of such places. Individuals may experience anxiety at the thought of leaving home, or when traveling alone, being apart from friends, or being in strange places. Agoraphobia is often associated with serious personal distress. In extreme cases, individuals may become completely "housebound" for prolonged periods.

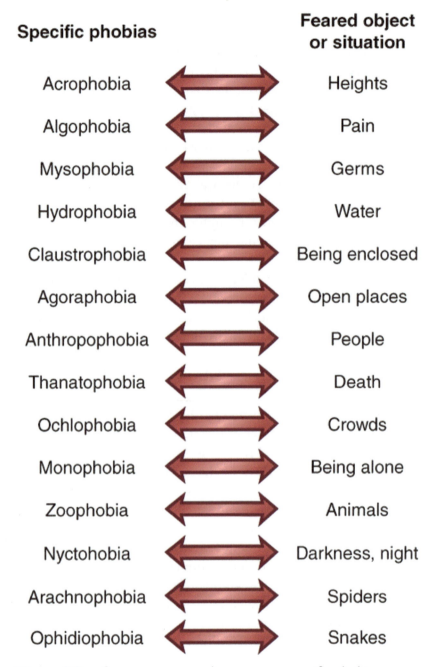

Figure 8.2 ⌊Some common and uncommon specific phobias.⌋

The prevalence of agoraphobia is uncertain, although some estimates suggest between 3% and 5% of the U.S. population may have the disorder (Kessler et al., 2009). Many people who experience panic attacks also later develop agoraphobia. The disorder is seen more frequently in women than in men, and most often begins in adolescence or early adulthood, although it may occur considerably later.

Social Anxiety Disorder (Social Phobia)

Social phobia involves a fear of social situations—that is, a fear of situations in which the individual is exposed to the judgment of others. The disorder's most common manifestations include avoidance of social situations and of public behaviors such as speaking formally to a group or giving a class presentation. Fear of using public rest rooms, washrooms, eating in public, appearing at certain social gatherings, and writing or performing in public are other manifestations of social phobia.

˪Social˩ phobias often lead the individual to adopt a lifestyle and occupational role that don't demand a great deal of social contact, thus permitting adequate adjustment and functioning. ˪Relatively˩ few people seek clinical help for this disorder.

© Vereshchagin Dmitry/Shutterstock.com

OBSESSIVE–COMPULSIVE AND RELATED DISORDERS

˪In addition to Neurodevelopmental Disorders and Anxiety Disorders, another classification of disorders in the *DSM-5* is Obsessive-Compulsive and Related Disorders. This classification includes disorders such as Obsessive-Compulsive Disorder, Body Dysmorphic Disorder, Hoarding Disorder, Trichotillomania (Hair-Pulling Disorder), and other obsessive-compulsive related disorders.˩

Obsessive-compulsive disorders (OCD) are defined by the presence of recurring thoughts or impulses that appear irrational to the person having them (obsessions) and/or behaviors that are not perceived as the result of the individual's wishes but that give rise to intense urges to engage in them and result in anxiety when they are resisted (compulsions). Thus, a compulsion is a behavior, and an obsession is a thought. Both obsessions and compulsions are perceived as incompatible with the individual's nature, but neither can easily be resisted. Other disorders in this category include body dysmorphic disorder, which is distress over perceived flaws or defects in one's physical appearance, causing significant impairment. Another example, hoarding disorder, is characterized by the abnormal and persistent difficulty discarding possessions. There is also trichotillomania (hair-pulling disorder) and excoriation (skin-picking disorder).

> **Obsessive-compulsive disorders:** A disorder characterized by recurrent and unwanted thoughts and/or the need to perform repetitive physical or mental actions.

The most common obsessions revolve around cleanliness; some examples include a fear of germs and of dirt, and fear of thinking evil thoughts and feeling guilty. They also sometimes take the form of repetitive thoughts of violence, accompanied by considerable fear of engaging in some highly undesirable behavior. Alternatively, obsessions may be marked by perpetual indecision and doubting, which can be severe enough to prevent reaching any decision.

Compulsions typically involve a strong impulse to repeat some senseless and meaningless act over and over again (e.g., checking drawers and locks or touching certain objects repeatedly). They are also often centered on washing and cleansing rituals. Less commonly, they might take the form of hoarding—as in the case of the man who had more than 100 cats in his home and one paranoid dog (Gerson, 2010). Evidence suggests about 1% of the adult U.S. population can be classified as obsessive–compulsive (NIMH, 2017b).

Treatment for OCD is similar to those treatments used for anxiety disorders. Some form of medication and psychotherapy is usually prescribed.

TRAUMA- AND STRESSOR-RELATED DISORDERS

In the *DSM-5*, the classification of Trauma- and Stressor-Related Disorders includes Reactive Attachment Disorder, Posttraumatic Stress Disorder, Acute Stress Disorder, and other stressor-related disorders. Psychological disorders that appear following exposure to an extremely traumatic event—such as war, rape, or a horrendous accident—sometimes take the form of **posttraumatic stress disorder** (PTSD). Symptoms may include flashbacks or nightmares during which the individual re-experiences the event. PTSD is often marked by sleep disturbances, anger and aggression, numbing/avoidance, hypervigilance, and significant impairment in social functioning. Compared with other military personnel, alcohol-related disorders are twice as likely for veterans who meet the criteria for PTSD (Jakupcak et al., 2010).

> **Posttraumatic stress disorder:** A disorder that appears following exposure to an extremely traumatic event where fear is experienced long after the traumatic event.

Estimates of the prevalence of PTSD vary widely. One study that looked at the results of 19 different investigations that had attempted to determine the prevalence of PTSD among veterans returning from Iraq found estimates ranging from a low of 1.4% to an astounding 31% (Sundin et al., 2010). It is estimated that 3.6% of U.S. adults had PTSD in 2016 (NIMH, 2017c).

Veterans are more educated in today's society about PTSD and are encouraged to seek treatment through their physicians and mental health providers as there are specific medications and therapies that can improve their quality of life and assist in the reintegration process.

In general, anxiety disorders are treated with medication, psychotherapy, or both. Treatment choices depend on the problem and the person's preference, although behavior therapy or cognitive–behavioral therapy (CBT) appear to be the most widely accepted. With CBT, the cognitive part helps people change the thinking patterns supporting their fears, and the behavioral part helps people change the way they react to anxiety-provoking situations. Medication will not cure anxiety disorders, but it can keep the symptoms under control. The most effective form of treatment tends to be a combination of medications and psychotherapy. Many people with anxiety disorders benefit from joining a self-help or support group; stress management techniques and meditation can also help.

The most commonly diagnosed mental disorders are anxiety disorders. Drug therapy is currently the treatment of choice.
© Andrey_Popov/Shutterstock.com

DISRUPTIVE, IMPULSE-CONTROL AND CONDUCT DISORDERS

Despite being most common during childhood, disruptive, impulse-control, and conduct disorders are almost as prevalent as anxiety disorders, occurring in approximately one in four people. These disorders manifest at about the same age. Disorders in this category are marked by failure to resist an impulse to engage in a behavior that is harmful either to the person or to others. They include a range of often aggressive behaviors. They are unique in that these problems are manifested in behaviors that violate the rights of others and/or bring the individual into significant conflict with societal norms or authority figures. Among the disorders in this classification are Oppositional Defiant Disorder, Intermittent Explosive Disorder, Conduct Disorder, and other impulse-control disorders.

Oppositional Defiant Disorder

Oppositional defiant disorder is characterized by a pattern of hostile, disobedient, defiant behavior toward authority figures. The disorder is sometimes apparent in children given to violent temper tantrums and persistent negative moods. Bullying, stealing, and vandalism are other possible symptoms.

> **Oppositional defiant disorder:** A disorder identified in childhood characterized by a pattern of hostile, disobedient, defiant behavior toward authority figures.

Intermittent Explosive Disorder

Intermittent explosive disorder is marked by the repeated failure to resist aggressive impulses. Children diagnosed with this disorder have typically engaged in a number of excessively violent acts against people or property, or both. As adults, they are at higher risk of aggression in their romantic relationships (Murray-Close et al., 2010).

> **Intermittent explosive disorder:** A disorder identified in childhood that is marked by the repeated failure to resist aggressive impulses.

Conduct Disorder

Conduct disorder, which is often preceded by oppositional defiant disorder, is a disorder that begins in late childhood and often becomes more severe in adolescence. A related disorder among adults is antisocial personality disorder.

> **Conduct disorder:** A disorder that begins in late childhood and often becomes more severe in adolescence that includes persistent pattern of behaviors violating the rights of others or socially inappropriate for the child's age.

The prevalence of conduct disorder appears to increase in older childhood, with 2% to 5% of children between 5-12 years demonstrating conduct disorder and 5% to 9% of adolescents between 13 and 18 years being diagnosed (Patel et al., 2018). Additionally, boys are more likely to present with symptoms of conduct disorder than girls. However, this gender difference does not appear until adolescence. In children under 5 years of age, there are almost no gender differences in conduct disorder. However, this changes in adolescence, where boys are two to three times more likely to be diagnosed with conduct disorder than girls (Patel et al., 2018). The disorder is marked by a persistent pattern of behaviors violating the rights of others or socially inappropriate for the child's age. Children with a conduct disorder are often selfish, relate poorly with others, and typically don't display a normal sense of guilt. They are frequently the school bullies, and demonstrate behaviors such as threatening, fighting, abusing animals, and vandalism.

Other Impulse-Control Disorders

There are a number of other impulse-control disorders, most of which are relatively uncommon. They include:

- **Kleptomania:** an irresistible urge to steal things even when they're not needed or particularly valuable
- **Pyromania:** a compulsion to set fires for personal pleasure and gratification
- **Trichotillomania:** marked by the recurrent pulling out of one's hair, resulting in noticeable hair loss and considerable tension if the individual tries to resist

Impulse control disorders are treated with medication and psychotherapy, usually some form of behavior therapy. These disorders often occur in conjunction with another condition, such as ADHD. Medication and therapy for that condition often helps alleviate the impulse-control disorder. Depression is often an underlying factor in some impulse-control disorders and consequently, treatment with antidepressants may be helpful.

DEPRESSIVE DISORDERS

A major change to classification of disorders in the *DSM-5* was the removal of the classification of "Mood Disorders" and development of two categories of mood disorders called Bipolar and Related Disorders and Depressive Disorders. Within the Bipolar and Related Disorders category you will find Bipolar I Disorder, Bipolar II Disorder, Cyclothymic Disorder, and other Bipolar related disorders. Within the Depressive Disorders category, you will find Major Depressive Disorder, Premenstrual Dysphoric Disorder, Persistent Depressive Disorder (Dysthymia), among other depressive disorders.

Major depressive disorder is the most common of all mood disorders, affecting an estimated 7.1% of the adult U.S. population in a given year (NIMH, 2019). It is characterized by a conglomerate of symptoms, including apathy, listlessness, despair, loss of appetite, sleep disturbances, unwavering pessimism, and thoughts of suicide (although not all of these symptoms need be present in every case).

> **Major depressive disorder:**
> A disorder characterized by a conglomerate of symptoms, including apathy, listlessness, despair, loss of appetite, sleep disturbances, unwavering pessimism, and thoughts of suicide.

DSM-5 criteria for major depressive disorder stipulate there be at least one major depressive episode. A depressive episode is defined as a period of at least 2 weeks during which the individual suffers from a depressed mood and/or loss of interest and pleasure in normal life activities. The depressed mood typically characterizes most or all of every day.

There appears to be a clear relationship between suicide and depression. In fact, more than 90% of people who commit suicide suffer from depression or some other mental disorder (Suicide in the U.S., 2010).

© travellight/Shutterstock.com

Persistent Depressive Disorder (Dysthymia)

While a major depressive episode lasts at least 2 weeks, **persistent depressive disorder (or dysthymia)** describes a chronically depressed mood that lasts at least 2 years and is present most days during that period. Except for its longer duration, dysthymia is marked by much the same symptoms as a major depressive episode, but of lesser severity. In effect, it is a lower-grade, chronic, long-term depression.

> **Persistent depressive disorder (or dysthymia):**
> A continuous, long-term form of depression, considered not as severe as major depression, in which individuals feel hopelessness, lack of interest in activities, and experience low self-esteem.

Premenstrual Dysphoria Disorder

An additional ⌐diagnosis⌐ added in the *DSM-5* is **premenstrual dysphoric disorder**. Symptoms must be present in the week prior to menses and become minimal or absent in the weeks post menses. The symptoms include marked mood swings or depressed mood, marked irritability or anger, marked anxiety or feelings of being keyed up, difficulty concentrating, decreased interest in activities, a marked lack of energy, specific food cravings, changes in sleep patterns, and physical symptoms such as breast tenderness, joint pain, or "bloating."

A person with depression can be treated in several ways. The most common treatments are medication and psychotherapy. For depressive symptoms, medications called **antidepressants** primarily work on brain chemicals called neurotransmitters, especially serotonin, norepinephrine, or dopamine. These chemicals are most involved in regulating our moods. **Electroconvulsive shock therapy (ECT)** is another very effective treatment for depression. This form of treatment creates seizures in the brain in a very brief and controlled situation. We are not sure how the ECT works but it seems to be just as effective as medications in many instances.

> ⌐**Premenstrual dysphoric disorder:** A severe extension of premenstrual syndrome (PMS) in which a woman experiences at least one of the following symptoms around her menstrual cycle: sadness or hopelessness, anxiety, extreme moodiness, or irritability/anger.⌐

> ⌐**Antidepressants:** A classification of medications that treats depression through regulating neurotransmitters like serotonin.⌐
>
> ⌐**Electroconvulsive shock therapy (ECT):** An effective treatment for depression where seizures are created in the brain in a very brief and controlled situation.⌐

BIPOLAR AND RELATED DISORDERS

⌐Bipolar and related disorders is a classification of disorders in the *DSM-5* that includes Bipolar I, Bipolar II, Cyclothymic disorder, and other bipolar related disorders.⌐

Bipolar I/II Disorder

Bipolar disorder, previously labeled manic depression, is in a category called Bipolar and Related Disorders. It is approximately half as common as major depressive disorder, affecting an estimated ⌐2.8%⌐ of the U.S. adult population (NIMH, 2017a). It is marked by recur-

> **Bipolar disorder:** A disorder characterized by mania and depression.

ring episodes of mania or depression, although both are not always present. Occasionally the attacks are cyclical; that is, mania is followed by depression, which may then be followed by another period of mania, and so on. More frequently, individuals experience a single episode of mania and one of depression, not necessarily in that order, and may then be free of both for long periods—sometimes even decades. At other times, the condition is characterized principally by mania and is labeled ⌐Bipolar I Disorder. Bipolar II Disorder⌐ refers to a mood disorder where depression rather than mania dominates.

Mania contrasts sharply with periods of depression. It is characterized by periods of extreme and intense activity, irrepressible good humor, grandiose plans and involvements, and overwhelming displays of energy and joie de vivre.

Family and twin studies provide strong evidence of a genetic basis for bipolar disorder, where the heritability coefficient has been estimated at approximately 59% (Karege et al., 2010; Lichtenstein et al., 2009). In this context, heritability coefficient means the extent to which the variability in a characteristic is due to genetics.

Although a mood disorder, bipolar disorder is very different from depression and cannot be cured; ⌐however,⌐ it can be treated effectively over the long-term. Proper treatment helps many people with bipolar disorder gain better control of their mood swings and related symptoms. Drugs called mood stabilizers are most effective. When combined with medication, psychotherapy can be an effective treatment for depression or bipolar disorder.

SUBSTANCE-RELATED AND ADDICTIVE DISORDERS

The *DSM-5* provides criteria for diagnosis of substance use disorders, along with criteria for intoxication, withdrawal, substance/medication-induced disorders, and unspecified substance-induced disorders. There is a continuum between mild, early use to more severe and serious addiction.

There is evidence that some behaviors, such as gambling, activate the brain reward system with effects similar to those of drugs of abuse. The symptoms resemble substance use disorders to a certain extent; consequently, there is also a nonsubstance-related disorder—gambling disorder.

Substance Use Disorders

Substance use disorder is a continuum of drug use defined mainly in terms of **drug intoxication** and **withdrawal symptoms**. With increasing use, many drugs have diminishing effects. This is due primarily to the fact that most abused drugs are effective precisely because they increase the release of dopamine, the neurotransmitter associated with pleasure and reinforcement, or block its reuptake. One consequence is the brain produces *less* dopamine naturally as it becomes increasingly dependent on external sources. Hence the apparent increased tolerance and the need to use more of the drug.

Withdrawal, the physiological and psychological effects of stopping drug use, results from a sudden reduction in stimulation of those areas of the brain associated with pleasure and typically leads to feelings of dysphoria—the opposite of *euphoria*. Withdrawal symptoms vary depending on the drug, its manner of ingestion, and the individual. Withdrawal is often marked by depression and anxiety, as well as by a strong craving, ⌐which is⌐ the hallmark of addiction. Sudden and complete withdrawal from alcohol dependence can be fatal.

> **Drug intoxication:** Recent use of a substance that induces a maladaptive and impairing state but is reversible.
>
> **Withdrawal symptoms:** A state occurring when an individual who regularly uses a drug, stops or reduces drug use, and can have unpleasant and sometimes dangerous reactions.

Prevalence and Types of Drug Use

As Figure 8.3 indicates, nearly half (46%) of all Americans aged 12 and up have tried one or more drugs, although only 8% describe themselves as current users (those who have used the drug in the last 30 days). Nicotine and alcohol continue to be the most widely used drugs.

Drugs are typically classified in terms of their effects rather than their composition. There are **narcotics** such as morphine and opium, addictive drugs that produce sensations of well-being; **sedatives**, such as tranquilizers and barbiturates; **stimulants**, such as the amphetamines and cocaine; and **hallucinogens**, such as LSD, ecstasy, and

> **Narcotics:** A drug type producing sensations of well-being.
>
> **Sedatives:** A drug type causing drowsiness.
>
> **Stimulants:** A drug classification causing excitement and joyfulness.
>
> **Hallucinogens:** A drug type causing hallucinations.

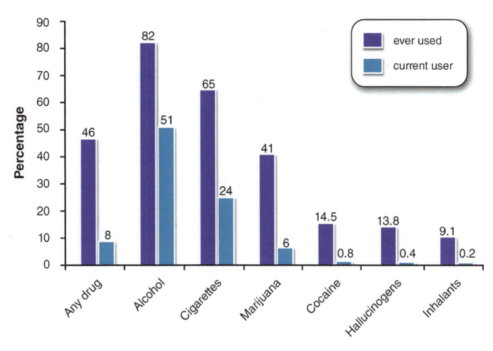

Figure 8.3   Drug use in the United States based on interviews of around 68,000 participants aged 12 or more.

Rohypnol. Marijuana is also ordinarily classified as a hallucinogenic drug, although its effects are seldom as dramatic as those of LSD or mescaline (see Table 8.3).

Medication and behavioral therapy, especially when combined, are frequently used for treatment. The process often begins with detoxification, followed by treatment and relapse prevention. Treatment for addictive disorders is not simple, or brief. Addiction treatment must help the individual stop using drugs, maintain a drug-free lifestyle, and achieve productive functioning in the family, at work, and in society. Most substance abusers require long-term or repeated episodes of care to recover and stay drug free. And sometimes, as with other chronic conditions, episodes of relapse may require a return to prior treatment components.

Table 8.3   Symptoms of Drug Use and Their Effects on the Nervous System

Drug	Early Symptoms	Long-Term Symptoms	Effects on Nervous System
Narcotics (opium, morphine, heroin, codeine, methadone)	Medicinal breath Traces of white powder around nostrils (heroin is sometimes inhaled) Red or raw nostrils Needle marks or scars on arms Long sleeves (or other clothing) at inappropriate times Physical evidence may include cough syrup bottles, syringes, cotton swabs, and spoon or cap for heating heroin	Loss of appetite Constipation	Bind to painkilling sites to dull sensation of pain; block reuptake of neurotransmitters such as dopamine. Mimic endorphins (cause sensations of pleasure and well-being). With chronic use, the brain may stop producing endorphins so user develops tolerance and craves more drugs to feel good.

(Continued)

Table 8.3   Symptoms of Drug Use and Their Effects on the Nervous System *(Continued)*

Drug	Early Symptoms	Long-Term Symptoms	Effects on Nervous System
Sedatives (barbiturates, tranquilizers, alcohol, Rohypnol, and GHB [the "date-rape" drugs])	Symptoms of alcohol consumption with or without odor: —Poor coordination and speech —Drowsiness —Loss of interest in activity	Withdrawal symptoms when discontinued Possible convulsions	Activate GABA receptors (which are inhibitory and cause drowsiness). GHB increases dopamine levels in the brain (associated with sense of well-being).
Stimulants (cocaine, crack, amphetamines, caffeine, nicotine)	Excessive activity Irascibility Argumentativeness Nervousness Pupil dilation Dry mouth and nose with bad breath Chapped, dry lips Scratching or rubbing of nose Long periods without sleep Loss of appetite	Loss of appetite Possible hallucinations and psychotic reactions	Caffeine and amphetamines promote release of noradrenaline (causes excitement and wakefulness). Cocaine and crack promote release of dopamine and inhibit its reuptake (causes sense of euphoria); leads to tolerance and addiction.
Hallucinogens (marijuana, LSD, PCP, mescaline, psilocybin)	Odor on breath and clothing Animated behavior or its opposite Bizarre behavior Panic Disorientation	None definite for marijuana Possible contribution to psychoses and possible recurrence of experiences later	Stimulate serotonin activity. Interfere with noradrenaline activity (produces hallucinations).
Inhalants (glue, paint thinner, aerosol sprays, solvents, other combustibles)	Odor of glue, solvent, or related substance Redness and watering of eyes Appearance of alcoholic intoxication Physical evidence of plastic bags, rags, aerosol glue or solvent containers	Disorientation Brain damage	Long-term use can break down myelin, leading to muscle spasms, tremors, and other physical problems.

Medications can be used to help with different aspects of the treatment process. Medications are used for withdrawal to suppress the withdrawal symptoms. After withdrawal, medications can also help to reestablish normal brain functioning to prevent relapse and reduce cravings.

Psychotherapy, especially behavioral therapy, helps patients engage in the treatment process, change their attitudes and behaviors related to drug abuse, and increase healthy life skills.

DISSOCIATIVE DISORDERS

The groupings of mental disorders we've considered so far are the most commonly diagnosed in the United States. The *DSM-5* lists a large number of additional categories. Among them is the category of Dissociative Disorders. Three principal dissociative disorders are described in the *DSM-5*: Dissociative amnesia, Dissociative identity disorder, and Depersonalization/Derealization disorder. They are called dissociative because they involve the splitting or separating of aspects of personality and functioning. Dissociative symptoms are sometimes seen in patients with PTSD.

Dissociative Amnesia

Dissociative amnesia is defined by a sudden and temporary loss of memory not attributable to any organic cause. Typically, the memory loss is for some unusually stressful or traumatic event. Some instances of dissociative amnesia involve loss of memory of violent outbursts or suicide attempts.

> **Dissociative amnesia:** A sudden and temporary loss of memory not attributable to any organic cause.

Dissociative amnesia may take different forms, distinguishable in terms of the type of material that cannot be remembered and the time period covered by the amnesia. In *localized* amnesia, the individual is unable to recall anything for a period of time following some event, such as a car accident. In *systematized* amnesia, some events may be recalled during the circumscribed period, but many others will have been completely forgotten.

Dissociative amnesia can include **dissociative fugue**, which involves a loss of memory. In addition, it involves wandering and sometimes assuming a new identity. People suffering from a fugue state undergo an episode during which they have forgotten who they are but are unaware of having been anyone else. During this time,

> **Dissociative fugue:** A loss of memory characterized by wandering and sometimes assuming a new identity.

they may leave their homes and even establish very different lives somewhere else. Both onset and recovery are usually rapid, but the individual may then be left with a feeling of disorientation and confusion.

Dissociative Identity Disorder

The dissociative aspects of amnesia and fugue states are obvious: In both cases, it is as though parts of the individual's personality and memory become separated from one another, some parts remaining temporarily inaccessible to the individual. **Dissociative identity disorder**, previously called *multiple-personality disorder*, involves a more complex type of dissociation in which individuals are from time-to-time dominated by distinctly different, complex, highly integrated personalities. Typically, domination by one personality is complete

> **Dissociative identity disorder:** A complex type of dissociation in which individuals are from time to time dominated by distinctly different, complex, highly integrated personalities.

and does not involve any memory of other personalities, although it sometimes does. Shifts from one personality to another may be sudden and dramatic.

The Three Faces of Eve (Thigpen & Cleckley, 1954) presents a classic illustration of dissociative identity disorder. "Eve White," who had been in psychotherapy for a period of time following complaints of severe headaches and blackouts, was a quiet, demure, soft-spoken woman. The therapist had no reason to suspect a multiple personality, until one day:

> As if seized by sudden pain, she put both hands to her head. After a tense moment of silence, both hands dropped. There was a quick, reckless smile, and, in a bright voice that sparkled, she said, "Hi, there, Doc!" The demure and constrained posture of Eve White had melted into buoyant repose (p. 137).

The "new" woman had no doubt that she was "Eve Black." Later, "Jane" emerged as a third personality.

The repeated shifts of personality that occur in a dissociative identity disorder do not occur in the fugue state. In addition, the two or more personalities that alternately dominate the individual diagnosed as having a dissociative identity disorder are complete personalities with well-integrated identities.

There is sometimes confusion between schizophrenia and "dissociative" or "multiple" identities, but the two are quite different. None of the schizophrenias involve dual (or triple) personalities in the sense of well-integrated, apparently normal, but separate manifestations of identity. In addition, the schizophrenias typically involve serious problems of perceptual or cognitive distortion.

Multiple personality, a popular fiction theme, is a rare condition now labeled *dissociative identity disorder*. In a few classic cases, it manifests itself almost as clearly as this doctored photo indicates.

© Stepan Kapl/Shutterstock.com

Depersonalization/Derealization Disorder

This is a disorder characterized by feelings of unreality. Those with depersonalization/derealization disorder often feel they are in a dreamlike state, and perhaps their body does not belong to them. Adam Duritz, front man for the rock group Counting Crows, says of his depersonalization disorder, "[It] makes the world seem like it's not real, as if things aren't taking place. It's hard to explain, but you feel untethered" (Celebrities with Dissociative Disorder, 2010). The disorder is uncommon and often disappears on its own.

Effective treatments for dissociative disorders include psychotherapy, medications, and hypnotherapy. Often the symptoms of dissociative disorders occur with other disorders, such as anxiety and depression; so the disorder may be treated using the same drugs prescribed for those disorders.

SCHIZOPHRENIA SPECTRUM AND OTHER PSYCHOTIC DISORDERS

This ⌞classification of disorders⌟ includes a variety of disorders characterized by *psychotic* symptoms such as **hallucinations** (perceptions of experiences without corresponding external stimuli together with a compelling feeling that these are real) and **delusions** (false beliefs or opinions). These disorders are severe, debilitating conditions and are defined by abnormalities in one or more of the five domains: delusions, hallucinations, disorganized thinking (speech), grossly

Hallucinations: Perceptions of experiences without corresponding external stimuli together with a compelling feeling that these are real.

Delusions: False beliefs or opinions.

disorganized or abnormal motor behavior (catatonia), and negative symptoms. Negative symptoms include diminished emotional expression, lack of motivation to do anything, and inability to experience pleasure and lack of interest in social interactions.

Schizophrenia

Among the most severe and the most common of the psychotic disorders, **schizophrenia** is characterized by emotional, cognitive, and perceptual confusion and a consequent breakdown of effective contact with others and with reality.

> **Schizophrenia:** A psychotic disorder characterized by emotional, cognitive, and perceptual confusion and a consequent breakdown of effective contact with others and with reality.

Schizophreniform Disorder

Schizophreniform disorder has the same kind of symptoms as schizophrenia but is different because it is brief and symptoms last only 1 to 6 months. **Brief psychotic disorder** is even shorter, lasting 1 day to 1 month.

> **Schizophreniform disorder:** Same symptoms as schizophrenia but the only differences are symptoms last only 1 to 6 months.
>
> **Brief psychotic disorder:** Similar to schizophrenia; however, symptoms can last from 1 day to 1 month.
>
> **Schizoaffective disorder:** Includes symptoms of schizophrenia in addition to a mood disorder such as depression or mania.

Schizoaffective Disorder

Schizoaffective disorder includes symptoms of schizophrenia in addition to a mood disorder such as depression or mania.

This classification of schizophrenias is not nearly as clear in practice as it might appear in theory. Numerous apparently schizophrenic patients cannot easily be classified within a single division, since symptoms often overlap or change over time.

Various psychotic disorders appear to be related to malfunctions in the metabolic processes involved in the essential transformations that occur among synaptic neurotransmitters such as dopamine, serotonin, and epinephrine. The effectiveness of many psychotherapeutic drugs appears to result from their effects on neurotransmitters, providing added evidence that these are implicated in some mental disorders. In addition, research with animals has shown stressful environmental events may adversely affect essential metabolic processes in the brain.

Genomic research provides very strong evidence that schizophrenia in particular has a genetic component. Lichtenstein et al. (2009) summarized a large number of studies looking at incidence of schizophrenia among twins, full and half siblings, and parents and estimated the contribution of genetics to the disorder was approximately 64%. This finding is consistent with the belief that neurotransmitters are implicated in these mental disorders (Gray et al., 2010).

There is no cure for psychotic disorders, so treatments focus on managing the symptoms of the disease. For the more serious forms such as schizophrenia, treatments include antipsychotic medications and various psychosocial treatments. Antipsychotic medications have been available since the mid-1950s. The older types are called conventional or "typical" antipsychotics and newer medications are called second generation, or "atypical" antipsychotics. The newer medications are much more effective and have fewer side effects. Psychosocial treatments can help people with psychotic disorders once stabilized on medication. Psychosocial treatments help these patients deal with the everyday challenges of the illness, such as difficulty with communication, self-care, work, and forming and keeping relationships.

SOMATIC SYMPTOM AND RELATED DISORDERS

Another grouping of disorders included in the *DSM-5* is the **somatic symptom disorders**. These include a variety of conditions in which the patient has symptoms suggestive of some medical problem, but no such problem can be found. People with this disorder are often very anxious about their health. The condition is not a result of consciously fabricating or exaggerating symptoms (called *malingering*) or what are called *factitious disorders* (where the patient deliberately produces or feigns symptoms). Those with somatic symptom disorders genuinely believe they are physically ill. Individuals with **illness anxiety disorder** have a preoccupation with having or acquiring a serious illness. They worry about their health and may perform excessive behaviors to avoid illness and focus on their health. **Conversion disorder** is similar to somatic symptom disorder but individuals with this disorder have one or more symptoms of altered voluntary motor or sensory functioning such as paralysis, weakness, tremors, or problems with vision or hearing.

> **Somatic symptom disorders:** A disorder in which the patient has symptoms suggestive of some medical problem but no such problem can be found.
>
> **Illness anxiety disorder:** Extreme worry about having or acquiring a serious illness.
>
> **Conversion disorder:** A disorder similar to somatic symptom disorder but individuals with this disorder have one or more symptoms of altered voluntary motor or sensory functioning such as paralysis, weakness, tremors, or problems with vision or hearing.

Treatment for somatic symptom disorders usually involves some form of psychotherapy. If anxiety or stress is a factor, treatments for dealing with anxiety may also be used.

PERSONALITY DISORDERS

Personality disorders are evident in behaviors that are socially inappropriate, inflexible, and often antisocial. Most of these behaviors typically become apparent during childhood or adolescence and are manifested as relatively stable, although sometimes highly maladaptive, personality characteristics.

> **Personality disorders:** Behaviors that are socially inappropriate, inflexible, and often antisocial that typically become apparent during childhood or adolescence and are manifested as relatively stable.

Unlike those with more serious mental disorders, persons suffering from personality disorders usually continue to function in society. Often, too, they experience little anxiety over their behaviors since they are ordinarily unaware of their maladaptive nature. Most are unlikely to seek help on their own. Many individuals diagnosed with other forms of mental disorder have a long-standing history of personality disorders.

The personality disorders identified in the *DSM-5* are the following:

- *Paranoid personality disorder* is marked by a profound, long-term, and unjustified conviction that other people are hostile, dangerous, and out to get them. It often leads to social isolation.
- *Schizoid personality disorder* is characterized by a disinterest in social relationships and a limited range of emotional reaction. It is sometimes evident in emotional coldness and a solitary lifestyle.
- *Histrionic personality disorder,* primarily a female disorder, is evident in excessive emotionality, attention seeking, and inappropriate flirtatiousness. People with histrionic personalities typically want to be the center of attention and are often egocentric and self-indulgent.
- *Narcissistic personality disorder,* primarily a male disorder, is evident in excessive self-love. Narcissus of the Greek legend loved himself above all else. Extreme arrogance, cavalier disregard for social

convention and the rights of others, supreme confidence, and selfish exploitation of others are the principal characteristics of the narcissistic personality. Not surprisingly, such individuals appear only rarely in clinics.

- *Antisocial personality disorder* displays a pattern of pervasive disregard for, and violation of, the rights of others. Common characteristics might include lack of remorse for actions that hurt others, lack of empathy, cruelty to animals, poor and abusive relationships, and frequent problems with the law.
- *Borderline personality disorder* is evident in fluctuating and unpredictable moods that are often extreme. Those with borderline personality disorder tend to alternate between idealizing and devaluing, and they often have unstable and chaotic interpersonal relationships.
- *Schizotypal personality disorder* is marked by a need for social isolation, by what are often very different convictions and beliefs, and sometimes by odd or eccentric dress and behavior. Because the disorder is very similar to some forms of schizophrenia, its inclusion as a personality disorder is controversial.
- *Avoidant personality disorder* is characterized by an extreme and pervasive pattern of social inhibition evident in feelings of inadequacy and avoidance of social interaction.
- *Dependent personality disorder* describes a chronic and long-term condition in which the individual manifests excessive dependence on others for physical and emotional needs.
- *Obsessive–compulsive personality disorder (OCPD)* is different from obsessive–compulsive disorder (OCD) described earlier. Whereas OCD is an *anxiety disorder* marked by recurring obsessions (thoughts that won't go away) and compulsions (behaviors that must be carried out repeatedly), OCPD is a *personality disorder*. It is marked by a chronic and persistent maladaptive pattern of interacting with other people and with the environment. Among its manifestations are excessive preoccupation with orderliness, perfectionism, and details and a need to control all aspects of the environment.

There is a danger, when reading quick descriptions of disorders, to recognize clusters of symptoms among people we know and wonder whether they might have this or that disorder. For example, we all know people who are neat and orderly, but the fact is that probably none of them would come close to satisfying the criteria for OCPD. Nor are all people who are shy candidates for a diagnosis of *avoidant personality disorder.* Note that for all other personality disorders, diagnosis is made only on the basis of specific combinations of *persistent, prolonged,* and/or chronic beliefs and behaviors.

Personality disorders are commonly viewed as difficult, if not impossible, to treat. However, two interventions in particular—dialectical behavior therapy (DBT) and cognitive therapy (CT)—show promise, especially for one of the more common and most persistent, borderline personality disorder (Beck & Freedman, 1990; Leichsenring & Leibing, 2003). Psychotherapy is the main way to treat personality disorders. There are no medications specifically approved by the FDA to treat personality disorders. However, several types of psychiatric medications may help with various personality disorder symptoms.

THERAPIES

People decide to seek mental health treatment in the form of **therapy** for a variety of reasons. Some individuals are dissatisfied with their level of satisfaction in life and may seek assistance in evaluating goals in their life. This may be related to relationship issues, career or

Therapy: Systematic processes for helping individuals overcome their psychological problems.

educational issues, or interpersonal struggles. Some individuals may be court ordered to seek services due to their involvement with the legal system, such as an arrest for domestic violence, a parenting evaluation due to being reported for abuse or neglect of a child, or because of an ongoing custody battle from a highly conflictual divorce. Others may seek treatment for a mental health disorder mentioned previously in the chapter. Some individuals are referred for services by their primary care physician, their pastor or priest, a friend or family member, or, in the case of a youth, school personnel may suggest services.

└There┘ are three broad approaches to treating mental disorders. In many instances, these reflect the therapist's basic model, as summarized in Table 8.1. Thus, if the therapist views the disorder as being the result of a system malfunction (medical/biological model), drug therapy, electroconvulsive shock therapy, or, more rarely, surgery will be the therapies of choice. If the therapist thinks the disorder is a result of learning or inappropriate cognitions (behavioral and cognitive model), learning-based therapies may be employed. And if the therapist views disorders as resulting from psychic conflicts (psychodynamic model), some form of psychoanalysis may be used. It should be noted that traditional psychoanalysis is rarely used in today's society due to the emphasis on briefer types of treatment as a result of managed care issues in health care. In conclusion, most therapists use a variety of approaches in dealing with mental disorder. Only rarely are the nonmedical approaches used without also using some form of drug therapy (antidepressants, sedatives, antipsychotic drugs, and so on).

Medical Therapy

Science has provided practitioners with chemicals and surgical procedures that can sometimes rectify a condition before its more extreme results appear. Syphilis, for example, can, if unchecked, lead to neurological impairment and the manifestation of various mental disorders. Simple and highly effective treatment of syphilis with penicillin or related drugs in its early stages prevents their appearance. Similarly, thyroid problems, insulin problems, and a variety of metabolic and glandular problems can be controlled chemically.

What Does the Bible Say?

Should a Christian take medication for mental disorders?

└There is much controversy within churches and Christian circles surrounding the use of medication for mental disorders, and individuals fall on both sides of the argument. On one side of the argument, you have individuals who believe that mental illness is a spiritual issue in which treatments should be focused on improving one's faith to improve one's mental condition. On the other side of the argument, you have individuals who believe that mental illness, like physical illness, can have physical causes that need to be treated with physical techniques. Ultimately, it comes down to the question: Are mental illnesses a physical issue or a spiritual issue?

Recent Christian approaches to mental illness seem to favor an approach that integrates physical and spiritual treatments. This is based on the perspective that humans have both a body and a soul that work together in life.

Genesis 2:7 ESV

"Then the Lord God formed the man of dust from the ground and breathed into his nostrils the breath of life, and the man became a living creature."

Matthew 10:28 ESV

"And do not fear those who kill the body but cannot kill the soul. Rather fear him who can destroy both soul and body in hell."

Mental health issues can originate from a person's psyche or from physical causes, both of which need to be explored if we are going to help people struggling with mental disorders. Furthermore, even if a mental health issue originates in a person's psyche, there may also be physical causes that made one vulnerable to the mental illness or perpetuate the mental illness. Therefore, most current Christian approaches favor the use of medication when physical causes are suspected in conjunction with spiritual treatment to grow one's psyche and soul to deal with the mental disorder at hand. ⌐

Drug Therapy

Drug therapy for mental disorders involves psychiatric medications, sometimes called psychotropic or psychotherapeutic medications. These drugs have dramatically changed the face of mental health treatment and reduced the number of people who suffer serious and disabling symptoms and the severity of the symptoms. Medications treat the symptoms of mental disorders, but they do not cure the disorder. They work differently for different people. Some people get great results from medications and only need them for a short time ⌐while⌐ other individuals

© Kirill__M/Shutterstock.com

have to take them for a long time or even a lifetime. As with all drugs, there are often side effects. Factors that can affect how medications work in people include:

- Type of mental disorder, such as depression, anxiety, bipolar disorder, and schizophrenia
- Age, sex, and body size
- Physical illnesses
- Habits like smoking and drinking
- Liver and kidney function
- Genetics
- Other medications and herbal/vitamin supplements
- Diet
- Whether medications are taken as prescribed (NIMH, 2014).

Mild tranquilizers (Valium, Librium, Xanax, Ativan) reduce anxiety and are useful for phobias, panic disorders, PTSD, and so on. Drugs known as antidepressants (Celexa, Lexapro, Prozac) are widely used in the treatment of depression. Most are not effective for several weeks or even months after starting treatment. They

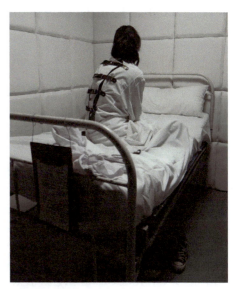

Treatment of mental disorders has changed dramatically with drug therapy. Calming medications can now accomplish what required a straitjacket only a few decades ago.

© Alvaro German Vilela/Shutterstock.com

work well for about a third of patients with major depression. Major tranquilizers (Haldol, Navane, Thorazine), called antipsychotic drugs, are used extensively with schizophrenic patients. Lithium and other drugs are widely used for bipolar disorder. Disulfiram (Antabuse) is sometimes used with alcohol addiction. There is some controversy over the effectiveness of these chemical substances. Most can have serious side effects; overdoses can sometimes be fatal. Their use frequently accompanies other forms of therapy where they might be employed simply to control anxiety or depression sufficiently so that the therapist can more effectively employ other treatments.

Psychosurgery

Another medical therapy involves surgical intervention. Among the most highly publicized of the surgical treatments is that of excising (removing) or making lesions (cuts) in the frontal lobes of the brain **(prefrontal lobotomy)**, a procedure that is sometimes successful in reducing anxiety and alleviating depression. Among its frequent side effects, however, are a general dulling of emotional reaction, occasional epileptic seizures, listlessness, and sometimes stupor (Jones, 2009). The procedure is now seldom used and is, in fact, illegal in many states and countries (Mashour et al., 2005).

> **Prefrontal lobotomy:**
> A surgical treatment that removes or makes lesions (cuts) in the frontal lobes of the brain to reduce anxiety and alleviate depression.

Electroconvulsive Therapy (ECT) Treatment

ECT or shock therapy involves the use of a brief burst of electric current aimed at inducing a seizure in the brain. ECT treatment is used most commonly in treating severe depression. This procedure is typically performed in a hospital setting and may involve a series of six to ten treatments spaced over a few months. Side effects can include short-term memory loss, confusion, and disorientation. Typically, these side effects subside in a short time period, but can linger and become problematic for the patient. ECT is rarely used and usually only in situations in which drug therapy is not effective.

Insight Therapy

The major insight therapy is *psychoanalysis*, which is based on Freudian theory. Its identifying characteristic is the belief that alleviating mental disorders depends upon achieving insight into the causes of present behavior. Freud believed mental disturbances result from conflict between basic impulses (id) and conscience (superego) that gives rise to anxiety. The ego's role is to find ways of reducing this anxiety. The psychoanalyst's main task is to uncover basic sources of conflict, many of which will have a sexual basis.

One of the techniques used in psychoanalysis is **free association**, where the patient is encouraged to say whatever comes to mind without evaluating or discarding material. The hope is these associated ideas will eventually lead therapist and patient back to a fundamental source of conflict or, failing that, the therapist will recognize where blocks to association occur. These **mental blocks** are assumed to be the ego's defenses against revealing sensitive issues. Through repeated verbal probing, the analyst may eventually be able to understand these blocks and perhaps even remove them.

> **Free association:** A technique used in psychoanalysis where the patient is encouraged to say whatever comes to mind without evaluating or discarding material.
>
> **Mental blocks:** The ego's defenses against revealing sensitive issues.

The analysis of dreams is another technique employed in psychoanalysis. Freud believed that ego defenses are at their weakest during sleep, and that sources of intense psychodynamic conflict are therefore often revealed during dreams. He distinguished between the apparent (manifest) meaning of dreams (a baseball bat is a baseball bat, whether in a dream or in a batter's hand) and their symbolic meaning (for all you and I know, a baseball bat might be a symbol of penis envy in a dream).

In the course of repeated psychoanalytic sessions, the therapist pays particular attention to the relationship that develops between analyst and patient. According to Freud, this relationship often illustrates **transference:** the therapist becomes somebody of importance in the patient's life, perhaps embodying a source of historical conflict. Thus, patients react to their therapists as they would to a parent or a lover, displaying in their behavior many of the attitudes they might

> **Transference:** Redirection of feelings directed toward the therapist that are associated with important figures in the patient's life.

have had toward that important person, perhaps at a time when conflict was being born. In effect, attitudes and feelings that might be the basis of conflict are transferred to the analyst. Recognizing this, the analyst may then interpret this transference, along with information derived from analysis of dreams and of association, thereby arriving at some insight into the source of the patient's conflict.

Learning-Based and Cognitive Therapy

Therapies based on learning theories stand in sharp contrast to psychoanalysis. The learning therapist is concerned mainly with the manifestations of disorders rather than with their causes and assumes that these manifestations can be unlearned or that more acceptable forms of behavior can be learned in their stead. Accordingly, these therapies make extensive use of learning principles.

Behavior Modification

Although there are a variety of approaches to **behavior modification**, most are based on the general principle that people are influenced by the consequences of their behavior—that their immediate environmental circumstances are more relevant than early experiences or psychic conflicts.

In a procedure called **systematic desensitization** (or *counterconditioning*), the therapist tries to replace an undesirable response with another incompatible and more desirable response. The procedure is particularly effective for phobias (Head & Gross, 2009). When treating a severe bird phobia, for example, the therapist begins by training the patient in relaxation. Once she has learned to relax, she is presented with the least frightening item on an ordered list of fear-inducing situations that she has previously described—perhaps just an outdoor scene with no birds and no bird noises. She is asked to imagine this scene while relaxing, relaxation being incompatible with anxiety and fear. In successive sessions, the patient is encouraged to imagine other situations until she can imagine a bird without any anxiety. Eventually, she might be able to hold one in her hand.

Closely related to systematic desensitization is **exposure therapy**, where the patient is simply exposed to fear- or anxiety-producing

> **Behavior modification:** The idea that people are influenced by the consequences of their behavior and their immediate environmental circumstances are more relevant than early experiences or psychic conflicts.

> **Systematic desensitization:** A type of therapy where the therapist tries to replace an undesirable response with another incompatible and more desirable response. The procedure is particularly effective for phobias.

> **Exposure therapy:** When a therapist exposes a patient to fear- or anxiety-producing stimuli.

stimuli. The procedure is much faster than systematic desensitization because it is not based on the notion that the patient should feel no fear. Rather, it is based on the belief that simply exposing the patient repeatedly to the fear-related stimulus will lead to reduction and eventual elimination of fear reactions. Research indicates that exposure therapy, sometimes using computer-based *virtual reality* simulations, can be highly effective in treating anxiety disorders such as PTSD (Reger et al., 2011).

Aversive conditioning, another learning-based approach, attempts to attach negative feelings and bring about avoidance behavior with respect to certain situations. For example, patients might be subjected to a mild electric shock or other aversive stimulus when they engage in, or think about, some inappropriate behavior. Some sexual disorders such as fetishes can be effectively treated with this approach.

> **Aversive conditioning:** When a therapist attempts to attach negative feelings and bring about avoidance behavior with respect to certain situations.

Positive Reinforcement

Another learning-based approach uses positive reinforcement for desirable behavior, sometimes combined with the withdrawal of reinforcement for undesirable behavior. For example, highly withdrawn patients might be given tokens, which can be exchanged for meaningful rewards, for social interaction. Instead of tokens, verbal reinforcement (praise) might be used.

Rational Emotive Behavior Therapy

Ellis's (1974; Ellis & MacLaren, 2005) **rational emotive behavior therapy (REBT)** is a *cognitive* therapy. It is premised on the assumption that our cognitive interpretations of events and situations are the root of emotional turmoil. Accordingly, therapy shouldn't focus on obscure historical causes but on the individual's immediate interpretation of the meanings of environmental events.

> **Rational emotive behavior therapy:** Therapist has the patient focus on his or her immediate interpretation of the meanings of environmental events, rather than obscure historical causes.

Ellis lists a number of erroneous assumptions that people make. When these assumptions are violated, the individual is anxious and unhappy. The goal of the therapist is to direct the patient's attention to these irrational ideas and to change them. The whole point is to replace irrational beliefs with more rational ones through cognitive and verbal means. Ellis lists many irrational beliefs, but he describes the following three as the main ones (Ellis, 2003):

1. I must always perform outstandingly well and win everybody's complete approval or I am bad, incompetent, and unworthy.
2. Other people must always treat me well and fairly; otherwise they are rotten and bad and don't deserve a good life.
3. My life must always be favorable, safe, hassle free, and enjoyable; if it isn't, I won't be able to bear it and it won't be worth living.

Ellis describes these irrational ideas as beliefs (B) in his A-B-C theory of disturbance. According to this theory, an emotional reaction or consequence (C) is usually ascribed to some specific experience (A, for activating event). In fact, however, the emotional consequence (C) is not a function of the event (A), but of the beliefs (B) the individual has. Since the majority of these beliefs are irrational (if they were rational, the emotional consequences would not ordinarily be disturbing), the goal of therapy is to replace irrational with rational beliefs (Figure 8.4).

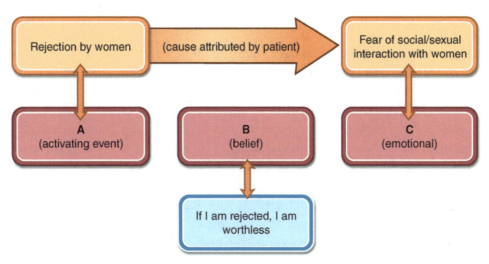

Figure 8.4   Ellis's A-B-C theory of disturbance.

Cognitive-Behavioral Therapy

CBT is a combination of behavior therapy and cognitive therapy and is a common mode of therapy used today. The premise behind this treatment modality is for a therapist to help the client identify distorted or unhealthy thinking patterns and work toward changing these patterns. The belief is as you change your thoughts, then a change in behavior often ensues.

The Effectiveness of Therapies

A large number of outcome studies have been conducted to look at the effectiveness of different therapies. Some look at improvements in morale—in the individual's sense of well-being and happiness. Others look at symptom reduction or at the reduction of impairment and at improvements in level of functioning. Many use highly objective measures, such as time spent doing compulsive behaviors, duration of abstinence from alcohol or drugs, incidence of gambling, or number of panic attacks.

Studies suggest some form of therapy is more helpful than no treatment (Smith et al., 1980). Sharf (2012) and Bickman (2005) also found people in treatment improved more quickly than those people who did not seek treatment. Although it is argued that no particular form of treatment is better than the other, research has shown that each major form of therapy is superior to no form of treatment or placebo (Prochaska & Norcross, 2010).

Outcome studies indicate clearly that therapies are often remarkably effective for pretty well all mental disorders, including substance abuse (Sledge & Hutchinson, 2010), borderline personality disorder (Waldinger, 2010), depression (Richards & Perri, 2010), and many other disorders. The move today is toward evidence-based treatment approaches, which have clear research support for best practices. Some therapies are clearly more effective than others for specific purposes. For example, *exposure therapy* has been shown to be highly effective in treating or preventing PTSD (Reger et al., 2011). Similarly, there is evidence that rational emotive behavior therapy is effective for depression—as are drug treatments (Sava et al., 2009). And drug therapies are effective for an enormous number of mental disorders, including bipolar disorders, anxiety disorders, personality disorders, and psychotic disorders. A few additional types of therapy include: light therapy, Eye Movement Desensitization Reprocessing (EMDR), art therapy, play therapy, and animal-assisted therapy.

Spirituality and Religion in Therapy

Although many psychological therapies have been shown to be effective in treating various mental disorders, studies over the past 30 years that have examined treatments that took patients' religious beliefs into account in therapy have shown results superior to secular treatments or usual care (Azhar et al., 1994; Azhar & Varma, 1995; Coelho et al., 2007; Razali et al, 1998; Xiao et al., 1998). Furthermore, studies have shown that a majority of adults suffering from mental disorders prefer to include religion in their therapy (Stanley et al., 2011). Research at Duke University's Center for Spirituality, Theology, and Health has consistently shown that incorporating spirituality into treatment improves outcomes. For example, in the *Handbook of Religion and Health, Second Edition* (2012), researchers from the Center for Spirituality, Theology, and Health reviewed 299 quantitative studies examining the relationship between religious beliefs, behaviors, and anxiety. In their review, they found that anxiety was reduced by religious/spiritual interventions in nearly 50% of the studies reviewed. Furthermore, when they reviewed the quality of the research studies (defined by rigorous methods and control of extraneous variables), the percentage of studies finding an inverse relationship between anxiety and religious/spiritual interventions rose to 60%. Additionally, of the 41 experimental studies or randomized clinical trials reviewed in their book, 71% reported that interventions involving religiosity or spirituality lowered anxiety.

While the body of research seems strong regarding the importance of including spirituality/religion in therapy, investigation of these studies reveals that spirituality is a complex construct and not one that is uniformly applied across studies. In fact, in interviews of clinical psychologists, Crossley and Salter (2005) found that clinicians find spirituality to be an elusive concept and one that is diverse across clients. Although interviewed clinicians supported the use of spirituality to help clients reach harmony, they reported it was a difficult concept overall to incorporate. Similarly, Barker and Floersch (2010) reported social workers claim that spirituality is a complicated and sometimes a vague construct in practice.

Typically, when spirituality and/or religion is used in therapy it is designed to match the preferences of the individual seeking help and thus, spiritual practices and truths vary largely. In their Religiously Integrated Cognitive Behavioral Therapy, Pearce and colleagues from Duke University's Center for Spirituality, Theology, and Health have developed a therapy that combines cognitive behavioral therapy with religious teachings and practice of five religions (Christianity, Judaism, Islam, Buddhism, and Hinduism). Depending on the client, a different religious version of the therapy is used and tested. Research on this therapy has shown it to be efficacious in treating mental illness outcomes and further suggests that incorporating one's religion into therapy is more effective than traditional therapies (Pearce et al., 2015).

There is a great need to continue the investigation of the spiritual and religious practices that are most effective in therapy. Furthermore, for Christian researchers and psychologists, it is important that terms be well defined and practices be clearly outlined when studying spirituality or the use of religion in therapy.

SUMMARY

A mental disorder includes patterns of behavior or thought that are not reasonable or easily understood and are associated with "clinically significant" distress or impairment in coping with the environment. Many individuals in the United States are impacted by a mental disorder every year. Psychologists use the

DSM-5 to help diagnosis a multitude of disorders and a wide variety of effective treatment approaches and therapies exist to help individuals diagnosed with disorders continue to lead happy and productive lives. ⌐Furthermore, integration of spiritual elements into therapy has shown effectiveness in improving mental health. As with all areas of Psychology, more research is needed to understand and treat mental disorders, and Christian psychologists should continue to study how faith and the Bible can be used, in conjunction with psychological and biological therapies, to improve well-being.⌐

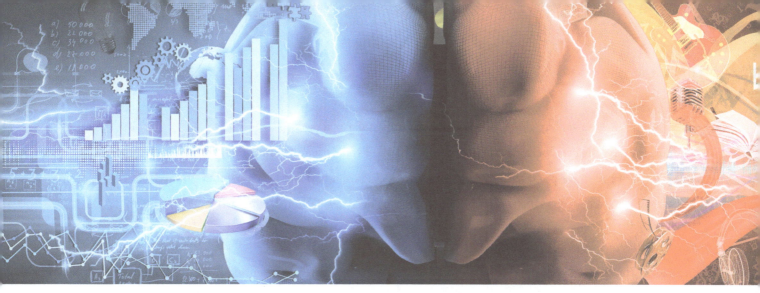

Glossary

Absolute threshold   A method used to study the limits of sensation; the smallest amount of a physical stimulus that can be correctly detected 50% of the time.

Accommodation   The process of adapting the current schemas to match the new information or experiences.

Acetylcholine   A neurotransmitter present in the peripheral as well as central nervous system, involved in voluntary activity as well as physiological functions (such as heart and respiration rates).

Action potential   A pulse-like electrical discharge along a neuron. Sequences of linked action potentials are the basis for the transmission of neural messages.

Active Deception   Active deception is deception by commission

Active vocabulary   Words actually used in speech.

⌐Acuity   The level of detail in a picture or the sharpness of an image.⌐

Adaptation   In perception, refers to a change in sensitivity resulting from stimulus conditions.

⌐Adaptive functioning   An inability to meet developmental and sociocultural standards for personal independence and social responsibility in activities of daily life such as communication, social participation, and independent living.⌐

Adrenal glands   Endocrine glands situated at the top of the kidneys, involved in releasing hormones at times of stress.

Adrenaline   Also called *epinephrine*. A substance produced by the adrenal glands, released in response to stress.

Afterimage   A visual image that continues after the stimulus that caused it is no longer present.

Aggression   Actions with the intent to harm others.

Agonists   An agent or drug that enhances the activity of some naturally occurring substance. For example, cocaine is a dopamine agonist in that it appears to stimulate the activity of dopamine.

Agoraphobia   Intense anxiety about, or avoidance of, unfamiliar places.

Agreeableness   A "Big Five" personality factor comprised of the traits friendly, compassionate, and cooperative.

Alleles   Each of two corresponding forms of a gene, one being inherited from each parent.

Alpha waves   Slower, deeper brain waves characteristic of deep relaxation, having a frequency of 8 to 13 cycles per second.

Altruistic behaviors   Self-sacrificing and helpful behaviors.

Amnesiacs   Those who experience partial or total loss of memory, sometimes resulting from head trauma.

Amok   A primarily male disorder common to Malaysia and other Southeast Asian countries, characterized by violent, homicidal episodes followed by amnesia.

Amplitude   ⌊The amount of vibration or pressure in a sound wave often referred to as loudness.⌋

Amygdala   A small structure in the limbic system (part of the forebrain) that is involved in emotion and aggression and that plays an important role in the processing and storage of memories that have to do with emotion.

Androgens   Male sex hormone.

Animistic thinking   Attributing lifelike qualities to inanimate objects.

Anonymous Research   Research that has ensured no identifying information is gathered and participants cannot be identified once the study is concluded

Anorexia nervosa   Psychological disorder characterized by being significantly underweight.

Anosmia   Inability to detect odors.

Antagonists   A drug that blocks the effectiveness of a neurotransmitter. For example, *beta blockers* are antagonists that reduce blood pressure by impeding receptivity of adrenaline receptors.

⌊Antidepressants   A classification of medications that treats depression through regulating neurotransmitters like serotonin.⌋

APGAR scale   Assessment scale used right after birth to determine the condition of the baby.

Aphagia   Undereating.

Archetypes   Literally, the first or original model. In Jung's theory, a universal thought or shared historical memory which is largely unconscious.

Archival research   Describes research that relies on preexisting records such as census counts, birth records, and school achievement records.

Army Alpha   The test given to literate military personnel to determine rank.

Army Beta   The nonverbal test given to illiterate military personnel to determine rank.

Arousal theory   A theory stating that individuals behave in a way to maintain an optimal level of arousal.

Arousal   ⌊The physiological aspects of emotion that can be detected and measured.⌋

Artificial insemination   The process of introducing sperm in a female's reproductive tract without sexual intercourse.

Asperger's syndrome   A developmental disorder characterized by impaired social interactions and repetitive behavior patterns. Now considered one of the *autism spectrum* disorders.

Assimilation   The process of ⌊integrating⌋ new information in a form to match the current schemas.

Association areas of the brain   Parts of the four cerebral lobes involved in higher mental processes like thinking, learning, and remembering.

Assumption   A belief that guides reasoning and research, accepted as fact, but often unprovable.

Attachment   The ˌemotionalˌ bond that ties two people together.

Attention deficit hyperactivity disorder (ADHD)   A disorder marked by excessive general activity for a child's age, attention problems, high impulsivity, and low frustration tolerance. Also termed hyperactivity.

Attention   A concentrated mental effort that functions as a filter to ignore unimportant events and focus on important events.

Attention deficit/Hyperactivity Disorder   A persistent pattern of inattention and/or *hyperactivity*-impulsivity interfering with functioning or development.

Attitude   Prevailing and consistent tendency to react in a given way.

Attribution theory   ˌThe causes that people attach to the behaviors of themselves or others.ˌ

Attributions   Inferences regarding the causes of behavior.

Auditory cortex   The part of our brain that is primarily responsible for processing the auditory information.

ˌAuthoritarianˌ parenting style   Parenting characterized by low warmth and high demands.

ˌAuthoritative parenting style   Parenting characterized by high warmth and high demands.ˌ

Autism spectrum disorder ˌ(ASD)   A neurodevelopmental disorder of varying severity characterized by persistent, pervasive, and sustained impairments in how an individual interacts with or communicates with others, often accompanied by repetitive patterns of thought and behavior.ˌ

Autism   A complex developmental disability marked by impairments in social interaction and communication skills. Classified as a *pervasive mental disorder*.

Autobiographical memory   A type of declarative memory consisting of knowledge about personal experiences, tied to specific times and places.

Autonomic nervous system   That part of the peripheral nervous system that is not ordinarily under conscious control. It regulates physiological functions such as respiration, heart rate, temperature, and digestion and includes the sympathetic and parasympathetic systems.

Average   A mathematical indication of central tendency, obtained by summing the numbers that describe a characteristic and dividing by the number of cases involved. Although averages are often good descriptions of the characteristics of a group, they frequently do not describe individuals at all well.

Aversive conditioning   When a therapist attempts to attach negative feelings and bring about avoidance behavior with respect to certain situations.

Axon   The elongated part of a nerve cell. Axons ordinarily transmit impulses from the cell body to adjoining dendrites.

Barnum effect   The tendency to accept vague personality descriptions of oneself as accurate.

Basic orienting system   The perceptual system whose principal function is to provide the organism with information about position of the body, movement, and relation to the gravitational plane. Sometimes called the *vestibular sense*.

ˌBehavior   An action; something observable and measurable.ˌ

Behavior modification   systematic application of learning principles to change behavior

Behaviorism   The scientific study of the prediction and control of behavior

Behavioristic theories   Theories concerned with objective evidence of behavior rather than with consciousness and mind.

Beta waves   Typical shallow and rapid brain waves of person who is awake, having a frequency of 13 to 30 cycles per minute.

Biblical worldview   A comprehensive and integrated view of the world from a biblical perspective. Also defined as a conceptual framework centered on the Bible by which people consciously or unconsciously interpret or judge reality; the Bible is viewed as the written Word of God.

Big Five factors   A widely accepted personality typology that includes extraversion, openness, conscientiousness, agreeableness, and neuroticism.

Binaural cues   Auditory depth perception that occurs with the use of both ears.

Binge-eating disorder   Psychological disorder characterized by excessive binging; however, the individual does not engage in purging behaviors.

Biological constraints   Limitations on learning that result from biological factors rather than from experience.

Bipolar disorder   A disorder characterized by mania and depression.

Birth of the placenta   The third stage of the process of delivery in which the placenta and other supporting structures detach from uterine wall and pass through the birth canal.

Blind spot   A gap in the retina due to the exit of the optic nerve where no photoreceptors are located; this causes a blind spot in the visual field during sensation.

Blocking   A phenomenon in classical conditioning in which conditioning to a specific stimulus becomes difficult or impossible because of prior conditioning to another stimulus.

Body senses   Sensory systems involved in perceptions of our body. Include the vestibular sense (balance and movement), skin senses (pain, temperature, and touch), and the kinesthetic sense (awareness of limb and body position and movement).

Bottom-up processing   An information-gathering process starting from each individual stimulus.

Brain fag   A form of study-induced mental exhaustion found primarily in West Africa, evident in depression, insomnia, anxiety, and learning problems.

Brain stem   Part of the brain that connects the spinal cord with the higher brain centers. Includes the hindbrain (medulla, pons, cerebellum) and the midbrain (reticular formation).

Brain   A complex clustering of nerve cells that is centrally involved in coordinating activities and events in various parts of an organism. The human brain is reputedly the most complex structure in the universe.

Brief psychotic disorder   Similar to schizophrenia; however, symptoms can last from 1 day to 1 month.

Bubba psychology   An expression for folk beliefs in psychology; also referred to as naive or implicit theories. *Bubba* (or sometimes *bubbe* or *bubbie*) means grandmother.

Bulimia nervosa   Psychological disorder characterized by binging and purging.

Bulimia   An eating disorder characterized by episodes of binge eating followed by severe dieting and sometimes purging or the use of laxatives and diuretics or extreme exercise.

Bystander effect   The more people who witness an event, the less likely they are to get help.

Case study   An in-depth observation of an individual, animal, event, or treatment method

Central executive system   In Baddeley's model of working memory, the system concerned with regulating the flow of information from sensory storage, processing it for long-term storage, and retrieving it from long-term storage.

Central executive   A part of Alan Baddeley's working memory model responsible for coordinating the input and output of information to working memory, as well as to integrate the separate pieces of information from the visuospatial sketchpad and phonological loop; the "CEO" of working memory.

Central nervous system   The human nervous system, which includes the brain and the spinal cord.

Centration   The fixation on one characteristic of an object at the exclusion of other characteristics.

Cephalocaudal   Pattern of development from head to toe.

Cerebellum   A major brain structure attached to the rear of the brain stem, the principal functions of which appear to be coordinating motor activity and maintaining balance.

Cerebral cortex   The convoluted outer covering of the cerebrum, the main functions of which have to do with higher mental processes like thinking and imagining. (See *cerebrum*.)

Cerebrum   The main part of the human brain, consisting of the two cerebral hemispheres and covered by the cerebral cortex.

CHC Theory of Intelligence   The most researched and widely supported theory of intelligence.

Chemical senses   Senses that respond to the chemical properties of substances and gases: namely, taste and olfaction.

Chemoreceptors   A class of receptors that detect water-soluble, lipid-soluble chemicals.

Chromosomes   In the nucleus of all cells, the microscopic bodies that contain genes, which are the carriers of heredity.

Chunking   A memory process whereby related items are grouped together into more easily remembered "chunks" (for example, a prefix and four digits for a phone number, rather than seven unrelated digits).

Ciliary muscles   The muscles within the eye that stretch or compress the lens for the purpose of focusing the visual image.

Circadian rhythm   A biological/behavioral cycle that is approximately 1 day long. It describes our sleep/wake and temperature cycles.

Classical conditioning   Learning through stimulus substitution as a result of repeated pairings of an unconditioned stimulus with a conditioned stimulus

Clinical psychologists   Trained psychologists specializing in helping people with emotional and behavioral problems. (See *counseling psychologists*.)

Cochlea   The spiral structure in the inner ear that contains both fluid and the basilar membrane; the latter houses sensory receptors for audition.

Cocktail party phenomenon   The fleeting and unconscious availability for processing of stimuli to which the individual is not paying attention.

Cognitive apprenticeship   Novice learners are paired with older learners, teachers, or parents who serve as mentors and guides.

Cognitive dissonance   A conflict between cognitions regarding behaviors, beliefs, values, desires, and so on.

Cognitive schemas   Pattern of thought, based on experience, which organizes information about objects, events, and things in the world.

Cognitive theories   Theories that look at processes such as those involved in thinking, problem solving, imagining, and anticipating.

Cognitive overload   The amount of working memory resources dedicated to a specific task with the idea that there is a limit to the amount of processing load the brain can manage.

Cognitivism   An approach concerned mainly with intellectual events such as problem solving, information processing, thinking, and imagining.

Commitment   The decision-making aspect of Sternberg's theory of love; involves deciding that one is in love and resolving what to do about it.

Complexity   With respect to sound waves, defined in terms of the mixture of waves emanating from vibratory sources, giving rise to subjective impressions of timbre.

Compliance   Changing one's behaviors due to an explicit (verbal or nonverbal) request from a nonauthority figure.

Conception   When a sperm fertilizes an egg.

Conceptual facts   Things we assert about the way the world operates based on strongly held views often derived from experience.

Concurrent schedule of reinforcement   A situation in which two or more different reinforcement schedules, each typically related to a different behavior, are presented at the same time.

Conditioned response   Previously the UR that is now given in response to the CS

Conditioned stimulus   A once neutral stimulus that becomes conditioned after repeated pairings with the US

Conduct disorder   A disorder that begins in late childhood and often becomes more severe in adolescence, which includes persistent pattern of behaviors violating the rights of others or socially inappropriate for the child's age.

Cones   A specific group of photoreceptors that are specialized to process color and are useful for daylight vision and high visual acuity.

Confederate   A participant in the study who is also part of the research team

Confidential Research   Research in which participants can be identified by information that is gathered. However, this information is kept in a manner that participant responses are not shared with others and the participants cannot be identified

Conformity   Changes in behavior due to unspoken group pressure.

Conscientiousness   A "Big Five" personality trait, it includes awareness of one's personal identity and mental processes like thinking, imagining, and feeling.

Consciousness   Awareness of one's personal identity. Self-awareness. Awareness of mental processes like thinking, imagining, and feeling.

Conservation task   A technique used to display limitations in thinking during the preoperational stage.

Constructivism   A general term for student-centered approaches to teaching, such as discovery-oriented approaches, reciprocal learning, or cooperative instruction—so called because of their assumption that learners should build (construct) knowledge for themselves.

Consummate love   Love that has all three components from the triangular theory.

Contiguity   Closeness in time of the stimulus and response

Control group   Group of participants not exposed to the independent variable

Conventional moral reasoning   Kohlberg's second stage of moral development when people focus on maintaining social order.

Converge   The ability of the two eyes to move, rotate inward toward the nose; this is often referred to as being cross-eyed.

Conversion disorder   A disorder similar to somatic symptom disorder but individuals with this disorder have one or more symptoms of altered voluntary motor or sensory functioning such as paralysis, weakness, tremors, or problems with vision or hearing.

Cornea   The transparent coating that covers the eyeball.

Correlation fallacy   The mistaken belief that if two variables are correlated, they must be causally related. Correlation is not proof of causation.

Correlation   A statistical relationship between variables. High positive correlation means that high scores on one variable are generally accompanied by high scores on the second. A high negative correlation means that high scores on one are typically associated with *low* scores on the second.

Correlational research methods   Provides information on the initial link between variables of interest

Correlational research   Research designed to uncover relationships between variables without determining cause and effect.

Counseling psychologists   Psychologists whose main function is to *counsel* individuals regarding issues relating to vocational or educational choices, learning problems, relationships, and mild emotional, physical, and mental disorders. (See *clinical psychologists*.)

Creationism   The belief that present life forms were created by a supreme being.

Criterion   (plural *criteria*) A standard, value, or goal by which something is judged; a necessary condition.

Cross-sectional design   Research design that collects information from different groups of people of different ages.

Cross-sectional study   Method of investigation that involves observing and comparing different subjects, usually at different age levels.

Culturally biased   A term used when an intelligence test gives an unfair advantage to White, affluent, male test takers.

Culturally loaded   A term used when many of the items on the intelligence test are derived from the mainstream culture.

Cutaneous sensitivity   Cutaneous senses (skin sense) refers touch, pressure, temperature, and pain (nociception).

Daydreaming   Engaging in waking dreams or reveries that are mainly under the dreamer's control.

Decibel   The scientific unit of measurement for loudness.

Declarative memory   Explicit, conscious long-term memory; may be either semantic or episodic.

Defense mechanisms   An unconscious mental strategy designed to avoid conflict and anxiety; examples include denial and repression.

Delivery   The second stage of the process of delivery in which the fetus passes through the birth canal.

Delta waves   Very slow brain waves (frequency of up to 4 per second) characteristic of deep sleep.

Delusions   False beliefs or opinions.

Demand characteristics   Hints and cues participants use to tell themselves how the researcher wants them to behave

Dendrites   Hair-like extensions emanating from the cell body of the neuron. Dendrites ordinarily receive impulses from adjoining axons.

Deoxyribonucleic acid (DNA)   A substance assumed to be the basis of all life, consisting of four chemical bases arranged in a mind-boggling number of combinations in the form of a double spiral (helix).

Dependent variable   Variable observed or measured

Depersonalization disorder   An Axis I DSM-IV-TR disorder marked by feelings of unreality, as though everything were a dream.

Depressant   A type of drug that slows down physiological functions. Alcohol is a commonly abused depressant and it slows down respiration.

Descriptive research   Describes the characteristics of an individual or of a group. Designed to answer one or more questions relating to who, what, where, when, and how (for example: What is the average age at which North American children say their first word?).

Deterministic   Having to do with the belief that every action has an identifiable cause that can be predicted given sufficient knowledge about prior events and their effects. Often contrasted with belief in free will.

Developmental psychologists   Study cognitive, physical, and emotional changes that occur between conception and death.

Developmental psychology   The study of change across the life span.

Diagnostic and Statistical Manual of Mental Disorders   A handbook used by health care professionals in the United States and much of the world as the authoritative guide to the diagnosis of mental disorders by classification in terms of categories, severity, and distinguishing characteristics of each disorder.

Difference threshold   A method used to study the sensitivity of sensation; the smallest difference between two stimuli that can be correctly detected 50% of the time; this is also called the just-noticeable difference.

Difficult infants   A type of temperament characterized by irregularity with respect to things like eating, sleeping, and toilet functions; withdrawal from unfamiliar situations; slow adaptation to change; and intense as well as negative moods.

Dilation and effacement   The first stage of the process of delivery in which the fetus turns head down and the cervix begins to expand.

Direct reinforcement   Results from the consequences of the act itself.

Discovery learning   A learner-centered approach to teaching in which the acquisition of new knowledge comes about largely through the learner's own efforts.

Discriminative stimulus (SD)   Skinner's term for the features of a situation that an organism can discriminate to distinguish between occasions that might be reinforced or not reinforced.

Disequilibrium   A state of cognitive imbalance, in which information does not match current cognitive schemas.

Dispositional attributions   Causes of behavior related to characteristics of an individual.

Dissociative amnesia   A sudden and temporary loss of memory not attributable to any organic cause.

Dissociative disorders   Disorders that involve separating certain memories or thoughts from normal consciousness.

Dissociative fugue   A loss of memory characterized by wandering and sometimes assuming a new identity.

Dissociative identity disorder   A complex type of dissociation in which individuals are from time to time dominated by distinctly different, complex, highly integrated personalities.

Distortion theory   A theory of forgetting that recognizes that what is remembered is often changed or reconstructed.

Dizygotic twins   Twins that result from two separate eggs and that are therefore fraternal (nonidentical).

Dominant gene   A gene that takes precedence over other genes in determining a related trait.

Dopamine   A neurotransmitter centrally involved with pleasure and reinforcement and also implicated in some instances of drug addiction as well as in conditions such as Parkinson's disease.

Doppler shift   The change in pitch emitted by an object moving horizontally in space, in relation to a stationary observe.

Double blind study   Neither the participant nor the researcher knows to which group the participant has been assigned.

Double-blind procedure   An experimental procedure in which neither the subjects nor the examiners know who is in the experimental group and who is in the control group.

Drive reduction   Behaviors that reduce an individual's drive state.

Drive   A state of motivation to act in a particular way to satisfy a need.

Drug intoxication   Recent use of a substance that induces a maladaptive and impairing state but is reversible.

Drug tolerance   Habituation to a drug. Evident in the observation that the effects of a drug often lessen with increasing use.

Dual or two-process theory   The idea that we localize low-frequency sounds by using time or phase differences, or both.

Dyadic interactions   Interactions involving two individuals.

Dysphoria   The opposite of euphoria; a common feature of drug withdrawal.

Dysthymic disorder   Marked by a serious, chronic depression lasting at least 2 years.

Eardrum   The thin membrane at the end of the ear canal that vibrates at a specific frequency when bombarded by sound waves.

Easy infants   A temperament type marked by high regularity in behaviors such as eating and sleeping; high interest in novel situations; high adaptability to change; and a preponderance of positive moods, as well as low or moderate intensity of reaction.

Echolocation   The use of sound to localize objects, based on the amount of time it takes an echo to return to the sound source.

Ectomorphs   According to Sheldon, a frail, thin body type, described as withdrawn and concerned with intellectual matters.

Educational psychologists   Are concerned with issues relating to understanding and improving teaching and learning in educational settings.

Effector   A specialized cell or organ that carries out a response to a nerve impulse.

Ego   In Freud's theory, the rational, reality-oriented level of human personality, developing as the child becomes aware of what the environment makes possible and impossible.

Egocentrism   The inability to see the world from another person's point of view.

Elaboration   A memory strategy that involves forming new associations, linking with other ideas or images.

Elaborative rehearsal   A type of rehearsal in which a person actively tries to tie new information to pre-existing information already in long-term memory. The net effect is to increase the likelihood that the new information is retained in long-term memory.

Electra complex   A Freudian stage (around 4 years) when a girl's awareness of her genital area leads her to desire her father and to become jealous of her mother.

Electroconvulsive shock therapy (ECT)   An effective treatment for depression where seizures are created in the brain in a very brief and controlled situation.

Electrodermal response   Electrical conductivity of the skin.

Eliciting effect   Imitative behavior in which the observer does not copy the model's responses but simply behaves in a related manner.

Embryo   The developing fetus, between 2 and 8 weeks after conception.

Embryonic period   Second period of prenatal development from implantation to 2 months.

Emotions   Complex feeling states that include predictable physiological arousal, cognitions, and behaviors.

Empirical facts   Things we can assert about the way the world operates based upon observational evidence.

Encoding   The process of transforming experienced information into a form that can be later stored and used by the brain.

Endocrine system   A system of glands that secrete hormones whose functioning affects things such as growth, maturation, behavior, and emotion. Includes the pituitary, the adrenal glands, and the gonads.

Endomorphs   Sheldon's large somatotype, believed to love comfort, be relaxed, good natured, and sociable.

Entity theory   The belief that intelligence is fixed and unchanging.

Episodic memory   A type of long-term memory (explicit memory, to be exact); conscious recollection of one's personal experiences that took place at a specific time in a certain place.

Equal loudness contours   Lines measuring the function of loudness and frequencies of sound waves.

Equilibrium   A state of cognitive balance, in which information matches current cognitive schemas.

Eros   A term employed by Freud to describe the life instinct, the urge for survival and procreation.

Estrogen   Female sex hormone.

Ethnic psychosis   A mental disorder such as Windigo that is specific to an ethnic group.

Ethologist   One who studies the behavior of animals in their natural habitats.

Event-related field (ERF)   A measure of magnetic fields at the scalp relating to neural activity typically associated with specific stimuli.

Event-related potential (ERP)   A measure of electrical activity in identifiable areas of the brain, corresponding to specific stimuli.

Evolution   A scientific theory that holds that present life forms have developed from preexisting species through a series of modifications governed by laws of natural selection and diversification of species.

Evolutionary psychology   An approach in psychology defined by its attention to biology and genetics as sources of explanation for human learning and behavior.

Ex post facto study   A study in which the experimenter does not assign subjects to experimental conditions or exercise control over these conditions; the experimenter simply studies participants on the basis of differences that already exist among them.

Expectancy-value theory   The belief that motivation is determined by the expectancy of success and the value of the reward.

Experimental group   Group exposed to the independent variable

Experimental psychologists   Psychologists involved in the use of experimental (scientifically controlled) research.

Experimental research   Involves the manipulation of a variable of interest and assignment of participants to treatment conditions

Experimenter bias   An unconscious phenomenon whereby experimenters' expectations influence their observations. Not to be confused with experimenter dishonesty.

Explicit memory   A type of long-term memory; conscious memory about facts or experiences.

Exposure therapy   When a therapist exposes a patient to fear- or anxiety-producing stimuli.

Exteroceptors   Receptors that respond to environmental energy or stimuli that are occurring from the outside of one's body, such elements include light, sound, touch, and chemical agents.

Extinction   Process by which classically conditioned responses are eliminated

Extraversion   This "Big Five" personality factor includes traits of outgoing, positivity, and energetic.

Extrinsic reinforcement   Reinforcement to increase a behavior in the future that comes from an external source (e.g., reading to earn a reward)

Factor analysis   A statistical procedure for reducing correlational data to a smaller number of dimensions by grouping closely related variables.

Fading theory   The belief that the inability to recall long-term memories increases with the passage of time as memory traces fade. Also termed *decay theory*.

Fallopian tube   One of two tubes that link the ovaries and the uterus, where conception ordinarily occurs.

False memory syndrome   Describes the possibility that a memory—especially of a highly traumatic event—may be a memory of something that has not actually occurred.

Falsifiable   The quality of being able to be tested through scientific methods and shown to be false or true.

Fast mapping   The learning of a concept, like a word, in a single trial.

Fetal period   Third and final period of prenatal development from 2 months to birth.

Fetus   An immature child in the uterus.

Fixation   A developmental delay due to unsuccessfully developing through a stage, sometimes manifested in personality characteristics and emotional disorders relating to the earlier stage.

Fixed interval (FI)   A reinforcement schedule provides reinforcement for the first response made after a certain time period has elapsed since the last reward, regardless of how many responses have been made during the interval.

Fixed ratio (FR)   A reinforcement schedule provides reinforcement after a specific/defined number of responses are made.

Flashbulb memories   A type of long-term memory. Memories formed by dramatic and surprising public or personal events; typically known to be immune from forgetting.

Flynn effect   The observation that there are gains in measured IQ over generations.

Forgetting   Loss from memory over time; contrasted with extinction, which occurs as a result of cessation of reinforcement.

Fovea   An area at the center of the retina that contains the highest density of cones; visual acuity is highest in this region.

Free association   A technique used in psychoanalysis where the patient is encouraged to say whatever comes to mind without evaluating or discarding material.

Frequency   With respect to sound waves, the number of waves per second in Hertz units, giving rise to the perception of pitch.

Frontal lobes   Frontal part of the cerebral cortex, centrally involved in higher thought processes.

Frustration   Occurs when someone is prevented from achieving a goal.

Frustration–aggression hypothesis   Hypothesis that frustration leads to anger, which will result in aggression if a suitable object or person releases the aggression.

Functionalism   The study of how the mind of an organism adapts to its current environment

Gender identity disorder   Persistent, overwhelming cross-gender identification and discomfort with one's anatomical gender.

Generalize   To engage in a process whereby conclusions derived under one set of circumstances are extended to other similar circumstances. The objective of most scientific investigations is to arrive at conclusions that can be generalized.

Generalized anxiety disorder   A disorder marked by excessive anxiety and worry, as a general state rather than episodic subjective sensation of anxiety, in the absence of specific situations or objects that might be associated with anxiety reactions.

Genes   The carriers of heredity.

Genetic makeup   The assortment of genes that compose the individual's genetic code.

Genome   The complete set of chromosomes of an organism. All of an organism's inheritable traits.

Genomics   The discipline studying genomes in an attempt to establish relationships between genes and characteristics.

Genotype   Genetic makeup. The assortment of genes that compose the individuals genetic code.

Germinal period   First period of prenatal development from conception to implantation

Glare   An uncomfortable level of brightness.

Glial cells   Cells that support neural functioning. Among other functions, they clean out debris and form protective coatings around nerves. (See *myelin sheath*.)

Gonads　Hormone-producing sex glands. Testes in the male; ovaries in the female.

Group test　A type of test usually used to measure intelligence that may be given to large groups at one time.

Habituation　A decrease in response to a stimulus following repeated or prolonged exposure. Also used to describe *drug tolerance*.

Hair cells　Thin, hair-like structures that are the sensory receptors for audition; these are located on the basilar membrane inside the cochlea.

Hallucinations　Perceptions of experiences without corresponding external stimuli together with a compelling feeling that these are real.

Hallucinogens　A drug type causing hallucinations.

Hawthorne effect　Describes the observation that individuals who are aware that they are members of an experimental group sometimes perform better simply for that reason.

Hering's opponent process theory　A theory that suggests we perceive color in terms of paired opposing groups of colors: red-green, yellow-blue, and black-white.

Heritability coefficient　The proportion of the total variation in a trait that is due to heredity. *High heritability* means that a large proportion of the variation in a characteristic is caused by a variation in genes.

Hippocampus　A limbic system structure in the forebrain, which is primarily involved in learning and memory.

Holistic education　A label for educational approaches that attempt to remedy what is seen as the failure of traditional education to educate the whole brain—especially the right hemisphere, which is speculatively linked with music, art, and emotion.

Holophrase　A word the child uses to convey as much meaning as an adult would convey with a much longer phrase.

Homeostasis　The body's ability to maintain a relatively stable physiological equilibrium under changing circumstances.

Hormones　Chemicals that have a pronounced effect on growth, maturation, behavior, and emotions and that are produced by endocrine glands and secreted directly into the bloodstream.

Humanism　A philosophical and psychological orientation primarily concerned with our worth as individuals and with those processes that are considered to make us more human.

Humanistic psychology　A branch of psychology whose primary concern is with the development of the self and with the uniqueness of the individual. Sometimes referred to as *third force* psychology; the other two forces are behaviorism and Freudian theory. (See *humanism*.)

Hyperphagia　Overeating caused by intense sensations and hunger drives.

Hypnosis　A state characterized by heightened suggestibility (willingness to do and to believe what is suggested by the hypnotist).

Hypothalamus　A small structure at the base of the brain involved in the functioning of the autonomic nervous system and in temperature regulation.

Hypothesis　An educated guess, often based on theory, which can be tested. A prediction based on partial evidence of some effect, process, or phenomenon, which must then be verified experimentally.

Hypothetical thought　The ability to think about possible solutions and outcomes to problems or abstract ideas.

Id   In Freudian theory, all the instinctual urges that humans inherit, including eros and thanatos.

Identification   Refers to the process of assuming the goals, ambitions, mannerisms, and so on of another person.

Identity   In Erikson's theory, a term closely related to *self*. To achieve identity is to arrive at a clear notion of who one is.

Illness anxiety disorder   Extreme worry about having or acquiring a serious illness.

Imaginary audience   An egocentric tendency to assume that we are the focus of other people's attention, that everyone is aware of and interested in our dress and behavior.

Imaginary playmate   My imaginary playmate is my best friend and goes everywhere with me and likes a lot of the same things I do and gets upset if I don't say hello and ...

Imitation   Copying behavior. To imitate a person's behavior is simply to use that person's behavior as a pattern.

Implicit memory   A type of long-term memory; memory about how to perform a task (usually accessed unconsciously).

Impulse-control disorder   Marked by the repeated inability to refrain from a behavior that is harmful or seriously distressful.

In vitro fertilization   The fertilization of egg cells outside the womb—literally in glass (in *vitro*).

Inattentional blindness   Diverted attention resulting in failure of accurate scene detection as if we are blind to that event.

Incentive motivation   The greater the subjective value of an item or reward, the more someone is motivated to achieve the item or reward.

Incremental theory   The belief that intelligence is ⌐not fixed⌐ and can be improved upon with effort.

Independent variable   Variable manipulated by the researcher

Individual test   A test, usually used to measure intelligence, that can be given to only one individual at a time.

Industrial/organizational psychologists   Psychologists concerned with applying psychological principles to workplace-related issues.

Infancy   The first 2 years of life.

Inhibitory/disinhibitory effect   The type of imitative behavior that results either in the suppression (inhibition) or appearance (disinhibition) of previously acquired deviant behavior.

Insanity   A legal term defined by law and determined by a court in consultation with mental health experts.

Insight   The sudden recognition of relationships among elements of a problem.

Instinctive drift   Refers to the tendency of organisms to revert to instinctual, unlearned behaviors.

Instincts   ⌐An innate, consistent tendency or compulsion in response to stimuli.⌐

Institutional Review Board (IRB)   A committee that reviews proposals of intended research and evaluates if the research is ethical and if the rights of the participants are being protected

⌐**Interaural intensity difference**   The slight difference in sound volume as it reaches one ear compared to the other.⌐

Interaural time differences   The slight difference in time sound arrives at one ear before the other ear.

Intellectual disability   Commonly called *mental retardation,* a significant general depression in the ability to learn, usually accompanied by deficits in adaptive behavior.

Intellectual developmental disorder (IDD)   A neurodevelopmental disorder characterized by deficits in general intellectual functioning, involving things such as reasoning, problem-solving, abstract thinking, judgment, academic learning, and learning from experience.

Intelligence quotient   The global score derived from standardized intelligence tests.

Intelligence   The overall capacity to think and act logically and rationally within one's environment.

Intermittent explosive disorder   A disorder identified in childhood that is marked by the repeated failure to resist aggressive impulses.

Internal working model   The expectations and understanding of the world formulated by the first attachment with caregivers.

Interoceptors   The receptors that are able to respond to materials inhaled, ingested, or passed, and to changes in chemical surroundings, mechanical pressure, or shearing force.

Interpersonal attraction   Positive thoughts of another person that are strongly influenced by proximity, similarity, and physical attraction.

Intimacy   In Sternberg's theory of love, refers to emotions that lead two people to want to share things.

Intrinsic reinforcement   Reinforcement to increase a behavior in the future that comes from an internal source (e.g., reading because one loves to read)

Introspection   The examination of one's own mind to inspect and report on personal thoughts or feelings about conscious experiences

Introversion   The opposite of extraversion   withdrawn, shy, and reluctant to engage in social interaction.

Intuitive thinking   Thought based on immediate comprehension rather than logical processes.

Iris   The colored part of the eye; a muscle in the center of which is an opening that forms the pupil.

Kinesthetic sense   One of the body senses, often referred to as the "muscle and joint sense," consisting of receptors sensitive to movement of muscles, joints, and tendons.

Kinesthetic sensitivity   Kinesthetic sense refers to knowledge about spatial position and movement information occurring from mechanical stimulation of mobile joints, muscles, and tendons.

Law of effect   Behaviors followed by reinforcement are more likely to be repeated and behaviors not followed by reinforcement are less likely to recur.

Learning   A process resulting in a relatively consistent change in behavior or behavioral potential and is based on experience.

Lens   A biconvex crystalline structure that helps focus the visual image onto the retina in the back of the eye.

Libido   A Freudian term for sexual urges.

Limbic system   A grouping of brain structures located beneath the cerebral cortex, associated mainly with emotion, memory, and reinforcement and punishment.

Link system   A mnemonic system that requires forming linked visual images of what is to be recalled.

Loci system   A mnemonic system in which images of items to be recalled are "placed" in familiar locations.

Locus of control ⌐When people attribute their successes or failures to internal or external factors.⌐

Logical thought The ability to rationally think about problems and situations.

Longitudinal design Research design that collects information from the same group of people across time.

Longitudinal study Psychological investigation in which the same subjects are examined over a period of time.

Long-term memory One of the human memory systems that can store information for a long-period of time.

Love The province of poets rather than scientists. A strong, interpersonal attraction, says science: a combination of passion, intimacy, and commitment.

Magical thinking Thinking, often characteristic of preschoolers and young children, that is not entirely logical or scientifically valid, but rather inventive and surprising and sometimes bizarre—hence *magical*.

Magnocellular pathway A visual pathway for peripheral vision and low spatial resolution images from the retina.

Major depressive disorder A disorder characterized by a conglomerate of symptoms, including apathy, listlessness, despair, loss of appetite, sleep disturbances, unwavering pessimism, and thoughts of suicide.

Major depressive episode At least 2 weeks of significantly depressed mood, loss of interest, and other symptoms of depression.

⌐**Mechanoreceptors** Receptors that sense deformations and motion of solids, liquids, and gases. Mechanical forces are those that tend to deform or accelerate objects possessing mass.⌐

Medulla The lowest part of the brain, found at the very top of the spinal cord and containing nerve centers involved in regulating physiological activity such as breathing, digestion, and heart functioning.

Melatonin A natural hormone closely tied to sleep/wake cycles. Also called the *sleep hormone*.

Memory The process of encoding, storage, and retrieval of any piece of information obtained through conscious experience; a memory can also be an individual instance of encoded, stored, and retrieved information.

Menarche A girl's first menstrual period.

Mental age The age given at which a child is currently performing intellectually.

Mental blocks The ego's defenses against revealing sensitive issues.

Mental disorder ⌐A major disturbance in an individual's thinking, feelings, or behavior that reflects a problem in mental function.⌐

Mesomorphs Sheldon's moderate somatotype, believed to love adventure, exercise, and activities that demand boldness and courage.

Meta needs Higher-level needs related to an organism's tendency toward ⌐psychological⌐ growth.

Mind A term referring primarily to human consciousness. Often defined as originating from or resulting in processes of the brain associated with activities like thinking, imagining, and perceiving.

Mnemonic aids Systematic aids to remembering, like rhymes, acrostics, or visual imagery systems.

Mnemonist Professional memorizer.

Modal model of memory A widely accepted model of memory that describes three types of storage: sensory, short-term, and long-term.

Model   A pattern for behavior that can be copied by someone. Also refers to descriptions of objects or phenomena. In science, models often serve as a sort of mental guide.

Modeling effect   The type of imitative behavior that involves learning a novel response.

Models   Guides or ways of looking at whether a behavior is abnormal or not.

Molecular genetics   The branch of genetics that deals with hereditary transmission. Concerned with how genes are copied, how mutations come about, and how genes are expressed in species characteristics.

Monaural cues   Auditory depth perception that occurs with just one ear.

Monozygotic twins   Twins resulting from the division of a single fertilized egg—hence *identical twins*.

Mood disorders   Mental disorders involving mood disturbance—for example, bipolar disorder and major depressive disorder.

Motivation   Conscious and unconscious forces that initiate and direct behavior.

Multiple intelligences   A theory suggesting that intelligence is a product of a number of abilities rather than one ability.

Myelin sheath   An insulating, protective coating that surrounds nerve fibers and facilitates neural transmission.

Naïve realism   A philosophical idea that states the world should exist in only one form and therefore all the viewers should see the world as it exists.

Nanometer   One billionth of a meter.

Narcotics   A drug type producing sensations of well-being.

Naturalistic observation   Observe people or animals in their natural settings

Nature-nurture controversy   The debate over whether heredity or environment is most influential in determining developmental outcomes.

Need for achievement   A strong desire to excel, meet some inner standard of excellence, and do well.

Negative reinforcer   Unwanted or painful stimulus is removed and consequently, the probability that the behavior will be repeated is increased

Nerve   Bundles of fibers consisting of neurons, whose functions is the transmission of neural impulses.

Nervous system   All parts of the body composed of nerve cells, the function of which is to transmit messages. The major components of the human nervous system are the brain, the spinal cord, receptor systems associated with the major senses, and other nerve cells implicated in the functioning of muscles and glands.

Neurogenesis   The active production of new neurons. Most prevalent during the prenatal period but also occurs in adulthood.

Neurons   Specialized information processing cells that make up the brain; they control sensations, thinking, and movement. A single nerve cell, the smallest unit of the nervous system, and its basic structural unit. The function of the neuron is to transmit impulses that are basically electrical but are made possible through chemical changes.

Neuroscience   A biologically based science that looks at the nervous system—especially the brain—to understand consciousness and higher mental processes.

Neuroses   A once common label for a variety of milder mental disorders characterized by anxiety and fear.

Neuroticism   This "Big Five" personality factor includes the traits nervous, sensitive, and moody.

Neurotransmitters   Naturally produced chemicals that are released by nerve cells and that initiate or facilitate transmission of messages among nerve cells (e.g., serotonin, dopamine, norepinephrine, and acetylcholine).

Nociceptors   ⌐A type of receptor that responds to painful stimuli or stimuli that are capable of causing tissue damage.⌐

Nominal fallacy   The ⌐faulty⌐ assumption that naming something explains it.

Nondeclarative memory   Unconscious, nonverbalizable effects of experience such as might be manifested in acquired motor skills or in classical conditioning.

Nonexperimental research   Makes observations about how variables are related to one another and describes the findings

Nonnaturalistic observation   Observations that occur in a laboratory or in other circumstances where the investigator deliberately manipulates or otherwise affects the phenomena being observed.

⌐Nonprojective tests   Personality tests that measure personality through straightforward questions or statements on which individuals report.⌐

Nonsense syllables   Meaningless combinations of vowels and consonants, like gar, lev, and kur, often used to study memory.

Norepinephrine   A neurotransmitter linked with arousal, memory, and learning. Anomalies in the functioning of the norepinephrine system may be linked to manifestations of depression. Also called *noradrenaline*.

Normal distribution   A probability distribution that takes the form of a symmetrical bell-shaped graph and that describes the expected distribution of many events and characteristics.

⌐Nuclei   Groups of neurons working together.⌐

Obedience   ⌐Changing one's behavior due to a direct request from someone in authority.⌐

Obesity   ⌐A disorder involving excessive body fat that can lead to significant health issues.⌐

Object concept   Piaget's expression for a child's understanding that the world is composed of objects that continue to exist when they aren't being sensed.

Object permanence   The understanding that objects exist even when out of sight.

Observational learning   Bandura's theory involving learning through observing and imitating models

⌐Observer bias   An error due to the personal motives and expectations of the viewer.⌐

Obsessive-compulsive disorders   A disorder characterized by recurrent and unwanted thoughts and/or the need to perform repetitive physical or mental actions.

Occipital lobe   The part of our brain responsible for processing the visual information.

Occlusion   A phenomenon in which an object closer to a viewer appears to block another object that is farther away from the viewer.

⌐Ocular lubrication   Our visual system is able to make its own surface liquid that serves to keep the eye moist; natural tears are the mechanism for this process.⌐

Oedipus complex   A Freudian concept denoting the developmental stage (around 4 years) when a boy's increasing awareness of the sexual meaning of his genitals leads him to desire his mother and envy his father.

Olfaction   The sense of smell.

Olfactory epithelia   Thin mucus membranes located in each nostril, containing odor-sensitive cells.

Openness   A "Big Five" personality factor consisting of the traits inventive, curious, and unconventional.

Operant conditioning   (Skinner) describes changes in the probability of a response as a function of its consequences

Operant   An apparently voluntary response emitted by an organism.

Operation   Piaget's term for a thought process characterized by certain rules of logic.

Opinion   Evaluations, which lack the strong motivational consequences of attitudes.

Oppositional defiant disorder   ⌐A disorder identified in childhood characterized by a pattern of hostile, disobedient, defiant behavior toward authority figures.⌐

Optic chiasm   The point in the brain at which the optic nerves from each eye meet and partly cross over to the other side of the brain.

Optic nerve   A large bundle of axons that leave the back of the eye and carries visual information to the visual cortex of the brain.

Organization   A memory strategy involving grouping items to be remembered in terms of similarities and differences.

Overjustification   Large external rewards reduce the intrinsic value of a behavior.

Ovum   The sex cell produced by a mature female, consisting of 23 chromosomes rather than 23 pairs of chromosomes.

⌐Pacinian⌐ corpuscles   The sensory receptors for touch located under the skin; these sensory receptors respond to pressure applied to the surface of the skin.

Panic attacks   An episode occurring for no apparent reason involving intense fear and anxiety, often accompanied by physical symptoms such as shortness of breath and heart palpitations.

Panic disorder   A disorder characterized by recurrent and persistent panic attacks.

Paradoxical effect   Literally, a surprising or contradictory effect; used to describe the apparently sedating effect that some stimulants (such as Ritalin) have on children who suffer from excessive activity.

Paradoxical sleep   Another label for REM sleep, so called because during this stage of sleep physiological functions such as heart and respiration rate are very similar to those of a waking state.

Paraphillias   Variety of sexual deviants such as exhibitionism, fetishism, and sadism.

Parasympathetic nervous system   Part of the autonomic nervous system that regulates physiological reactions that accommodate emotional reactions.

Parietal lobes   Cerebral lobes located just above the temporal lobes, between the frontal and occipital lobes. The parietal lobes are involved in sensation.

Parkinson's disease   A central nervous system disease characterized by tremors, slow movement, and other symptoms; associated with low dopamine levels in the brain.

Parvocellular pathway   A visual pathway for central vision and high spatial resolution images.

Passion   In Sternberg's love theory, a strong, often sexual, and sometimes overwhelming desire to be with another person.

Passive Deception   Passive deception is deception by omission

Passive vocabulary   Words that are understood but that may not actually be used in speech.

Perception   ⌐Psychological processes whereby meaning, past experience or memory, and judgments are used to evaluate the significance of particular stimuli.⌐

Peripheral nervous system   The neural networks that fan out from the central nervous system to various parts of the body.

Permissive parenting style   Parenting characterized by high warmth and low demands.

⌐Persistent depressive disorder (or dysthymia)   A continuous, long-term form of depression, considered not as severe as major depression, in which individuals feel hopelessness, lack of interest in activities, and experience low self-esteem.⌐

Personal fable   An expression of adolescent egocentrism marked by the elaboration of fantasies, the hero of which is the adolescent.

Personality disorders   Behaviors that are socially inappropriate, inflexible, and often antisocial that typically become apparent during childhood or adolescence and are manifested as relatively stable.

Personality   The set of attributes that characterize an individual, including temperamental, emotional, mental, and behavioral tendencies, influenced by genetics, learning, and social experiences.

Persuasion   Deliberate attempts to alter behavior or beliefs.

⌐Phase difference   The slight difference in the degree the sound wave is moving through its wave when it reaches one ear compared to the other.⌐

⌐Pharmacodynamics   The mechanism of action of drugs and their corresponding effects.⌐

⌐Pharmacokinetics   The path that drugs take through our body, from start to finish.⌐

Phenomenology   Concerned with the world of appearance—that is, the world as it appears to the individual.

Phenotype   A person's manifested characteristics, resulting from the interaction of genotype with the environment. (See *genotype*.)

Phi phenomenon   The illusion of motion created by presenting a rapid succession of slightly different static images.

Philosophy   The pursuit of wisdom; the study of reality in an attempt to arrive at an accurate and unified conception of the universe and its nature. Because people are part of the universe, philosophy originally included attempts to understand humans—which is now the discipline of psychology.

Phobias   Intense, irrational fears, recognized by the person as unreasonable, and often leading to avoidance of certain objects or situations.

Phonetic system   A powerful mnemonic system in which previously learned associations between numbers and mental images are used to recall large numbers of items forward, backward, or in any order.

Phonological loop   A part of Alan Baddeley's working memory model specialized to process verbal and auditory information.

Photons   A visible light particle. In *quantum physics,* an elementary particle that is the basic unit of light and other forms of radiation.

Photoreceptors   ⌐Receptors that are sensitive to radiant electromagnetic energy (light).⌐

Physiological basis of aggression   Biological factors impacting aggression such as hormones.

Physiological needs   Basic needs to satisfy internal functions of an organism.

Pibloktoq   Arctic hysteria, a 19th-century form of madness found almost exclusively among the Inuit, marked by bouts of screaming and crying and sometimes shedding one's clothing.

Pinna   The outer funnel-shaped structure of the ear; normally, this is what people refer to as their ear.

Pituitary gland   A small endocrine gland found as a protrusion off the hypothalamus. The *master gland* involved in controlling functioning of other endocrine glands.

Pixilation   A physical measure of resolution on a screen.

Placebo control group   Participants are exposed to a placebo

Placebo   An inert substance or object

Placenta   A flat, thick membrane attached to the inside of the uterus during pregnancy, connected to the fetus by means of the umbilical cord.

Plasticity   The ability to change.

Play   Activities with no goal other than the enjoyment derived from them.

Polymodal nociceptors   Nociceptors activated by a variety of high-intensity mechanical, chemical, and very hot or very cold stimuli.

Pons   A small brain structure that appears as a bulge at the front of medulla. Part of the brain stem involved in breathing and arousal.

Population   In an experiment, the group to which results are to be generalized.

Positive reinforcer   Pleasing or positive stimulus is given and consequently, the probability that the behavior will be repeated is increased

Postconventional moral reasoning   Kohlberg's third stage of moral development when people focus on equality and the greater good.

Posttraumatic stress disorder   A disorder that appears following exposure to an extremely traumatic event where fear is experienced long after the traumatic event.

Potential stimulus   Physical energy that has yet to be detected, but is in fact detectable.

Preconventional moral reasoning   Kohlberg's first stage of moral development when children focus on receiving rewards or avoiding punishments.

Prefrontal lobotomy   A surgical treatment that removes or makes lesions (cuts) in the frontal lobes of the brain to reduce anxiety and alleviate depression.

Prejudices   Personal beliefs about groups based on illogical reasoning or faulty generalization.

Premenstrual dysphoric disorder   A severe extension of premenstrual syndrome (PMS) in which a woman experiences at least one of the following symptoms around her menstrual cycle: sadness or hopelessness, anxiety, extreme moodiness, or irritability/anger.

Prenatal development   Period of development from conception to birth.

Primary reinforcers   Stimuli that are naturally rewarding for an organism.

Proactive interference   This is when old information prevents the formation or recall of newer information.

Process of delivery   The three-stage process of giving birth.

Projective tests   Personality tests in which stimuli are ambiguous and testees' responses are interpreted as reflecting unconscious aspects of personality.

Propinquity   Physical proximity; factor related to physical attraction.

Proprioceptive sensation   Sensation relating to bodily position and movement arising from receptors within the body.

⌐**Proprioceptors**   Are sensory receptors that are activated by muscular movement or passive displacement of body parts.⌐

Protowords   The infant's first wordlike sounds used to signify a specific person or object.

Proximodistal   Pattern of development from core out to appendages.

Psychiatrists   Medical doctors with extensive additional training in the identification and treatment of mental and emotional disorders.

Psychoactive drug   A chemical substance that has the ability to alter perception, mood, behavior, and/or physiological function.

Psychoanalysis   A psychotherapeutic technique based on the belief that humans face psychological distress as a result of unconscious conflicts and desires (primarily sexual or aggressive) brought on during childhood

Psychodynamic theory   The elaborate theory developed by Freud, based on his notion that behavior and personality are developed by unconscious urges and motivations.

Psychodynamic   Relating to conscious and unconscious forces that influence behavior and personality.

Psychological hedonism   ⌐A psychological approach suggesting that humans are ultimately motivated by a desire for pleasure and the avoidance of pain.⌐

Psychological needs   The need for affection, belonging, achievement, independence, social recognition and self-esteem.

Psychology   Systematic investigation of human behavior and thought

Psychometric _g_   A term coined by Spearmen regarding a person's general or overall intelligence.

Psychosocial development   Erikson's phrase to describe human development as a sequence of stages involving the resolution of crises that are mainly social.

Puberty   Sexual maturity following pubescence.

Pubescence   Changes of adolescence leading to sexual maturity.

Pupil   The opening in the iris that allows light to pass through the lens and into the eyeball.

⌐**Pupilloconstrictor zone**   The part of the midbrain responsible for controlling the diameter of the pupil.⌐

Random sampling   A sampling procedure in which each member of the population has an equal chance of being selected for the sample.

Rapid-eye-movement sleep (REM sleep)   Sometimes referred to as the stage 5 of sleep, the stage during which most of our dreaming occurs.

Rational emotive behavior therapy   Therapist has the patient focus on his or her immediate interpretation of the meanings of environmental events, rather than obscure historical causes.

⌐**Rebound effect**   Drugs exert acute, immediate effects as the drug wears off, an equal but opposite effect generally takes place. Taking a drug that produces sedation can result in increased arousal when it is deactivated by the body.⌐

Receptors   Specialized cells or groups of cells that respond to sensory stimulation.

Recessive gene   A gene whose characteristics are not manifested in offspring when paired with the corresponding dominant gene.

Reciprocal altruism   An explanation for altruistic behavior that asserts individuals are helpful to others because of the expectation this will be reciprocated.

reciprocal teaching   a method designed to improve reading comprehension

Reflex   A simple, unlearned behavior like blinking in response to something coming toward the eye.

Reflexes   Stimulus–response associations

Refractory period   A brief period after firing during which a neuron is "discharged" and is incapable of firing again.

Regression   A Freudian expression for the phenomenon of reverting to some of the activities and preoccupations of earlier developmental stages.

Rehearsal   The process of repeatedly introducing new information in order to retain the information in short-term memory, or to introduce into long-term memory.

Reinforcement   The effect of a reinforcer.

Reinforcer   any stimulus condition or consequence that increases the probability of a response

Rejecting/neglectful parenting style   Parenting characterized by low warmth and low demand.

Reliability   Consistency of your measure to produce similar results on different occasions

Repression   A Freudian term for the process by which intensely negative or frightening experiences are lost from conscious memory.

Respondent   A response elicited by a known, specific stimulus. An unconditioned response.

Response   A muscular, glandular, or mental reaction to a stimulus.

Reticular formation   (*Reticular activating system; RAS*) That portion of the brain stem assumed to be responsible for the physiological arousal of the cortex as well as for the control of sleeping and waking.

Retina   A light-sensitive membrane at the back of the eye that contains the sensory receptors for vision.

Retrieval cues   Stimuli like sounds, words, locations, smells, and so on that facilitate recall (that remind the individual of something).

Retrieval   The process of recognizing and then correctly recalling a piece of information from storage in long-term memory.

Retrieval-cue failure   Inability to remember due to the unavailability of appropriate cues.

Retroactive interference   A theory of forgetting in which more recent information gets in the way of trying to recall older information.

Reuptake   The process by which a nerve cell recaptures some of the neurotransmitters it has released. Some medications and drugs function to increase neurotransmitter effectiveness by blocking reuptake.

Rods   A specific group of photoreceptors that are specialized to process dim light and are useful for night vision and peripheral vision.

Sample   A subset of a population. A group with characteristics similar to those of the larger group from which they are selected.

Sapir-Whorf hypothesis   The belief that language is essential for and determines thought (strong form); or the belief that language limits but does not determine thought (weak form).

Schema (also scheme or schemata)   The label used by Piaget to describe a unit in cognitive structure. A scheme is, in one sense, an activity together with its structural connotations. In another sense, a scheme may be thought of as an idea or a concept. It usually labels a specific activity: the looking scheme, the grasping scheme, the sucking scheme.

Schemas   A cognitive framework placing information into classifications and groups.

Schizoaffective disorder   Includes symptoms of schizophrenia in addition to a mood disorder such as depression or mania.

Schizophrenia   A psychotic disorder characterized by emotional, cognitive, and perceptual confusion and a consequent breakdown of effective contact with others and with reality.

Schizophreniform disorder   Same symptoms as schizophrenia but the only differences are symptoms last only 1 to 6 months.

School psychologists   Psychologists who deal with behavioral and learning problems affecting schoolchildren and issues relating to testing and placement of gifted or challenged children.

Science   An approach and an attitude toward the search for knowledge that emphasize objectivity, precision, and replicability.

Scientific method   ⌐A set of orderly steps used to analyze and solve problems universally applied across scientific disciplines. The framework for the systematic study of behavior and mental processes.⌐

Secondary reinforcers   stimuli that may not be reinforcing initially but that eventually become reinforcing as a function of having been associated with other reinforcers.

Secure base   A safe, supportive relationship that infants use to explore and understand their world.

Sedatives   A drug type causing drowsiness.

Self-actualization   An ongoing process in which an organism attempts to reach its ⌐full⌐ potential.

Self-efficacy   ⌐Judgments and personal evaluations of one's own competence.⌐

Semantic memory   A type of long-term memory (explicit memory, to be exact); it is one's general knowledge about the world and specific concepts.

Sensation   ⌐Certain, immediate, and directly qualitative experiences or produced by simple isolated physical stimuli. Sensations always travel in an ascending fashion, starting from a particular sensory receptor and terminating in the brain.⌐

Senses   Specialized organs by means of which stimulation is received and felt (for example, organs related to sight, smell, touch, taste, and hearing.)

Sensitive period   Time when the major systems are being formed and are most vulnerable to damage.

Sensorimotor stage   Piaget's first stage of cognitive development.

Sensorimotor   First stage of Piaget's stages of cognitive development. It describes how infants understand their world. They understand their world mainly in terms of the activities they perform and the sensations that result.

Sensory adaption   A decline in a sensation's sensitivity resulting from the presence of a constant stimulus.

Sensory memory   A form of memory that holds large amounts of sensory information such as sights and sounds for a very brief amount of time, normally only a few seconds.

Serotonin   A neurotransmitter, the bulk of which is found in the gut, where it regulates intestinal activity. Too low levels of serotonin may be associated with depression.

Seven deadly sins of memory   A term coined by Schacter to illustrate the forgetful nature of human memory systems.

Sex chromosome   A chromosome in sperm and egg cells responsible for determining the sex of the offspring.

Sex-linked defects   Defects due to the action of a gene located on the sex chromosome, most often on the X chromosome, and most often manifested in males.

Sexual dysfunctions   Problems relating to sexual desire or response.

Shaping   Reinforcing small sequential steps in a chain of behaviors, leading to the desired final behavior

Short-term memory   A type of temporary memory used to hold information long enough for an individual to process it, and make sense of it; also called working memory.

Significant   In research, refers to findings that would not be expected to occur by chance alone more than a small percentage (for example, 5 or 1 percent) of the time.

Single blind study   Only the researcher knows to which group the participant has been assigned

Single-blind procedure   An experimental procedure in which either the investigators or the participants are not aware of who are members of the experimental group and who are members of the control group.

Situational attributions   Causes of behavior related to characteristics of the situation.

Skin senses   Also called the cutaneous senses, the body senses consisting of skin receptors sensitive to touch, temperature, and pain.

Skinner box   an experimental chamber used in operant conditioning experiments

Slow-to-warm-up infants   An infant temperament type marked by low activity level; high initial withdrawal from the unfamiliar; slow adaptation to change; and a somewhat negative mood, with moderate or low intensity of reaction.

Social cognitive theory   An explanation of learning and behavior that emphasizes the role of social reinforcement and imitation as well as the importance of the cognitive processes that allow people to imagine and to anticipate.

Social learning theory   Argues aggression is a result of learning from models in our environment.

Social phobia   Excessive fear of embarrassment in social situations, often leading to avoidance.

Social psychology   Studies the relationships among individuals or between individuals and groups.

Socialization   The process of learning behaviors that are appropriate and inappropriate for a given culture.

Sociobiological altruism   An explanation for altruistic behavior that asserts organisms are helpful to others to ensure survival of the species.

Solipsism   A philosophical idea that states the world exists by the viewer's conscious state and may be different from the objective state of this world.

Somatic symptom disorders   A disorder in which the patient has symptoms suggestive of some medical problem but no such problem can be found.

Somatic system   Part of the peripheral nervous system concerned with bodily sensations and muscular movement.

Somatoform disorders   A grouping of mental disorders characterized by physical complaints that appear to be medical in nature but cannot be explained by injury, disease, drug abuse, or other mental disorders.

Somesthesis   Bodily sensations.

Sound shadow   The difference in sound intensity due to head blocking/deflecting some of the sound waves.

Sound waves   Displacements of molecules caused by vibratory events whose subjective effect is the perception of sound.

Specific learning disabilities   A developmental disorder marked by impairments in cognitive skills such as reading, writing, arithmetic, or mathematical skills.

Specific phobia   Excessive and unreasonable fear brought about by a specific stimulus.

Sperm cell   The sex cell produced by a mature male, consisting of 23 chromosomes rather than 23 pairs of chromosomes.

Spinal cord   Main link between the brain and sensory and motor systems, closely involved in reflexes such as the knee-jerk reflex.

Spontaneous recovery   Is a classical conditioning-related behavior referring to the rapid reemergence of a previously extinguished behavior.

Statistical procedure   A way of analyzing data (observations). Typically used in scientific investigations to determine whether a set of observations might have been expected to occur by chance.

Stereotypes   Widely held beliefs about groups based on illogical reasoning or faulty generalization.

Stimulant   A type of drug that speeds up physiological functions. Cocaine is an abused stimulant and it speeds up the heart rate.

Stimulus (pl. stimuli)   A quantifiable pattern of physical energy, which is able to interact with an organism and produce a change in the condition of the organism. That is, a stimulus is a type of environmental energy, like light, that we are capable of detecting and responding to.

Stimulus discrimination   Involves making different responses to highly similar stimuli

Stimulus generalization   Involves making the same responses to different but related stimuli

Storage   The process of storing.

Strange situation   The procedure developed by Ainsworth to assess different attachment styles.

Stratified sampling   A sampling procedure that takes steps to ensure that subgroups of the population are represented proportionally in the final sample.

Structuralism   The study of breaking down conscious experience into its fundamental elements: sensations, feelings, and images

Structures   Formed when nuclei are grouped.

Subject variable   Characteristic or attribute of a participant that can impact the participant's behavior or thoughts

Substance-related disorders   Disorders related to drug abuse or to the effects of various chemical or gaseous substances, including medications.

Suggestibility   A characteristic of a hypnotic state wherein subjects become exceedingly ready to believe whatever is *suggested by* the hypnotist and willing to perform whatever activities are asked of them.

Superego   The personality structure that defines the moral or ethical aspects of personality.

Survey research   A questionnaire is designed to obtain information regarding individuals' behaviors, attitudes, or opinions

Survey   A research method that involves sampling a large group of individuals.

Susto   A Latino disorder marked by listlessness, muscle tics, and anxiety and attributed to the loss of one's soul following some trauma.

Symbolic model   A model other than a real-life person. For example, books, television, and written instructions are important symbolic models.

Symbolic thought   The ability to mentally use one object to stand for another.

Sympathetic nervous system   Part of the autonomic nervous system that instigates the physiological responses that accompany emotional behavior.

Synapse   A microscopic gap between the end of an axon and an adjacent dendrite, axon, or other cell across which neural impulses (neurotransmitters) travel.

Synaptic knob   Slight enlargements on the wispy branches at the ends of axons.

Synesthesia   A condition in which different sensations overlap and are processed simultaneously. A person with synesthesia might see a musical note or *hear* a color.

Systematic desensitization   A type of therapy where the therapist tries to replace an undesirable response with another incompatible and more desirable response. The procedure is particularly effective for phobias.

Systems   Many structures working together.

Taste buds   The sensory receptors for gustation that are located deep within porous structures on the tongue; there are five basic types of taste buds.

Temperament   Infants' and children's biological predisposition to respond to the world in predictable ways.

Temporal lobes   Cerebral structure located on either side of the cerebrum, associated primarily with speech, language, and hearing.

Teratogens   Any substances ingested, consumed, or experienced by the mother that can cross the placental barrier and damage the developing organism during pregnancy.

Territoriality   Example of an innate or biological aggressive tendency.

Thalamus   A small brain structure that serves as a major relay center for incoming sensory signals.

Thanatos   A Freudian term denoting the death wish or death instinct.

Therapy   Systematic processes for helping individuals overcome their psychological problems.

Thermal or mechanical nociceptors   Nociceptors associated with sensations of sharp, stinging pain.

Thermoreceptors   Receptors that are sensitive to changes in temperature.

Theta waves   Slow brain waves (4 to 7 per second) characteristic of the early stages of sleep.

Third force psychology   Maslow's term for the humanistic movement in psychology—so labeled to differentiate it from the *first force* (behaviorism) and the *second force* (Freudian psychodynamic theory).

Top-down processing   An information-gathering process starting from an individual's knowledge, expectations, and prior experiences.

Trait   Any distinct, consistent characteristic that can vary from one person to another.

Transduction   The process of converting a physical stimulus into a meaningful and useful neural signal capable of being interpreted by the brain.

Transference   Redirection of feelings directed toward the therapist that are associated with important figures in the patient's life.

Transitive inference   A type of logical thinking in which an inference is made about the relationship of two objects or events by comparing them with a third rather than by comparing them directly.

Triadic reciprocal determinism   Describes the three principal features of our social cognitive realities our personal factors (our personalities, our intentions, what we know and feel); our actions (our actual behaviors); and our environments (both the social and physical aspects of our world).

Triangular theory of love   Sternberg's theory of loving involving commitment, passion, and intimacy.

Triarchic theory of successful intelligence   Sternberg's view that intelligence involves analytical, creative, and practical abilities, as well as skill in selecting and shaping environments to maximize adaptation.

Type   A related grouping of personality traits.

Umami   One of the five distinct tastes humans can distinguish, variously described as *savory* or *meaty*.

Umbilical cord   A long, thick cord attached to the placenta at one end and to what will be the child's navel at the other.

Unconditioned response (UR)   The automatic, unlearned response an organism gives when the US is presented.

Unconditioned stimulus (US)   A stimulus that elicits an automatic, unlearned response from an organism.

Uterus   The womb, where the infant develops prenatally.

Validity   Ability of your measurement to accurately measure what it is supposed to measure.

Variable   An event or characteristic with at least two possible values.

Variable interval (VI)   A reinforcement schedule provides a reinforcement after the first response is made after some period of time has elapsed, but the time changes or varies from reinforcer to reinforcer.

Variable ratio (VR)   A reinforcement schedule provides reinforcement after a certain yet changing number of responses are emitted.

Vestibular organ   The part of the inner ear, consisting of the semicircular canals, involved in balance, body orientation, and movement.

Vestibular sense   The sense, highly dependent on the semicircular canals in the inner ear, that provides us with information about balance and movement.

Vicarious reinforcement   When you see someone doing something repeatedly, you unconsciously assume that the behavior must be reinforcing for that person.

Visual constancies   Properties of visual perception that enable us to perceive color, size, and shape as being constant under a variety of different conditions.

Visual-spatial sketch pad   One of the slave systems in Baddeley's model of working memory, concerned with the processing of material that is primarily visual or spatial.

Visuospatial sketchpad   A part of Alan Baddeley's working memory model specialized to process visual and spatial information.

Wavelength   The linear distance between two successive compressions or peaks in light waves.

Weber's law   A principle in sensation that suggests that the size of the difference threshold is relative to the strength of the original stimulus.

"What" pathway   A visual pathway projected into the temporal lobe that responds to and integrates information about the size, color, and/or the identity of an object.

"Where" pathway   A visual pathway projected into the parietal lobe that integrates information about the location of an object.

Windigo   A primarily male disorder found among some Native American tribes in which the victim becomes convinced that he will become a *Windigo*—a person-eating creature.

Withdrawal symptoms   A state occurring when an individual who regularly uses a drug, stops or reduces drug use, and can have unpleasant and sometimes dangerous reactions.

Working memory   The Baddeley model describing how information is processed in short-term memory by means of a control system (central executive system) and systems that maintain verbal material (phonological loop) and visual material (visual-spatial sketch pad).

Yerkes–Dodson Law   An optimal level of arousal exists for different behaviors and that this level varies both for different individuals and for different behaviors.

Young-Helmholtz trichromatic theory   A theory that recognizes the existence of three cone systems whose different responses to light waves determine perception of color.

Zygote   The fertilized egg that starts to divide.

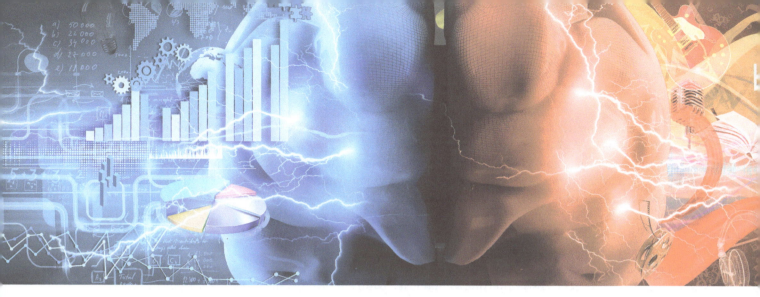

References

Abdala, G., Kimura, M., Koenig, H., Reinert, K., & Horton, K. (2015). Religiosity and quality of life in older adults: Literature review. *Life Style, 2*, 25–51. doi:10.19141/2237-3756/lifestyle.v2.n2.p25-51

Abelson, M. B., & Ousler, G. W., III. (1999). How to fight computer vision syndrome. *Review of Ophthalmology, 6*(7), 114–116.

Adolfsson, B., Andersson, I., Elofsson, S., Rossner, S., & Unden, A. L. (2005). Locus of control and weight reduction. *Patient Education and Counseling, 56*(1), 55–561.

Agency for Toxic Substances and Disease Registry (ATSDR). (2017). Lead toxicity: What are U.S. standards for lead levels? *Environmental Health and Medicine Education.* https://www.atsdr.cdc.gov/csem/csem.asp?csem=34&po=8

Ai, A. L., Tice, T. N., Peterson, C., & Huang, B. (2005). Prayers, spiritual support, and positive attitudes in coping with the September 11 national crisis. *Journal of Personality, 73*, 763–792. doi:10.1111/j.1467-6494.2005.00328.x

Ainsworth, M. D. S. (1973). The development of infant-mother attachment. In B. M. Caldwell & H. N. Ricciuti (Eds.), *Review of child development research* (Vol. 3, pp. 1–94). Chicago, IL: University of Chicago Press.

Ainsworth, M. D. S., Blehar, M. C., Waters, E., & Wall, S. (1978). *Patterns of attachment: A psychological study of the strange situation.* Hillsdale, NJ: Erlbaum.

Allport, G. W. (1968). The historical background of modern social psychology. In G. Lindzey & E. Aronson (Eds.), *Handbook of social psychology* (Vol. 1, 2nd ed.). Cambridge, MA: Addison-Wesley.

Allport, G. W., & Odbert, H. S. (1936). Trait names: A psycho-lexical study. *Psychological Monographs, 47*, 2–11. doi:10.1037/h0093360

Almas, E., & Landmark, B. (2010). Non-pharmacological treatment of sexual problems—A review of research literature 1970–2008. *European Journal of Sexology and Sexual Health/Revue europeene de sexology et de santé sexuelle, 19*(4), 202–211.

Altman, J., & Bayer, S. A. (1990). Migration and distribution of two populations of hippocampal granule cell precursors during the perinatal and postnatal periods. *Journal of Comparative Neurology, 301*(3), 365–381. doi:10.1002/cne.903010304

Alzheimer's Association. (2015). 2015 Alzheimer's disease facts and figures. *Alzheimer's Association Report.* https://doi.org/10.1016/j.jalz.2015.02.003

American Academy of Neurology. (2009, March 17). Shrinking in hippocampus area of brain precedes Alzheimer's disease. *Science Daily.* http://www.sciencedaily.com/releases/2009/03/090316173214.htm

American College of Obstetricians and Gynecologists. (2015). The Apgar score. Committee Opinion No. 644. *Obstetric Gynecology, 126*, 52–55.

American Optometric Association. (2020). *Computer vision syndrome.* https://www.aoa.org/patients-and-public/caring-for-your-vision/protecting-your-vision/computer-vision-syndrome

American Psychiatric Association. (2013). *Diagnostic and statistical manual of mental disorders* (5th ed.). Arlington, VA: American Psychiatric Publishing.

American Psychiatric Association. (2015). *Understanding mental disorders: Your guide to the DSM-5.* Washington, DC: American Psychiatric Publishing.

American Psychological Association. (2020). *About APA.* https://www.apa.org/about/

Amsler, S. J. (2010). Energetic costs of territorial boundary patrols by wild chimpanzees. *American Journal of Primatology, 72*(2), 93–103.

Anacker, C., Zunszain, P., Cattaneo, A., Carvalho, L. A., Garabedian, M. J., Thuret, S., . . . Pariante, C. M. (2011). Antidepressants increase human hippocampal neurogenesis by activating the glucocorticoid receptor. *Molecular Psychiatry, 16*, 738–750. doi:10.1038/mp.2011.26

Anderson, J. R. (1990). *Cognitive psychology and its implications* (3rd ed.). New York, NY: W. H. Freeman and Company.

Anderson, R. (2013). Positive sexuality and its impact on overall well-being. *Bundesgesundheitsbl, 56*, 208–214. https://doi.org/10.1007/s00103-012-1607-z

Antheunis, M. L., Valkenburg, P. M., & Peter, J. (2010). Getting acquainted through social network sites: Testing a model of online uncertainty reduction and social attraction. *Computers in Human Behavior, 26*(1), 100–109.

Anton, S. D., Martin, C. K., Han, H., Coulon, S., Cefalu, W. T., Geiselman, P., . . . Williamson, D. A. (2010). Effects of stevia, aspartame, and sucrose on food intake, satiety, and postprandial glucose and insulin levels. *Appetite, 55*(1), 37–43.

Arnone, D., Horder, J., Cowen, P. J., & Harmer, C. J. (2009). Early effects of mirtazapine on emotional processing. *Psychopharmacology, 203*(4), 685–691.

Arnulf, I., & Leu-Semenescu, S. (2009). Sleepiness in Parkinson's disease. *Parkinsonism & Related Disorders, 15*(Suppl. 3), S101–S104.

Asch, S. E. (1955). Opinions and social pressure. *Scientific American, 193*(5), 31–35.

Asensio, S., Romero, M. J., Romero, F. J., Wong, C., Alia-Klein, N., Tomasi, D., . . . Goldstein, R. Z. (2010). Striatal dopamine D2 receptor availability predicts the thalamic and medial prefrontal responses to reward in cocaine abusers three years later. *Synapse, 64*(5), 397–402.

Ashcraft, M. H., & Radvansky, C. A. (2010). *Cognition* (5th ed.). Upper Saddle River, NJ: Prentice Hall.

Atkinson, R. C., & Shiffrin, R. M. (1968). Human memory: A proposed system and its control processes. In K. W. Spence & J. T. Spence (Eds.), *The psychology of learning and motivation* (Vol. 2). London, England: Academic Press.

Azevedo, F. A. C., Carvalho, L. R. B., Grinberg, L. T., Farfel, J. M., Ferretti, R. E. L., Leite, R. E. P., . . . Herculano-Houzel, S. (2009). Equal numbers of neuronal and nonneuronal cells make the human brain an isometrically scaled-up primate brain. *Journal of Comparative Neurology, 513*(5), 532–541.

Azhar, M. Z., & Varma, S. L. (1995). Religious psychotherapy in depressive patients. *Psychotherapy & Psychosomatics, 63*, 165–173.

Azhar, M. Z., Varma, S. L., & Dharap, A. S. (1994). Religious psychotherapy in anxiety disorder patients. *Acta Psychiatrica Scandinavica, 90*, 1–3.

Baio, J., Wiggins, L., Christensen, D. L., Maenner, M. J., Daniels, J., Warren, Z., . . . Dowling, N. F. (2018). Prevalence of autism spectrum disorder among children aged 8 years — autism and developmental disabilities monitoring network, 11 sites, United States, 2014. *Morbidity and Mortality Weekly Report: Surveillance Summaries, 67*(6), 1–23. doi:http://dx.doi.org/10.15585/mmwr.ss6706a1

Baker, M. (2016). A Nature survey lifts the lid on how researchers view the 'crisis' rocking science and what they think will help. *Nature, 533*, 452–454.

Balaban, M. T., & Reisenauer, C. D. (2005). Sensory development. In N. J. Salkind (Ed.), *Encyclopedia of human development*. Thousand Oaks, CA: Sage. http://www.sage-ereference.com/human development

Bandura, A. (1977). *Social learning theory.* Englewood Cliffs, NJ: Prentice Hall.

Bandura, A. (1997). *Self-efficacy: The exercise of control.* New York, NY: W. H. Freeman.

Bandura, A. (2001). Social cognitive theory: An agentic perspective. *Annual Review of Psychology, 52,* 1–26.

Bandura, A., Ross, D., & Ross, S. A. (1961). Transmission of aggression through imitation of aggressive models. *Journal of Abnormal and Social Psychology, 63,* 575–582.

Bandura, A., & Walters, R. (1963). *Social learning and personality development.* New York, NY: Holt, Rinehart & Winston.

Banks, M. S., & Ginsburg, A. P. (1985). Early visual preferences: A review and new theoretical treatment. In H. W. Reese (Ed.), *Advances in child development and behavior* (Vol. 19, pp. 207–246). New York, NY: Academic Press.

Barbaresi, W. J., Colligan, R. C., Weaver, A. L., Voigt, R. G., Killian, J. M., & Katusic, S. K. (2013). Mortality, ADHD, and psychosocial adversity in adults with childhood ADHD: A prospective study. *Pediatrics, 131*(4), 637–644.

Barber, T. X., & Westland, S. (2011). *Thinking therapeutically: Hypnotic skills and strategies explored.* Norwalk, CT: Crown House Publishing.

Barker, S. L., & Floersch, J. E. (2010). Practitioners' understandings of spirituality: Implications for social work education. *Journal of Social Work Education, 46,* 357–370. doi:10.5175/Jswe.2010.200900033

Barreto, A., Zhai, J., Rishe, N., & Goa, Y. (2007). Significance of pupil diameter measurements for the assessment of affective state in computer users. *Advances and Innovations in Systems, Computing Sciences and Software Engineering, 43,*146–151.

Bartels, M., Rietveld, M. J., Van Baal, G. C., & Boomsma, D. I. (2002). Genetic and environmental influences on the development of intelligence. *Behavior Genetics, 32*(4), 237–249. doi:10.1023/A:1019772628912

Bartone, P. T. (2010). Preventing prisoner abuse: Leadership lessons of Abu Ghraib. *Ethics and Behavior, 20*(2), 161–173.

Batista, J., & Freitas-Magalhaes, A. (2009). The recognition of basic emotions in temporal lobe epilepsy. In A. Freitas-Magalhaes (Ed.), *Emotional expression: The brain and the face* (pp. 24–56). Porto, Portugal: Edicoes Universidade Fernando Pessoa.

Baumrind, D. (1973). The development of instrumental competence through socialization. In A. D. Pick (Ed.), *Minnesota symposia on child psychology* (Vol. 7, pp. 3–46). Minneapolis, MN: University of Minnesota Press.

Baumrind, D. (1991a). The influence of parenting style on adolescent competence and substance use. *Journal of Early Adolescence, 11,* 56–95. doi:10.1177/0272431691111004

Baumrind, D. (1991b). Parenting styles and adolescent development. In R. M. Lerner, A. C. Petersen, & J. Brooks-Gunn (Eds.), *Encyclopedia of adolescence* (pp. 746–758). New York, NY: Garland.

Bayer, S. A., Yackel, J. W., & Puri, P. S. (1982). Neurons in the rat dentate gyrus granular layer substantially increase during juvenile and adult life. *Science, 216*(4548), 890–892. doi:10.1126/science.7079742

Bays, J. (1990). Substance Abuse and Child Abuse: Impact of Addiction on the Child. Pediatric Clinics of North America, 37(4), 881-904. https://doi.org/10.1016/S0031-3955(16)36941-3

Beach, S. R., Schulz, R., Yee, J. L., & Jackson, S. (2000). Negative and positive health effects of caring for a disabled spouse: Longitudinal findings from the Caregiver Health Effects Study. *Psychology & Aging, 15*(2), 259–271. doi:10.1037//0882-7974.15.2.259

Beaver, K. M. (2010). The biochemistry of violent crime. In C. J. Ferguson (Ed.), *Violent crime: Clinical and social implications* (pp. 75–98). Thousand Oaks, CA: Sage.

Beck, A. T. (2008). The evolution of the cognitive model of depression and its neurobiological correlates. *American Journal of Psychiatry, 165*(8), 967–977.

Beck, A. T., & Freedman, A. (1990). Cognitive therapy of personality disorders. New York, NY: Guilford.

Beck, R. (2006). God as a secure base: Attachment to God and theological exploration. *Journal of Psychology and Theology, 34,* 125–132.

Belin, P., Zatorre, R. J., Lafaille, P., Ahad, P., & Pike, B. (2000). Voice-selective areas in human auditory cortex. *Nature, 403,* 309–312. doi:10.1038/35002078

Bellavite, P., Conforti, A., Piasere, V., & Ortolani, R. (2005). Immunology and homeopathy. 1. Historical background. *Evidence-based complementary and alternative medicine. eCAM, 2*(4), 441–452. https://doi.org/10.1093/ecam/neh141

Bender, J. A., Pollack, A. J., & Ritzmann, R. E. (2010). Neural activity in the central complex of the insect brain is linked to locomotor changes. *Current Biology, 20*(10), 921–926.

Benjamin, L. T., Jr. (2008a). The Pulfrich pendulum effect: When to and fro is roundabout. In L. T. Benjamin Jr. (Ed.), *Favorite activities for the teaching of psychology* (pp. 79–82). Washington, DC: American Psychological Association.

Benjamin, L.T., Jr. (2008b). Psychology before 1900. In S. F. Davis & W. Buskist (Eds.) *21st century psychology: A reference handbook* (pp. 2–11). Thousand Oaks, CA: Sage.

Berlyne, D. E. (1960). *Conflict, arousal, and curiosity.* New York, NY: McGraw-Hill.

Bermudez-Silva, F. J., Viveros, M. P., McPartland, J. M., & de Fonseca, F. R. (2010). The endocannabinoid system, eating behavior and energy homeostasis: The end or a new beginning? *Pharmacology, Biochemistry and Behavior, 95*(4), 375–382.

Bernard, L. L. (1924). *Instinct: A study in social psychology.* New York, NY: Holt, Rinehart & Winston.

Bhaduri, N. P., Sarkar, K., Sinha, S., Chattopadhyay, A., & Mukhopadhyay, K. (2010). Study on DBH genetic polymorphisms and plasma activity in attention deficit hyperactivity disorder patients from Eastern India. *Cellular and Molecular Neurobiology, 30*(2), 265–274.

Bickman, L. (2005). A common factors approach to improving mental health services. *Mental Health Services Research, 7*(1), 1–4. doi:10.1007/s11020-005-1961-7

Blake, R., & Sekuler, R. (2005). *Perception* (5th ed.). New York, NY: McGraw-Hill.

Blakemore, C. (1977). *Mechanics of the mind.* Cambridge, MA: Cambridge University Press.

Blakemore, S. J., Burnett, S., & Dahl, R. E. (2010). The role of puberty in the developing adolescent brain. *Human Brain Mapping, 31*(6), 926–933.

Blehm, C., Vishnu, S., Khattak, A., Mitra, S., & Yee, R. W. (2005). Computer vision syndrome: A review. *Survey of Ophthalmology, 50*(3), 253–262. doi:10.1016/j.survophthal.2005.02.008

Block, J. (1995). A contrarian view of the five-factor approach to personality description. *Psychology Bulletin, 117*(2), 187–215. doi:10.1037/0033-2909.117.2.187

Blouin, A. G., Blouin, J. H., Iversen, H., Carter, J., Goldstein, C., Gary, G., . . . Perez, E. (1996). Light therapy in bulimia nervosa: A double-blind placebo-controlled study. *Psychiatry Research, 60*(1), 1–9. doi:10.1016/0165-1781(95)02532-4

Boake, C. (2002). From the Binet–Simon to the Wechsler–Bellevue: Tracing the history of intelligence testing. *Journal of Clinical and Experimental Neuropsychology, 24*(3), 383–405. doi:10.1076/jcen.24.3.383.981

Bohannon, J. (2015). Many psychology papers fail replication test. *Science, 349*(6251), 910–911. doi:10.1126/science.349.6251.910

Bolles, R. C. (1970). Species-specific defense reactions and avoidance learning. *Psychological Review, 77,* 32–48.

Bolton, P. F., Golding, J., Emond, A., & Steer, C. D. (2012). Autism spectrum disorder and autistic traits in the Avon Longitudinal Study of Parents and Children: Precursors and early signs. *Journal of American Academy of Child and Adolescent Psychiatry, 51*(3), 249–260. doi:10.1016/j.jaac.2011.12.oo9

Borrero, J. C., Frank, M. A., & Hausman, N. L. (2009). Applications of the matching law. In W. T. O'Donohue & J. E. Fisher (Eds.), *General principles and empirically supported techniques of cognitive behavior therapy* (pp. 415–424). Hoboken, NJ: John Wiley & Sons.

Bowlby, J. (1953). *Child care and the growth of love.* London, England: Penguin Books.

Bowlby, J. (1969). *Attachment and loss: Vol 1. Attachment.* New York, NY: Basic Books.

Bransford, J. D., & Stein, B. S. (1993). *The IDEAL problem solver* (2nd ed.). New York, NY: W. H. Freeman.

Bregman, J. (2005). Apgar score. In N. J. Salkind (Ed.), *Encyclopedia of human development.* Thousand Oaks, CA: Sage. http://www.sage-ereference.com/humandevelopment

Breslau, N. & Peterson, E. L. (1996). Smoking cessation in young adults: age at initiation of cigarette smoking and other suspected influences. *American journal of public health, 86*(2), 214–220.

Bright, C. N., & Penrod, B. (2009). An evaluation of the overjustification effect across multiple contingency arrangements. *Behavioral Interventions, 24*(3), 185–194.

Brown, D. C. (Ed.). (2009). *Advances in the use of hypnosis for medicine, dentistry and pain prevention/management.* Norwalk, CT: Crown House Publishing.

Brown, R., & Kulik, J. (1977). Flashbulb memories. *Cognition, 5,* 73–99. doi:10.1016/0010-0277(77)90018-X

Bruer, J. T. (2006). Points of view: On the implications of neuroscience research for science teaching and learning: Are there any? *CBE Life Science Education, 5*(2), 104–110.

Brumariu, L. E., & Kerns, K. A. (2010). Parent–child attachment and internalizing symptoms in childhood and adolescence: A review of empirical findings and future directions. *Development and Psychopathology, 22,* 177–203. doi:10.1017/S0954579409990344

Buchanan, K. I., & Bardi, A. (2010). Acts of kindness and acts of novelty affect life satisfaction. *Journal of Social Psychology, 150*(3), 235–237.

Burger, J. M. (2009). Replicating Milgram: Would people still obey today? *American Psychologist, 64*(1), 1–11.

Burger, P. H., Goecke, T. W., Fasching, P. A., Moll, G., Heinrich, H., Beckmann, M. W., . . . Kornhuber, J. (2011). How does maternal alcohol consumption during pregnancy affect the development of attention deficit/hyperactivity syndrome in the child. *Fortschitte der Neurologie-Psychiatrie, 79*(9), 500–506. doi:10.1055/s-0031–1273360

Burke, K. C., Burke, J. D., Regier, D. A., & Rae, D. S. (1990). Age at onset of selected mental disorders in five community populations. *Archives of general psychiatry, 47*(6), 511-518.

Busby, D. M., Carroll, J. S., & Willoughby, B. J. (2010). Compatibility or restraint? The effects of sexual timing on marriage relationships. *Journal of Family Psychology, 24*(6), 766. doi:10.1037/a0021690

Bush, D. E. A., Schafe, G. E., & LeDoux, J. E. (2009). Neural basis of fear conditioning. In G. G. Berntson & J. T. Cacioppo (Eds.), *Handbook of neuroscience for the behavioral sciences* (Vol. 2, pp. 762–764). Hoboken, NJ: John Wiley & Sons.

Butler, T., Schofield, P. W., Greenberg, D., Allnutt, S. H., Indig, D. C., Vaughan, D'Este C., . . . Ellis, A. (2010). Reducing impulsivity in repeat violent offenders: An open label trial of a selective serotonin reuptake inhibitor. *Australian and New Zealand Journal of Psychiatry, 44*(12), 1137–1143.

Buysse, D. J., Strollo, P. J., Jr., Black, J. E., Zee, P. G., & Winkelman, J. W. (2008). Sleep disorders. In R. E. Hales, S. C. Yudofsky, & G. O. Gabbard (Eds.), *The American Psychiatric Publishing textbook of psychiatry* (5th ed., pp. 921–969). Arlington, VA: American Psychiatric Publishing.

Cacioppo, J. T., Petty, R. E., Kao, C. F., & Rodriguez, R. (1986). Central and peripheral routes to persuasion: An individual difference perspective. *Journal of Personality and Social Psychology, 31,* 1032–1043.

Cain, D. J. (2010). *Person-centered psychotherapies.* Washington, DC: American Psychological Association.

Cajochen, C., Munch, M., Kobialka, S., Kräuchi, K., Steiner, R., Oelhafen, P., . . . Wirz-Justice, A. (2005). High sensitivity of human melatonin, alertness, thermoregulation, and heart rate to short wavelength light. *Journal of Clinical Endocrinology & Metabolism, 90*(3), 1311–1316. https://doi.org/10.1210/jc.2004-0957

Caldwell, A. B. (2006). Maximal measurement or meaningful measurement: The interpretive challenges of the MMPI-2 Restructured Clinical (RC) Scales. *Journal of Personality Assessment, 87,* 193–201. doi:10.1207/s15327752jpa8702_09

Cannon, W. B. (1929). *Bodily changes in pain, hunger, fear, and rage* (2nd ed.). New York, NY: Appleton Century Crofts.

Cannon, W. B. (1939). *The wisdom of the body.* New York, NY: Norton.

Cannon, W. B., & Washburn, A. L. (1912). An explanation of hunger. *American Journal of Physiology, 29,* 441–454.

Carlson, E. A., Sroufe, L. A., & Egeland, B. (2004). The construction of experience: A longitudinal study of representation and behavior. *Child Development, 75,* 66–83. doi:10.1111/j.1467-8624.2004.00654.x

Cartwright, R. D. (2010). *The twenty-four hour mind: The role of sleep and dreaming in our emotional lives.* New York, NY: Oxford University Press.

Cartwright, S. (2008). Economic costs of drug abuse: Financial, cost of illness, and services. *Journal of Substance Abuse Treatment, 34*(2), 224-233.

Cash, S. J., & Wilke, D. J. (2003). An ecological model of maternal substance abuse and child neglect: Issues, analyses, and recommendations. *American Journal of Orthopsychiatry, 73*(4), 392-404.

Cassia, V. M., Turati, C., & Simion, F. (2004). Can a nonspecific bias toward top-heavy patterns explain newborns' face preferences? *Psychological Science, 15*, 379–383. doi:10.1111/j.0956-7976.2004.00688.x

Cassidy, J. (1994). Emotion regulation: Influences of attachment relationships. *Monographs of the Society for Research in Child Development, 59* (2–3 Serial No. 240), 228–249.

Cattell, R. B. (1946). *Description and measurement of personality.* New York, NY: Harcourt Brace & World.

Cavaiola, A. A., & Strohmetz, D. B. (2010). Perception of risk for subsequent drinking and driving related offenses and locus of control among first-time DUI offenders. *Alcoholism Treatment Quarterly, 28,* 52–62. doi:10.1080/07347320903436169

Celebrities With Anxiety. (2018). https://www.webmd.com/anxiety-panic/ss/slideshow-celebrities-anxiety

Celebrities with Dissociative Disorders. (2010). http://www.associatedcontent.com/article/5734796/celebrities_with_dissociative_disorders.html?cat70

Centers for Disease Control and Prevention. (2010). *10 leading causes of death by age group, United States – 2010.* https://www.cdc.gov/injury/wisqars/pdf/10lcid_all_deaths_by_age_group_2010-a.pdf

Centers for Disease Control and Prevention. (2015). *A 2005 message to women from the U.S. Surgeon General: Advisory on alcohol use in pregnancy.* https://www.cdc.gov/ncbddd/fasd/documents/surgeongenbookmark.pdf

Centers for Disease Control and Prevention. (2018a). *Alcohol use in pregnancy.* https://www.cdc.gov/ncbddd/fasd/alcohol-use.html

Centers for Disease Control and Prevention. (2018b). *Autism spectrum disorder.* https://www.nimh.nih.gov/health/statistics/autism-spectrum-disorder-asd.shtml

Centers for Disease Control and Prevention. (2018c). *Youth Risk Behavior Surveillance System (YRBSS).* https://www.cdc.gov/healthyyouth/data/yrbs/index.htm

Centers for Disease Control and Prevention. (2019a). *Obesity.* https://www.cdc.gov/healthyschools/obesity/index.htm?CDC_AA_refVal=https%3A%2F%2Fwww.cdc.gov%2Fhealthyschools%2Fobesity%2Ffacts.htm

Centers for Disease Control and Prevention. (2019b). *Preventing intimate partner violence.* https://www.cdc.gov/violenceprevention/intimatepartnerviolence/fastfact.html

Chambers, R. A., Taylor, J. R., & Potenza, M. N. (2003). Developmental neurocircuitry of motivation in adolescence: a critical period of addiction vulnerability. *American Journal of Psychiatry, 160*(6), 1041-1052.

Chance, T., & Scannapieco, M. (2002). Ecological correlates of child maltreatment: Similarities and differences between child fatality and nonfatality cases. *Child and Adolescent Social Work Journal, 19*(2), 139-161.

Chaplin, T. M., & Aldao, A. (2013). Gender differences in emotion expression in children: A meta-analytic review. *Psychological bulletin, 139*(4), 735–765. https://doi.org/10.1037/a0030737

Chaudhuri, A. (2011). *Fundamentals of sensory perception.* New York, NY: Oxford University Press.

Chen, J., & Millar, W. J. (1998). Age of smoking initiation: implications for quitting. *Health reports-statistics Canada, 9,* 39-48.

Chen, K., Kandel, D. B., & Davies, M. (1997). Relationships between frequency and quantity of marijuana use and last year proxy dependence among adolescents and adults in the United States. *Drug and Alcohol Dependence, 46*(1–2), 53–67.

Chen, W. C. (2009). Test anxiety and under-performance: An analysis examination process. *Bulletin of Educational Psychology, 40*(4), 597–618.

Cho, I., Jia, Z. J., & Arnold, F. H. (2019). Site-selective enzymatic C–H amidation for synthesis of diverse lactams. *Science, 364*(6440), 575–578. doi:10.1126/science.aaw9068

Choi, K. H., Higgs, B. W., Wendland, J. R., Song, J., McMahon, F. J., & Webster, M. J. (2011). Gene expression and genetic variation data implicate PCLO in bipolar disorder. *Biological Psychiatry, 69*(4), 353–359.

Choquet, H., & Meyre, D. (2011). Genetics of obesity: What have we learned?. *Current Genomics, 12*(3), 169–179. https://doi.org/10.2174/138920211795677895

Christian Association for Psychological Studies. (2020). https://www.caps.net/

Clark, D. B., Kirisci, L., & Tarter, R. E. (1998). Adolescent versus adult onset and the development of substance use disorders in males. *Drug and Alcohol Dependence, 49*(2), 115–121.

Coelho, H. F., Canter, P. H., & Ernst, E. (2007). Mindfulness-based cognitive therapy: Evaluating current evidence and informing future research. *Journal of Consulting and Clinical Psychology, 75*, 1000–1005.

Cohen, D. (2006). Critiques of the "ADHD" enterprise. In G. Lloyd, J. Stead, & D. Cohen (Eds.), *Critical new perspectives on ADHD* (pp. 12–33). New York, NY: Routledge.

Cohen-Yavin, I., Yoran-Hegesh, R., Strous, R. D., Kotler, M., Weizman, A., & Spivak, B. (2009). Efficacy of reboxetine in the treatment of attention-deficit/hyperactivity disorder in boys with intolerance to methylphenidate: An open-label, 8-week, methylphenidate-controlled trial. *Clinical Neuropharmacology, 32*(4), 179–182.

Compton, W. (2018). Self-actualization myths: What did Maslow really say? *Journal of Humanistic Psychology*, 1–18. doi:10.1177/0022167818761929

Conway, M. A., Anderson, S. J., Larsen, S. F., Donnelly, C. M., McDaniel, M. A., McClelland, A. G. R., . . . Logie, R. H. (1994). The formation of flashbulb memories. *Memory & Cognition, 22*, 326–343. doi:10.3758/BF03200860

Coplan, R. J., & Bullock, A. (2012). Temperament and peer relationships. In M. R. Zentner & R. L. Shiner (Eds.), *Handbook of temperament* (pp. 442–461). New York, NY: Guilford Press.

Coren, S., Ward, L. M., & Enns, J. T. (2004). *Sensation and perception* (6th ed.). New York, NY: Wiley.

Corkin, S. (1984). Lasting consequences of bilateral medial temporal lobectomy: Clinical course and experimental findings in HM. *Seminars in Neurology, 4*, 249–259. doi:10.1055/s-2008-1041556

Corral, M., Kuan, A., & Kostaras, D. (2000). Bright light therapy's effect on postpartum depression. *American Journal of Psychiatry, 152*(2), 303–311.

Costa, P. T., Jr., & McCrae, R. R. (1992). *Revised NEO personality inventory (NEO-PL-R) and NEO five-factor inventory (NEO-FFI manual)*. Odessa, FL: Psychological Assessment Resources.

Cowan, N. (2001). The magical number four in short-term memory: A reconsideration of mental storage capacity. *Behavioral and Brain Sciences, 24*, 87–185. doi:10.1017/s0140525x01003922

Cowan, N. (2010). The magical mystery four: How is working memory capacity limited, and why? *Current Directions in Psychological Science, 19*, 51–57. doi:10.1177/0963721409359277

Craig, C. R. (2006). *Modern pharmacology with clinical applications* (6th ed.). Philadelphia, PA: Lippincott.

Craik, F. I. M., & Lockhart, R. S. (1972). Levels of processing: A framework memory research. *Journal of Verbal Learning and Verbal Behavior, 11*, 671–684. doi:10.1016/S0022-5371(72)80001-X

Crossley, J. P., & Salter, D. P. (2005). A question of finding harmony: A grounded theory study of clinical psychologists' experience of addressing spiritual beliefs in therapy. *Psychology & Psychotherapy, 78*, 295–313. doi:10.1348/147608305X26783

Curtin, M. (2017, December 29). *The 10 top skills that will land you high-paying Jobs by 2020, according to the world economic forum*. https://www.inc.com/melanie-curtin/the-10-top-skills-that-will-land-you-high-paying-jobs-by-2020-according-to-world-economic-forum.html

Darley, J. M., & Latané, B. (1968). Bystander intervention in emergencies: Diffusion of responsibility. *Personality and Social Psychology, 8*, 377–383.

Darwin, C. (1859). *On the origin of species by means of natural selection, or the preservation of favoured races in the struggle for life*. London, England: John Murray.

Dawkins, R. (1976/2006). *The selfish gene*. New York, NY: Oxford University Press.

DeCasper, A., & Fifer, W. P. (1987). Of human bonding: Newborns prefer their mothers' voices. In J. Oates & S. Sheldon (Eds.), *Cognitive development in infancy* (pp. 111–118). Hillsdale, NJ: Erlbaum.

DeLisi, M., Umphress, Z. R., & Vaughn, M. G. (2009). The criminology of the amygdala. *Criminal Justice and Behavior, 36*(11), 1241–1252.

Denis, P. L., Morin, D., & Guindon, C. (2010). Exploring the capacity of NEO PI–R facets to predict job performance in two French-Canadian samples. *International Journal of Selection and Assessment, 18*(2), 201–207. doi:10.1111/j.1468-2389.2010.00501.x

Dennis, D. J. (2009). Review of the Cattell controversy: Race, science, and ideology. *Journal of the History of the Behavioral Sciences, 45*, 390–392. doi:10.1002/jhbs.20399

Dethier, V. G. (1976). *The hungry fly: A physiological study of the behavior associated with feeding*. Cambridge, MA: Harvard University Press.

Deuchar, R., & Holligan, C. (2010). Gangs, sectarianism and social capital: A qualitative study of young people in Scotland. *Sociology, 44*(1), 13–30.

Dew, J., & Wilcox, W. B. (2013). Generosity and the maintenance of marital quality. *Journal of Marriage and Family, 75*(5), 1218–1228. https://doi.org/10.1111/jomf.12066

DeZalia, R. P. (2009). A sociocultural perspective on genocide: A review of the psychology of genocide: Perpetrators, bystanders, and rescuers by Steven Baum. *Culture Psychology, 15*(3), 349–362.

DiFranza, J. R. (2008, May). Hooked from the first cigarette. *Scientific American*, 82–87.

Digman, J. M. (1990). Personality structure: Emergence of the five-factor model. *Annual Review of Psychology, 41*, 417–440. doi:10.1146/annurev.ps.41.020190.002221

Dionisio, D. P., Granholm, E., Hillix, W. A., & Perrine, W. F. (2001). Differentiation of deception using pupillary responses as an index of cognitive processing. *Psychophysiology, 38*(2), 205–211.

Distracted Driving. (2017). *National highway traffic safety administration*. https://www.nhtsa.gov/risky-driving/distracted-driving.

Dollard, J., Miller, N. E., Doob, L. W., Mowrer, O. H., & Sears, R. R. (1939). *Frustration and aggression*. New Haven, CT: Yale University Press.

Dweck, C. S. (2006). *Mindset: The new psychology of success*. New York, NY: Random House.

Dweck, C. S., & Grant, H. (2008). Self-theories, goals, and meaning. In J. Y. Shah & W. I. Gardner (Eds.), *Handbook of motivation science* (pp. 408–416). New York, NY: Guilford Press.

Eccles, J. S., & Wigfield, A. (2002). Motivational beliefs, values, and goals. *Annual Review of Psychology, 53*, 109–132.

Ego-Stengel, V., & Wilson, M. A. (2010). Disruption of ripple-associated hippocampal activity during rest impairs spatial learning in the rat. *Hippocampus, 20*(1), 1–10.

Eisenberg, N., Fabes, R. A., Shepard, S. A., Guthrie, I. K., Murphy, B. C., & Reiser, M. (1999). Parental reactions to children's negative emotions: Longitudinal relations to quality of children's social functioning. *Child Development, 70*, 513–534.

Ekman, P. (2005). Conclusion: What we have learned by measuring facial behavior: Further comments and clarifications. In P. Ekman & E. L. Rosenberg (Eds.), *What the face reveals: Basic and applied studies of spontaneous expression using the facial action coding system (FACS)* (2nd ed., pp. 605–626). New York, NY: Oxford University Press.

Elder, T. E. (2010, June 17). The importance of relative standards in ADHD diagnoses: Evidence based on exact birth dates. *Journal of Health Economics*. http://www.ncbi.nlm.nih.gov/pubmed/20638739

Elkington, J. R. (1966). Medicine and quality of life. *Annals of Internal Medicine, 64*, 711–714.

Ellers, J., & van der Pool, N. C. E. (2010). Altruistic behavior and cooperation: The role of intrinsic expectation when reputational information is incomplete. *Evolutionary Psychology, 8*(1), 37–48.

Ellis, A. (1974). *Humanistic psychotherapy: The rational-emotive approach*. New York, NY: Julian Press.

Ellis, A. (2003). Early theories and practices of rational emotive behavior therapy and how they have been augmented and revised during the last three decades. *Journal of Rational-Emotive & Cognitive-Behavior Therapy, 21*(3/4), 219–243.

Ellis, A., & MacLaren, C. (2005). *Rational emotive behavior therapy*. Atascadero, CA: Impact Publishers.

Emmons, R. A., & Mishra, A. (2011). Why gratitude enhances well-being: What we know, what we need to know. In K. M. Sheldon, T. B. Kashdan, & M. F. Steger (Eds.), *Series in positive psychology. Designing positive psychology: Taking stock and moving forward* (pp. 248–262). New York, NY: Oxford University Press. https://doi.org/10.1093/acprof:oso/9780195373585.003.0016

English, D. J., Marshall, D. B., Brummel, S., & Orme, M. (1999). Characteristics of repeated referrals to child protective services in Washington State. *Child Maltreatment, 4*(4), 297-307.

Erikson, E. H. (1950). Growth and crises of the "healthy personality." In M. J. E. Senn (Ed.), *Symposium on the healthy personality* (p. 91–146). Josiah Macy, Jr. Foundation.

Erikson, E. H. (1959). *Identity and the life cycle: Selected papers*. New York, NY: International Universities Press.

Erikson, E. H. (1963). *Childhood and society*. New York, NY: W. W. Norton.

Erikson, E. H. (1968). *Identity, youth and crisis*. New York, NY: W. W. Norton.

Eriksson, S., Palsdottir, V., Garemo, M., Mellstrom, D., & Strandvik, B. (2010). Metabolic profiles of fat and glucose differ by gender in healthy 8-year-olds. *Acta Paediatrica, 99*(1), 78–82.

Estrada, A., Keeley, J. A., & Leduc, P. A. (2007). Facilitating aviation emergency procedure recall using a pictorial mnemonic system. *International Journal of Applied Aviation Studies, 7*(1), 11–27.

Estroff, T. W., Schwartz, R. H., & Hoffmann, N. G. (1989). Adolescent cocaine abuse: Addictive potential, behavioral and psychiatric effects. *Clinical Pediatrics, 28*(12), 550–555. https://doi.org/10.1177/000992288902801201

Eysenck, H. J. (1947). *Dimensions of personality*. London, England: Routledge & Kegan Paul.

Eysenck, H. J. (1967). *The biological basis of personality*. Springfield, IL: Charles C. Thomas.

Eysenck, H. J., & Eysenck, S. B. G. (1976). *Psychoticism as a dimension of personality*. London, England: Hodder and Stoughton.

Eysenck, M. W., & Keane, M. T. (2005). *Cognitive psychology: A student's handbook* (5th ed.). New York, NY: Psychology Press.

Fagan, T. K., & Wise, P. S. (2007). *School psychology: Past, present, and future* (3rd ed.). Bethesda, MD: NASP Publications.

Fajkowska, M. & Kreitler, S. (2018). Status of the trait concept in contemporary personality psychology: Are the old questions still the burning questions? *Journal of Personality, 86*(1), 5–11.

Famularo, R., Kinscherff, R., & Fenton, T. (1992). Parental substance abuse and the nature of child maltreatment. *Child abuse & neglect, 16*(4), 475-483.

Farooqi, S. (2010). Genes and obesity. In P. G. Kopelman, I. D. Caterson, & W. H. Dietz (Eds.), *Clinical obesity in adults and children* (3rd ed., pp. 82–91). Hoboken, NJ: Wiley-Blackwell.

Faye, C., & Sharpe, D. (2008). Academic motivation in university: The role of basic psychological needs and identity formation. *Canadian Journal of Behavioural Science, 40*(4), 189–199.

Federal Bureau of Investigation. (2019, September 30). FBI Releases 2018 Crime Statistics. *FBI News*. https://www.fbi.gov/news/pressrel/press-releases/fbi-releases-2018-crime-statistics

Feldman, B. (2001). *The Nobel Prize: A history of genius, controversy, and prestige*. New York, NY: Arcade Publishing.

Feng, B., & MacGeorge, E. L. (2010). The influences of message and source factors on advice outcomes. *Communication Research, 37*(4), 553–575.

Ferguson, C. J., Miguel, C. S., & Hartley, R. D. (2009). A multivariate analysis of youth violence and aggression: The influence of family, peers, depression, and media violence. *Journal of Pediatrics, 155*(6), 904–908.

Ferrari, P. F., Paukner, A., Ruggiero, A., Darcey, L., Unbehagen, S., & Suomi, S. J. (2009). Interindividual differences in neonatal imitation and the development of action chains in rhesus macaques. *Child Development, 80*(4), 1057–1068.

Festinger, L. A. (1957). *A theory of cognitive dissonance*. Stanford, CA: Stanford University Press.

Festinger, L., & Carlsmith, J. M. (1959). Cognitive consequences of forced compliance. *Journal of Abnormal and Social Psychology, 58*, 203–210.

Fields, G. (2010). Enclosure: Palestinian landscape in a "not-too-distant mirror." *Journal of Historical Sociology, 23*(2), 216–250.

Fields, R. D. (2008). White matter matters. *Scientific American, 298*(3), 54-61.

Fischer, P., Krueger, J. I., Greltemeyer, T., Vogrincic, C., Kastenmuller, A., Frey, D., . . . Kainbacher, M. (2011). The bystander-effect: A meta-analytic review on bystander intervention in dangerous and non-dangerous emergencies. *Psychological Bulletin, 137*(4), 517–537. doi:10.1037/a0023304

Flavell, J. H., Miller, P. H., & Miller, S. A. (2002). Cognitive Development (4th ed.). Upper Saddle River, NJ: Prentice Hall.

Fletcher, H., & Munson, W. A. (1933). Loudness, its definition, measurement and calculation. *Journal of the Acoustical Society of America, 5*, 82–108. doi:10.1121/1.1915637

Foltran. F., Gregori, D., Franchin, L., Verduci, E., & Giovannini, M. (2011). Effect of alcohol consumption in prenatal life, childhood, and adolescence on child development. *Nutrition Reviews, 69*(11), 642–659. doi:10.1111/j.1753-4887.2011.00417.x

Foo, P., Warren, W. H., Duchon, A., & Tarr, M. J. (2005). Do humans integrate routes into a cognitive map? Map- versus landmark-based navigation of novel shortcuts. *Journal of Experimental Psychology: Learning Memory and Cognition, 3*(2), 195–215.

Forbes Finance Council. (2018, June 5). *Eight essential college classes for those considering a career in finance.* https://www.forbes.com/sites/forbesfinancecouncil/2018/06/05/eight-essential-college-classes-for-those-considering-a-career-finance/#548d15ce5f33

Forray, A., Merry, B., Lin, H., Ruger, J. P., & Yonkers, K. A. (2015). Perinatal substance use: A prospective evaluation of abstinence and relapse. *Drug and Alcohol Dependence, 150,* 147–155. doi:10.1016/j.drugalcdep.2015.02.027

Fortin M., Bravo G., Hudon C., Lapointe, L., Almirall, J., Dubois, M. F., . . . Vanasse, A. (2006). Relationship between multimorbidity and health-related quality of life of patients in primary care. *Quality of Life Research, 15*(1), 83–91. doi:10.1007/s11136-005-8661-z

Foschi, R., & Cicciola, E. (2006). Politics and naturalism in the 20th century psychology of Alfred Binet. *History of Psychology, 9*(4), 267–289. doi:10.1037/1093-4510.9.4.267

Fraley, R. C. (2002). Attachment stability form infancy to adulthood: Meta-analysis and dynamic modeling of developmental mechanisms. *Personality and Social Psychology Review, 6,* 123–151. doi:10.1207/s15327957pspr0602_03

Freud, S. (1914/1955). On narcissism: An introduction. In J. Strachey (Ed. and Trans.), *The standard edition of the complete psychological works of Sigmund Freud* (Vol. 14, pp. 67–103). London, England: Hogarth.

Freud, S. (2003). *An outline of psychoanalysis* (H. Ragg-Kirby, Trans.). New York, NY: Penguin Books.

Friedman, D. (2003). Cognition and aging: A highly selective overview of event–related potential (ERP) data. *Journal of Clinical and Experimental Neuropsychology, 25,* 702–720.

Friedman, R. A. (2006). Uncovering an epidemic-screening for mental illness in teens. *New England Journal of Medicine, 355*(26), 2717.

Froehlich, T. E., Lanphear, B. P., Auinger, P., Hornung, R., Epstein, J. N., Braun, J., . . . Kahn, R. S. (2009). Association of tobacco and lead exposures with attention-deficit/hyperactivity disorder. *Pediatrics, 124*(6), e1054–63. Epub 2009 Nov 23. PubMed PMID: 19933729; PubMed Central PMCID: PMC2853804

Gaffrey, M. S., Luby, J. L., Belden, A. C., Hirshberg, J. S., Volsch, J., & Barch, D. M. (2011). Association between depression severity and amygdala reactivity during sad face viewing in depressed preschoolers: An fMRI study. *Journal of Affective Disorders, 129*(1–3), 364–370.

Gafner, G. (2010). *Techniques of hypnotic induction.* Norwalk, CT: Crown House Publishing.

Gagné, M., & Deci, E. L. (2005). Self-determination theory and work motivation. *Journal of Organizational Behavior, 26*(4), 331–362. doi:10.1002/job.316

Gallagher, K. E., & Parrott, D. J. (2010). Influence of heavy episodic drinking on the relation between men's locus of control and aggression toward intimate partners. *Journal of Studies on Alcohol and Drugs, 71*(2), 299–306.

Gansberg, M. (1964, March 27). 37 who saw murder didn't call the police; apathy at stabbing of queens woman shocks inspector. *The New York Times.* https://www.nytimes.com/1964/03/27/archives/37-who-saw-murder-didnt-call-the-police-apathy-at-stabbing-of.html

Garces-Bacsal, R. M. (2010). Tales gifted children tell: Exploring PTAT responses as path-ways to socio-affective concerns. *Gifted Child Quarterly, 54*(2), 138–151. doi:10.1177/0016986209358616

Garnham, A. (2009). Cognitivism. In J. Symons & P. Calvo (Eds.), *The Routledge companion to philosophy of psychology* (pp. 99–110). New York, NY: Routledge/Taylor & Francis Group.

Gelernter, D. (2019). Giving up Darwin: A fond farewell to a brilliant and beautiful theory. *Claremont Review of Books, 29*(2), 1-14. https://claremontreviewofbooks.com/giving-up-darwin/

Gerson, J. (2010, September 1). Animal hoarding a mental disorder. *Edmonton Journal,* A9.

Gianakos, I. (2002). Predictors of coping with work stress: The influences of sex, gender role, social desirability, and locus of control. *Sex Roles, 46,* 149–158. doi:10.1023/A:1019675218338

Gibbons, F. X., Eggleston, T. J., & Benthin, A. C. (1997). Cognitive reactions to smoking relapse: The reciprocal relation between dissonance and self-esteem. *Journal of Personality and Social Psychology, 72,* 184–195.

Giles, J. (2008). Sex hormones and sexual desire. *Journal for the Theory of Social Behaviour, 38*(1), 45–66.

Gilestro, G. F., Tononi, G., & Cirelli, C. (2009). Widespread changes in synaptic markers as a function of sleep and wakefulness in *Drosophila. Science, 324*, 109–112.

Gilligan, S. & Bower, G. (2013). Reminding and mood-congruent memory. *Bulletin of the Psychonomic Society, 21*, 431–434. doi:10.3758/BF03330000

Gleitman, L., & Papafragou, A. (2005). Language and thought. In K. J. Holyoak & R. G. Morrison (Eds.), *The Cambridge handbook of thinking and reasoning* (pp. 633–662). London, England: Cambridge University Press.

Gomez, S., & Queiroz, L. S. (1982). The effects of black widow spider venom on the innervations of muscles paralysed by botulinum toxin. *Quarterly Journal of Experimental Physiology, 67*(3), 495–506.

Goodwin, C. J. (2008). Psychology in the 20th century. In S. F. Davis & W. Buskist (Eds.) *21st century psychology: A reference handbook* (pp. 12–20). Thousand Oaks, CA: Sage.

Gottfredson, L., & Saklofske, D. H. (2009). Intelligence: Foundations and issues in assessment. *Canadian Psychology, 50*(3), 183–195. doi:10.1037/a0016641

Gottfried, J. (2010). Central mechanisms of odour object perception. *Nature Reviews Neuroscience, 11*, 628–641. doi:10.1038/nrn2883

Gouin, J. P., Hantsoo, L., & Kiecolt-Glaser, J. K. (2008). Immune dysregulation and chronic stress among older adults: A review. *Neuroimmunomodulation, 15*(4–6), 251–259.

Graf, P., & Schacter, D. L. (1985). Implicit and explicit memory for new associations in normal and amnesic subjects. *Journal of Experimental Psychology: Learning, Memory, & Cognition, 11*, 501–518. doi:10.1037/0278-7393.11.3.501

Gray, L. J., Dean, B., Kronsbein, H. C., Robinson, P. J., & Scarr, E. (2010). Region and diagnosis-specific changes in synaptic proteins in schizophrenia and bipolar I disorder. *Psychiatry Research, 78*(2), 374–380.

Gray, L., Watt, L., & Blass, E. M. (2000). Skin-to-skin contact is analgesic in healthy newborns. *Pediatrics, 105*, e14.

Greene, K., Krcmar, M., Walters, L. H., Rubin, D. L., & Hale, L. (2000). Targeting adolescent risk-taking behaviors: The contributions of egocentrism and sensation-seeking. *Journal of adolescence, 23*(4), 439–461.

Greenhill, L. L., & Hechtman, L. I. (2009). Attention-deficit/hyperactivity disorder. In B. J. Sadock, V. A. Sadock, P. Ruiz (Eds.), *Kaplan and Sadock's Comprehensive textbook of psychiatry* (Vol. 2, 9th ed., pp. 3560–3572). Philadelphia, PA: Lippincott Williams and Wilkins

Griffin, A. S., & Galef, B. G., Jr. (2005). Social learning about predators: Does timing matter? *Animal Behaviour, 69*(3), 669–678.

Gronfier, C., Wright, K. P., Jr., Kronauer, R. E., & Czeisler, C. A. (2007). Entrainment of the human circadian pacemaker to longer-than-24-h days. *The National Academy of Sciences of the USA, 104*(21), 9081–9086. http://www.pnas.org/content/104/21/9081.full.pdf

Guinness World Records. (2020). *Loudest crowd roar at a sports stadium.* https://www.guinnessworldrecords.com/world-records/loudest-crowd-roar-at-a-sports-stadium

Gulick, W. L., Gescheider, G. A., & Frisina, R. D. (1989). *Hearing: Physiological acoustics, neural coding, and psychoacoustics.* New York, NY: Oxford University Press.

Guo, O., Sun, P., & Li, L. (2018). Why neurotic individuals are less prosocial? A multiple mediation analysis regarding related mechanisms. *Personality & Individual Differences, 128*, 55–61.

Gupta, R., Gour, D., & Meena, M. (2013). Interventional cohort study for evaluation of computer vision syndrome among computer workers. *International Journal of Medical Research and Review, 2*(1), 40–44. doi:10.17511/ijmrr.2014.i01.009.

Gur, R. E. (2002). Functional imaging is fulfilling some promises. *American Journal of Psychiatry, 159*(5), 693–694. https://doi.org/10.1176/appi.ajp.159.5.693

Guskiewicz, K. M., Bruce, S. L., Cantu, R. C., Ferrara, M. S., Kelly, J. P., McCrea, M., . . . Valovich McLeod, T. C. (2004). National athletic trainers' association position statement: Management of sport-related concussion. *Journal of athletic training, 39*(3), 280–297.

Guthrie, E. R. (1935). *The psychology of learning.* New York, NY: Harper & Brothers.

Habashi, M. M., Graziano, W. G., & Hoover, A. E. (2016). Searching for the prosocial personality: A big five approach to linking personality and prosocial behavior. *Personality and Social Psychology Bulletin, 42*(9), 1177–1192.

Hakulinena, C., Jokelaa, M., Hintsanenb, M. Pulkki-Råbacka, L., Elovainioc, M., Hintsaa, T., . . . Raitakarif, O. T. (2013). Hostility and unemployment: A two-way relationship? *Journal of Vocational Behavior, 83*(2), 153–160. doi:10.1016/j.jvb.2013.04.003

Haley, W. E., LaMonde, L. A., Han, B., Burton, A. M., & Schonwetter, R. (2003). Predictors of depression and life satisfaction among spousal caregivers in hospice: Application of a stress process model. *Journal of Palliative Medicine, 6,* 215–224.

Harlow, H. F. (1953). Mice, monkeys, men, and motives. *Psychological Review, 60,* 23–32.

Harlow, H. F., & Harlow, M. K. (1965). The affectional systems. In A. M. Schrier, H. F. Harlow, & F. Stollnitz (Eds.), *Behavior of nonhuman primates* (Vol. 2, pp. 287–334). New York, NY: Academic Press.

Harlow, H. F., Harlow, M. K., & Suomi, S. J. (1971). From thought to therapy: Lessons from aprimate laboratory. *American Scientist, 59,* 538–549.

Harlow, H. F., & Zimmerman, R. R. (1959). Affectional responses in the infant monkey. *Science, 130,* 421–432.

Harmell, A. L., Chattillion, E. A., Roepke, S. K., & Mausbach, B. T. (2011). A review of the psychobiology of dementia caregiving: A focus on resilience factors. *Current Psychiatry Reports, 13*(3), 219–224. doi:10.1007/s11920-011-0187-1

Harper, F. D., & Guilbault, M. (2008). Maslow's hierarchy of basic needs. In N. J. Salkind (Ed.), *Encyclopedia of educational psychology* (Vol. 2, pp. 633–639). Thousand Oaks, CA: Sage.

Hartmann, E. (2007). The nature and functions of dreaming. In D. Barrett & P. McNamara (Eds.), *The science of dreams* (Vol. 3, pp. 171–192). Westport, CT: Praeger.

Head, L. S., & Gross, A. M. (2009). Systematic desensitization. In W. T. O'Donohue & J. E. Fisher (Eds.), *General principles and empirically supported techniques of cognitive behavior therapy* (pp. 640–647). Hoboken, NJ: John Wiley.

Healthy Aging Team. (2017, February 2). *Top 10 chronic conditions in adults 65+ and what you can do to prevent or manage them* [Blog post]. https://www.ncoa.org/blog/10-common-chronic-diseases-prevention-tips/

Hebb, D. O. (1972). *A textbook of psychology* (3rd ed.). Philadelphia, PA: Saunders.

Henriksen, M. G., Nordgaard, J., & Jansson, L. B. (2017). Genetics of Schizophrenia: Overview of methods, findings, and limitations. *Frontiers in Human Neuroscience, 11,* 322.

Hergenhahn, B. R., & Henley, T. (2014). *An introduction to the history of psychology* (7th ed.). Belmont, CA: Wadsworth.

Heron, W. (1957, January). The pathology of boredom. *Scientific American, 196,* 52–56.

Herrnstein, R. J. (1997). In H. Rachlin & D. I. Laibson (Eds.), *The matching law: Papers in psychology and economics.* New York, NY: Russell Sage.

Hess, A. (2019, January 6). *The 10 most in-demand skills of 2019, according to LinkedIn.* https://www.cnbc.com/2019/01/04/the-30-most-in-demand-skills-in-2019-according-to-linkedin-.html

Hipp, J. R., & Perrin, A. J. (2009). The simultaneous effect of social distance and physical distance on the formation of neighborhood ties. *City & Community, 8*(1), 5–25.

Hoefling, A., & Strack, F. (2010). Hunger induced changes in food choice. When beggars cannot be choosers even if they are allowed to choose. *Appetite, 54*(3), 603–606.

Holland, S. K., Vannest, J., Mecoli, M., Jacola, L. M., Tillema, J. M., Karunanayaka, P. R., . . . Byars, A. W. (2007). Functional MRI of language lateralization during development in children. *International Journal of Audiology, 46,* 533–551.

HooverInstitution. (2019, July 22). *Mathematical challenges to Darwin's theory of evolution* [Video]. Youtube. https://www.youtube.com/watch?v=noj4phMT9OE

Hopkins, G. L. (1998). Why people abuse drugs. *Vibrant Life, 14*(1), 4–6.

Horcajo, J., Petty, R. E., & Brinol, P. (2010). The effects of majority versus minority source status on persuasion: A self-validation analysis. *Journal of Personality and Social Psychology, 99*(3), 498–512.

Horn, J. L., & Blankson, A. N. (2012). Foundations for better understanding of cognitive abilities. In D. P. Flanagan & P. L. Harrison (Eds.), *Contemporary intellectual assessment: Theories, tests, and issues* (pp. 73–98). New York, NY: The Guilford Press.

Horowitz, T. S., Cade, B. E., Wolfe, J. M., & Czeisler, C. A. (2001). Efficacy of bright light and sleep/darkness scheduling in alleviating circadian maladaptation to night work. *American Journal of Physiology, Endocrinology, and Metabolism, 281*(2), 384-391. doi: 10.1152/ajpendo.2001.281.2.E384

Husain, M., & Jackson, S. R. (2001). Vision: Visual space is not what it appears to be. *Current Biology, 11,* 753–755. doi:10.1016/S0960-9822(01)00439-0

Hussaini, S. A., Komischke, B., Menzel, R., & Lachnit, H. (2007). Forward and backward second-order Pavlovian conditioning in honeybees. *Learning and Memory, 14,* 678–683.

Huttenlocher, P. R. (1990). Morphometric study of human cerebral cortex development. *Neuropsychologia, 28*(6), 517–527.

Indeed Career Guide. (2020, March 2). *10 best skills to include on a resume (with examples).* https://www.indeed.com/career-advice/resumes-cover-letters/best-resume-skills

Izard, C. E. (2009). Emotion theory and research: Highlights, unanswered questions, and emerging issues. *Annual Review of Psychology, 60,* 1–25.

Jacoby, L. L., Toth, J. P., & Yonelinas, A. P. (1993). Separating conscious and unconscious influences of memory: Measuring recollection. *Journal of Experimental Psychology: General, 122,* 139–154. doi:10.1037/0096-3445.122.2.139

Jakupcak, M., Tull, M. T., McDermott, M. J., Kaysen, D., Hunt, S., & Simpson, T. (2010). PTSD symptom clusters in relationship to alcohol misuse among Iraq and Afghanistan war veterans seeking post-deployment VA health care. *Addictive Behaviors, 35*(9), 840–843.

James, W. (1890/1950). *Principles of psychology* (Vol. 1). New York, NY: Holt.

Jang, K. L., Livesley, W. J., & Vernon, P. A. (1996). Heritability of the Big Five personality dimensions and their facets: A twin study. *Journal of Personality, 64,* 577–591. doi:10.1111/j.1467-6494.1996.tb00522.x

Jansson, L .M., Velez, M., & Marrow, C. (2009). The opioid-exposed newborn: Assessment and pharmacological management. *Journal of Opioid Management, 5*(1), 47–55.

Jarnecke, A. M., & South, S. C. (2017). Behavior and molecular genetics of the Five Factor Model. In T. A. Widiger (Ed.), *The Oxford handbook of the five factor model.* New York, NY: Oxford University Press.

Joanisse, M., Gagnon, S., & Voloaca, M. (2013). The impact of stereotype threat on the simulated driving performance of older drivers. *Accident Analysis and Prevention, 50,* 530–538. doi:10.1016/j.aap.2012.05.032

Johns Hopkins Medicine. (2020). *Mental health disorder statistics.* https://www.hopkinsmedicine.org/health/wellness-and-prevention/mental-health-disorder-statistics

Johnston, L. D., & O'Malley, P. M. (1986). Why do the nation's students use drugs and alcohol? Self-reported reasons from nine national surveys. *Journal of Drug Issues, 16*(1), 29–66.

Johnston, L. D., O'Malley, P. M., & Bachman, J. G. (1991). *Drug use, drinking, and smoking: National survey results from high school, college, and young adult populations: 1975–1990. Vol. 1.* High School Seniors. DHHS Pub. No. (ADM) 91-1813. Rockville, MD: National Institute on Drug Abuse.

Jones, E. (2009). Review of madness to mental illness: A history of the Royal College of Psychiatrists. *Psychological Medicine: A Journal of Research in Psychiatry and the Allied Sciences, 39*(4), 695.

Jones, N. (2015, August 19). *8 classes all college students should take.* https://www.usatoday.com/story/college/2015/08/19/8-classes-all-college-students-should-take/37405553/

Kahana, E., Bhatta, T., Lovegreen, L. D., Kahana, B., & Midlarsky, E. (2013). Altruism, Helping, and Volunteering. *Journal of Aging and Health, 25*(1), 159–187. https://doi.org/10.1177/0898264312469665

Kalat, J. W. (2009). *Biological psychology* (10th ed.). Belmont, CA: Cengage/Thomson/Wadsworth.

Kamin, L. J. (1969). Predictability, surprise, attention and conditioning. In B. A. Campbell & R. M. Church (Eds.), *Punishment and aversive behavior.* New York, NY: Appleton-Century-Crofts.

Kandel, D. B., Yamaguchi, K., & Chen, K. (1992). Stages of progression in drug involvement from adolescence to adulthood: Further evidence for the gateway theory. *Journal of Studies on Alcohol, 53*(5), 447–457.

Karege, F., Perroud, N., Schurhoff, F., Meary, A., Marillier, G., Burkhardt, S., . . . Malafosse, A. (2010). Association of AKT1 gene variants and protein expression in both schizophrenia and bipolar disorder. *Genes, Brain and Behavior, 9*(5), 503–511.

Katja, B. K., Pine, D. S., Lieb, R., & Wittchen, H. U. (2010). Incidence and risk patterns of anxiety and depressive disorders and categorization of generalized anxiety disorder. *Archives of General Psychiatry, 67*(1), 47–57.

Katon, W. (2003). Clinical and health services relationships between major depression, depressive symptoms, and general medical illness. *Biological Psychiatry, 54*, 216–226.

Keel, P. K., Eddy, K. T., Thomas, J. J., & Schwartz, M. B. (2010). Vulnerability to eating disorders across the lifespan. In R. E. Ingram & J. M. Price (Eds.), *Vulnerability to psychopathology: Risk across the lifespan* (2nd ed., pp. 489–494). New York, NY: Guilford Press.

Keith-Lucas, T., & Guttman, N. (1975). Robust single-trial delayed backward conditioning. *Journal of Comparative and Physiological Psychology, 88*, 468–476.

Kelley, B. M., & Middaugh, L. D. (1999). Periadolescent nicotine exposure reduces cocaine reward in adult mice. *Journal of Addictive Diseases, 18*(3), 27–39. doi:10.1300/j069v18n03_04

Kelley, B. M., & Rowan, J. D. (2004). Long-term, low-level adolescent nicotine exposure produces dose-dependent changes in cocaine sensitivity and reward in adult subjects. *International Journal of Developmental Neuroscience, 22*(5–6), 339–348.

Kelly, K.J., Comello, M.L., & Hunn, L.C. (2002). Parent-child communication, perceived sanctions against drug use, and youth drug involvement. *Adolescence, 37*(148), 775-87.

Kessler, R. C., Berglund, P., Demler, O., Jin, R., Merikangas, K. R., & Walters, E. E. (2005). Lifetime prevalence and age-of-onset distributions of DSM-IV disorders in the National Comorbidity Survey Replication. *Archives of General Psychiatry, 62*(6), 593–602. doi:10.1001/archpsyc.62.6.593

Kessler, R. C., Chiu, W., Demler, O., & Walters, E. (2005). Prevalence, severity, and comorbidity of twelve-month DSM-IV disorders in the National Comorbidity Survey Replication (NCS-R). *Archives of General Psychiatry. 62*(6), 617–627. doi:10.1001/archpsyc.62.6.617

Kessler, R. C., Patricia, P., Demler, O., Jin, R., Merikangas, K. R., & Walters, E. E. (2005). Lifetime prevalence and age-of-onset distributions of DSM-IV disorders in the National Comorbidity Survey Replication. *Archives of General Psychiatry, 62*, 593–602.

Kessler, R. C., Ruscio, A. M., Shear, K., & Wittchen, H. U. (2009). Epidemiology of anxiety disorders. In M. M. Anthony & M. B. Stein (Eds.), *Oxford handbook of anxiety and related disorders* (pp. 19–33). London, England: Oxford University Press.

Kirkwood, M. W., Yeates, K. O., & Wilson, P. E. (2006). Pediatric sport-related concussion: A review of the clinical management of an oft-neglected population. *Pediatrics, 117*, 1359–1371.

Klineberg, O. (1938). Emotional expression in Chinese literature. *Journal of Abnormal and Social Psychology, 33*, 517–520.

Koelsch, S. (2010). Towards a neural basis of music-evoked emotions. *Trends in Cognitive Sciences, 14*(3), 131–137.

Koenig, H., King, D., & Carson, V. B. (2012). *Handbook of religion and health*. Retrieved from https://ebookcentral-proquest-com.ezproxy.liberty.edu

Koerner, E. F. K. (2000). Towards a "full pedigree" of the "Sapir–Whorf hypothesis." From Locke to Lucy. In M. Pütz & M. H. Verspoor (Eds.), *Explorations in linguistic relativity* (pp. 1–24). Amsterdam, the Netherlands: H. John Benjamins.

Kohlberg, L. (1969). Stage and sequence: The cognitive-developmental approach to socialization. In D. A. Goslin (Ed.), *Handbook of socialization theory and research* (pp. 347–480). New York, NY: Rand McNally.

Kohlberg, L. (1976). Moral stages and moralization: The cognitive-developmental approach. In T. Lickona (Ed.), *Moral development and behavior: Theory, research, and social issues* (pp. 31–53). New York, NY: Holt, Rinehart, and Winston.

Kohlberg, L. (1978). Revisions in the theory and practice of moral development. In W. Damon (Ed.), *New directions for children and adolescent development: No. 2. Moral development* (Vol. 1978, pp. 83–87). San Francisco, CA: Jossey-Bass.

Kohlberg, L. (1981). *Essays on moral development, Vol. I: The philosophy of moral development*. San Francisco, CA: Harper & Row.

Köhler, W. (1927). *The mentality of apes.* New York, NY: Harcourt, Brace, & World.

Kokkinos, C. M., Panayiotou, G., Charalambous, K., Antoniadou, N., & Davazoglou, A. (2010). Greek EPQ-J: Further support for a three-factor model of personality in children and adolescents. *Journal of Psychoeducational Assessment, 28*(3), 259–269. doi:10.1177/ 0734282909351023

Koriat, A., Melkman, R., Averill, J. R., & Lazarus, R. S. (1972). Self control of emotional reactions to a stressful film. *Journal of Personality, 40,* 601–619.

Kroger, C., Schweiger, U., Sipos, V., Kliem, S., Arnold, R., Schunert, R., . . . Reinecker, H. (2010). Dialectical behaviour therapy and an added cognitive behavioural treatment module for eating disorders in women with borderline personality disorder and anorexia nervosa or bulimia nervosa who failed to respond to previous treatments. An open trial with a 15-month follow-up. *Journal of Behavior Therapy and Experimental Psychiatry, 41*(4), 381–388.

Lachman, M. E. (2004). Development in midlife. *Annual Review of Psychology, 55*(1), 305–331. doi:10.1146/ annurev.psych.55.090902.141521

Lajtha, A., & Sershen, H. (2010). Nicotine-alcohol reward interactions. *Neurochemical Research, 35*(8), 1248–1258.

Lam, R. W. (1998). Seasonal affective disorder and beyond: Light treatment for SAD and non-SAD disorders. Washington, DC: American Psychiatric Press.

Landers, D. M. (2007). The arousal-performance relationship revisited. In M. BarEli (Ed.), *Essential readings in sport and exercise psychology.* Champaign, IL: Human Kinetics.

Larkby, C., & Day, N. (1997). The effects of prenatal alcohol exposure. *Alcohol Health Research World, 21*(3), 192–198.

Lashley, K. S. (1924). Studies of cerebral function in learning. *Archives of Neurological Psychiatry, 12,* 249–276.

Latané, B., & Darley, J. M. (1968). Group inhibition of bystander intervention. *Journal of Personality and Social Psychology, 10*(3), 215–221.

Latané, B., & Darley, J. M. (1970). *The unresponsive bystander: Why doesn't he help?* New York, NY: Appleton-Century-Crofts.

Laumann, E. O., Gagnon, J. H., Michael, R. T., & Michaels, S. (1992). *National health and social life survey,* [United States]. Ann Arbor, MI: Inter-university Consortium for Political and Social Research [distributor], 2008-04-17. https://doi.org/10.3886/ICPSR06647.v2

Lawton, A. (1981). From here to infinity. *Science Digest, 89*(1), 98–105.

Lazar, R. M., Minzer, B., Antoniello, D., Festa, J. R., Krakauer, J. W., & Marshall, R. S. (2010). Improvement in aphasia scores after stroke is well predicted by initial severity. *Stroke, 41,* 1485–1488.

Lazarus, R. S. (1974). Cognitive and coping processes in emotion. In B. Weiner (Ed.), *Cognitive views of human motivation.* New York, NY: Academic Press.

Lazarus, R. S. (1999). *Stress and emotion: A new synthesis.* New York, NY: Springer Publishing Company.

Lear, J. (2005). *Freud.* New York, NY: Routledge.

Leclair-Visonneau, L., Oudiette, D., Gaymard, B., Leu-Semenescu, S., & Arnulf, I. (2010). Do the eyes scan dream images during rapid eye movement sleep? Evidence from the rapid eye movement sleep behaviour disorder model. *Brain: A Journal of Neurology, 133*(6), 1737–1746.

LeDoux, J. (2010). From the integrated mind to the emotional brain. In P. A. Reuter-Lorenz, K. Baynes, G. R. Mangun, & E. A. Phelps (Eds.), *The cognitive neuroscience of mind: A tribute to Michael S. Gazzaniga* (pp. 89–98). Cambridge, MA: MIT Press.

Lee, S., Colditz, G. A., Berkman, L. F., & Kawachi, I. (2003). Caregiving and risk of coronary heart disease in U.S. women: A prospective study. *American Journal of Preventive Medicine, 24*(2), 113–119. doi:https://doi.org/10.1016/S0749-3797(02)00582-2

Lee, Y. T., Jussim, L. J., & McCauley, C. R. (Eds.). (1995). *Stereotype accuracy: Toward appreciating group differences.* Washington, DC: American Psychological Association.

Leichsenring, F., & Leibing, E. (2003). The effectiveness of psychodynamic therapy and cognitive behavior therapy in the treatment of personality disorders: A meta-analysis. *American Journal of Psychiatry,* 160(7), 1223–1232.

Leman, J., Hunter, W., Fergus, T., & Rowatt, W. (2018). Secure attachment to God uniquely linked to psychological health in a national, random sample of American adults. *The International Journal for the Psychology of Religion, 28,* 162–173, doi:10.1080/10508619.2018.1477401

Lepper, M. R., & Greene, D. (1975). Turning play into work; Effects of adult surveillance and extrinsic rewards on children's intrinsic motivation. *Journal of Personality and Social Psychology, 31*, 479–486.

Lepper, M. R., & Greene, D. (1978). Overjustification research and beyond: Toward a means-ends analysis of intrinsic and extrinsic motivation. In D. Greene & M. R. Lepper (Eds.), *The hidden costs of reward* (pp. 109–148). Hillsdale, NJ: Lawrence Erlbaum Associates.

Levran, O., Londono, D., O'Hara, K., Randesi, M., Rotrosen, J., Casadonte, P., . . . Kreek, M. J. (2009). Heroin addiction in African Americans: A hypothesis-driven association study. *Genes, Brain and Behavior, 8*(5), 531–540.

Lewis, M. D. (2005). Bridging emotion theory and neurobiology through dynamic system modeling. *Behavioral and Brain Sciences, 28*, 169–194.

Lewis, M., Feiring, C., & Rosenthal, S. (2000). Attachment over time. *Child Development, 71, 707*–720. doi:10.111/1476-8624.00180

Lewis, N. A., Turiano, N. A., Payne, B. R., & Hill, P. L. (2017). Purpose in life and cognitive functioning in adulthood. *Aging, Neuropsychology, and Cognition, 24*(6), 662–671.

Li, C., Ford, E. S., Zhao, G., & Mokdad, A. H. (2009). Associations of health risk factors and chronic illnesses with life dissatisfaction among U.S. adults: The behavioral risk factor surveillance system, 2006. *Preventive Medicine, 49*(2–3), 253–259. doi:10.1016/j.ypmed.2009.05.012

Li, L., Shults, R. A., Andridge, R. R., Yellman, M. A., Xiang, H., & Zhu, M. (2015). Texting/emailing while driving among high school students in 35 states, United States. *Journal of Adolescent Health, 63*(6), 701–708. https://doi.org/10.1016/j.jadohealth.2018.06.010

Li, R., & Wong, W. I. (2016). Gender-typed play and social abilities in boys and girls: Are they related?. *Sex Roles, 74*, 10.

Li, Y., & Lei, X. (2010). Social support and personality of patients with suicide attempt without mental illness. *Chinese Journal of Clinical Psychology, 18*(2), 194–195.

Liben, L. S., & Bigler, R. S. (2002). The developmental course of gender differentiation: Conceptualizing, measuring, and evaluating constructs and pathways. *Monographs of the Society for Research in Child Development, 67*(2), vii–147.

Lichtenstein, P., Yip, B. H., Björk, C., Pawitan, Y., Cannon, T. D., Sullivan, P. F., . . . Hultman, C. M. (2009). Common genetic determinants of schizophrenia and bipolar disorder in Swedish families: A population-based study. *Lancet, 373*(9659), 234–239.

Liebe, U., & Tutic, A. (2010). Status groups and altruistic behaviour in dictator games. *Rationality and Society, 22*(3), 353–380.

Lilienfeld, S. O., Lynn, S. J., Ruscio, J., & Beyerstein, B. L. (2010). *50 great myths of popular psychology: Shattering widespread misconceptions about human behavior.* Malden, MA: Wiley-Blackwell.

Linder, J. R., & Gentile, D. A. (2009). Is the television rating system valid? Indirect, verbal, and physical aggression in programs viewed by fifth grade girls and associations with behavior. *Journal of Applied Developmental Psychology, 30*(3), 286–297.

Lipari, R. N., Ahrnsbrak, R. D., Pemberton, M. R., & Porter, J. D. (2017). *Risk and protective factors and estimates of substance use initiation: Results from the 2016 National Survey on Drug Use and Health.* https://www.samhsa.gov/data/sites/default/files/NSDUH-DR-FFR3-2016/NSDUH-DR-FFR3-2016.pdf

Loftus, E. F. (1975). Leading questions and the eyewitness report. *Cognitive Psychology, 7*, 560–572. doi:10.1016/0010-0285(75)90023-7

Loftus, E. F. (1979). *Eyewitness testimony.* Cambridge, MA: Harvard University Press.

Loftus, E. F., & Palmer, J. C. (1974). Reconstruction of automobile destruction: An example of the interaction between language and memory. *Journal of Verbal Learning &Verbal Behavior, 13*, 585–589. doi:10.1016/S0022-5371(74)80011-3

Lopez-Duran, N. (2011, October 18). Fifty percent (50%) of teens have experienced a psychiatric condition by their 18th birthday. *Child Psychology Research.* http://www.child-psych.org/2010/10/fifty-percent-50-of-teens-have-experienced-a-psychiatric-condition-by-their-18th-birthday.html

Lorenz, K. (1952). *King Solomon's ring: New light on animal ways.* New York, NY: Crowell.

Lucas-Thompson, R., & Clarke-Stewart, K. A. (2007). Forecasting friendship: How marital quality, maternal mood, and attachment security are linked to children's peer relationships. *Journal of Applied Developmental Psychology, 28,* 499–514. doi:10.1016/j.appdev.2007.06.004

Lustig, C., & Hasher, L. (2001). Implicit memory is not immune to interference. *Psychological Bulletin, 127,* 629–650. doi:10.1037/0033-2909.127.5.618

Lynn, S. J., Boycheva, E., Deming, A., Lilienfeld, S. O., & Hallquist, M. N. (2009). Forensic hypnosis: The state of the science. In L. Jennifer, K. S. Douglas, & S. O. Lilienfeld (Eds.), *Psychological science in the courtroom: Consensus and controversy* (pp. 80–99). New York, NY: Guilford Press.

Macfarlane, A. (2008). Olfaction in the development of social preferences in the human neonate. In R. Porter & M. O'Connor (Eds.), *Ciba foundation symposium 33—Paren–Infant interaction.* Chichester, England: John Wiley & Sons. doi:10.1002/9780470720158.ch7

Mack, A., & Rock, I. (1998). *Inattentional blindness: Perception without attention.* Cambridge, MA: MIT Press.

Macmillan, M. (Ed.). (2000). *An odd kind of fame: Stories of Phineas Gage.* Cambridge, MA: MIT Press.

Macmillan, M. (2008). Phineas Gage–Unravelling the myth. *The Psychologist, 21*(9), 828–831.

Madey, S. F., & Rodgers, L. (2009). The effect of attachment and Sternberg's Triangular Theory of Love on relationship satisfaction. *Individual Differences Research, 7*(2), 76–84.

Main, M., & Solomon, J. (1990). Procedures for identifying infants as disorganized/disoriented during the Ainsworth Strange Situation. In M. T. Greenberg, D. Cicchetti, & E. M. Cummings (Eds.), *Attachment in the preschool years: Theory research and intervention* (pp. 121–160). Chicago, IL: University of Chicago Press.

Manning, R., Levine, M., & Collins, A. (2007). The Kitty Genovese murder and the social psychology of helping. *American Psychologist, 62*(6), 555–562.

Maranon, G. (1924). Contribution à l'étude de l'action émotive de l'adrénaline. *Revue Française Endocrinologique, 2,* 301–325.

Marinkovic, K., Oscar-Berman, M., Urban, T., O'Reilly, C. E., Howard, J. A., Sawyer, K., . . . Harris, G. J. (2009). Alcoholism and dampened temporal limbic activation to emotional faces. *Alcoholism: Clinical and Experimental Research, 33*(11), 1880–1892.

Mark, A. L. (2013). Selective leptin resistance revisited. *American Journal of Physiology. Regulatory, Integrative and Comparative Physiology, 305*(6), R566–R581. https://doi.org/10.1152/ajpregu.00180.2013

Markham, A. (2013, February 15). The pain of positive stereotypes. *Psychology Today.* http://www.psychologytoday.com/blog/ulterior-motives/201302/the-pain-positive-stereotypes

Martin, L. E., Holsen, L. M., Chambers, R. J., Bruce, A. S., Brooks, W. M., Zarcone, J. R., . . . Savage, C. R. (2010). Neural mechanism associated with food motivation in obese and healthy weight adults. *Obesity, 18*(2), 254–260.

Mashour, G. A., Walker, E. E., & Martuza, R. L. (2005). Psychosurgery: Past, present, and future. *Brain Research Reviews, 48*(3), 409–419.

Maslow, A. H. (1970). *Motivation and personality* (2nd ed.). New York, NY: Harper & Row.

Mason, O. J., & Brady, F. (2009). The psychotomimetic effects of short-term sensory deprivation. *Journal of Nervous and Mental Disease, 197*(10), 783–785.

Masten, A. S., Faden, V. B., Zucker, R. A., & Spear, L. P. (2008). Underage drinking: A developmental framework. *Pediatrics, 121*(4), 235–251.

Maxouris, C., & Rose, A. (2020, January 8). Glacier National Park is replacing signs that predicted its glaciers would be gone by 2020. *CNN Travel.* https://www.cnn.com/2020/01/08/us/glaciers-national-park-2020-trnd/index.html?utm_content=2020-01-08T11%3A35%3A42&utm_source=twCNN&utm_term=link&utm_medium=social

McClellan, M., Stanwyck, J., & Anson, C. A. (1993). Social support and subsequent mortality among patients with end-stage renal disease. *Journal of the American Society of Nephrology, 4*(4), 1028–1034. http://jasn.asnjournals.org/content/4/4/1028.long

McClelland, D. C. (1958). Risk taking in children with high and low need for achievement. In J. W. Atkinson (Ed.), *Motives in fantasy, action, and society.* New York, NY: Van Nostrand Reinhold.

McClelland, D. C., Atkinson, J. W., Clark, R. A., & Lowell, E. L. (1953). *The achievement motive*. New York, NY: Appleton-Century-Crofts.

McCook, A. (2016, Sept. 1). *Whistleblower sues Duke, claims doctored data helped win $200 million in grants*. American Association for the Advancement of Science. https://www.sciencemag.org/news/2016/09/whistleblower-sues-duke-claims-doctored-data-helped-win-200-million-grants

McMahon, S., & Farmer, G. L. (2009). The bystander approach: Strengths-based sexual assault prevention with at-risk groups. *Journal of Human Behavior in the Social Environment, 19*(8), 1042–1065.

McWilliams, J. R. & Lynch, G. (1983). Rate of synaptic replacement in denervated rat hippocampus declines precipitously from the juvenile period to adulthood. *Science, 221*(4610), 572–574. doi:10.1126/science.6867730

Meadows, M. (2005, May–June). Dealing with dry eye. *FDA Consumer Magazine, 39*(3), 1–3.

Meletis, C. D., & Wood, S. G. (2009). *His change of life: Male menopause and healthy aging with testosterone*. Westport, CT: Praeger Publishers/Greenwood Publishing Group.

Mennella, J. A., Griffin, C. E., & Beauchamp, G. K. (2004). Flavor programing during infancy. *Pediatrics, 113*, 840–845.

Merikangas, K. R., He, J., Burstein, M., Swanson, S. A., Avenevoli, S., Cui, L., . . . Swendsen, J. (2010). Lifetime prevalence of mental disorders in US adolescents: Results from the National Comorbidity Study-Adolescent Supplement (NCS-A). *Journal of the American Academy of Child and Adolescent Psychiatry, 49*(10), 980–989. doi:10.1016/j.jaac.2010.05.017

Milgram, S. (1963). Behavioral study of obedience and disobedience to authority. *Journal of Abnormal and Social Psychology, 67*, 371–378.

Milgram, S. (1965). Some conditions of obedience and disobedience to authority. *Human Relations, 18*, 67–76.

Miller, G. A. (1956). The magical number seven, plus or minus two: Some limits on our capacity for processing information. *Psychological Review, 63*(2), 81–97. doi:10.1037/h0043158

Miller, H. C., Rayburn-Reeves, R., & Zentall, T. R. (2009). Imitation and emulation by dogs using a bidirectional control procedure. *Behavioural Processes, 80*(2), 109–114.

Miller, P. H. (2011). *Theories of developmental psychology* (5th ed.). New York, NY: Worth.

Milner, B. (1970). Memory and the medial temporal regions of the brain. In *Biology of memory*. New York, NY: Academic Press.

Minnes, S., Lang, A., & Singer, L. (2011). Prenatal tobacco, marijuana, stimulant, and opioid exposure: Outcomes and practical implications. *Addiction Science and Clinical Practice, 6*(1), 57–70.

Minnier, E., Misanin, J. R., & Hinderliter, C. F. (2007). Age and interstimulus interval in forward and backward long-trace taste-aversion conditioning. *Perceptual and Motor Skills, 105*(3, Pt 2), 1223–1226.

Mischel, W. (2004). Toward an integrative science of the person. *Annual Review of Psychology, 55*, 1–22. doi:10.1146/annurev.psych.55.042902.130709

Montoya, R. M., & Horton, R. S. (2013). A meta-analytic investigation of the processes underlying the similarity-attraction effect. *Journal of Social and Personal Relationships, 30*(1), 64–96. doi:10.1177/0265407512452989

Montoya, R. M., & Horton, R. S. (2014). A two-dimensional model for the study of interpersonal attraction. *Personality and Social Psychology Review, 18*(1), 59–86. doi:10.1177/108886831351887

Moors, A. (2009). Theories of emotion causation: A review. *Cognition & Emotion, 23*(4), 625–662.

Morcom, A. M., Bullmore, E. T., Huppert, F. A., Lennox, B., Praseedom, A., Linnington, H., . . . Fletcher, P. C. (2010). Memory encoding and dopamine in the aging brain: A psychopharmacological neuroimaging study. *Cerebral Cortex, 20*(3), 743–757.

Moulton, S. T., & Kosslyn, S. M. (2008). Using neuroimaging to resolve the psi debate. *Journal of Cognitive Neuroscience, 20*, 182–192. doi:10.1162/jocn.2008.20.1.182

Mulvaney, M. K., & Mebert, C. J. (2007). Parental corporal punishment predicts behavior problems in early childhood. *Journal of Family Psychology, 21*(3), 389–397.

Munch, M., Kobialka, S., Steiner, R., Oelhafen, P., Wirz-Justice, A., & Cajochen, C. (2006). Wavelength-dependent effects of evening light exposure on sleep architecture and sleep EEG power density in men.

American Journal of Physiology-Regulatory, Integrative and Comparative Physiology, 290(5), 1421–1428. https://doi.org/10.1152/ajpregu.00478.2005

Murphy, R., Straebler, S., Cooper, Z., & Fairburn, C. G. (2010). Cognitive behavioral therapy for eating disorders. *Psychiatric Clinics of North America, 33*(3), 611–627.

Murray, H. A. (1938). *Explorations in personality.* New York, NY: Oxford University Press.

Murray, H. A. (1943). *Thematic apperception test manual.* Cambridge, MA: Harvard University Press.

Murray-Close, D., Ostrov, J. M., Nelson, D. A., Crick, N. R., & Coccaro, E. F. (2010). Proactive, reactive, and romantic relational aggression in adulthood: Measurement, predictive validity, gender differences, and association with intermittent explosive disorder. *Journal of Psychiatric Research, 44*(6), 393–404.

Must, A., & Anderson, S. E. (2010). Childhood obesity: Definition, classification and assessment. In P. G. Kopelman, I. D. Caterson, & W. H. Dietz (Eds.), *Clinical obesity in adults and children* (3rd ed., pp. 375–391). Hoboken, NJ: Wiley-Blackwell.

Naifeh, S. C. (2011). Carl Gustav Jung, M.D., 1875–1961. *American Journal of Psychiarty, 158*(12), 1973. doi:10.1176/appi.ajp.158.12.1973

Naish, P. L. N. (2010). Hypnosis and hemispheric asymmetry. *Consciousness and Cognition: An International Journal, 19*(1), 230–234.

Narayan, V., & Haddad, P. M. (2011). Antidepressant discontinuation manic states: A critical review of the literature and suggested diagnostic criteria. *Journal of Psychopharmacology, 25*(3), 306–313.

Naseem, Z., & Khalid, R. (2010). Positive thinking in coping with stress and health outcomes: Literature review. *Journal of Research and Reflections in Education, 4*, 42–61.

National Comorbidity Survey Replication (NCS–R). (2010). http://www.hcp.med.harvard.edu/ncs/ftpdir/NCS–R_ Lifetime_Prevalence_Estimates.pdf

National Institute of Mental Health. (2008). *Attention deficit hyperactivity disorder* (NIH Publication No. 08-3572). http://www.nimh.nih.gov/health/publications/attention-deficit-hyperactivity-disorder/adhd_booklet.pdf

National Institute of Mental Health. (2014). *Autism spectrum disorder.* http://www.nimh.nih.gov/health/topics/autism-spectrum-disorders-asd/index.shtml

National Institute of Mental Health. (2017a). *Bipolar disorder.* https://www.nimh.nih.gov/health/statistics/bipolar-disorder.shtml

National Institute of Mental Health. (2017b). *Obsessive-compulsive disorder (OCD).* https://www.nimh.nih.gov/health/statistics/obsessive-compulsive-disorder-ocd.shtml

National Institute of Mental Health. (2017c). *Post-traumatic stress disorder (PTSD).* https://www.nimh.nih.gov/health/statistics/post-traumatic-stress-disorder-ptsd.shtml

National Institute of Mental Health. (2019). *Major depression.* https://www.nimh.nih.gov/health/statistics/major-depression.shtml

National Opinion Research Center. (2014, May). *Long term care in America: Expectations and realities.* http://www.longtermcarepoll.org/PDFs/LTC%202014/AP-NORC-Long-Term%20Care%20in%20America_FINAL%20WEB.pdf

Neonatal drug withdrawal. American Academy of Pediatrics Committee on Drugs. (1998). Pediatrics, 101(6):1079-88.

Neubauer, D. N. (2009). Asleep: Inside and out. *Primary Psychiatry, 16*(5), 17–18.

Newcomb, T. M. (1961). *The acquaintanceship process.* New York, NY: Holt, Rinehart & Winston.

Newman, S. M., Paletz, E. M., Obermeyer, W. H., & Benca, R. M. (2009). Sleep deprivation in pigeons and rats using motion detection. *Sleep: Journal of Sleep and Sleep Disorders Research, 32*(10), 1299–1312.

Nickerson, R. S., & Adams, M. J. (1979). Long-term memory for a common object. *Cognitive Psychology, 11*, 287–307. doi:10.1016/0010-0285(79)90013-6

Nicolas, S., & Levine, Z. (2012). Beyond intelligence testing: Remembering Alfred Binet after a century. *European Psychologists, 17*(4), 320–325. doi:10.1027/1016-9040/a000117

Nolley, E. P. & Kelley, B. M. (2007). Adolescent reward system perseveration due to nicotine: Studies with methylphenidate. *Neurotoxicology and Teratology, 29*(1), 47–56.

Norton, A. (2014, April 22). New drug may help prevent migraines. *WebMD.com*. http://www.webmd.com

Nowak, R. (1994). Nicotine scrutinized as FDA seeks to regulate cigarettes. *Science, 263,* 1555–1556.

Oakley, D. A., & Halligan, P. W. (2010). Psychophysiological foundations of hypnosis and suggestion. In S. J. Lynn, J. W. Rhue, & I. Kirsch (Eds.), *Handbook of clinical hypnosis* (2nd ed., pp. 79–117). Washington, DC: American Psychological Association.

O'Brien, C. P. (2001). Drug addiction and drug abuse. In *Pharmacological basis of therapeutics* (10th ed.) (Hardman, J. G., Limbird, L. E., & Gilman, A. G., eds.). New York: McGraw-Hill.

O'Brien, C. P., & McLellan, A. T. (1996). Myths about the treatment of addiction. *The Lancet, 347*(8996), 237–240.

O'Donnell, J. A., & Clayton, R. R. (1979). Determinants of early marijuana use. In: Beschner, G. M., & Friedman, A. S. (Eds.), *Youth drug abuse: Problems, issues, and treatment.* Lexington, MA: Lexington Books.

The Official Division 30 Definition and Description of Hypnosis. (2014). *The society of psychological hypnosis: Division 30 of the American Psychological Association.* Retrieved March 10, 2020, https://www.apadivisions.org/division-30/about

Öhman, A., Carlsson, K., Lundqvist, D., & Ingvar, M. (2007). On the unconscious subcortical origin of human fear. *Physiology & Behavior, 92*(1–2), 180–185.

Olds, J. (1956). Pleasure centers in the brain. *Scientific American, 195,* 105–116.

Olds, J. (1958). Self-stimulation of the brain. *Science, 127,* 315–324.

Oliaro, S., Anderson, S., & Hooker, D. (2001). Management of cerebral concussion in sports: The athletic trainer's perspective. *Journal of athletic training, 36*(3), 257–262.

Orne, M. T. (2009). On the simulating subject as a quasi-control group in hypnosis research: What, why, and how. In E. Fromm & R. E. Shor (Eds.), *Hypnosis: Developments in research and new perspectives* (2nd ed., pp. 519–566). Piscataway, NJ: Transaction Publishers.

Ortet, G., Escriva, P., Ibanez, M. I., Moya, J., Villa, H., Mezquita, L., . . . Ruiperez, M. A. (2010). The short version of the Junior Spanish NEO-PI-R (JS NEO-S). *International Journal of Clinical and Health Psychology, 10*(2), 327–344.

Paintner, A., Williams, A. D., & Burd, L. (2012). Fetal alcohol spectrum disorders—implications for child neurology, part 1: Prenatal exposure and dosimetry. *Journal of Child Neurology, 27*(2), 258–263.

Palmer, S. E. (1999). *Vision science: Photons to phenomenology.* Cambridge, MA: MIT Press.

Panic disorder. (2010). *NHS choices: Your health.* http://www.nhs.uk/conditions/panic–disorder/Pages/Introduction.aspx

Panksepp, J. (2010). Evolutionary substrates of addiction: The neurochemistries of pleasure seeking and social bonding in the mammalian brain. In J. D. Kassel (Ed.), *Substance abuse and emotion* (pp. 137–167). Washington, DC: American Psychological Association.

Parrott, W. G. (2004). The nature of emotion. In M. B. Brewer & M. Hewstone (Eds.), *Emotion and motivation* (pp. 5–20). Malden, MA: Blackwell Publishing.

Patel, R. S., Amaravadi, N., Bhullar, H., Lekireddy, J., & Win, H. (2018). Understanding the demographic predictors and associated comorbidities in children hospitalized with conduct disorder. *Behavioral Sciences, 8*(9), 80-88. http://dx.doi.org.ezproxy.liberty.edu/10.3390/bs8090080

Pavlov, I. P. (1927). *Conditioned reflexes* (G. V. Anrep, Trans.). London, England: Oxford University Press.

Pearce, M. J., Koenig, H. G., Robins, C. J., Nelson, B., Shaw, S. F., Cohen, H. J., . . . King, M. B. (2015). Religiously integrated cognitive behavioral therapy: A new method of treatment for major depression in patients with chronic medical illness. *Psychotherapy, 52*(1), 56–66. https://doi.org/10.1037/a0036448

Perou, R., Bitsko, R. H., Blumberg, S. J., Pastor, P., Ghandour, R. M., Gfroerer, J. C., . . . Huang, L. N. (2013). Mental health surveillance among children – United States, 2005–2011. *Supplements, 62*(2), 1–35.

Pew Research Center. (2009a, July 9). *Public praises science; scientists fault public, media: About the survey.* https://www.people-press.org/2009/07/09/about-the-survey-16/

Pew Research Center. (2009b, May 4). *Religion and science: Conflict or harmony?* https://www.pewforum.org/2009/05/04/religion-and-science-conflict-or-harmony/

Pew Research Center. (2020, February 15). *Public praises science; Scientists fault public, media.* https://www.people-press.org/2009/07/09/public-praises-science-scientists-fault-public-media/ 1/7

Pfeifer, J. H., & Blakemore, S. J. (2012). Adolescent social cognitive and affective neuroscience: Past, present, and future. *Social Cognition and Affective Neuroscience, 7*(1), 1–10.

Piaget, J. (1954). *The construction of reality in the child* (M. Cook, Trans.). New York, NY: Basic Books.

Piaget, J. (1963). *The origins of intelligence in children.* New York, NY: W. W. Norton.

Piaget, J. (1969). *The child's conception of the world.* Totowa, NJ: Littlefield Adams.

Piaget, J. (1973). *The language and though of the child.* New York, NY: Meridian World.

Piaget, J. (1999). The stages of intellectual development of the child. In A. Slater & D. Muir (Eds.), *Blackwell reader in developmental psychology* (pp. 35–42). Malden, MA: Blackwell.

Piaget, J., & Inhelder, B. (1977). *From the logic of the child to the logic of the adolescent: Essay on the shaping of the formal operative structures.* Klett-Cotta.

Piech, R. M, Pastorino, M. T., & Zald, D. H. (2010). All I saw was the cake. Hunger effects on attentional capture by visual food cues. *Appetite, 54*(3), 579–582.

Pinker, S. (1997). *How the mind works.* New York, NY: W. W. Norton & Company.

Plaisant, O., Courtois, R., Reveillere, C., Mendelsohn, G. A., & John, O. P. (2010). Factor structure and internal reliability of the French Big Five Inventory (BFI-Fr). Convergent and discriminant validation with the NEO-PI-R. *Annales Medico Psychologiques, 168*(2), 97–106. doi:10.1016/j.amp.2009.09.003

Popova, S., Lange, S., Bekmuradov, D., Mihic, A., & Rehm, J. (2011). Fetal alcohol spectrum disorder prevalence estimates in correctional systems: A systematic literature review. *Canadian Journal of Public Health, 102*(5), 336–340.

Porter, R. H., & Rieser, J. J. (2005). Retention of olfactory memories by newborn infants. In R. T. Mason, M. P. LeMaster, & D. Muller-Schwarze (Eds.), *Chemical signals in vertebrates 10* (pp. 300–307). New York, NY: Springer Publishing Company.

Posner, M. I. (1980). Orienting of attention. *Quarterly Journal of Experimental Psychology, 32,* 3–25. doi:10.1080/00335558008248231

Pothakos, K., Robinson, J. K., Gravanis, I., Marsteller, D. A., Dewey, S. L., & Tsirka, S. E. (2010). Decreased serotonin levels associated with behavioral disinhibition in tissue plasminogen activator deficient (tpa-/-) mice. *Brain Research, 1326,* 135–142.

Potter, S. J., Moynihan, M. M., Stapleton, J. G., & Banyard, V. L. (2009). Empowering bystanders to prevent campus violence against women: A preliminary evaluation of a poster campaign. *Violence Against Women, 15*(1), 106–121.

Presley, C. A., Meilman, P.W., & Lyerla, R. (1997). *Alcohol and drugs on American college campuses: Issues of violence and harassment.* Carbondale, IL: Core Institute, Southern Illinois University.

Prochaska, J. O., & Norcross, J. C. (2010). *Systems of psychotherapy: A transtheoretical analysis* (7th ed.). Pacific Grove, CA: Brookes/Cole.

Prokop, P., & Vaclav, R. (2008). Seasonal aspects of sexual cannibalism in the *praying mantis (Mantis religiosa).* *Journal of Ethology, 26*(2), 213–218.

Pullum, G. K. (1991). The great Eskimo vocabulary hoax and other irreverent essays on the study of language. Chicago, IL: University of Chicago Press.

Ranganath, K. A., Spellman, B. A., & Joy-Gaba, J. A. (2010). Cognitive "category-based induction" research and social "persuasion" research are each about what makes arguments believable: A tale of two literatures. *Perspectives on Psychological Science, 5*(2), 115–122.

Rauschecker, J. P., & Tian, B. (2000). Mechanisms and streams for processing of "what" and "where" in auditory cortex. *Proceedings of the National Academy of Science, 97,* 11800–11806. doi:10.1073/pnas.97.22.11800

Ray, O., & Ksir, C. (1990). *Drugs, society, and human behavior* (5th ed.). St. Louis, MO: Times Mirror/Mosby.

Razali, S. M., Hasanah, C. I., Aminah, K., & Subramaniam, M. (1998). Religious-- sociocultural psychotherapy in patients with anxiety and depression. *Australian & New Zealand Journal of Psychiatry, 32,* 867–872.

Reger, G. M., Holloway, K. M., Candy, C., Rothbaum, B. O., Difede, J. A., Rizzo, A. A., . . . Gahm, G. A. (2011). Effectiveness of virtual reality exposure therapy for active duty soldiers in a military mental health clinic. *Journal of Traumatic Stress, 24*(1), 93–96.

Revonsuo, A. (2000). The reinterpretation of dreams: An evolutionary hypothesis of the function of dreaming. *Behavioral and Brain Sciences, 23*(6), 1016–1017.

Revonsuo, A., Kallio, S., & Sikka, P. (2009). What is an altered state of consciousness? *Philosophical Psychology, 22*(2), 187–204.

Reynolds, B. A., & Weiss, S. (1992, March). Generation of neurons and astrocytes from isolated cells of the adult mammalian central nervous system. *Science, 255*(5052), 1707–1710.

Rezvani, A. H. & Levin, E. D. (2004). Adolescent and adult rats respond differently to nicotine and alcohol: Motor activity and body temperature. *International Journal of Developmental Neuroscience, 22*(5–6), 349–354.

Richards, C. S., & Perri, M. G. (Eds.). (2010). *Relapse prevention for depression*. Washington, DC: American Psychological Association.

Richman, J. E., McAndrew, K. G., Decker, D., & Mullaney, S. C. (2004). An evaluation of pupil size standards used by police officers for detecting drug impairment. *Optometry: Journal of the American Optometric Association, 75*, 1–8. doi:10.1016/s1529-1839(04)70037-8

Riediger, M., Schmiedek, F., Wagner, G. G., & Lindenberger, U. (2009). Seeking pleasure and seeking pain: Differences in prohedonic and contra-hedonic motivation from adolescence to old age. *Psychological Science, 20*(12), 1529–1535.

Roazen, P. (1975). *Freud and his followers*. New York, NY: Knopf.

Robbins, M., Francis, L. J., & Edwards, B. (2010). Happiness as stable extraversion: Internal consistency reliability and construct validity of the Oxford Happiness Questionnaire among undergraduate students. *Current Psychology: Research Reviews, 29*(2), 89–94. doi:10.1007/s12144-010-9076-8

Roberts, B. W., & DelVecchio, W. F. (2000). The rank-order consistency of personality traits from childhood to old age: A qualitative review of longitudinal studies. *Psychological Bulletin, 126,* 3–25.

Robins, L. N., & Przybeck, T. R. (1985). Age of onset of drug use as a factor in drug and other disorders. In C. L. Jones & R. J. Battjes (Eds.), *Etiology of drug abuse* (pp. 178-192). Rockville, MD: National.

Robins, R. W. (2005). The nature of personality: Genes, culture, and national character. *Science, 310*(5745), 62–63.

Rodieck, R. W. (1998). *The first steps in seeing*. Sunderland, MA: Sinauer Associates.

Rogers, C. R. (1951). *Client-centered therapy: Its current practice*. Boston, MA: Houghton Mifflin.

Roscoe, W. (1991). *The Zuni man-woman*. Albuquerque, NM: University of New Mexico Press.

Rosenzweig, M. R., Leiman, A. L., & Breedlove, S. M. (1999). *Biological psychology*. Sunderland, MA: Sinauer Associates.

Rothbart, M. K. (2011). *Becoming who we are: Temperament and personality in development*. New York, NY: Guilford Press.

Rotter, J. R. (1982). *The development and application of social learning theory*. New York, NY: Praeger.

Rowan, J. (1998). Maslow amended. *Journal of Humanistic Psychology, 38*, 81–92.

Rowell, A. M., & Faruqui, R. A. (2010). Persistent hyperphagia in acquired brain injury; an observational case study of patients receiving inpatient rehabilitation. *Brain Injury, 24*(7–8), 1044–1049.

Rubin, Z. (1970). Measurement of romantic love. *Journal of Personality and Social Psychology, 16*, 265–271.

Russell, B. (1927). *Philosophy*. New York, NY: Norton.

Saguy, A. C., & Gruys, K. (2010). Morality and health: News media constructions of overweight and eating disorders. *Social Problems, 57*(2), 231–250.

Sandin, S., Lichtenstein, P., Kuja-Halkola, R., Larsson, H., Hultman, C.M., & Reichenberg, A. (2014). The familial risk of autism. *JAMA, 311*(17), 1770–1777. doi:10.1001/jama.2014.4144

Sanz, J., Garcia-Vera, M. P., & Magan, I. (2010). Anger and hostility from the perspective of the Big Five personality model. *Scandinavian Journal of Psychology, 51*(3), 262–270. doi:10.1111/j.1467-9450.2009.00771.x

Sattler, J. M. (2008). *Assessment of children: Cognitive foundations* (5th ed.). San Diego, CA: Jerome M. Sattler Publisher, Inc.

Sava, F. A., Yates, B. T., Lupu, V., Szentagotai, A., & David, D. (2009). Cost-effectiveness and cost-utility of cognitive therapy, rational emotive behavioral therapy, and fluoxetine (Prozac) in treating clinical depression: A randomized clinical trial. *Journal of Clinical Psychology, 65*(1), 36–52.

Sawyer, S. M., Afifi, R. A., Bearinger, L. H., Blakemore, S. J., Dick, B., Ezeh, A. C., . . . Patton, G. C. (2012). Adolescence: A foundation for future health. *Lancet, 379*(9826), 1630–1640.

Schacter, D. L. (1999). The seven sins of memory: Insights from psychology and cognitive neuroscience. *American Psychologist, 54*, 182–203. doi:10.1037/0003-066X.54.3.182

Schacter, D. L., & Tulving, E. (1994). What are the memory systems of 1994? In D. L. Schacter & E. Tulving (Eds.), *Memory systems.* Cambridge, MA: MIT Press.

Schacter, D. L., Wagner, A. D., & Buckner, R. L. (2000). Memory systems of 1999. In E. Tulving & F. I. M. Craik (Eds.), *The Oxford handbook of memory.* New York, NY: Oxford University Press.

Schachter, S. (1971). Some extraordinary facts about obese humans and rats. *American Psychologist, 26*, 129–144.

Schachter, S., & Singer, J. E. (1962). Cognitive, social, and physiological determinants of emotional state. *Psychological Review, 69*, 379–399.

Scherer, K. R. (2005). What are emotions? And how can they be measured? *Social Science Information, 44*, 695–729.

Schredl, M. (2010). Explaining the gender difference in dream recall frequency. *Dreaming, 20*(2), 96–106.

Schredl, M., Atanasova, D., Hormann, K., Maurer, J. T., Hummel, T., & Stuck, B. A. (2009). Information processing during sleep: The effect of olfactory stimuli on dream content and dream emotions. *Journal of Sleep Research, 18*(3), 285–290.

Schwartz, C., Meisenhelder, J. B., Ma, Y., & Reed, G. (2003). Altruistic social interest behaviors are associated with better mental health. *Psychosomatic Medicine, 65*(5), 778–785. https://doi.org/10.1097/01.PSY.0000079378.39062.D4

The Science of Sleep. (2010). Science & Nature: Human Body & Mind. *BBC.* http://www.bbc.co.uk/science/humanbody/sleep/articles/whatissleep.shtml

Scoffier, S., Paquet, Y., & d'Arripe-Longueville, F. (2010). Effect of locus of control on disordered eating in athletes: The mediational role of self-regulation of eating attitudes. *Eating Behaviors, 11*(3), 164–169. doi:10.1016/j.eatbeh.2010.02.002

Scoville, W. B., & Milner, B. (1957). Loss of recent memory after bilateral hippocampal lesions. *Journal of Neurology, Neurosurgery & Psychiatry, 20*, 11–21. doi:10.1136/jnnp.20.1.11

Seidman, G., & Miller, O. S. (2013). Effects of gender and physical attractiveness on visual attention to Facebook profiles. *Cyberpsychology, Behavior, and Social Networking, 16*(1), 20–24. doi:10.1089/cyber.2012.0305

Sekuler, R., & Blake, R. (2002). *Perception* (4th ed.). New York, NY: McGraw-Hill.

Sela, L., & Sobel, N. (2010). Human olfaction: A constant state of change-blindness. *Experimental Brain Research, 205*, 13–29. doi:10.1007/s00221-010-2348-6

Self, D. W., & Staley, J. K. (Eds.). (2010). *Behavioral neuroscience of drug addiction.* New York, NY: Springer Publishing Company.

Selfhout, M., Burk, W., Branje, S., Denissen, J., van Aken, M., & Meeus, W. (2010). Emerging late adolescent friendship networks and Big Five personality traits: A social network approach. *Journal of Personality, 78*(2), 509–538. doi:10.1111/j.1467-6494.2010.00625.x

Sendin, M. C. (2010). Rorschach usefulness in treatment planning. *Rorschachiana, 31*(1), 70–89.

Seres, I., Unoka, Z., Bodi, N., Aspan, N., & Keri, S. (2009). The neuropsychology of borderline personality disorder: Relationship with clinical dimensions and comparisons with other personality disorders. *Journal of Personality Disorders, 23*(6), 555–562. doi:10.1521/pedi.2009.23.6.555

Sharf, R. S. (2012). *Theories of psychotherapy and counseling: Concepts and cases* (5th ed.). Pacific Grove, CA: Brookes/Cole.

Sheedy, J. E., Gowrisankaran, S., & Hayes, J. R. (2005). Blink rate decreases with eyelid squint. *Optometry and Vision Science, 82*(10), 905–911. doi:10.1097/01.opx.0000181234.63194.a7

Shepherd, G. M. (2006). Smell images and the flavor system in the human brain. *Nature, 444*, 316–321. doi:10.1038/nature05405

Siegel, S. (2001). Pavlovian conditioning and drug overdose: When tolerance fails. *Addiction Research & Theory, 9*(5), 503–513.

Siegel, J. M. (2003). Why we sleep: The reasons that we sleep are gradually becoming less enigmatic. *Scientific American, 5,* 92–97.

Simons, D. J., & Chabris, C. F. (1999). Gorillas in our midst: Sustained inattentional blindness for dynamic events. *Perception, 28,* 1059–1074. doi:10.1068/p2952

Skinner, B. F. (1953). *Science and human behavior.* New York, NY: Macmillan.

Skinner, B. F. (1969). *Contingencies of reinforcement: A theoretical analysis.* New York, NY: Appleton-Century-Crofts.

Skinner, B. F. (1971). *Beyond freedom and dignity.* New York, NY: Knopf.

Skinner, B. F. (1989). *Recent issues in the analysis of behavior.* Columbus, OH: Merrill.

Slanger, E., & Rudestam, K. E. (1997). Motivation and disinhibition in high risk sports: Sensation seeking and self-efficacy. *Journal of Research in Personality, 31,* 355–374.

Slater, A., Field, T., & Hernandez-Reif, M. (2007). The development of the senses. In A. Slater & M. Lewis (Eds.), *Introduction to infant development.* New York, NY: Oxford University Press.

Sledge, W. H., & Hutchinson, J. (2010). Psychotherapy and psychosocial interventions in the treatment of substance abuse. In S. G. Lazar (Ed.), *The committee on psychotherapy. (2010). Psychotherapy is worth it: A comprehensive review of its cost-effectiveness* (pp. 175–226). Arlington, VA: American Psychiatric Publishing.

Slomski, A. (2006). The addicted brain. *Proto: Massachusetts General Hospital dispatches from the frontiers of medicine.* http://protomag.com/assets/the–addicted–brain

Slotkin, T. A. (2004). Cholinergic systems in brain development and disruption by neurotoxicants: Nicotine, environmental tobacco smoke, organophosphates. *Toxicology and Applied Pharmacology, 198*(2), 132–151. doi:10.1016/j.taap.2003.06.001

Smeets, P. M., Lancioni, G. E., Ball, T. S., & Oliva, D. S. (1985). Shaping self-initiated toileting in infants. *Journal of Applied Behavior Analysis, 18*(4), 303–308.

Smith, M. L., Glass, G. V., & Miller, T. I. (1980). *The benefits of psychotherapy.* Baltimore, MD: Johns Hopkins University Press.

Smith-Machin, A. L. (2009). Reducing the risk of disordered eating among female college students: A test of alternative interventions. *Dissertation Abstracts International: Section B: The Sciences and Engineering, 70* (4-B), 2588.

Sokol, R. J., Delaney-Black, V., & Nordstrom, B. (2003). Fetal alcohol spectrum disorder. *Journal of the American Medical Association, 290,* 2996–2999. doi:10.1001/jama.290.22.2996

Soto, C. J. & John, O. P. (2017). Short and extra-short forms of the big five inventory-2: The BFI-2-S and BFI-2-XS. *Journal of Research in Personality, 68,* 69–81.

Sood, B., Delaney-Black, V., Covington, C., Nordstrom-Klee, B., Ager, J., Templin, T., . . . Sokol, R. J. (2001). Prenatal alcohol exposure and childhood behavior at age 6 to 7 years: I. dose-response effect. *Pediatrics, 108*(2), E34.

Spear, L. P. (2000). The adolescent brain and age-related behavioral manifestations. *Neuroscience and Biobehaviorial Reviews, 24*(4), 417–463. doi:10.1016/s0149-7634(00)00014-2

Spear, L. P. & Brake, S. C. (1983). Periadolescence: Age-dependent behavior and psychopharmacological responsivity in rats. *Developmental Psychobiology, 16*(2), 83–109. doi:10.1002/dev.420160203

Spelke, E. S., & Hermer, L. (1996). Early cognitive development: Objects and space. In R. Gelman & T. K. Au (Eds.), *Perceptual and cognitive development* (pp. 71–114). San Diego, CA: Academic Press.

Sperling, G. (1960). The information available in brief visual presentations. *Psychological Monographs, 74*(Whole No. 498), 1–29. doi:10.1037/h0093759

Spitz, R. A. (1949). The role of ecological factors in emotional development in infancy. *Child Development, 20,* 145–155.

Stanford Prison Experiment. (2011). Stanford prison experiment: A simulation study of the psychology of imprisonment conducted at Stanford University. http://www.prisonexp.org/

Stanley, M. A., Bush, A. L., Camp, M. E., Jameson, J. P., Phillips, L. L., Barber, C. R., . . . Cully, J. A. (2011). Older adults' preferences for religion/spirituality in treatment of anxiety and depression. *Aging and Mental Health, 15,* 334–343.

Steinberg, L. (2007). Risk taking in adolescence: New perspectives from brain and behavioral science. *Current directions in psychological science, 16*(2), 55-59.

Steinberg, L. (2008). A social neuroscience perspective on adolescent risk-taking. *Developmental Review, 28*(1), 78–106.

Steptoe, A., Deaton, A. A., & Stone, A.A. (2015). Subjective wellbeing, health, and ageing. *The Lancet, 385*(9968), 640–648. https://doi.org/10.1016/S0140-6736(13)61489-0

Sternberg, R. J. (1986). A triangular theory of love. *Psychological Review, 93*, 119–135.

Stockett, K. (2009). *The help.* New York, NY: Amy Einhorn Books/Putnam.

Strasburger, V. C. (2009). Media and children: What needs to happen now? *JAMA: Journal of the American Medical Association, 301*(21), 2265–2266.

Substance Abuse and Mental Health Services Administration. (2014a). *Projections of national expenditures for treatment of mental and substance use disorders, 2010–2020.* https://store.samhsa.gov/product/Projections-of-National-Expenditures-for-Treatment-of-Mental-and-Substance-Use-Disorders-2010-2020/SMA14-4883

Substance Abuse and Mental Health Services Administration, Center for Behavioral Health Statistics and Quality. (2014b). *The TEDS report: Age of substance use initiation among treatment admissions aged 18 to 30.* https://www.samhsa.gov/data/sites/default/files/WebFiles_TEDS_SR142_AgeatInit_07-10-14/TEDS-SR142-AgeatInit-2014.htm

Substance Abuse and Mental Health Services Administration. (2018). *Key substance use and mental health indicators in the united states: Results from the 2018 National Survey on Drug Use and Health.* https://www.samhsa.gov/data/sites/default/files/cbhsq-reports/NSDUHNationalFindingsReport2018/NSDUHNationalFindingsReport2018.pdf

Substance Abuse and Mental Health Services, Center for Behavioral Health Statistics and Quality. (2018). *Key substance use and mental health indicators in the United States: Results from the 2017 national survey on drug use and health* (HHS Publication No. SMA 18-5068, NSDUH Series H-53). Rockville, MD. https://www.samhsa.gov/data/

Suicide in the U.S.: Statistics and prevention. (2010). *National institute of mental health.* http://www.nimh.nih.gov/health/publications/suicide-in-the-us-statistics-and-prevention/index.shtml#factors

Sumter, S. R., Valkenburg, P. M., & Peter, J. (2013). Perceptions of love across the lifespan: Differences in passion, intimacy, and commitment. *International Journal of Behavioral Development, 37*(5), 417–427. doi:10.1177/0165025413492486

Sundet, J. M., Erikson, W., & Tambs, K. (2008). Intelligence correlations between brothers decrease with increasing age difference: Evidence for shared environmental effects in young adults. *Association for Psychological Science, 19*(9), 843–847. doi:10.1111/j.1467-9280.2008.02166.x

Sundin, J., Fear, N. T., Iversen, A., Rona, R. J., & Wessely, S. (2010). PTSD after deployment to Iraq: Conflicting rates, conflicting claims. *Psychological Medicine: A Journal of Research in Psychiatry and the Allied Sciences, 40*(3), 367–382.

Sung, S. Y., & Choi, J. N. (2009). Do Big Five personality factors affect individual creativity? The moderating role of extrinsic motivation. *Social Behavior and Personality, 37*(7), 941–956.

Szymborska, W. (1995). *View with a grain of sand: Selected poems.* New York, NY: Harcourt Brace.

Taioli, E. & Wynder, E. L. (1991). Effect of the age at which smoking begins on frequency of smoking in adulthood. *New England Journal of Medicine, 325*, 968–969.

Taupin P. (2006). Neurogenesis and the effect of antidepressants. *Drug Target Insights, 1*, 13–17.

Teglasi, H. (2010). *Essentials of TAT and other storytelling assessments* (2nd ed.). Hoboken, NJ: John Wiley & Sons.

Terman, M., & Terman, J. S. (2005). Light therapy for seasonal and nonseasonal depression: Efficacy, protocol, safety, and side effects. *CNS Spectrums, 10*(8), 647–663. doi:10.1017/s1092852900019611

Thigpen, C. H., & Cleckley, H. (1954). *The three faces of Eve.* Kingsport, TN: Kingsport Press.

Thomas, A., & Chess, S. (1977). *Temperament and development.* New York, NY: Brunner/Mazel.

Thompson, R. A. (1998). Early sociopersonality development. In W. Damon (Series Ed.) & N. Eisenberg (Vol. Ed.), *Handbook of child psychology, Social, emotional and personality development* (Vol. 3, 5th ed., pp. 25–104). Hoboken, NJ: Wiley.

Thomsen, M., Fink-Jensen, A., Woldbye, D. P. D., Wortwein, G., Sager, T. N., Holm, R., . . . Caine, S. B. (2008). Effects of acute and chronic aripiprazole treatment on choice between cocaine self-administration and food under a concurrent schedule of reinforcement in rats. *Psychopharmacology, 201*(1), 43–53.

Thorndike, E. L. (1898). Animal intelligence: An experimental study of the associative processes in animals. *Psychological Review Monograph Supplement, 2*(8), i-109.

Tolman, E. C., & Honzik, C. H. (1930). Insight in rats. *University of California Publications in Psychology, 4,* 215–232.

Toma, C. L., & Hancock, J. T. (2010). Looks and lies: The role of physical attractiveness in online dating self-presentation and deception. *Communication Research, 37*(3), 335–351.

Torabi, M. R., Bailey, W. J., & Majd-Jabbari, M. (1993). Cigarette smoking as a predictor of alcohol and other drug use by children and adolescents: Evidence of the "gateway drug effect." *Journal of School Health, 63*(7), 302–305. https://doi.org/10.1111/j.1746-1561.1993.tb06150.x

Total isolation. (2008). BBC. *Science and Nature.* http://www.bbc.co.uk/sn/tvradio/programmes/horizon/broadband/tx/isolation/

Tulving, E. (1972). Episodic and semantic memory. In E. Tulving & W. Donaldson (Eds.), *Organization of memory.* London, England: Academic Press.

Tulving, E. (2002). Episodic memory: From mind to brain. *Annual Review of Psychology, 53,* 1–25. doi:10.1146/annurev.psych.53.100901.135114

Turner, J. E., & Goodin, J. B. (2008). Motivation and emotion. In N. J. Salkind (Ed.), *Encyclopedia of educational psychology* (Vol. 2, pp. 692–696). Thousand Oaks, CA: Sage.

Twenge, J. M. (2009). Change over time in obedience: The jury's still out, but it might be decreasing. *American Psychologist, 64*(1), 28–31.

Twitmyer, E. B. (1905). Knee jerks without stimulation of the patellar tendon. *Psychological Bulletin, 2,* 43.

U.S. Census Bureau. (2010b). *International data base, June 2010 update.* http://www.census.gov/ipc/www/idb/world popgraph.php

U.S. Census Bureau Population Estimates by Demographic Characteristics. (2005). *Table 2: Annual estimates of the population by selected age groups and sex for the United States: April 1, 2000 to July 1, 2004* (NC-EST2004-02). http://www.census.gov/popest/national/asrh/./.

Ulas, H., Polat, S., Akdede, B. B., & Alptekin, K. (2010). Impact of panic attacks on quality of life among patients with schizophrenia. *Progress in Neuro-Psychopharmacology & Biological Psychiatry, 34*(7), 1300–1305.

van Honk, J., Harmon-Jones, E., Morgan, B. E., & Schutter, D. J. L. G. (2010). Socially explosive minds: The triple imbalance hypothesis of reactive aggression. *Journal of Personality, 78*(1), 67–94.

van Ijzendoorn, M. H., Schuengel, C., & Bakermans-Kranenburg, M. J. (1999). Disorganized attachment in early childhood: Meta-analysis of precursors, concomitants and sequelae. *Development and Psychopathology, 11,* 225–249.

Vargha-Khadem, F., Gadian, D. G., Watkins, K. E., Connelly, A., Van Paesschen, W., & Mishkin, M. (1997). Differential effects of early hippocampal pathology on episodic and semantic memory. *Science, 277,* 376–380. doi:10.1126/science.277.5324.376

Vasilenko, S. A., Lefkowitz, E. S., & Maggs, J. L. (2012). Short-term positive and negative consequences of sex based on daily reports among college students. *Journal of sex research, 49*(6), 558–569. https://doi.org/10.1080/00224499.2011.589101

Vernon, D. (2009). Human potential: Exploring techniques used to enhance human performance. New York, NY: Routledge/Taylor & Francis Group.

Vieira, M. M., Ferreira, T. B., Pacheco, P. A. F., Barros, P. O., Almeida, C. R. M., Araujo-Lima, C. F., . . . Bento, C. A. M. (2010). Enhanced th17 phenotype in individuals with generalized anxiety disorder. *Journal of Neuroimmunology, 229*(1–2), 212–218.

Viner, R. M., Ozer, E. M., Denny, S., Marmot, M., Resnick, M., Fatusi, A., . . . Currie, C. (2012). Adolescence and the social determinants of health. *Lancet, 379*(9826), 1641–1652.

Visser, S. N., Danielson, M. L., Bitsko, R. H., Holbrook, J. R., Kogan, M. D., Ghandour, R. M., . . . Blumberg, S. J. (2014). Trends in the parent-report of health care provider-diagnosed and medicated attention-deficit/hyperactivity disorder: United States, 2003–2011. *Journal of American Academy Child Adolescent Psychiatry, 53*(1), 34–46.

Vlessides, M. (2020). *Blue-light therapy helps heal the brain.* https://www.medscape.com/viewarticle/924216

Vonthron, A. M., & Lagabrielle, C. (2002). The influence of locus of control orientation and internal versus external causal attributions on obstacles during work, in professional integration strategies. *Psykhe: Revista de la Escuela de Psicologia, 11*(2), 197–205.

Vyazovskiy, V. V., Cirelli, C., Pfister-Genskow, M., Faraguna, U., & Tononi, G. (2008). Molecular and electro-physiological evidence for net synaptic potentiation in wake and depression in sleep. *Nature Neuroscience, 11*, 200–208.

Vygotsky, L. S. (1962). *Thought and language* (E. Hanfmann & G. Vaker, Trans.). Cambridge, MA: MIT Press.

Waldinger, R. J. (2010). Psychotherapy in the treatment of borderline personality disorder. In S. G. Lazar (Ed.), *The committee on psychotherapy. (2010). Psychotherapy is worth it: A comprehensive review of its cost-effectiveness* (pp. 61–86). Arlington, VA: American Psychiatric Publishing.

Walsh, T., McClellan, J. M., McCarthy, S. E., Addington, A. M., Pierce, S. B., Cooper, G. M., . . . Sebat, J. (2008). Rare structural variants disrupt multiple genes in neurodevelopmental pathways in schizophrenia. *Science, 320*(5875), 539–543.

Walster, E., Aronson, V., Abrahams, O., & Rottman, L. (1966). Importance of physical attractiveness in dating behavior. *Journal of Personality and Social Psychology, 4*, 508–516.

Wan, C. –S., & Chiou, W.-B. (2010). Inducing attitude change toward online gaming among adolescent players based on dissonance theory: The role of threats and justification of effort. *Computers & Education, 54*(1), 162–168.

Wasserman, J. D. (2012). A history of intelligence assessment: The unfinished tapestry. In D. P. Flanagan & P. L. Harrison (Eds.), *Contemporary intellectual assessment: Theories, tests, and issues* (pp. 3–55). New York, NY: The Guilford Press.

Watanabe, S. (2010). Pigeons can discriminate "good" and "bad" paintings by children. *Animal Cognition, 13*(1), 75–85.

Watson, J. B. (1916). Behavior and the concept of mental disease. *Journal of Philosophy, Psychology, and Scientific Methods, 13*, 589–597. doi:10.2307/2012555

Watson, J. B. (1928). *The ways of behaviorism.* New York, NY: Harper.

Watson, J. B. (1930). *Behaviorism* (2nd ed.). Chicago, IL: University of Chicago Press.

Weiner, B. (2008). Reflections on the history of attribution theory and research: People, personalities, publications, problems. *Social Psychology, 39*(3), 151–156. doi:10.1027/1864-9335.39.3.151

Wheeler, M. A., Stuss, D. T., & Tulving, E. (1997). Toward a theory of episodic memory: The frontal lobes and autonoetic consciousness. *Psychological Bulletin, 121*, 331–354. doi:10.1037/0033-2909.121.3.331

Whittington, B. & Scher, S. (2010). Prayer and subjective well-being: An examination of six different types of prayer. *The International Journal for the Psychology of Religion, 20*, 59–68. 10.1080/10508610903146316.

Whorf, B. L. (2012). In J. B. Carroll, S. C. Levinson, & P. Lee, (Eds.), *Language, thought, and reality: Selected writings of Benjamin Lee Whorf (2nd ed.)., introduction by John B. Carroll; foreword by Stephen C. Levinson.* Cambridge, MA: MIT Press.

Wigfield, A., Tonks, S., & Klauda, S. L. (2009). Expectancy-value theory. In K. R. Wenzel & A. Wigfield (Eds.), *Handbook of motivation at school* (pp. 55–75). New York, NY: Routledge/Taylor & Francis Group.

Williams, T., & Williams, K. (2010). Self-efficacy and performance in mathematics: Reciprocal determinism in 33 nations. *Journal of Educational Psychology, 102*(2), 453–466.

Wittchen, H. U. (2002). Generalized anxiety disorder: Prevalence, burden, and cost to society. *Depression and Anxiety, 16*(4), 162–171.

Wolfe, J. M., Kluender, K. R., Levi, D. M., Bartoshuk, L. M., Herz, R. S., Klatzky, R. L., . . . Merfeld, D. M. (2012). *Sensation and perception* (3rd ed.). Sunderland, MA: Sinauer Associates.

Wolters, A. M. (2005). *Creation regained* (2nd ed.). Grand Rapids, MI: William B. Eerdmans Publishing. ISBN: 9780802829696

Wolters, G., & Goudsmit, J. J. (2005). Flashbulb and event memory of September 11, 2001: Consistency, confidence and age effects. *Psychological Reports, 96*(3), 605–619.

Wood, J. M., Lilienfeld, S. O., Nezworski, M. T., Garb, H. N., Allen, K. H., & Wildermuth, J. L. (2010). Validity of Rorschach inkblot scores for discriminating psychopaths from nonpsychopaths in forensic populations: A meta-analysis. *Psychological Assessment, 22*, 336–349. doi:10.1037/a0018998

Woodman, T., Zourbanos, N., Hardy, L., Beattie, S., & McQuillan A. (2010). Do performance strategies moderate the relationship between personality and training behaviors? An exploratory study. *Journal of Applied Sport Psychology, 22*(2), 183–197. doi:10.1080/10413201003664673

Workman, L., Chilvers, L., Yeomans, H., & Taylor, S. (2006). Development of cerebral lateralisation for recognition of emotions in chimeric faces in children aged 5 to 11. *Laterality: Asymmetries of Body, Brain and Cognition, 11*, 493–507.

World Health Organization. (2005). The World Health Organization Quality of Life assessment (WHOQOL): Position paper from the World Health Organization. *Social Science and Medicine, 41*(10), 1403–1409.

World Health Organization. (2006). *Constitution of the World Health Organization.* http://www.who.int/governance/eb/who_constitution_en.pdf

Worldometers. (2010). *Worldometers: World statistics updated in real time.* http://www.worldometers.info/weight-loss/

Worrall, E. (2016, September 3). Two hundred million dollar scientific grant fraud case. *Watts Up with That.* https://wattsupwiththat.com/2016/09/03/two-hundred-million-dollar-scientific-grant-fraud-case/

Xiao, S., Young, D., & Zhang, H. (1998). Taoistic cognitive psychotherapy for neurotic patients: A preliminary clinical trial. *Psychiatry & Clinical Neurosciences, 52* (supplement), 238–241.

Yamagata, S., Suzuki, A., Ando, J., Ono, Y., Kijima, N., Yoshimura, K., . . . Jang, K. L. (2006). Is the genetic structure of human personality universal? A cross-cultural twin study from North America, Europe, and Asia. *Journal of Personality and Social Psychology, 90*(6), 987–998.

Yerkes, R. M., & Dodson, J. D. (1908). The relationship of strength of stimulus to rapidity of habit formation. *Journal of Comparative Neurological Psychology, 18*, 459–482.

Zatorre, R. J., Belin, P., & Penhune, V. B. (2002). Structure and function of auditory cortex: Music and speech. *Trends in Cognitive Sciences, 6*, 37–46. doi:10.1016/S1364-6613(00)01816-7

Zeaman, D. (1949). Response latency as a function of amount of reinforcement. *Journal of Experimental Psychology, 39*, 466–483.

Zee, P. C. (2010). Shedding light on the effectiveness of melatonin for circadian rhythm sleep disorders. *Sleep, 33*(12), 1581–1582.

Zeki, S. (1993). *A vision of the brain.* New York, NY: Wiley.

Zhang, L. J., Xiao, Y., Qi, X. L., Shan, K. R., Pei, J. J., Kuang, S. Z., . . . Guan, Z. Z. (2010). Cholinesterase activity and mRNA level of nicotinic acetylcholine receptors (alpha 4 and beta 2 subunits) in blood of elderly Chinese diagnosed as Alzheimer's disease. *Journal of Alzheimer's Disease, 19*(3), 849–858.

Zhu, J.-N., & Wang, J.-J. (2008). The cerebellum in feeding control: Possible function and mechanism. *Cellular and Molecular Neurobiology, 28*(4), 469–478.

Zimbardo, P. G. (2007). *The Lucifer effect: Understanding how good people turn evil.* New York, NY: Random House.

Zinchenko, Y. P. (2009). Mass media as an effective tool for prevention of socio-psychological factors in the development of terrorism. *Psychology in Russia: State of the Art, 2*, 459–476.

Zubek, J. P. (1973). Behavioral and physiological effects of prolonged sensory and perceptual deprivation: A review. In J. E. Rasmussen (Ed.), *Man in isolation and confinement* (pp. 9–84). Chicago, IL: Transaction Books.

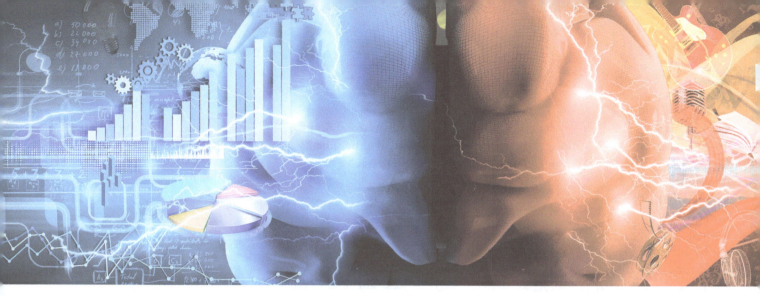

Index

Y